Death of an Era

Memoirs of Andrew E. Long

BALBOA.
PRESS
A DIVISION OF HAY HOUSE

Balboa Press books may be ordered through booksellers or by contacting:

Balboa Press
A Division of Hay House
1663 Liberty Drive
Bloomington, IN 47403
www.balboapress.com
1 (877) 407-4847

Print information available on the last page.

ISBN: 978-1-5043-8261-8 (sc)
ISBN: 978-1-5043-8263-2 (hc)
ISBN: 978-1-5043-8262-5 (e)

Library of Congress Control Number: 2017909612

Balboa Press rev. date: 07/20/2017

Table of Contents

Chapter One

As I Remember

Wesley Brooks Long and Annis Marie Henderson Long, Andy's parents

I, ANDREW EDWARD LONG, WAS born November 17, 1924 in Bartlesville, Washington County, Oklahoma. I was born at my grandparents Mr. and Mrs. Andrew Henderson's home at 3rd and Santa Fe Streets in Bartlesville. Dr. Smith, who had delivered hundreds of babies, delivered me. My mother had weighed only 98 pounds before she became pregnant and I weighed 10 pounds at birth. I was named for my mother's father as I was their first grandchild. My mother and father lived just a few blocks down the street. I was the first of three children born to my parents. My father was Wesley Brooks Long, born Oct. 23, 1890 in Rolla, Missouri and my mother was Annis Marie Henderson, born, in 1900 in Osage County, Indian Territory. I had one sister and one brother — Marjorie Marie Long, born June 12, 1927 and John Wesley Long, born Jan 16, 1937. My first memory is of going to the dentist, a Dr. Edgerton. I must have been about four years old. Dad bought me an ice cream cone afterwards for being such a big boy and not crying. I also remember about this same time that my Dad's mother, Grandmother Stark, made me some mince meat pie. I ate so much that I got sick, and I still don't like mince meat pie!

My grandparents lived on a farm and I lived with them on the farm my first three school years. The Great Depression had just started and my grandparents and my parents lived together in a large 2-story house on the 360 acre farm. The farm was owned jointly by my grandparents and my uncle, Jack Henderson, and his wife, Cora Tinker Henderson. At the early age of six I learned to do many things. My grandfather taught me how to hunt and shoot. He was a lawman in his younger days— sheriff, deputy U.S. marshall, and chief of police in Bartlesville. He always seemed to me to be bigger than life itself. My grandmother, Gertrude Henderson, taught me how to plant and raise a garden, how to hatch baby chickens and ducks, and how to clean fish, squirrels and rabbits. We were such good friends, and were until she died in 1958.

Cora Tinker Henderson was part Osage Indian. She was a very beautiful young lady, and like all the Osages of that day, she received a large amount of money as an Osage Indian Headright from the oil that was discovered in huge abundance on Osage land. The money enabled Uncle Jack and Aunt Code (as Cora was called) to buy another 65 acres of rich farm land on Turkey Creek, just one mile south of the town of Dewey, and about five miles north of my grandparent's farm. Both farms were farmed by the family. Jack and Code built a large red brick house with a clay tile roof. It had just about everything you could want in a home, including a large garage and servant's quarters. A large colored man who called himself "Negro George" (approximating the expression of the time) worked for them and he helped out on both farms. They had a large barn for the horses, a hay loft and grain storage. Jack and Code used to have barn dances in those days that were great fun. The grounds surrounding the home were beautiful, with a large circle drive in front. Roses were planted in the circle and the drive was lined with poplar trees.

Jack and Code's first child was a beautiful baby girl, Dorothy Jeanne, with coal black hair, an olive complexion and blue eyes. She was about a year younger than me. We had a great time growing up together, riding our ponies and playing. Their second child was a son, named after his father and called Jackie. Jackie was about a year younger than my sister Marge.

We cousins also had another uncle, who was only seven years older than me. I loved my uncle L. D. Henderson, and stuck to him like glue. L. D. taught me how to ride a horse, milk a cow, raise pigs and goats, how to butcher a hog, dehorn cattle, build fences, hoe corn, drive a tractor, a car and a pickup truck, how to saddle a horse and herd cattle, and how to fight, wrestle, drink whiskey and show great respect for my elders.

I started school at the age of five, attending the Rice Creek School, a rural elementary school, and Highland Park School, both in Bartlesville. On the farm we lived only a quarter mile from Rice Creek School, my grade school, and L. D. and I rode his horse back and forth to school, and since we lived so close, home for lunch. My closest friends from school were Junior Sears, Ann Boxwell, Naomi Medcalf, Jackson Milam, Jack Stout, Stanley Moran, Carl Statts, and Clara Jean Dilley. My favorite teachers were: Maude Darnell, she was about 17 or 18 years old when she taught me the first and second grade at Rice Creek School (she was also my daughter Andra's first grade teacher many years later) and Mrs. Pound, Mrs. Kahill, and Mr. Myers (he had only one arm and was the principal) at Highland Park School.

Something I remember about first grade is when school was out for Election Day and Franklin D. Roosevelt was elected President of the United States. Also, in first grade I remember very well when our teacher, Maud Darnell, spanked the whole school because no one would tell who toilet papered the trees on Halloween night. Miss Darnell taught all eight grades. I was on the first seat in the front row of first grade, so she asked me if I wanted to be the first one to be spanked or the last one. I said, "I want to be the last one, Miss Darnell." So, she started with the eighth grade students first. She used a wooden paddle and the big boys got a pretty hard spanking. The little girls didn't get spanked hard, but they cried anyway.

Another thing I've never forgotten is that I wore a little skull cap to school. Most all the boys had one of these at one time or another. You made them out of a man's felt hat crown, cutting the brim off, and with the scissors you cut half-diamonds all around the edge, then turn the edge up all around. Anyway, I came in from recess one day and the teacher called the class together and said, "Andrew, what do you have on your head?" I had a mosquito bite on my head and had been scratching it all day and it had gotten infected. So, I said, "A mosquito bite, teacher." All the kids laughed and when they did, I realized that I had forgotten to remove my scull cap when I came in from recess. Then in the fourth grade I had my first fist fight, against Jackson Milam. My dad taught me how to box at an early age. He and I got tired of me being chased home from school — and we did put a stop to that! I enjoyed school, made good grades and had lots of friends.

Summers were great! I practically lived on a creek that ran through the farm. I would catch fish, frogs, and crawdads. I was only six or seven years old and my grandmother would help me clean them. I roamed up and down Rice Creek for about a half mile on our place. I knew every inch of it.

In those days we farmed with horses and mules. Later they got a tractor, but when the Depression was on, everyone farmed with horses and mules so it was necessary to grow lots of corn in order to have plenty of feed for the horses, cows, hogs, chickens, ducks, geese and guinnies. When the farm was first purchased it was in disrepair, so after they got the crops planted, the men and my young uncle, L. D., started working on all the things that had to be repaired or replaced. To name a few — rebuilding all the fences (and there were a lot of them), setting posts after cutting them from the timber along the creek, stringing barbed wire, putting in a new foundation under the large barn (what a job!), cutting large trees with a long, two-man crosscut saw, loading the large logs onto the wagon and hauling them to the sawmill to have them cut into large 2-inch thick boards to build new horse stalls and cow stantions for the milk cows in the barn, and repair the smokehouse that was used to store the hams and pork sausage from the hogs we would butcher. The men worked very hard as there was so much to do. I was right there with them, helping if I could, watching and learning. It was natural that I would learn to cuss. My uncle L. D. was a teenager and boy, could he cuss! I didn't cuss much in those early days, but I sure learned how.

My dad worked right along with my grandad, Uncle Jack and Uncle L.D. He was a small man, about 5'3" and about 120 pounds, so he couldn't do too much heavy work, but he tried. He had been a car salesman and had owned a tire store before the Depression, and was an avid baseball fan, knowing the stats for every player on every professional team. I was always with the men when they were working and I was a "go - fer." If they forgot to bring a small tool or wrench or something, they would tell me where to find it in the barn or shed and send me after it. They would say, "Now, Andy, don't stop and look for a crawdad under a rock when you cross the creek, just hurry up and come straight back." I was always underfoot and I loved them all dearly — and vise-versa. I learned so much. When my young uncle, L.D. would drive the team of mules pulling the corn cultivator, I was right up there on the seat with him, or following right behind them picking up fishing worms from the freshly cultivated soil.

When noontime came, L. D. would unhitch the team from the cultivator and we would each ride one, water them in the creek and then on to the barn to feed them corn. We would have our lunch (which was called "dinner" in those days), then back to the field after about an hour afternoon's rest. One day I remember I was riding one of the horses and we were watering them in the creek when the horse walked under a treelimb. I grabbed the limb to keep from getting knocked off. The horse kept on walking and I held onto the limb and then dropped off into the creek. The water was not deep, so no problem and L. D. and I had a good laugh.

I was old enough to hoe corn and there was plenty of that to do, day after day in the hot sun. I learned to work hard and to do a lot of things. I' ve never forgotten that about an hour or so before sundown we would come in from the field, then saddle the horse and ride to the pasture to drive the milk cows into the cow pen and shed. We would milk about five or six cows, then carry the milk pails to the smoke house and pour the milk into the separator to separate the cream from the milk. By turning a crank on the separator, one spout would pour out the cream and one spout would pour out the milk. We would dip out one quart of milk before separating to we would have milk to drink and cream for coffee with our meals. We would carry the separated milk down to the hog pen and this was feed for the hogs, along with some ears of corn. This is how we fattened our hogs. The cream would be kept in our large ice box until Saturday. Grandmother would save enough cream out to churn for butter for our use, then put the rest of the cream in a couple of large, tall buckets with tight lids. They would be taken to town, along with a couple of large baskets of country fresh eggs to the grocery store each Saturday. My grandmother would tell the grocer how many dozen eggs she had and he would weigh the buckets of cream. She would hand the grocer her list of groceries and he would add up the groceries and subtract the charge from the amount she had coming from her eggs and cream.

L.D. would drive Grandma and me, and sometimes Grandpa, into town every Saturday afternoon. L. D. and I would first go to the Silver Dollar Bar where he would order a quart of beer and a bottle of pop for me. Then we would go to the Saturday afternoon picture show (now the "movie theater"). A ticket was five cents and five cents for a sack of popcorn. This was our Saturday afternoon treat while Grandmother would do a little shopping at the Five and Dime Store, clothing store, etc. But not much because money was so scarce. I remember a pair of bluejeans for me was forty-nine cents and a pair or tennis shoes were forty-nine cents. I got one pair of each every year. The minute I came home from school, I would take off my jeans and put on some old ones and take off my good tennis shoes, and go barefoot.

After Saturday's trip to town, it would be home again to start milking those old cows. Later on when I grew up and became a teenager, the Depression was over. My folks moved away from the farm and my Dad got a job selling Dodge and Plymouth cars. We moved to Tuxedo, a suburb of Bartlesville, and I went to Highland Park School. However, each year I would spend the summers on my Grandparent's farm. We always had one cow and some chickens and my job was to milk the cow and take care of the chickens. I would spend those summers working with L. D. bailing hay and shocking wheat, barley and oats. By this time things had gotten better as the country was beginning to come out from the Depression. My Grandad bought a tractor and we did not need to use as many horses and mules. Also, we did not need to plant as much corn to feed the livestock (some, of course, for the milk cows and hogs) and we started raising more wheat, oats and barley, as well as alfalfa hay. I was always a slender kid. No fat. Just muscle and bone. I could buck those 100 pounds hay bales and stack them in the barn loft right along with the men. I was a strong kid.

When my sister and I were very young — I was about six or seven, and she was three or four — my Uncle Jack bought us a very young goat. We named her Nanny. She was white and fun to play with. As the weeks went by, she grew to about waist high and her little horns grew almost straight up and were about four or five inches long. Just right for me to hold her by and play with her. My sister liked to play with her too but she was not strong enough to hold her and sometimes the goat would back up a little, then run and butt Marjorie in the stomach and knock her on her little butt. My Grandmother would say, "That goat is going to hurt that baby! We had better get rid of it before she does." Shortly after that my Uncle Jack drove up in a brand new Model A Ford Roadster. It was lemon yellow and was new and shiny. It wasn't long until Nanny had jumped up on the running board, then climbed up the front fender and was jumping up and down on the hood of the car. Jack saw her and he said, "Now that does it! I'm going to get rid of that damn goat for good!" He called 'Negro' George to help him and they tied her hind legs to the garden fence and George took his razor that he always carried and cut Nanny's throat. To this day I can still hear that little goat say, "Baa, baa, baa, baa." Marge and I cried and cried and after they skinned and dressed the goat, Grandma roasted her for supper. They all enjoyed the roasted goat supper, except my little sister and me. In those days people were all very practical. They knew that goat was going to seriously hurt our little girl and the escapade with Uncle Jack's new car was what was needed to take care of the problem. A sound lesson in common sense, I think.

Our Aunt Code always drove a new car because having her Osage Indian Headright, she got a big check every month. Each year for Christmas my sister and I would always get nice gifts from Aunt Code. We could always count on it. We would go visit our cousins, Dorothy and Jackie Henderson and sometimes stay all night in their big, beautiful home and have a great time. Uncle Jack loved us. He would call me "Andy Pain" after the famous race car driver of that time. He would call Marjorie "Red" even though she was a blond.

I remember that they had a very large refrigerator in their pantry and there was always a case of Pepsi Cola in it, so we knew we would get a bottle of pop whenever we wanted it — a great treat for us in those days!

My mother was always there on the farm to help my grandmother with whatever she was doing, but no question about it, grandma ruled the Roost! In the summer there was lots of work to be done. Mostly gardening and canning. We would pick peas, green beans, sweet corn, black-eyed peas, and all kinds of fruit. Then can all we could and store it in our storm cellar, which was located just off the back porch.

My grandpa's sister, Lizzie Elam, lived in Bartlesville and she and Uncle Matt Elam ran a large rooming house. They provided rooms and meals. Lizzie always helped grandmother plant a large garden and then all pitched in at canning time. We always had plenty to eat. They used a large pressure cooker to can the food. One time Aunt Lizzie managed to get a tin canning machine, so they experimented on canning corn with it. They canned many, many cans of corn and worked their butts off with this! We'll never figure out what they did wrong, but a few days after they finished canning the corn, the cans started exploding all over the smoke house! Oh, Lordie, how it did stink! That ended the canning in a hurry!

As I said before, the farm was badly in need of repair when they bought it. Fortunately, we did have natural gas that was piped to the house from a nearby oil well just across our back garden fence. So, we had gas for heating, cooking and gas lights with gas piped to the ceiling of each room in the large, two-story house. It did provide pretty good light. We had a battery-powered radio and we could get programs like Amos and Andy, Gildersleves, soap operas like Ma Perkins, the Farm Market Report and of course, Franklin Roosevelt's Fireside Chats, as he called them. My grandparent's were staunch Republicans, but my Mom and Dad had had enough of Hoover and the Depression, so they were Democrats. They did have some serious arguments! Us kids were too young to know about those things.

My grandpa had been a lawman all his adult life. First a city policeman on horseback. One of a dozen of them all on white horses in those early oil field days in Washington County, Oklahoma. Then he was Assistant Chief of Police, then Chief of Police, then Deputy Sheriff, then Sheriff for two four-year terms (about the time I was born), and then U. S. Marshall. He caught lots of bad guys: Henry Starr, Blackie Thompson, Red Andrews, and many more. This is when they lived in town before the Depression and before the farm.

My grandfather, as I said, was a staunch Republican and he had run for Sheriff on the Republican ticket, so he was not about to accept any handouts from the Government or welfare or W.P.A., etc. You can imagine how rough and tough the town of Bartlesville was in the early oil field days. This was at the very beginning of statehood. My mother, Annis Marie, was actually born in Indian Territory before Oklahoma became a state.

My grandmother's parents were Thomas Nathaniel Moon and Delila Jane Johnston Moon. They had three boys and three girls and were farmers northwest of Bartlesville in Indian Territory. They had traveled in a covered wagon several times back and forth from Oklahoma to New Mexico looking for just the right place to farm.

My grandfather's parents were Andrew Jackson Henderson and Sarah Catherine Ferguson Henderson. He became an Indian Agent and adviser to the Indians. The Great Osage Tribe was the most prominent tribe in this area of the Indian Nation, but there were also Deleware and Cherokee tribes. They had three children. He leased farmland from the Indians which later became the townsite of Dewey, Oklahoma. I don't know exactly how my grandparents met, but they got married and lived a short time at the homestead of my grandmother's parent's place. My mother had told me many times when she was just a baby, born in 1900, that the Indians would come to their place and lay out under a big shade tree and bounce her on their stomachs. My mother had dark, black hair and black eyes. My great-grandmother Moon would tell her daughter, Gertrude, "Those Indians are going to steal that baby girl!" It never happend, but they tried to trade my grandfather a string of Indian ponies for that baby girl — but my grandmother said "no deal".

My grandfather's mother died at age 36 and left my great-grandfather with three children; my grandfather was about nine. His older sister, Elizabeth Henderson Elam, was just a teenage girl and she took charge of raising the others with her father. My great-grandfather, Andrew Jackson

Henderson, was born in 1851 and died in 1989 at the age of 47. My grandfather was about nineteen years old. A few years later he and my grandmother married and in 1900 my mother was born.

My mother, Annis Marie Henderson was born in Indian Territory in 1900. In 1907 Oklahoma became a state and big things began to happen in Washington, Osage and Tulsa counties. In Washington County, Bartlesville and Dewey and Osage County to the west became oil boom towns. People came from everywhere! Several of the large oil companies got started in Bartlesville. Frank and L. E. Phillips, brothers, started Phillips Petroleum Company. Henry Sinclair, Mr. Skelly and Mr. Getty all started oil companies in their own names. Also, this is where in Osage County, Conoco Oil Company was started at Ponca City, Oklahoma. These towns grew very fast. People came from all over to work in the oil fields and start up businesses.

All the numbered streets in Bartlesville ran east and west and all the streets that ran north and south were named after the various Indian Tribes: Osage, Delaware, Cherokee, Creek, Chocktaw, Chickasaw, Quapaw, Comanche, and so on. Phillips Petroleum Company still has it's world headquarters in Bartlesville, Oklahoma. There is a saying among the employees that when they retire and finally die, instead of going to Heaven, they all want to go to Bartlesville.

Bartlesville was a very fast growing town and a rough, tough town with all the tough oil field workers, boiler makers, and rig builders, etc. So you can see it was a hard job to keep the peace. My grandfather's job as a lawman was a tough and dangerous one. Andy Hendreson was kind of a legend in those early days. He was a fair man and had more common sense than any man I have ever known, and he had to be super tough. In later years he would show us his right hand and the knuckles had been knocked back about a half inch. They would say to him, "Andy, why don't you use your Billy Club or Black Jack or your pistol barrel on those tough guys instead of your fists?" His answer was, "Sometimes you don't have time."

One interesting story my grandfather used to tell was that Frank Phillips came to Bartlesville as a barber and he would stop by his barber shop for a shave on his way to work as Sheriff. Frank Phillips got a lot of oil leases from the Indians, struck it big, and thus became Phillips Petroleum. The same thing happened with all the other above-mentioned men.

My father's parents, Moses Long and Melissa Reynolds Long were married in 1875. He was eighteen and she was seventeen. They had a farm in Henry County, near Rolla, Missouri. Both came from farm families, as did most of the population in those days. To this young couple came nine children — six boys, and three girls. The boys were Thomas, Arthur (Pat), Neam, James Lou, Wesley and Walter. The girls were Alma, Harriett (Hattie), and Mattie. My father, Wesley, was the eighth child.

My grandfather was a strong, hard-working man and he died of a heat stroke in the month of July 1892 at the age of 36, leaving a beautiful widow with eight children, and one more due in February. Melissa sold the farm and moved the youngest six children to Cherryvale, Kansas. The three older boys went their separate ways. Tom stayed in Missouri. Arthur Long (called 'Pat') joined a cattle drive outfit. He was just a young teenager and he probably joined them in Kansas City, Missouri where the stock yards were. Texans drove their cattle there to be shipped out on the railroads to the eastern cities. He started out as a young cowboy and had a very colorful life. He spent his early years on these many cattle drives and he became an expert cowboy. While working on the 101 Ranch near Ponca City he becames the first white man to bulldog a steer. He was taught by a black man by the name of Bill Pickett. He became World Champion Bulldogger and was asked to join Buffalo Bill's Wild West Show. They traveled all over, even to Europe where he performed his famous Bulldogging talent with large steers, not like the small steers that you now see on TV Rodeos. Sometimes he would have to bite a large steer on the lip to help throw him down. Later on, he worked as a ranch foreman for the owners of several famous ranches in Oklahoma, like the Will Rogers Ranch near Clairmore, the Cross Bell Ranch owned by the Nullendorfs, and a huge ranch near Hula Lake (pronounced "Hugh-la"), northwest of Copan and Dewey, Oklahoma.

An interesting story told by my dad was one day on the Cross Bell Ranch he had some young cowboys bailing hay and when they got back to the bunkhouse one of them picked a fight with Uncle Pat. At that time Uncle Pat was 65 years old, but that didn't matter at all. He grabbed the young cowboy and turned him over his knees and spanked his ass for him in front of the other cowhands, then told him to go to the office for his last paycheck and leave. After that he also was ranch foreman for the Adams

Ranch, northwest of Bartlesville. At that time the owner was Boots Adams, who was then the president of Phillips Petroleum Company. After that Pat retired to Claremore, Oklahoma where he had worked for many years and raised his family. His wife was always the ranch cook on the ranches where Uncle Pat was foreman. They raised five girls and two boys. The boys were the youngest children. Uncle Pat finally passed away at the age of 86 in 1968. The last time I saw him was at my Dad's funeral at Dewey, Oklahoma in 1962. I always thought he was a wonderful man. He and my grandfather on my mother's side, Andy Henderson, used to ride broncos together when they were both young.

Having a grandfather that was a famous lawman and an uncle who was a famous cowboy, it's no wonder some of the wild things I have done in my lifetime. Understandable, don't you think? I have heard a number of times that a man is not like his father, he is more apt to be like his grandfather. It jumps a generation. I think this is true because I was much more like my Grandpa than my Dad.

So, Moses Long's young widow, Melissa Long, moved to Cherryvale, Kansas and bought a large rooming house with the money she received from the sale of the farm in Missouri. This was a way to make a living for her and her six remaining young children. Two of the three girls were old enough to help her with the rooming house chores — keeping the rooms clean, the washing, ironing, and cooking. Lots of families were moving west in those days and rooming and boarding houses did a good business. Lots of cowboys and outlaws stayed at the rooming house in the days nearing the turn of the century.

The second oldest con of Moses Long was Neam. He died a fairly young man. He was working on an eastern Colorado farm and one day while hauling hay be got down off the wagon to check something that was wrong with the way the harness was hooked up to the wagon. For some reason, the team bolted and he was knocked down. The wagon ran over him and crushed his chest.

Young Harriett (Hattie) was a very pretty young girl of fifteen and a very handsome young cowboy and her fell in love. He wanted to marry Hattie and told Grandma Long that he would pay up all of her bills if she would give her permission for them to marry. Well, Grandma being a very practical woman, knew if she refused them that her daughter would run off and get married anyway, so she said, "All right." This is about the time that the Dalton Gang had robbed the two banks in Coffeyville, Kansas. The townspeople and the law had been tipped off somehow that the robbery would take place and they were ready for them. They thought that they had killed all of them except one, and he was wounded and went to prison, but apparently one had escaped. The young cowboy's name who married my Aunt Hattie was Bill Wolfenbarger. This was a short time after the robbery. The newlyweds moved to Guthrie, Oklahoma, a town that had just become the first state capital of Oklahoma (the capital was later moved to Oklahoma City). The oil boom was on in a big way there also. As the story goes, my Great Uncle Bill and Aunt Hattie opened a saloon and restaurant. Uncle Bill ran the bar and Aunt Hattie did the cooking. Their business prospered as Uncle Bill Wolfenbarger was very smart, as well as tall and good-looking and Aunt Hattie was a beautiful young woman.

Uncle Bill was a born promoter. He would arrange westling matches and boxing matches with the young farm boys and oilfield workers, and horse races in and around Guthrie. This would draw some good crowds for his bar and restaurant business. When my dad was just a boy he was always small and could really ride a horse very well. He traveled to Guthrie by train and became a jockey in the horse races for Uncle Bill. All these were legitimate businesses, quite different from his previous occupation when he was known as Bill Dalton and escaped from the Coffeyville bank robberies. When he married my aunt he took his mother's maiden name of Wolfenbarger.

I don't know how many years they were in Guthrie, as this all happened before my time, but I do remember in 1936 when I was in the Fourth Grade my Uncle Bill and Aunt Hattie Wolfenbarger came to visit us in Bartlesville, Oklahoma. They were then living at Farley, New Mexico. It was a very small town in the southeast corner of New Mexico, several miles west of Cimmaron. They asked my folks if I could go back with them to their home in Farley and stay for the summer. They had no children except an adopted son about my age. My folks would not let me go.

It was about 40 years later before I found out why I could not go with my Uncle Bill and Aunt Hattie. Many years later, in 1948, when I was 23 years old, married and with a young son named Timothy, we moved to Oklahoma City and discovered that Aunt Hattie and Uncle Bill were living there. His adopted son and wife lived there also. I was surprised to find that my Grandmother Long, who was now in her ninteies was living with Uncle Bill and Aunt Hattie, who were then in their late 70's. Uncle Bill stayed in bed most of the time, until his old-age pension check (now called "social security") would arrive, then he would dress up in his black suit and big black hat. He had long black hair and a big black handlebar moustache. A handsome old man. He would walk down to the neighborhood bar and have a few drinks, play the jukebox and visit with the girls. Occasionally they babysat Tim for us — once putting him in a dark closet for misbehaving.

Several years later they all passed away, and the great Bill Dalton secret died also. This secret about Uncle Bill was never known outside the family and I did not learn of it until I was about fifty years old. One day while I was visiting with my Aunt Alma's three daughters, my cousins in Bartlesville, I asked about Uncle Bill. The oldest of the three, who is now dead, said, "Andrew, he was nothing but an old outlaw!" And then she told me the whole story.

After Hattie moved away, Melissa Long continued to run the rooming house for several more years. She was a very striking woman and she had a good head for business. As the story goes, Melissa married twice more, but the husbands were not good to her and the boys ran both of them off.

Later, as the three remaining children grew into their teens, Widow Long did find the right man for husband #4 — his name was J. G. Stark. He and his brother ran a grocery store in the nearby town of Niotaze, Kansas. J. G. sold his half of the grocery store to his brother, and Jacob G. Stark and Melissa Long got married. They sold the rooming house and the newlyweds and Melissa's youngest three children — Alma, Wesley, and Walter — all moved to Bartlesville, Oklahoma.

Mr. and Mrs. J. G. Stark opened a small grocery store and the children went to work. Alma worked in the grocery store and later married an oil-field worker name Bill Nelson and raised four beautiful daughters — Oletha, Opal, Dorothy, and Annabelle. The two boys found jobs in the prosperous and fast-growing oil boom. World War I was looming in Europe and in a year or so, the U.S. would get involved.

Young Wesley and brother Walter volunteered for the Army. I don't know what part Walter served in, but my father, Wesley Brooks Long, served in the Balloon Battalion. He left Newport News, Virginia by ship and arrived in France when things were going hot and heavy. It was an exciting time for him, as it was for all the young men of the time. Dad said one of his jobs was riding in a side car of a motorcycle and he used a mounted machine gun. Both boys survived the war and were fortunate enough not to get wounded or gassed with the German's poison gas.

When they came home, Bartlesville, Oklahoma was still growing and both boys got pretty high-paying and dangerous jobs — driving nitro-glycerine trucks, hauling the liquid explosive to the oil fields. Nitro is very volatile and the hard rubber tired trucks traveling over the rough roads of those days (no asphalt paving) made it dangerous! There were three drivers, the Long brothers and one of their friends. The story goes that one day it rained and Dad had a delivery to make. As his truck was climbing "44 Hill" in the Osage Hills west of Bartlesville, the slick clay road caused his truck to start sliding backwards. He applied the brakes, but it kept sliding on back, veered off the road and the back of the truck bed bumped into a tree. He said he just sat there and shook for a few minutes. When he returned to town after being pulled up the hill and making his delivery, he was told that his friend, not his brother, had been killed when his truck had exploded that morning at another location. He said they told him the only thing they found of the driver was one of his thumbs. When Dad and his brother Walt got over the shock, they went to work the next morning and handed their truck keys to the boss and started looking for another job.

Uncle Walt loved horses and mules and got a job hauling oil field pipe on wagons pulled by six-mule teams. He traveled all over that part of Oklahoma doing this for a number of years. He was one hell of a mule skinner! He was a big and tall man, while my Dad was a small, short man. They nicknamed my Dad, "Shorty Long." I think that stuck with him all his life. Dad worked at several jobs then he decided to go into business for himself. He rented a good-sized building on West 3rd Street, a good business location, and opened a tire store. He also sold gasoline and oil from his filling station. Bartlesville was a pretty prosperous town because of the oil boom, so lots of cars were being sold. Business was good at Dad's store and station. This was before Western Auto, Goodyear Tire Stores, Montgomery Ward and Sears. They all came along later selling tires. So business was good.

A story Dad used to tell was that the Osage Indians were pretty rich with oil money and they would buy a new Buick or other new car and then when their milk cow would get out, they might just drive their new car to try to get her back. If they scratched their car up pretty badly, they would just go to town and buy a new one. Or maybe, they would get drunk and get their car stuck and just sit there and try to get it out of the mud until they burned up the engine. Wild times, huh?

Along about this time, my Grandfather Henderson was in his second 4-year term as Sheriff and his daughter, my mother, had learned to drive. She would buy the gas for her car at Dad's station. This is how my Dad and Mom met. She and Dad were about the same height. Mom weighed only 98 pounds when she was married and was about 5'1" or 5'2" tall. They made a well-matched pair. About a year later, Andrew Edward Long was born on November 17, 1924 and weighed ten pounds. Hard to believe, huh? Their business was good for four or five years until our country went into the grips of the Great Depression.

When the Depression grew worse is when my Grandmother and Grandfather and Uncle Jack and his wife, Cora, bought the big farm and this is when my Mother and Dad and my sister, Marjorie, and I all moved into the large, two-story farm home. I was about five years old and Marge was about three. Marge had long blond hair, and Mom would spend a lot of time curling it. She was a pretty little girl. She grew into a beautiful young lady with a very winning personality. Times were tough, but we had plenty to eat on the farm and an abundance of family love.

When I was 7 or 8, I fell from an apple tree at my grandparent's home and caught my chin on a nearby clothesline. My mouth was snapped shut so hard it chipped part of my lower front tooth. (This tooth remained chipped all my life, until I had all my teeth pulled at age 76 in 2001.) This fall could easily have broken my neck! I was very lucky! Then when I was twelve, I was visiting my cousin, Dorothy Jean Henderson, in Dewey, Oklahoma in 1936 when she and I climbed onto the roof of my uncle's garage. When we decided to get down, I eased down to the edge of the roof, then I bent my legs back to touch the wall, but it was too far from the wall to the edge and I fell straight down and landed on the top of my head. I didn't hurt my head, but I did dislocate my right elbow, and the elbow was slightly broken. I carried a bucket of sand around with me all summer, but my arm did not ever straighten out fully. This ruined my dad's dream of me becoming a big league baseball pitcher. My right arm is still about a half inch shorter than my left arm. Luckily, the fall did not break my neck — I cheated death for the second time at 12 years of age.

I was baptized in the First Christian Church in Bartlesville. I was too young to remember, but I do know that I was baptised. The thing I remember most of my early childhood is that every Sunday morning, rain or shine, hot or cold, my mother dressed up my sister Marjorie Marie and me and the three of us went to Sunday School (but rarely to church when we were young). When I was in Junior High School I attended the First Christian Church at Dewey, Oklahoma, a town about four miles north of Bartlesville where we lived. Reverend Venable furnished the car, a 1935 Ford, and our male teacher drove our class to Silom Springs, Arkansas to a church camp. I remember that he drove so fast he burned up the engine!

I attended the Limestone Junior High School at Bartlesville, and the Bartlesville Junior High School. My special friends in Junior High were Neil Montgomery, Dick McCarthy, Paul Fipps, Clara Jean Dilley, Imogene Fox, Stanley Moran, Bob and Ben Toth, Fred Skinner, John Earl Ness, Jack Stout, Troy White, Lester Warner, Buck Jacobson, Bob Scruggs, and Carl Statts. A Junior High teacher that I remember was Mrs. Littlejohn at Limestone School. Memories I have of this time are playing with my friends on Coon Creek, fishing, hunting rabbits, and catching frogs, playing rubber guns, Neil Montgomery and I getting sick drinking his dad's home brew, and the day I whipped the neighborhood bully, Billy Stinger, a fat kid. I hit him hard in his fat belly and knocked the wind out of him and it was all over. Also, the night Duck Jacobson, a left-handed kid, whipped me. This was my first experience with a left-hander. What a fight!

When I was around 14, in the 8th grade at Limestone School in Bartleville, Oklahoma, I was pitching a softball and Jack Stout, a large kid, batted the ball very hard straight back at me and struck me in the heart. It knocked me out and they thought it had killed me, but I regained conciousness and for the third time I survived death. Then, when I was a young boy scout we all went for an overnight campout at Sandcreek Boy Scout Camp west of Bartlesville. I was just learning to swim and the other boys and I went into the creek, but as we tried to swim across the creek, I couldn't make it. I was struggling and thought I was going to drown when an older Eagle Scout dove in and saved my life and once again I cheated death.

I attended Dewey High School in Dewey, Oklahoma. Special friends were Bill Claibourne, Cal Claibourne, Kenneth Monroe, Ray Amos, Wally Lacefield, Winefred Lusk, Bob and Ray Johnson, and Carl and George Ropp. Teachers I remember are Miss Jane Mathis for math and algebra, Miss Reaves for English, Mr. Hill for American history, Mr. Pope for shop, Mr. Houlk for mechanical drawing, Mr. George Tiner was the principal, Mr. Millard Means for music, and Mr. Clodfelter, the superintendent. Outstanding memories from High School are of playing in the band (drums), riding our bikes, and on Halloween ringing the fire bell at City Hall and driving the town marshall, Bill Smith, nuts turning over outdoor toilets, hunting and fishing with my friends, our pool games on Saturday nights and getting a pint of bootleg whiskey or going to the Preview picture show.

In November of 1941 I was a 17 year old senior at Dewey High School in Dewey, Oklahoma. The school had a program for seniors to work half-days at a local business and get school credit, if their grades were good enough to qualify. It was called Occupational Education. My job was working at the local cleaners and pressers, run by Liter and Mildred Bothe. I worked from 1 pm to 6 pm weekdays and all day on Saturdays. All the students earned the same pay, which was $2 per week. I was happy with my job and eager to learn an occupation. One day I had a terrible stomach ache. Liter suggested I go across the street and have the druggist mix me some caster oil in a coke. So I did. Well, it got worse. Much worse. So away we go to the hospital in Bartlesville. I had a ruptured appendix. My parents were panicked! (Just a few years earlier my little five-year-old cousin, Phyllis Joy Henderson, had died of a ruptured appendix.) Dr. Weber said he would have to operate immediately. It was a mess! A new experimental drug, called sulfa, had just been developed, so Dr. Weber filled my lower stomach cavity with the sulfa drug and he miraculously saved my life. I cheated death again at age 17. While I was convalescing, the Japs bombed Pearl Harbor on December 7th. I was just starting to walk a little and I remember I was walking across the living room when the announcement came over the radio about Pearl Harbor.

I graduated from Dewey High School in the Spring of 1942. As a result of my experience at Bothe Cleaners, I was able to get a real job at an old established cleaners in Bartlesville called Bateman Cleaners. From $2 a week to $20 a week, driving the delivery truck and meeting customers. This lasted a few months. By this time the war was in full swing, and all the young men wanted to do their part. Some of my buddies came by where I worked and talked me into going with them to Parsons, Kansas some forty miles from Dewey. There was a munitions plant there and we all thought that we could help out in the war effort and make some good money at the same time. I was still only 17 1/2 years old.

So, I quit my job at the cleaners and we all packed our $3 suitcases and hopped a freight train from Dewey, Oklahoma to Parsons, Kansas. We were nearing Parsons in the late afternoon when we got to talking to a hobo and he told us that we had better get ready to jump off the train before it got all the way in because of a very tough old railroad bull that was there to protect the trains around Parsons from sabotage. He scared the hell out of us, so as the train slowed to around 10 miles per hour we tossed out our suitcases and we followed. All four of us — Andy Long, Wally Lacefield, Ray Amos, and Winefred Lusk (nicknamed "Weinie"). Clothes scattered and skinned up some, we went on in to Parsons and got a room for the night. The next morning we inquired at the unemployment office about a job. We were told we were all too young, but that they were building an air force training base at Independence, Kansas a few miles away and maybe we could get work there. So, we caught a streetcar to Independence and sure enough, we got jobs.

They were building large concrete sewer pipes, about 6-8 feet in diameter. My job was to build the lip on the top edge of the large concrete pipes. We had to lift a large steel ring from on top of the pipe, then pour concrete in the ring form so the pipes would fit together. One day I was working with a big, young black guy and we were tilting the large steel ring in place (it weighed about 300 lbs.). We were lifting together, when for some reason he turned loose, and I was left trying to hold the whole thing. I felt a terrible sting in the lower right side of my stomach. A trip to the Lock Joint Pipe Company's doctor in Independence, Kansas confirmed I had a hernia. I told the lady where the four of us had room and board that I would have to leave and go to Bartlesville and tell my folks of my pending operation. I stepped to the phone and asked what time the next freight train went south and they said in about 30 minutes.

I caught it and showed up at my dad's office with coal dust and cinder smell and announced that I had a rupture and would have to go back to Independence for an operation. Quite a shock to Mom and Dad! In a day or two, Mom and I caught a passenger train to Independence and I had the operation. Everything went well and they told me that I would have to be in the hospital for two weeks with the foot of my bed raised 14 inches higher than the head. The first day I was in the hospital, they moved in a 7 or 8 year-old boy screaming from a broken leg. He was a momma's boy deluxe, and he bawled and squawled continuously. The wailing threw me into shock, and a perfectly good operation suddenly became a very serious situation. They said they almost lost me. They bathed me in alcohol and managed to save my life and moved the spoiled kid out of my room. So, again at 17 1/2 I cheated death one more time.

While I was convalescing from my hernia operation, I turned 18 on November 17, 1942. A lot of my friends were joining different parts of the armed forces. I thought I preferred the navy instead of the army or marines. I had become an accomplished drummer. Since I was a young teenager I had been taking drum lessons from an old music teacher, Isaac Allen Delano Luther (who also taught my son, Tim, many years later). Ike was a real character. He took me on as a student when I was a drummer with the Sons of the American Legion Drum and Bugle Corp. (My father was a World War I veteran and a member of the American Legion.) Anyway, Ike suggested that I try to get into the Navy School of Music and perhaps be stationed on a large cruiser, battleship or aircraft carrier, as those are the only ships that had a band on board. I did inquire, and I passed their test with a "B" grade. While I was waiting for futher instructions, the armed forces decided to close enlistments in the navy, as they needed more men in the army. So that blew up my dream of getting on a large ship in the Navy Band. By this time I was draft age, and I was very disappointed.

In the meantime though, my grandfather was getting old and sick and he needed help on his farm. He said he could get me a deferment from the draft if I would come and work on the farm. I grew up on the farm when I was a young boy and I knew how to do most of that kind of work as I had spent most summers helping out working with my favorite uncle, L.D. Henderson. He was only seven years older than me and he taught me about all kinds of farm work. How to milk a cow, ride a horse, harnace a team of horses, shoe a horse, build fences, bale hay and drive a tractor. So, at 18, I could take his place. He had gotten married and had a couple of beautiful baby girls. He also wanted to help in the war effort and moved to California to work as a welder in the shipyards. So, I would be taking his place on the farm. $30 a month and room and board — $1 a day. This worked out fairly well for several months, but I became more and more bored. I would go to town on Saturday afternoon with my grandmother to sell her eggs and cream, and my grandparents would let me take the car on Saturday nights to go to the picture show or to a dance.

Almost all the young men I knew were in the service and I felt out of place. People would look at me like I was a shirker or draft dodger. I wasn't, I was on a deferment, but that didn't help my feelings, though. One Saturday night I ran into a classmate of mine from high school, Jack Bales, at a dance. We had a great visit and he spent a couple of days with me on the farm. He had joined the Merchant Marines. He told me all about it and I knew almost immediately that I would like to do that too. Especially when he told me how much money they paid! He said it was dangerous and that is why it paid so well. He said he could make a three month trip and come home with $1,200. And, if he got sunk, he would get $600 to replace his clothes. Wow, I thought! When you compare that with the $30 a month I was earning on the farm, I knew what I wanted to do!

My grandfather's health became worse and the farm was put up for sale. I knew that a younger cousin of mine, Jackie Henderson, could take my place on the farm, so I announced I was planning to join the Merchant Marines and see the world. A letter to their address in Oklahoma City produced a train ticket to sign my enlistment papers and to take my first physical exam. I passed and a week or two later another train ticket to Oklahoma City arrived to take me to join about two dozen other young enlistees. We were on our way to Kansas City, Missouri for a more rigid physical and then on to New York City. The date was the last part of June 1943. I was 18 1/2 years old, fresh off the farm and green as goose poo-poo. I will never forget seeing the sights of New York City for the first time — Times Square, The Empire State Building, the Statue of Liberty, Coney Island, and the opening up of a world I had never dreamed existed, let alone ever seen before.

Chapter Two

The World War II Years

Andrew Edward Long

Bonnie Jeanne Scott 1943 graduation photo

ABOUT JULY 1ST, 1943 I arrived in New York City with 20 or 30 other young guys on the train from Oklahoma City via Kansas City. We went to the U.S. Maritime Training Center at Sheep's Head Bay for our 3rd and last physical examination. There were about three or four hundred new recruits there. I passed my physical okay and we began our training.

It was just like Boot Camp in the Army or Navy. Lots of marching and obedience training. Learning to take orders, etc. Then we began our swimming training (very strenuous!). We had to learn to swim every which way — how to come up with very vigorous splashing to keep water away from our head, like you would if the surface was burning oil on the water, so that you could get a breath of air, then go back under again and swim under water for several feet to get further away from the burning water surface, and come up for air again and again splashing. Also how you would tie a knot in the legs of your jeans, hold them over your head and try and quickly pull them forward in the air to fill the legs full of air, gather the waist together then pull your upper body up between the legs, thus forming a sort of life support. This was quite a feat, but it would work for a while if the water temperature in the North Atlantic was not freezing cold. Next we had to jump off of a 30-40 foot tower into the water. This is about the height of the ship's deck from the surface of the ocean. This was pretty scary for the first few times! With all of this strenuous training some of the "momma's little darling boys" just couldn't take it. I didn't have too much trouble with it, though, as I was in good shape from the farm work I had done. Then came the lifeboat training. Each ship had two lifeboats on each side of the ship. Each would hold about 15 men. We had to learn how to row in unison and how to rig the sail to make it into a sailboat (no motors!). We did not get shore leave for two weeks and it was very welcome when it did come! This is when those young guys from the southwest and midwest got a chance to see the sights of New York City. This training went on for six weeks, then we were ready to be assigned to a ship. About four new recruits were all they would put on a ship; the rest were old and experienced seamen. The Liberty Ships and older ships the same size only carried 27 men, so about 3 or 4 new ones were about all the old salts could put up with. Two to four new seamen would be thrown in with some of the roughest, toughest older seamen that you can imagine! They couldn't understand why all these "landlubbers" were going to sea anyway. It was tough on the young ones and we grew up fast. My nickname for the first month or so was "you dumb Oklahoma son-of-a-bitch." After a few months it was okay and with a total of 27 to 30 men on board you became pretty darn close.

When my six-week training was over, I received my lifeboat ticket showing I had had the lifeboat training. I was sent on the train from New York City to Boston with six or eight other young ones to ship out from there. I was there about a week or so and then I got the call with one other guy to go to Portland, Maine to go aboard the S. S. City Service Kansas that was discharging its oil cargo and would be sailing in a couple of days. The ship was an old World War I tanker that was owned by the City Service Oil Company and leased to the U. S. Government, running coast-wise from ports in the northeast United States to the Dutch West Indies (Aruba and Curacao) and the northern coast of Venezuela to load oil, then deliver it to New York City, Philadelphia, New Jersey, etc. Each ship could carry about 100,000 barrels of liquid oil or gas. In those days they would try and use any large ship that would float and run half satisfactorily. We would usually run in a convoy with other ships, but this "old rust-bucket," as we called her, would have engine trouble once in a while and then it did get spooky. (To say the least!)

When I first boarded the Kansas, my job was to be the officer's pantryman. I was to work with another young seaman who was the waiter for the officers. His name was Bill Dewald from Vandalia, Illinois. Bill was about 23 years old, an older guy since I was only 18 1/2. We bacame very good friends and our friendship lasted for many, many years until he died in 1995. He had made a trip or two before I came aboard and he taught me my job and what I was supposed to do.

There were three different departments on the ship: the deck department, the engine department, and the stewarts department, headed by the Chief Stewart. Our Chief Stewart was Philip Adrian who was my boss. Then there was the Chief Cook, Karl Hagenback (nicknamed "Dutch"). Karl was German born and came to Chicago and Philadelphia as a young man. His father was wealthy and he sent young Karl to the United States to become a doctor. But, as the story goes, it was during the time of prohibition and Dutch got in with the wrong crowd and fast money and at one time he was with the Dillinger Gang. He was a tough old guy that spoke broken English. I say old, I think he must have been 45-48 years old then. He was a very good cook and he and the Captain of the ship were good friends. The Captain was a young Italian, I don't remember his name, but I do remember he was the youngest captain going to sea on a Merchant ship at that time. He was about 40 years old. He would buy a case of Scotch whiskey when we left port in the States and it would last him for two weeks unitl we would hit port in Aruba or Curacao, etc. Then he would buy a case of Rum to last him until we got back to a U.S. port. He was so scared, he would stay drunk most of the time.

One of the funniest stories about Dutch and the Captain is this: Once in a while he would have breakfast, not often, but when he would Bill Dewald would order his breakfast, such as two eggs over easy, crisp bacon, buttered toast, etc. Dutch would fix it up just perfect for his friend, the Captain. Sly Bill Dewald one day thought he would have some fun. The Captain didn't come in for breakfast that day, but Bill gave Dutch the breakfast order as the Captain would order. And when he got everyone else served, he ordered this like it was for the Captain. Dutch fixed it up so nice this morning and Bill proceeded to eat it himself. Well, Dutch came into the officer's salon (dining room) and no Captain was there, but Bill Dewald was eating the beautiful breakfast that Dutch had prepared for the Captain. Was he pissed off! Dutch and Phil Adrian were alcoholics, but they did not drink on board ship (only the Captain). However, when we would hit port and when Dutch got supper prepared and over with, then he would take off for some drinks — lots of drinks. Dutch's helper, the Galley Boy, was a large young Dutch boy and when we would hit port Dutch would come to me and say, "Andy, I will have Hans do your work at supper time and you can go ashore and here is some money. You bring me back a quart of Gin." So that is what I would do. I would catch a cab and go to a liquor store for his Gin and, of course, I would take time for a drink or two myself before returning to the ship with Dutch's Gin. This way Dutch could start drinking early and be half-crocked by the time he got everyone served. Then he would take me with him to make sure I could take care of him and make sure he would get back to the ship. We had some great times. He knew lots of places along the waterfront and lots of people. One time in Philadelphia he took me with him. He said we were going to "2nd and Pine Street in Philly" to visit Polack Annie. She had been Dillinger's girl friend at one time.

My second trip on the S. S. Kansas was around the first part of October 1943 and we left port from Philadelphia and in a couple of weeks we were in Puerto La Cruz, Venezuela. By this time all the crew knew each other pretty well, especially in the Stewards Department. Each night after supper we would meet in the cook's cabin — Dutch Hagenback, Phil Adrian, Bill Dewald and Andy Long - and the four of us would play Poker. I did not know how to play and it took me the whole of the first trip to learn. So most of my pay was spent learning and quite a lot of my second trip's pay was lost also. Dutch would keep book of how much each one would win or lose each night and when we would make port we would pay up or collect our winnings. I didn't win much the second trip, but I did finally become a pretty good Poker player by the third trip. (I remember Dutch had a small portable record player, but only one record. I can't remember the song but it was a very pretty love song and we would play it over and over.)

The trips to the West Indies and Venezuela were in very hot weather and with no air conditioning on the ship. A lot of times we would sleep out on deck on folding cots. One time I took my cot on deck and put it in the shade of one of the large liferafts (They were set up on an angle so they could be released in case the ship was hit and in danger of sinking.) Well, I went to sleep in the shade but when the sun moved around, I was in the sun in my shorts and the backs of my legs got very, very sunburned. I learned how to put vinegar and soda on sunburns, it literally boils out the heat. Once in the pantry where I worked, one of the deckhands was going to get a cup of coffee out of the large coffee tanker. He turned it up some way or another and hot coffee spilled out all over his bare chest. They treated his scalded chest with vinegar and soda. That happened before my sunburned legs, so I knew what to do when it happened.

To give you an idea of just how old and filthy this old ship was, at night when the cook would clean out the Galley he would take a gallon fruit tin can, grease the inside with butter and put some bread crumbs in the can - and the next morning he would have an inch or more of cockroachs in the can to dump over the side of the ship.

My job, as I said, was pantryman and my duties were to make coffee in the large coffee maker twice a day, wash the officer's dishes, dish up the desserts, etc., slice the grapefruit or oranges of a morning, and assist Bill Dewald, my buddy, who was the officer's messboy, or waiter. Also Bill took care of cleaning the Captain's cabin. I took care of cleaning the Chief Engineer's cabin.

The last trip I made on the Kansas (third trip) was to Los Piedras, Venezuala. Well, Dutch and the galleyboy, Hans, and I went ashore. It was just a very small village and the mountains seemed to start up almost from the seashore. Huge mountains and beautiful. Anyway, we caught a little sort of an old panelled Ford taxi up the mountain to a small bar with a shady thatched roof outside where the natives played music. Well, we all three had more to drink than we should have and we all passed out. The next morning we were awakened by the same little car and the driver, who was honking the horn and yelling "the ship she pulled out, the ship she pulled out." We panicked and down the mountain we went in the taxi, over the very bumpy road. Well, the ship was blowing its whistle a lot and very lucky for us it was another ship that had pulled out, not ours. (If Dutch had not been with me and Hans, we would have been left, but our ship had to have a cook so they could not leave without Dutch.)

I was still pretty green, not yet 19 years old. One day we were near port and the Steward, Phil Adrian, was cleaning out the big walk-in ice box. No refrigerator, it was just a huge ice box with big cakes of ice. Dutch told me to go down below and tell Phil to give me that rabbit and that we were going to have Welch Rabbit for supper. Well, I did go and tell Phil that Dutch wanted him to send up the rabbit for supper. He said, "What rabbit?" I said that Dutch said he was going to cook Welch Rabbit for supper. He said, "You dumb Oklahoma son-of-a-bitch! Welch Rabbit is not made with rabbit meat." So, I still had my nickname.

We docked in New York City and I had a 30-day leave coming, so I caught a train home for Christmas with my mother, dad, sister, and little brother in Wichita, Kansas. Dad had gotten a job at Boeing Aircraft Plant building bombers. My sister was a senior in high school and my brother was in the first grade. I had a wonderful leave time and I drove down to Bartlesville, Oklahoma to visit my grandmother and uncles. My grandfather had passed away in September while I was on my second trip. I went to a Saturday night dance at the Silver Castle nightclub and ran into one of my friends from Bartlesville, and low and behold, found out that he had joined the Merchant Marines shortly after I had. He asked me where I was shipping out of and I said New York. He suggested we both ship out together from Galveston, Texas, as it would be closer and warmer than New York City in the winter. So, that is what we did. Mack Blevins and I started a close friendship in January 1944 that has lasted for 57 years.

We joined the National Maritime Union in Galveston, Texas and it opened up a much better deal for us. The old City Service Kansas was an old non-union ship and from this time on we sailed more modern ships, both tankers and freighters, and troop ships; all in good shape and our pay was also better. We caught a brand new troop ship that had just been fitted out and sailed from Galveston, Texas to New York without any troops to load troops bound for England. Her name was the Sea Porpoise and she was owned by the United States Lines. She could hold 6,000 troops plus the ship's crew of 34 seamen to run her. We were only on her from the first part of February 1944 to the middle of February 1944. We signed off in order to avoid the very cold North Atlantic and signed on a ship that would be in warmer water.

We signed on the S. S. Winchester February 17, 1944. She was a wonderful ship — a large new tanker that was powered by a steam turbine engine and was much faster than the old ships and the Liberty Ships whose top speed was around 11 knots (about 12 miles per hour). The S. S. Winchester could go at a top speed of 19 knots (around 20 miles per hour). Nice and clean and air conditioned! We caught her at Hoboken, New Jersey and sailed right away for Curacao, Dutch West Indies to load 280,000 barrels of airplane gasoline and a deck cargo of Air Force fighter planes. They were P-38's and P-51's. This time Mack and I signed on as wipers in the engine room. Wipers were maintenance men who worked a straight eight hour shift, 8:00 AM to 5:00 PM, with an hour off for lunch and two 15 minute coffee breaks, one at 10:00 AM and one at 3:00 PM.

It took a couple of days to pump off our gasoline cargo and before sunup we left Curacao and ran together with nine other fast tankers just like ours off the north coast of Venezuela. That made up the convoy of ten fast tankers loaded with gasoline and deisel fuel for planes, trucks, and tanks. At sunrise we left in a north-easterly direction without escort of any kind. Because of our 19 knots speed we could outrun the submarines.

Several days of sailing and we were at the Azores, islands off the coast of western North Africa. At this time we realized the convoy had picked up an escort of small destroyers known as "D.E.'s" They were outside our view on the perimeters of the convoy. One morning we passed a Spanish fishing boat and one of our escorts circled it for a while, and it took off in a soutwestern direction. We were then several hours away from the Straits of Gibralter where you enter the Mediterranean Sea from the Atlantic. This ship channel begins to narrow somewhat in this area. Of course, none of us crewmen knew our destination, but by this time we knew we had to be headed for North Africa. Around 3:00 PM, Mack and I were on the fantail of the ship having our coffee break when we heard a tremendous explosion and the tanker on our port side was totally engulfed in flames and was sinking. Well, all the other ships were blowing their steam whistles, sounding alarms and started a zigzagging course. Several of us started running down the stairs to get our life jackets and we were locked up in the stairway with our gun crew who were trying to come up on deck to get to their gun locations. We backed up and let the gunners come up, then we went below to get our life jackets. The few minutes that followed were the most fearful and exciting time of my life, before and since. As I said, the Strait had narrowed and the 10 tankers were in close proximity to each other. Later we deduced that the Spanish fishing boat had radioed our course to a German submarine and that they located themselves on the ocean bottom where our convoy would have to pass over them. All they had to do was to come up to periscope depth and fire a torpedo into the tanker on our port side. Several of the small D.E. escorts came in among the convoy and started throwing depth charges and, indeed, they were successful in sinking the German submarine. So, I cheated death once again. We were relieved that we were not hit because we would have all been killed. With 280,000 barrels of airplane fuel there would have been no escape. The ship that was hit was lost with all hands.

This called for some soul-searching for Mack and I, and we had heard that there was a recruiting place in New York City and that they were hiring truck drivers to sign up to drive trucks to haul supplies over the Burma Road in China and the Pacific Theater. We decided that we would port in New York. That was sort of a "soldier of fortune" job and shouldn't be any more dangerous that sailing tankers. Anyway, we steamed on into our destination in the Mediterranean Sea — Algiers, North Africa, where they started pumping off our cargo of airplane fuel.

On our last leave before we sailed on the S. S. Winchester, June 1944, I had met the most beautiful girl I had ever seen, Bonnie Jeanne Scott, at my parent's home in Wichita, Kansas. She was my sister Marge's best friend. I was nineteen years old and she was eighteen years old. I had dated her several times and had even taught her how to dance while on leave. I even had marriage on my mind. So, when we went ashore in Algiers the first thing I did was send a telegram to Bonnie in Wichita, Kansas. It was a short one, as I couldn't say where I was. All it said was "Do nothing unitl I get home." There was a soldier that also thought she was something special, and I wanted her to know I was very interested in her.

The reason the fast tanker convoy had entered the Mediterranean was that the Armed Forces were ready to open a second front on the so-called "Soft Underbelly of Europe" and this fuel we carried, as well as the fighter planes, were badly needed. Mack and I went ashore in Algiers for the day and had a ball! We had strapped four cartons of cigarettes to our legs, and wrapped two sheets (which the Arabs liked to use as robes) each around our waists and filled our pockets with bars of soap. We were able to get a very good price from the Algerian peddlers to trade them for souveniers to take home. We had quite a time in Algiers! We even went up into the Casbar, which was off limits to the Army and Navy, but not to the merchant seamen — an unforgetable experience. We were told to be sure we had some sort of a weapon when we went ashore, so I had a large knife that my dad had made me from a file and with a poured aluminum handle on it. Luckily, I never had to use it, but it did allow comfort.

When our ship returned to New York City we checked into the Burma Road idea we had. They said that, indeed, they were hiring and the first thing they asked us: "Are you married?" Because of the danger they did not hire married men. Mack and I said that we would think it over. Well, both of us sort of had marriage on our minds, at least I did, and after talking it over we decided that what we should do was start sailing freighters or troop ships instead of tankers. They were safer. The troop ships had better protection and freighters cargo in most cases, unless they were carring munitions, were a lot safer than tankers loaded with gasoline.

Mack Blevins and Andy Long had a well-deserved leave coming and we caught a train home. Mack came to Wichita and dated my sister, Marjorie, and Bonnie and I made a foursome. We had a wonderful time! Marje had just graduated from high school and had accepted a job at the Pentagon in Washington, D. C.

When our 30-day leave was about over, Mack and I had heard that sometimes service men could hitch a ride on brand new Army airplanes. So, we checked this out and sure enough, Beach Aircraft in Wichita, Kansas was building small 5-passenger, twin-engine planes and they were being flown to the east coast. We took our sea bags out to the Beach plant and they had one ready to go. A young Airforce lieutenant was the ferry pilot. He asked if we had parachutes. Our answer, of course, was "no." We decided we probably would not need them anyway. After some hesitation, the young lieutenant said, "Well just remember you guys told me you do have parachutes." We said, "okay, let's go." This was a brand new plane and the lieutenant had never flown one of this particular type of plane. Off we go into the "wild blue yonder!" We sure didn't want to ride the train back to New York, because when we left New York City to come home on leave the train was so crowded we had to stand up all the way from New York to Chicago, where we finally got seats. We figured we would take our chances without parachutes rather than maybe have to stand up going back to New York City.

Shortly after we left Wichita, we ran into the darndest rain storm, thunder and lightening. That little plane was all over, up and down. What a wild ride! We wondered if we had made the right choice or not. It was very dark and it was getting late in the afternoon when we were nearing Kansas City, Missouri. The pilot said, "Boys, we are going to set her down here and we will take off in the morning at 8:00 AM." So Mack and I got us a room, had supper, and a couple of drinks. We took in a movie and after a good night's sleep had breakfast and a taxi ride to the airport. We boarded the little plane and were off again in a light rain. Well, as we continued on east, the storm grew more intense, up and down, sideways — by late afternoon the pilot said, "Boys we are going to have to set her down in Pittsburg, Pennsylvania." This suited us just fine! We had all we wanted that day.

We stayed all night in Pittsburg about the same as we did in Kansas City the night before and bright and early the next morning we were on our way again to Atlantic City, New Jersey. The storm was over and we had a nice bright day. We arrived in Atlantic City around noon, thanked the pilot and shortly thereafter we took a bus from Atlantic City, New Jersey to New York City that afternoon. So you could say Andy Long had cheated death once again.

While Mack and I were on our 30-day leave and I was in Wichita and Mack was in Bartlesville, Oklahoma, I went down to Dewey, Oklahoma (just outside Bartlesville about four miles). Our leave was about half over and I was visiting my Aunt and Uncle and two cousins at their home in Dewey, Oklahoma. I was standing in their kitchen, the radio was on and they announced that the Americans and British had landed at Normandy and other beaches in France and D-Day had begun. The date was June 6, 1944. Mack and I had arrived at Atlantic City and New York City around June 18, went to the National Maritime Shipping Hall and, as we had planned, signed on a large troop ship, the Sea Serpent. She held around 6,000 Army troops and about June 21, 1944 we headed for England, again as wipers in the engine room, to unload the troops. The trip was fairly uneventful, and about five weeks later we were back in New York on July 27, 1944. The Sea Serpent was a very good, fast ship and made it over to Europe in about two weeks or so. Our job as wipers was fairly easy and we did a lot of painting and I had by now become a pretty darn good painter. It was very hot in the engine room, but we had good quarters and always had good food.

The Merchant Seaman's life was very dangerous, but we felt somewhat better on a troop ship than on the tankers and slower Liberty Ships. They were real sitting ducks! All us seamen had about the same feeling concerning the circumstances and the only way we could cope with the constant fear was to say to ourselves, "If we get torpedoed, our fear and troubles are over. And, if we didn't get hit, we didn't have any thing to worry about." This was our standard attitude. Otherwise, we couldn't have stood the constant fear.

On August 4th we were on our way to England with another load of troops, unloaded them and on our way back to New York City for the second time on the U. S. S. Sea Serpent. Mack and I decided that since it took about 30 days to make the round trip to England, and we had about 30-days leave coming, why didn't we go home on leave and catch the Sea Serpent after she makes another round trip to England.

It was around the middle of September, 1944 when we headed home once again on the train. As always, my Dad, Mom, sister Marge and little brother, John (seven years old), would meet me at the train station in Wichita, Kansas. Bonnie and I had grown quite fond of each other and my whole little family just loved her. I knew she was the girl I wanted to marry. We had written to each other very regularly and I would get quite a stack of letters went I would hit port. When I got home we were inseparable.

We were married on September 27, 1944 at 927 Faulkner Street in Wichita, the home of Mr. and Mrs. McGruder. Bonnie and her sister Dorothy rented the basement apartment from the McGruders. They treated those girls like they were kids of their own. My future brother-in-law, Dwight Stanfield, was my best man. My sister was there as Bonnie's bridesmaid, along with her older sister, Dorothy. My parents and brother, John, and Bonnie's mother were also there. Bonnie's mother, Viola Scott, came to Wichita from Galena, Kansas on the train.

Everything went very well, even though it started raining hard about the time the wedding ceremony began. For years later I would say that if it hadn't been raining, I might have run out, but that was never true. I didn't seize the moment, and as of this year 2001, I have now served sixty-one years of a life-term of marriage with no time off for good behavior! Bonnie was nineteen August 11, 1944 and I would be twenty about six weeks after the wedding.

After the wedding, I drove us to the train station in Dad's car and we almost got hit by a train at a crossing! I slammed the brakes on hard to avoid getting hit and my little brother, John, bumped his head so hard on the windshield that it cracked the glass. No damage to his head except a large goose egg! Bonnie and I and her mother, Viola, boarded the train for Galena, Kansas, about a 100-mile trip, to spend our short honeymoon there with her folks and meet Bonnie's dad and six other sisters, ranging in age from four to fifteen. (Her two brothers were in the army.) John and Viola had ten children in all, healthy and nice looking. Not a dud in the bunch! The three smallest ones were amazed at their big sister's new husband. I had a good time kidding them and teasing them. I had just been paid off from my last trip. I made good money in the Merchant Marines, and I had some one hundred dollar bills in my billfold. I pulled one out and showed it to them and asked them if they had ever seen one before. They immediately ran into the kitchen and said, "Momma, Momma, sister has married a rich man!" Bonnie's dad was quite a character. Very personable, and very smart. He could do about anything he set his mind to do. He had worked in the lead mines in the Galena, Kansas and Joplin, Missouri area. During the depression years he layed rock, block and brick while with the C. C. C. work camp. He was actually an artist with his rock laying ability. I will write more about her dad and mother as this story progresses. We stayed in Galena for seven days and returned to Wichita to Bonnie's apartment. She was then working as a bookkeeper for McKesson Robbins drug store. Soon after that I had to return to the sea.

Mack and I headed back to New York City. We arrived there on the train around the first week of October, 1944. We went to the shipping hall to check on the U.S.S. Sea Serpent, as we had planned when she got back from England. For the next few days we kept a close eye on the large board where they posted the ships that were in port and were hiring. When the Sea Serpents name didn't appear on the board we went to the inner office and inquired as to when she would be in port. The man said, "Haven't you heard about the Sea Serpent being sunk?" He said she had unloaded her troops in England and as she was coming back through the English Channel, she hit a German mine and had gone down all hands. Mack and I were shocked! Had we not gotten off and gone home on leave, we would have been on her and would have been two more dead seamen. My Guardian Angel saved my life one more time!

It was decision time once again for 'ol Mack Blevins and me. Mack said he thought he would quit sailing for a while and go back to Bartlesville. He did and soon after, he got married. I decided to ship out alone and went to the shipping hall and took a job as wiper in the engine room again on a Liberty Ship named The Eugene T. Chamberline. I signed on October 17, 1944. The entire ship was loaded and the cargo was U. S. Army winter gear. Everything the soldiers would need to keep as warm as possible: army blankets, tents, tentstores, combat boots, army overcoats, etc. We headed into the North Atlantic with winter soon approaching.

The U. S. Forces were making good progress since the invasion of Europe at Normandy in June and it was now around the middle of October. After sailing a week or so at 10 or 12 knots we hit the darndest winter storm! It was so bad we lost four or five days making it across the Atlantic.

Our destination was Antwerp, Belgium but, of course, none of the crew knew exactly where we were going. It was secret. There were about 30 or so ships in the convoy with all kinds of war material and armement. The German's probably knew where we would be docking and there were good docking facilities at Antwerp. Well, the Germans rained a tremendous number of V-2 rockets on Antwerp, Belgium and many, many ships were sunk or destroyed in this 'Battle of the Belgium Bulge.' If it had not been for the winter storm that slowed us down getting there, our ship would have been right in the middle of this tremendous disaster. So we pulled into LeHarve, France with our cargo of winter equipment, clothing, etc. Our ship was saved and Andy Long survived another near death experience. LeHarve, France had almost been completely destroyed as our armed forces drove the German's out of that part of France, and from the U. S. bombing raids on the Germans while they were there. All of the bridges were destroyed by the Germans as they evacuated and all the loading docks had been destroyed also. We had to unload our entire cargo with our own steam-driven booms and the Army drove the Army ducks alongside the ship just like an army of ants working. It took about two weeks to unload our cargo. Then homeward bound.

While we were in LeHarve I never went ashore much as the city was obliterated. I did, however, buy a German soldier's helmet and a German hand grenade from a Frenchman. The explosive part of the grenade had been emptied out to make it harmless, but it sure looked real! It was called a potato masher — it had a round wooden handle about 10 inches long fastened to a thin metal canister, about the size of a pork & bean can, that held the explosives. The German soldiers would stick the wooden handles in their belt so they had easy access when they wanted to throw it. The German helmet had the name "Esser." in the inside headband. I still have the helmet as a keepsake, but the potato masher somehow got lost many years ago.

When we left LeHarve we sailed across the English Channel to refuel and take on ballast to make our otherwise empty ship ride much, much smoother. Otherwise she would roll and toss like a bobbing cork. Also we had to pick up clean linen and a new supply of food for our voyage home to New York City. The port we stopped at was the Ilse of Wight, which is just off the southern coast of England. This was not a fun trip by any stretch of the imagination and I have very vivid memories of it. About all there was to do was to work eight hours a day as a wiper cleaning and painting in the engine room. I wasn't too terribly hot this trip as it was in November and into December coming home to New York. It was pretty dangerous as the ship was constantly moving back and forth and up and down. There was lots of climbing around, getting a secure place for your paint bucket, holding on with one hand, trying to reach all the steampipes and plumbing pipes to be painted. We had one rule and it was "one hand for the ship and one hand for yourself to hold on." On this trip there were two wipers, as usual, on a Liberty Ship. Since Mack was not with me this trip, I boarded alone and found out that the other wiper and my roommate for the whole trip was a young kid from New York City. What a blow! This guy had never worked at all! He didn't know how to do anything. He was seasick most of the time, in fact his nickname became "Seasick." He was supposed to do everything I did, but it was almost impossible to get him going.

One day early, as we were in the paint room mixing paint for the day, I couldn't get him to help me do anything and I drew back my fist like I was going to smack him (which was a "no, no" on the ship). My boss, the First Engineer, walked through the door to the paint room and saw me with my fist drawn back and to my surpise he said, "Go ahead and hit him, Andy, I didn't see a thing." The other thing about this guy was that he was so lazy he hardly ever took a shower and hardly ever changed his clothes or did his laundry. You can imagine how our room, "folksel" (as we called our quarters), smelled! The whole room was about ten feet wide by twelve feet long. It had two bunks, an upper and a lower. He was in the upper and me, the lower, so I wouldn't have to look at his messy bed. I spent most of my time writing letters to my new sweet wife and my folks, reading some and most evenings playing Poker in the mess hall. I even made myself a sort of make-shift desk, fastening it to the wall and supported with two legs, so I would have a place to write letters. Bonnie was so good at writing me, I always had several letters when we would get to port.

Our food on the ships was usually very good. Since there were only twenty-seven men plus our gun crew of about ten Navy gunners, it wasn't too much work for one cook and one galley boy. On Thanksgiving Day we had turkey and dressing and all the trimmings and on Christmas Day the same. We were at sea both days. One going and the other coming back to New York.

On New Year's Eve we were about a day from the end of our trip. One of our firemen on this trip, the 8:00 PM - 12:00 Midnight watch, invited me to join him and the oiler and the 3rd Engineer to help them celebrate New Year's Eve with a bottle of gin. No drinking was allowed on the ship, but they figured this was an exception to see the New Year of January 1945 in. So I thanked them and we had quite a bull session and said our "goodbyes" as the next day, January 1st, we would anchor in the Hudson River at the George Washington Street Bridge. We were unable to dock because of the late hour and holiday.

The next day we did dock and I went ashore to celebrate and call home and let Bonnie and my folks know that I would be home in a few days. I had a very good paycheck coming, so I had a "Grand Plan." On the trip that I had taken before this one, on the tanker U.S.S. Winchester, I had gone ashore in Curicao and purchased a very large suitcase — about 10 inches thick, 18 inches high and about 36 inches long made of really good leather. I was always thinking of how I could make some extra money to put away for us to use when the war was over — if I was lucky enough to still be alive. Well, I figured that if I shipped all my belongings home in my seabag and shipped it on my train ticket and not have to carry it, that I could take my large leather suicase empty on the train and when I got to Chicago and had to change train stations, I could catch a taxi cab and take the empty suitcase and have the taxi driver stop at a liquor store and I would buy enough whiskey to fill it up. This is exactly what I did. I got out of the cab and told the driver I would be right back and for him to wait. So, the liquor store man filled it up with Fifths of Old Crow, Four Roses, Seagrams and Jack Daniels. Then the liquor store man said, "You are 21, aren't you?" And I said, "Sure I am." I felt his was a necessary lie under the circumstances. He said, "Have you got something to show me that you're 21?" Well, when I pulled out my I.D. He looked at it and promptly said, "You lying son-of-a-bitch!" I quickly said, "Now wait just a minute and I will be back." I walked to the taxi driver, gave him a hundred dollar bill to take to the liquor store man and to bring back the suitcase of eighteen bottles of whisley to put in the trunk of the taxi, then on our way to the train station. I paid the taxi driver well and got a young black Red Cap, as the porters were called. This suitcase was so heavy that he could hardly carry it. He said, "What in the world have you got in here?" I said, "I have all of my clothing and gear. I'm a seaman and I'll give you $10 (which in those days was about like $100 now) if you can get my bag and suitcase on the train. He looked at my ticket and said, "Come on, follow me and don't say anything." So we headed for the check-in gate and there was such a crowd, as there always was at the train stations as everyone traveled on the trains in those days. The Red Cap told the ticket man that his man has a wife and baby up ahead and he has to get to them. The ticket guy said, "He better have!" We finally got to my train car and he helped me lift the heavy suitcase up on the overhead rack. I moved back about three seats and across the aisle so I could keep an eye out on my booty.

It was all night and the next day on the train before I got to the train station in Wichita. Bonnie, Dad, Mom and John all met me. I had not seen them since the middle of October, 1944 after our wedding September 27th. So being home again was wonderful! I could not let any of them know what was in my suitcase. I also said that I would pick up my sea bag with my gifts for them and all my clothing in the morning and not to take time to get it tonight. Well, we drove to my folk's house, then Bonnie and I took the car to her apartment. I slid the big suitcase under our bed for safe keeping. The next morning I was awakend by my sweet Bonnie's crying, "I've married a bootlegger!" The tears and snot flew for quite a while as Bonnie had been raised as a good little Baptist girl. Even though her dad liked his booze as well as any man, she couldn't stand it that her new husband not only drank some whiskey, he was going to sell the rest! Kansas and Oklahoma were both "dry" states and the only way you could buy whiskey in those states was from a bootlegger by the bottle.

That suitcase was worth a lot of money, as bootlegged whiskey sold for as much as $9 per pint and my bottles were all Fifths, almost twice the size of a pint. Well, finally I convinced her that I would only keep a couple or three bottles and sell the other fifteen Fifths as soon as I could. So early that morning I loaded the suitcase of whiskey in Dad's car and went to downtown Wichita. I went into a barber shop for a haircut and during the haircut I asked the three barbers if they wanted to buy some whiskey very reasonably. They agreed to buy two bottles each, which was $20 each. And I still have eleven Fifths left! The barbers told me the guy next door to the Barber Shop ran a pawn shop and drank a lot of whiskey, so I went in to see him and sure enough, I made a deal on the remaining eleven bottles for $75. So I had gotten out of the whiskey business real fast, but with very little profit after paying the taxi driver and the Red Cap. Harldy worth the effort. But, I was able to glue my new marriage back together!

We had a wonderful time while I has home on leave. We went down to Oklahoma to visit my grandmother and my uncle and his wife. My uncle had taken off work at his job in the shipyards in California until they could get the farm sold. Bonnie had her first experience riding a horse. She would not get on one by herself, so we rode double and I've never gotten her on a horse since. Strictly a city girl! During my trip with Bonnie to Oklahoma, I looked up my old shipmate, Mack Blevins, and he was ready to go back to New York City with me to ship out again. So we arrived in New York at the Shipping Hall around the middle of February, 1945.

Before going home after the Eugene T. Chamberlain got back to New York City from LaHarve and England, I signed on a large diesel freighter. It was by far the best ship I had sailed on! I cannot remember her name for the life of me, but she was a large refrigeration ship. The entire hold of the ship (the large cargo space) was like a very, very large deep freeze; the cargo was sides of hanging beef for the army. The Armed Forces were then in England. Being a diesel-driven ship the engine was huge. The crank case was so large you could stand up in it (if you could get inside the engine!). For 24 hours a day we had to listen to "boom, boom, boom, boom, boom." It was deafening! All day and all night! Instead of two wipers, she had six and we all worked in the engine room all day, 7 days a week. She was as fast as ships go, I think in excess of twenty knots an hour. I feel that the constant noise may have contributed to my hearing loss.

On our trip home she joined about forty other freighters and she was the Commodor, as the master ship of a convoy is called. Quite a few of the other ships in the convoy were loaded with German prisoners the U.S. Army had captured and were to be interred in the U.S. until the "end of this damn war."

The large ship was very clean and the food was good. The wipers were in two cabins, three in each. Each cabin had a port-hole about fourteen inches in diameter. The 1ˢᵗ Engineer was a little guy and like most little men I have known, was a pain in the ass. He was a stickler for cleanliness! That kept all six of us wipers constantly painting and cleaning.

The trip was fairly uneventful until we were about three or four days out of New York. We ran into rough seas and were headed due west when the storm we were in turned into a hurricane coming up the U.S. coastline, offshore some distance. Well, the storm was fierce and worse that any I had experienced before. With the storm moving north and the ship going west it became necessary for us to turn into the storm and change our course to go south, turning right into it and, maybe ride it out. When we did the seas were so high, 25 to 30 feet, it would cover the whole ship! The bow would go down and our stern would go up. When the stern would go up, the twin screws that propelled the ship would come out of the water and would literally thrash the air. Then the bow would come up again and the propellers would be down again propelling us along. It was like riding a pitching horse. As night fell on the worst night, it was difficult for the convoy to stay in formation. Our radio man had many S.O.S. calls from some of the ships. I am sure several of the ships went down and I am also sure some of them were loaded with German soldiers.

Two things I remember most about this was, just before dark the three guys in our cabin decided to unbuckle the hinges on our port-hole to take a look outside. Well, when we did the force of the water coming through the fourteen-inch port-hole was like fourteen inches of water coming out of a firehose! It flooded our cabin with about eight inches of water before we could get the port-hold fastened back. We had single bunk beds with pine railings and we had to tie ourselves in with the ropes crossed over us from side-to-side of the bunk.

Our cabin was not far down the hall (or "gangway" as it is called on ship) from the Mess Hall. All the long tables were bolted to the steel deck and so were the swivel chairs. I sat down with my back to the table and when a huge wave hit the side of the ship, it pitched me out of my chair about eight feet. I just barely got my hands out to cover my face before I slammed into the wall. I have never been as frightened — before or since.

After a very wild night, the seas clamed and there were only nine ships that we could count — out of the forty that were there before the storm. I don't know if the rest of them all sank or just became separated, but since we were the largest and strongest ship in the convoy I know several of them must have sunk. What a way for those prisoners to die! Of course, in those days none of this kind of thing was reported to the press because of news blackouts, so we never heard anything about this. And, 'ol Andy Long escaped death one more time.

The name of this ship, as I mentioned, I cannot remember. It is not even listed on the record of all the other ships I sailed. As I said, forty ships started out and only nine were together when the storm subsided, two days and two nights later. The other thirty-one ships could have easily gone down and this is information that was top secret.

It was after this trip that Mack Blevins and I got back together again and on February 16, 1945 we signed on at the National Maritime Shipping Hall in New York City as firemen and water tenders. This is a combination job on Liberty Ships. Her name was The Casper S. Yost. We had both been studying some books in order to pass the test to get our certificates to sail as firemen-water tenders and oilers. With this designation came the prestige of Petty Officers.

I had the 8:00 AM to 12:00 Noon watch and Mack the 12:00 Noon to 4:00 PM watch. The 4:00 PM to 8:00 AM watch was a large Greek fellow. A tall, good looking guy with a black handlebar mustache. He was always smiling and friendly and we all three became very good friends. He could speak pretty good English. He had gotten his citizenship papers by serving in the U.S. Army before war time and then he joined the Merchant Marines. He had been in about a year longer than Mack and me.

We had signed on the Casper S. Yost February 16, 1945 and it was June 6, 1945 before we arrived back in the U.S.A. We did not know where we were going or how long we would be gone. We didn't know what our cargo was, but a little later we found out that it was general cargo such as typewriters, kegs of nails, corregated sheet metal, and things like that. About the safest cargo that we had carried of all of the other voyages. We sailed south from New York to Trinidad in the Caribbean to refuel, then east into the south Atlantic. We ran a zig-zag course as we were running alone. This would make it harder for a German submarine to get a bead on us. We could not cover too many miles in a day because of zig-zagging, but it was safer. This was the middle of February and the war was still going on in Europe, more of the German subs were operating in European waters, so we didn't have as much to worry about, but if we had any kind of trouble we would be all alone in a hell of a big area of ocean. We didn't go ashore in Trinidad as we had just a day or two to refuel, then we never saw land again for 39 days from when we left on February 16, until we got to Cape Town, South Africa. The waters of the Caribbean and the South Atlantic were indigo blue, which is very deep and the weather was absolutely beautiful! All we ever saw in the 39 days were porpoises and flying fish. No birds, no ships. We just hoped that we wouldn't have any serious engine trouble. Of course, none of the Merchant ships had a doctor of any kind on board. So naturally, you were forced to be very careful. If you were sick you worked anyway. It was one job, one man. No replacements, seven days a week.

In those days South Africa was beautiful, but was pretty much segregated — a way of life there. The city of Cape Town was very old and beautiful. We were there a couple of days and I only went ashore once. I was alone and I spent several hours sight-seeing. We sailed on around the Cape of Good Hope, after unloading some of our cargo at Cape Town, to Port Elizabeth, a beautiful seacoast town on the east coast of South Africa. We were then in the Indian Ocean. We unloaded some more of our miscellaneous cargo, then on up the east coast to New London, South Africa to unload more cargo. I enjoyed sight-seeing and visiting with some of their wonderful people. They are very much like Americans, very friendly, of English, French and European ancestry. Port Elizabeth had a lot of tall apartment buildings where people lived and was a very clean town. Walking down the street at night, the entrances to the apartment buildings would all have a tall, black native with a long spear holding it straight up guarding the entrance of the building. The apartment buildings all had elevators that the residents used. Then, we went further up the coast to Durban, South Africa, the largest of the cities we visited.

When we were in port, the firemen doubled the time we were on watch, as there was not much to do. Instead of working four hours, and having eight hours off, we would work eight hours and have sixteen hours off. This way we could spend six or eight hours ashore and still have time for eight or so hours of sleep. This worked well as this way two of us three firemen could go ashore together and not have to go alone. One bright morning John the Greek, as we called him, and I went in to downtown Durban. John dealry loved his beer so the first thing we did was get a whole case of long neck beer and hire a rickshaw, just like the ones the Chinese have except all decorated up with a tall, black native pulling it. The native had a headdress and leggings with bells and feathers and he whistled loudly — very picturesque! We really had a ball going all over downtown Durban.

We decided to go to the beach and swim in the surf. We had drunk most of the beer by this time and were feeling no pain. It was Friday the 13th of April, 1945, but we didn't give that a thought. So we rented bathing suits. They were the kind that are one piece, just like a woman's, and black in color. The beach was beautiful with almost-white sand, and that day there was three or four feet of surf. We didn't read any signs, we just went directly to the water's edge and waded out a ways and started swimming farther on out. The surf would knock us down and we would get through it and swim on out.

We were out about 50 yards or so, far enough that when we stopped to rest we realized that we could not touch bottom. We decided to start swimming back. About that time we saw people on the beach hollering and waving their arms trying to motion us to come back. If we had stopped long enough to read the signs before we went in, we'd have seen the warning "dangerous undertow." I started swimming as hard as I could, but couldn't seem to gain any distance. I would turn over on my back and swim a little while, but the surf would take me under. I was getting so exhausted! I could just barely touch bottom, but the undertow would pull me farther on out. I looked around for John and couldn't see him anywhere. I thought, "What am I going to tell the guys on ship? What happened to John the Greek?" The next thought I had was that it didn't look like I was going to get back either!

I made one final try to swim as hard as I could and I could just touch the bottom for an instant, then the surf would carry me out a little further. I was so exhausted, I was almost unconscious. Oh, yes, I should have mentioned this before, but earlier that morning we had gotten word that President Franklin D. Roosevelt had died in Hot Springs, Georgia on April 12th. (South Africa time was about twelve hours ahead of the U.S., so it was already Friday the 13th of April in Durban, and the 12th of April in the States.) The thought that ran through my mind as I was struggling for my life was that "Mr. President, it looks like we will meet in hell very shortly." I had never been this close to death and this time, I had time to think about it — and let me tell you, that it is true that your whole life seems to flash before your eyes like a very fast newsreel. This is the only way I can describe what was happening to me.

I would go down and touch bottom, barely, but my head would go under. I was just about gone when I felt someone take hold of my hand or arm and drag me into a boat. This is when I passed out. The next thing I remember was I awoke laying on the beach on my stomach, sunburned somewhat, and the sand was wet around my head where I had vomited salt water. I had never been so tired before. Beside me lay John the Greek. One of the straps on his rented bathing suit was broken. John was a very powerful individual and he had swum so hard that he broke the strap, if you can imagine that!

We were laying side-by-side in the sand and no one else was around. I told him I thought he had drowned and he said when he couldn't swim straight back like I was trying to do, he swam at an angle and was able to make it back to where he could walk almost out, when he passed out. We were both sunburned and so very tired. It was then that we saw the sign that said, "Dangerous Undertow. No Swimming." We dressed in the dressing room and caught a taxi back to the ship.

We both went to bed to rest and to sleep until I was to relieve Mack in the Engine Room. In port, as I said, the fireman was the only one in the entire Engine Room that was on duty. The only thing that we had to do was build enough steam to run the electric generators to furnish electric lights and hot water for the ship. We called it "donkey watch." So, it was very lonesome down there, about five flights of steel stairs, by yourself. I relieved Mack at 4:00 PM and John was still asleep. I would go down to check my pumps and gages, stay about ten minutes, then climb the stairs up to the Mess Hall, stay about ten minutes, then go back down to the Engine Room. This was a "no, no" but I was so nervous I just couldn't stay down there very long. Finally it was time to wake John so he could relieve me. I went into our cabin and found John lying on his stomach. I hollered and touched him, but he would not wake up. I checked to see if he was breathing and, yes he was. He was lying on his stomach as I said, and I could see his heart beating through his back! Well, I went straight to the Chief Engineer's cabin, woke him up, and told him that I could not wake my relief fireman. I also told him what had happened. He immediately went to the Captain and they called an ambulance and took John to the hospital. John remained in the hospital with pneumonia for a week or so while our ship was being loaded with bulk coal. At the same time, Mack and I handled the "donkey watch" in the Engine Room and I began getting my strength back — and my nervous system back to normal!

We were surprised one morning when a family of four — a man, wife, boy and little girl — all Americans, came aboard as passengers. They were missionaries. We enjoyed visiting with them. They had been in South Africa for some time and they enjoyed talking with some Americans. They were on their way to Rio de Janeiro for further service. However, as usual, none of the crew knew where we were going until we were at sea.

We left mid-morning, right after John the Greek was brought back to the ship. We sailed along the east coast of South Africa in the Indian Ocean, went around the Cape of Good Hope past Cape Town, into the south Atlantic Ocean, plugging along at around 10 to 11 knots, with a very heavy shipload of coal, still on a zig-zag course, still mourning the death of our beloved President Franklin D. Roosevelt.

About two weeks later we arrived at Rio de Janeiro, the most beautiful harbor we had ever seen. The skyline of hotels on the white sand beach and the majestic Sugar Loaf Mountain rising high above the coastline. It took a week to ten days to unload the coal, then we moved a short distance to another dock and started loading manganese iron ore — a very heavy cargo.

We had ample time to go ashore and a lot to see. Naturally, the first thing we did was to visit the Chicago Bar (as it was named) for lots of beer. Then on the streetcar to the main part of the beautiul city and arrange to take the cable car up to the top of Sugar Loaf Mountain. It is actually two mountains — the cable car goes to the top of the first mountain where there is a very nice restaurant. We took a second cable car on further up to the top of the second mountain. No businesses there — just for observation and picture taking, which we enjoyed very much. You can see the entire city, the blue beach with white sand shore and the purple and green mountains. Remembering back I must have felt like "Now I have seen it all!" The ride down was breathtaking to say the least.

We spent most of the day touring the city by street car, stopping often to take pictures and shop for gifts to take home (Butterfly trays, which Bonnie and my mother really enjoyed). We also took a cog rail car up to the top of a mountain north of the city where there was a huge statue of Christ called the "Corcovado." The statue was so large that it rose above the clouds on top of the mountain. I have a picture of this — it is amazing! The mountain was so steep that only a cog rail car could be used to go to the top. It was an unforgettable experience.

A night or two later the Marti Gras celebration started. The crowds were tremendous, so very colorful, beautiful costumes, music, singing and dancing. I have never seen anything like it since.

One night I remember I was ashore by myself and it got late. I had a couple of beers too many, maybe. Anyway, I couldn't remember just how to get back to where my ship was docked. I saw a Brazilian policeman. He couldn't speak English, nor could I speak Portugese. So I thought for a minute and I thought about how to say "street car." I said, "Ding, dong, ding, dong." He said, "Ding, dong, ding, dong." I said, "Ship." We both rejoiced and I got back to my ship okay. Another strange thing I remember was so few cars. They did not run on gasoline then, they ran on charcoal. I don't know how it worked. All I know is that it did work.

When our ship was finally fully loaded with manganese ore, we left bright and early. Sad to leave such a beautiful place, but also very happy to be headed home to see my beautiful wife and my family and friends. When we left Rio, it was almost June and we were below the equator and working down in the Engine Room. The heat was almost unbearable! The temperature was around 120-130 degrees and it never cooled off. The fireman/watertender on watch has one place to work, which was about a 12 ft. x 15 ft. space. The floor was steel boiler plate to stand on and we had to position ourself where we could constantly watch our water sight glasses — they were oblong about 14 inches long, positioned about eight feet off the floor, so we could see any fluctuation. There were two sight glasses and that told us how much water that was in each of the two boilers. We didn't dare let it get too low or we could blow up the boiler if we were careless. Constant vigilance, so to speak!

Each of the two boilers, which were about twelve feet square and eight feet tall, was filled with water — fresh water, not salt water (we had to carry a supply on the ship). It took great care to watch our two water pumps that supplied water to the boilers. Each boiler had a firebox that contained four burners that sprayed pre-heated oil thru an atomizer at the end of the burner into a fine spray mist. The pressure of the oil was controlled by a fuel oil pump, a pressure gauge and a temperature guage. The oil went to the burners and through the little atomizers and sprayed in a fine mist. It immediately became a white hot, very bright, ignited spray. Each fireman on his watch had to pull four burners from one firebox each watch. As he pulled each one, one at a time, he immediately replaced it with one that had been cleaned by the fireman on the previous watch. For each burner we changed I had to look through a small peephole to make sure the oil of the new burner lit properly. Most important, or equally so, was to make sure that the steam pressure we were supplying to the engine was of proper pressure. This controlled the speed of the ship.

The difficult part of all this was when, or if, there was an emergency or when the Captain was manuevering the ship, preparing to dock her. He would have to go from full speed to, say, half speed, then maybe slow speed. The firemen would have to really be on the ball to shut off enough burners to reduce the pressure in order to not blow the boilers. This could get a little tricky and it took a lot of concentration to pull it off. The signal would come down to the Engine Room Engineer who was on the watch and near the throttle, so as the signal from the Captain would register on the device that the Captain had, it would show the same to the Engineer in the Engine Room. They tried not to change speed too quickly in order not to blow the boilers. This is why it takes a ship quite a while to stop. There is one hell of a lot of weight in forward motion. It has to take time to slow down and then go into slow, then into stop, then if necessary, into slow astern (reverse). So you see, the firemen has a lot of responsibility. There are only three men in the Engine Room on any watch besides the Wipers — the Engineer, the Oiler, who checks the temperature on all the large engine bearings to make sure they are not overheating and maybe freeze up, and the Fireman-Water tender. All of this is while there is one hell of a lot of constant noise. One day when I first started sailing as a Wiper, I was painting some steam pipes near the boilers and I was just whistling sorta to myself, when the 1st Engineer, who was on his way up hollered, "You dumb son-of-a-bitch! Stop that whistling! I've been looking all over for a steam leak! Don't you know you are not supposed to whistle in the Engine Room?" A steam leak with the high pressure could get very serious! So no more whistling.

It was so hot in the Engine Room, as I said, particularly in the summer, and especially this trip — a lot of it near the Equator. All the firemen only wore their dungarees — no shorts, no shirts, no socks, only shoes. When our watch was over at the end of each four hours, our pants were sopping wet and our shoes were slushing with sweat. When I would get off my watch at 12:00 midnight, I would go out on deck outside of our cabin and sit on a hatch cover and cool off in the cool breeze. There was always a breeze because the ship was moving forward at about ten miles per hour. Up on the top deck there were big round metal wind scoops. They were about two feet in diameter, curved at the top end. The top was about eight feet off the top deck and ran down to the Engine Room. This was how we got fresh air to the Engine Room. It did help. Anyway, after several months of this sweating every day and every night, then cooling off in the cool breeze, I developed some pretty severe bronchitus. I will tell more about this later on in the book. I did enjoy sitting on deck though and cooling off and thinking of home and my beautiful young wife, looking at the moon and the stars and longing for the war to be over so that we could get on with our married life and start a family. This was around the middle of June 1945. The war had just about stopped in Europe, but things were still a mess and things were uncertain.

It was rumored that our destination was probably Baltimore, Maryland near smelters where our cargo of manganese iron ore was headed. We docked on the 20th of June, 1945 and Mack and I went ashore while John the Greek stood his watch. Along the waterfront in Baltimore was a pretty rough area. We stopped at a bar to have some drinks and being young and foolish as we look back now, we didn't take any precautions. We had one beer each and ordered another and got up and walked back to the restroom with our beer glasses full of beer sitting on the bar. When we returned to our barstools and started drinking our beers, we drank those and ordered two more. I started feeling very bad, and felt like I was about to pass out. Mack felt bad also and had one hell of a headache. Mack said, "I think we have been given a mickey, let's get out of here fast!" We did and lucky for us a cab was just driving by. We hailed it and told the driver to take us to our pier number where our ship was docked. I was so sick I started throwing up and the cabbie would stop, then we'd go a little way, then stop again for more vomiting. Mack started doing the same thing. We were so lucky to have gotten out of that bar when we did as we had just been paid off in cash from our long, long voyage and we both had quite a lot of money! We spent the rest of the day and night sleeping and resting and the next day we left for home on the train.

Our trip on the Liberty Ship, the Casper S. Yost, ended June 21, 1945. We had a nice payoff from the long trip, some very nice gifts and souvenirs, and a 30-day leave coming. Being Petty Officers now we were entitled to wear our officer's uniforms and did we look handsome! At least, we thought so. We had a long train ride home to Wichita and Mack came home with me so he could meet my sister. I bought Dad a different car — a 1937 Pontiac. A good one and Bonnie and I and Marge and Mack double-dated. We had some good times, partying and dancing. Then Bonnie and I drove Mack to Bartlesville, Oklahoma to his home and Bonnie and I visited my grandmother and other relatives for a few days.

Dad was still working at Boeing Aircraft and Mom and my little brother, John, were enjoying their summer with me. Bonnie was still working at McKesson Robbins Wholesale Drug Company. Before I got home on this leave, Bonnie had rented her own apartment. We had a more private place to spend our time while I was home on leave. The apartment was near Riverside Park in Wichita. She had a bicycle and it was pleasant for her to walk and ride her bike around in the park, which was very pretty with lots of big trees, etc.

My leave was up around the 20th of July, so Mack and I once again took that long train ride back to New York City and to the Shipping Hall and signed on a large troop ship named the U.S.S. Marine Panther on July 24, 1945.

We had enough of those hot engine rooms, so we signed on as Deck Seamen. Most of our duties were out in the open air standing watch on the bow and climbing up the very high crows nest to stand a four hour watch each day; and also plenty of painting and assisting with the work on deck when leaving the dock and coming into the dock at port time. Pretty enjoyable most of the time, even when it was raining. It was summer, so it was pretty nice work. We had a ship load of army troops to help with the mop up in Germany. We landed in Glasgow, Scotland and we had a day to go ashore to the beautiful city on the sea coast with lots of mountains — very scenic. The troops were unloaded there. Most probably were to be used for occupational duty.

Our Marine Panther then steamed on around the west coast of France and Spain and entered the Mediterranean at the Strait of Gibraltar and docked at Marseille, France. We didn't have much time to see the city as we were loading troops to go to help with the coming invasion of Japan. I remember going ashore during the day. The main street was a tree-lined boulevard and very beautiful. The city had escaped any major damage from the war.

It took three or four days to load 6,000 army troops and these guys were all very upset because all of them had almost enough points to be discharged, but not quite enough. Now that most of the fighting was over in Germany, they were going to have to go and join in on the invasion of Japan. Sad sacks to say the least! After loading was complete we steamed out of the Mediterranean into the Atlantic in a south-western direction and headed for the long journey toward the Panama Canal.

Just before we had reached Marseille, we had gotten information from the radio operator (our only means of news) about the United States testing an enormous bomb in the New Mexico desert. Several days later we heard more news — the U.S. had dropped an atomic bomb on Hiroshima, Japan. We kept steaming southwest for several more days, then another bit of information that another bomb had been dropped on Nagasaki. We kept on steaming the same direction. Then in a few more days, we got news that the Japs had surrendered and the war was over. Naturally, everyone, including the soldiers, were very happy. The soldiers were relieved as they knew a large number of them would have been killed otherwise, but now they were sad that they would have to go over and serve occupational duty and that was a bummer as we kept on steaming southwest. About three days later (as I recall it was cloudy and with no sun shining to tell us which direction we were headed) we heard the loudest cheering you can imagine. A lot of the soldiers were on deck and they noticed the wake of the ship was making a sweeping half-moon turn to the right — which meant we were changing course from a southwest direction to a northwest direction — the direction of New York City. Everyone was estatic! They all had ran to the right side of the deck of the ship — the gruff old Captain got on his bull horn and yelld, "You sons-of-bitches! You're going to turn the ship over! Move out all over the deck and keep the ship upright!" So they did. We were still about three or four days out of New York City but it was so wonderful that the World War was over. At least, the fighting part.

It was August 21st when Mack and I signed off the U.S.S. Marine Panther and the celebration had subsided by then. We spent a few days in New York City after calling home and were trying to decide what we were going to do. We went down to the waterfront and the shipping hall to see what jobs were available. On September 8th we signed on the largest tanker in the world at the time — the S. S. Phoenix, a huge ship. We signed on her as firemen/watertenders for her first trip. She was going coastwise to Houston, Texas to load oil and return to New York. We made the trip and decided it was time to go home. We signed off on September 18, 1945. My bronchitus had not improved, so I decided to check with the Coast Guard Hospital on Ellis Island; they handled the Merchant Seamen's medical problems and had their records of service. I made an appointment for a month later, and then Mack and I immediately went home.

I needed to do some deep thinking about my future. I knew that I did not want to be drafted into the army for possible occupational duty in Japan and I did not want to keep on sailing. When I got home I found that Boeing Aircraft Company had completely shut down as the war was over and there was no longer any need for flying fortresses, heavy bombers. The Enola Gay had taken care of that. Dad was out of work.

The four of us — Dad, Mom, Bonnie and I had a very serious discussion. Dad said that with so many people laid off at the airplane factories, it probably would be difficult for him and me to get a job. I agreed and that is when I mentioned that I had been riding the train between New York City and Wichita for the past three years and had noticed the most beautiful cornfields, with cornstalks 10 feet high, in Indiana. I had always said to myself that if I lived through this war I wanted to live in Indiana where the tall corn grows. I also thought that the midwestern area would have lots of manufacturing jobs manufacturing all kinds of things that people would need — like cars, trucks, tractors, washers, dryers, refrigerators, and many other things — whereas Wichita was an airline manufacturing city and now that the war was over, they wouldn't be making many airplanes.

We all decided that we would try Indiana. None of us had lived in Indiana and neither Dad, Mom, nor Bonnie had ever even been there. It would be a big adventure. So we started planning. Dad suggested that we travel as light as possible, just our suitcases. It would be a comfortable trip for the five of us (my brother, John, was in the 2nd or 3rd grade then). We took just what clothes we could get in our suitcases. My folks said they would store their furniture and after we found a place to live they would have it shipped to us in Indiana. I sold my set of trap drums that I had in high school as I decided I didn't need them any longer. The money I got for them helped with our expenses for the trip.

Bright and early one morning we headed northeast to Indiana. I think we made it to St. Louis, Missouri the first night and then to Anderson, Indiana by the next night. This was late September of 1945. The weather was pleasant and it was a nice time to travel. The others saw why I loved Indiana so much. Anderson was a medium-sized town and, indeed, had a lot of automobile manufacturing jobs.

After we looked the town over, we decided this would be the place for us to try and locate. Dad applied for a job the next morning at a company called Delco Reamy. They made car and truck batteries. He got the job and next Monday morning went to work. The next thing was to find a place for us to live. We saw a new two-bedroom house, almost finished, and stopped to talk with the man that was building it. He was living in a small trailer house on the site. He agreed that he would rent it to us. So, we were quite lucky to find a new house to rent, even though it was small. Bonnie had a job at Safeway checking out customers when she first went to Wichita before she worked at McKesson Robins Drug Company, so she easily got a job at Safeway as a checker. Within a few days everything was working out. John was settled in school, too.

It was time for me to return to New York City to keep my appointment at the Coast Guard Hospital. A Dr. Lang examined me. I really liked him. After the examination, he admitted me to the hospital at Ellis Island, just offshore of New York City, for further tests and for observation for 30 days. They were checking for tuberculosus. I called home and explained to Bonnie and my folks and promised to keep them informed by mail. I was very concerned as I had lost a lot of weight (down to 130 lbs.) and was smoking like a chimney. I certainly wanted to find out if I was sick or not.

Ellis Island as you may know is where all of the immigrants were stopped for processing when entering the United States by boat. The hospital was pretty large and well-staffed and a large area around it was nicely landscaped. I was free to roam around outside and it was a fairly pleasant place to be. I got permission two or three times to go into the city by subway. After three years being in and out of New York I was quite capable of going anywhere I wanted to go. The time passed slowly, however, and at the end of 30 days and a lot of tests, Dr. Lang paid me a visit. He gladly informed me there was no tuberculosus, that the spot on my right lung that had showed up on my x-ray must have been from having pheumonia when I was young. I might add the spot was about the size of a quarter and after numerous x-rays since then, it has not changed a bit. The doctor told me my blood was very strong and that my bronchitus had improved and that I should quit smoking.

I then told the doctor that I had been in the Merchant Marines about three years and that I thought that was long enough to serve my country, but that I was only 22 years old and I was still draft age for the army until I was 26 if I quit sailing in the Merchant Marines. He agreed with me that I had served long enough. He scratched his head and was quiet for a couple of minutes. He said that I should not go back to sea for a while and then said, "I am going to give you a medical discharge saying that you are no longer fit for sea duty. This will take care of you not being drafted in the army." I thanked him very graciously and the very next day I caught a train for Anderson, Indiana. I arrived in Anderson on Thanksgiving Day and I realized when my family met me at the train station how much I had to be thankful for. A new life was about to start. It was simply wonderful to be home again with Bonnie and my folks.

Chapter Three

From Our New Life In Indiana To The Cookware Years

Bonnie and Andy with Tim

A FEW DAYS LATER WE met the family that lived next door. Real, nice people. She was a large, fat gal who was very friendly. He was a large man and a building contractor. I asked him if he needed any help. He asked if I had any experience. I told him about my painting experience in the Merchant Marines and that I had experience with all kinds of iron work. He said he would give me a try — the job paid 60 cents an hour. I agreed and the three of us — Dad, Bonnie and I — were all working. John was in school, and Mom kept the place "spic & span" and enjoyed her visits with Mrs. Poore, our new neighbor. Christmas came and went, as did New Years.

Winter had set in and the midewest did have some cold weather. The ground froze hard and digging footings for a house was very difficult. In those days they didn't have backhoes like they do now, and we had to dig the footings for the concrete foundations by pick and shovel. I only weighed about 130 lbs. and I would hit the frozen ground with a pick and it would either sting my hands or the pick point would bounce. It was very hard work. I did enjoy the inside painting, however, especially when the weather was too bad to work outside and I would get to paint inside. With the weather like it was, I didn't get very many hours in, so I didn't make much money at 60 cents an hour! Things were about to change.

Sometime in March of 1946 Dad and Mom got a letter from my Grandmother that the farm had finally sold and that Uncle L.D. Henderson, his wife and two small girls were moving back to California to work in the shipyards that he had worked in before he came back to run the farm after my Grandfather had died in 1943. My Grandmother wrote my mother that she had bought a house and was living alone in Dewey, Oklahoma, a small town north of Bartlesville. She said she would like my Mom and Dad and John to come back to Oklahoma and live with her. It was decision time. Mom was very homesick by this time. The only place that she had ever lived was Oklahoma until moving to Wichita, Kansas during the War. Her mother was not in good health, so she dearly wanted to return to Oklahoma. We all talked it over and decided that it was the thing for them to do. So they moved back to Dewey to be with my Grandmother. Bonnie and I hated to see them leave, but we understood.

I was tired of not making much money due to the cold weather and decided to see about getting another job. I read an ad in the local paper that the Great American Tea Company was looking for a route salesman. The Great American Tea Company was owned by A & P (Atlantic and Pacific Grocery Company) and was very similar to the Jewel Tea Company with which everyone is familiar. I didn't know it at the time, but my career as a salesman was to last for many, many years to come. I got the job at about the time the folks left for Oklahoma. Bonnie and I found the nicest little one-bedroom duplex apartment and rented it. It was located on Highway #67 at the edge of town with a small grocery store and the city bus stop nearby. And, oh, yes...Bonnie announced that she was pregnant! A brand new chapter in our lives was about to begin.

The routes were already established and there were about thirty families that I called on each day, Monday through Friday. There were ten routes, and I called on each route every two weeks. Our mainstay was selling fresh, ground, bagged coffee, among several other items such as soap powders, handsoap, perfumed soap, perfume, powder, small kitchen gadgets, shampoo, candy, spices, etc. I would deliver their order that they gave me the previous time, collect their money, then take their order for the next two week delivery. The district manager's office and warehouse was in Indianapolis about thirty miles away. It was run by a man named Riley, a big, tall Irishman, and his son. They were really nice people. We hit it off immediately and I loved my job. Riley would come up to our house every Saturday and bring up the orders I had sold the week before, pick up the money I had collected and go over the specials that we could offer on the coming week's routes.

I would spend part of Saturday and Sunday loading my truck with the next week's deliveries. Several of my routes were in small towns around Anderson and Muncie, Indiana. I got to know my customers pretty well as I saw them every two weeks. I had to go in a run sometimes to call on that many people each day and it would be dark each night as I would get home to my lovely wife. I would have to send in my weeks report every Saturday night, so we would go downtown in the truck to the Post Office and also take in a movie. No television in those days. Bonnie would have to sit on a wooden box as the panel truck only had one seat for the driver, but we didn't mind. We had no other car.

Bonnie was quite happy as we had another young couple living in the apartment next door and she was pregnant,too. Their names were Merle and Rita Beller. A funny thing we remember was that Rita had a lot of gas on her stomach and she told Bonnie that when she passed gas at night Merle would pull the sheet up over her head so she wouldn't fart in the bed. Bonnie never told me about this for a long, long time because she thought I might do the same thing to her. We remained friends for many years after we moved away.

Another family lived across the highway #67 from us. Wonderful folks. They were in their late 30's or early 40's. They were Alva and Grace Riley with a son and daughter that were young pre-teens. They took us young folks under their wings and were the dearest friends we ever had at that time. Alva ran his auto repair business at his home. He had a small shop and he stayed busy. They always planted a very large garden, so we shared fresh vegetables and watermelon with them often. Grace was a wonderful wife and mother and became a role model for Bonnie. We played a lot of dominoes and cards with them. When our son was born it was Grace that drove Bonnie to the hospital. I followed in the route truck. Grace and Alva fell in love with our baby boy.

I must tell you this funny story. Just a short time before Tim was born, and she was due any day, Bonnie screamed and I just knew it was time. I said, "Is it time, is it time?" She said, "No, I think there's a bug in the bed!" It scared me so bad, I rolled her over, pulled up her nightgown and with my hand, I paddled her butt good. This is the only time I have ever laid a hand on her and she has never has forgotten this little spanking, but she is still afraid of bugs.

A few days later it really was time to go to the hospital and we called Grace Riley and away we went early in the morning. I stayed until the baby was born at 7:15 AM, then I left the hospital and started the day's coffee route. I was so proud of that 7 lb. 2 oz. beautiful baby boy that I told every customer I called on that day and for the rest of the week. His name was Timothy Edward Long, born September 17, 1946. Bonnie had just turned 21 on the past August and I would be 22 years old in two months. Our little family had gotten off to a good start.

Things were going pretty well for us. I liked my job. We had some fine friends. Bonnie had started saving her money for the doctor's bill back in January when she found out she was pregnant. Smart girl! Of course, we had the hospital's bill to pay and we were able to take care of that. She was in the hospital ten days, which was standard procedure in those days.

When we rented the duplex aparmtent, we had to buy some new furniture as we had none. We went to Montgomery Wards, opened a charge account, and got a living room suite, bedroom suite, baby bed, small refrigerator and a little two burner kerosene cook stove with a little portable oven for it. There was no gas utility where we lived, so everyone heated with coal. Even our hot water tank, which we shared with the other apartment heated with coal. Sort of inconvenient, but it worked. We had a large, round coal stove for heat with a round metal chimney from the stove through the ceiling and through the roof. A real dirty "pain in the ass" to build a fire for heat and take a bath, but we managed.

It was beginning to get cold by now in October and November, and one evening the metal round stovepipe to the ceiling was about to come loose. So, I started to fix it and in the process I had coal soot all over my hands and face, and having a hell of a time. Timmy was having the colic and had been crying most of the day and Bonnie was worn out taking care of a sick, crying baby. It was unusual for him to cry, but he was sick. I took the baby from her and sent her to bed. I had coal dust all over my hands, so right away it was on his little blanket, etc. and he cried and cried and cried. I had heard somewhere that if you take a teaspoon of whiskey and light a match under it to burn off the alcohol and give it to the baby it would stop his colic. So, I happened to have a pint of whiskey and decided to try it. I did and it didn't work; he didn't belch any gas, just kept on crying. Well, in a little time I tried it again. Still no luck, he kept crying. So, after a while I thought I would give him another teaspoon full and not burn off the alcohol. I did and he gaged, turned red faced then turned blue faced and I was scared to death. I shook him hard and he let out the loudest belch, like an adult. His color came back and in a few minutes he quit crying, smiled and in a while he was asleep. He never had colic again. I thought for a while I had lost my precious little baby boy. No more colic, and no more whiskey!

I haven't mentioned it before, but there was another Great American Tea Company route and driver besides mine in the Anderson area: Lesha Sears, a very large woman. She had been with them for a long time. She was a great old girl and we got along fine. Lesha lived alone with her beautiful daughter. Her daugher and boyfriend were about to get married. She asked me if I knew of anywhere they could rent an apartment. Well, it so happened that Bonnie and I were getting a little homesick and her folks and mine had been writing us, asking if we could possibly come back to Wichita and Dewey before Christmas. My folks still lived with my Grandmother in Dewey and Bonnie's folks had moved from Galena, Kansas to Wichita. Also, winter was approaching and we remembered how cold it was last winter with the very damp wet cold of Indiana. Bonnie suffered with sinus problems and it seemed to be getting worse, so we got to thinking if we had a car, we might just move back to Wichita. I got my thinking cap on and thought I would talk to Lesha Sears about her daughter.

I asked Lesha if her daugher had a car and she said, "Yes, a little 1936 Plymouth Coupe, a real nice car." I asked her if she and her husband to be had any furniture. She said, "No." Then I asked if she would ask her daughter if she would trade her little car to Bonnie and me for our furniture, and if so, they could take over our duplex apartment and not even have to move the furniture and have a very nice place to live. She said, "Andy, I think this would be great. Let's make it happen." So, about the middle of December 1946 we folded up the baby bed and our clothes and personal belongings and got in our little black 1936 Plymouth Coupe and headed west to Wichita, Kansas after saying goodbye to our friends.

Our first night we stopped in Indianapolis, Indiana at the request of my boss, Mr. Reilly. They had a really nice dinner for us and a great visit. They were such nice folks. He hated to lose me as a driver/salesman, but having children of their own and grandchildren, they understood what we were doing. In our conversations that evening, Mr. Reilly asked me what I was going to do when I got to Wichita. I said, "I don't know yet." He said when he was a younger man he sold Club Aluminum Cookware on the dinner demonstration plan. He said, "Andy, I think you would make a good salesman doing this and you should check this out when you get to Wichita." I thanked him and bright and early the next morning we headed west to Wichita.

My Merchant Marine buddy, Bill DeWald, who I sailed with on my first three trips lived in Vandalia, Illinois. So, we called him up and he said to come on out and spend the night. It had been three and a half years since I had seen him. We had a wonderful visit with him and his wife and the next morning we took off and drove all the way to Galena, Bonnie's hometown, to visit her older brother, Robert Scott, and his wife, Inas, and their little baby boy, David. Bob had been discharged from the Army about the same time as I had gotten out of the Merchant Marines.

The next day we drove to Dewey, Oklahoma (just south of the Kansas line) to see my folks and grandmother. They were so glad to see us and their first grandchild. What a wonderful homecoming! That little Timmy was the most beautiful baby. When we went somewhere, like a restaurant, people would stop and look at him and say, "He is the most beautiful baby we have ever seen." This happened many times and I know Bonnie and I just beamed. I had said several times the reason I married Bonnie was that we would have very good-looking children and grandchildren, and that turned out to be true.

After visiting my folks in Dewey, we drove north about 125 miles to Wichita to Bonnie's mother and dad's home. It was a small two-bedroom home that Bonnie's mother's brother and his wife had bought so that her folks could get out of Galena and relocate to Wichita, where there was more opportunity for them and their other children. Bonnie's mother had wanted to go back to college and get a teaching degree. She had had about one year of teaching before she had married Bonnie's dad. There were six of bonnie's younger sisters still at home— the youngest was in the first grade. Four were out of the nest and married, and six were still at home and in school. The house was small for the eight of them and there was not much room for Bonnie and I and little Timmy.

Right away I bought some material and some linoleum for the floor and Bonnie's dad and I proceeded to make us a little apartment out of their one-car garage. We celebrated Christmas 1946 with them and the next day Bonnie's dad took me to work with him. He was a very good concrete mason and block and brick layer. He had a job for me to mix his mortar for him to lay brick. There was a great need for new housing everywhere and in Wichita especially. A new housing project was just getting started on South Waco Street by Snow Construction with about eighty new homes to be built, all needing concrete block foundations and brick chimneys. All of them had basements and the basement walls were to be concrete block also. So there were a lot of blocks and bricks to be laid. My job paid eighty cents per hour. In an eight-hour day I made $6.40 a day, less withholding. Some job! And hard work, too. Things had to get better.

The superintendent on the job was a big red-nosed Irishman that liked to drink his whiskey, but never on the job. However, Kansas being a "dry state," whiskey was expensive and hard to get. Me being 22 years old and willing to take chances since my days in the Merchant Marines, I had a thought. I had a little money saved, about $100, so I figured if I drove to Joplin, Missouri (near Galena) on the weekend and bought $100 worth of whiskey, all in pint bottles, and drove back to Wichita with the whiskey in the trunk of my little Plymouth Coupe, that I could make a deal with the big Irish superintendant. The deal I had in mind was that I would give him a pint if he would let me go around and take orders with some of the other workers. There must have been fifty or sixty of them to sell a bottle to right after they got off work. I explained that I could mix up my last mortar box full of mud to hold John Scott until quitting time, and give me time to take my orders. The super liked the idea so I put the plan to work. I knew I couldn't keep my scheme from Bonnie's mom very long, but it did last long enough for us to get ahead financially for a while. I was smart enough to know this couldn't last, so I stopped. About this same time I read a want ad in the paper that would, ultimately, make a tremendous change in the life of Andy Long.

I knew I really wanted to get a better job than I had mixing mortor for my father-in-law, John Scott. I had no deisre to be a brick mason, so I started to read the want ads in the Wichita paper. Under Salesmen Wanted the following ad appeared:

"$150 a week easy. Car and sales experience essential." A phone number was listed.

This was February of 1947. When I called, a man answered, "Hello," and I said, "Hello, have you hired that salesman yet?" The man said, "Yes, but I can always use another good salesman." He told me where his office was located on north Market Street and asked me to come in to talk to him about the job the next morning.

The next morning I dressed up in my best outfit and drove to the appointment about the sales job. The man's name was Bill Sontag and the product was Lifetime Stainless Steel Cookware. He said, "This is not aluminum cookware, it is stainless steel. It comes with a lifetime guarantee." He explained that it was sold on the dinner demonstration plan. He was just getting started in his business as the distributor of this new product manufactured by the Reynolds Metal Company in Chicago, Illinois. He said he had just recently hired four other salesman and they were all doing well. He showed me the whole set on a beautiful red spread cloth and explained that the cookware was made of the same metal that doctor's and dentist's surgical instruments are made of. It doesn't stain, rust, crack, warp or wear out. Guaranteed for life.

I was quite impressed. He introduced me to the other four salesmen that he had recently hired and he had their names on a blackboard showing how many dollars and how many sets each salesman had sold the past week. He told me the percentage of the total sales each salesman earned in commission and I was very impressed. He suggested that if I wasn't busy that evening that I go with one of the salesmen who had a dinner demonstration that night to see if he did anything that I couldn't do. If not, then I could go with him the next evening when he made his sales appointments and calls and I could see if he was making any money.

I remember very clearly the names of the four other salesmen — Jerry Herrington, Lloyd Messmer, Vaughn Loomis and Jim Craft. Three of these stayed with Bill and sold lots and lots of cookware and the other one was one of the best salesmen I have ever known — Jerry Herrington. He later changed to selling real estate and started his own company, J. Herrington and Associates.

Anyway, I did go with Jerry Herrington that evening and he was so smooth I just didn't know if I could do like he did or not, but on his sales calls the next night he sold three sets of cookware from the four calls he made. The next night I went with Jim Craft. He was about my age, which was 21. He had just gotten started a couple of weeks earlier, so he wasn't so smooth yet. I felt that I could learn to do as well as Jim Craft. He sold a couple of sets the next night on his sales calls — and I was hooked.

I went with Lloyd Messmer the next night and he was also very good. He had sold WareEver Aluminum Cookware before the war, so he was an experienced cookware salesman but now with a much better product. He was a very good salesman and an excellent detail man so I went with him several times and tried to pattern my style after his. And it worked!

Lloyd was about ten years older than me, Herrington was also about ten years older than I was.

Vaughn Loomis was the other salesman, about five years older than me. He had been a farm boy early in his life like me, so we related well. He had worked at Boeing Airplane Company during World War II and they were laying off workers, so he was trying cookware. He had four kids at this time. Vaughn was probably the hardest worker of us all. He was strictly a country boy, plenty smart, but had a speech impediment, sort of buck-toothed and had the prettiest wife that I had ever seen by this time of my life. He and I and Bonnie and Pauline became very good friends over the many years we sold cookware together, and after that also. (Tim even moved their daughter, Glenda, to Santa Fe in 1973 and they almost got married.)

Vaughn, being a country boy, was much more comfortable selling to the farm families than to city folks. It wasn't long before he was leading all the other salesmen in sales, week after week. Almost all his sales were cash sales because farmers don't get paid by the month like city folks. Cash sales also carried ten percent more in sales commissions than time payment sales.

I started out selling in town because Bonnie and I were still living with Bonnie's folks. Our baby boy was only five months old, so she had to take care of little Timmy. Bonnie's mother agreed to go on my demonstrations as my helper and dishwasher in the kitchen. She was going to Friends University at the time, which was near their home. Her last of ten children was in the first grade and she was finally going back to college to get her teaching degree. What a woman! More about her later. Anyway, she needed a little extra money, so I paid her for about six hours work each of the three nights per week I had a dinner booked. I made my sales on the other three nights of the week — no work on Sundays. This worked out very well until summer, and I noticed Vaughn Loomis's sales were picking up — and all cash sales.

One day I said to Vaughn, "How do you manage to get almost all cash sales?" His answer was a very logical farm boy's answer. "Andy, if you are going to dig tatters, where do you go?" I said, "Where do you go, Vaughn?" He said, "You damn fool, you go to the tater patch, that's where!" He was selling at that time around Cherokee and Alva, Oklahoma. I asked Vaughn if he cared if I went down to the same general area. He said, "I'll do better than that. You go with me on my next dinner party, give the after dinner talk and I will let you have the sales calls and see if you can sell farmers." I jumped at the chance and that is the kind of people that I sold most of my cookware to for a long, long time. I had five calls that next day and I sold five sets, all cash. And booked three more dinners from that first one. It happened to be at a very small town, Burlington, Oklahoma. I promptly rented a furnished apartment for Bonnie and Tim and me and we moved to Cherokee. One reason for my early success was that the price of wheat which the farmers grew was $4 per bushel. And they had a bumper crop that year. Most were getting 100 bushels per acre. I was elated to say the least!

Bill Sontag was a very happy man. Also, all his boys were doing good. Messmer was also selling mostly in the rural areas around Haysville and other small towns closer to Wichita. The Cherokee area where Vaughn and I were selling was about 100 miles from Wichita. We would see our folks every other weekend or so. That was nice for all of us. They were, naturally, happy for us.

Sontag was always trying to get us to hire more salesmen and we would draw a 10% override on their sales. So, I trained a young one who lived at Jet, Oklahoma and his dad also went to work. The father had been selling Rex Air Vacuum Cleaners so I traded him a set of cookware for a Rex Air Vacuum for Bonnie. Their names were Cefus DeFever and Alex DeFever. They both became pretty good salesmen. So, I then had two salesman working under me drawing override. I also traded a small set of cookware to a jeweler in Cherokee for a beautiful chime clock, the kind that sets on a mantle and a circular fan that we certainly enjoyed in our apartment. (There was no air conditioning in those days, so we really needed it.)

The area was getting a little crowded with salesmen by this time, as Vaughn had hired a man, also. Sontag suggested that I move to Blackwell, Oklahoma and so we did. Blackwell was a small town surrounded by wheat country. We had some difficulty finding a place to live, but finally I found a duplex. Each side of it was just alike — two bedrooms, bath, living room, and kitchen. Quite nice as I remember, with a park across the street and about six blocks to downtown. We still had our little black Plymouth Coupe but I thought it was time we got a better car. The Plymouth was a 1936, and it was now the fall of 1947. Cars were pretty scarce then as the war had only been over two years and the supply of new cars had not caught up with the demand. We found a 1941 4-door Chrysler that was in very good shape and we were very happy with it as it was the second car that we had since we left Indiana, about a year earlier.

There were good wheat farms in every direction around Blackwell. I cold-canvassed for a couple of days and booked three dinner parties. From these I sold several sets, all cash, and I was on my way, in a big way, in my brand new territory. A short time later a young couple with a new baby moved in the other side of the duplex. He had just recently been discharged from the Navy and had married his wife in Pittsburgh, Pennsylvania. Strange girl, at least to us, as we weren't used to eastern people. All she did was hold the baby and read love story magazines. When the baby would wet his pants, she would just sit there and read and not bother to get up and change him. So their home had a pretty strange odor as I remember. The husband's name was Max Hawkins. He was about my age, but seemed younger. Anyway, he did not have a job, so I decided I would hire and train him to be a cookware salesman. He picked it up pretty quickly and I had my third salesman under me that I was getting an override on besides my own sales.

Vaughn and Pauline would come over to see us once in a while, as Vaughn was working around Enid, Oklahoma, not too far away. We would go to dances and visit for a day or two and enjoy each other's friendship. We were only a couple of hours from Wichita and Vaughn still lived there. Vaughn would drive out to his territory each week and go home on weekends. We would go to Wichita quite often and with the Loomis's, the Messmer's, and Bill Sontag, go dancing. The men enjoyed doing some drinking, the women didn't drink much. Bill Sontag, our boss, was single, so he would have a lady friend each time we would go out. All four couples became very close friends.

Bill Sontag made us three salesmen his "district managers." We were all making money and having fun. How much better could it get? Working very hard, too, I must say. But we loved it!

I must tell a little story: Christmas time was approaching and we planned on going to Wichita for Christmas to be with our folks and my sister, Marge, and her husband, Dwight Stanfield. So, Christmas morning we got up very early and Bonnie fixed us oatmeal for breakfast. Timmy was about eighteen months old, sitting in his highchair with his bowl of oatmeal with cream and sugar. For some reason he decided to lift his bowl of oatmeal up and turn the bowl over on his head like a hat. He thought he had done something very funny and started laughing. Naturally I started to laugh, too. Well, my sweet wife lost her temper with both Tim and me! Oh, yes! I almost forgot...Bonnie had fixed me some fried eggs and bacon for breakfast and had the plate in her hand when Tim pulled his little stunt. She was so mad at us for thinking it was funny, she threw the plate of eggs and bacon at me and then we really had a mess! I was laughing so hard she drew back her fist and said, "I've just got to hit you!" And, then she hit me on the shoulder. Not real hard, but hard enough to get satisfaction out of her frustration and the mess. Then we all three had another good laugh. What I thought was so funny was that she had to apologize to me before she hit me!

We headed to Wichita and had a wonderful Christmas. It was the first time we had enough money to buy everyone some nice Christmas gifts. We spent the whole week visiting and partying with family and friends — then back to work and getting 1948 started.

Business was still pretty good around Blackwell, but I was beginning to think about where I could find a new territory. I had been there about four or five months. The telephone rang one morning and it was Bill Sontag calling. He said he was getting ready to leave Wichita for Tulsa in a few minutes and said if I wasn't busy he would come through Blackwell and I could go with him. He had gotten a couple of inquiries from two different men about going to work selling Lifetime in the Tulsa area. So, he came by and we both went to Tulsa and met these two fellows at the Tulsa Hotel.

One of them was a young guy about my age that had lived in California for a short time and he had sold Lifetime Stainless Steel there before he moved back to Broken Arrow, Oklahoma. His name was Herman Bowline. The other one was Frank Garrison and he lived in Turley, Oklahoma, also near Tulsa. Bill agreed to hire them, provided they would agree to let me train them. Bill had talked about this while we were driving from Blackwell. He told me that if I would train these guys, and more in Tulsa, he would give me them to add to my override commission. I now had five salesman under me.

I took Bonnie and Tim to Wichita to my folks for a while and I went to Tulsa and checked into the Bliss Hotel, a medium-priced hotel where I would spend the next month. When I started training Bowline, he said he had three buddies who wanted to start training, also. They were Charlie Vaughn, Doc Dodd and Tip Wood. I said, "Ok," and called Frank Garrison at Turley to tell him that it would be two weeks before I could start with his training.

The first night the four new men from Broken Arrow met in my hotel room. We talked cookware and had a few drinks and then Bowline pulled a deck of cards out of his pocket and said, "How would you guys like to play some poker?" We all agreed. Now understand, none of us were over 23 years old. What these guys didn't know was that I had a lot of experience playing poker on the tanker S.S. City Service Kansas during the War. So we started and about two or three hours later I had all of them broke and each one had written me a hundred dollar check to cover their loses.

During the time I was winning their money, the three young wives of these guys started looking for their husbands. They knew that the boys had gone to the Bliss Hotel to meet this cookware man who was going to train them. Well, with all the bawling and squalling and cussing, these girls were upset! Remember, a hundred dollars in those days was like a thousand dollars today. I could see right away that if I wanted to keep these four families interested in becoming cookware people, I had better do something in a hurry. So I said, "Folks, to show you I am a pretty good guy, I'm going to give each of you your checks back." The guys were very happy, and the girls were too, but they did say they had already stopped payment on the checks in the morning anyway. So, no more poker games!

I did get them all trained, including Frank Garrison in Turley, in the next month but in a short time all of them had petered out except Herman Bowline. The rest just weren't old enough to use good judgement in handling their finances to be in business for themselves in the cookware business.

Bowline did very well and sold cookware for several years. He and I became the best of friends and Bonnie and his wife, Wanda, also became very close. Herman's nickname was "Tony," and all his friends call him that. Tony was my friend for 47 years and there will be many, many more stories about Andy Long and Tony Bowline throughout the rest of this book. He was the most unforgettable character I ever met.

There was not much farmland around Tulsa, and I longed to find a good territory with lots of wheat farmers whose wives liked to cook. Their husbands had plenty of money to buy them a good set of Lifetime Stainless Steel Cookware. I contacted my old friend, Mack Blevins, from my Merchant Marine days in Bartlesville (just fifty miles north of Tulsa). I found out he was selling tires for the General Tire Company, so I told him about how well I was doing selling cookware. He got interested and we took off the next morning for Oklahoma City. We drove on through Oklahoma City to El Reno, Oklahoma, thirty-five miles west. We stopped to fill up on gas and I booked a cookware dinner with the fellow that ran the Phillips gas station. The dinner party was to be the following night. That dinner was a huge success! We sold three sets and booked two more parties for the next week. We took off for Blackwell, picked up Bonnie and Tim, and went back through Bartlesville. Mack followed us up to Oklahoma City in his car. We found a nice 2-bedroom garage apartment in Oklahoma City with room for Mack to stay with us.

We put on those two dinner parties, sold more sets and booked more dinners. The second dinner party that was booked from the first one was with a fellow by the name of Lloyd Howard and his wife, Anna Lou Howard. He was a huge man and a tractor mechanic at the local John Deere Implement Company. I had sold him a set off the first dinner in El Reno, so after he had his party and sat through another demonstration, he was really sold on Lifetime. I asked him how he would like to have a job selling Lifetime — he jumped at the chance! I not only hired him to sell, I also hired his mechanic buddy who was single and crippled from polio. So, I had me two more salesmen — and was off and running in my new territory. My buddy, Mack Blevins, just didn't work out. It wasn't his bag. He got a job in Bartlesville selling Chevrolet automobiles. The new salesman with polio didn't work out either, but Lloyd Howard sure did and he worked for a year or two, doing quite well. Lloyd and Anna Lou and Bonnie and I all became very good friends, and our friendship lasted fifty years. They loved little Tim as they did not yet have any children of their own. Lloyd's nickname was "Red." He had red hair and was always very jovial. And, as I said earlier, he was a very big man — 280 pounds and 5'10." We both worked south, east, and west in the rural farm area. There was lots of it! Farmers were all doing well, and I was selling like hell, averaging about 80% of sales from each of the three dinners I had per week. Bonnie and Tim and I still lived in Oklahoma City, but had rented a small 2-bedroom house with a carport and it was an improvement over the garage apartment.

One day I had a dinner party cancel so I called the Howards and asked them if they wanted to go with us to visit my mom and dad who had moved to Albuquerque, New Mexico. They agreed and I said, "We will pick you folks up in one hour and head right on west of El Reno on Highway 66." It was 6:00 or 7:00 PM when we left El Reno and we drove all night. None of us had every been west of Oklahoma. We were about to Clines Corners on Highway 66 around sun-up and we were all enjoying the wide open spaces and clear blue sky, and the Sandia Mountains as we approached Albuquerque. This was a first for all four of us. My folks were delighted to see us! It was a surprise visit as we had come on the spur of the moment when my dinner demonstration cancelled. We had a joyous visit. Mom, Dad, and my little brother, John, had never met the Howards. We had a great visit and didn't go to bed until that night — we were dead on our feet, too! So, early to bed and then we started our long drive back to El Reno the next morning.

Earlier in this story I mentioned that I would tell more about Uncle Bill Wolfenbarger and Aunt Hattie in Oklahoma City. We decided to let Aunt Hattle babysit Timmy while Bonnie assisted me on my cookware demonstrations. (This is when Bill locked Timmy in the closet, as mentioned earlier.) It would let Aunt Hattie earn a little money and I needed Bonnie's help in the preparation, dishwashing, and kitchen cleanup. Bonnie and I would drive thirty to forty miles to the dinner and then drive back to Oklahoma City, pick up Timmy, and finally get home about midnight or later to catch a few hours sleep. Then, I would leave the house around 6:00 AM and start making my sales calls, sometimes as early as 7:00 AM — especially if it was harvest time for the wheat farmers. It was necessary to have both the man and his wife present when I was trying to write up an order, as it was a considerable amount of money that they would be spending.

I prided myself on being one of Sontag's top salesmen. I would certainly sell 80% of my prospects. I will try and tell you what all of us cookware salesmen had to do, from start to finish. I first started selling Lifetime Stainless Steel in January 1947. I stopped selling cookware in the fall of 1961 after moving the family to Los Alamos, NM. This was almost fourteen years. The first thing I would do was canvas a rural area until I found a nice farm lady that would be really interested in finding out more about Lifetime Stainless Steel. I would show her one of the pans and some of our lovely premiums that she would receive by letting me hold a dinner demonstration in her home. All she had to do was to invite four or five other couples to come to her house the next Monday night to eat the food that I would prepare in my Lifetime Cookware. I would furnish all the food except the bread and butter and cream and sugar for the coffee. All I would ask her to do was to invite couples that had not recently bought a good set of cooking utensils and invite people that she thought could afford to buy a set if they wanted to. You see, if she did this, then all I had to do was put on a good demonstration to sell these farmers who were making a very good living selling their wheat, or in their other occupations. I told the hostess that when the party was over, I would leave her kitchen as clean as I found it, and that I would not quote any prices at the party, but if the couples were interested, I would make appointments with the individual couples for the next day or evening to see them in their own respective homes.

So, all I had to do was to furnish all the food and show up at the hostesses home around 4:30 PM in the afternoon with my cookware set and with all the food, consisting of a 5-6 pound seven-bone chuck roast for the five-six couples plus their children, if they brought them along. In addition to the roast, I would bring 2 or 3 bunches of carrots, two medium heads of cabbage, about a dozen medium potatoes, a box of graham crackers, a box of rice, a box of frozen green peas and a box of frozen corn, one big onion and one stick of butter for seasoning. All the hostess had to do was to set her dining room table with plates, cups, saucers, and silverware. I would ask her to pull up a chair and watch me prepare the meal and tell her that if her husband would be kind enough to purchase a set of Lifetime for her, then she would know how to use it. So, usually, she would watch every move I made. I would place the large six-quarter roaster (a Dutch Oven) on the stove burner on a medium flame, empty with only a small piece of the butcher paper the meat was wrapped in on the bottom of the pan. When the paper turned brown, I would place the meat in and sear it well. The meat would stick real tight, as I would show her, but as soon as it was seared for five minutes or so, I would take a meat fork and show her how it would turn loose and I could move it around, explaining that once the pores of the meat had seared and closed that it had turned loose from the pan, as stainless steel cookware had no pores for food to get trapped in, being a non-porous material.

As soon as the meat was seared and browned on the first side, I would turn it over to sear the other side. As soon as the second side seared, I would put the dome cover on and turn the heat down very low. No water or shortening was in the roaster except maybe a small piece of suet (pig fat pronounced: "sue-it") the butcher would give me with the roast if it didn't have much fat on it. In other words, it would be cooking in its own juice and as long as the fire was not too hot and had steam escaping from under the lid, it would continue to cook in it's own juice.

Next I would wash the potatoes with a brush and cook them with their jackets on. The only water on the potatoes was the water that would cling to them when I would fill the pan with water, then turn it over and pour all the water off. Maybe a tablespoon of water, or so, would be clinging to the potatoes. I would start them off on a medium-low fire and as soon as the lid on the pan was hot, I would turn the fire down to the lowest I could get. This was very important because with very little water to begin with on the potatoes, you couldn't afford to lose any. The carrots would be brushed or peeled with a carrot peeler, then sliced into pieces about 1/8" or 1/4" thick. Then I'd place one half stick of butter in the bottom of the 2-qt. pan, salt them a little and start them cooking with the heat on a medium-low fire until the lid was hot to the touch, then I'd turn the fire as low as possible for 20 or 30 minutes, remove the pan from the burner and place the carrot pan on the top cover of the roaster where they would finish.

For the cabbage I would take a few of the outside leaves off the heads, then quarter it, then start slicing it into a 3-qt pan with the other half stick of butter, seasoning with a little salt. I pressed it down as I placed it in the pan, filling it with water, and like the potatoes, poured the water off — the only water in the pan was what would cling to the cabbage. I would show the hostess how I would slice a couple of the outside green leaves of the cabbage in the form of a large star and place it on top of the sliced cabbage, then start it on a medium-low fire just like the carrots until the lid was hot, then turned the fire to low to finish cooking. It didn't take long.

I told the hostess that the color of the green star would be as green as it was when I placed it in the pan when we were ready to serve. Also, when I put the carrots on to cook, I placed one larger slice of carrot, about the size of a quarter, on top and poured a half-teaspoon of salt on it. This salt is not for seasoning, but to show that if the cooking process did not even dissolve the mineral salt, then that is proof that the method of cooking in Lifetime could not have cooked away any of the natural minerals or vitamins that are in each food. The same things happens with the cabbage. You do not smell cabbage cooked this way when it is cooking, therefore, anyone can eat this cabbage and not have to worry about indigestion or gas or taking Tums. I would tell the people this, and for some who could not eat cabbage without indigestion, I would tell them to eat it anyway, and I would pay the doctor's bill if it made them sick. I would explain to them that when cooking with this method, they were not destroying any of the food value that was in the raw food. The reason this is true is that this food never reaches the boiling point. Instead of being boiled and destroying half the taste and half the vitamins and minerals, it is cooked with steam at a temperature of 160-180 degrees, not 212 degrees where it is boiled and thereby destroys the food value and it goes down the drain. The drain says "good, good, good." While the roast is cooking on one side, I have got the carrots and potatoes started cooking and now it is time to stir up a graham cracker steamed pudding for the dessert. I would crumble up the crackers, add 2 eggs, 1 cup of water, 1 teaspoon of baking powder, put it in a buttered pan and place it on a rack with holes in it and cook it on top of the roast.

Having salted the roast and turned it over to cook it on the other side, I cut a large onion in half and placed it on top of the roast. I do this to show the people that the same steam that cooks the roast also cooks the steam pudding and the onion, but none of the onion taste leaves the onion and it does not affect the taste of the pudding. When the steam pudding was done, it would be sliced like cake and served with a sauce that I made with lemon juice, red cake coloring and flour and spooned out on the slice of cake for dessert. Very tasty!

I also would wash a cup of rice, rubbing it with my hand in order to rub a lot of starch from it so the grains would separate when cooked. The reason I cooked rice was to show how fast our cookware cooked, as everyone knew how long it took to cook rice in those days. The hostess would have been watching me do all this and by now it would be about time for her guests to arrive. When all the guests were there and seated in the living room, the hostess would take me into the living room and introduce me to them. I would welcome them and give them a short talk about what they would be seeng in the kitchen shortly.

Then into the kitchen we would all go, and I'd show them what I told them about in the living room. I'd first show them the rice I was going to cook, add water to the rice, 2 cups to one cup of rice, and tell them, "We all know how long rice takes to cook." I'd tell them to bring it to a boil, then turn the fire down and let it cook for three minutes, and tell them, "This is regular rice, not Minute Rice that you buy." When the rice has simmered for three minutes, I then explain I am going to place it in the refrigerator to finish cooking. They would all gasp at this. "Folks, I will now show you all the food I have prepared for dinner tonight." I'd first take the 2-qt. pan with the carrots in it off of the top of the domed cover of the roaster. I'd say, "I know some of you men probably don't like carrots, but notice the deep rich orange color of these. I know you have not seen carrots like these or tasted carrots like these. If you like the taste of raw carrots, please try these tonight. You will be very pleasantly surprised." Then I would turn to the hostess and say, "Mrs. Jones, when did I put this salt on this carrot slice on top here?" She would say, "When you put them on to cook." "That's right. The reason I put it there was just to show that I haven't cooked any of the minerals out of these carrots because salt dissolves very easily, even in cold water. Now, take a look in the roaster." I would lift the tall cover and remove the pan off the rack above the roast. "Here is our dessert for tonight. I think you will enjoy it." I would remove the rack and say, "See this big onion on top of the roast? Yes, the same steam that cooked the roast and this onion also cooked the steamed pudding. But you will not taste the onion taste when you eat dessert. Again, proving none of the food value or vitamins or minerals leave the food. Our bodies get it all."

"Now here is our roast. Cooked in its own juices. Notice it is still touching the sides of the pan, no shrinkage, and notice how much broth we have for making gravy. This is not an expensive cut of meat, it is a chuck roast. It will have a very good flavor and will be nice and tender. Quite a savings by not having any shrinkage. Now, here are our potatoes, cooked with the jackets on. Eat them skin and all, if you like, as most of the iodine in a potato is in the skin and just under the skin. Let me show you this with one slice of the potato and this flashlight. See, it's about a quarter inch deep all around the potato. Now, let me put a few drops of iodine on this slice of potato and drop it into this small pan of boiling water. You see, it only took a couple of minutes to boil away the mineral iodine from the potato. So again, you see how a lot of the real food value is destroyed by the boiling water and goes off in the air or down the sink drain and what our body gets is mostly bulk."

"Okay, folks, give me just a few minutes to slice the roast and dish up the vegetables and make the gravy. By the way, try the gravy on the potatoes, rice and also on the cabbage — it's delicious. Oh, yes, let's check the rice we have cooked that's in the refrigerator. Yes, it looks done. I will turn the rice pan over on this plate; notice how it comes out like a cake. The reason it doesn't stick to the bottom or the sides of the pan is because stainless steel has no pores in it for food to get down into like soft aluminum pans or cast iron which has pores that open when the pan is hot and close when the pan cools, thereby locking a little bit of food in the pores until the pan is used again in several hours, or sometimes days." After we finish eating, I will tell you more about this during some of the tests we will show you. The food will be served shortly, so please be seated around the table."

While the people were eating I was busy dishing up the rest of the food from the pans for second helpings, and getting my cookware washed and put away in their cases. Also I was getting the things ready to make the tests for the 'after dinner talk' that I make when the guests finish their steamed pudding desert. At this time I ask if anyone can guess the flavor of the red sauce on the slices of pudding cake. One or two of them will say cherry because of the red color. I say, "No, it's lemon with a little red cake color." We all retire to the living room for the after-dinner talk while Bonnie, or my assistant, cleans the table, leaving the rest of the leftover food in bowls for the hostess to serve at another meal. We also washed the dishes and tidied up the kitchen and left it spotless, as promised. This is so very important as everyone notices and they may like to have a dinner party in their home if they purchase a set of Lifetime tomorrow.

The after-dinner talk is when the important selling points must be made, and it usually takes about 30 minutes or so. "Folks, did everyone get enough to eat? You may notice that you may not be as hungry at breakfast in the morning as you usually are. I will explain more about this and also why this is especially true when you ladies season the food the way your family likes it. The only seasoning I used this evening was a little salt. When you go to the grocery store you pick out the food that looks fresh and nourishing, but when it is boiled in the cooking process 30-40% of the food value is lost. I imagine most of you folks raise cattle and hogs and I am sure you are careful to make sure they get the proper feed that have the right amount of minerals in order to raise healthy animals. The same thing is true with our own diets. The only difference is that most of our food has to be cooked. So this is where the proper tools are required to do the best job."

"That's about the same with everything we work at. Without good tools you men couldn't do a good job with your work. Thousands of dollars are spent on farm tools, as you know. Pickups, tractors and combines are so expensive, but you have to have them to get the job done. All too often our wives are called on to do one of the most important jobs she does using 49-cent, 79-cent or $1.29 cooking utensils in preparing tasty and healthy meals for her family. That's three meals per day, 365 days per year and that adds up to 1,095 meals per year."

"Just for the fun of it, let's use a little 6th grade arithmetic in our heads and see how the savings can easily add up. Three meals a day using a savings of only 10 cents a meal is a very minimal amount. Counting the meat shrinkage and food value loss would add up to 30 cents per day, $9 per month or $108 per year. This goes on for a lifetime when you do your cooking with the best cookware in the world, which is Lifetime Stainless Steel, guaranteed for life — preparing the most nutritious food for your family's health.

"Now I want to tell you how Lifetime is made. It is manufactured by Reynolds Metals Company in Skokie, Illinois, a suburb of Chicago.

The metal used is called 18-8 stainless steel: 18 percent chrome, 8 percent nickle and 74 percent regular steel. The identical metal that is used to make doctor and dentist's surgical instruments. There is absolutely no chemical reaction with this metal and any food chemicals. It is absolutely pure and sanitary. It will not rust, stain, pit, warp, or chip, like all other cookware metals do."

"I have here our one-and-a-half-quart pan and I will tell you how it is made. First, the pan is made of heavy single-ply stainless steel. Then, another piece of stainless steel is electrically seam-welded onto the bottom of the pan with a piece of soft, mild steel (similar to the steel used in the heating element of your electric iron or in the heating element of your electric stove burner) sandwiched in between. This layer of mild steel holds and distributes the heat evenly all across the bottom, eliminating hot spots on the pan. Then, the outside layer of steel comes up about one inch on the rest of the pan. All the pans are made this way except the baking pans and coffee maker, which is a dripolator. You see, this pan is about three inches high and eight inches across."

"I want the heaviest man here to help me for a minute or two. Sir, I will place this pan on it's edge on the floor and ask you to balance yourself on my shoulder and step up on the edge of the pan on one foot, and put your full weight on the pan with your other foot." Everyone is surprised that the pan does not collapse. I then bang the lid on the edge of the pan real hard to show it does not dent the lid or the pan. I pass the pan around so everyone can examine it and also feel the heavy weight of the utensil. The people have been very attentive, so far. Things always go good, as none of them have ever seen anything like this. I am very polite. I have on the pants to the suit I arrived in and a starched white shirt with my tie tucked in between the buttons of my shirt so it will not get in the food or be swinging around.

"Now, folks, I have a chart here. I want to show you how important it is for our bodies to get the vitamins and minerals they need to keep working for a long period of time. There are sixteen minerals that make up the human body to make it function well, plus all the vitamins. These minerals are absolutely necessary to let the body function properly: the eyes, ears, liver, blood, heart, lungs and stomach. We either get them from our properly prepared food, or in the form of pills of minerals and vitamins. Too much neglect means having to spend the time and expense of going to the docctor."

"We know how important it is to see that our dog, cat, and our livestock get the proper food, but all too often we do not pay enough attention to what we eat, as long as it tastes good and fills us up. Does anyone know what the only perfect food is?" Usually, several say "milk."

"Well, it is very important, but the only perfect food that contains all sixteen minerals is wheat." This makes all the farm families feel real good, and all the other families are surprised, too.

"Wheat is the only food that contains all sixteen minerals that the body requires. Now, we all know that by the time the wheat is ground and processed into cereal, flour for bread, and various vitamins and medicines, often times there is not too much food value left in the flour that winds up in a loaf of bread." At this point I take a slice of white bread from the loaf the hostess brings me. I peel the crust off of one slice and begin to make a small round ball out of it, about the size of a ping-pong ball. I simply bounce it on the carpet or floor and it bounces up to about waist high, and I ask,

"How would you like to try and digest this?" This always gets a good laugh from everyone. By this time, we are all on pretty good common ground, so I say,

"Folks, this just about completes our program. Has everyone had a good time? Good, good. I have, too. My job is divided into two parts. The company pays me for putting on these demonstrations and they also pay me for each call that I make the next day after the dinner. So, if you have enjoyed the program so far, I am sure you will extend me the courtesy of a few minutes in your homes tomorrow when you wives and husbands are both home to show you the full set of Lifetime and tell you more about it and also the price and terms should you be interested. If you are, fine and dandy, and if not, I assure you we are just as good of friends as we ever were. I will pass out these little cards for you to put your name and address on. Someone here is going to win a little gift. I want each of you to write on your card how many grains of wheat are in this small bottle. The one closest to the number will win the prize." They do this and I collect the cards and tell them who won the prize, and hand a little stainless steel cake server to the winner. Then I start making my appointments. I try and pick out the couple who seem to be the most interested to see first, then if they buy it is always easier for the second one to sell if I can say to them that Mr. and Mrs. "Sample" bought a set a few minutes ago, and so on, until I have made my four, five, or six appointments for the next day or evening. It takes about 30 minutes to show the set and go through all the combinations.

I carried a large spread cloth, either navy blue, a pretty red or maroon, about four by five feet square. Each pan was packed in a separate soft cloth bag and I wiped each pan with the cloth to remove any finger prints from it. I displayed the whole set on the spread cloth like each is a separate jewel. It was beautiful!

As a little side note, I'd like to expain to you readers some of the basic features in selling. There are selling factors and buying factors and we used to sell a high percentage of our sales calls by holding demonstration after demonstration and by the many, many sales calls made over a number of years. The ones of us cookware salesmen that survived had the sales pitch memorized so well that it didn't sound memorized. So, in order to get positive answers we would have to ask positive questions. By this time the question of how much the set cost had been asked by the couple. It was now time to go into what we called the "Bear Trap Close." I had already told them $136.50 and I quickly stated that "it's about the same price as you would pay for a very good cookstove, refrigerator, washer and dryer, a good sewing machine, or vacuum cleaner, but this Lifetime Stainless Steel, remember, is guaranteed for life. You will be using it long after all these other things will have been replaced, plus the fact it will pay for itself over and over each year that you own it."

Now, the Bear Trap Close: "Mrs. Kircher, if your husband would be kind enough to get (NOT "buy") this set for you, ma'm would you use it correctly, like I showed you last night — appreciate it, and take care of it?" Usually she would say, "Oh, yes." and, if so, I would then turn to the man and say, "Mr. Kircher, you look to me like the kind of man that would like to see her have it, right?" Usually, he would turn to his wife and ask, "Do you want it?" and I would butt in and say, "Sure she wants it. You might as well ask if the Pope is Catholic. She likes good tools to do her work just like you do." He usually says, "Well, hell, get the checkbook." It hardly ever fails if the salesman has done his work well and has been a real gentleman and been calm and cheerful.

To back up a little bit, while I was unpacking the cookware on the spread cloth, I would take out my order book that's right on top and hand it to the couple saying, "I have listed all the names of the people that have bought our cookware in the community. You probably know some of them." If I have been working in a community very long, they will usually know several of the people. Ocassionally, the man will say, "You mean old Tom Householder, that old tightway, bought a set?"

"Oh, yes, he did, like the rest of them too." What he is telling me is that if he didn't buy, then he is tighter than the old "tightwad Householder." So, after they made the check out to Andrew Long, I would say, "When would you folks like to have your dinner?" Sometimes they would say, "Do we have to have a dinner?" and I would say, "Oh, no, but remember when you arrived at the dinner last night everything was already cooked. When you have your dinner, you will get to see me cook the whole meal from start to finish on your own stove. Thereby, you will be able to remember how to use your set properly, right from the start. I happen to have next Monday or Wednesday nights open, which one would be better for you folks?"

"Next Monday will be fine, all you have to do is invite four to six couples that can afford to buy a set if they want to. You will have your choice of one of our nice premiums for being host and hostess and, what's more, if three or more couples buy a set from your dinner, you get an extra premium. Of course, I furnish all the food."

"Thank you folks very much. Your set will arrive in about ten days to two weeks, and I will see you next Monday around 4 or 5 o'clock."

This is the way we did it, and it was wonderful. It wasn't easy to do all the things necessary to be a top producer year after year. First, you had to have a good autmobile as you could not cancel or be late and be successful. You had to be responsible enough to always have the money to finance your traveling expenses, car, gasoline, motel, meals, dinner groceries, premiums and any other emergencies. Once in a while I would give a free dinner, as we called it, when no one bought — it didn't happen often, but sometimes it did — and we had to be prepared.

When the day was over, I would cash all the checks made out to me, and buy a money order to Sontag's Company, Lifetime Midwestern

Stainless Steel Co., and mail it to Wichita, Kansas. Bill Sontag had become a great success in the Lifetime Cookware Distribution Business and Reynolds Metals Co., the manufacturer, had rewarded him a total of six states as exclusive distributor. By this time, his district managers, such as myself, had hired lots of salesmen. Some were successful, and some were not, but within about two years he had about 50 or 60 salesmen and additional district managers. Bill was good to his men and his men were loyal to him. Everyone was making money that could do the job. Others fell by the wayside. Every few months or so, Bill would have a sales meeting in Wichita, Kansas at the Lassen Hotel, the best hotel in Wichita at that time. Most all of us would attend and all would have a wonderful time. He would have a really good sales specialist to teach us sales techniques; the best was Frank Kaplan. He would hold us spellbound! Things like teaching us to present positive questions to get positive answers, as I mentioned before, and things like saying to your prospect, "Now this is the size set that the Jone's bought." Don't say this is the set I sold the Jone's. He said people don't like to be "sold." Also, I remember he would say that people buy for two reasons: one, because of self approval, and two, because of the approval of others. This explains the reason I wrote everyone else's name in the community who had bought a set on my order book, the approval of others. There are several of those type of sales techniques, but the ones above are the ones I remember and have used all of my life in things I have done in my different businesses. Believe me, they work!

We had lots of fun at these sales meetings. Some would drive a long, long way to get to Wichita, arriving usually on Saturday afternoon. There would be several couples in a group that knew each other well, and Saturday evening we would go out to dances and nightclubs and stage shows and do some drinking. All good salesmen drank whiskey and our group was no exception!

From time to time I would think of trying something else besides selling cookware, and I would for short periods of time, but all in all, I probably spent around 12 years exclusively in the cookware business. I was always trying to get enough money to get out of the business, then when I did it seemed that I was trying to get enough to get back into it. For a short time I tried selling electrical and plumbing supplies on the road. I would leave home Monday morning and not get home until Friday night.

I didn't make much money and was gone from my family all week. Then I finally got a job in Bartlesville, Oklahoma selling fine men's apparel for a little Jewish man, about 4'10" tall, by the name of Martin Zofness. He had been in that same location on Johnston Street in Bartlesville for 47 yars, and his son, who was about my age, worked with him. Mr. Zofness was a nice man and he had known my Dad when they were both young men, so he trained me well. I was happy with my job, no more night work and no more traveling. This was the year 1958. I earned $75 a week. This is just one of the jobs I had, but there were a lot more cookware experiences before I got to the year of 1958.

Throughout my long life I have found there are two kinds of people, ones who think the cup is half full, and ones who think the cup is half empty. Positive people, or negative people, extroverts, or introverts. Race horses or plow horses is the way I like to describe them. I would describe a good salesman as always positive by nature. He is like a race horse, high strung and usually tempermental. A go, go, go type. Some describe him as full of "piss and vinegar." Drinkers, smokers, wild, hard driving individuals, who usually die fairly young. I can't figure how I have survived so long other than that I quit smoking when I was 33 years old. I am now 77 years old, so I have not smoked for 44 years and am still in good health.

I've always drank some whiskey, a little, since I was 15 years old. I would slip in my grandmother's cupboard, where my granddad kept his pint bottle to make himself a drink before supper. I would swipe a little drink of his whiskey and no one knew. Then, when I was a little older, I would get to go with my Uncle L. D. Henderson on Saturday nights when he would take his girlfriend dancing. He would drop me off on the main street of Dewey, Oklahoma where the picture show was across the street from the local pool hall. One of my best school friends, Kenneth Monroe, and I would play ten ball pool against some of the other guys for 50 cents a game until we won two or three dollars — enough to buy a pint of bootleg whiskey (Oklahoma was a "dry state", so the only place to buy whiskey was from a bootlegger. Cheap whiskey was $2.50 to $3 a pint).

One night we had won $3, enough for a pint of Sunny Brook. The bootlegger's house was a yellow house with a pink fence (so it would be easy to find) about two blocks off of Main Street. I had stuck the pint in the waist of my pants and pulled my shirttail out over my belt to hold the whiskey and Kenny and I started walking back to Main Street. About halfway back we looked up and here came 'ole Bill Smith, the town marshall, who was making his rounds. Just about the time we got to him the pint began slipping down my pants leg and it popped out flat on its side and broke.

'Ole Bill said, "Oh, boys, quite a loss! $2.50, huh?"

Kenny said, "Hell no, Bill — $3!"

He said, "You pissants, get the hell to home before I put you in jail!"

"Oh, Bill! We were planning to go to the preview tonight and its about to start. Can't we go to the picture show?"

"Well, okay." He said. "But you better not let me catch you drinking again!"

When the preview was over, about midnight, my uncle would drive by the picture show to pick us up after he took his girlfriend home. He would drive us home to Grampa's farm, and have a big bowl of Post Toasties and cold milk before bed.

To go back a little here to my cookware days of sales meetings, even though I drank a little whiskey all my life, the reason it has not killed me is that I never ever drank in excess and for long periods, like a lot of people have done. I never drank enough that I couldn't get up and go to work every morning of my life. No excess in anything is what I try to do and it has worked well for me. I think this is why I have outlived all the other salesmen that I have known. My old boss, and my dear friend, Bill Sontag, lived to be 93 years old. He told me that he and I were the only cookware men from his cookware company that were still living.

I want to tell you a few stories about Bill Sontag and our exploits and fun times over the years. On December 31, 1949 Bill Sontag married his wife Maxine. He was about 40 and she was 25 — a beautiful lady. He joked that the reason they got married on New Years Eve was that he had a tremendous year in the cookware business and he wanted to take advantage of being able to file his income tax jointly with his wife for the year 1948. So, on New Years Eve they tied the knot. Bonnie and I and Lloyd Messemer and his wife, Audrey, were jointly Best Men and Bride's Maids. What a celebration that night! After the wedding we all went to their apartment for drinks. We kept them up and wouldn't go home — we laughed about this for many years to follow.

In 1948 I had also had a tremendous year in sales! We were still living in Oklahoma City and working all the small towns around the city for a 60-mile radius. I had quite a few men and had trained them. I had 9 salesmen under me and I was only 23 years old. It was the first year that I was concerned about paying income tax. So I contacted a young tax attorney in Oklahoma City to figure my taxes. He and I were certainly surprised when he told me I had earned $13,000 taxable income. To give you an idea how much money this was in those days, in 1948 you could buy a brand new Oldsmobile Rocket 88 for $1,400. Today a new Oldsmobile is more than ten times $1,400, more than $14,000. So, my earnings of $13,000 for the year 1948 would be comparable to around $130,000. Not bad for a 23 year old salesman, huh?

In November of 1948, though, something disasterous happened. Sontag was having one of our big sales meetings in Wichita. I had to pick up a new salesman that I had just hired, who lived in Guthrie, Oklahoma, about 30 miles to the north, to ride with us. Bonnie, Tim and I would also pick up Lloyd Howard, another salesman, at El Reno, about 34 miles west of Oklahoma City, So we went out of Oklahoma City on U.S. Highway 66 about 4:00 AM and at the west side of Oklahoma City there was a nightclub called The Silver Spur. Well, it was still dark and a car full of drunks were just leaving The Silver Spur and they ran through the stop sign at a high speed and hit our car broadside. As their car hit our car, I had tried to turn sharply to the right, but it was too late to avoid the crash. The new salesman was in the front seat with me, and Bonnie was in the back seat behind me holding little Timmy on her lap. Tim was just two years old. Our car turned over two and a half times. The back seat became dislodged and Bonnie and Tim were under it. I just knew they were killed! But, I quickly found they were alive. Someone had called an ambulance, but it seemed like forever before they got there. The people were also getting out of their car and they had no apparent injuries, but one woman was crying and sreaming as she thought that someone had been killed in our car. Well, the injuries were that Tim had a broken leg, Bonnie had two black eyes, and a big knot on the side of her head. She had had her legs crossed holding Tim on her lap and her right foot was against the left side of the car, so her right foot was hurt, but not broken and she had to have cruthces for quite a while in order to walk. The salesman's left knee broke through the plastic speaker of the car radio, but no bones were broken. I suffered no apparent injuries, but for years now I still have a problem with my right hip that often pinches the nerve. I have to lay on my back, raise my right leg straight up and swing the leg around several times until it makes a "pop" and stop hurting.

Anyway, the police came and took the information from everyone, and the four of us went to the hospital in the ambulance and found the extent of our injuries. Bonnie's right foot still bothers her when she is on her feet for long periods of time. We found out that the driver of the other car was a 25 year old budding cowboy actor from Oklahoma that lived in Hollywood, California and had just broken into the movies. His name was James Drury. He became quite famous as he starred in the television series, The Virginian. Later he appeared in movies with John Wayne several times. His insurance paid for our car, which was totalled and we replaced it with a dark green 1948 Dodge Club Coupe. We contacted the young tax lawyer that had figured our taxes, the only lawyer that I knew, and he flew to California on our behalf. He was green and we were greener and he came back with just the amount of money to cover our hospital examinations and Tim's broken leg. So that was that.

When they examined Bonnie at the hospital with x-rays on her head and foot, they asked her to tell them her name and she looked at me and said, "I don't know." Also she didn't know her address. She said, "Andy, what is our address?" She did know my name, but not hers. Naturally, we did not go to the sales meeting in Wichita that day.

When we got through with the examinations at the hospital, we went home by taxi. We lived about one block from a large Walgreens Drugstore. They had lots of toys there, so I hobbled over and came back with a big arm load of all kinds of toys for my baby boy. I was so grateful that none of us were killed!

December 1948 was a good month for cookware sales because of Christmas gifts for the farm ladies and we had a good Christmas in Wichita with both Bonnie's and my folks and then Sontag's wedding to top off a week's worth of celebrating. I want to tell you more about the sales meetings Sontag had in Wichita and stories about some of the characters that attended. It gave us not only sales techniques, but lots of stories and happenings that we shared with each other. So get ready for some fun:

One story I remember very well about a tall good-looking Irish fellow from Nebraska, who dressed like a model. His name was Kelley. His brother-in-law, Lewis, sold Lifetime. Sontag had Kelley scheduled to speak on how to book a cold turkey dinner demonstration. Kelley happened to be sitting in the row right in front of me and his suit coat was on the back of his chair. I happened to have a simulated plastic pile of dog crap with me, so I slipped in into his coat pocket. I remember that when Kelley spoke he had a habit of putting his hand in his left-hand suit coat pocket from time to time, quite a stance.

He was into his talk a few minutes when he put his hand into his left suit coat pocket. He stopped talking for a moment, then pulled out his hand with the plastic dog turd. It really cracked him up and everyone in the room died laughing! He said, finally, "Who is the god-damned clown that did this?" and I had to confess so I could get my plastic dog crap back. I got quite an applause when I confessed that I did it. At the same meeting, prior to the meeting getting started, several of us guys were visiting. As I remember the three Comeau brothers, all Lifetime salesmen, from Kays, Kansas were there, also Lloyd Messmer, Tom Oliver from San Antonio, and me. R. J. Comeau had just had a fabulous week in sales and he was really bragging just how he did it. All of us were listening intently, especially Tom Oliver. We were all seated in sort of a huddle and Tom was real close to R. J. Well, I happened to know that Tom Oliver was very goosey, so I goosed Tom and he raised his hand and pointed it in R. J.'s face, and I said, "What do you say, Tom?" and he said, "It's a lie, it's a lie, it's a lie!" R. J. didn't know what to say or think, but all of us laughed our asses off! I think all of us were thinking the same thing to ourselves. Good salesmen are often "primadonnas" at times and all of us recognize this.

A salesman from Oklahoma City by the name of I. W. Chance, who we called Ike for short, was quite a character. A big, tough guy and when he put on a demonstration you would swear he was a holy-roller preacher! He always had his share to drink at these meetings. Once when he was walking down the hall to his room in the hotel, he passed on open door and a woman was screaming. Her husband, or boyfriend, who was a brand new salesman, was really slapping the woman around. Ike Chance stepped in the room and decked the guy real hard — and low and behold the gal took off one of her high-heeled shoes and started hitting Chance in the face! He slapped her, stepped out of the room and pulled the door shut. He said, "That's the last time I will ever butt into a family argument!"

Sontag was always having sales contests of some kind and one winter he had a contest where any of the salesmen who had a $1,000 week within the month could all go on a deer hunt with him at his cabin in Buena Vista, Colorado. So, my good friend Lloyd Messmer, who was an excellent hunter, me, and Harry Duster from Topeka, Kansas (who Lloyd and I didn't know very well. He was a real "blow hard" as I remember) and a couple of other fellows all qualified. Anyway, we were all excited. Lloyd and I were both working in the Altus, Oklahoma area and he and his wife Audrey were great friends of Bonnie and me. Audrey was a jokester deluxe, so she said, "Andy, I want to play a joke on Lloyd so I have sewed the bottom hole closed around the bottons on the trap door on his longjohn underwear." She said, "You take your camera and get Lloyd's picture when he goes outside Sontag's cabin in the morning." Naturally, I thought this was a good idea. So, sure enough, come morning, Lloyd was right on schedule with his morning crap. It had snowed about six inches during the night, so he poked out a place to squat and I slipped to the back corner with my camera. Well, he fumbled and fumbled trying to get the trap door of his longjohns open and finally gave up and ripped the trap door open and at the same time I snapped his picture and couldln't help laughing. I thought he was going to kill me! I explained, "I didn't do it, Lloyd! All I did was get a good picture. Your sweet wife was the one who thought up the idea." His answer was, "I should have known it was her idea." We always had great times.

We hunted that day and after supper we were all sitting around the fireplace drinking and visiting. When old Harry Duster who had never been deer hunting said, "Lloyd, I saw you on the side of the mountain across the canyon from me today." Lloyd thought for a minute, then replied, "How did you know it was me?" Buster said, "I was scoping you." Lloyd said, "You were what?" Buster replied, "I was scoping you." Lloyd was a tough guy and he jumped up and said, "I am going to tear your ass up, you SOB. You could have killed me!" Harry thought real fast to save himself and said, "Oh, I had the bolt out. I couldn't have shot you." Lloyd said, "I don't believe that but I'll tell you one thing for sure, if you ever scope me again I will whip your fat ass and that is a promise."

The next day we all agreed that Lloyd and I could position ourselves at one end of a canyon and the other guys would spread out across the canyon and walk several yards apart and try to drive the deer up the canyon to where Lloyd and I were perched up high above the floor of the canyon on a big rock. It wasn't long until there came a doe with her two, three-fourth's-grown, fawns. They didn't see us, but the doe smelled us. She bolted, but Lloyd said, "On the count of three you take the one on the left and I'll take the one on the right." So we each got our young tender deer and the next morning we headed back to Altus, Oklahoma happy hunters.

Going back now to February 1949 in Oklahoma City (after the car wreck when Bonnie and Tim got hurt) and after winding up the tremendous year of 1948, I decided to find us a better place to live. We had been living in a furnished place for two years and usually moving a lot, so it was now time we found an unfurnished place and bought some furniture of our own. We found a real nice looking two bedroom duplex about three blocks from where we were living. Happiness had arrived! Little did we know that our lives were about to change.

The phone rang one day and it was a fellow by the name of Netherton calling. I can't remember what his first name was. But he was Sontag's office manager. Everyone called him Net for short. I had seen him several times in the Wichita office but did not know him well. He told me that he and Sontag had had a disagreement and that he was leaving Sontag. I said, "I am sorry to hear that." And he said, "Don't be sorry. I think I have found something that could make us a lot of money. Big money." That quickly got my attention. So I said, "Tell me about it." He told me that Lifetime Stainless Cookware now had a competitor, that Allegany Ludlam Steel Corporation of Pennsylvania had invented a steel process where they could mold 3-ply stainless steel sheets with two layers of 18-8 stainless steel with a layer of soft mild steel and the whole pan could be made of the 3-ply steel. Not only the bottom of the pan, like Lifetime's, but the bottom and the sides would all be of 3-ply with even heat distribution. The name of the new set of cookware would be called "Permanent", which would also be covered with a lifetime guarantee like Lifetime's was. He said that Allegany Ludlum was looking for distributors. Net certainly was not a salesman, but he really knew his bookkeeping and had handled Sontag's business very well with one other man and three women working under him. So I thought this might be a good chance to form a partnership and build a company of our own. I called him back later, after I called Jim Craft who was still selling and was one of the men that had trained me to sell Lifetime in the beginning.

We decided for the three of us to meet in Oklahoma City and make our plans. We did just that and, after a couple of telephone calls to Pennsylvania, we told them about our interest in forming a company of the three of us — one to run the office and two to train salesmen and to handle all the sales. We asked if Arkansas and Louisiana were open for franchising and they said that they were. We informed them that the three of us would leave right away and make a tour of both states and decide which city we would pick for our headquarters. We detailed our experience and it indeed looked like we could have a good business "marriage." So, one morning in late February the three of us got into my Dodge Club Coupe and headed to Arkansas from Oklahoma City. The highway was covered with about two inches of ice all the way to Little Rock! Cautious, slow going but we got there before dark and stayed overnight and looked it over really well. Neither Net nor I had ever been to Arkansas, but Jim Craft was born and raised in Jonesborough, a small town in the northeastern corner of the state. After we looked Little Rock over for a few hours, we headed south on snow-covered roads to the town of Alexandria, Louisiana, in the west central part of Louisiana. We liked the town, but decided it was a little small for our headquarters and we would be better off picking a larger city like Baton Rouge or New Orleans. So we went on to Baton Rouge which is the state capital and liked it very much because of its size and location.

We thought we had better go on to New Orleans and at least look it over as none of us had been in Louisiana before. It was still cold as hell. It was one of those freak snowstorms that normally do not hit Louisiana, but this one did. The whole place was almost shut down because of the slippery streets and most people didn't know how to drive on snow or ice. They didn't even put antifreeze in their cars and it was interesting for us to watch. We stayed all night there and at breakfast an interesting thing happened. The waitress said, "Do you want grits with your eggs?" And we said, "What are grits?" She explained, so we said, "Okay." When she served coffee I added the usual amount of cream to mine and it hardly colored it at all. I called the waitress over and said, "Miss, would you pour this out and bring me some fresh coffee, this cup must be what was leftover from last night." She said, "Sir, that is fresh coffee." I said, "It can't be, just look. The cream hardly colored it." She said, "Sir, Lousiaina coffee is made with chickory in it. That's the way everyone here drinks it." So, this introduced us to Lousiana coffee.

We didn't waste much time looking over New Orleans as we decided it was not centrally located enough and was too large a city for our headquarters. We then went back up country to Baton Rouge and this time looked it over real good and decided this is where we would put our headquarters. The state capital is there, L.S.U. is there, located on the Mississippi River, and the State employed a lot of workers as well. We looked around for an office location and found a good one located on Plank Road which is one of the main arteries of the city. We liked it, so I put up a deposit and I told them that we would see them in a week or so. I found a nice two-bedroom duplex near the Mississippi River and also near L.S.U. We could even hear the tugboat whistles on the river. I put a deposit on it. Net's wife had to give her notice to the dentist she was working for as a dental tech before she and their eighteen month old little boy could move down. So, Net rented an apartment and told Jim Craft that he could bunk with him until his wife and baby could get moved down. Jim was single, so this worked out fine. Net had been a bombadeer in the Air Force in Europe during the War. While in training in the states he had met his wife in Las Vegas, Nevada working as a cocktail waitress. She was a real pretty blond. Craft was single, so he was quite mobile.

Back, then, to Oklahoma City and Wichita for us all, and we set a date to head down to Baton Rouge, Louisiana. We had our new furniture that we had recently purchased that would just fit in the duplex in Louisiana, so we set the date for the movers to pick it up and take it to Baton Rouge. Net was driving an old black Packard Coupe, a powerful old car so he and Jim left wichita and we started our trip south: Net, Jim, Bonnie, Tim, and me. Well, on our way into Dallas, Nets old Packard started having trouble. We were almost to the Oklahoma-Texas state line when it just quit. We tied a log chain to his Packard and I pulled him into a garage in Dallas to have it worked on. We got on our way about noon the next day and on into Baton Rouge by nightfall. Our furniture arrived the following day and we were soon settled in and about ready to set the woods on fire in our business, so to speak.

We had to sign a six-month's lease on our duplex, but that didn't create a problem at the time. We liked it, and the young couple next door (students at L.S.U.) had a little girl that was the same age as Tim. They hit it off really good and she could hold her own with Tim. The lady next door's sister was single, and she took care of the little girl while the lady was in school at L.S.U. She wasn't real good looking, but not bad either as I remember and Jim Craft had a chance for a little indoor recreation from time to time.

The couple next door owned an old Model Ford car and it was parked in front of the duplex most of the time. Well, one day Bonnie looked out the front window and the little Ford was sort of jumping and bucking down the street. She could see the top of Tim's head in the front seat of the car and the little girl was pushing the starter button located on the floor panel of the car. The key was not in the car, so it couldn't start, of course, but it still bucked and jumped. Our duplex was only about a half-block from the dike that holds the Mississippi River back and the street dead ends at the dike. I was not home but Bonnie questioned both kids about this, and they said they just wanted to go see "Scuffy the Tug Boat" that Bonnie had been reading to Tim from one of the Little Golden Books. They could hear the tug boat's whistle, so they wanted to see Scuffy. Another time, she and the neighbor lady were both home when they missed the kids and looked out towards the river where they could see the kids heads bobbing along in the tall grass that was growing on the dike. Again, they just wanted to see Scuffy. I think they both got their little butts spanked this time.

The lady that lived next door's husband was studying child psychology at L.S.U. as one of his subjects and he told Bonnie there were two ages that were the worst for a child to go through: 2 1/2 years (and the only thing that was good about this age was that they would soon be three); and fifteen years old was the other worst year.

Since Jim Craft didn't have a car then, we decided to work together. We would split up the demonstration talks and it worked out pretty good until he got a good car. One of the big shots with the Allegany Ludlum Corporation decided to come down to visit us at Baton Rouge as we had never met anyone in person from the factory. He came down on the train and we showed him our office and around town and then went by our house to meet Bonnie and Tim. He was a very nice guy and we hit it off well. He said he had no idea that we were all so young. We did know our business, and he realized it, and it was not belabored. He said, "If you guys will drive us to New Orleans I will take you out to dinner and entertainment at the Fairmont Hotel." So we said, "Okay," and we did. The Fairmont is the most famous hotel in New Orleans. It was where Sammy Kay, the famous band leader did all his broadcasts and he drew large crowds. He stayed around a couple of days and attended one of our demonstration dinner parties. He was impressed and he went back to Pennsylvania well pleased.

In a couple of weeks Net's wife and baby arrived and they were happy as she got a job right away working for a dentist similar to the job she had in Wichita. A few things were different in Lousiaina than in Kansas or Oklahoma. In Louisiana, instead of having counties they have parishes. Similar, but different, folowing French law instead of English. We had to go to a lawyer to have our time payment contracts changed. They were a lot different than the ones we had used in Oklahoma, Kansas, and Texas. After considerable expense we finally got this worked out. We had to change our demonstration a little, also. Hardly anyone in Louisiana eats Irish potatoes. They all eat sweet potatoes instead. So, we changed the way we cooked them and they all loved them. They really loved the way we fixed the rice as they grow a lot of rice in Louisiana and eat a lot of it.

I hired a prospective salesman by the name of Russell Scott. He was working for Fuller Brush Company and the company had sent him to Louisiana to open up the territory at Baton Rouge. He was not doing too well and I think he was getting tired of knocking doors all day long selling Fuller Brushes. He was a good looking guy and I was glad to hire him as I thought he would make a good cookware salesman. By the way, he had family in Enid, Oklahoma, where he had come from, so we hit it off well.

We had been rolling along pretty good by this time. A couple or three months had passed and we were enjoying driving around our new town and the beautiful L.S.U. campus grounds, the State Capitol Building, a highrise that overlooked the Missossppi River, and the hugh Huey P. Long Bridge. We toured the capitol one weekend and saw the bullet holes in the marble wall by the elevators where the Governor's body guards shot the bastard that shot Governor Long. I found out one thing right away, the people in Louisiana either loved Huey P. Long or hated him. Not much in between. So with a name like Long I would hasten to say when introduced on my cookware dinners that I was not related to Governor Long as I was born and raised in Oklahoma, and that worked. The time of year was late spring and summer of 1949. Our country had prospered well after the war years as not much private merchandise had been manufactured during 1942-45, so there were jobs for anyone willing to work. During the war years most everything manufactured was war material. No private cars, furniture, appliances, nothing except war material. After the war people were introduced to new types of washing machines, dryers (which were never heard of before the war), refrigerators, deep freezers, and modern cook stoves. Just about everything. Lots of homes were being built and the economy was pretty good.

By 1949 the country was beginning to get caught up selling all these things and the new word of "recession" was being bantered around. We had never heard of this new word or what it meant, but we were soon to find out. A large percentage of the people living in Baton Rouge were employed at the very large Esso Oil Refinery located there on the Misssissippi River. The headlines in the local paper one evening read that due to the recession Esso Oil Co. would lay off 450 workers at the refinery. What a shock for everyone! There was no unemployment benefits in those days, it had not even been thought of. So it was just like a wet blanket had been spread over the entire town.

450 families in trouble didnt' seem like too many people considering the population of Baton Rouge, but the big problem was everyone else thought they might be next. So the economy just about dried up. People quit buying anything they didn't really need. Naturally, it affected sales of our Permanent Cookware. After two or three weeks we all realized we would have to do something in order to exist. It certainly didn't look like we were going to build the great business that we had planned on. Net pointed out that his function in the business did not produce any income to the company, as his job was to run the office and do the bookkeeping. Jim Craft said, "Well, I am single and I don't require much money to keep me." He was living with the Nethertons in their extra bedroom so he didn't have much expense and still no car. So, the big monkey was on old

Andy's back. I had a great thought about how I could keep things going long enough for us to make some different plans. Net's wife was working in the dental office, so her paycheck helped them a little.

My thinking was this: in southern Arkansas, about 150 miles north of Baton Rouge, there were some prosperous looking farms that we had seen when we were looking for our headquarters. Their main crops in the farm area were cotton, rice, sweet potatoes and cattle. So I suggested that Jim and I head up that way and try and book some farm dinners. I had done very well working with farmers as I mentioned before, and I felt this is how we could get enough money to wind down our big venture that we had dreamed about. Well, we booked two cold turkey dinners and we made six sales, all cash — and did we need it! We did the same thing the next week, and sold six more sets, all cash.

Since Net's apartment was only rented, not leased, he didn't have any problem and he still had a couple of week's rent paid up. Jim lived with Net, so no problem there. Our office was not on a lease either, and our landlord understood our problem and was very nice about it too. However, Bonnie and I had signed a six-month lease, and it was about two weeks before our rent was due for the next month. There was enough money to pay our current utility bills and this sort of thing, so our only big problem was the lease on the duplex. I told Bonnie there is only one thing for us to do — we'll have to jump this damn lease. Niether of us liked this sort of thing, but it was absolutely necessary. We had some money left, but we had to make it last. Net took off for western Kansas where his folks lived. Jim got a job there in Baton Rouge. I don't remember what, but it was a job.

We called a trucking company to come out and load our furniture and belongings: practically new furniture — living room sofa, bedroom suite, kitchen furniture; no stove or refrigerator, but a new spin dry washing machine, Tim's baby bed, play pen and all our clothes and personal cookware and dishes and kitchen furnishings, and four brand new sets of Permanent Stainless Steel that I had payed for that we hadn't sold. The truck and men showed up around 1:00 PM and by 4:00 PM we were all loaded up and ready to roll. The truck driver said, "We only allow 10 cents per pound insurance, is that okay?" And old dumb Andy said, "Well, okay," as I was in a hell of a hurry to get out of there and on the road. The driver never said I could buy more insurance if I wanted to. It was panic time as we were jumping our lease and we needed all our money to travel on. We paid the truck driver for the moving charges and were on our way to where my folks lived in Albuquerque, New Mexico.

I told Bonnie that since we had such a long way to go, to pack everything except one good leather suitcase and a little .22 caliber automatic rifle that I had traded for a set of cookware. Just a limited amount of clothing for all of us in our suitcase. It was mid summer, so it was summer clothing.

Well, we made it all the way to Houston, Texas around midnight, stayed all night and left early the next morning. We had never been in that part of Texas going to El Paso, and as you know, it is one hell of a long way! So, hardly able to stay awake, we made it to El Paso about midnight the second night. Up early again the next morning and on into Albuquerque that afternoon. We had made the whole trip in two and a half days! My folks were delighted to see us and their little grandson, who would soon be three years old. They had a very small place, as they had moved out to Albuquerque for dad's health. Mom made room for us and we planned to make do out of our one suitcase until the truck arrived with our furniture and things, hopefully in a few days.

Well, a few days passed and no truck; then in about 10 days we got a letter from Jim Craft who had our address at my folks. He had stayed in Baton Rouge and he said he'd run into one of the guys who helped load our furniture on the truck and that it had turned over and burned in a creek bed while trying to avoid hitting a calf on the road. I'll tell you, that news was shocking to all of us, especially Bonnie. She just collapsed and sat down in the dirt and cried and cried. Everything we had was lost. Not only our furniture, but all our clothes, baby things, dishes, bedding, pictures, keepsakes and gifts, yearbooks, and souveniers I had bought while in the Merchant Marines. Everything was just gone.

With some of the money we had left, we bought clothes for all of us. I bought two new suits and shoes, shirts and underwear, the same with Bonnie and Tim. We called the F.B.I. in Albuquerque and they checked it out and said, "Yes, that is what happened." I couldn't say for sure how well they checked, or whether they just called and were told the same thing. Anyway, in a few days we received a check for $118, which was the insurance amount of ten cents per pound for 1180 pounds. The value of our things were at least three or four thousand dollars, even in those days.

There were also four new sets of Permanent Cookware worth about $600 that I planned to sell later. Not much money and no job, so the ordinary family would say it's about panic time, but not us. I have always said, and I still do, "When the going gets tough, the tough get going." I answered an ad in the paper for a sales job and it was a new vacuum cleaner company that was just getting started in Albuqeurque, Filter Queen, and it was a very good one.

They hired about six salesmen, including me, and started our training. The young distributor had just arrived from California to start his business in the State of New Mexico. To make a long story short, I just didn't have my heart in it — but I tried hard to get going. I sold a couple of sweepers in two weeks or so and it was all cold turkey knocking doors all day long. The pressure was getting to me and I decided to call Bill Sontag in Wichita. He was glad to hear from me and held no animosity towards me for leaving to try my wings in Louisiana with Permanent. Bill said he would get two sets of Lifetime (one to sell, one to cook with) in the mail to me right away along with some premiums with which to book some dinners. I told him there was a possibility I could hire the sales manager with the vacuum cleaner company to train as a cookware man. He was a good vacuum salesman, but he just couldn't get any good men to stick with it. So, I thought I could maybe make a cookware man out of him. This guy was also a part-time preacher and a tall geeky looking character. So, I arranged to have my first dinner demonstration at his house and he invited some of the other vacuum salesman to attend so that they could see if they might want to start selling Lifetime Cookware. Well, the way it worked out, only the sales manager wanted to try it, so he and I started his training.

One of the other salesmen and I hit it off pretty good, but he decided to take an insurance selling job. He mentioned that his Mom and Dad lived on a ranch near the little town of Corona, New Mexico. So, I decided to go see them since I knew their son and was his friend. Their names were Mr. and Mrs. Jim Rogers. It turned out they were wonderful, salt of the earth, small-town ranch people and had lived there most of their lives. They were in their sixties and had a teenage grandson living with them.

Well, I booked a dinner with the Rogers and the following week Preacher Simmons and I returned to Corona and I put the dinner on and sold five sets of Lifetime! Jim and his wife bought one and all four couples they invited also bought. I booked three more dinners for the following week and I was off and running. Just like "Damn, the torpedos, full speed ahead." My finances were beginning to pick up and things looked real good for the immediate future. Bonnie and I found us a small furnished apartment just big enough for the three of us.

I got a bright idea about how we could move very easily since we didn't have a lot of furniture and things to move except my sample cases of cookware, our clothes and a limited amount of dishes, sheets and pillow cases, three plates, 2 cups, 3 glasses, 3 knifes, forks, and spoons for the three of us. I bought a large trunk with the outside covered with blue metal, about three feet long and two feet wide. It fit perfectly in the trunk of our Dodge Club Coupe, along with Tim's baby bed and our new Filter Queen vacuum cleaner that I had to buy for my demonstration when I was selling them. It was a good one and we used it for years. We still have the blue trunk and for years now have used it for keepsakes and pictures, etc.

The little apartment was a small motel apartment right on West Central Avenue and further on out West Central was a nice roadhouse lounge called The Peacock Lounge owned by a well-known radio disk jockey (like a talk show host these days on television). His name was Dick Bills — some name, huh? His son-in-law was a young singer and guitar player by the name of Glen Campbell. I know most of you remember him as he became a big country western star for many years, and also made a few movies. One was True Grit, with John Wayne and Katherine Hepburn. We would go out there once in a while to relax and get out of our small apartment, leaving little Tim with a neighbor couple that had a little girl.

One day the Preacher and I were on our way to Corona to put on a dinner party and it was getting a little cold. Corona was about 100 miles from Albuquerque and we were out about 25 miles or so east on Highway 66 before we turned south on a gravel road. Anyway, we blew out a tire. No problem as we had a spare, so we changed the tire and proceeded for another 50 miles or so on a good gravel road, and low and behold, we blew out another tire! We must have ran over a nail or something. Anyway, all we could do was keep driving with the wind to our back. The car began to get hot and ran out of water, so we had to stop. Boy, were we in trouble! Well, we looked through the fence and in the pasture there was a small pond with water in it to water the cattle. So Preacher and I took four of our largest pots and climbed throught the fence, walked about 100 yards, got four pots of water and filled our dry radiator, and in about two or three miles down the road there was a small country filling station. We made it! We explained that we were going to Corona and they said it was about 15 miles farther and maybe someone would come by going to Corona — so nothing to do, but wait for a ride to take our wheel in to get a tire put on it. Like I said, the weather was cold and the station had a pot belly wood stove, so we stood around it to keep warm and somehow I backed up too close to the stove and burned a hole about 2 inches square in the tail of my new suit coat. I was sick about this! It certainly wasn't my day.

A short time later a pickup came by and we caught a ride with him and bought a couple of tires and hired the man at the station to take us back to our car. While we were getting the tires mounted I called the hostess where we were to have the dinner party that evening and explained to her that since it was toolate to have time to get to our car and get back that I would like to have the dinner at her house the day after tomorrow. She readily agreed and that is what we did. It was the only time I had cancelled a dinner the entire time I sold cookware. The Preacher and I were tired out and it had been a very exhausting day for me. Two tires and a suit coat burned. Later I had the tail of the coat reweaved, but it was not a real good job and it didn't look very good. I was always particular about my clothing in those days. It was a quiet evening on the drive back to Albuquerque and Preacher Simmons said, "Andy, I really don't think I will ever be a very good cookware salesman. I think I had better get back to selling vacuum sweepers." So I said, "If that's what you want to do, then that is what you should do." So that was that.

That suited me fine as I about had a belly full of trying to hire good salesman, and now since we were lean and mobile because of our few belongings, I looked forward to just taking care of my own sales and building up our bank account again. Corona was, and still is, just a little bitty town. One grocery store, sort of a general store where I could get my groceries to put on three dinners a week and go home Saturday night after I made my calls from Friday night's dinner party. That made it a lot easier on me. That is when I switched to those hard-surfaced and partitioned paper plates to serve the food in so I could put on a dinner and not have to wash so many dishes and still get away from the host's house by 11:00 PM find a place to sleep and get ready to make my sales calls the next day instead of driving all the way back to Albuquerque on the dinner nights, then back to Corona the next day to make the sales calls. The only place to stay all night was a small hotel. It had about four rooms upstairs with a bathroom down the hall. Very reasonable rent at $2.50 per night. The lady that rented the rooms ran a little one-person cafe and I could get breakfast and occasionally other meals when necessary. This worked out well. I had everything I needed, with Sundays and Monday until noon at home, as well as Saturday and Sunday nights to be with Bonnie and Tim. Fortunately, there was a good grocery store near the motel where we lived.

I always sold a high percentage of my calls as I had my sales pitch razor sharp because of the many, many times I had performed it. I remember I had traded for lots of different things from time to time. One time there was a little old ranch woman who lived alone. She didn't have much money and she asked me if I would trade a set for a beautiful hand made quilt she had quilted. It was someting we certainly needed, so we made a deal and she and I were both happy. This sort of thing would happen from time to time and everyone always liked Andy Long. I had a wonderful product and I was always fair with people and always tried to be calm and cheerful. I had several good stories, some funny and a few tear-jerkers. Some who would say, "Andy, you backed the hearse right up to the front door," when I would talk about people's health, and other things that they seldom thought about, during the after dinner talk. They always enjoyed these stories and jokes as I never overdid them.

Old Jim Rogers became a great friend and several different times he would just show up at the homes where I was putting on a dinner. He would say, "Andy, I didn't come to eat, I just came to watch the show." Of course, he knew everyone for miles around Corona as he also drove the school bus and had lived there for many years. There was no television in those days, so the performance I gave was appreciated by all. Most of the time, the hostess would ask me if it was okay if Jim ate with the rest of them and, naturally, I said, "Oh, yes, there is plenty of food." He invited me to go deer hunting with him and I jumped at the chance. When I showed up to go hunting, there were four other hunters besides Jim and me. His wife and grandson were visiting away from home, so it was just us six men. The other four hunters were all airmen stationed at the Roswell, NM bomber base. It was where the huge six-motor piston engine aircraft were stationed. It was the largest plane in the service at that time. It was before they had jet airplanes. It's the one that carried a fairly large crew and it was the beginning of the cold war era with Russia and they would make that long, flight over Russia and back without refueling. The planes were huge and it was a large base in Roswell, and an important one. Some of you may remember that period was about the time of the much published crash of the flying saucer that took place around Corona, which is not too far from the Roswell Base where the headquarters for the investigation was held. The famous UFO Museum is still located in Roswell, and an annual UFO convention is held every year.

Anyway, this is where these four hunters were stationed and the night before the hunt I went to the grocery store and I bought food just like I would do to put on a dinner party, and using Jim Rogers set of Lifetime I had sold him, I cooked supper for all of us and had enough for supper the next night after we had hunted all day. Everyone really appreciated me doing this and we had a wonderful visit and hunt. Old Jim was 65 years old, but he could out-climb all of us in those mountains on his place. He was used to the high altitude as he had lived there for most of his life — the rest of us were not as acclimated as he was.

I had about sold this territory out, so I had been thinking about where I would find a new territory. I had been working there two or three months and Bonnie and Tim were getting tired of the small motel apartment and me being gone most of the time. Things were about to change. We put our blue trunk, and what little bit of other things we had, in our Club Coupe and our little family drove to Clovis, New Mexico about 175 miles east of Albuquerque. We were very pleasantly surprised with how clean Clovis was and all the farm land and cattle land for miles around. Also Portales, New Mexico, was about 15 or 20 miles south of Clovis. There was a lot of wheat land and irrigated farm land of sweet potatoes and peanuts. The towns were very close to the New Mexico and Texas state lines. Clovis was also a railroad town which provided quite a lot of jobs. There was a railroad roundhouse there where they had facilities to work on the train engines and do a lot of railroad repair, so all in all it was a very prosperous town of around 30,000 people.

I was elated with what I saw and we decided to find a furnished apartment and get to work. We found a nice apartment across the street from the city park and a small zoo. I explained to the landlady what I did for a living and asked if she knew of anyone I could get to watch our little boy about three nights a week, from about 4:00 PM until around 10:30 or 11:00 PM. She said she could do that, so we had a real handy set-up there and it worked very well. The very next day I drove out northwest of Clovis to a small community named Pleasant Hill, booked a dinner for two or three days later and sold three sets of Lifetime and booked two more dinners for the next week. I was thrilled to death with our new territory. One nice plus about this territory was the wheat farms were large and the houses far apart, so on the drive back to town after the dinner parties, I put my little .22 caliber rifle in the car and when we saw a rabbit in the headlights and I had a little recreation and also some rabbit meat for us to eat for a change of our menu at home.

Things went well there and we were beginning to pump up our bank account. We would drive back west to Albuquerque to see the folks on some weekends. Dad was feeling better and Mom had gone to work at a little sundry store within walking distance of their little pueblo style house. The sundry store was on the south side of East Central, across the street from the Fair Grounds. The owners were Mr. and Mrs. Rudy. Real nice people. Everyone called the man Rudy, ha, ha! There was his one-chair barber shop at one end of the little store, and his wife and Mom Long ran the store and soda fountain.

Dad got a job selling cars at the Lincoln Mercury place on North 4th Street. Business continued to be good and we met one young farm couple that we hit it off with and we became good friends. Their names were Coy and Martha Gooch. Coy's folks had been wheat farmers when he was young and Martha's grandparents had also owned a farm next door to the Gooch's farm. So in the summer time, Martha would get to come out from Dallas and visit her grandparent's farm for the summer and she and Coy became good friends. Years later Coy joined the Army in World War II and Martha grew up in Dallas and married a young man who became a pilot in the War. Anyway, during the war, Martha's pilot husband was killed, so later she and Coy renewed their acquaintance and had gotten married. She was a pretty thing, tall and slim and so very funny. She could put a lunch together so fast you couldn't believe it, bake a pie and have things ready to go in no time. They were big farmers then and we enjoyed visiting with them.

Coy and I would go duck hunting and rabbit hunting. There were numerous large ponds for cattle watering, so we had plenty of places to hunt ducks. We exchanged lots of war stories and one in particular I really enjoyed (since I was a "dumb-Oklahoma-son-of-a-bitch"). Coy said he was in an Army training camp in California, a farm boy fresh off the farm and had a job as bartender in the Officer's Lounge. His buddy was a waiter in the Officer's Dining Room, so they would change off with each other when they would want to go to town on leave. One time he was taking his buddy's place as Officer's Waiter. He was serving soup to a Major and the Major asked him, "What kind of soup is this, Private?" And Coy said, "It's Milk Soup, Sir." The Major stirred it up a little and said, "You dumb son-of-a-bitch! It's Clam Chowder!" So, Coy said he was shipped out to the Pacific Theater the next day!

Another funny story was one day they had been working in the wheat fields sowing wheat and Martha worked right along side of Coy. They came in for lunch and they noticed that a large snake had gotten into her china cabinet! She had a lot of really beautiful furniture from her first marriage; her husband was a Captain before he was killed. Anyway, Martha screamed and Coy got his shotgun and shot the snake in the china cabinet — he killed the snake, as well as all the crystalware in the cabinet.

Like I said, Martha worked with him on the farm all the time. They would only go to the help-yourself laundry when all the clothes they had were dirty. One day we went out to see them and they had their pajamas on while working. Martha told Bonnie that all their other clothes were dirty and they were going into town this afternoon to do their laundry. They would fill up four or five washers at a time, then dry them and then come home and have lots of clean clothes.

Coy and Martha had a small, old 25 ft. trailer house in their yard, a fairly good one, but small, so I traded them a big set of Lifetime for it and pulled it to Albuquerque. The day we left to go, it had snowed during the night, but I was going to go anyway. No brakes on the trailer, of course! We made it okay, by being very careful. Hell, I was 24 years old then and I wasn't afraid of anything then! I thought I could do about anything I set my mind to. I wanted the trailer to have in Albuquerque at the folk's place so Tim, Bonnie and I would have a place to sleep when we went to visit Mom and Dad. A little later on I had a set of good, electric brakes put on it.

A few months later, after I had sold quite a lot of Lifetime around Clovis and Portales, Sontag called me and said, "Andy, how would you like to be Regional Manager for me?"

I said, "What would be my territory?"

He said, "Oklahoma, Texas and New Mexico. Do you remember Tom Oliver?"

I said, "Oh, yes, I remember old Goosey Tom in San Antonio."

Bill said he needed someone to help Tom get started again, "He's in a slump."

Then Bill said he had an inquiry from a young fellow in Arlington, Texas, just north of Dallas that needs to be trained and wondered if I remembered I. W. Chance in Oklahoma City. I said, "Oh, yes, I remember him. The guy the woman hit in the face with her high-heeled shoe at the Lassen Hotel." Bill also said that Bowline in Broken Arrow needed to get started again.

Bill said, "If you will do this I'll raise your commission on your sales from 50% to 55% and you can draw a 5% override on those fellows and any other ones you hire and train."

So, I said, "I'll give it a try."

Back to Albuquerque to park Tim and Bonnie in the trailer at Mom and Dad's place and I took off for San Antonio. I left Albuquerque early that next morning and drove into a hotel in San Antonio late that night. I called Tom Oliver and told him, "Sontag asked me to come by and perk you up and help you get started again."

Tom was sure glad to see me! It gets very lonesome when a salesman gets down on his luck and it's like going out every day looking for a new job. I told Tom that I had been having really good luck selling farm people and maybe we should try to find a good rural area. He suggested that we go to Kerrville, Texas — thirty or forty miles northwest of San Antonio. So that is what we did. By noon I had booked a dinner for the next day and another one that afternoon for the next week. Old Tom began to get his enthusiasm back and we put that first dinner on and sold four sets of cookware. This put some money in his pocket and he was on his way.

One of the couples that came to the first dinner were young and had a couple of small kids. They were obviously pretty poor, lived in a real small house with single-ply wooden floors. Anyway, we sold them a small set on time payment. But the funny thing about the sale was when I had spread the blue spread cloth out to place my show set on it and started to show the various pans, I noticed the spread cloth moved up and down a little in the middle. I couldn't figure it out, so I moved some of the pans over and lifted up the cloth and a pig was under the house and had stuck his snout up through a knot hole and that was what was making the spread cloth move! We had a good laugh at that!

I got Tom started, then on to Arlington, Texas to interview the young man that had inquired about Lifetime. I arrived late that afternoon, checked into a motel and gave the young fellow a call. He came down and I showed him and told him all about Lifetime and explained to him that the only way for him to decide would be for us to book a dinner and for him to go along with me and watch what I did, and then to go with me on the calls the next day and see if I made any money. I told him that is the way I started in the business. He said okay and we booked a dinner and I put it on, sold a couple of sets but didn't book any other dinners off of it.

I asked him what he had been doing for a job. He said, "I recently got discharged from the Navy and got married and went to work for my father-in-law who is the Ford dealer in Arlington, Texas." He said he did not like working for his father-in-law and wanted to do something else. He just didn't think he could do all the things I had done, so I said "Maybe you should have stayed in the Navy." He said, "Maybe so."

So, the next morning I took off for Oklahoma City and I. W. Chance. I had asked him once what the "I. W." stood for and he said, "I want a chance." I remembered that so when I called him on the phone, I said "This is Andy Long," and he remembered me and asked what I was doing in Oklahoma City. I told him Bill Sontag wanted me to come down to see him and offer him that chance that his I. W. stood for. "So, here I am to help you get started back in the cookware business."

He had really hit bottom. He had gotten a divorce and had a job as a fry cook in a small restaurant. He had been a good cookware man with Lifetime and had also sold Wearever Aluminum Cookware before the war when was he was a young man in Roswell, New Mexico.

I said, "I'm here to do whatever it takes to help you get started."

He said, "Okay," and picked up the phone and called the cafe where he worked and said, "I'm long gone, get a replacement for me." He was living with his girl friend in an upstairs apartment, so the next day he and I took off to Guthrie, Oklahoma, in some of my old territory that I had sold in before the Louisiana venture. We booked a dinner and sold three sets, then two more dinners and sold seven more. I. W. Chance was rolling again! He didn't even have a car. He was behind on his rent a couple of weeks, so now he had money in his pocket. We split the commission on the sales we made, so we had to be very careful with the money.

We talked it over and he said, "Andy, I have so many bills. I have got to get out of Oklahoma City."

I said, "Where would you like to go to start over?"

He said, "If it was okay with you, I'd like to go to El Paso, Texas."

I said, "If that's what you want, that's what we'll do." So he and his girlfriend put their things in cardboard boxes and about three in the morning, when everyone was asleep — including the landlady — we quietly made a few trips with their things to the trunk of my little Dodge Club Coupe, jumping his rent. When the sun came up we were ready to cross the Oklahoma State Line into west Texas on our way to El Paso. We got as far as White City, New Mexico that night, stayed all night and made it into El Paso around noon.

Apartments were scarce, but we finally found an upstairs one. The landlady said, "You're lucky! We were full up but last night an old man died and as soon as I clean the room you can have it." It was small, but the price suited Chance as he knew they could get something nicer later on. Then we went car shopping and found a real old one for $150, but it looked and ran pretty good, and at today's prices would be equal to around a thousand or so.

We booked a dinner and sold three sets. I gave Ike the whole commission and he was happy that he was back in the cookware business to stay. Mission accomplished! Old, young Andy Long headed for Albuquerque in a couple of days to see my little family and Mom and Dad.

Sontag was frantic that he hadn't heard from me for quite some time. I had been very busy and I hadn't taken time to write or call. When I did and told him that I had gotten Tom Oliver started and also Chance, he said,

"Oh, yes, I have been receiving your contracts and shipping the sets out to the people you sold." I also told him that the young fellow at Arlington just wasn't cookware material, so don't waste time on him, and he agreed. He told me that he had made arrangements to take ten of his top producers on the train to Chicago to visit the factory where Lifetime Cookware was made. He wanted me to be one of the ten men going. I readily agreed, as Bonnie was anxious to see her folks in Wichita, also.

We soon left Albuquerque for Wichita, Kansas. We visited a couple of days and Bill Sontag had a lead that some lady wanted to buy a set of cookware like her sister had. She lived at Arkansas City, Kansas, about fifty miles or so east of Wichita. I went down and sold her and booked a dinner for the next night so she would know how to use her set. I usually didn't book a dinner the very next night, but I didn't have much time to put one on before the train left for Chicago. Anyway, it was a success and I sold three more sets the following day.

The next afternoon the pullman train left with ten salesmen, each with a bottle of booze, and Bill Sontag for Chicago. We had a great dinner in the dining car and it took about two hours, as most of us had a pretty good head of booze on. Not any of us falling down drunk, but just happy as hell, and silly.

Herman Bowline and I had become very good friends by then, over the many months of cookware association. His nickname was Tony — everyone called him that instead of Herman. Tony was half Irishman and half Native American Indian. It is true that Indians can't hold their liquor, none of them, and Tony was proof of that, but he was also half Irish and you know how Irishmen like to drink. So, Tony really did get loaded. He was a big guy and had a big, loud voice to match. So, Tony decided he'd be the lcomotive engineer and said, "Andy, you be the caboose." We started up the aisle on the train, Tony yelling, "Woo, woo, woo, woo, woo" and with me holding Tony's coattail, saying "Chucka, chucka, chucka, chucka." We had gone through several cars of the train and were waking people up that had already gone to sleep in their pullman beds. The conductor caught up with us and said, in no uncertain terms, "You sons-of- bitches get back to your seats and if you don't stay there I'm going to put you off the train in Kansas City!" So, that took care of that. No more playing train.

After a good night's sleep and after breakfast, we pulled into Chicago and to the Stephen's Hotel, the tallest hotel in Chicago. Very nice. We got settled into our rooms and gathered to take the taxi ride out to Skokie, Illinois, a suburb of Chicago where the factory was located. We enjoyed meeting the people who made the cookware and they enjoyed meeting the people who sold the cookware so they could have jobs. It was a very interesting afternoon.

We all paired off into two's to go to our rooms and get ready to go out to see the nightlife of Chicago, all but the Comeau brothers of Hays, Kansas; they said they'd never seen television and they were going to stay in their room and watch TV. The rest of us "high rollers" all laughed at this! Most salesmen are race horses, not work horses, and this bunch was certainly no exception.

Tony and I found a nice bar and had a couple of drinks, then took a cab ride along Lake Shore Drive to see the Chicago skyline. Beautiful! Then, we went to a very nice restaurant and lounge for a great meal and stage show of dancing ladies and strippers. Tony decided he wanted to go backstage and visit with some of the dancing girls, so we did. Try to, that is. There were a couple of bodyguards that had better ideas for us! We darn near got into a fight, but I finally got Tony out of there.

Tony needed to get some toothpaste or something, and we went past a drug store on the corner as we were walking back to the hotel. I noticed they also sold whiskey, so without him knowing it, I bought a pint of whiskey so we could have a drink in the morning to sober up with. We walked a couple more blocks back to our hotel, took the elevator to the 19th floor and got ready for bed. He had more to drink that night than I had so he went to bed and was asleep right away. It was about midnight. I got ready to go to bed, but I thought I'd better hide the pint of whiskey so Tony wouldn't find it. I put it on the top shelf of our closet, then went to bed.

Well, we must have slept a couple of hours or so when there was knock on the door, "Hey, you guys awake?" I said, "We are now! What is it?"

"It's Kelly and Lewis, the two brother-in-laws from Nebraska. Do you have any whiskey?" they asked when they got into the room. I said, "Yeah, on the top shelf of the closet." One of them got the pint, took a drink and passed it around to the rest of us. We each had two or three drinks, straight and it wasn't long before they left to go back to their room.

Then Tony decided he would go to the bathroom. He staggered around drunk, all over again. Well, he thought he was in the bathroom, but he had opened the closet boor instead. I looked up and he was pissing on my topcoat!

I said, "You drunk SOB, you are pissing on my topcoat, damn you!" Well, he staggered out and I pushed him towards his bed, but he kept on going. The room was sort of small and he staggered and started to fall through the window! I jumped to grab him and he grabbed hold of the drapes and fell backwards away from the window, thank God! But the drapes had been torn down from the wall! Well, I got him back in bed, and about 9:00 AM we came alive. Hung over, but alive. We had a good breakfast and found out that we would be leaving from the train station about noon. I never mentioned to Sontag or anyone about the condition of our room and drapes! We all checked out, Sontag payed the bill, and we went to the train station and home to Wichita. I never heard whether he ever got billed for the drapes.

It was a quiet trip home on the train. Everyone had a good time. Sometime during the night or early morning we arrived in Wichita. When Tony and I woke up in our pullman beds the train car was on the railroad siding and everyone else was gone. All the salesmen got their cars and headed back to their respective towns to go back to work after a really fun trip. Bill Sontag loved his men and we all loved Bill. The trip was great and appreciated by all.

Bonnie and I spent a few more days in Wichita visiting with her folks and I went car shopping. I found a white, four-door 1950 DeSota demonstrator that was about six months old. So, I traded my little Dodge Club Coupe for it and surprised Bonnie and her family there in Wichita. I can't remember what time of year this was, but it must have been winter as I had worn my top coat. When Bonnie, Tim and I returned to Albuquerque after the Chicago trip, I was longing for a new territory and for some reason I thought I would like to work around San Angelo, Texas. Dad said, "I have an idea that I would like for Mom and I to live in San Angelo, too."

Dad loved me, Bonnie and Tim so much that he always wanted to be near us. Anyway, I suggested that he drive his Chrysler that he had just traded for and follow us to San Angelo. We were still living out of our blue trunk, but the larger 4-door DeSota gave us more room to move our belongings. Dad sold their little house and the large lot is was on and decided Mom could live in the little trailer, that I had traded for in Clovis. We found a trailer space for it near where Mom worked at Rudy's Sundry Store in Albuquerque.

One bright, early spring morning we took off for San Angelo, us in the DeSoto and Dad in the Chrysler. Everything went well and we arrived in San Angelo later that afternoon, found a room to spend the night and the next day looked for a furnished apartment. We found a nice two bedroom duplex with the landlady living in the other half. The next day Dad and I went out in my car. He wanted to see how I booked my demonstration dinners.

One of the reasons I had chosen to try San Angelo was that they raised a lot of cotton that the farmer's sold in the fall. There was also more sheep raised in that area of Texas than in the whole state of Wyoming. Very big business in that part of Texas. San Angelo had the reputation of being the wool capitol of the U.S.A. In the spring of the year they sold the year's lambs as well as the wool they sheared from the sheep before the hot weather. Some farmers sold both cotton and sheep, but more of them were either sheep ranchers on the rougher land, or cotton farmers on the flatter, richer land. There was plenty of both.

We settled in and everything was going well. Dad watched Tim while Bonnie went with me on my dinners, which was much easier on me. Something I remember that was interesting was there was a lady who tooled leather purses, billfolds, belts and pistol scabberts. She wanted to trade some tooled leather things so I made a deal with her for a purse for Bonnie and an agreement that she would teach Bonnie how to tool leather. The lady got a nice set of Lifetime and Bonnie got a nice purse and learned how to tool leather. She took lessons for a couple of weeks and became very good at it. She made Timmy a pistol holster and belt for his toy pistol. About this time, my Dad nick-named Tim his "San Angelo Buddy" and this stuck for several years.

Bill and Maxine Sontag had been married for a year or so when one day they drove up to see us. They stayed for two or three days and Bill went with me on one of my dinners and calls the following day. The hostess's family did their cooking on a wood stove. I had never cooked on a wood stove, but I had told her that if she could, then I could. So I did.

113

Everything came out very well. I had cooked on every other kind of stove: gas, propane, electric and kerosene. All I had to do was start the cooking on the hot part of the stove and simply slide the pans to the back to finish cooking. I used the theory that what couldn't be done by some folks was being done by others all the time. Bill and I had a great time that night, cooking on that wood stove! These were sheep and goat-farm people — real "salt of the earth" folks.

All of us, including Dad, went fishing while Bill and Maxine were there. Bill had a little long-barreled .22 pistol that we were playing with that day. We saw a large snake in a tree not very high up. Bill said, "Andy, see if you can shoot it." Well, I did — to his surprise, and he mentioned it several times during the years that followed.

He and Maxine then went down to see Ike Chance and his new wife in El Paso and the Chances took them across the border to Juarez to entertain them. There were stage shows and everything there. They had a ball! I. W. Chance had found his nitch and was very grateful that I had taken him and his girlfriend there from Oklahoma City. Bonnie and I visited them a couple of times later on and really enjoyed them and the time we spent in Juarez.

As always, it came time for us to be moving on. Mom had enough of New Mexico and Dad's health was better. They wanted to move back to Wichita. They were homesick to see my sister, her husband and their new baby son, and Mom's mother in Dewey, Oklahoma. To show you how I had to think on my feet most of the time, I could see that I had a potential problem getting out of my lease with the landlady next door. So while I was on my sales calls in a small town 50 miles or so from San Angelo, I got an idea that I would send myself a telegram to San Angelo and it would say, "Andy, you are being promoted to a management position provided you can be in Wichita and ready to go to work on the 1st of the month. Bill Sontag." Well, it was the 26th that day and rent was due on the 1st. I sent the telegram to myself. When it arrived, back at our house, I knocked on my landlady's door and, holding my thumb over the name of the town that I sent the telegram from, I show her the telegram that I had received from Wichita, Kansas. She was a real nice lady so she agreed to let me out of my lease since it only had a couple of months to go. I thanked her very much and the next day we all took off for Albuquerque — Dad in his Chrysler and us in my DeSoto.

The little trialer house that I had traded for from Coy and Martha Gooch was going to come in handy now! I had electric brakes installed on it as I planned on taking it to Lamar, Colorado to live in while working the sugar beet and wheat farmers in that area. As soon as my folks headed back to Wichita, Kansas we took off for Colorado. We headed north to Santa Fe, then through Las Vegas, New Mexico and on through Raton. It was dark by this time and it was a little spooky pulling that trailer through Raton Pass! But, we made it and on through Trinidad, Colorado. We had been looking for a place big enough to pull off the highway so we could get some sleep but had not seen any place at all. About this time we blew the right front tire on the trailer and, low and behold, I looked up and right ahead was a nice place to pull off the highway. It was too dark to do anything, so we went to sleep and early the next morning I jacked the trailer up and took the tire back to Trinidad, about five or six miles behind us. I bought a tire and returned, put it on the trailer and we were on our way to Lamar, Colorado to find a trailer park and see if I could book some dinners.

One of Bonnie's younger sisters, then about thirteen years old, was on summer vacation from school and wanted to come visit us for part of the summer of 1950. So, young Janice Scott had a chance to make herself a few bucks babysitting Timmy, who was then about three and a half. I worked about as hard as I could for three days and couldn't book a single demonstration dinner! It so happened that the whole farm area had been saturated with a competitor's stainless steel cookware called "Low Heat," a good set made of the same kind of 3-ply steel like the Permanent Stainless Steel sets I sold in Baton Rouge, Louisiana. Nothing to do but to go somewhere else.

We headed east to Wichita. The folks with my younger brother, John, who was about 13 or 14, bought a new two-bedroom house with a small down payment from the sale of their property in Albuquerque. Dad had already gotten a job at the Cessna Aircraft Plant, which was busy building small private planes. He had worked for Boeing Aircraft during the War and was experienced, so that helped him get on with Cessna right away. They were happy to be back in Wichita and to be there with my sister,

Marjorie, and her little family. Of course, Mom's mother also lived only 125 miles south of Wichita at Dewey, Oklahoma. So, that was nice.

After we spent a couple of days in Wichita visiting my folks and Bonnie's folks and Sontag, we pulled our trailer on to Dewey, Oklahoma to visit my Grandmother, who I loved dearly. We then went on to Tulsa, Oklahoma to see the Bowlines at Broken Arrow, now a suburb of Tulsa. Tony and I, and Bonnie and Wanda were such close friends we all decided that they and their little girl, Penny (who was the same age as Tim), would go down to El Reno, about 150 miles southwest of Tulsa. This is the farm area where I had done so well a couple of years earlier. So the six of us took off for El Reno, Oklahoma and Tony and I decided to work together and split the commissions and Bonnie wouldn't have to go on the dinners to help.

The little trailer had two beds — one at each end. So, since the kids were small it worked out okay with a couple and one kid in each. This lasted for about a month or so and Tony was getting very lonesome for his folks and friends in Broken Arrow. He just never was able to move around from place to place like we were. Tony and I were the best of friends for 47 years and we still are with his wife, Wanda, and their three children. He was the most unforgettable character I have ever met in my whole life!

While in El Reno, I even booked dinners with families that I had sold a few years before and some of them had grown children that they bought sets for now. Everyone loved their cookware! I remember what one fellow told me. He said, "Andy, the best thing that I ever bought was this Lifetime Cookware. The next best thing was the insulation in our house. Both of these things have more than paid for themselves and are in very good shape. Everything else we have bought we have had to replace: cars, furniture, refrigerators, cookstoves and damn near everything else." After that, I told this story many times and it helped.

Sontag taught me so much about life and selling. He grew up in a small town east of Wichita in prairie and farm country. The whole area stretches from central Kansas clear south past the Oklahoma border, called The Flint Hills. There are many, many cattle ranches there. His family were German folks, as many of the early Kansas settlers were. He studied to be a teacher and a coach, played basketball, and loved it until he died at the age of 93. His teaching background helped him a lot in training salesmen.

116

He was in the army during World War II serving in China. While there he met another fellow soldier with whom he had a good friendship, and somehow helped him get the Lifetime distributorship, which wound up being six states. He would always say, "All you have to do is find a need, and to fill that need, and then work like hell." That is certainly what he did.

Sontag would drive all night to go see one of his salesmen. Then go on a dinner with him to see how he could help cheer him up or just to keep up the friendship with him. He came to see us lots of times. If we had room enough, he would stay all night with us; if not, he would get a hotel room. He would always eat with us and enjoyed Bonnie's cooking when he could. He didn't have to have anything fancy and liked anything she fixed. He didn't have a phony bone in his body.

I think I mentioned that Bonnie's family was large — ten children in all. For the 58 years I have been in the family they have had a family reunion every Thanksgiving, long after both her parents passed away. We have attended 90 percent of them, no matter where we were living at the time. Bill Sontag always lived in Wichita and each time we would come back for Thanksgiving, we would stay for a few days. I would always spend the day after Thanksgiving with Bill, from early morning until late evening, while the girls would go to the after-Thanksgiving sales. Bill and I would either go hunting or fishing, weather permitting; if not, we'd just sit and reminisce. This went on for years and years until he died.

With some of his money, Bill would buy land. He bought a pretty large piece of land at the eastern edge of Wichita on Kellog Street (also Highway 54) going east — about 40-50 acres. It had a four-acre lake on it, so he subdivided it into about two-acre homesites for large homes, each facing the lake. He had a water well drilled in the center so the lake was filled with fresh water constantly. It was a beautiful site to see. Then he built a large family home for his family. It even had a cement fallout and storm cellar in the basement. It wasn't long until a large home builder traded Bill a very large ranch home, fairly old but with a square mile of pasture land, 640 acres, near Derby, Kansas. It also had a small wooded creek running through it. A magnificent old place.

Derby, Kansas is a suburb of Wichita and was a fast-growing little town. So, it didn't take long until his ranch land was about to be surrounded with houses, schools, and some businesses, driving the price sky high. He remodeled the big house and by this time Bill and Maxine had five or six children. This home was large and perfect to raise his family. About this time he went into the cattle business and it flourished. He then also bought a very large ranch, just land, with a large lake on it. He was really into the cattle business by this time. Later he leased this big ranch out and sold his cattle off. A horse fell on him and crippled him up some, but he fully recovered in time. He was still in the cookware distribution business and his salesmen were going very well. Maxine Sontag had a four or five year old son when Bill and her got married, then she and Bill had four girls in a row, then along came Bill, Jr. During this period you might say Bill Sontag was raising cookware, salesmen, kids and cattle.

He still had time to take his family to Buena Vista, Colorado for summer vacations and fall hunting trips with some of his salesmen. One time he had Lloyd and Audrey Messmer and Bonnie, Tim and I meet him and Maxine and her son, David (who was about five years old and the same age as Tim) at their cabin. We had a great time fishing for trout in the creek that ran through his property. We also fished at a large lake that was several miles away. I can't remember the name of it, but us three men had a wonderful time and caught several really large lake trout. The funniest thing that happened that trip was we were all sitting around visiting after a wonderful trout supper. It was dark and Messmer went outside. He had found an old bearhide, large enough to cover his body, so he put it over his head and slowly walked by one of the windows, making noises like a bear outside of the cabin. Our two 5-year old little boys saw him go by the window, then back again. Then Lloyd went around to the door and scratched on the door and opened it — the boys really got scared! Little David Sontag had a real deep voice for a little kid and he let out a large deep "Momma" and ran around the room and jumped up in Maxine's lap. Lloyd knew it was time to take off the bear skin and we all had a real good laugh. None of us ever forgot this.

Another very good deer hunting story was with just Bill and me. I was working in Altus, Oklahoma at the time and Bill called me and said, "How would you like to go deer hunting in Colorado?" Naturally, I said "Okay." Bill said it was a post season hunt that was at Pagosa Springs, Colorado and asked if I would drive to Wichita to his place. He was living in the large house he had built on the 40 acres with the small lake at that time. I left Altus that morning and got to Wichita in the afternoon. We left about 4:00 PM in his new Lincoln. Out across western Kansas about 10:00 PM or so, Bill got real sleepy. I had been dozing so I was awake and he said, If you will drive, I'll get into the back seat, lay down and sleep awhile." Wetsern Kansas is flat as a pool table and I was glad to be driving his new Lincoln. In an hour or so all of a sudden an old cow on the edge of the shoulder started walking onto the highway. Well, I immediately put on the brakes and swerved to miss her! The only problem was that I had never driven a car that had power brakes, so when I tromped the brake peddle like I would have on my car, this Lincoln really stopped quickly. Well, our two deer rifles had been laying above the back seat in front of the rear window. When I put the brakes on, Bill wound up in the floor of the back seat and the deer rifles were on top of him. He yelled, "What happened?" I said, "I damn near hit an old cow." So, no more sleep until we got into Buena Vista, Colorado. We got to bed very late, but about mid-morning we got up and had our breakfast and got his open-topped Jeep, that he kept there, out and hitched it to the back bumper of the Lincoln.

It had come a snow during the very early morning while we were sleeping. Buena Vista is in the central part of Colorado and Pagosa Springs is in the southern part, so we had quite a bit of driving yet to do. And, we had to go over Wolf Creek Pass to do so. It is very mountinous in that part of Colorado. The road was covered with snow on the Pass, so we put on snow chains and continued on until about midway on the Pass. The Lincoln just couldn't make it. Of course, it was colder than hell and here we were. So, I told Bill, "I'm going to put on all the warm clothes we have and I'll get in the Jeep, put it in four-wheel drive and push while you drive and see if we can make it up and over the Pass." Of course, the Jeep was open-air and it was dark. This was probably a good thing because we couldn't see the deep canyon just off the edge of the icy road. Well, this plan worked and in a few miles we got to the crest of the Pass and started down the other side and I was so glad to get back in the Lincoln so I could get warmed up.

We made it into Pagosa Springs, where we were going to hunt, in time to get a good night's sleep. It had stopped snowing in the night and the sun came out. It was early December. We separated to hunt, so I walked down the side of one mountain across a little valley, or canyon, then part way up the other side so I could see the mountainside where Bill was about a half-mile away and also see the bottom of the canyon. About an hour later I heard a shot and I hoped it was from Bill. I looked across the canyon and then I saw a very large buck. I had not seen one this size before or since. He was standing under a large pine tree with his head down where his nose almost touched the ground. He was about 150 or 200 yards away and I didn't have a scope on my rifle, but it was a very good 30.06 ("thirty ought six") custom made from an Army Springfield rifle with a walnut stock. I could hit about anything I could see with it. (I had traded a set of Lifetime Cookware for it from a couple in Clovis, New Mexico two or three years earlier. The guy that made it was a brakeman on the railroad there at Clovis. I had heard that after he had traded me the rifle, he had been killed in a trainwreck near Vaughn, New Mexico.)

Anyway, I took careful aim because it was a pretty long shot without a scope on my rifle. I squeezed it off and the big deer dropped in his tracks! I was excited! It took me about ten minutes to get to him as it was rough terrain. I was so happy and what a huge rack! A tremendous deer, the biggest one I had ever seen. When I got to him I went "from the very pinacle of enthusiasm to the depths of despair in thirty seconds," as Sontag used to say when a cookware sale cancelled once in a great while. Anyway, I could see the deer was all swelled up and there was a hole in his side and stomach where a lot of muck and blood had been running out. It was obvious the deer had been shot during the regular season. He had not died but he was very sick and badly wounded. So, it was a blessing that my shot put him out of his misery. He had a tremendous rack and would have made a great trophy on the wall. I don't know how I would have gotten hm out of that canyon as it was too steep and rough for the Jeep to get to where he was. So, I went back to see where Sontag was at, and he had his deer gutted and bled and in the Jeep. So, we decided to get back to town and make arrangements to have his deer cut up and shipped in dry ice to Wichita (as they did in those days).

We went back over Wolf Creek Pass in the daylight to see where we had been through two nights before and we couldn't believe how dangerous it was! No guardrails, and steep, bottomless canyons and roads covered with ice. We made it on into Buena Vista, stayed all night, unhooked the Jeep to leave it there and took off for Salida, Colorado and on home to Wichita. The next day I drove onto Altus, Oklahoma and back to work again.

Now I want to back up a year or so to the time period when the Bowlines and Longs had been living in the little trailer house in El Reno and Tony decided to go back to Broken Arrow. We stayed in El Reno, Oklahoma for a short time and then decided to pull the trailer to my folks' back yard in Wichita. Bonnie, Tim and I drove on back to New Mexico. We had never been to Roswell, so we drove there. It was a nice town but we didn't like it as well as we did Clovis. So we did not stay in Roswell except for a couple or three hours and drove on to Clovis. We really liked that town.

We found a small house this time that was furnished. A real nice little brick place, so we rented it by the month, no lease for us from now on. Around the middle of July, 1950 Bonnie informed me she was pregnant. This is about the time we were in El Reno with the Bowlines with all of us in the little trailer. How in the world she could have gotten pregnant then I'll never know, but she was. This probably was the reason we took the little trialer to Mom and Dad's in Wichita and left it, and wound up back in Clovis in the little brick house knowing that we would be needing more room with a baby coming. Tim was about four years old then. Anyway, business was as good, as usual, and we were happy. Our 1950 DeSoto was a good car and performing well. A good car was a must in the cookware business. One day a knock came at the door and low and behold, there was Bonnie's Dad, John Scott, standing there! John had decided to hitchhike to see us in Clovis. What a surprise! The next day I drove him around town and he saw where some houses were being built and we stopped and John asked them if they could use a good brick and block layer. The answer was "yes" and the next morning he went to work.

We enjoyed him for about a month. One weekend, the four of us had driven over to the little town of Fort Sumner to go fishing at Lake Sumner. Then one Friday night after John had got paid, he didn't show up for supper and later that night a knock at the door produced a local police officer. He told us John Scott was in jail for being drunk. This surprised us somewhat, but not too much as John had done this sort of thing a number of times over the years. So I drove to the police station the next morning to get him out of jail, but he would not let me pay his fine or bail. He said,

"They have already made me a trustee." So in a few days they let him out and he asked me to drive him to the highway so he could hitch a ride. I was upset with him so I agreed. I drove him about ten miles east to the state line of Texas, where the highway to Amarillo, Texas junctioned, and let him out. The little town of Texico, New Mexico was there, so I drove around for about five minutes and went back where I had let him out and he was gone. He had caught a ride right away.

John Robert Scott and Viola Lula Gwinup were both born in the year 1900, the same as my mother. So at this time he was about fifty years old. He and Vi, as everyone called her, had ten children. Most of them were either born during the Depression years or were growing up during that time, just like I was. Can you imagine the struggle this family must have had! John tried hard during those years. Viola was raised on a farm near Alva, Oklahoma, where they were married. She had taught school for about 12 months before they were married and later just being a mother didn't leave any time to teach.

John and Vi were very intelligent people. John could play the violin, guitar, piano and could even build crystal set radios for their home entertainment. He never had any lessons on how to play any of these instruments. The Depression years were so very hard! John learned to lay rock and brick with the W.P.A. Camps in those early Depression years, so this was good training. It came in mightly handy in later years. He was also a very good salesman and in the early years he and his brother ran a fruit and vegetable market in Wichita. His brother, Walter Scott, was crippled so when the Depression hit John gave Walter his half of the market and he and Viola took their five children (at that time) to Galena, Kansas. Galena, Kansas was a small town in Kansas just across the state line from Joplin, Missouri. They had lead and zinc mines there and jobs were available. John Scott worked in the mines for quite a while and he and Vi were still making babies. Times were tough and they were just barely getting by. Then, John got "leaded" (lead poisoning) by working in the mines and had to quit. He started selling fruits and vegetables. He would hang around the Joplin Market until late and when the growers would pack up to leave he would offer to buy what they had left at a real cheap price. Then he would take it home and cull out anything that was over ripe. The family would have it to eat, or if too ripe, they'd throw it away. Then with the good stuff he

122

would go out the next day door-to-door and sell it. Sometimes two or three of the older kids would go along to help. Bonnie hated to do this.

During the wheat harvest in western Kansas, John and a buddy would go out and work the harvest. It was so tough to make a living in those Depression years. The three oldest kids, Robert, Dorothy, and Bonnie, got little jobs to help buy their school clothes and things they needed. Bonnie worked at Eckels Grocery. She would open the store early, then go to chool, then after school she would work until closing time. They all three learned how to work hard. They were all smart and Bonnie was Salutatorian her senior year of high school and earned a college scholarship, but still didn't have enough money to attend. Bonnie's mother took in washing and ironing and sewing for people. It was a struggle but they managed. Then when World War II started, Robert, the oldest boy, joined the Army and Dorothy, Bonnie's older sister, got married and moved to Wichita and got a job.

Bonnie graduated in 1943 and moved in with Dorothy in Wichita. Dorothy's husband, Garnet Sawin, was in the Army then, so the girls lived together sharing the rent. Bonnie got a job as a checker in a Safeway Store and that is where she met my sister, Marjorie. They became the best of friends. This is how I met Bonnie while home on leave when I was in the Merchant Marines. Marjorie was Bonnie's Maid of Honor, and her boyfriend and future husband, Dwight Stanfield, was my Best Man at our wedding.

In the meantime, Bonnie had gotten a better job with McKesson-Robins, a wholesale drug company in Wichita, as a bookkeeper. Sometimes she would catch the train to Galena for the weekend and help her Mother with her bills. That family was close to each other and by this time there were ten children in all. After the War was over the family moved back to Wichita.

Bonnie's uncle, her mother's brother, Gene Gwinup, was a Safeway manager in Wichita, so he and his wife, Fern, bought a small house for John and Viola to live in with the six children that were still in school and living with them. It was crowded, but it worked. The house was near Friend's University, a religious college. The youngest child, Beverly, was in the first grade, so Viola enrolled to finish her education that she had just started when she and John Scott got married. How about that! She had ten children, then returned to college and got her teaching degree. She taught school in Galena, Kansas and was a teaching elementary school principle for 20 years at Spring Grove Elementary School. She finally retired at age 72 with high honors from the school board and the parents. Viola also taught the Adult Sunday School class in her church in Galena and she was listed in "Personalities of the West and Midwest." This is proof of one of Bill Sontag's favorite sayings: "All it takes for a smart person to make a success of himself (or herself) is to work hard, have strong desire, and stick with it." When Viola, John and the younger children lived in the little house in Wichita is when Bonnie and I returned to Wichita from Anderson, Indiana.

Back to Clovis, New Mexico in the fall of 1950: The Korean War had started and I became worried that I could be drafted into the army; at that time they were drafting men as old as 26. Men that had served as Merchant Marines during World War II were not considered veterans at that time. They were considered as sea-going civilians who had not served. Well, since I had been a good-thinking man all my life, I put my brain to work and came up with this idea. If I could get my Merchant Marine papers that I had during the war and pass the physical showing that I was again fit for duty, then Mack and I could go back into the Merchant Marines and not have to be drafted into the army. I couldn't stand the thought of having to go into the army after having already served three years of the war in the Merchant Marines. So, I wrote to the National Maritime Service in Galveston, which was run by the U.S. Coast Guard. I sent them all my records of all the ships I had served on during the War and told them I would like to ship out again. They informed me by letter to come to the National Maritime Hospital in Galveston and take a physical examination and, if I passed, all my papers and licenses would be re-issued. Bonnie and I had a serious talk aobut this and we agreed that this is what I should do.

She, Tim and our child that was due in March could stay with my folks in their new house in Wichita. So, I left Clovis one January morning and arrived in Houston, Texas that night and the next morning I caught the bus to Galveston Island. I passed the physical exam with flying colors. I had quit smoking some time back after I was originally discharged and had gained about thirty-five pounds in weight — up until then I had not weighed over 130 pounds! The normal weight for my height of 5'10 1/2" was 165 pounds, just what I weighed. I was probably in better health then I had ever been.

I made a phone call to Mack Blevins telling him what I had done and was answered with, "Hell yes, let's go!" I then called Bill Sontag, informed him of my situation and he understood. In fact, he told me that it looked like he might not receive enough Lifetime from the factory to keep his business going because of the shortage of steel caused by the war effort in Korea.

Mack came to Wichita and the two of us caught the train the next day for Galveston. As soon as I realized I would be leaving for Galveston, I sold our little trailer that was parked in the folk's side yard and traded my 1950 DeSoto for a Frazier automobile, so Bonnie would have transporation and some money for her and Tim to live on while I was gone. After Mack and I got to Galveston, we re-joined the National Maritime Union and went to the shipping hall. Sure enough, they were needing two firemen/watertenders and we received two railroad tickets for New Orleans to catch a Liberty tanker by the name of the U.S.S. Sea Dream.

We rode that train all night and went aboard the ship and we sailed up the Mississippi River to Baton Rouge and started pumping on a cargo of oil at none other than the Esso Refinery that I have written about earlier in this narrative. It was just about two years to the day when Net, Jim Craft and I started our venture in Baton Rough with our cookware company. Quite a coincedence, I thought. Mack and I went ashore and took a cab down Plank Road where our office had been and, sure enough, the big sign was still there. Across the top it read Permanent Stainless Steel Company. It was still vacant after almost two years. The recession at Esso Reginery and Baton Rouge was not over yet. It probably was a good thing we left there when we did!

Well, in a day or two when we were fully loaded with oil, we steamed down the river and into the gulf and back up the east coast to Charleston, South Carolina. The U.S.S. Sea Dream Liberty Ship was so misnamed! I had never seen such an oily, dirty ship! Everything I touched on deck would get you dirty with oil. What a mess!

The word got out that we were waiting for a convoy of several ships to gather, then we would head for the Panama Canal and the convoy would head for Japan. This didn't sound too bad, we thought, but when the time came to leave they mustered us all to come into the Officer's Lounge to sign on for the trip. It was then we found out that when we got to Japan our ship was going to be there for nine months before returning to the U.S. We would be shuttling oil from Japan to Korea for nine months! I just couldn't stand the thought of being away from Bonnie and Tim and the new baby. Mack felt the same way, because he was planning on getting married to a beautiful girl in the spring. This nine months deal just wasn't in our plans at all! So, we both told the Captain we were not going to sign on for this trip. Oh, he raised some sort of hell! He was the largest man I had ever seen at that time and he was a mean old SOB! He cussed us with every word he could think of, but we told him the only way we would be making this trip was that we would have to be shanghied. He knew he would be in big trouble, so he told the rest of the crew the ship could not leave until he got replacements for these "god damn firemen." We packed our bags and to the train station we went.

No train from Charleston was going west, so we caught a bus to Birmingham, Alabama, then a train to Little Rock, Arkansas, then to Bartlesville for Mack and Wichita for me. Surprise! Surprise! When I took a cab from the train station and knocked on the folks' front door, they couldn't believe that I was home — and Bonnie was about two weeks or so from having the baby. A call to Sontag was good news to him also. He said he was still getting enough cookware to stay in business and he welcomed me back by saying he had a hot lead on someone that wanted a set of Lifetime who lived in Herrington, Kansas and another one in El Reno, Oklahoma.

These two towns were about 250 miles apart, so I called Mack Blevins and told him this news and suggested he come up and we sell together for a while. He said, "Okay." While I was waiting a day or two for him to arrive on the bus, I decided I needed a better car to sell cookware in than the old Frazier, so I traded it in for a high-powered Torpedo — a 2-door 1948 Oldsmobile 98. It was a very pretty car, dark green. The trip to Kansas produced two or three very good dinners and several sales and we were off and running again. We lived right in downtown Herrington in a hotel. It was a small town right in the heart of wheat country about fifty miles or so north of Wichita. One of the "Dinners" in Herrington wanted to postpone her dinner party for three or four days, so I said, "Okay" and with about three or four days on our hands I called the lady in El Reno, Oklahoma, the other lead that Sontag gave me, and booked a dinner with her for the next night. We took off the next morning, got to El Reno that afternoon and had a four-couple dinner that night. We made the calls the next morning and sold four sets of cookware! Hooray! We had a dinner that next day with the lady that postponed in Herrington, so we stayed all night in El Reno in an old wooden two-story hotel across from the Railroad Depot. The telephone was down the hall. I called the folks and Mom said, "Bonnie is very nearly ready to have the baby." I gave her the number on the phone in the hall outside our room.

The phone woke us up early that morning and we were informed that Bonnie had delivered us a little baby girl, which she really wanted, as we had one boy already. I told Mom of our situation, that we were in El Reno and had a dinner in Herrington that night and had to be buying groceries in Herrington around 3:30 or 4:00 PM, so I would be coming through Wichita on highway 81, but I would not have time to stop at the hospital. I asked her to explain to Bonnie, give her my love, and tell her that I would see her in a couple of days or so. This didn't go over too well — with my mother or with Bonnie! But, that's the way it had to be under the circumstances. I'm not sure that Bonnie agreed with that, even to this day, which will be 51 years later this March 13th, 2002 in just about a month from now.

Mack and I continued to work around Herrington for a couple of months and his girlfriend would come up to Wichita on weekends to see him. Bonnie and I had rented a cute little furnished house with two bedrooms and a garage on Poplar Street in Wichita, just a few blocks from her sister's house. This was company for Bonnie and also Mack's girlfriend, Betty Jane. Betty Jane came up for a week and helped Bonnie with the new baby girl, who had whooping cough. These two young girls had quite a time with this!

Mack became restless; he felt he was not doing his fair share just helping me on the dinners, as we were splitting the commission. Neither of us was getting very far ahead. This had served the purpose when we came back from Charleston and the U.S.S. Sea Dream, but it was time for something else to happen. Mack went back to Bartlesville and a short time later he decided to go back to sailing ships again. He postponed his and

Betty Jane's wedding and took off. Neither he nor I knew it at the time, but the ship he caught did go to Japan and did shuttle back and forth to Korea for nine months. It was good that he had postponed the wedding. After Mack left, I continued to sell around Herrington.

Let me back up a bit. After our precious little baby girl, Andra Jeanne Long, was born on March 13, 1951, I had come in for the weekend a couple of days later to see Bonnie and Andra. Bonnie was still in the hospital until Sunday, March 18th. On Saturday night, my brother-in-law Dwight Stanfield and I went out to the Calico Cat Nightclub to have a few drinks and to watch the dancing girls. He took me home to Mom and Dad's house (we hadn't moved yet) and Mom was waiting up for Dwight and me. She said, "I have some really bad news for you, son."

I said, "Oh, my, what happened to Bonnie or the baby?"

She said, "They are okay, but Bonnie's dad got hit by a car and killed tonight." He was 51 years old. It was the night of March 17th; Bonnie was to go home in a day or two. Never before or after in my lifetime have I ever had to do anything as hard as to tell Bonnie that her dad was dead. He was walking across the street to a liquor store to get a bottle of wine and it was misting rain. A 17-year-old kid was driving an old Ford with a cracked windshield and it was hard to see through, especially in the rain. He ran over John Scott, dragging him for a way. They caught the kid, took John to the hospital and gave him a blood transfusion. They must not have known that he was Rh-negative; they apparently gave him Rh-positive blood and that is what killed him. It was not general knowledge in those days — he might have died of his injuries anyway, but we will never know for sure.

At least Bonnie was able to go to the funeral a few days later. This was in the middle of March, 1951. Bonnie's mother was ready to graduate from Friend's University at the end of May with her teaching degree. She and the three remaining girls who were still living at home all moved back to Galena, Kansas.

About this time her second son, J. R., got out of the Army. He was just younger than Bonnie. He was named after his dad, but did not go as John, just J. R. He was entitled to a G.I. loan, so he and his mother made a deal. J. R. was newly married, and had a job, but no real money. So, he bought a house with his G. I. loan, not a new one, but a large old two-story home. Mom had a little life insurance policy on John Scott, so she paid for the remodeling that it took to fix the upstairs room so she and the girls would have a place to live. J. R. did the work and Mom paid for the materials.

Mom got a job teaching in the Galena School System and this career lasted until she was forced to retire at the age of 72. Several years after moving into the house with J. R., the last of the three girls got married and left the nest. Viola Scott went back to the college in Pittsburgh, Kansas on nights and weekends and got her Masters Degree. Later she was made a teaching principal. What a woman! I loved her dearly, as did all her children, including her sons-in-law and daughters-in-law. I like to think I was her favorite son-in-law. There are several more stories about Viola L. Scott that I will tell as we progress.

At this juncture, I do want to tell you about her two sons. The oldest son, Robert, had built him and his wife a large new home with his own hands, just a block from his brother's two story house. Robert Scott had several acres of land, so he furnished the lot for a small two-bedroom house to be built on it. Mom got a loan to buy all the material, and the youngest son, J. R., did all the labor and built her the cutest little new home next-door to Robert. This is where she lived until she passed away with all her living children there, and she told them all that day that she was dying and she quietly passed away on June 25, 1976, twenty-six years after her husband, John Scott. She was a remarkable woman, and, as I mentioned before, was listed in "Personalities of the West and Midwest."

Now, back to 1951 and Poplar Street in Wichita. In early September, my very good friend, Lloyd Messmer, was still selling cookware. Lloyd came by my house and said he was getting ready to go up to Bismark, North Dakota. He said Tom Oliver was up there in Bismark and was really selling a lot of Lifetime Cookware. There were lots of very large wheat farms there that ran all the way to the Canadian border. Tom had moved his whole family up there: himself, his wife and three daughters. I don't know whether he was running from the Law or not, but North Dakota is a hell of a long way from San Antonio, Texas. Anyway, he was doing really well.

Lloyd was taking his wife, Audrey, and his little three year old boy, Dale, and planned on renting a furnished apartment in Bismarck. He also was pulling a small 4'x 8' trailer with things they needed to keep house.

Since we were such good friends, Lloyd said to me, "Why don't you and Bonnie go to Bismarck with us?"

I thought it over for 5 or 10 minutes and said, "When are you leaving?" It was almost September 1st, 1951 and the rent was due in a day or two. So, I bought a small trailer from the neighbor across the street and on September 1st, both the Messmers and the Longs took off. We had to cross all of Kansas from south to north, then Nebraska and South Dakota, and across North Dakota to Bismarck. It was a long trip and I think it took us two days. We both found apartments the next day, got settled in, and both went out to book dinners. Tom and his family were glad to see us. The weather was beautiful, but a little cool. Little did we know that it can get really cold in North Dakota! Things went well for a couple of months, thru October. On Sundays, the three men would go duck hunting and pheasant hunting and always get plenty of birds and ducks. We would all go to Tom's house Sunday night and eat duck or pheasant, fried potatoes, and salad. All the women were good cooks and we really enjoyed stuffing outselves. Good whiskey, good food and good friendship. Hard to beat!

The territory was big. Tom was working far north, all the way to Minot, North Dakota and Lloyd and I were working together then as we had a new baby and a 4 1/2 year old and the Messmer's had a 3 year old. When it starts snowing in October, it doesn't melt for the rest of the winter until spring. So, it was good that Lloyd and I were going to our dinners together and, that way, if we had trouble with the car we wouldn't be alone on snow-packed roads.

One night, I remember we were coming home from our sales calls and, all of a sudden, Lloyd stopped the car. I said, "Why did you stop?"

He said, "For two things. I want to have a drink of whiskey." He always kept a pint between his feet, under his front seat. "The other thing is, I think we have been driving on black ice!" He opened his car door and slid his left foot back and forth, and sure enough, it was indeed black ice. So, we slowed down for the rest of the way to town and home.

One "Dinner" I remember well. We had six couples in all but only one family spoke English. All the rest spoke Russian. There were lots of Russian farm families in North Dakota, especially near the Canadian border. We put on our regular dinner talk and the host and hostess translated for us and we sold a set to all the couples. It was the first time we had cooked on a coal stove, but I had cooked a dinner one time in San Angelo, Texas on a wood stove, so it worked out okay.

Well, November came and the roads were snow packed, but passable. In town they put coal splinters on top of the packed snow and it helped. It was around the middle of November and one evening Lloyd called me on the phone from his apartment and said, "Andy; Audrey, Dale and I just got home from the picture show. I did not take my topcoat — I only had my suit coat on and I about froze to death just driving home! I turned the radio on and they announced that the present temperature in Bismark is 27 degrees below zero! We need to be getting the hell out of here, or plan on staying inside for the rest of the winter!"

I responded with, "What say that we give Sontag a telephone call in the morning and see if he can find us a new territory where the weather is warm."

He said, "Good idea!" So the next morning a call produced the following:

Bill agreed right away asking, "Where would you like to go? We chose Ardmore, Oklahoma near the state line between Oklahoma and Texas. In two days we wre loaded and we both took off, each pulling a little two-wheeled green trailer. Lloyd in his big Buick and me in my big Oldsmobile. We didn't stop but one night until we got to Wichita to see our families. Then on to Ardmore the next day and each of us found a nice comfortable small furnished house. Believe it or not, we were both fishing for croppie on Thanksgiving Day on Lake Murry, south of Ardmore, enjoying the weather.

When Lloyd and I called Bill Sontag from North Dakota, he told us that he was not going to be able to get very much more Lifetime cookware because the Korean War was going full blast by now and the factory was really cutting back due to a steel shortage. However, he had found a source of new cookware made of three-ply steel similar to the kind that I had sold in Louisiana, except that it was a thinner three-ply steel called Eternal Ware. He thought it would cook just about like Lifetime except it might not hold heat as long. He said it would sell for a lot less money than Lifetime. Lifetime had a price increase a year or so earlier and was selling for $161.85 instead of the $126.50 when I started selling it five years before. He said, "This set has one pan less than Lifetime but the price would be only $104.85 and your commission will stay the same. Fifty percent for cash sales and forty percent for payment sales." We agreed to give it a try as we really didn't have a choice.

It worked out okay. The price was not as high, and this was a big plus in selling around Ardmore, Oklahoma as it was pretty poor country. Mostly Black Jack Oak-covered hills and rocky pasture land. Quite a lot of oil play had been there years earlier, but not much new drilling and it was not a boom type town at all. So, the price reduction on our stainless steel product was certainly a plus.

We told the same stories, with the same demonstrations. Nothing changed except a lesser quality product and a lower price. Well, we tried it and everything went very well. We were selling and putting on the dinners together and still splitting the commissions so that our wives could be at home taking care of our little children. Andra Jeanne was now just one year old, Tim was about five and a half and Dale Messmer was about four.

We were not making much money working together, but it was easier and we enjoyed doing quite a bit of fishing. Lloyd had a small aluminum boat and small boat motor that had been stored with his things in his dad's barn on their farm near Wichita. So we would take the boat and were really enjoying fishing in the warmer weather, and with spring coming on, it would soon get better. Little Dale was getting old enough that Lloyd could take Audrey and Dale with him and she really enjoyed this as she loved to fish and also to hunt.

He was perfectly happy to stay right in Ardmore, but I was getting restless to find some good wheat farm country were I could make cash sales, instead of time payments. I told Lloyd I was going to get in my car and drive due west. We had been in Ardmore since Thanksgiving and now it was around April 1, 1952. So, I packed up my suitcase, cook set, show set and several premium gifts for the hostesses, and headed west early one morning.

I got to Lawton, Oklahoma, the home of the Army's Ft. Sill military base. A real nice town but very little farm country. Lots of pasture. I had lunch and went on west around Snyder, Oklahoma and the wheat and cotton land began to look pretty good. Then on west and a little south and I came to Altus, a nice-sized town of around 12,000 people and lots of wheat and cotton farms, some irrigated land, some not.

I really liked Altus. Nice and clean and also the county seat of Jackson County. I had Altus in my mind, that this was probably where I would want to find a house for us to live in. I decided that since it was still early in the afternoon, I would drive on west on Highway 62. About ten miles or so west I came to Duke, Oklahoma, then on west another eight or ten miles was the small town of Gould, Oklahoma — all surrounded by farms of wheat and cotton land. Wheat was up and growing good and the cotton had just been planted in March and April.

Then I drove on to the town of Hollis, Oklahoma, still on Highway 62 — plenty of nice farms. I began to get pretty excited over what I had found. Hollis is located just a few miles north of the Texas line, and almost due west of Ardmore, Oklahoma; about 150 miles or so from where Lloyd and I had been working and living. It was nearly dark, so I fould a cheap motel and checked in.

I got up early the next morning, filled up with gas, had breakfast and drove west of Hollis to the Texas line, still in cotton and wheat country. Hollis was a nice small country town I would judge to be about 5,000 - 10,000 people, but with a large trade area. So, I could see a new territory that was about forty square miles. I was so enthused! I placed a call to Bonnie and said, "Start packing, I have found our new home."

The next thing I did was to go back to Altus from Hollis and look for us a furnished house or apartment. Sure enough, there it was in the newspaper the previous evening — a two-bedroom furnished house with garage and nice yard. It was just what I was looking for, so I rented it and another big plus was that two doors north was a small neighborhood grocery store that handled meats, vegetables, and everything I needed for my demonstration dinners. This was also great for Bonnie when I was gone with the car (which was most of the time). She was within one-half block to the grocery store on Lee Street, down the sidewalk. The house had a nice shade tree in the front yard and a nice front porch.

I had not driven north of Altus yet, so I did and this is where I found miles and miles of irrigated farms. Then I found out why Altus looked like a very prosperous town. I kept driving north a few more miles in the irrigated farm country and then I saw where the irrigation water was coming from. All of a sudden the flat irrigated farm land turned into some large rock mountains and a big dam and a large lake. I couldn't believe what I was seeing! It was the Sweetwater River dammed up to make a lake. It was called "Lake Lugert" by some, and by others "Lake Altus." It was a really beautiful setting and at that time, a diamond in the rough, so to speak.

Just to jump ahead 40-50 years, Lake Altus is now a resort lake with a large lodge motel. It hosts conventions, vacations, and sportmen from all over Oklahoma and north Texas. We visited it recently and I think they talked about the price tag that the State Park Dept. spent on upgrading it was around $40 million dollars. Fabulous for fishing, water skiing, boating, golf, tennis and all kinds of recreational activities. A really beautiful playground.

Now, back to 1952. Well, it was a diamond in the rough for sure! I couldn't have been happier about finding our new place to live and work. The small town of Granite, Oklahoma was near the Lake (because of the granite mountains that border the lake), where granite products like tomb stones and grave markers are manufactured. I realized the ingenuity of the people that made Oklahoma, who located a state penitentiary there and put the prisoners to work in the granite mines. This may have been the place where the saying got started, "Send those prisoners to the rock pile, and see if they will make the decision to change their lives." The town of Granite is small and has been there a long, long time.

I arranged a demonstration dinner with a nice farm couple for the following night. They invited six other couples and the next day and evening I sold six sets of Eternal Ware Cookware — four which were cash and two on time payment. Talk about ecstatic! I arranged three more dinners from that one for the next week.

Another thing that Bill Sontag says is, "If you don't find the circumstances you want, then make them to suit you. You must first know them, second, you must do. Doing one or the other will not make the results you are after." I thought of this that day. I could have stayed in Ardmore and struggled and be frustrated or I could get in my car and find a wonderful new territory to work and prosper. I have never forgotten the teachings Bill taught us young guys, and the older ones too.

The one that he taught me that I practiced for many years, and still do to this day, and have taught my children and grandchildren is "Plan your work, then Work your plan." So simple, but you will be surprised how effectively it works. Believe me!

When I got back to Ardmore to get Bonnie, Tim and baby Andra to move them to Altus, we went over to see Lloyd and Audrey Messmer and tell them all about Altus and to say goodbye.

Lloyd had bought himself a little larger outboard motor — a 7 1/2 horsepower Scot-Atwater and so I bought his old 4-horse little Scot-Atwater. I told him all about Altus and the nice lake and told him to come on over and share this good territory with me. He said, "I'll think about it and let you know." He liked Lake Maury so much that he just wasn't ready to make a move.

So away we went the next morning and by evening we were through unloading the small trailer and moved into our furnished house and settled in. Everything went well and I was selling like hell! I would get up early and drive to Lake Altus about 17 miles and rent a small boat for $2 and buy 3 dozen minnows for $1 from the guy that ran the boat and tackle shop. The little 4-horse motor was just what I needed. I would fish until around noon, drive home, leave the fish for my sweet wife to clean, than step over to the corner grocery and buy my groceries for my cookware dinner that night. I would now take a two-hour nap while Bonnie would wash and brush my potatoes, wash and peel and slice my carrots, slice up my cabbage and put them all in plastic refrigerator bags. I would awake from my nap, shave, shower, dress and boogie out of there to go to work for the evening, arriving at the host and hostess's home around 4:30 PM and start the dinner — cooking and showing the hostess how to do it. Then, have the dinner as usual, using the big hard surface paperplates, which made it a lot easier on me working by myself. Then I'd make my appointments for the next day and evening as usual and then "Sell, Sell, Sell."

Since I was selling most of my sales for cash, Sontag made me a better deal on buying my cookware from him. He would send me six or eight sets at a time. I would pay for them in advance. This made it easier on him and also on me, as I could deliver each set as I sold it. The people didn't have to wait a week or two for delivery. Also there was never any doubt in their minds that they might never get their cookware that they had paid for. This got me about a $10 or $15 raise on what I was making on each sale.

So, making money and having fun, and don't forget — working hard. Bill Sontag was still handling my time payment orders for me.

It was looking like both the wheat and cotton farmers were going to have a very good crop. This made selling a lot easier! It got so good that I sold almost 100% of my sales in this new territory. One Sunday, Bonnie took the kids to church, just up the street a couple of blocks. When she got home she said that she met the nicest lady about her age with two children about the ages of ours. The girl was Tim's age and the boy was Andra's age. Her name was Myrtle Jones. She talked on and she said that they visited about what their husbands did for a living and other things. Myrtle said her husband had a small acreage at the east edge of town and was building some buildings for a small shopping center. After we had our Sunday dinner, we went for a drive and took a look at this guy's project.

Well, it consisted of one pretty nice wooden building that was a beer joint, a nice looking one with a bar and small dance floor with booths around it. Right behind the bar he had built three nice little one-bedroom cottges and one two-bedroom one. Then, across the parking area from the bar, he had a small service station. Next door to it was a block building about 25' x 60' that was a used furniture store run by the wife of the station owner. Next to the furniture store was a new block building that was the same size as the furniture store that was still vacant. It had a nice glass front and door; there was still not floor covering or paint as yet. The man's name was Bobby Jones and he called this little venture, Jonesville. At this juncture I'm going to tell you about Bobby Jones. Get ready for quite a true story!

"Jonesy," as well call him, joined the U. S. Marine Corps in 1940, a year or so before World War II started, along with some other guys who were all in the National Guard. He served in northern China, up near the Russian border. He used to tell me that he and the Russion girls would talk through the fence and that some of them were beautiful girls, a cross between Chinese and Russian. Anyway, when the Japs bombed Pearl Harbour he was stationed on Corregidor Island and was almost immediately involved in some very fierce fighting. They hadn't had time to build up a large number of soldiers or Marines yet, so when they were attacked, they were greatly out-numbered. So, Gen. Skinny Wainwright, as they called him, had to surrender the Island upon Gen. Douglas MacArthur's orders.

MacArthur escaped by P.T. boat to Australia and this is when the well-known phrase, "I shall return." was born.

The Marines held out as long as they could, but it was inevitable what had to be done at the time. This was when the infamous "Battan Death March" started. Jonesy was right there, right in that march and became a Japanese prisoner of war for four years. He suffered, as all of them did that managed to survive this long march of eighty-five miles. Lots of men died on the march. The ones that did survive were put to work in the mines, constantly under guard. Made into slave laborers, they were given very little food, beaten often and endured horrible treatment. Any excuse the Japs had, they took. There was never a good meal, most of what they ate was a thin soup of water and caffer corn, as we call it in the States — sort of like we see now in chicken and bird feed.

All the prisoners soon looked like walking skeletons. All they had to wear was their tattered uniforms, just what they had when they were captured. Malnutrition was rampant and it seemed, according to Jonesy, that it attacked the weakest part of each soldier's body — for some it affected their lungs, some their hearts, some their brain, eyes, or stomach. It affectd Bobby's eyes and ended up killing the optic nerve in each eye. There is no treatment for this "dry" type of macular degeneration, then or now. Bobby is blind, for when he looks straight ahead, he can see only at the sides of his eyes. So, there is very little he can do. Naturally, he cannot drive and read like anyone else. The average guy would just give up, but not Jonesy.

The Japs had intended to just blow shut the entrances to the mines while the soldiers worked them, but our forces rushed in so fast they were able to save many of the prisoners before the Japs could accomplish this.

A story that Jonesy told me is about one of the Marine Captains. The Captain was some kind of a prick before the capture, and still was afterwards. He had a little dog somehow and he loved that dog. Well, one day three or four of the guys decided they would skin the little dog and roast him, so they did. The Captain said, "What are you guys cooking?" One of them answered, "We caught a rabbit. Would you like some of it?" The Captain answered, "You boys mean you would share it with me, are you sure?" They said, "Oh, yeah. You can have some." Well, they all enjoyed having a little bit of meat for a change as the only meat they got was if they happened to find a nest of baby mice or if they pulled some bark off a tree to get some bugs. This is true.

Anyway, the Captain had not missed his little dog as yet, but in a while he did and he called and he called, but no dog did he find. Well, it finally dawned on him that he had eaten some of his little dog. Jonesy said, "He liked to went nuts!" They were all too weak to fight so no "fisticuffs" occurred, but this was a real payback for this prick Captain. They enjoyed the payback as well as the meal. Bobby also said, "If they stole anything at all from the Japs, they were shot," so not many of them did.

V. J. Day came and Bobby and his two brothers got home alive. One of his brothers was also a Marine and was shot and wounded by a Jap soldier. As the Jap lunged into Harold's fox hole to finish him off with his bayonette, Harold shot the Jap dead. He survived in pretty good shape. The other brother was in the Merchant Marines and he came home okay, with no injuries.

The boy's dad had ran a combination pawn shop and small clothing store before, and during, the War. The three boys grew up helping their dad in the store so two older boys went back to work with their dad, but with Bobby's eyes he wouldn't have been able to read the price tags. So he had to do something else. Well, the first thing he did was buy a nice corner lot in Altus and a small concrete block machine, with the money he had coming from the four years back pay he got for the time spent in the Jap prison. He made enough blocks to build his house, one-at-a-time. He said that the one thing he learned in prison camp was patience. He did have that. When the house was finished he married Myrtle, who was working at the telephone company and they moved into their new home. He bought her a brand new convertible, the prettiest little black and white Ford Victoria. Of course, she had to do all the driving, and still does. He was restless and went far and wide searching for something that would help him see, but to no avail.

Altus was the home of an Air Force base that was used to train pilots during World War II and they were ready to tear down all the, more or less, temporary buildings. One very large building was used for Air Force troops to play basketball and various other large gatherings and so on. They put it up for bids and Bobby submitted the high bid. He always thought his War record and being a prisoner of war had a lot to do with his getting the building. What his plan was, was to move it into town from the base intact, but it was just too large for any house moving company to move. He planned to use it for a sports center. He planned to have boxing and wrestling matches and all kinds of sporting events and contests. When it was too heavy and large to move, he had to change his plans as to how he could use the building.

Jonesy, being very smart and with an inventive nature, decided to hire a bunch of guys to tear it down, clean the lumber and haul it to town, a truckload at a time. He had to do something. He had three or four acres on the highway east of town, so this is when he decided to build the bar and lounge and the four little cat houses behind it with the lumber. He named the bar The Pink Elephant. Being a Marine he recognized every bar and lounge needed some little houses or cabins nearby. Then he built the filling station and the other buildings and rented them out. All except the one that wasn't quite finished when I met him.

I was still selling Eternal Ware and fishing and enjoying my little family and nice house. My sister, Marjorie, and brother-in-law, Dwight, decided to drive down from Wichita to visit us. Dwight and I naturally went fishing that next morning and Marge and Bonnie stayed home. Bonnie had seen what I am going to tell you before and mentioned it to me, but I thought she didn't know what she was talking about and didn't pay much attention. Maybe it had only happened once or twice, I don't know. Anyway, she told Marge about it and they laughed and talked about it. Our kitchen window over the sink looked out over our side driveway into the neighbor's back yard. They were both in the kitchen and Bonnie looked out the window, and said, "Marge, quick, look he's doing it again!" The old boy was the grocery man's father-in-law and lived in the house next door to us, in between our house and the grocery store. Well, the guy was around 45-50 years old and he was standing in his back yard in full view of our kitchen window and he had his pecker out, swinging it around and round and it was a dandy, a real whopper. Marge said, "Oh, my God! I never saw anything like this — and so big!" This is what Bonnie had been trying to tell us, but none of us would believe her. The girls were flabbergasted and Bonnie said to Marge, "Well, enough is enough! I'm going over and knock on their front door and talk to his wife about this." Well she did. The lady just couldn't believe it and denied it. So Bonnie said, "If it happens again I'm calling the police." Well, it didn't happen any more.

The old boy was a watchmaker and had a little watch shop in his son-in-laws grocery store and I would see him every time I bought my Dinner groceries. I would not have thought it would happen. Our girls laughed about this for many, many years. Well, a few years later after we left Altus it happened again. Except at The Pink Elephant bar and lounge. Jonesy was not there at the time it happened, but the waitress told him about it. This same old boy was sitting in a booth by himself and when the girl brought him his beer he had his big old thing out and laying on the table. She told Jonsey that she was speechless. Finally, she told the guy that he had better put that thing away or she was coming back with a butcher knife to cut it off. I guess he was just so proud of it he just had to show it off.

One day later, after all this had happened, I told Bonnie what we should do was to talk to Mr. Jones (we had just met him at this point) and see how much rent he was charging for his new building that was just about ready. Bonnie said, "What would you do with it?" I said, "Remember the little dry sundry store mom worked at in Albuquerque when the folks lived there? Well, we could open a sundry store, have a soda fountain for cokes, make malts, shakes, coffee and sell candy, gum, cigarettes, magazines, comic books and all the other things drug stores handle, except prescriptions."

I said, "You could run this store and I will help you until I go on my dinners in the evening. I will keep on selling cookware and maybe someday I'll go to college and study to be a pharmacist." There was a college at Wetherford, about 85 miles from Altus, that taught pharmacy. Well, we talked about this some more and decided to see how much Jonesy wanted for rent and what he thought about our idea. Realize, I was now 26 years old. I thought, like most of us do at that age, that I knew about all I needed to know. With a sparkle in my eyes, the whole world was our oyster. I just knew I could do about anything that I really wanted to do.

Jonesy said, "Okay." I think the rent was about $75 a month then, but I'm not sure. Coffee and cokes were a nickel, cigarettes 20 cents, so I'm not sure about how much the rent was then. Anyway, he said, "I'll buy the tile for the floor covering if you will help me lay it." I said "Yes," and then Bonnie and Myrtle decided to help us too. We did a good job. Then we built a partition all the way across, separating the front part from the back part, for a store room and bathroom. We installed the bathroom fixtures and then I decided to buy a soda fountain and ice cream case, back bar, long counter, and set of ten stoools for the counter. What a job!

We looked in the Oklahoma City paper and found a soda fountain, carbinator and the works for our soda bar. Our good friend, Lloyd Howard, who lived in El Reno, about 35 miles west of Oklahoma City, was no longer selling cookware. He was living on a wheat farm share-cropping for the old couple that owned the farm and milking a whole bunch of cows. He had recently gotten a job as a guard, or a security officer as they call them now. So, in fact, he had three incomes: one from his share of 1/2 of the crop from the wheat, another from the sale of milk from his cows, and the third from his job at the El Reno Federal Prison. He was doing well, and we were still very good friends. I called Red Howard and said, "My friend Bobby Jones and I are on our way to try and buy a used soda fountain in Oklahoma City. Red, could you drive us over from your house in your pickup and bring it back to Altus?" He said, "Sure, glad to do it." So we did. I negotiated a pretty good deal for the works and got it for $250, about two-thirds of his asking price.

Jonesy and I had our work cut out for us plumbing the carbinator, but we prevailed and also hooked up a new evaporative cooler for air conditioning. It took us a month or so before we got our sign up across the top front of the building, "Andy's Sundries." Then the same thing on a big sign in the front drive near the highway. By the time we got it all done, it must have taken two months. I was still putting on my Dinners as our need for money was great in order to get our stock and get started. Jonesy took me into the bank where he did his business. He introduced me to the old president of the bank. His name was Bellinger — I will never forget him. I had never borrowed money from a bank before. The only thing I had ever financed was when I traded cars, so this was a first for me. Jonesy had known this old man for a long time. He told him what I wanted to do and that he was my landlord. Now, Jonesy was about two years older than me, and that wasn't very old. The banker asked how much money I would need. I said about $1,500 would do it and I could pay it back at $100 per month.

141

"Well, go home boys and count the silverware, and I'll make you this loan." It was the first money I had ever borrowed in my life. This doesn't seem like a lot of money today, but then you could buy a new car for that amount of money. In fact, about four months before all this, I had bought a new four-door Plymouth for $1,650. So, it was a lot of money in those days. (I was becoming quite an entrepreneur, buying cookware ten sets at a time from Sontag and getting ready to open a new business.)

My lucky star was about to shine once more. About a hundred feet east of our store was a butane company office. And right behind the office was a good-sized house for rent. We had to buy some furniture, but not too much, and this was a real deal for us because Bonnie was to run the store while I was selling cookware and we only had one car. This was a big problem with us living on the other side of town, about two miles away. Living next door to our business would be just fine. The five guys that worked at the butane company all became good friends and good customers at our sundry store. Another plus was that Lloyd and Audrey were about ready to join us in Altus, over from Ardmore, Oklahoma. Well, the house we had next to the grocery store on Lee Street was just what they needed.

My Mom and Dad, and little brother, John, decided to move down and for mom go to work in our new store and help Bonnie and also help take care of our little baby, Andra, who was about 18 months old. Tim was almost six and Dad and him were such good friends. We had three large wire-round turning racks chocked full of comic books for sale as well as other magazines. Tim would sit down on the floor between the three tall racks and spent damn near all day in the summer time reading them. The school bus picked him and his uncle John up right in front of our house and dropped them off after school. No problem there. Oh, yes. Bobby Jones' two bedroom house was vacant so this is where my folks and brother lived — very convenient.

There was a vacant lot between the butane office and our store building, so Jones rented it to a company for a used car sales lot. Dad had sold cars for 27 years before the War so he got a job selling used cars. They had a small trailer for an office. This was just fine, as it gave Dad something to do. His health wasn't very good, but the work wasn't hard either. Dad had emphysema and couldn't do any physical work to speak of. Jonesy and

Dad became good friends also and, as I told you earlier, Dad was a World War I veteran. So, Bobby, having pull with the local American Legion in Altus, somehow got Dad set up to get a Veteran's pension. What a help this was! The folks really needed this income and it lasted Dad the rest of his life. What a blessing. He never forgot Jonesy for what he did for him. I don't know what string he pulled, but it worked.

Things were going well, except we were working very hard and long hours. Bonnie and I both grew up working so we knew how, but this was taking it's toll on us both. We would open the store at 8:00 AM and close at midnight. Sixteen hours every day, except Monday which we would take off. Lots of days while I was gone selling, which was most of the time, Bonnie was doing it all at the store. Something had to change.

Bonnie's sister, Juanita, had married and her husband was stationed at Ft. Sill, Oklahoma near Lawton, just sixty miles from us. They had a newly born baby boy. Bonnie wrote to Juanita and told her that if she came down from Wichita, Kansas and stayed with us, she could bring her baby, Michael, and Andy would pick up her husband, Cliff Johnson, every Friday evening and he could visit her and the baby for the weekend. Then Andy would take him back to Ft. Sill on Sunday night. Juanita and the baby could live with us and she could take care of little Andra, who was now about 2 1/2 years old. Juanita could feed the kids and keep house and help Andy prepare his vegetables for his Dinner demonstrations. Well, this suited them just fine! I even let Cliff use my car when I wasn't using it while he was there for the weekend. They enjoyed this. So, we made it work.

Bonnie was on her feet for such long periods that she miscarried our third child. It was an early miscarriage, so no great deal of damage to my Bonnie. I don't know how we would have handled another child at this particular time. I guess we would have somehow. We always did.

As the months passed, the Jones and the Longs became better and better friends. And, as of right now, this friendship has lasted fifty years, from 1952 to 2002. About once a month in those days Jonesy and I would drive across the Oklahoma and Texas state line to a little village in Texas called Punkin Center. Well, I don't think I mentioned that Oklahoma was a dry state, except for beer. So, we would go down to Punkin Center about twenty miles, buy some whiskey and brandy and hide it in the weeds out behind my building. We didn't drink much wiskey or brandy, but we had it when we wanted it. Most of our casual drinking was at Jonesy's club, The Pink Elephant, that served only beer.

One day, Bobby and I were sitting at the counter drinking coffee when a big old boy came in and ordered a malt. We didn't know him. Bonnie made the best malts and shakes anywhere — so thick that when you turned the plastic cup upside down, it wouldn't fall out. Real thick. Anyway, we kept the different flavors in a big ice cream chest against the wall and it kept the ice cream real hard. When she dipped it out with the round dipper, she really had to press hard to get the ice cream into the steel mixer for the malt.

Bonnie was always good-looking, especially in those days. Well, in the process of dipping the ice cream, her whole rear end was somewhat in motion. This old boy, about 30 or 35, said "You are getting kind of heafty there, aren't you gal?" Well this set her off! She told him in no uncertain terms, "Well, if I am it is no concern of yours!" The old boy paid for his malt and got the hell out of there right quick!

Jonesy and I were laughing our asses off, and then Bonnie really got pissed off at us for not doing anything to this big guy. Later we were glad we didn't try, as after he left, someone else said "Did you guys know that old boy is a deputy sheriff?"

Several months later Mom and Dad informed us they needed to go back to Dewey, Oklahoma as my grandmother was not doing too well and she wanted them to move in with her. So this is what they did.

Later, Timmy almost choked to death. He had gotten a 2" cardboard whistle, in a box of candy at the Saturday morning movie show, with a small round metal insert that had sharp edges wedged into one end of the cardboard. The sides of the little metal was crimped like a pop lid, only much smaller. Well, he would blow through the whistle and suck in a big breth to blow it again. By putting the cardboard in his mouth a number of times, it became wet and the little metal piece that was crimped came out of the cardboard and Tim swallowed it. Well, Dr. Abbernathy, our doctor, had his office next door to his house — we got Tim there within five minutes. The doctor could see where it was stuck in Tim's throat, but he could not get hold of it with his instrument — shaped like a pair of scissors but with plyers on the blades — without the sharp crimped edges of the whistle tearing Tim's throat and esophygus. Of course, we were there along with Jonesy. I was right beside Tim and the doctor. Well, Tim started choking and turned colors and couldn't breathe. I grabbed Tim up in my arms and said, "Doctor, don't let him die..." I started shaking him vigorously and all of a sudden he vomited and out came the whistle. "Thank you, God" was the only appropriate thing to say. What a scare!

We were into our second year in the sundry business and it was taking all I could make selling my cookware, with Bonnie working herself to death. That meant something had to change again. Well, we decided to remove almost all of the drug store type stock we were trying to sell because we didn't have many customers for this type of merchandise. Most of our business was coming from our soda fountain, candy, cigarettes, coffee, milk shakes, hamburgers, soups and sandwiches. So what I did was sell off all this slow moving stuff. We then had a carpenter build a bunch of booths with a sizable area for a little dance floor, partitioned it off with a half wall so the teenagers would have a place of their own to hang out, dance, visit and play the jukebox.

Then we added a grill and went into the hamburger and sandwich business. As cheap as everything was — like cokes five cents, coffee five cents, malts 25 cents — Bonnie was putting in sixteen hour days and the take in the cash register was only around $20. I had just been subsidizing the store with my cookware sales. In order to increase business further we decided to hire some cute girls to curb hop. This drew quite a bit of extra business. We changed the name of the place to Andy's Drive-in. This all helped, but we could see that it was never going to do enough business for me to stop selling cookware.

The old airbase was torn down, as I told you about earlier, and by this time the Korean War was over. Then the Cold War was beginning to warm up, so we got word that they were going to re-open the base with permanent-type structures, most of which would be brick buildings and housing. The planes would be B-47's and also air-to-air tanker refueling planes to train the airmen for this work. They moved in quite a lot of young, new airmen and as it so happened, our drive-in was half way between town and the air base on the highway. So, with the pretty little curb hops, business did improve.

Again, I used Sontag's teaching: if you don't like the circumstances you are in, then make them — by making a change — which I did. We were in our third year and old Lloyd Messmer and I had really saturated our farm family territory and it became necessary for us to again work together. So we ranged far out and would be gone a week at a time. I would come to town on weekends and stock up on groceries and things for our homes for a week, then take off again for another week. We were working out as far as 150 miles from Altus. Lots of driving. We would take one of our cars one week, then the other car the next week. One weekend, Bonnie and I had a long talk about our future and decided what we needed to do was sell our drive-in and locate in another good territory to sell cookware.

I finally had an answer — after trying to sell the store for several months to no avail. This old farmer had a couple of teenage daughters around 18 or 19 years old. They were definitely ripe and ready for picking. He stopped in one day and asked me if I would consider trading my business for a farm. I answered that I might be interested — "Tell me about it".

So he said, "It is 80 acres located up in the sand hills north of Gould, Oklahoma." This is an area where I had sold lots of cookware (except in this part, being located in the sand hills). No chance of irrigation and a dry land farm was not worth too much, I thought. He said he had an offer to sell it to a neighbor for $4,000 but he and the neighbor had never gotten along and he said he didn't want to sell it to that SOB.

Well, the light came on in Andy's head! I thought, I don't know his neighbor. So why don't I trade the farmer for his 80 acres then after the deal is made, sell it to the neighboring farmer. Oh, the girls were so happy and so was their daddy. There was nothing for them to do out there on the farm and the old man knew this. He was looking for a place where the girls would be exposed to the possiblity of getting married. The little drive-in was just the thing that would make this possible as we had quite a lot of airmen stop in for pie, coffee, soft drinks and hamburgers.

Jonesy was a smart guy and he said, "Andy, they won't last long, I don't think, but I am your friend and I can see you do need to get rid of this place. If they don't make it, I can always rent the building for some other type business, so I won't hold you up. Make the deal."

Well, we made the deal and in a few days I sold the little farm for around $4,000, which is not a lot of money nowadays, but in those days it was. Today the $4,000 would be like $40,000 today. At least ten times. Remember, I had bought a new Plymouth three years earlier for $1,650 and today it would get a least $16,000. So looking at it this way, it wasn't too bad a deal.

So, again putting Sontag's teachings to work, I made better circumstances. We said our goodbyes. Bonnie's sister Juanita's husband was being transferred so she and her little boy moved back to Wichita. We decided to move to Oklahoma City. Once again, three long years of hard work were behind us. Lots of memories and some very good, long-lasting friendships.

We had mixed emotions about leaving but we knew it was time to go on to, hopefully, greener pastures. We located a nice two-bedroom brick duplex, on the same street that we had lived on when we lived in the brick duplex just before we went on the Baton Rouge, Louisiana venture. There was a nice school, Thomas A Edison Elementary, nearby for Tim, who was now in the third grade. This was in January 1955. Andra would soon be three years old in March. We had the money that we got from the sale of the 80-acre farm in the bank and our little Plymouth that we had bought in Altus in 1952, which had a lot of miles on it. So we went car shopping and bought a very beautiful red and white Desoto 4-door sedan.

Television sets had only been on the market for a year or so and we had not bought one yet, so bought a nice 25-inch set. My Dad loved us all so very much that he drove down from Dewey to stay with us for a while. He was not able to work, but my mother got a job in Bartlesville working the front counter of a cleaning shop and laundry. She had done this type of work years earlier in her life before she got married, so she had plenty of experience. Of course, she was also there with my grandmother to look after her. Dad loved the new television set! He would turn it on in the morning and it was on all day until late at night!

Sontag was getting good deliveries on Lifetime Stainless Steel sets from the factory again, so I went back to selling Lifetime again instead of the cheaper Eternal Ware. I was beginning to tire of selling cookware. I had been selling it for seven or eight years and just couldn't get too excited about it. One day we got a letter from my sister in Wichita and she suggested that I move to Wichita and see about getting a job selling real estate. She said, "Andy, you would make a good real estate salesman, I think." This was about three months after we had moved to Oklahoma City from Altus.

One little story that I must tell you now is about little Andra Jeanne. Our neighbors had a little girl about the same age. They were playing in our front yard. We lived about three houses down the street form the busy Lincoln Boulevard. Well, the girls decided to walk up to Lincoln Blvd. and play. Anyway, Bonnie got a knock on the door and it was a policeman with both girls in tow. He said, "I found these two running back and forth across Lincoln Boulevard." Bonnie couldn't believe Andra had gotten out of her sight so quickly! She thanked the officer very much and set our little girl down for a long serious talk.

The more I thought about my sister's suggestion, the more I wanted to give it a try. So we drove to Wichita for a visit with my sister and Bonnie's sister, Dorothy. Dorothy was now divorced and had three small children — two boys about Tim's age and one little girl a year younger than Andra. Dorothy had a good job that she had had for a long time as bookkeeper for a furniture store. She was the sole breadwinner for her flock, so she had her hands full. However, she had bought a small two-bedroom house in a large subdivision called Meadowview. She had her two little boys in some sort of a home (I never understood how that worked) and she would see them every weekend. To make a long story short, while Bonnie was telling her that we were thinking of moving back to Wichita and maybe Andy would sell real estate, Dorothy came up with this idea:

She said, "You folks, move in with me. Pay the grocery expenses and take care of my daughter Bonita for me and it won't cost you anything until Andy sees if he want to sell real estate or not. Give it a try." We talked it over and decided it was a good idea.

So, here we go again. We moved in and I studied like mad for a couple of weeks for the real estate salesman's license exam. I took the exam and passed. With license in hand and a nearly new car which was an essential in the real estate business, I approached the Graham Realty Company. The company was owned by Allan Graham and his brother-in-law, who was a housing contractor of subdivisions. We had plenty of new homes to sell. Allan's younger brother, Bob Graham, was also working as a salesman along with with a couple of other young guys. All of us were pretty young, including the boss. I jumped right in, and in the first three weeks I sold a house each week. Boy, I got excited! But something bad was about to happen — and did. Boeing Aircraft Co., which was the major employer in Wichita then, had a major layoff. That shook up the entire city. It was very similar to what had happened to us in Baton Rouge, Louisiana about seven years earlier.

To make a long story shorter, I stayed with it for two or three months longer and didn't sell another house. It was time to change our circumstances again. We had been in Wichita about four or five months. I hadn't had time yet to figure out just what I would do. Early one evening in the summer, a big storm came up. Kansas was famous for having lots of tornados and it looked like we could be getting one now. My old friend, Lloyd Messmer, was now living in Wichita with his sister, mother, his old father, and his little boy, Dale in a large two-story home on South Broadway about three miles from Bonnie's sister. Lloyd was now out of the cookware business also.

Now, bear with me for a very important and serious thing that happened to the Messmer family. While we were struggling with getting rid of our business venture in Altus, Oklahoma, Lloyd, Audrey and little Dale (who was now about five years old) moved to Venita, Oklahoma. Remember how Lloyd loved to fish? Well, Lake Afton, was a great, big lake near Venita. Lloyd was enjoying fishing and hunting and selling cookware in the area. He was living in a trailer house with his wife and son.

Audrey had just had another baby boy. She liked to fish and hunt and hadn't had much time to do so with having to raise little Dale. Dale was now big enough to go with Lloyd and her quite a bit and she was happy about this, but when she found out they were going to have another child it threw her into a tailspin, so to speak. Here she is with another baby to raise and leading a lonesome, hum-drum life with a five year old and a baby. She just couldn't handle it. (This was all happening while we were in Oklahoma City, just a month or so before we moved to Wichita.)

She called Bonnie one day and asked her if we could come up to Venita to visit them. It was about 150 miles to Venita (north of Tulsa) from Oklahoma City. Lloyd and I went fishing early the next morning while Bonnie and Audrey and the children stayed there in the trailer and visited and the little boys played. She and Bonnie talked about lots of things — as we had known them since 1947 — and Lloyd an I had sold cookware together for so long and had lots of good times together. When Lloyd and I arrived back to their trailer from fishing we ate lunch and then Audrey asked Bonnie if she would drive her to downtown Venita, just a few blocks away. So they did, and Audrey said "Bonnie, stop here at the Western Union office. I want to send my dad a telegram." He lived in southern Oklahoma in a small town named Wapanuka.

Lloyd used to laugh and say his wife came from Wapanuckie, that always got a good laugh. They had met in Wichita, and gotten married there, when they worked at the Boeing Aircraft Plant during World War II.

While the girls were driving around and talking after she sent the telegram to her dad, she was so upset with her situation that Bonnie was getting very concerned about her. She told Bonnie that she wanted her dad to come see her — this is why she sent the telegram. Well, an hour or so later, we left for Oklahoma City. Bonnie told me she was worried about Audrey, and she thought she had tried to commit suicide but was scared and didn't do it. We were worried.

Audrey's brother and his family lived in Tulsa. He was a big wheel in the oil field pipe- line workers' union. Well, when we got to Tulsa it was late afternoon on Sunday. We found his address in the phone book and drove to his house. They were not at home, so we left him a note telling him how much we were concerned and continued on to our house in Oklahoma City.

We tried to call Audrey's dad that evening and got no answer. They were gone, so the next morning we called him and Bonnie told him her concerns. He said they were not home yesterday and they had not received any telegram. He also told Bonnie that he planned to go see Audrey and Lloyd and the new baby in a few days and he would have a talk with Audrey. We had tried hard to alert them, but to no avail.

I had a Dinner demonstration party that night which was Monday. Lloyd had told me that he had one booked for Monday night also. Anyway, while we were eating breakfast Tuesday morning, the phone rang and it was Lloyd. He told us that Audrey had shot herself with his twenty-two rifle while he was putting on his Monday night demonstration. The little boy, Dale, was playing outside. She had tried once and shot herself in the upper shoulder and then tried again and got the job done. We were so sad to hear this, but we tried our best to let them know. They just didn't think anything like this could happen.

Bill and Maxine Sontag in Wichita were as shocked as we were. Bill said that they would drive to Oklahoma City and pick us up and we could all go down to Wapanuka together. So sad.

Lloyd was left with a five year old boy and a new baby that had a lot of things wrong with him. I don't remember all of the baby's problems but they were such that there was no way Lloyd could cope with them. The baby was adopted and Lloyd had no way of finding out who had taken him. This is when Lloyd took Dale and they moved to Wichita with his folks and older sister in their big house on South Broadway.

It wasn't long after this that we moved from Oklahoma City to Wichita and started selling real estate and lived with Bonnie's sister, and when the storm came up that I wrote about earlier, we went to Lloyd's folks' house in order to share their storm celler — a large one.

As Lloyd and I were standing outside the cellar watching the clouds, I got a bright idea. I said to Lloyd, "Why don't you and I go into the storm cellar and bomb cellar business?" At this time in the U.S., the whole country was concerned about all the missile silos that we had pointed at Russia and I'm sure that Russians had them pointed at the U.S., too. So, we figured as long as we lived in so-called "tornado alley", we might as well sell bomb shelters.

The more we thought of it, the more we decided this is what we should do. Lloyd said, "My nephew is about your age, Andy, and a sharp, slick guy. Let's the three of us go in together. That will help our finances." I agreed. His name was Les Black and he had a used car lot and owned a nightclub — a wheeler, dealer type. So, we rented a house near Harry Street and S. Broadway in a busy part of town for our office and headquarters.

I don't remember just how we found these guys, but they were from Arkansas. Both big and strong, one was the other's father-in-law. They had a set of steel forms that bolted together in about 3 foot by 5 foot sections. They would dig a large circular hole, then get inside of the hole and bolt all these forms together, set it up about 4-6 inches off the dirt floor, then put on the round stectioned pieces that made the ceiling of the cellar, bolt it all together from the inside, so when they poured the cement from the ready mix truck using a concrete vibrator, the cellar would not have any seams and would be completely waterproof. Then we would use waterproof paint so the inside would be nice and clean and bug-proof. Then, we would make the steps and build the door with 3/4 inch marine plywood and cover it with sheet metal. Also we would install a vent in the roof for air. Very nice, very tight. These sold for around $550 for the one that was flush with the top of the ground, to be used for tornado protection. For a more expensive one for $650, we would dig the hole three feet deeper and put three feet or dirt over the top in order to be safe from radiation from an atomic bomb. We figured that these two models should sell well as the storm Lloyd and our families were watching when we got this bright idea did indeed hit the small town of Udal, Kansas that very night and killed a lot of people.

So, we had a pretty large sign made, hired a sign painter to paint a picture of a tornado cloud and a bomb explosion going off, etc. It went quite well for a couple of months but when the tornado season was past people just lost interest in storm cellars. Heck, they could buy a good used car as a second car for $500 or $600. So, our good intentions and hard work didn't pan out. Les did keep the thing going for a while and also added the contruction of concrete swimming pools to the storm and bomb shelter business.

Lloyd got a steady job with Cessna Aircraft Company that gave him a regular income and regular hours to better care for his little boy, Dale, who he was raising by himself. He bought himself a nice trailer home located at the edge of a large pond. The pond was previously a sand pit. There are lots of them around Wichita. You can dig down anywhere in Wichita about ten feet and hit water. Wichita has had the large Arkansas River running through it for centuries with lots of sand, so the pits are deep and filled with water, and the fishing is good at most of them. This trailer park was the ideal one for Lloyd, as his love for fishing made it the perfect spot to park his trailer. He worked his hours so that he could take Dale to school and pick him up. They lived at this place for years.

Our own kids were getting older now and we could see the need to get in one spot and stay there so that they would not be changing schools all the time. Andra was about to start in First Grade and Tim was getting ready to start the Fourth Grade. Back to Dewey, Oklahoma we went. We found an almost new, nice two-bedroom house at 102 Herford Street, across the street from Bluestem Elementary School and only about four blocks from my Grandmother's house and my Mom and Dad. I was back into the cookware business with Sontag and Lifetime Cookware.

We planned on staying put for some time, or at least where Bonnie and the kids were concerned. If I had to travel later on I could, and come home on weekends. It was time to buy some furniture and settle into the little house. It was pretty nice when I think about it — back where I started high school and graduated in May 1942. Close to schools and my folks could enjoy their grandchildren, too.

It was a hot summer of 1956, almost too hot to book any cookware dinners. I had my work cut out for me to figure out a plan of survival! The stint in Wichita in the real estate business and the expense of buying furniture had taken it's toll on our finances. I somehow got hold of a sales training manual teaching encyclopedia salesmen how to get appointments and to make sales of sets of encyclopedias by the referral method. I figured if it worked on books I might be able to modify the pitch to fit cookware. This way I would not have to put on dinners to make sales and it would be a lot less expensive to run my cookware operation; no food or premiums to buy and not the long trips driving, plus I could be at home most every night. So, you can see there were lots of reasons for me to try hard to write and memorize this new selling technique.

I planned on selling to single working girls for most of my sales, and some young married couples, occasionally. The thought behind this was two-fold: young ladies usually get a job of some kind when they graduate and make some money. Most of them live at home with their parents. They usually have more disposable income than married folks with families to support. Their mom and dad usually provide their shelter and food, so they have money to buy some things for their hope chests, like linens, dishes, silverware, cookware and so on. Bartlesville happened to be the world headquarters for Phillips Petroleum Company and they employed many, many office workers. Most of the young girls all wanted to go to work for Phillips. The problem was how to get the appointments to show my Lifetime set of cookware.

I studied the encyclopedia plan diligently and began to formulate it to fit my Lifetime set. Bonnie typed it up for me and a week or so afterward I had it memorized; it was time to give my plan a try. The first problem was how to get the first sets sold in order to get some referral names? I picked out a nice looking apartment house close to the Phillips Petroleum building. Sure enough, I hit the jackpot on the first door I knocked on. A young lady came to the door and I gave her my memorized pitch, "Hello, my name is Andy Long. I work for the advertising department of Reynolds Metals Company of Chicago, Illinois. We are now advertising a new product and I have a gift for you, just to look at it and give me your honest opinion. I won't ask you to buy anything. Could you spare me just a few minutes of your time?"

She said, "Okay, won't you step in."

Again, I said, "My name is Andy Long and I work for the advertising department of Reynolds Metals Company. What is your name?"

She said, "Mary Jane Williams."

"Well, Mary Jane, let me give you the little gift I promised. Here it is." I had it in my inside suitcoat pocket and I took it out; a nice engraved stainless steel pie and cake server. "You know, most companies spend their advertising money either in magazines or newspaper ads or on the radio or television. That costs thousands of dollars when you think about it, right?" I'd then had her first affirmative answer. The first "yes." Very important at this stage of the pitch.

"Mary Jane, our company does it differently. They spend their advertising money on things like the cake server I gave to you and other things also. By the way, do you have your hope chest started yet?" Then I'd get her second "yes" answer.

"By the way, Mary Jane, do you happen to work for Phillips Petroleum Company?" Then, I'd get the third important "yes" answer I really was looking for. I had not previously opened my cookware sample case as yet, but it was now time.

I said, "I am going to show you the most beautiful things you can imagine, as well as useful." I would spread out my pretty maroon-red spreadcloth and start placing the pans in their proper places.

"This product I am advertising (not selling) is made of the very finest stainless steel there is — the same material used in doctor's and dentist's surgical instruments. It will never stain, rust, wear, pit or chip. In fact, it is guaranteed for your lifetime (Get the idea why I said "your" lifetime instead of "a" lifetime?) "Isn't it beautiful?" The fourth "yes" answered my question. I would then hand her the smallest pan and usually they would "ooh and aah…it's so heavy and strong" and I would say, "Oh, yes, it is because it is made to last you a lifetime and guaranteed to do so."

Then I would go through the rest of the set. "Now, that pan is the 1 1/2-quart pan and these other three sauce pans are the 2-quart, 3-quart and 4-quart. This one is our 6-quart roaster, for all kinds of meat roasting and stews, chili and large servings of food. This is the small fry pan and this one the large fry pan and egg poacher rack. It is used on the fry pan for poaching eggs and also the roast pan to place this steamer pan on the rack to steam another vegetable in while you are using the roaster to cook your roast. This dome cover fits both the fry pan and the roaster. Isn't it beautiful, Mary Jane?" "Oh, yes" she said; the fifth "yes."

Usually by this time she will ask, "What does a set like this one sell for?" Answering her, I would say, "Well, there are sets similar to this Lifetime set that sell for as much as $300, $400, or $500. Our company is advertising (not selling) this set of Lifetime for only $285. Isn't that wonderful, Mary Jane?" She is thinking about what I just asked her about the price, if it is wonderful or not. Sometimes they would say, "yes" and sometimes they wouldn't answer. If she said, "yes" for the sixth time, I am getting close to having myself a really good prospect.

Now comes the clincher! "Well, Mary Jane, I'm going to tell you something you are not going to believe. Remember, we talked about how much some companies spend on advertising?. Well, we spend quite a lot also, but we do it differently. It's a good thing that you are sitting down because if you weren't, you would probably fall down when I show you this beautiful 52 piece set of stainless steel tableware. Isn't it beautiful, Mary Jane?" This usually always draws a "yes." That's seven yeses that I've gotten her to say.

"Well, getting back to what we were saying about advertising, Mary Jane. This 52-piece set comes with the cookware without a penny extra charge. Isn't that wonderful?" This usually draws "yes" #8 to my question.

"Now, I haven't told you the best news yet. Mary Jane, if you qualify to participate in this program I am authorized to include with your set of cookware and your 52-piece set of tableware this service for eight of beautiful imported china dishes. All at no extra charge. Isn't this a wonderful way to advertise our new product — the Lifetime stainless set of cookware? You get the cookware, the tableware, and the service for eight china dishes all for the low, low price of $285. I think you'll agree that this is a very good way to advertise, don't you?" Then, with an answer from her, I have gotten my ninth "yes."

"Now, the qualifying part of this I told you about is this: If you can give me five names of young ladies, like yourself, that are working and have not purchased their cookware yet for their hope chest, we will not only include the tableware, we will include the dishes at no extra charge. This is provided that you purchase today, now. I don't have time to come back over and over to the same place. The company wants me to keep moving on to see as many people as possible."

"One of the best parts about this wonderful offer is you don't have to pay it all now. All you need to do is pay $20 down now and pay $10 per month. In a short time it will be paid for. That won't inconvenience you would it, Mary Jane?"

Well, I then get the answer when she says, "No, that won't inconvenience me at all. I can handle that." So I have gotten my final yes when she said "no." How about that!

I then hand her the five cards to write the names of her friends who are working and have not yet purchased their sets of cookware. I quickly fill out the time payment contract and tell her to be expecting all of her things in about two weeks. The cards I gave her for the names of her friends all say "This card is to introduce Andy Long who has a free gift to give you. He will not ask you to buy anything, but please let him explain the advertising program that I think is wonderful."

Then I pack up my samples and bid her goodbye and good luck. I only carry one wrapped up china plate and one cup and saucer as I really didn't need the whole set of dishes. This worked like a charm! I found a way to sell a very high percentage of the prospects and didn't have to cook a single potato!

I later taught my very good friend Tony Bowline how to do this and on our first appointment in Bartlesville that he went with me, we found a nest of three girls, all working for Philips Petroleum Company, in the same apartment. Well, we sold all three at once and Tony was sold to the hilt for the referral plan of mine right quick. Bill Sontag thought it was great also. He would order lots of the tableware and sets of china and sell it to me at a very low price. I would buy it from him and, of course, add it to the normal selling price of the Lifetime set, and still have a very good price to offer the young hopefuls and young couples.

Sontag ran a contest for the months of October and November 1956. The top ten salesmen in dollar volume for the two months would win a free trip for the man and his wife to fly to Acapulco, Mexico along with him and his wife, Maxine, all expenses paid. I guess I started a revolutionary way to sell cookware without putting on a cooking demonstration — I was lucky enough to win and be one of the ten winners! I asked Bill if I could have a check from him for the amount of the ticket. He asked why and I said I wanted to drive to Mexico City and take Bonnie and our two kids with us. He immediately said "yes" as I knew he would. We picked our time to go and decided on the day after Christmas of 1956. The kids were on Christmas vacation so they didn't miss any school. Andra was six and in the first grade and Tim was ten and in the fifth grade.

Before we left Dewey, Oklahoma on the trip to Mexico, I had our DeSoto all tuned up so that I could be sure we would not have any car trouble. We took off south early one morning and late that afternoon we drove into San Antonio, Texas where my mother's sister and family lived. Uncle Mack McKinney, Aunt Belle, their son, Jim, who had recently joined the Naval Air Force as a pilot, their daughter, Barbara Ann, who was a teenager and their youngest little baby boy, Mike. We stayed all night with them and the next morning Jim and a buddy pilot flew their jets into San Antonio for a visit. He did not know we would be there so it was a pleasant surprise for us all.

Jim was so handsome and proud in his uniform, just like you would imagine a young fighter pilot to look like. Sadly about eight or nine years later when he was in Florida stationed aboard the aircraft carrier Theodore Roosevelt his plane had a flameout as he was taking off. He cleared the deck and pulled his ejection seat, but it ejected him into the water as he hadn't had time to rise high enough into the air. His family was devastated by his death and soon after moved to Florida to be near where Jim died. They stayed some five years or so then moved back to Ingleside, Texas. This is now the home port of the battleship Wyoming and where Barbara and her husband, Remy Ashley, live. They run an automobile repair shop and garage. Mike McKinney is a police officer in Corpus Christie, Texas.

Aunt Belle and Uncle Mack lived in Ingleside until their deaths. She died at age 66 and he at age 93. We manage to see Barbara and Remy and Mike every five years or so. In fact, Barb and Remy stopped by our house in Alamogordo this past summer of 2001 to visit us on their way to Colorado.

Now, back to our trip to Mexico: We left San Antonio and crossed the border at Laredo, changed our money into pesos, then drove till dark and spent the first night in Ciudad Victoria, Mexico. The next day was a long day of driving and we arrived at the small town of Zimapan, about three hours north of Mexico City. The place we spent the night was gorgeous! It was a large two-story Inn, or Hacienda, with nice, large rooms and a restaurant. We had a wonderful meal at the restaurant and we enjoyed the Mexican music as we were seranaded by four Mexican Mariachis playing their instruments and singing, all dressed up in their Mariachi clothes and big Mexican hats. So colorful! This was a first for us to see this sort of thing.

The next morning after breakfast we talked to the proprietor and his wife. They were educated in the United States and spoke excellent English. We asked them where a good hotel was in Mexico City. He recommended the Hotel Frances — like `Frances the Talking Mule', a popular television program starring Donald O'Conner that was showing in the states, so we could remember that name. He wrote a note in Spanish that said, "Please lead us to the Hotel Frances." and told me to give the note to a taxi driver when we got into Mexico City. This worked like a charm and we got settled into our room at the hotel about 3:00 PM.

It was Sunday, and the bullfights started at 4:00 PM, so we had just enough time for our taxi to get us there — what a wild ride that was! The bullfight was quite an experience. To hear the cheering, and the colorful costumes of the Matadors, as well as the majestic music of the trumpets. We got some very good pictures of the ceremony, the Matador, the Picadors, the Toreadors, and, of course, the bulls.

An interesting thing happened that night at dinner. Andra ordered Rainbow Trout. I can't remember what we ordered, but when the waiter brought the trout, it still had the head on it and the eyes were open! It took some kind of doing to get her to eat it! The next morning she woke up with a sore throat, so we had the hotel call a doctor and he came and gave her a penicillin shot. Tim stayed in the hotel with her and Bonnie and I did a little shopping; by evening Andra was okay and there was no more sickness for any of us after that.

Mexico City is a beautiful city, and so big. In fact, it is now listed as the world's largest city. We visited many local attractions. The Mexico City Cathedral is magnificent (the only way to describe it) and the University of Mexico City is also very large, beautiful and impressive. There are large, colorful panoramic murals on the outside walls and manicured landscaping. Across the street from the Hotel Frances is the famous Sanborn Restaurant, reportedly the finest in Mexico City. We enjoyed eating there — HOT seasoning and, afterward, a huge plate of strawberries and shortcake.

The Mexican's celebrate Christmas in Mexico City on January 6th, so we got to see all this. It is sort of like Christmas Eve in the United States. We enjoyed seeing Santa all dressed up, talking to the little children on the streets and in the stores. We were there for a couple more days, then we drove on south to the town of Tasco, where the famous silver mines and shops are. We toured a mine and shopped there, drove around, then drove back to our hotel and a good night's sleep.

Heading home the next day, we detoured to the backroads to see the pyramids, climbing up one, then drove all the way to Monterrey, Mexico by nightfall. On the way to the pyramids a mail truck passed us. It was being chased by Federales in a tan coupe. The Federales were shooting at the truck from their moving vehicle and for a while, we were between them! More excitement!

Then on the drive back the next morning, we were going along and all of a sudden our car lost power. We were out in the middle of nowhere and it was getting very serious. We were just crippling along when we passed an old man and a donkey pulling his cart. I asked him if he knew where I could find a mechanic. He directed me to a little village about a mile ahead and I found a sign saying "Mechanic." I honked the horn. It was 8:30 or 9:00 AM. An old boy came out of a little adobe shack rubbing his eyes, as the chickens came out with him. I said, "Are you a mechanic?"

He said, "Si, me master mechanic." He fiddled around a few minutes and all of a sudden the car started running just fine. He said, "Points she...." and he held his finger on his thumb showing me the points were closed shut. This was the problem and he had solved it. I handed him a hand full of Mexican paper money and he and I were both very happy. This was a miracle!

As we traveled on up north we would be going down through the jungle, then in a few minutes, we would be high in the mountains again. One extreme to the other. No four-lane roads in Mexico in those days, and no guard rails. The canyons were deep and the roads were dangerous at times. As I said earlier, Andra was almost six years old. She was looking out the window in the back seat and all of a sudden she said, "Daddy, this road is not very healthy is it?" We laughed and said, "Sis, you are so right!" She then sat down in the back floorboard and stayed there until we were out of the mountains.

We were driving slow in the mountains and the road was very curvy. We came around one curve and there was a woman and several little kids that had stretched a rope across the road. We stopped and she said, "Pesos" and held out her hand. So I gave her some pesos and they all laughed and were happy and so were we. They lived in a straw hut perched on the "Y" of a huge tree growing straight out over a deep jungle cliff — no plumbing necessary! We stayed all night in Monterrey and then drove back into the States the next day. We drove all the way to El Reno, Oklahoma, our old stomping ground from cookware days and got a motel for the night and the next evening we were back in our little home on Herford Street in Dewey, Oklahoma. A lot wiser than before our trip to Mexico City. We had an unforgetable trip.

So once again back to selling Lifetime Cookware on the referral plan. My travels took me far and wide, all around the small towns within 50 miles of home. It's kind of like hunting for a new job every day. One of the easiest ways to get started in a new town was to go into a drugstore or cafe for a coke or a cup of coffee and strike up a conversation with the waitress. If she didn't have a wedding ring on, I would ask if she had started her hope chest yet. If she was single and living at home without expenses, she had some disposable income and could afford $10 a month payments. I'd sell her, then she would give me five more names of her friends and I was on my way again.

Business was good, but I was beginning to get tired of it and was longing for something different. So, I had my eyes open all the time. I remember I was driving over to Pahuska and Hominy, Oklahoma, about twenty or thirty miles, when I stopped at a drive-in for lunch. I was sitting in my car eating a hamburger and drinking coffee. I had the radio on when all of a sudden the announcer came on with an emergency message. He said the local Safeway grocery had just been robbed by a young man driving a green four-door car with a Kansas tag. About this time I looked out my side window and, low and behold, there was man driving by on the highway not fifty feet from me in a dark green car. I put my sandwich down, started my car and slowly drove onto the highway to Pahuska. I let him get a couple of hundred yards ahead of me and about five miles on down the highway was a filling station. I stopped and told the station owner what I heard and asked if I could use his phone to call the Pahuska police. He said, "Yes, I'll dial it for you." I told my story quickly and told them he would be in Pahuska in five or ten minutes.

Well, I got back into my car and drove on to Pahuska and to the police station — just as they were getting the guy in handcuffs out of their police car. They had acted very quickly and had blocked the highway at the Sand Creek Bridge where it curved and narrowed to one lane. That's where they had caught him. Well, I went into the police station and announced that I was the guy that had called them. The local newspaper reporter was there also, so I told my whole story to him. I got a very nice write up about this, and how it had all happened, in the local newspaper. I still have the clipping. I was a big hero, but I hadn't had time to sell anything that day. However, it was fun and there would be other days for selling..

The newspaper reporter had written that I said I had to drive eighty miles per hour in order to get close enough to tell if the dark green car had a Kansas tag, like they had said on the radio. The cops didn't say anything about my driving that much over the speed limit — they were just happy to make the arrest!

Another interesting story is about our first grader, Andra. Back many years earlier, my teacher for first, second, and third grades at the Rice Creek School was a young eighteen-year-old teacher by the name of Maude Darnell. Well, it just happened that our Andra's first grade teacher at the Bluestem Elementary School across the street from our house on Hereford Street was the same Maude Darnell. She had taught me in 1930 — and Andra in 1957, twenty-seven years later. How about that? Small town living. The schools were only about six miles or so apart.

One day I was home early and I heard some car brakes. I looked out and my next door neighbor had my little girl in his arms. She was crying and I met them in my front yard. I asked, "What happened?" and he said, "She ran across the street from school right in front of me." Luckily, he didn't run over her, but it did bump her and knock her down, skinned her knee and legs some. But she was not hurt badly. What a scare! All three of us were just scared to death — what a tragedy it could have been.

We were generally pretty happy. My folks, and my grandmother that I dearly loved, lived just a few blocks away. Tim had a good dog, Tuffy (half collie and half coyote, from Red and Anna Lou's farm in El Reno where he worked summers) and the two of them, along with his BB gun, would roam up and down Coon Creek, which was about a quarter mile away. Tim was ten or eleven years old. He was very trustworthy, so we didn't worry about him much. I had grown up in the same area when I was his age. I think the worst thing about my being gone most every night was I never got to go to a Little League ballgame, Scout meeting, or P.T.A. meeting with him. Bonnie did all this by herself. She never complained, as she knew it couldn't be helped. But it did bother me and I kept thinking about doing something else for a living.

I would go down to Broken Arrow, Oklahoma, about sixty miles away to see my old cookware buddy, Tony Bowline, once in a while. I had taught him how to sell on the referral plan and sometimes we would go out together so it wouldn't be so lonesome for each of us. I remember one time in particular in the summertime, when it was hot as hell and the cars were not air-conditioned in those days, we got the bright idea of making our own air conditioner from a block of ice layed on a cookie sheet and put on the floorboard in front of the heater blower. Well, it didn't work, it was just a big mess. We drove on up to Sallisaw Lake outside of Broken Arrow a few miles, driving down a country road when we saw a young lady sitting on a big rock by her mailbox reading a letter. I stopped and said, "Hi. Are you reading a letter from your boyfriend?"

She said, "How did you know?"

"It was just a guess." My next question was, "Do you have a hope chest?"

She said, "I've been thinking about it."

"Well, this is your lucky day! Me and my friend here work for the advertising department of Reynolds Metal Company and we have some free gifts for girls like you for giving us your opinion on a new product we are advertising. It will only take a few minutes of your time. Is your mother home?"

"Yes, she is," she said.

"Well, I have a gift for her too. Let's go up to the house, okay?"

To make a long story short, we wound up making two sales and both of them were very happy and so were we. Anyway, it was still hot as hell and at about 4:00 PM. Tony said, "There is a beer joint over by the lake dam. Let's go over for a cold one." Good idea.

So, we opened the front door and some big lanky old boy was dusting himself off and said, "Does anyone else want some of me?" Two guys were laying on the floor. One was out cold and the other was down and bleeding.

Well, Tony says, "Yeah, I'll take a little of it." That old boy hit Tony so hard, down he went! Just as he did, I hit the guy as hard as I could. He was not looking at me so he didn't see it coming and he went down in a heap. About that time his buddy hit me and down I went. I think we all had all we wanted, so Tony and I quickly got back into my car and drove to the nearest motel, got a room, got some ice and I had a pint of whiskey in my trunk so we washed up, fixed ourselves a good big drink each, then took some of the whiskey on a clean washcloth and tenderly patted it on our cuts and bruises.

I said, "You big dumb SOB. All you would have had to say when he asked if anyone else wanted any was 'I don't want any,' and none of this would have happened." Well, this is what happens when you're young and foolish and full of piss and vinegar, huh?

It wasn't long after that Tony and Wanda bought a small neighborhood grocery store and filling station from his uncle, located on the east edge of Broken Arrow. There were a lot of truck farms there growing all kinds of vegetables on a large scale and they employed a lot of people — Blacks, Whites, and Indians. Tony had a lot of these people trading with him. He got along well with all of them and he would let them charge groceries when they needed to. Some of the customers would steal from him and he knew most of the ones who would, so he would watch them closely and when they did, he would just put it on their bill and usually add a little extra to make up for the times he didn't catch them. They never cheated 'ole Tony and got away with it.

Tony had one big old black grandmother that would always bring her little grandson with her and she would always bug 'ole Tony about this drinking and cussing. She would tell him if he didn't change his ways and start going to church he was going to hell. Well, one day he rigged up a string across the ceiling back to the wall and down to the cash register where he always stood. He tied a large wooly spider, fake of course, and pulled it up to the ceiling in the aisle. The old black gal came in and right away she started ragging 'ole Tony about religion. When she was right under the spider, Tony turned loose of the string and the spider dropped right into her grocery cart. Well, she screamed out loud and said, "Tony Bowline! You are going to hell, you SOB! She never ragged on him again after that.

He was such a funny guy. Another of his black customers came in, and Tony said, "John, you haven't been in for quite a while. Where've you been?"

John said, "I've been sick, Tony, been in the hospital, but I'm feeling alright now."

And Tony said to him, "Yes, John, you look like you are getting your color back." They both laughed at that, as did everyone else in the store.

Tony had finally gotten out of the cookware business, but we still stayed best friends no matter where we lived. Our families visited with each other for the next forty-five years, and there will be more stories about Tony to come.

One day I was selling, still on the referral plan, and roamed on southeast to Sallasaw, Oklahoma in an area known as Cookson Hills in southeast Oklahoma — Pretty Boy Floyd country. It has alway been considered the outlaw country of Oklahoma. These hills are where most of the whiskey stills were when Oklahoma was a dry state. Bonnie has three neices and a nephew there and, counting the children and grandchildren of her sister, Willadean, they number into the thirties in all. Willadean's husband died. They had met in Wichita during the War years then moved to southeastern Oklahoma and started their family there. Well, husband John Lee died when the children were young adults and Willadean married a big, old, rough, wild S.O.B. that had a wrecking business: houses, buildings, etc. He salvaged anything that was good, and had a second hand store across the Arkansas border in Ft. Smith where he and Willadean worked. He did well for a man who could neither read nor write.

One day while her husband, Big Bob, and a couple of the kids were working on a building, Willadean was running the store by herself. A young punk came into the store and said, "I'm robbing you," and pulled out a pistol.

She said, "I'm not giving you my money. I work hard for my money." With this said, he pulled out the pistol, put it to her head and shot and killed her. Bob and Willadean were not getting along well at that time and Bob had a fairly lage insurance policy on her. So, for years, all of Willadean's family and sisters and brother were suspicious that Bob had had her killed. The police finally caught the man that killed her and while he was in jail he admitted he killed her. He never implicated Bob in the murder. It took seventeen years after Willadean's death before the Ft. Smith, Arkansas officials finally executed the man that had shot her. This was during the time that our good 'ole boy Bill Clinton was governor of Arkansas. By this time, Bob was killed in an apparent accident. He was moving a large refrigerator down some stairs in a house and he was in front of it and supposedly slipped and fell. The refrigerator fell on him and killed him.

Bonnie and I visited Willadean's children and grandchildren every five years or so. The last time was in January, 2001. They had a big cookout that evening, about thirty in all. Bonnie stays in touch by e-mail. That is still a very rough part of the USA.

I continued to sell Lifetime in 1957 on the referral plan, but, God, I was getting really tired of it and I did not want to leave Dewey because I didn't want the children to have to change schools. They were both doing really well and my dad and mom, and grandmother were nearby and we all enjoyed that. One day I ran into an old boy that was selling airline correspondence courses to young girls, as well as to young men. The girls were training to become airline hostesses, ticket counter clerks, and reservationists, and the boys were training for ticket counter work, baggage handling, and the like. The bulk of the work was selling to the young girls that were just graduating from high school. They would take the correspondence part for several months and then finish with two months of training in Kansas City, Missouri to learn how to walk, talk, put on makeup and fix their hair, etc. This job appealed to me as it was similar to selling cookware on the referral plan and to the same type prospects that I had been working with. So, this old boy trained me for about a week and away I went.

The way this worked was the airline course company would mail all senior girls and boys an attractive brochure about hiring young people (mostly to the girls). They would pick small towns to mail to because most small towns don't offer the possibility of many jobs for young people just out of high school and a lot of them don't have the opportunity to go to college either. Anyway, the mailer that was sent to them had a questionnaire card that asked a few questions for the girls to fill out and to return to the school. Questions like, "What is your weight? Height? Eye color? Hair color?," etc. The return card would have their name, address, and all of this information on it.

The company would then mail a stack of these cards to the salesmen and they would have a stack of leads to call. When the salesman would hit town, he would check into a hotel or motel with a phone and spend some of the day on the phone. This is what he would say, "Could I speak to Peggy Ann Hughes?"

"Oh, this is Peggy?"

"Peggy Ann, this is Mr. Andy Long. I work for the airlines and I am in town for a few days to interview girls like yourself." You can imagine what an exciting response I got to the above call! I then would say, "Let me ask you some questions. First, Peggy Ann, I see on the card that you have blond hair, is that right? ("Oh, yes.") "Then, you have blue eyes?" ("Oh, yes.") This would go on with the height and weight, etc. Then I would say, "I need to interview you. Could I see you, and your mom and dad this evening? I can see you at 5:30 or 7:00. Which would be better?" "Okay, I'll see you at 5:30 this evening. You still live at 301 Maple Street don't you?" ("Yes.") "Okay, I'll see you then." You can imagine how pretty she would be looking, all dressed up in her best dress and so excited to see me.

At this point, I will explain that we salesmen actually work for the airline training school. If and when the students finish their correspondence part of the course, then they go to Kansas City for the final two months training that I mentioned. For the ones that pass both courses, the school tells all the different airline companies that they have a graduating class ready for them to pick the graduates that they choose to hire.

Now getting back to my presentation to Peggy Ann and her parents: I open my briefcase. I first lay out my pad of contracts in full view so they become familiar with it, so as not to spook her mom and dad when the time comes to start writing them up (this is important!). Then I open a large hardcover 3-ring binder with lots of colored photos: pictures of different airliners and pictures of the handsome captains, pretty hostesses, girls behind the ticket counters, pictures of football teams boarding the planes, baseball players, politicians, well-dressed business people, etc.

"Now, Peggy Ann, I want you to imagine yourself working behind the ticket counter and a big league baseball team comes in to get tickets and then find out that their plane is socked in and they will not be able to fly out until the next day. What do you think they will ask you? Well, I'll tell you. First, they will ask you 'What is there to do tonight in Dallas?' You might say, 'I know of a place to dine and dance that is real nice if you fellows would like to go there.' Well, what do you think the next question is going to be asked of you? I'll tell you what it is. 'Would you enjoy going with us to show us around and bring two or three of your friends with you?'"

"This is just one example, Peggy Ann, of what can happen. You are exposed to lots of nice people. Not only sports types, but also captains of business and industry, and all kinds of people with money to spend."

"Now, Mom and Dad, let me ask you a question. Don't you think it would be better to have your little girl in a position to meet someone someday to present you with grandchildren than wind up marrying the boy that works in a little one-horse filling station here in town and in a few years wind up on a dead end street?" They may not answer this question, but you know damned well it sure as hell hit home. Of course, you have to pick the right time to bring this up. If everything looks promising, it is time to say, "The cost of this whole course, including Kansas City, is only $395 and we have a real nice payment plan so you can pay it out by the month. If you don't already have a college plan for Peggy Ann, don't you folks think you should give her a chance to give herself a good start in life?"

Usually it is time now to pick up the order pad and ask, "Which plan would you folks prefer — cash or time payment?" or "What is your first name, Mr. Hughes?" Sale made. You can easily see that selling these airline courses was very similar to selling cookware on the referral plan. So it didn't take long and I had it down pat.

I think it's time now to tell you some important things about salesmanship. A good salesman is in great demand. Not a mediocre one, or a lying one, or an obnoxioius one. Good salesmen are in great demand. Nothing happens until a sale is made. Each and every product that is manufactured has to be sold for the manufacturer or company to exist, grow and prosper. A good, dependable salesman, one that knows his product, and will get off his ass can just about name his price. All companies have to have them to exist. Anything you can think of has to be sold first. Mediocre salemen won't get the job done, the same as any other profession. A good, friendly, honest one is, and always will be, in demand. Almost every head of any company started out in the sales department and worked his way up to the top management jobs. They are thinkers, dreamers, and usually high-strung individuals — like race horses, not plow horses. They are tempermental and intelligent "go, go, go" individuals. Every successful company has to have them and pay them very well; otherwise, their company would not grow and prosper, and would soon be out of business.

I still longed for a daytime sales job so that I could enjoy my family and not have to travel all the time. Very soon I found that I preferred selling stainless steel cookware to airline corespondence courses — I could make a lot more money selling cookware. After all, I had been selling Lifetime Stainless Steel for close to 11 years.

I made a decision when I had the chance to go to work as a salesman for the leading men's clothing store in Bartlesville. The company was Zofness Brothers Mens Clothing. Mr. Martin Zofness was a little Jewish man about 5 ft. tall. He had been in business in Bartlesville in the same location for 47 years. His brother had long since passed away and his only son, Charlie, was now with him. They handled the best-named brands of everything they sold: suits, coats, topcoats, pants, sweaters, shirts, underwear, socks, ties, shoes and hats. Mr. Zofness had an excellent reputation. My dad has known him since they were both young men. (I think this might have had something to do with my getting the job. Of course, my years of salesmenship had a lot to do with it also.)

The job didn't pay much — I think about $75 a week. That was not bad then, as things are about ten times that amount now. Inflation, you know. And it was warm in the winter, cool inside in the summer and no on-the-road expenses; home every evening. Working 9:00 AM to 6:00 PM, except on Saturdays when you closed after the last customer left.

Mr. Zofness took a liking to me. He taught me how to dress and how to really sell clothes. The first thing he did was get me dressed up like a walking, talking model. He said, "Andy, we are going to pick you out two good-looking suits, four ties, shirts, socks, shoes and hat. You are going to be a walking model." He said, "You get a 20 percent discount on all this and you can use our revolving charge plan."

I said, "How does it work?"

He said, "For example, you can buy $120 worth of clothing and pay only $10 per month, or $240 worth and pay only $20 a month. You can add or take away from the total as you pay and whatever the balance is just divide by the number of months. No interest or carrying charges." This was great and it was offered to all of our customers. No discount to them, of course, but also no carrying charges. This worked so well, especially for the young men just out of college that were going to work at Phillips Petroleum Company, whose world headquarters was then in Bartlesville. There were hundreds and hundreds of them that Martin Zofness had trapped with his famous "no interest or carrying charges revolving charge plan."

Jokingly, I would say to those young men when they asked how the revolving charge plan worked, "Well, you pick out whatever you want in order to dress well and you pay so much per month — and if you don't pay, then you and Mr. Zofness go around and around." Then we would both laugh. But it did work well and it had been tested over many, many years. Keep in mind that I was only 33 years old and had eleven years of sales experience. I now often refer to this 11 years as the equivelent of two PhDs in Sales Education.

Now I was a 33-year-old good-looking, well-dressed new salesman in a fine habadashery, ready for a new challenge. Mr. Zofness knew everything there was to know about the men's clothing business after 47 years, and he taught me how to dress and properly coordinate colors.

I had sold my 1955 DeSoto and purchased a 1949 Mercury — just something to drive back and forth to work four miles each way from Dewey to Bartlesville. I started my work day at 9:00 AM, and at 10:00 AM we got a 15-minute coffee break, with a 30-minute lunch at 11:30 AM. Then back to work at noon in order to take care of the Phillips shoppers on their lunch break from noon to 1:00 PM. Now, when I would go on my coffee or lunch breaks, Mr. Zofness would say, "Get your hat on, Andy, get your hat on." He always wanted me to look my best when I went out as I was representing the store. Another lesson was when a customer would come in, and then when they would leave without buying anything, like a lady "just looking," he would ask me, "What was the name of the lady?"

I would say, "I didn't get her name."

He said, "The first thing you do when you greet a customer is to introduce yourself and ask their name." I didn't dare tell him a name if I didn't know it, because he knew all of his customers. We never sat down and smoked a cigarette. He wanted us on our feet all the time — straightening the socks, suits or ties on the racks, etc. He said, "If you are sitting down in the back of the store and smoking, and a customer comes in the front door, you are like an old-fashioned radio. Like the ones that would have to warm up after turning on. I want you turned on all the time so when a customer comes in you are warmed up and ready to help them."

Sometimes I would bring my lunch. Bonnie would pack me a couple of sandwiches and I would walk up the street three blocks to the city library and eat my lunch there. We had come back home from Mexico just a new months earlier and we were so impressed with it that I told Bonnie that if we were ever able to accumulate $20,000, we would plan to retire in Mexico. So I would find every book I could on Mexico to learn as much as I could and would take some of them home and the four of us started trying to learn the Spanish language. Realize, of course, that $20,000 then would be about $200,000 now. We would study so many words each week and then add some more the next. We even got a set of Spanish teaching records. This gave our family something to do together. We never did learn enough that we could carry on a conversation — of course, the kids were both in grade school.

Mr. Zofness hired another young salesman named Marvin Smith. Mr. Z. said it was his greatest challenge to make a salesman out of Marvin as his former job was working in a funeral home, where he was supposed to look sad and solemn, not smile or laugh like the average salesman should. So after a while, Marvin came around and replaced the look of an undertaker with that of a smiling salesman. Charlie Zofness was about our age also, and we all became good friends.

One day my Bonnie girl decided she would like to get a job at Phillips Petroleum Company. The kids were old enough to be home from school by themselves until she got home at 5:00 PM. So, I bought a little Chevrolet sedan from the old lady, Mrs. Clara Weber, who lived across the street from my Grandmother's house. Mrs. Weber had gotten too old to get a driver's license — then about 91 years old. She used to take my Grandmother for a drive once in a while. One day they were out driving around and when Grandma got out, she said, "Weber, I'm not going to ride with you any more. You scare the life out of me!"

Mrs. Weber's daughter lived in Tulsa. She was the widow of a rich oil man named Bovaird. He owned a chain of oilfield supply houses all over the country. So when he died, Mabel Bovard took it over. She had helped him build the business so she was plenty capable with her lawyer's help. Mabel lived in a beautiful two-story brick home on a large landscaped lot in a prestigious area of Tulsa. She lived there by herself until her death.

When we met Mabel at her mother's home in Dewey, she was in her early 60's and was very worried about her mother's driving. So she told Bonnie that if she would take her mother to the grocery on Saturdays, she would sell her Grandma Weber's car very cheaply. Bonnie said, "Sure, I will take her to the grocery store." We had become good friends of Mrs. Weber, Tim even mowed her lawn every week. So, for $150, Bonnie had some wheels. The little car ran like a sewing machine as it only had about 12,000 miles on it.

My Grandmother Henderson passed away in the fall of 1957 at the age of 79. Bonnie was not working then, so she had the day duty to stay at the hospital with Grandma, then my Uncle L.D. would stay part of the night. Grandma's four grandsons — me, my brother John, and my Uncle Jack's two sons, Jackie and Johnny Henderson were the pallbearers at her funeral. My two uncles presented Bonnie with $100 for staying with Grandma at the hospital while she was so sick. Bonnie put the hundred to good use — she rented a typewriter and started brushing up on her typing to prepare for a job interview at Phillips Petroleum Company. She passed with "flying colors" and went to work about the same time I started working at Zofness Brothers in the fall of 1958.

School started in September and Bonnie working was a big help — now we had two incomes. One day when she came home from work Bonnie told me she saw a "for sale" sign on a big two story house close to the new Phillips building, the Adams Building. Phillips had outgrown their original building and added this new one — all offices. They needed the land where some older homes were located for a parking lot. I called about it the next day and the man who owned it, Howard Cannon, came by were I worked at Zofness. He had known Martin Zofness for many years, so the three of us had a talk. Cannon was on the board of directors of the Home Savings and Loan Association. He said he could get me a loan to buy his house and move it, so with Mr. Zofness's blessing, the loan was approved. About the same time we found out about the house, we inquired about the vacant lot next door to my Grandmother's house, which she had willed to my mother. With money I saved from the sale of my 1955 DeSoto, I purchased the lot next door to my parents. Then I found a contractor who agreed to move the house from Bartlesville to Dewey, build a new foundation for it, and do some remodeling for $2,500. Now enters Mabel Bovaird into our lives.

Bonnie and I drove to Tulsa to see her that Sunday and she agreed to loan us the $2,500 for the moving and repair money. Our first home. A couple of months later, we moved from the little rental house on Hereford to our big house at 501 E. Third Street, Dewey, Oklahoma. We both worked at our jobs in the day time and at night we would work on the inside of the house until about midnight, then get up and do the same thing — day after day. Scraping paint off the trim and really refinishing the large stair case bannister. Then I hired a local one-man carpenter to sand and refinish the hardwood floors and re-sheetrock and paint. We bought some beautiful hanging chandeliers for the big living and dining rooms, and when we finally got through with it, after about six months, it looked like a palace. All four of us were happy as larks to have a nice place of our own. Our folks were happy for us too.

My mom still worked at the cleaners and my dad was retired and did not work, so he was there next door to look after the kids after school until we got home from work. I stayed with Zofness and Bonnie stayed at Phillips Petroleum and the kids were a year older. This "ho hum" deal had gone on for another year and in the spring of 1960 this "race horse" was beginning to get figgity and needed to get out and about. It was just too confining for me. I read an ad in the paper that Plaza Realty was looking for someone to sell real estate. You know, I was doing okay back in 1955 in Wichita selling real estate until Boeing started laying off lots of people and the real estate business went to hell fast and I had to go back to selling Lifetime. So I went for an interview with the real estate broker, Lee Skinner. He liked me and said, "When can you go to work?" I said I would have to study for my real estate license and give notice to Mr. Zofness. I did, and a month later I started work for Plaza Realty of Bartlesville, Oklahoma. I had enjoyed working for Mr. Zofness. He taught me a lot and I will never forget my time working there, but now I was in the real estate business for the second time.

Lee Skinner was a fairly large man in his middle fifties. He looked a little like a snapping turtle, if you can picture that. He had a speech impediment and talked slow. He had been in the business for a long time and knew a lot about it. He worked with two or three young builders and sold several homes to be built from a selection of plans and the young builders would build them. He had recently hired another young man to sell for him that had two older brothers also building homes. So, with some resales and new homes to be built, we had plenty to sell. I passed my real estate exam, but before they issued me my license, the real estate board called me in and started questioning me pretty strongly. I expained that I had been selling for quite a few years and had been born and raised in Bartlesville and my parents and grandparents and my great-grandparents were old settlers there, too. This gave me the okay. I asked "Why all these questions?" They said that the guy Lee Skinner was under suspicion by the Oklahoma Real Estate Commission and they wanted to find out if I knew him or not. I said I had never met him before I answered his ad in the paper. They told me, "Mr Long, he will bear watching."

Anyway, I started my new job after I got a better looking car. A nice little 4-door Plymouth — a 1956 model. Nice car! I started off with a bang! — selling three houses in two weeks. I met with all the young builders that Skinner represented — and young Bill Hawkins, the other salesman, and I hit it off real well. The weeks rolled on and things were going okay. Bonnie had received a promotion and was in charge of Phillips Petroleum's liquid fertilizer rail tanker cars, routing them all over the U.S. Quite an important job with a nice raise in pay. She was happy and I was happy — and our two kids were doing well in school and growing.

Tim had started taking drum lessons from the same old German teacher — Isaac Allen DeLano Luther — that had taught me years earlier. Young Tim ate it up and was soon First Chair Drummer in the Dewey High School Band (while only in Jr. High), just like I was when I was in high school there many years earlier. This was in 1958, and he started playing at the Starlight Club, a nightclub in the Tuxedo area of Bartlesville with guardianship papers as he was only 12 years old. So as of this year, 2002, Tim has been playing trap drums for some 44 years and he is a much better drummer than I ever was.

It looked like I had the world by the tail! A job that I liked without leaving home, Bonnie and the children all doing well and my folks living next door to our newly remodeled home. This was about to change just a few months later. Some of the sales that I made on houses that had to be built took several months to close before I got paid my commission. One in particular was almost complete when I found a buyer. I sold it and figured in a month or so I would get paid. When I asked Lee Skinner, my broker, when this home was going to close, he kept making all kinds of excuses why it hadn't closed. Finally, about a month or six weeks later, I ran into the old man that had the house built for sale. I asked him when his house was going to close. He promptly said, "Andy, it closed a month or so ago." I was shocked!

I went straight to Lee Skinner and jumped right in the middle of his crap! I said, "Why haven't you paid me my commission?" With his stuttering speech-impediment he said, "Well, Andy, I had to pay my office rent and pay my advertising bill and I just didn't have the money to pay you."

I said, "Why didn't you tell me this instead of lying to me that it hadn't closed? I saw the owner uptown and he said it had closed weeks ago. I want my money right now. All $1,100 of it."

"I don't have the money now, Andy." he said.

I said, "Then you get your checkbook out, you crooked son-of-a-bitch, and write me eleven post-dated $100 checks." He promptly got the checkbook, then said, "Okay, but let me date the first one thirty days from now, then one each month thereafter."

"Well," I said, "Okay." I gathered up my things and left.

I went to the broker that had warned me about Lee Skinner and who questioned me when I started to work for Lee. "Andy, I told you he was a crooked guy." he said. He went on to say that when Lee Skinner was a younger man, just after World War II was over, he started a subdivision, in Bartlesville, of small two-bedroom houses with Federal Housing Administration financing and started building a bunch of these F.H.A. homes. For some reason or other he decided to abscond to Mexico with $60,000. After he got to Mexico he changed his mind and managed to get back to the United States and avoided having to go to prison. How in the world he managed to keep his Real Estate License I never found out.

Well, the story gets worse. The Sunday just before my first $100 check was cashable, Lee Skinner dropped dead. They listed his death as an apparent heart attack. It was speculated that he was about to have his current real estate license revoked and that he committed suicide. Anyway, I never got any of my $1,100 in checks cashed.

"Once a crook, always a crook." my old grandfather Andy Henderson used to teach me. He would always say, "Son, never lie, cheat or steal. Lying is as bad a stealing. You can put a thief in jail, but you can't do much with a liar." I listened to everything my grandfather told me and have followed this good advise as close as I could all my life so far, and I see no reason to change now. I am teaching my little ten-year-old grandson this very same thing, and right now he is listening. I hope he continues to listen to me. I think he will. My daughter, Andra, says that my grandson, Davis Grayson Riordan, is me reincarnated. He thinks he knows everything and won't shut up. So, maybe he is. And if he is, that can't be too bad, can it?

It had been about two years since I had stopped selling cookware and had started with Zofness Brothers Men's Clothing, then with my latest venture with Plaza Realty and Lee Skinner. So, I thought maybe I should see how I could do, now that I was a little older, selling cookware again. I thought that I would sell on both plans — the Dinner Demonstration Plan, and the Referral Plan when I didn't have a dinner booked. I had never done this before, just one or the other, but not both at once. I decided to not try and do both in the same immediate territory but within thirty miles or so apart. So I put this latest idea to work. This way if I didn't have a dinner booked for the evening or until the next week, I could always call on a single girl or two and make some sales. This worked pretty well. I could work close enough to Dewey that I wouldn't have to stay overnight and I could be home every night.

A call to Bill Sontag as usual and the idea was readily accepted. I don't think he had any other salesmen who were selling on both plans. He was, as usual, well pleased to hear from me and the feeling was mutual. I had always made good money in the cookware business and I was looking forward to getting started again. I first started a Dinner right there in Dewey. Then spread out to Nowata, about twenty miles east, then on to Claremore, Oklahoma, the home of Will Rogers, and then on to Miami, Oklahoma, then on to Grove, Oklahoma near the Grand Lake of the Cherokees. I would work Bartlesville, Pahuska, Ponca City and small towns south and west of Bartlesville. Soon I was putting money in the bank once again. Thinking back, it now seems like I was always trying to make enough money to get out of the cookware business, or trying to get back into the cookware business.

I had never bragged how good a cookware man I was in those days but looking back now I see clearly that I was one of the best, if not the best. Many years later, after Bill Sontag and I both had retired, he told me several times I was the best Lifetime Cookware man he had ever had. It made me feel very good and our long friendship was rock-solid, mutually.

I remember something that happened twenty years or so later. Maxine Sontag had gotten cancer in her leg and died, leaving Bill and their six adult children. We naturally attended the funeral and were warmly welcomed, coming all the way from Los Alamos, New Mexico to Wichita. The funeral was over and we were at the cemetary standing next to Bill and he said to Bonnie, "That Andy has certainly done well in his business, Bonnie."

Bonnie said, "Yes, if he could only have been a little more successfull."

And Bill said, "Bonnie, I don't see how he could have been any more successful."

I have thought of this many times since. And our friendship lasted another twenty years, seeing each other almost every Thanksgiving when we would come to Wichita to Bonnie's family reunion when the weather permitted us to travel.

The time was the summer of 1960. I had been hitting it pretty hard and Bonnie was doing well in her job at Phillips. School was out for the summer. We had not seen the Jones family in Altus for a long time, so a phone call of considerable length produced an agreement that if we would drive to Altus from Dewey with the kids, the Jones family and the Long family would all get in Bobby's big, new Dodge stationwagon and take us a cross-country vacation. The car had a luggage rack on top of it, so this is where we could put all our luggage, covered with a water-proof tarp and have plenty of room for all eight of us — four adults and four kids in the big car. Andra, and their son, Gary, were only nine or ten years old, so it worked out okay.

Bobby never could see well enough to drive so the driving was all up to me. We split the cost of gas, food and lodging and we took off bright and early one morning from Altus and headed for Amarillo, Texas, then on up to Colorado and planned on staying in a recreational campground for the night. We had our camping gear on top of the stationwagon along with our luggage. Well, when we arrived at our first night's destination, which was the Royal Gorge in Colorado, it was raining like hell. So we got a motel room for the night. (And from then on we stayed in motels every night for two weeks — except for one night at Yellowstone National Park on our way back home.) The drive across the Royal Gorge was quite a scary experience for us all. I had heard before about how a guy will get cold feet when they get scared. Well, I'm here to tell you driving across that bridge, my legs were numb, so indeed, I had cold feet! It was one of the scariest experiences I ever had!

Then onto Colorado Springs, a place all eight of us enjoyed. None of us had been to any of the places that we were going to visit. Oh, how all of us were enjoying this trip, as well as our super friendship. Their girl, Shirley, was Tim's age, and their boy, Andra's (as previously stated). Then, on to Denver were we drove around the whole town and visited the U. S. Government Mint. Quite an interesting place for all but the young ones. Then, on to Salt Lake City, Utah. Driving late that night we were able to get to Salt Lake City for our second night's sleep. The next morning we visited the beautiful Mormon Tabernacle, quite an experience for us all.

None of us had really been much of anywhere, except Bobby and I during World War II, at that time of our lives, except for Bonnie and me and our Baton Rouge, Louisiana adventure.

The next morning, Day Three, we drove past the salt plains and the Great Salt Lake, and drove on through to Reno, Nevada — a very long way. But, we were young and strong so we kept on driving until the next afternoon when we finally arrived and started looking for a room. We really had trouble fnding a place to stay, and when we did it was all in the very same large room — as we were somewhat short of money since we originally had planned on camping out. We did okay and had no disagreements to speak of, because in those days Bobby and I made all the decisions and they all went along with what we said.

The only problem we had was that when we got the room, it was only about 3:00 PM and so warm that we left our door open and only closed the screen door. Well, we were so very tired, having driven all night, that we were just worn out and everyone fell right to sleep. None of us woke up until the next morning and we couldn't believe that we hadn't even locked the door! We got up and drove around Reno and went downtown where all the casinos were. We couldn't take the kids in so we just looked inside in amazement, then back on the road to Tahoe. We drove around the beautiful lake, enjoyed the big pine trees (which none of us had ever seen before) and were just in awe at all the mountains. We were all "rock struck," so to speak.

Then on to Sacramento, California and to San Francisco. We enjoyed the waterfront, especially me, being an old seaman (or rather a young seaman at the time). We enjoyed eating lots of seafood. The next evening we got into Los Angeles and finally found a place to stay all night that was close to Disneyland. This was my first experience with driving on a freeway! I would drive by the exit that I needed to turn off, then try to find my way back to try it again. How frustrating! But, we all really enjoyed Disneyland the next day! We really had a great time and took in everything they had. The day before we had gone through the Redwood Forest. What huge trees! One was so big and old they had cut a hole through it that we drove our car through! Amazing.

After leaving Los Angeles, we went on to San Diego. We really liked this city, so clean and so pretty and the climate was wonderful. Then we caught a large passenger boat (not a ship) to Catalina Island, about an hour ride. Myrtle Jones and their little son both got seasick for a while. We had a wonderful time on Catalina swimming and playing on the beach. Then back to San Diego and on to Tijuana, Mexico across the border. We did some shopping in the Mexican market, and the next day headed north thru Arizona to see the Grand Canyon. These eight Okies all were very impressed with this big gash in old Mother Earth! The only time we used our camping gear that we had carried on the top of the car the entire trip was the night we spent at the Grand Canyon. After this, it was time we headed for Oakie Land and home. We had a well-needed rest for a day and a night and the four Longs headed for Dewey, Oklahoma. What a wonderful trip! All of us still remember it. Bonnie had a two-week vacation from Phillips and it had taken all of it for this vacation.

When we had been living in Altus in 1952 until 1955 we used to go up to Lake Altus and all eight of us go swimming. Bobby and Myrtle were such good friends, and still are in 2002 — fifty years later. From young friends to old friends, and not one single argument and no fights. This may not be a record, but it's a pretty good average, huh?

When we left Altus that morning after our vacation was over, we decided to look around Altus and the surrounding farm land. We were very impressed by the fine irrigated farm country and not only that, since we had left, the Air Force had built a permanent airbase there. This time they had built all brick homes and buildings and had made a long-term commitment. They were training airmen to fly these giant planes, the C5A and other huge ones that can carry several hundred troops and equipment — ones that today are used to fly tanks, trucks, and large cargos all over the world wherever they are needed. Ft. Sill at Lawton, Oklahoma is where a very large fort is located, training soldiers with tanks and heavy artillery and is only 50 or 60 miles from the airbase at Altus. A large six-lane straight new highway had been built so that they could move many soldiers and their equipment to about anywhere they are needed in a hurry. So, the quiet sleepy little town of Altus was on the move. Not only prosperous from the farm country, but having a thriving business community, too. We liked what we saw and thought if we ever left Bartlesville and Dewey, Altus might be a very good place to live again.

I was still selling Lifetime now and since it was hot weather in July and August, as it always is, it was too hot to be cooking demonstration dinners. I was selling on the referral plan almost exclusively, and still driving the little 1954 Plymouth which was air conditioned and comfortable. I was in need of a new territory that was good, preferably good farm country where I could make a lot of cash sales. Sontag had a sales meeting in Wichita and we went up for the weekend. I visited my old friend Vaughn Loomis and he said he was working in far west Texas around Dumas. He said he had been doing really well and mostly all cash. Huge wheat farms and huge cattle feed lots. He said it runs for miles and miles. He said, "Andy, you should come on out there. There is another town about twenty miles from Dumas by the name of Dalhart. I'm getting damn lonesome out there by myself." He said he came home every weekend and I could do the same and we could see each other once in a while. So in January of 1961 I enter Dalhart, Texas.

On my first Dinner, I sold four sets, all cash. I found a small motel right across the street from a small cafe for my breakfast and an occcassional lunch on the days that I had a dinner party that night. The motel room had a refrigerator and a large sink so I had a good place to prepare my vegetables in advance and put them in plastic bags which helped me work alone on the dinners. I stayed in this same little motel in Dalhart, Texas for a couple or three months and was really selling and making money. Vaughn and another salesman were still in the general area, so once in a while we would meet halfway, in the town of Stratford, Texas for lunch and a visit. It gets lonesome way out there in west Texas by yourself, so this was good.

I was doing well enough that I could comfortably trade for a newer car. One weekend in Bartlesville I found one. It was a black four-door Dodge demonstrator. Boy was it pretty! It had everything on it you could imagine. It was the most beautiful car I had ever seen — prettier than a Cadillac or Lincoln and even more expensive. They had ordered it special, but the year had changed, so they wanted to sell it bad. The price was $5,700.00, a hell of a lot then for a car. But I had to have that car! Twin radio antennas coming out of the rear fenders, the driver-side seat would swivel and turn a quarter turn. When you opened the door you just stepped out and swung the seat easily back into place. It was super powerful and the speedometer showed a top speed of 140 miles per hour— unheard of in those days! This car made it a lot more enjoyable trip when I would come home on weekends.

Then I found out that Phillips Petroleum Co. had a company plane, a C-45 I think it was, the twin-engine old workhorse plane of World War II that was so popular during those years. Anyway, this plane flew twice a day from Bartlesville to Borger, Texas where Phillips had a carbon black plant. So I checked this out and the result was that I could leave Dalhart, Texas Saturday morning to Bartlesville, then leave Bartlesville on Monday morning and fly to Borger, Texas. I would leave my Dodge at the Borger Airport which was almost thirty miles from Dalhart and Bonnie would pick me up in Bartlesville a couple of hours later. Then, my dad would drive me to Bartlesville from Dewey four miles on Monday morning. This was wonderful! It was about 350 or 400 miles to drive each week one way, so I became the only flying cookware man that I know of. Those long drives were wearing me out. The flying helped a lot. I wasn't tired all the time anymore from those long drives each weekend.

This worked out well on into the spring of 1961 and I knew it would soon be time to try and find a new territory as good as the one I had in west Texas. Also, it didn't allow much of a family life for us, so Bonnie and I had a long talk: whether to maybe move back to Altus, Oklahoma just for the summer. We could rent a small place there so I could sell in the Altus area, mostly around Fredrick, Oklahoma. I hadn't worked in that area when we lived there in the 1952, 1953 and 1954.

Fredrick is the real good looking farm country that we saw the day we started home from our vacation with the Jones family. I thought then: "I might just come back here someday and work this fine farm area again." Well, the time had come for a move for the summer months.

We both had really been working hard these past few years and we sure enjoyed our vacation. Bonnie longed to become a housewife again after doing a good job of getting us on our feet financially. We agreed to go to Altus for the summer while the kids were out of school and she would go with me again as my assistant putting on my dinner demonstrations. When we got to Altus we saw a brand new mobile home park owned by a guy by the name of Hoyt Shadid. He also owned the Plymouth Dodge Agency where I bought my new 1952 Plymouth when we came to Altus the first time back in 1952. He still remembered me after nine years and was happy to rent us a new trailer that was plenty big enough for us and the two kids.

Tim was old enough to watch Andra while Bonnie was working with me so things were great. We had a TV and this helped, and the mobile home park was near the city park and zoo. Tim had a fall trying to ride Andra's bicycle to band practice. He broke his ankle, requiring that he play his bass drum with his left foot at the "Starlight Club" in Tuxedo, near Bartlesville. He had a walking cast on his broken ankle, so he didn't go too far away from the trailer that summer.

I booked a couple of Dinners near Tipton and Fredrick, Oklahoma right in the heart of wheat and cotton country. Now, me being nine years older, a polished old cookware salesman, 36 years of age, and still my calm and cheerful self, I really 'set the woods on fire' so to speak.

I need to back up a bit in order to explain something important that had happened before I left Dewey for Altus: I was no longer selling Lifetime Cookware. The Reynolds Metals Company had sold their manufacturing business to the West Bend Cookware Company in Wisconsin. For years and years they had been in the aluminum cooking utensil business, making all kinds of cookware utensils. They could see the handwriting on the wall that stainless steel was fast taking over the fine cookware business, so they decided to quit trying to compete with their aluminum products and join in on the stainless steel market. West Bend started producing a very good and very beautiful new set made of heavy 3-ply stainless steel, similar to the Permanent Stainless Steel that Allegany Ludlum was making (the one that we had a franchise with in Louisiana and Arkansas in 1949). So, here came big competition in the fine expensive cookware business.

At the same time, Bill Sontag was getting older and tired. He had been working in a very high-pressure business for many, many years. He had made a lot of money and had invested it wisely in land — a very large ranch near the small town of Layton, Kansas, where he had been raised from birth and had lived until he entered college and then served in World War II. He also had recently gone through heart bypass surgery; one of the first ones that was performed. He wisely decided to get out of the cookware business and spend more time at the ranch with his cattle business — and be of more help to his wife, taking care of their six children. (As I mentioned earlier, she developed cancer and passed away several years later.) They were such good people and Bonnie and I loved them dearly.

I realized it was time for me to look into this new product of West Bend Stainless Steel called Luster Craft. There was a young fellow by the name of Vance Rule who was a distributor for Luster Craft in Tulsa. He lived in Broken Arrow, a suburb of Tulsa, and his home was on the golf course outside of Broken Arrow near Tony Bowline's convenience store. He had heard that Tony had sold cookware before, so he stopped by Tony's store one day to meet him and talk cookware with him. They enjoyed talking to each other and Vance said he didn't know how to do a cookware demonstration, but would like to learn. He had been training college boys how to sell single girls on the referral plan.

Well, my old friend Tony Bowline told him that the guy he needed to meet was his old friend and cookware buddy, Andy Long, now living in Dewey, Oklahoma. He also told him that I could sell on both plans, the dinner party and the referral plan and had been in the business since 1947, some thirteen years. So, Tony stepped to the phone and called me to see if I could come down to meet this guy, Vance Rule. I said, "yes" and the next morning I was in Vance's office talking cookware.

I liked him and could see he was a good salesman, about my age. He showed me the Luster Craft and all the various premiums that he had as gifts for dinner parties. Well, I saw a real opportunity for old Andy Long. He did not have a local finance plan. Their financing was all handled through the West Bend Company in Wisconsin. This did not attract me at all. I had been handling my own time payment sales through the 1st National Bank of Dewey, Oklahoma. The current president was Jimmy Dick McQuarry, an old high school friend of mine that had graduated with me. Jimmy Dick liked these contracts as the stainless steel cookware was a very good product, so he handled these contracts just like he would do on vacuum cleaners, furniture, cars, and other products. He would go ahead and pay me just like I had made cash sales, then the bank would make the interest and also, perhaps gain another customer for the bank. He never had any of these loans go bad.

So, I told Vance that I would train him how to put on a dinner party if he would just sell me the sets of Luster Craft and some premiums for cash in advance, as a sub-distributor. We knocked this idea around and after a day or two of negotiating, I had me one hell of a deal. I would buy the cookware, twelve sets at a time, cash in advance, for only 25% of my retail selling price. I didn't tell him how much I would mark it up, as it was none of his business.

I told him I was going to sell in southern Oklahoma for the summer and whenever I wanted product, for him to send me twelve sets. Do so and I would pay the shipping charges. Well, he jumped at this and I was in business headed for Altus, Oklahoma. This friendship lasted for years and years, even long after we were both out of the cookware business.

In the middle of June, 1961 the wheat harvest was in full swing, with abundant crops. And the cotton was about half grown and looked like an abundant crop would be harvested in the fall. So for the next six weeks, through July, I was giving three dinner parties a week and selling almost 100% of my parties, paying off like never before! We were making plenty of money and having a ball, enjoying Sundays at Lake Altus with our friends, the Joneses.

Bonnie's birthday was coming up on August 11th, and the days were getting hotter and hotter. So, I said to her, "I'm going to take you on a birthday vacation somewhere it is nice and cool." The August days in Oklahoma are usually around 110° - 115° and she said, "Where could you find a cool place in August?"

I said, "Remember one time we were in Albuquerque in the summer, in June, and I went fishing in northern New Mexico with Rudy, the man that mom worked for in the little sundry store in 1950? Well, he took me fishing. I drove my car and we went to Eagle's Nest Lake, northeast of Taos, New Mexico. I remember laying down on the sandy lake shore and looking up at the snow capped mountains and it was nice and cool. So, let's all go to Taos, New Mexico."

About this time my new friend and Luster Craft distirubtor, Vance Rule, had tallied up all my sales for the month of July and had sent me a copy of the Luster Craft bulletin that West Bend mailed out from West Bend, Wisconsin once a month and a picture of me was on the front page of it, saying "Andy Long of Oklahoma is the top salesman of our company for all of the United States for the month of July. Never before has any of our salesmen sold $6,100 worth of Luster Craft in one month." It also said that "he sells both on the dinner party plan and the referral plan, however, he prefers the dinner party plan." I was so happy with his write-up! I said to Bonnie, "This does it. Get ready for our vacation!" (I still have a copy of this bulletin.)

Well, we headed west one morning in early August and made it to Clovis, New Mexico by early evening. Our good friends we wrote about earlier that were big wheat farmers, Coy and Martha Gooch, were still farming but had moved to town in Clovis. After a surprise phone call (after 10 years without any contact) they were happy to hear from us and invited us to have dinner with them. Coy grilled steaks and after a good meal and wonderful visit, they invited us to stay all night with them. The next morning we headed to Taos and checked into a very nice motel with a swimming pool. We all donned our swimming suits, went out to the pool, got in the water — and it was too cold to swim! Believe it or not! Taos is high in the mountains and when to sun starts going down it gets really cool, even in the summer time.

We spent a wonderful day in Taos looking in the various shops and visiting the indian pueblos that were still occupied by indians, as they had been for centuries; that's why they call it 'old Taos.' Kit Carson Park was there, as well as his grave. I will talk more about this much later in this book when we would build a large pueblo style condominium complex in Taos years later, 1973.

We spent the night in a different motel that was larger and had guitar entertainment that we all enjoyed. The next morning it was raining, which was not unusual because July and August is their rainy season. It usually rains a little each day, then the sun comes out, and the days are wonderful after the rain, usually around 80°. We decided to drive on south to Santa Fe, about fifty miles along side the rapids of the Rio Grande as it runs between the highway and the moutains. Again, we were 'rock struck' by the beauty of the moutains.

About 15 miles northwest of Santa Fe there is a little town, or village, I should say, by the name of Pojoaque. State Road 4 intersects the Santa Fe Hightway 285 there, and there was a sign saying, "Los Alamos 18 miles." Well, we were surprised to see that we were so close to Los Alamos. I said to Bonnie, "Lets go up there." Indeed, it is 'up there' as it is, for sure, high in the mountains!

She said, "I'll bet you it will be closed to the public."

I said, "Maybe not. It is 1961. Let's see if we can go into the town. We can always turn around if we can't go in."

Chapter Four

Enter Los Alamos Into Our Lives

Governor Bruce King and Andy

WE DROVE ACROSS INDIAN LAND for about ten miles or so, then we crossed the Rio Grande River at Ottowi Bridge, which is the beginning of Los Alamos County, the smallest county in New Mexico. I think it is only around 44,000 acres if my memory serves me right. Anyway, we really start climbing here and we were amazed at the canyons, cliffs, and views.

Los Alamos County never even existed before World War II. The government needed to find a place that they could locate a secret scientific laboratory, in a place that was both remote but still accessible, and protected from the general public. It was bordered on the east and west by indian land, south and southeast by the banks of the Rio Grande and north and west by the Jemez Mountains. Very rugged and almost impassible except by one little dirt and gravel road that, at the time, was a continuation of Route 4. The elevation of Los Alamos is 7,300 feet, and the most beautiful mountain scenery you have ever seen. When they were trying to locate a place to build this secret laboratory, physicist Robert Oppenheimer suggested Los Alamos to President Franklin D. Roosevelt. He had attended an exclusive rich man's summer school for boys in the mountains of New Mexico. The boys were housed in a huge building built of giant ponderosa pine logs, with a tremendous fireplace and on a beautiful site with a small artesian pond in the center. It froze over in the winter and they would quarry large chunks of ice that they stored in a small insulated building to keep for their summer needs. The boys that attended this school were such as the son of the president of Quaker Oats Company and others like that. It was a very exclusive place in those days.

It is said that later, when the final assembly of the first atom bomb was made, it was assembled in the old ice house which was still in good shape.

The military that protected Los Alamos had horse-mounted patrols. They patrolled the mountains that practically surrounded Los Alamos and it was also well fortified by high chainlinked fences.

Anyway, that morning in early August of 1961 we came to a large chainlink gate on the blacktop road about a mile east of downtown Los Alamos. The gate was open and the guard house was not occupied, so we slowly proceeded. The local airport was on the right up about a mile. The town is located on several plateaus with large bridges connecting the laboratory sites in one direction and the housing sites in the other.

The first, most beautiful sight we saw was the high mountain range, half-moon in shape, extending on the west from south to north. The whole western horizon was covered with dark green pine and large bright yellow areas of the fall Aspen groves. The aspens always turn golden in August and September when the mountain temperatures drop coming into the fall.

As we got to the west end of the airport we started seeing the houses. They were all painted white, with various trim colors. All the lawns were simply manicured with green grass, and flowers and plants in brilliant colors. I had never seen a more beautiful neighborhood in my life, with clean streets and no litter of any kind. Bonnie and I looked at each other in amazement and disbelief. Then we drove on into the business district and found the buildings kept in the same manner with landscaped lawns, shrubs and brilliant flowers. The buildings were stucco, trimmed with cut stone and very neat.

We drove on and looked the town, neighborhoods and streets over. The large pines were everywhere. The boys school had been turned into a lodge and it was the town's only hotel.

I said to Bonnie, while thinking about a place to live and work in my cookware business, "There is no poverty, no slums, no unemployment, only highly paid people and no competition, I think." We were taken agast!

The business community was sort of a large square with all the entrances facing a huge landscaped area of walks, flowers, and grass. Simply gorgeous. We found a small restaurant and since it was noon, we went in for a bit of lunch. I struck up a conversation with some of the people there and asked who I could talk to about renting a place to live. Someone said, "Go over to Trinity Drive, about two blocks away, and talk to the folks at the County Building."

So, after lunch I went into the County Clerk's office and introduced myself to a lady named Jessie Siglock. She was the County Clerk. She said, "Will you be working at the Laboratory?

I said, "No."

She said, "In order to live in Los Alamos you must be project-connected, as we call it. You see, Mr. Long, the Atomic Energy Commission (AEC) owns and maintains all the housing here. Everyone rents from the government and has since the beginning in 1942. Now, there are some new homes being built down the mountain about nine miles at a place called White Rock."

When Los Alamos was being built, the laboratory buildings, the townsite buildings, schools and houses, and many apartment building had to be constructed. The White Rock community was a large trailer park where the workers that built Los Alamos lived. All the trailers were gone and the land had been cleared except for some old abandoned blacktop roads. They were going to build several hundred new homes in order for the people of Los Alamos who wanted to buy their own home could do so, and no longer have to rent to the government.

The County Clerk continued, "All that is there presently are four model homes and some bulldozed streets, but there's no paving, sewer, and only temporary water and gas service for the model homes. They have just gotten started this summer, but some day it will be a very nice place to live." She said I might drive down to White Rock and talk to them and see if I could buy a home there. She then asked me what kind of buisness I was in. I explained to her briefly about Lifetime Stainless Steel and how I demonstrated it in order to sell it. Jessie got real interested in what I was telling her. So I said, "If I can find a place to live, I will talk to you about having one of my demonstration dinner parties and I will have a real nice hostess gift for you."

On that, I left and drove a couple of blocks further down Trinity Drive to the Atomic Energy Commission headquarters. Jessie had said that I could talk to a nice fellow by the name of Herman Rosen, who was the assistant director of the AEC. The townspeople all called the building "The Kremlin" in jest. Anyway, I had a very good and interesting conversation with Mr. Rosen. Nice guy. Unbeknownst to either of us that day, but it did happen that months and years later, we became good friends.

Well, when I met him he explained what "project-connected" meant. He said that the long-range plan for the future of Los Alamos was to change it over from a private government town to a public town, just like all the other towns in the United States. He said, "In a few years we are going to offer the dwelling units for sale to the people that have been renting them all these years. Almost twenty years in fact. Eventually, all the business buildings will also be offered for sale." He said that the gates to the town were opened in 1957. It was now 1961. So, this is why we were not stopped when we drove in earlier. After I told him what I did for a living, he said that my business would be welcomed. "In fact, eventually any business that is in any other American city will be welcomed here. We want our town to be like any other American city."

The business community was run by individuals like myself and they, of course, had to rent their business buildings from the AEC. The people that ran the bank, clothing store, drugstore, gas stations, were all considered "project-connected," so they got to rent their housing from the AEC. He also said, "This will be a wonderful place to live and work when the change-over comes. We already have our own ski run up on the mountain, which can be seen from the town and our ice-skating rink, movie theater, two or three restaurants, cleaners, liquor store, and one large grocery store." All the proprietors rented their buildings from the A.E.C.

Well, he told me what I wanted to know. It didn't look too promising for me to find a place to live, but we drove on down to White Rock anyway. The area of White Rock is on a large plateau of several hundred acres, bordered on the west by State Road 4 coming from Los Alamos and going to Bandelier National Park, ancient Indian ruins and artifacts, and by Pajarito Road going from White Rock to laboratory sites that are located in the vicinity of the road, all surrounded by tall chainlink fences. This road allowed easy access to those sites when the town of White Rock was built, and people started living there. The area was large enough for 2,000 or more homes in years to come. The plateau is bordered by the Rio Grande River and gorge on the north and east. The view is spectacular looking east at the snow-capped mountain of the Sangre de Cristo mountains that ring Santa Fe.

Like we were told, there wasn't much to see in White Rock then — a dirt and gravel road and new furnished model homes. A sales office located in the garage of the first home and next door, in the second one, was the construction office on the lower floor, one executive office and one bookkeeping office upstairs Both of these homes were split level. There were two single level furnished models as well. Three were pre-fabricated homes manufactured by the National Homes Corporation, and one was what is called in the trade "stick built," built entirely from start to finish on the site. All were very well built and attractive.

We were met by the young sales manager, Barry Banducci, and he showed us through the models. As I mentioned before, all the services were temporary at that time. We were asked if I worked with the Lab. I said "no" but that I was looking for a place to live. Well, naturally, there wasn't much interest in us then, but he explained again what we had heard from Herman Roser earlier, that you had to be project-connected to live here. I asked the salesman, "Where do you live?"

He said, "Well, I have an apartment for my wife and me and our baby in Los Alamos. Working here makes me project-connected." The sales manager then asked me, "What kind of work do you do?"

I answered that I was a salesman. He then asked, "Have you ever sold houses?"

I said, "Yes, I have, but I'm not doing that now."

He asked, "Did you like selling houses?"

"Yes," I said, "I did."

He then said, "We sure do need a good salesman or two."

I then asked, "Do you mean that if I would sell houses for you, I could get a place for me and my family to live in Los Alamos?"

He said, "I think so. Let's talk to my boss if you have the time."

I said, "We have the time. We're on vacation." He picked up the telephone and called over to the house next door and talked for a minute to someone, and in a few minutes a man came into the sales office.

He was the business manager and PR man for the project, his name was Doyle Kline. The sales manager introduced us and again I answered the same questions as I had with Barry Banducci. He asked, "What are you selling now?"

I said, "I am selling the finest stainless steel cookware in the world. I have been doing this for around thirteen or fourteen years, except for about one year of selling real estate and new homes. In fact, I make a lot of money selling and demonstrating this cookware. I have a bulletin in my car showing that I was awarded the top salesman with my company in the whole United States for last month."

Mr. Cline said, "I would like to see this." So, I got it and showed it to him and the sales manager, and to say the very least, they were impressed!

He then asked, "What would it take for you to take a job with us?"

I answered, "Well we came to Los Alamos by accident. We were vacationing in Taos and decided to take a side trip to Santa Fe this morning and saw the sign that said 'Los Alamos 18 miles' and decided to take a look." I explained that we were so taken with it all — the climate, the beauty and cleanliness, and we thought it would be such a great place to raise and educate our children — so we decided to find out how we could live here. "We were told that you folks were building some houses in White Rock, so here we are. What you have just asked is certainly worth me giving it some serious thought. I'll tell you what, we are going on to Santa Fe to spend the night. I'll discuss it with my wife and maybe see you tomorrow."

With that, we said our good-byes and drove to Santa Fe, looked around for a while, had supper and found a motel for the night. I didn't get much sleep that night! I kept thinking about what a beautiful place Los Alamos would be to live. My thoughts ran to what Bill Sontag had told me, 'when I wanted to change my circumstances, to try and make the circumstances that I wanted.' Sometime in the night I came up with a great idea. My cookware business requires me to work at night on the dinner parties and the sales calls, so why not explain this to the man I talked with in White Rock. My daytime hours could be spent selling houses for them. Also my weekends would be available to sell houses. This just might work out.

The next morning we drove back up the mountain to White Rock from Santa Fe. It's about 34 miles from Santa Fe to Los Alamos, a little less to White Rock. I told Barry Banducci that I wanted to talk to him and Doyle Kline about an idea that I had come up with the night before. I explained that I could sell houses during the daytime and on weekends, and sell my cookware at night. They pondered this for a while and then I found out about their part-time broker and his part-time salesmen. All the salesmen that were currently working, except for Barry Banducci, the sales manager, were all part-time. One of them was a real estate broker by the name of Gayle "Pat" Patterson. He worked at the Los Alamos Lab and he had hired four others as salespeople, three men and one woman. One of the men was a school teacher and the rest work at the laboratory.

Doyle Kline said, "I think this will work. Barry, you and Andy can sell days and Patterson and his people can sell nights. Then, on weekends all of you can be selling. This would give us real good sales coverage." Then he said, "You will have to be licensed by the New Mexico Real Estate Commission under Patterson's broker's license. So, you will need to talk to him about this." I agreed to see him that evening.

I said, "If Mr. Patterson agrees to this and you can give me your assurance that you can find me a place to live, we will be back out here in a couple of weeks. I would prefer a furnished place so we would not have to move our furniture so fast. Besides this, we need to start our kids in school on the first of September. We will have to work fast, but I'm pretty sure we can make it happen."

Doyle said, "I'll get right onto finding you a place to live."

So, we said, "We'll be going home in the morning so we will say 'good-bye' now."

Barry said, "Andy, there is a little trail where you can drive to the canyon rim of the Rio Grande River. You should take the time to see this fabulous view before you drive home." So we did. It was even more spectacular than we could have imagined. You look down the steep canyon walls about a quarter of a mile and see and hear the mighty Rio Grande River. This was really the clincher that sold us on believing that this was the thing we should do.

So, back up the mountain nine miles to Los Alamos from White Rock. I say "up", because the elevation at White Rock is 6,300 feet and Los Alamos is 7,300 ft. The first stops were the schools. Tim would start into the 10th grade, and Andra into the 5th grade, beginning September 2nd. The next stop was to see Mrs. Jessie Siglock at the County Building, to tell her the good news about us finding a place to live and having become 'project connected' by going to work selling homes in White Rock, and since I would be working days and weekends, I could still sell my cookware at night. She said she had been thinking about what I had told her about my stainless steel cookware and she was interested in finding out more about it. Well, this really turned on the light in my head!

I said, "Mrs. Siglock, what you need to do to really find out all about it is to let me put on a dinner party in your home next week. This way you will find out all there is to know. Just invite three or four couples over to your house next Monday evening for dinner. I'll furnish all the food and you will get a real nice gift being hostess. There will not be any prices quoted at your dinner and if the folks are interested, I will call on them the next evening in their homes."

"Oh," She said, "This would be great, Mr. Long."

"I'll see you next Monday evening around 5:00 PM at your house," I replied. It was now Tuesday, the week before the Dinner on the following Monday.

The next stop was to go to the local bank in Los Alamos, which was the Santa Fe National Bank, Los Alamos branch, and introduce myself to the president and manager of the bank, John Helms. I told Mr. Helms that I was moving to Los Alamos and that I planned on selling my cookware here and was looking for a bank that would handle my time payment contracts. I had a beautiful picture of Luster Craft and one pan in my briefcase. I showed these things to him. He, like all bankers, was hesistant to make any commitments, but I kept selling him on me and my wonderful product and that I was the top producer last month in the nation and that I also could give him the name and phone number of Jimmy McQuarry, who was president of the Dewey, Oklahoma First National Bank, who handled all my time payment contracts over the whole state of Oklahoma. He agreed to call him. I said, "I'll see you next week when I get back to Los Alamos." This introduction to Johnny Helms became a friendship that lasted many, many years.

The next stop was the Pattersons, to meet Pat Patterson, the broker, and his wife, Clara. Well, it so happened that Doyle Kline had called Pat at work that day and told him that I probably would be by to meet him and give him the details on his meeting with me. We hit it off right from the start. He was a tall, lanky, good-looking guy about 50 with gray wavy hair and his wife, a little-bitty gal who he called "Petie," as everyone did. To make a long story short, I wound up booking another dinner for the following Wednesday night. So, this gave me two dinners to test the market before we finalized our plans to move to Los Alamos, New Mexico. This is only the end of the second day since we drove into beautiful Los Alamos the morning before.

I was planning my work and working my plan. Everything seemed to be working out beautifully. Before we left Los Aalmos we drove to the Los Alamos Lodge and made reservations for the following Monday night so we'd have a place to sleep after our Monday night dinner party at the

Siglock's. Bonnie and the kids were getting a little tired of waiting in the car while I had been talking to people all day long, so we drove back to Santa Fe, had a nice Mexican dinner and on to bed for a real early start for the drive home to Dewey in the morning.

Noon-time came when we got to Guymon, in Western Oklahoma. It was already 110 degrees and climbing. We had been enjoying the 80 and 85 degree days for the past few days and when we hit 110 degrees, we realized we were making the right choice in planning the move to Los Alamos, and a job, a new prosperous cookware territory, a place to live with good schools, a good climate and beautiful surroundings. We were all happy with the way things were going.

We drove to Dewey that night and informed my folks of our plans and they understood the opportunity that we had. I explained that what I had in mind was to let them move into our big house with our furnishings and they could rent their house out to someone else for an extra income. This met with mixed feelings. They hated to see us move that far away, but they could see that it was going to be good for us and if it didn't work out, we could always move back.

I drove to Tulsa the next morning and bought a dozen sets of Luster Craft from Vance Rule and told him all about our coming venture. I asked him to find out what trucking line he could use to ship my cookware to Santa Fe, New Mexico. Yellow Truck Lines was chosen and that was set up for future deliveries. I told him all the details including the two cookware parties I had booked for the next Monday and Wednesday. He said, "Andy, you are a 'wheeler-dealer' deluxe!"

When our mail came the next day, a letter arrived from Doyle Kline of the Noxon Construction Company in White Rock. He informed me of our new living quarters that he had found for us. A nice two-bedroom duplex, all furnished. He said he had a nine month's sub-lease for us to sign when we got back. It so happened that a young scientist was being sent back for some advanced education. He apparently was an exceptional student and they had more important plans for him at the lab. They did this sort of thing when they found the right people. I will go into more detail about how the laboratory functioned and was operated by the Atomic Energy Comission later. Anyway, the duplex was available September 1st, now about two weeks away. Doyle also put in writing what we had discussed and had it approved by Noxon Construction Company's president in Los Angeles, California where they were headquartered.

I hadn't used my little two-wheel trailer (that I had bought in the fall of 1951 when we moved to Bismark, North Dakota) very much, so I bought some paint and gave it a nice new paint job and started to get things ready that we would need to occupy our furnished place in Los Alamos. We told my folks that we would not be leaving until September 1st to move, but Bonnie and I would be leaving this weekend to go back to Los Alamos to put on two dinner parties next Monday and Wednesday, then return Friday or Saturday and pack our little trailer with our things. Anyway, Bonnie and I were going out first to 'test the market' before we actually would permanently leave for Los Alamos with our kids and our little dog.

We planned on putting on the two dinner parties that I had booked with the Siglocks and Pattersons for Monday and Wednesday, make the sales calls on Tuesday and Thursday, then return on Friday to Dewey and start moving my folks into our house and getting our things ready to put in our little two-wheeled trailer, that we would need to keep house in our furnished duplex in Los Alamos when we arrived the following week of September 1st. Everything was well planned, so all we had to do was make it work.

We loaded our car with my cookware set and show set and several of the sets I had bought from Vance Rule in Tulsa, so that I could make immediate delivery on the sales that I hoped to make on the two up-coming dinners. This would show the people that, indeed, they would be getting what they paid for. Just good business. Bonnie and I started out on Sunday and drove half-way and got a good night's sleep so we wouldn't be worn out when we drove in and started putting on the Monday evening dinner party. We arrived at the Lodge in Los Alamos about noon, ate lunch and took a two-hour nap. We bought our groceries for the dinner and showed up at the Siglocks around 4:30 PM to start preparing the food for the guests that would arrive at 7:00.

Everything went extremely well. I got appointments from everyone easily and went back to the Lodge feeling pretty confident that I would make some sales. There were four couples including the host and hostess, Mr. and Mrs. Siglock. When I finished my last sales call the next evening, I had sold and delivered all four sets of Luster Craft to four happy customers. We were elated!

The next dinner was Wednesday and to make a long story short, I did the very same thing on my calls from the Patterson's dinner, except that they had five couples instead of four and I sold all five of them and delivered their sets. Oh, yes, I booked two more dinners for the latter part of the next week after that. Wow! Was I pumped up! Bonnie and I both knew that we had made the right choice when we decided to make Los Alamos our new home!

Before I left for Dewey I stopped in to see the banker, John Helms, and he was glad to see me. He reported that my friend and banker Jimmy Dick McQuarry in Dewey, Oklahoma had given me a glowing report. He told me his bank would be happy to finance my time-payment contracts. Another positive thing in our plans had just happened. However, after I had just sold these nine sets, all for cash, I didn't expect to have many contracts to take to the bank. The reason was that almost everyone in Los Alamos worked for the Laboratory and the Laboratory had their own Federal Credit Union. So, the people simply paid cash, then borrowed the money from their credit uinon, which was what they preferred to do. Another good thing.

We also stopped by White Rock and talked to Doyle Kline and Barry Banducci to tell them of my good luck in my cookware sales and that we were getting ready to head back to Oklahoma to get our things and our kids and would see them on the 1st or 2nd of September, 1961. We asked for the address of the duplex so we could take a look at the outside of it and see how far it was to the two schools our kids would be attending We thanked them for the duplex instead of an apartment. They were pleased to see me and get a report on our progress. We were well-pleased with the location and the fact that it had a fenced back yard so we could bring our little miniature black poodle with us.

As soon as we got back to Dewey, I called Vance Rule and told him I would send him a check for another dozen sets of Luster Craft and to ship them right away to Santa Fe as I would be putting on two more dinners the next week. He was happy as could be, and would ship them that day. Well, we closed our bank accounts, thanked Jimmy Dick for his recommendation to Mr. Helms in Los Alamos and bid him goodbye. Mom said that she would take care of getting the utilities changed to their names and change our address at the post office as soon as we sent her our new one in Los Alamos and start finding a renter for their house. We finished her and Dad's move into our big house and it was all working out as planned.

Looking back now I get tired just thinking about how much we had done in the two weeks when we got back from our vacation to Taos, New Mexico! Whew!

Bright and early the morning of August 31, 1961 with our little newly-painted green trailer hooked onto our good-looking black Dodge, two kids and their dog, Bonnie and I were at the very beginning of a venture that would last for twenty years. We drove all day and at one minute after midnight, September 1, 1961, we drove into the town of Los Alamos, never dreaming that we would spend the next twenty years in this beautiful place.

We got the kids started in school and moved into our duplex home and rested and got ready for my dinner party on the next day. It, and the one that Friday, were equally as successful. Two of the guys that had attended the Patterson's Dinner were part-time salesmen for Pat Patterson. So that gave me the opportunity to get acquainted with them. One of them, Summers Cox, worked in the Health Lab for the Laboratory and the other one, Cal Etherly, was a high-school science teacher. We became good friends. Both of them lived near our duplex — and Cal took me deer hunting. We lived only one-half block from the mountains — some of the most rugged ones in the county. I didn't get a deer, but Cal did and I helped him drag it out. So this was another thrill that made me even happier than I already was, if that was possible.

Pat Patterson was a wonderful guy and so was his wife, Petie. He helped me study for my up-coming real estate salesman's exam. He and I studied every evening because if I didn't pass the first time I took the exam, I would have to wait six months before I could sit for it again. Well, I did pass, as I thought I would, because I had passed the one I took in Kansas and also the one in Oklahoma. I was legal by the 1st of October.

Now I want to describe the work structure and situation of the Noxon Consturction Company of Los Angeles. It was owned by a young man I would judge to be about 35 years old at that time — a college graduate from a wealthy family that had just recently inherited $750,000. This three-quarters of a million dollars today would equate to about $10,000,000 today. His father had founded The Purina Dog Food Company. This inheritance was what put Sandy Noxon into the construction business in California. His school chum, J. B. Brown was the lawyer, a figure-head type, and was made vice-president of the company. They had been in business for a relatively short period of time, no more than three or four years and mildly successful, when they decided to bid on a government contract in Los Alamos, New Mexico.

So, Sandy and J. B., along with their architectural and engineering departments, put together a proposal with the proper drawings, layout and all the other particulars, and submitted their proposal to the Atomic Energy Commission for the White Rock, New Mexico project. Probably the smartest thing they did was to contact the senior U. S. Senator from New Mexico, Clinton P. Anderson who, at that time, was about as important to New Mexico as God.

I have no direct knowledge, then or now, as to what was discussed, but the Noxon Construction Company's proposed plan was awarded the contract and Mr. Doyle Kline was hired by Noxon to be the man in charge of the negotiations with the AEC once the project got under way. Doyle Kline had been, or was at the time, an aide to Clinton P. Anderson. Doyle had been a trusted employee of the Senator for several years and was very close to him. So, I personally think this had a lot to do with Noxon getting the contract for White Rock. Doyle handled all the public relations for Noxon in New Mexico, dealing with the AEC, the banks, the newspapers, radio, etc. He didn't try and run the construction department, but he did oversee the sales and financing for the sales we made and shared the necessary work with the F.H.A. and the Bank of New Mexico in Albuquerque. This was shared with Chuck Coutts, the project construction manager, who also worked with FHA and the Bank.

The agreement with the Bank of New Mexico was that as soon as the company had twenty-five firm contracts for new homes, then, at that time, the bank would release $3,000,000 of development money for the streets and all utilities to be installed for White Rock: sewer, water, power and telephone, all underground. The Grand Opening of the project had taken place in the early summer of 1961, and, to date, they had only about fifteen firm sales. Not too good.

Winter was approaching in New Mexico. September had already produced some light snow and a lot more to come. This is not something that the California home-builders were familiar with, but they were getting close to finding out about how severe the winters were in the mountains.

The project manager, Chuck Coutts, was only 27 or 28 years old and plenty sharp! He had considerable large production home building experience and plenty of drive. Jack Tobin was his assistant and was liason between the sales force and the construction department. Once the sale was made, he took over working with the customers about color selections, any minor changes, appliances, etc. He was a pretty good-looking blond guy, about 24 years old, with a pleasant personality. Both he and Chuck were college graduates. Jack drove a little Porsche sportscar and was single. Chuck Coutts, on the other hand, had a very nice wife, Pat, and three young kids who were all in grade school.

Jack Tobin had a girlfriend that was a very beautiful young German girl who worked for a scientist and his wife as a nanny for their kids. Her name was Christa. Jack and her made a beautiful couple. They both liked to ice skate and ski. They were really looking forward to the snow that would be coming soon.

The engineer and surveyor was a guy named Mark Hooper. His wife was named Sue. The purchasing agent that ordered all the materials for the construction was Ted Wilkie. These men were all the department heads responsible for the construction of the homes.

Chuck Coutts, as project manager, had to negotiate with all the sub-contractors who would do the various phases of building the houses, including all the grading and dirt work to prepare the streets and then the individual lots and building sites. Other sub-contractors were the plumbing, concrete, electrical, drywall, framing & finish carpentry work, roofing, fireplace masonry and brickwork, and so on. Chuck was responsible for all the contracts made with these various subs, a very responsible job for a guy of 27 or 28 years old.

Doyle Kline's wife was named Nelba. They had two young daughters.

Let me take a minute to explain something I think is important. Like I said, 99% of the people worked at the laboratory, most of which were married and had worked and lived in Los Alamos since the early 1940's. For those of you that don't know much about the scientific-type of people, (such as all of us that were working for Noxon Construction) let me tell you they are a different kind of folk. They had been pampered and sheltered for years and the ones who were young married couples or single new-hires were the same breed of cats. Almost all were over-educated and geniuses in their particular fields. So you see, all of us "common working class" Americans were beginning to find out what we had to deal with!

Getting back to our sales department, Barry Banducci was a young Italian American from San Francisco, about 23 or 24 years old. Most of our prospects were about that age or a little older, most of which were just out of graduate school from various colleges, all of them were very intelligent young scientists. Barry was really not yet qualified to deal with most of these young scientific types. He won more arguments than sales, and the part-time salesmen, as well as Pat Patterson, just didn't have enough time to get the sales production up and going. I could see all this taking place after I was there a while, so I had to make an adjustment. Even though I was an excellent salesman with fourteen years experience, I could readily see, after working a month, that if this project was going to succeed, the sales production was going to have to pick up considerably, and pretty quickly, with all the overhead and payroll expenses that the Noxon Co. was funding. Sales had to increase.

One thing that I was experiencing in my Luster Craft sales was the fact that my main sales pitch about the health benefits I was stressing with this method of cooking was going in one ear and out the other with most of these young scientific types. They were young and healthy — why worry about that? They were not the older farm families I had been used to selling, but an entirely different bunch of folks. I was making some sales, but not like I had started out. What most of these young lab people wanted to know was "how are these pans made?" My answer was, after my usual explanation about being surgical steel and so on, I would then say "I don't know any of the scientific details. All I know is, it works. You know, our factory pays the engineers that design our product $20,000 per year and I'm only a ragged-ass salesman." Of course, that wasn't much of an explanation, but this is what I would say. Later on I will explain what I have just said above in selling these same type people.

Now back to the sales force — things did not look too good. It was the middle of November 1961. On the morning of November 15th, Doyle Kline asked me to come over next door to his office and that he had something to talk with me about. He said Berry Banducci was leaving Los Alamos and moving his wife and baby back to California. The pressure was getting to young Barry, his wife was very homesick to see her mom and dad, and they were anxious to see their new grandbaby. Doyle said he had a letter from Sandy Noxon offering me the sales manager's job.

My pay would be $150 per week and $25 for each sale that was made by me and my salespeople. Also a credit card for gas and oil for my car. Doyle asked, "Andy, what do you think about this?"

I said, "You call him and tell him I will give it a try for two weeks. This will give us a chance to see if it is working out. If we are both satisfied with my performance after this two weeks, then we have a deal. If either of us is not satisfied, then the deal is off."

A short time later Doyle called me again and said this was a good idea. So, around Thanksgiving Day I became the new sales manager for the Noxon Construction Company in White Rock. The first thing I decided was that this had to be my full-time job. I stored my cook set and show set of Lustercraft permanently.

The entire Noxon staff congratulated me and offered me their total support. I talked with Pat Patterson about this and he was happy also. His sales people had just about petered out anyway, except for himself, so he and I started out working together on our sales calls just like I had done with some of my cookware buddies before. It worked very well. I would make two appointments for each evening if I could: one for 6:30 PM and one for 9:00 PM in Los Alamos. Usually they would be people that had already looked at the lots and had one or two favorite ones in mind.

I had initiated a new idea and it was working. When I would show the various lots to a prospect I would say, "Now folks, let's not get into a hurry about bagging a home. You need to give a lot of thought to which one you like best and the size and all."

"I have a suggestion. In order to take time to decide which house plan to buy, you need to tie up the favorite lot you want so someone else doesn't buy it before you decide which house you want to build on it. We have a new plan where you can reserve the lot you want for two weeks so you don't have to be in a big rush in getting the right house to have built. You can reserve a lot for the two-week period for $50. In the event you change your mind about buying a house, you can get your $50 back. We don't want to keep it. It is for you to have time to make your decision on the right house. Then you sign the building contract on the home you want to have on the lot you want."

This new idea I had worked like a charm! Sales began to pick up.

Doyle Kline and Chuck Coutts both lived in single family homes in Los Alamos. One day Pat Coutts told Bonnie and Sue Hooper that she had been invited to coffee and to also bring some of the other Noxon wives to a get-acquainted party to meet some of the laboratory wives. The three Noxon girls thought this would be nice. Now, remember, all these lab women were college graduates just like their husbands, and being young educated women, they hadn't really gotten to know anyone that wasn't just like them.

Bonnie said the conversations went quite well until one of them asked Bonnie what her alma mater was. Well, Bonnie told her that she had not attended college and the conversation went flat in a hurry. (Bonnie had been the Salutatorian for her high school class but even though she had a scholarship to go to college, her family could not afford her board and expenses.) This ended any other similar get-togethers with these stuck-up laboratory wives. This closed the ranks of the Noxon people and there were enough of us that we had lots of good times among ourselves without doing any social mixing. In time, we did get acquainted with quite a few of the business people in the town and they were good folks to know. Altogether different from the average laboratory family.

Some of these lab folks were brilliant in what they were educated to do, to the point of being geniuses, but had little common sense. The ones we were selling houses to were mostly younger people. Some of them working at their first job. The general mindset was that these business people were just trying to make a profit off of them, and they resented that. They thought they should buy everything at cost. The only way they could make any extra money was by buying everything as cheaply as possible. It didn't take long for me to realize this.

Here are a few examples that I heard about as time passed in talking with other business people: If a fellow was a mathematician at the lab, he would argue with the banker about how the bank figured his interest. If he was dealing with a service station, he would tell the station owner that he checked out the oil that he carried and that he tested it and it was not what was advertised on the oil can. One guy bought a diamond ring for his wife and he took it back and wanted his money back from the jeweler because he had put it under a very large microscope and it showed that the diamond had a flaw in it. I had a personal experience with one of my home buyers. He said, "Mr. Long, I want to make sure the noise level on my furnace doesn't exceed 16 decibels on the A scale." Naturally, this dumbfounded me.

I thought I knew what he meant, but my answer was with a question. "Jezebels, jezebels, what the hell are Jezebels?"

"No, decibels," he said.

Then I said, "Is this with carpet on the floors, with the closet doors closed, or just how would you be satisfied?" He looked dumb-founded, and I am sure he thought I was a dummy.

Anyway, I said, "Mr. Mitchell, you see the way the company arrives at the price of the house we are selling you is from the F.H.A., who does the financing and has these homes appraised. All the things in the building of these homes and your house, is priced in accordance with our standard furnace. However, if you want to upgrade your furnace or anything else, we will have to charge you more."

"Oh, I don't want to pay any more so I guess that is okay."

They were just as green as goose shit about business. So it was good, I guess, to have the A.E.C. babysitting them. Later on I will get into more of this sort of thing when I start having to deal with the lab employees who served on the County Planning Committee and County Council.

In December the weather had turned bad and by Christmas it had snowed a total of 36 inches! The coldest night was 30 degrees below zero!!! None of us had seen cold weather like this, especially the California folks. Construction on the homes that we had sold slowed down because of the weather. Jack and Chris were enjoying the skiing and all of us went ice skating and the kids played in the snow. I think this 30 degrees below zero was the coldest day on record there and in the Espanola valley. Large old apple trees, some of which were 100 years old, just burst. The battery on my Dodge burst as there was no garage to keep the car in at night at the house where we lived. We had bought an old Jeep station wagon for a second car and had to shovel both of them out every morning.

I had gotten new insurance from an Allstate Insurance man in Santa Fe, so he came up to our house to talk to our young new driver, Tim, who had just gotten his driver's license. He took time to talk to Tim about being very careful, which I really appreciated. It wasn't long until Tim had a wreck. It wasn't his fault, and the woman driver was not hurt badly, thank God. Tim was coming down a small hill that was covered with ice when this old gal made a left turn right in front of him. He braked his car, but on the ice it kept on sliding and popped her right on the passenger side of her car. Her driver's side door came open and out on the street she went. It was a blessing in disguise, however, because Tim became a very careful driver after that. He and Carmen Zielinski, his girlfriend at the time, even introduced and passed a bill in the YMCA's Youth in Government mock legislature at the state capital requiring automobiles to have seat belts.

Getting back to Pat Patterson and me, I found out in our conversations that he had been in the Merchant Marines also. So, we were real blood-brothers, so to speak. We were doing really well on our sales calls in the people's homes each night. Thinking about it now, what we were doing was exactly what I had done for years on my sales calls from my cookware dinners when I called on the individual couples the next night after the dinner party. They couldn't get up and leave because we were in their house, and had plenty of time to talk and do some real selling. So, it was paying off.

Each night after we would finish our sales calls, we would stop by the Carriage Inn. This was a beautiful new restaurant and lounge, with a piano bar, padded seats and the works. It was a very popular watering hole. Pat loved his booze! He would drink about three drinks for my one. He would say, "Barkeep, give me another one, so I can catch up with Andy."

A couple of days before New Year's Eve, we finally produced the 25 firm contracts that would release the $3,000,000 in development money that Noxon so badly needed for the streets, utilities, and to keep the company solvent.

At our New Year's Eve celebration party at the Carriage Inn, old Andy Long was the hero. Our reservations included a bottle of champagne for each person. We had a wonderful time. There was a small band, so Chuck Coutts talked them into them letting me play the trap drums. I had not forgotten how to play even though I had sold my drum set when Bonnie and my folks moved to Anderson, Indiana from Wichita, Kansas after World War II. The party got wild, but no trouble. Everyone was having a ball. Mostly business people and Noxon people. A great guy by the name of Bun Ryan and his wife, Jean (still good friends of ours), owned the bar and lounge. They were about our age, around 37-40 years old. Jean got a little too much champagne, so she climbed up on the bar and did a dance for us. What a night! Chuck Coutts also did a solo dance that night.

Not long after that the construction really picked up as sales had improved and this made it easier to sell our home prospects as they could see that the project was really going to succeed.

One night, the Coutts and the Longs went to Santa Fe for a night out. The Patterson's agreed to babysit our little girl, Andra, who was in the 5th grade, until we got home. There was a famous nightclub in the village of Tesuque, outside of Santa Fe, called El Nido. So, this is where we went for dinner, dancing, and drinks. Chuck and I were feeling no pain, all of us really enjoying each other and Chuck and I had a pretty good load on. Finally, when it came time to leave, we had to cross the dance floor to the front door. There was a room about 8 ft. x 10 ft. that is just through the door onto the dance floor, then another door opening to the outside. This is to keep some of the cold and snow out before coming into the club. When we opened the outside door, standing there in about six inches of snow was an old bay mare, with the halter rope hanging down. Well, when we saw her, one of us, and I don't remember which one, said, "Let's put her inside." Oh, this was a great idea we thought. Well, we put her in the little room and closed the door. The four walls of this little entrance room was covered with mirrors except for the two doors, and it had quarry tile floors. When the horse entered, the snow on her feet got her to slipping and sliding on this tile floor. Well, we quickly got into our car and drove up the street about a half block to the corner and turned around and drove back across the street from the front door. Old Chuck was laughing so hard the tears were streaming down his face. I was laughing also. Anyway, it took about five or ten minutes and the door opened and the big fat Mexican chef, with his apron and big chef top hat on, came leading the horse out, and about a dozen or so people followed — all wondering how the horse got into El Nido!

We drove on back up the mountain to Los Alamos, dropped the Coutts off at their house and the next morning we went to the Patterson's to pick up Andra. To our surprise, Petie told us that earlier that morning Pat had a heart attack and the ambulance came to pick him up. (The hospital was only about three blocks from their apartment, and Pat was doing fine.) Petie said, "Bonnie, Andra slept through the whole thing and never woke up at all."

Sunday was my busiest day at White Rock. We had three furnished models, all open for inspection and I was now all by myself with Pat in the hospital. I spent my time in the largest model, the Glenwood. The people would usually go through all the models, then wind up in the Glenwood and I would hand out literature and a plat showing all the lots numbered and the proposed street names, so they could, hopefully, find a lot they liked.

By me working six days a week, including weekends, I had my day off on Monday. This particular Sunday, Doyle Kline happened to be in White Rock and while we were visiting, I told him about Chuck and I putting the horse in El Nido. He also thought this was funny as hell. Well, the best is yet to come.

Chuck told me later on Tuesday that he was in his office working and Doyle came in to see him. He told Chuck that there was a special deputy from Santa Fe County, by the name of Martinez, up in his office and that he wanted to talk to a feller by the name of Coats or Cots, or Coutts, about a couple of guys that put a horse in the El Nido Club on Saturday night. He said he didn't know what the other guy's name was. You can imagine how Chuck's head started spinning about how in the hell this guy could have found out his name! Well, old Doyle just couldn't hold his serious composure any longer and Chuck noticed just a little bit of a smile on Doyle's lips and Chuck then said, "That damn Andy told you about this didn't he?" Then both of them started laughing, as well as the guys in the large room.

We made our own fun in those days. Everyone was working hard, fighting the cold and mud. A big burden on me was beginning to ease up a little as we had the critical 25 firm sales made and building was under way on several homes. Chuck had started a house for himself and his family on a nice corner lot. It was called the Valle Grande, our largest home offered. It was a four bedroom, about 2400 sq. ft. The selling price to the public for this home was around $24,000. Imagine what it would sell for at today's prices! (The average income for all the lab employees at the time was $12,000 per year.)

On Mondays, my day off, Bonnie and I would leave the house early and spend the whole day usually together, enjoying all the places within easy driving distance. About once a month we would drive to Albuquerque. It was not a large city like it is today. It was around 100,000. Today it is around 500,000.

One day we drove up into the mountains and didn't turn around soon enough. There was still some snow on the ground and as far as we went, the snow was on the frozen dirt trail. We kept going because we couldn't get to a place to turn around. Finally, we got stuck! It was still freezing at the altitude where we were. Well, I worked and worked and just about the time I was about to give out, I finally got us unstuck. I had gotten the car hot trying to get it turned around, so thankfully, we were going down-grade back down the mountain. We made it but it was a lesson well learned. Never drive in the high mountains in the snow in a two-wheel drive vehicle.

One day in the fall of 1962 when the deer season was on before the snows came, I went hunting by myself on my day off. I drove up in the high mountains to a place called the Valle Grande. I was walking down a jeep trail and there came a big, tall fellow coming toward me. Well, we introduced ourselves and this big cowboy type's name was Bruce King. I told him who I was and he said that he had a large area leased to run cattle on here and they had just loaded all of them last week and took them off the mountain before the snows came. He had come back today to see if his cowboys had happened to leave any strays but he hadn't seen any. He said he and his two brothers had several ranches and their headquarters was in Stanley, New Mexico, close to Moriarty. We must have stood there in the middle of the trail for 30-45 minutes and had a great conversation. I told him he reminded me of Will Rogers, my grandfather's good friend. He talked a lot like him. I told him I was raised on a farm and ranch when I was young, so we seemed to hit it off and both of us enjoyed our visit. I didn't see him for several years, but there will be much more to write about Bruce King and Andy Long later on.

The company decided that I needed a secretary to help me with the typing of the contracts. I had been doing them all in longhand. I was also doing the loan applications since the financing was done by the bank in Albuquerque which was too far away for people to have to travel to make applications for their FHA loans. I had to take all the information from the buyers for the loans and their credit reports. By doing this, I knew everything about each family, their finances and all. In those days, the down payment on these FHA homes was only around $400 - $500. Some of these young couples did not always have the necessary money available. When you stop and think about it, that was the equivalent to around $4,000 - $5,000 today. So, old Andy put his creative mind to work once again.

I asked them, "Is it possible to borrow this down payment from your folks?" In most cases they would say that they probably could. The problem was with FHA financing you could not borrow your down payment because when the bank and FHA would calculate how much money the family would have to make their monthly house payment, there might not be enough to go around.

So, this is what I would say to my buyers. "Folks, you call or write your parents explaining about how you want to buy a new home and that you need to borrow some money for part of the down payment. Now, folks, FHA will not allow us to borrow this down payment money. So your parents will have to write a letter back which will say that they are making you a gift of this money and no repayment or interest is expected. Of course, your mom and dad trust you to do the right thing about whether you intend to pay them back or not. This is entirely up to you and your parents, whatever you tell them verbally about payback."

When we got this letter back from the buyer's parents explaining what they said about a gift, we would include the letter in the loan package and show the amount on the credit financial form as a gift. So, once again, old Andy made some circumstances fit the need. About a third of my sales had to use this tactic.

Our California construction company began to find out about pouring concrete in cold weather. This was not a problem in California where it never freezes, but it damn sure is in the mountains of New Mexico! After two or three concrete jobs froze, and then a week or so later they were jack-hammering the frozen concrete out, they finally learned how to pour concrete in freezing weather. Spring would soon be here so I was beginning to see that I needed to get a couple more salesmen as the part-time people just couldn't do the job and Pat couldn't work anymore as his heart doctor said, "No." He had to be satisfied with just his job at the laboratory.

I talked to Doyle Kline about hiring another salesman or two and he said he knew of a guy in Albuquerque, named Joe Monack. Joe came up to talk with me and we found him an apartment to live in. Joe had an old car that was not in very good shape so, on some cold mornings, I would have to push him to get it started. His wife was still in Albuquerque working and did not plan on moving up to Los Alamos, so he was "Baching." Bonnie fixed my lunch as White Rock had no stores of any kind. She would also fix Joe a lunch.

Joe was about five years older than me and I had turned 37 the past November. He was a pretty good "bullshitter," so I thought I could train him to be a salesman. He had a little bit of experience working for a home builder in Albuquerque some time back. He had presently been working as a masseur in a health club. So I started training him to do everything I was doing, including taking the loan application and credit report information, etc. I took him with me every night on my sales calls and in about two weeks, I had me a pretty fair salesman. When we would finish our last sales call at night, we would stop by the Carriage Inn for a couple or three drinks. Joe had a great singing voice and he knew a lot of songs. So the gal at the piano bar would play and Joe would sing. We had a good time and were getting to be pretty well known. Joe Monack was of Hungarian nationality and was originally from Pittsburg.

I recall one loan closing in particular: Allan Conner and his wife, Sue, who we also got to know very well as the years rolled by. This was the first house that Allan and Sue had bought, so he decided to read every word of the disgustingly long F.H.A. mortgage. I think his 6th grade teacher must have told him to be sure to read everything before he signed it. Anyway, this was going to take about an hour for him to read it and would play hell with the mortgage lender, Joe Pierce's schedule, so he called me at the other office where I was and said, "Andy, I need you over here right away."

I high-tailed it over and saw the problem. I said, "Allan, let me suggest something to you. You know all these loan papers are just alike, and they

211

are not going to change anything for anyone, so if you want to buy this home you have to sign these papers. I suggest that one of these cold nights when you have nothing better to do, just build you a nice big fire in your fireplace and get comfortable in your favorite easy chair and read every word of this mortgage that you have signed." Allan thought for a moment and then said, "Andy, that is a good idea." So Joe's problem was over and he was able to keep his schedule on track with the other buyers.

One other funny thing I will share with you. I told you previously how tight some of those young scientists are, well this one takes the cake! It was time for him to write the check for the down payment so he started to make it out and he made an error in the figures. Oh, he was so upset! So he took another check and then made an error in the written amount. Oh, this really made him upset. He said, "Can I mark this out and start over?"

I said, "No, that isn't legal. You need to write another check."

He said, "I don't want to do that. The bank charges me for each check I write."

I said, "Well, I guess we will have to sell your house to someone else." I normally didn't lose my patience with these folks, but this time I did.

He just sat there and I said, "There is another alternative. Here, I will give you this dime and we'll let your wife make out the check for you to sign."

Joe looked at me and smiled, and said, "Andy, I think you have solved our problem." And it did.

When I was young I had lots of patience, but as the years rolled on my patience wore very thin. I will tell you many more stories about dealing with these over-educated people.

Now, for a bit of good news. The Lab had decided to let the young scientist, from whom we were sub-leasing our duplex, continue his schooling for an additional nine months, so this let us stay in the same place for almost another year. By this time we decided to take the offer that Noxon made to their main employees about buying a home at cost. We picked a nice lot on Rover Blvd. and started a Briarcliff model. Each lot in the subdivision was 100 feet wide and 125 feet deep, approximately one-quarter acre.

The first increment of the subdivision was 209 lots. The government had charged the bidder, which was Noxon in this case, $25 dollars per acre for the raw land. This is with no utilities, no streets, no amenities of any kind, but it was one hell of a deal because they were trying to make the project attractive to all the various bidders, with the condition that if they completed 209 homes on all the lots, the could buy more land at the same price and start on a second increment.

Things were going very well. Sales were good. We were selling four to six per week and closing four to six loans per week. The first twenty-five homes were completed and the families had moved in. Things looked very, very good.

Noxon had another large project going in California — a 400 lot subdivision. I don't know any of the details about it except that they decided to have the Los Alamos project manager, "boy wonder" Chuck Coutts, transferred back to take over the project. It was rumored that the project was in trouble. I sold Pat and Chuck's house to Guy and Flo Elliott, and the Coutts finally moved to California for good. Noxon sent in another project manager, Bill Heath. He was a little older than me and probably about 40-45 years old, a real drinker and carouser. He just didn't seem to take care of business like he should. The bookkeeper he hired was way behind in her books and construction slowed down. Now, understand that we had about thirty or forty houses under construction in various stages, so the load was heavy on the guy doing the building and we were still selling more and more homes.

I got so concerned about the houses not getting finished on schedule that I talked to Doyle Kline about it. He said, "Yes, Andy, I am worried too."

I said, "Doyle, I have an idea that may show Sandy Noxon what is going on here." I told him I had a Polaroid camera and I would have my salesman take a picture of each house that was under construction each Friday afternoon and date the pictures, show the lot #, address, and customer's name, put them in a large picture album and we could then see if the homes were getting worked on, week by week. He said, "Good idea. Make it happen."

Joe Monack and Bill Hawkins, my two salesmen would take the pictures and in about three weeks there was hardly any appreciable progress made. I showed this album to Doyle and he said Sandy Noxon was coming to town soon and he would show it to Sandy.

Old Bill Heath found out about what we were up to and he blew his top at me. He stopped just short of a fist fight, but he was hot, as the pictures didn't lie. Well, the result of this was young Sandy Noxon and his wife decided to temporarily move into our Manor House model, as it was furnished, of course. He called in his head bookkeeper from the Los Angeles office, Hazelle Bradshaw, a great gal and very smart and competent. Their bookkeeping was all done on computers and with the White Rock records lagging way behind, things were going to hell.

We were not finishing the homes fast enough, and closing the loans on them, to generate enough money to buy the materials and pay the subcontractors. So, when the material suppliers and subs were not getting paid, things were going from bad to worse.

I am not a hundred percent sure about this next part, but I am pretty sure that I am right. The project in California was in financial trouble and I think funds were siphoned off the Los Alamos job to keep the California job afloat. The bookkeeper lagging behind caused some "second guessing" by the top management at the company in California. So, after Sandy Noxon spent a month or so in White Rock, he was convinced that what I was telling them was true. So some things in the bookkeeping in White Rock changed. They hired an additional gal, Jolene, to help LeAnn so they could get current.

It was around the middle of June, 1962 when I got a letter from my mother that my dad had gone to Wichita where my sister, Marjorie, and her family lived and their doctor examined my dad and found that he had prostate cancer. What a blow to me and my little family! They were preparing to operate, so in a few days we headed to Wichita, Kansas. I was devastated to say the least. Dad and I loved each other so much. The cancer had spread throughout his body and the doctors said that he was not going to live. His kidneys were not working, so it was just a matter of a day or two. He was suffering so much, his body was jumping and jerking. There was nothing I could do to help him, so I prayed to God to take my dad and stop his suffering. Later that day, June 25, 1962, I was standing at the foot of his bed looking at him and he opened his eyes. Dad had bright blue eyes and our eyes met and he fixed his eyes on me and in a few seconds he was gone, still looking straight at me. I will never forget that last look as long as I live.

Dad had a talk with me just before he went to the hospital in Wichita. Just he and I. He told me the hardest thing he had to go through was when his dear old mother died. She had lived to be 93. He had never known his dad as he had died when Wesley was only two years old. I had mine 37 years. We talked a long time and I am so glad that we had time for that long talk. He told me that my mom had our big house looking like a palace and, indeed, she did. This is where all the family and friends gathered for the funeral in Dewey at the First Christian Church, followed by the burial at the Dewey Cemetery. Dad was a World War I veteran, so the Bartlesville American Legion provided an Honor Guard and the service was very nice. Dad's last two brothers and his last two sisters were there and lots of his friends and other relatives. To my surprise, my two very good friends, Lloyd Howard from El Reno and Bobby Jones from Altus, and their wives, were there and that meant so much to me. They each had come over 200 miles to be there.

A couple of days later we headed back to Los Alamos, pretty mixed up as to whether we should stay in Los Alamos or return to Dewey to be near my mother and closer to Bonnie's mother and the rest of her family. It was decision time.

When we got home to Los Alamos and started back to work, everyone that I had sold new homes to were so nice to me and so sympathetic. It made me feel better. I got so many sympathy cards and calls from the people I that had sold homes to, that it sure made me feel good about White Rock. The White Rock Noxon gang were all worried that I might go back to Oklahoma, as they knew I was thinking about it. Doyle called me over to his office and said that Sandy Noxon and J. B. Brown wanted him and me to fly to Los Angeles for a few days. I had never flown on a jet plane, so it was quite a thrill.

For the next two days they wined and dined Doyle and I and took us around their projects, offices, and architect's office and explained that they had four new models on the drawing boards and wanted me to approve them if I thought they would be good sellers. They said that the four that we had were fine, but we were getting just too many of the same plans and we needed some new models to stimulate my sales. We could still sell the old plans if anyone wanted one of them. They could take the furniture out of the old models and use it to furnish the new ones with some changes and I could sell the four old models in order to pay for the cost of the new ones. This was agreed on by all.

The next day we just toured around, the four of us, Doyle, Sandy, J. B and I. They were so very friendly. What I hadn't realized as yet was that they were giving me their very best California sales pitch! When we were driving back to Los Angeles from the suburbs of Riverside, California, they popped the big question to me, "Andy, are you going to stay with us in White Rock or are you going back to Oklahoma?"

I said, "Well, I have been giving it a lot of thought and I think that after our visit today and the new models and all, that if I can buy a home like the other Noxon employees have done, I will stay in Los Alamos. My family all like it very much. As soon as the AEC decides to sell the government houses in Los Alamos, I will move my mother and younger brother out to Los Alamos and buy them a small government house." This is what they were waiting to hear ever since Doyle and I landed in Los Angeles.

J. B. said, "Boys, shall I take you right to the airport, so you can be home by tonight?" and that is what we did. Their sales pitch had worked and now that many years have passed, I'm glad that it did.

Understand that the White Rock buyers had no contact with any of the other Noxon people who built their homes. We sales people were the only ones that they had to deal and converse with. So my phone hardly every stopped ringing. I had two lines and before I could hang up one, the other would be ringing. This was especially true when the work had stopped or slowed down on the finishing of their homes. You could imagine when their homes would sit day after day and no work had been done on their house. They would call Andy and start asking questions. I had just about run out of answers. Especially when the weather was good and there was no reason why they were not finishing their home. This was what was upsetting me so much.

After my visit to Los Angeles I think some major decisions were made. Noxon had come up with a large chunk of money from somewhere. I imagine he had pulled it out of their other project that I suspected had gotten money out of the White Rock project (that I told you about earlier). Anyway, the homes started getting finished faster and sales also picked up. The new models were still three or four months away from being finished because we didn't dare finish our new models while the people weren't getting their homes worked on.

Another change was made. My secretary was nervous with all of us salesmen and customers in the garage sales office where all four of us had to work. She was ready to quit. You see, in those days no one had copy machines or computer printers to make copies, so everything had to be typed with two carbon copies plus the original. She wasn't an expert typist and if she had to work late typing a contract for signatures, she would get upset and get carbon paper marks on her face and hands mixed with tears. So, I saw some changes were necessary.

Doyle's office was in the model next to the sales office, upstairs in one of the three bedrooms. The other bedroom was for the two construction lady bookkeepers, so this left one other bedroom that wasn't being used. I talked with Doyle about replacing my secretary with Bonnie. She and I would share this third bedroom for a sales manager's office and Bonnie could do my typing — of the credit reports and loan application papers — and schedule the closings with the buyers and the title company in Albuquerque. This smoothed things out considerably as the other sales office was just not big enough for the salesmen, Bonnie and I to do all of our work.

I was now just across the upstairs hall from Doyle's office and just down the stairs from the draftsman making changes, for extras that the customers wanted, to their plans. This was great because then I could check on them regularly and make sure the changes were made before the blueprints were printed and copies sent out to the various subcontractors. It sure did eliminate a lot of mistakes having all the changes in writing on the building plans.

I just can't tell you how close I was with these first buyers, especially the first twenty-five that were necessary to spring the $3,000,000 for the development costs of the streets, utilities and services. I still remember almost all of their names.

One day, out of the blue, my thoughts ran to the other salesman, Bill Hawkins, who had worked with me when I worked for that crooked broker in Bartlesville, Oklahoma. Bill was a young home-builder, along with his two older brothers. I called Bill one evening and he was surprised to hear from me, and excited about the opportunity to come to work in New Mexico.

Through the summer and into the fall of 1962, sales continued to be good. The new models came on line and my two starting salesmen, Bill Hawkins and Joe Monack, were producing well, and White Rock was really beginning to grow. A new fire station was being built. Previously, it was a small trailer house for the three firemen and one truck. We could even buy cigarettes, candy bars and gum at the fire station! Nothing else, just yet, for sale in White Rock.

Bill Hawkins and I would go deer and antelope hunting in season and occasionally go fishing.

Harry Allen and his wife, Marion, bought the Manor House model. Harry was probably the most well-known man in White Rock at the time. His job at the Lab was as head of the purchasing department. It was through Harry S. Allen that every thing, from nuclear reactors down to birdseed for the birds at the experimental health lab, flowed. For some reason, Harry and I hit it off really well, as did Bonnie and Marion Allen.

Every Thursday night about five or six of us would meet at Harry's house for a poker game. If any one won more than $25 it was a miracle. But we had a lot of fun.

Remember I told you about the tall, good-looking 24-year old girlfriend of Jack Tobin? Well, these two decided to get married. They made a very handsome couple. They both loved to ski. Well, Chris was trying to figure out how she was going to get a wedding dress, so she and Bonnie made a deal. Chris said to Bonnie, "I'll teach Andra to ski if you will make my wedding gown." Deal made!

The wedding came off beautifully, and Bonnie and I presented them with one of the three sets of LusterCraft Stainless Steel that I had left when I went to work with Noxon and quit the cookware business. Bonnie and Chris had some good times going to Santa Fe shopping occasionally. One day they decided to walk 9 miles to White Rock from Los Alamos to lose weight. Well, when they were ready to leave Los Alamos for White Rock, Bonnie said, "Chris, what shall we take to eat?" Chris thought that was so funny. Walking to lose weight, but taking something to eat. I heard her tell this several times later as the years rolled on. Really, it was just a joke between the four of us.

In the fall of 1962 Jack Kennedy was elected president and the next spring he visited the Los Alamos Scientific Laboratory and the town. We, like most everyone else, attended the speech he gave at the Los Alamos High School football field. The kids especially enjoyed seeing a real live president. Shortly afterwards the Cuban missile crisis was upon us. And being a likely target, Los Alamos Scientific Laboratory started survival preparations.

Bill Heath and Doyle Kline called all of the Noxon people together to give us our assignment of where we should go in the event of an alert or an attack. More than a little fear ran up our necks and for a while we were all pretty nervous.

There was plenty of room in the strong concrete buildings at the Laboratory for all the townspeople, but the most concern was the length of time it would take to drive nine miles up the mountain to Los Alamos from White Rock. Thank God within a few days our fears subsided as our gutsy young president stared old Khrushchev down.

Soon, January 1963 came upon us with the usual cold temperatures. Sales slowed and completions slowed, naturally. But by this time we were about half sold out of our 209 lots and houses in Increment #1. Our four new models were finished and they looked good. The AEC was finally convinced that White Rock was going to be a real community before long, so their thoughts turned to an elementary school. It was up to Andy and Bonnie Long to take a telephone poll to find out how many people had children and their ages, and if they didn't have any, did they plan on having children. All the school children who lived in White Rock before the schools were built had to be bussed nine miles up to Los Alamos. So a school was needed. Doyle Kline told me that the AEC had asked him if someone at the Noxon Company could take a survey of 1) how many of the families had now bought homes in White Rock, 2) the ages of their children, and 3) how many more intended to have children within the next five years. They planned to build an elementary school first, so the youngest children would not have to ride the bus to Los Alamos. He said that yours truly was the logical one to do this job as I knew all the buyers by name and could get the information easier than anyone else. Joe, Bill and I called the people we had sold, and in a few days we had the needed information. This was very important and everyone was very cooperative.

A couple of our most valued and fondest friends were Peggy and Roger Corbett. Peggy was so helpful in all community affairs. She and Galen Felt came to Los Alamos with the very first people on the scene. He was a physicist and she was secretary to Robert Oppenheimer, the first director of the Lab. Later, she divorced Galen Felt and, with three young children, married Roger Corbett, the local owner and operator of the Corbett Cleaning Company. Roger, his dad and brother ran the cleaning and laundry business. They were our dearest friends in Los Alamos for all of the years we were there. She was the local representative and reporter for the Santa Fe New Mexican, the Santa Fe newspaper. There is much, much more to write about Peggy Corbett as the years continue on. They were one of the first couples to buy a home in White Rock and the first to move in. She kept all the important happenings in White Rock in the newspaper, and reported on all the happenings with the Laboratory and the A.E.C. Both she and Roger were very political. The Corbett family had come from Hereford, Texas and were among the first families to open a business in Los Alamos. Real pillarsof the community.

Having been a secretary to Oppenheimer and the wife of a leading scientist, she knew most of the important people in the Lab, as well as the local business people. She liked to throw parties and did so quite often. We became very good friends. She and Roger had another baby boy, Mark, that we watched grow up. He was six when we first met the Corbett family.

Let me explain how the County government in Los Alamos worked at this time. There were no county taxes because up until this time no one owned their home or any of the commercial buildings. Uncle Sam owned the whole town — lock, stock and barrel. So the A.E.C. paid an equivalent amount of money to run things, such as schools, police and fire departments — everything. Of course, everyone paid sales tax on things they purchased and this went to the state, but no one had paid property taxes to the county except the ones that had just bought new homes.

House sales were brisk, for the more people that moved in, the more people decided that White Rock was really going to survive and keep growing. They had gotten started on our house and we were happy. By this time we had sold around 100 to 125 homes, of which about 100 were occupied.

Our home was finished in June of 1963 and we moved in. When the new models were finished, we bought some of the old model homes' furniture. We made some very good buys on things they couldn't use in the new models. Everything was just like new. Our furniture was still back in Dewey in our big house that Mom and my brother, John, were living in. The home we had built was the most popular model, the Briarcliff. It had three bedrooms and a bedroom-sized den that could be used as a fourth bedroom, living room/dining room combination with a fireplace and a sliding door that led to a 12 ft. x 20 ft. covered patio. There was a nice galley kitchen with an eating space looking out onto a half-moon driveway with two curb cuts and a two-car garage. It was 1,372 sq. ft. with three mature pinon trees in the front yard. The address is 112 Rover Blvd. It had white stucco trimmed with brick and red trim with a light gray shingled roof. All deluxe appliances for a total cost to us of $21,500 — a savings of about $2,000 off of our regular price.

Rover Boulevard was not named after someone's good old dog. It was named after one of the most important projects that the Lab was working on. It was a spacecraft that would be powered with nuclear fuel and could roam all over the universe in outer space for a long, long time. This is why the entrance street of the subdivision was named Rover.

The other entrance street, on the other side of the subdivision of 209 lots, coming off of State Road #4, was named Sherwood Boulevard. This was for another project the Lab was working on, namely how to make fresh water out of salt water. So, you see, not all the projects at Los Alamos were about weapons.

We would occasionally drive to Albuquerque on our day off and we enjoyed it. Once in a while we would go to El Paso and cross into Juarez for a weekend, load up on booze, frozen fish and shrimp, souvenirs, etc. Sales were good, but construction was still slower than it should have been. Financial problems were still plaguing the Noxon Company in California and I think this is why they were short on being able to pay for materials and labor on time in White Rock.

We stayed in touch with Chuck and Pat Coutts in Los Angeles by letter and telephone and one day I got a call from Chuck and he told me that he had quit Noxon as the company was in trouble and he thought I should know. He had taken a job on a huge project a few miles north of

Los Angeles near the town of Oxnard, on Hueneme Bay (pronounced: "Y-nee-me"). The name of the project was "Joe E. Brown's Twenty Million Dollar Condominium Project." A young Jewish guy by the name of Joe Bolker was the owner. The Joe E. Brown name was just for promotion, as is common in tinsel town.

The Hueneme Bay project was 500 two-and three-bedroom condos built on speculation. Joe Bolker's father-in-law was Mark Taber, who was chairman of the First Charter Corporation, a savings and loan association in Los Angeles. Can you imagine spec-ing five hundred condos? Very big bucks! A big project. Chuck was project construction manager of this baby and all of 30 years old. He and I had a two-man admiration for each other — me for his project managing ability in construction, and he for my sales ability.

Chuck told me to come out and look the deal over, and he thought I might get a job as sales manager. Well, I could see the storm clouds building with the Noxon Construction Company so I told Doyle that we were taking a few days off for Thanksgiving and traveling to Dewey, Oklahoma. I left Bonnie and the kids to visit my mother and I drove to Tulsa, left my car at the airport and flew to Los Angeles. The plane had a scheduled stopover at Denver, but the airport was socked in because of a snow storm, so all the people who were going to get off at Denver had to get off at Colorado Springs, Colorado. Well, with the stewardess feeding me plenty of drinks, we made it to LA okay, but I was now three sheets to the wind when I met Chuck at the airport. We had a couple or three more in Los Angeles when we got to his new home in Malibu. We had a nice dinner and a great visit. Chuck said, "Andy, you sleep-in tomorrow morning. I have to go in early and Pat is going shopping with a couple of her girlfriends." He said, "I'll call you later and we will have lunch and I'll show you around our project after lunch." This was just fine with me as I was a little hung over from the trip.

This was November 23, 1963. The phone woke me about 10:00 AM. It was Chuck. The first thing he said was that he had just heard on the radio that President Kennedy had just been shot and killed in Dallas, Texas. What a way to wake up and what a shocker. Later Chuck picked me up at his house and we had lunch and toured the project. It was big alright —and just getting started. He said it would be a while before they would have the models and the clubhouse, pool and a small golf course finished. The models would face the golf course and I could see it was going to be a first class project. He said, "Andy, this is where you should be — out here with us. California is really a great place to live." Their home was about two blocks from the beach. He said, "I'm going to tell Joe Bolker about you and I'll be in touch." I said, "Okay."

He took me back to the airport and I took a direct flight from L.A. to Tulsa and was back in Dewey that night, having a wonderful Thanksgiving dinner that next day. The following day, Friday, we headed back to our new home in White Rock and back on the job from Saturday and Sunday. I was glad I had taken the time to look the Hueneme Bay project over and thought to myself that if things didn't straighten out in White Rock for the Noxon Company I would have a place and a job to go to.

Doyle Kline called me into his office on Monday morning and said, "Andy, we need to talk." He looked shook up, so I said, "Okay. What's happening?" Doyle said, "The banks have gone as far as they can with Noxon and the creditors, suppliers, and subs have formed a creditor's group and are taking control of the White Rock project. The bank has hired a man by the name of Kenneth Mount as General Manager and his former partner, a top notch project manager, for the construction by the name of Charley Bernitz."

He said, "Everyone with Noxon here is getting laid off at the end of this week except for you and Bonnie. Tell Joe Monack and Bill Hawkins the bad news." What a shock! I could see it coming, but it was still a shock! Doyle continued, "All the creditors and the bank of New Mexico have formed a creditor's group and the name of the project is now The White Rock Development Company."

I met Kenny Mount and Charlie Bernitz the next morning and the first thing that he said was "Andy, Doyle Kline has told me what a fine job that you and Bonnie have been doing with sales and getting the loans closed and the bank has been well satisfied with the job you have done." Kenny was a little guy with glasses and he talked so fast it was hard to keep up with what he was saying. He was about 5'4" and about 125 pounds, but he seemed okay. Like a lot of little men, he wanted everyone to know he was in charge. (He had been a submarine commander during World War II.)

Kenny also had a lady with him from the Bank. He explained that this lady would be working with Bonnie until she got the books in order, and that the girls with Noxon had them in a mess. He said, "Mr. Long, I have found out there are 47 houses under construction and we are going to have to work our way out of all those sales that you have made. So, I want you to slow down on your sales."

I said, "Mr. Mount, I have been selling for many years, but I have never in my life been told to slow down on sales. It's always been 'Andy, we need more sales.' What's going on?"

"Well, it's going to take some time to get new subs lined up and hire our own carpenters and concrete men, and get lumber and material storage sheds built and get our feet on the ground. Charley Bernitz and I built a lot of houses in Farmington and we are bringing in our own engineer-surveyor, John Mendius, and our plumbing sub, Bo Stoker and Gus Olminson, our stucco sub — all from Farmington. It will be a somewhat different type of operation than the Noxon Company. Charley Bernitz is my construction superintendent and manager. He is a big tough Bohemian and he knows his business. He is a good guy and you will like him, I'm sure. He builds real fine homes. It will be different. He has known all his subs for a long time and they are all dependable."

"One of the first things we are going to do is run a new cost estimate on all the plans of the models you are selling, and the prices may be increased, so this is why you should slow down on your sales until we get our new prices. We will all be in this one model home. You will have the whole garage for your sales office and Bonnie and the lady from the bank will use the inside of the house. Bonnie can do the work she has been doing for you and will also be my right hand gal. This should work out fine."

"Andy, I am in the market for a home to move my family into if I can buy a resale from one of your customers."

I said, "I happen to have one house for sale right now. It's the largest model we sell, the Valle Grande, a four bedroom. The lawn is in and it will be available next week. I will have the guy come in to talk to you about it." He was delighted to hear this and did indeed move his wife and children in soon thereafter. Problem solved.

The first thing that Charley Bernitz did was have four flatbed wagons built with rubber car-type wheels on them. They would load the blocks on one of the wagons and the framing materials on another one and pull them to the lot site — and the material the workmen needed was right there ready to use. This really did work well. It eliminated shortages and a lot of coming back and forth to the storage sheds.

All of our buyers and prospects were wondering what was going on, so a meeting was held in one of the school's auditoriums in Los Alamos and Kenny Mount gave a really good talk and explanation as to what was happening in White Rock. People were uneasy, to say the least, until he explained that all of Noxon's construction people were being replaced but that Andy and Bonnie Long were going to be staying with them and had a done a very good job and they were happy to have them with the new organization of The White Rock Development Company. Boy, Bonnie and I got a standing ovation from everyone there and we certainly did enjoy that, plus the fact that Kenny Mount knew then that the people were very glad that I was not leaving. After all, we were the only contact that the buyer's had had with the Noxon Company. When they had a problem, they called Andy. So this sealed the deal of the transfer of ownership of the company.

Things began to smooth out in the construction part and indeed, the homes took a price increase of about 15% and that didn't cause me too much of a problem. I was still making sales and by this time I was pulling the creditors 'chestnuts out of the fire', so to speak, and they were not going to lose a lot of money. Up to that time, I had sold approximately 150 homes, a lot of which were still under construction.

In any neighborhood there is usually about a 5% turnover in houses being resold. There was no difference here. So I went to Albuquerque and sat for my real estate broker's license. This made me eligible to handle the resales. I told Kenny Mount that I could provide this service to our customers should any of them need to leave town and no other outside Realtors would be involved to muddy up our operation in White Rock. There were no other real estate people in the County at this time and I was the only one. I also explained to him that I thought I had proven myself to Noxon as well as to the creditors and that I wanted a new deal. I would handle all the sales from now on and all the closings with Bonnie's help and not draw a salary, but I wanted a 3% commission on all my sales from now on.

Well, he said he would have to talk to the creditor's group about this. So I said, "Okay. I will need to know your decision by June 1st." It was then May 15, 1964. I then said, "That gives them two weeks to decide and if not, I have the possibility of a good job in California that I can go to." This shook Kenny Mount pretty good, so we left it at that.

School was almost out and Tim had graduated and had been accepted by the Foreign Language League to study German in Seefeld, Austria. At that time he thought he might become a German language teacher. (Some time later he changed his mind, however, and got a masters degree in Philosophy of Science and graduate minor in Physics, as well as an Electronics degree specializing in Laser Optics at the UNM-LA Graduate Center with an overall 3.6 GPA). Tim had never been away from home alone, and at seventeen he was going to Austria.. He took a piece of trinitite from the site of the first test of the atomic explosion at Trinity Site, New Mexico which he was to present to the Mayor of Seefeld, Austria near Innsbruck.

One guy in the creditor's group, Richard Cook of the Espanola Mercantile Co., where Noxon had bought a lot of lumber and roofing materials, was a hard-nosed SOB. His father had ran the business for many years and was a good old man, but this son was a real hard ass. He said, "No raise for Andy Long." This was about a week from my deadline of June 1.

I said, "You guys have one more week to make up your mind, and then I'm gone." I don't know what went on behind the scenes, but the morning of May 31, Kenny said, "Andy, Cook gave in. He thought you were bluffing. Were you really bluffing?"

"Hell, no! I was dead serious. I think I have done one hell of a job and will continue to do so until this project is sold out." So back to work as usual and by this time, I was getting along real well with all of Charley's subs as well as Charley himself. I have a few good stories to tell to lighten all this up. Charley had a trailer on one of the vacant lots about a block away from Kenny's office and the sales office. He had his phone there. It was not his living quarters, just a construction office and the subs also used it. They all had apartments in Los Alamos during the week and on weekends they drove back-and-forth to Farmington. All except the engineer, John Mendius, who bought a big, new home down the street from me in White Rock where he and his wife and two children lived. We came friends as well as me and Bo Stoker, the plumbing sub and Gus Olminson, the stucco sub.

The first story is about Gus. He was from Farmington and there are a lot of Navajo Indians there and they are very, very good stucco hands. So, he let them camp out in the pinon trees in some of the nearby vacant land which would be Increment #2 when it was finished. Gus would bring a lot of groceries that his wife would buy in Farmington when he would come back to White Rock on Monday morning. Well, one Saturday morning (they did not work weekends) a knock came to my front door and four Navajos were standing there and one of them said, "Andy, need five bucks, need groceries, Andy. Need groceries." Well, I gave him $5 and they went on their way. I told Gus about this as I thought they were telling me the truth. Well, he gave me the $5. He said, "I don't think they need groceries."

The next Saturday the same thing happened and I gave them $5. I told Gus he owed me another $5. He said, "Andy, my wife buys them plenty of groceries. Those damn Indians are lying to you. They are buying wine with your money. I will give you this $5 but if you give them any more, I'm not going to pay you." I said, "I believe you, Gus." So I told Bonnie to buy a pound of weenies and a loaf of bread and, if they came this Saturday, to give it to them. Well, she did and we didn't have any more requests of $5 for groceries after that.

Another thing that happened with Gus's crew — we were losing some bathroom fixtures out of the houses that were still under construction: sinks, toilet stools, etc., that had not been installed yet. So, Charley said to Gus (they were the best of friends for many years), "Let your men stay in one of those unfinished houses at night." So he did. Well, the windows had not been installed as yet, so in the dark of night the thieves came in through the windows and in the dark stumbled over one of the Indians. There were thieves and Indians jumping out of the windows. I don't know which were scared the worst! But it stopped the thievery.

Kenny Mount owned an old one-tone blue van type truck with seats, and once in a while he, Charley and Gus would drive it down the mountain to the town of Española and have a few drinks at the Grand Hotel bar. Los Alamos was not the place for these rough construction types to do any heavy drinking. Well, one evening I was going home and I drove by

Charley's little trailer office and he waved me down and said, "Andy, how about a drink of vodka?"

I said, "Sure." and went in and he poured me a big drink. Well, I had forgot that I had a very light lunch that day at noon, just a bowl of tomato soup. After a couple of vodkas, I called Bonnie and told her that I was going to Española with Kenny, Charley and Gus and would see her later tonight. Well, by the time we got there we were all feeling very loose. Realize that all of us were working our asses off and a chance to relax with a few drinks was sure welcomed, so after a drink or two at the bar we retired to the dance floor and got a booth for the four of us. By this time we were all drinking beer and Charley was dancing with a big old gal — and Charley was big, 6' and 250 lbs., and she was close to that. Well, old Gus for some reason decided to tackle old Charley and just as he did another gal was walking across the dance floor from the bar and she had two five-gallon buckets of empty beer cans to take out the back door. She didn't make it. Just as Gus tackled Charley, all four of them went down and beer cans scattered all over the dance floor!

Kenny was drunk but had sense enough to say, "Don't call the police. I'll get them out of here. Give Gus a broom and we'll try to sweep up the cans." But he wasn't doing a very good job. This only lasted a couple of minutes and we all went out the back door and started getting into the truck. It was slow going up the mountain as Kenny was trying to be very careful as that mountain road was pretty dangerous even when you are sober.

I went to sleep. Later on I figured out that I had only had a bowl of tomato soup for lunch and no supper at all. So it hit me pretty hard. They woke me up when Kenny drove into my driveway. He got me up on my feet. I looked up over my shoulder and old Gus was standing on the street curb hosing down the street in front of our house. Kenny was helping me get to my front door and I was sick and I was holding onto one of the pinon trees that was close to the front door to keep from falling down.

The porch light came on and Bonnie opened the front door. She didn't say anything, just shaking her head. Kenny looked at her, put his hand in his pocket and said to me, "Here, eat some of these Chlorettes and she won't know you've been drinking." Even to this day, I think this is the funniest thing I've ever heard! I didn't dare turn loose of that tree or I would have fallen on my ass. To this day I swear Bonnie pushed me as I as going down the hall to our bedroom, but she swears she didn't. Well, this was the first and last time I went drinking with these construction guys.

One other story that involves Charley Bernitz. Mr. and Mrs. Al MacKnight's house was under construction and Charley drove down the street and saw the lady had two of Charley's carpenters out at the curb looking back at the front of the house. She was waving her arm a little, so Charley stopped to see what was taking place. He said to one of his carpenters, "What are you guys doing?"

He said, "The lady is trying to decide if she wants to have us lower all the front windows on the front side of her house or not."

Old Charley said, "Well, lady those men make $6.50 per hour, so we'll keep track of their time and send you a bill."

"Oh," she started crying and Charley drove off. It wasn't long until she came to tell me how rudely she was treated by this mean old man. After twenty or thirty minutes of soothing her hurt feelings and a lot of finesse, everything was all right and the windows were left like they were. We never had any more trouble from this little lady.

Another customer was a nice little Mormon lady with her two little kids and their wagon. They had it loaded with bricks that they had picked up from another house that was under construction down the street from her house. She had made several trips with the wagon and was planning to make a flower bed with these bricks. Well, it so happens the bricks were just enough to build the fireplace on the other house and it would make it short on finishing the fireplace. I didn't get involved in this one, but Charley sent one of his young laborers up to pick up the bricks she had stacked up in her yard and he hauled them back to where she had gotten them.

Another story involves Bo Stoker, the plumber. Bonnie got a call, from another nameless gal, that her pilot light had gone out and asked if she would have the plumber come by and light it for her. Bonnie said, "Sure." Well, old Bo came back by the office about 30 minutes or so later and was carrying a pie. He said, "Bonnie, I brought you a piece of pie this nice lady gave me for lighting her pilot light." Funny thing though, every couple of weeks her pilot light would go out and Bo would have to go by and light it.

We had fun, and these lonely little housewives would enjoy the little Peyton Place now and then. Some of those high-powered young scientists sometimes would work all night on a project and just didn't have time to take care of their homework properly. But it never got out of control.

One time, Bonnie's sister Juanita and her husband, Cliff, who lived in Wichita came to visit us. Well, Charley said, "If you want to take him fishing, Andy, come to Farmington and stay all night with me, and Bo will pick you up early and take you up to Vallecitos Lake in Colorado fishing. Bo knows where to catch trout." So we did. While driving up, when we were out in the open spaces, we looked out and there were four wild horses jumping around and playing. Cliff and I had never seen any of these wild horses and we got a kick out of them.

Charley got us up early and his wife fixed us a big breakfast and a lunch each and Bo, Cliff an I took off for the lake. Bo had a 14' aluminum boat and motor and knew where to go. To make a long story short, we caught trout like I've never caught them before or since. We wound up with a huge catch!

Cliff hooked one and it jumped out of the water and landed in the boat! Cliff laid his rod down and I said, "Why aren't you fishing? And he said, "I want to smoke a cigarette. I haven't had time to smoke." What Bo did was take a couple of small salmon egg bottles and pitch salmon eggs out all around the boat. He said, "I have to be careful doing this as the game warden might be nearby looking at us with his field glasses".

Well, we didn't get caught and we caught a lot of fish! I thought we never would get them all cleaned when we got back to Bo's house. Charley and his wife, and Bo and his wife, and Cliff and I ate fish and French fries and salad until we were all stuffed. Neither Cliff nor I have ever forgotten this fishing trip. We still talk about it almost every time we get together.

I was still selling quite a few houses as well as several resales. My commission on the resales was 5%, and still 3% on the new homes, so I was accumulating some nice savings. By mid-summer, our net worth was around $30,000 which by today's standards would be a hell of a lot more. The White Rock Development Company was finally beginning to get their financial affairs in order and the bank and other creditors were ready to find a company to buy their interests out as well as the option to get started on Increment #2 and four additional acres that had been set aside for commercial development. This was quite a plan.

Big changes were coming! The Roswell, New Mexico airbase, which was the home of the giant piston engine B-36 Bomber, was being shut down by the Lyndon Johnson administration for two reasons. One being that Roswell was basically a Republican stronghold in New Mexico and they hadn't supported the Democrats in the last election that elected Kennedy as President and Johnson as Vice President. The second reason was that jet bombers, namely the B-47 Jet, was going to replace the big B-36's. So as a result, the base closure caused this little town of Roswell to go into a very serious financial slump or recession, as they call it nowadays. Businesses were closing and relocating to keep from going broke. It so happened that a construction company called Home Planning and Development Company, owned by a young man named Ed Leslie, exactly the same age as me at 39, and his wife, Shirley, and his wife's mother, Mrs. Chapman (the Chapmans were formerly ranchers so they were pretty well fixed), had been developing land and building homes in Roswell and they needed to relocate their company.

The first thing we knew, they were entering negotiations to take over all of White Rock Development Company's holdings in White Rock and form Home Planning & Development Company. It didn't take long for this to take place and Ed Leslie had all of his own subs that would relocate with him. His plumbing sub was the Jasper Conner Co., his electrical sub was R. D. Morehead, his framing sub was R. C. Dennis, his concrete sub was Clyde Roach and his architect was Elwood Cardin. All of these guys were very capable and experienced and were eager to move as their businesses in Roswell had evaporated.

It didn't take long for the transition to take place from the White Rock Development Company to the Home Planning & Development Co., and with the A.E.C.'s blessings. Kenny and Charley's subs and Bo's would finish the houses that were still yet unfinished and not start any more. The time period of this was around August 1, 1964. Ed and Shirley Leslie were very likable people and, as I said, about Bonnie's and my age. Ed and Kenny Mount and Bonnie Long worked several days getting Ed familiar with the White Rock Development Company's financial procedures and accounts payable, and receivable, that would have to take place. The Leslies and the Longs were to become good friends later in the years to come.

Shirley Leslie later mentioned that Ed said Bonnie Long was the smartest white woman he had ever seen and we would all have a good laugh. In these transitional days, we got to know the Leslies quite well and one day Ed said, "Andy how about you and Bonnie going to work with us?" I said, "Tell me more about your sales organization, Ed."

"Well," he said, "My sales manager is my brother-in-law, Walt Chapman." I said, "Who is your construction superintendent?" He said, "Oh, that is my mother-in-law." I said, "Who works with the customers on their colors and selections of countertops, appliances, decorating, etc.?" He said, "Oh, my wife, Shirley, does that." I said, "Ed there is no way that I could please the whole family and besides that, I have a job to go to in California, I think. But thank you very much for asking me."

So a new day was dawning. I called Chuck Coutts and said, "Do you think I could go to work at Hueneme Bay?" He said, "I am pretty sure you can get the sales manager's job as Joe Bolker has gone through eight or nine sales managers in this past year and I have told him that anyone that can sell homes to those Los Alamos egg-head scientists can sell these condos. He said he would talk to Bolker and call me back. Bonnie and I had discussed whether or not we should sell our new home in White Rock or just lease it. We finally agreed to lease it if we could.

When Chuck called back he said, "Can you come out for an interview?" I said, "Yes, I'll fly out, rent a car, and see you Monday." So I did. I met Joe Bolker and he explained my duties — that I would be managing ten other salesmen: eight men and two women, most of whom were older real estate people as they would be working with older retired prospects and would have a better rapport with them than young salesmen would.

Bolker said he was prepared to pay me $1,500 per month and to rent me a new 3-bedroom condo at a very reasonable rent for my family and also pay for my moving expenses to California. I was shown around the project and saw that almost all of the 500 condos were finished, as well as the large clubhouse, pool, and golf course. Very few of the condos were sold. So, I could see why he had gone through so many sales managers during the past year. Of course, I also realized how hard it is to get very many places sold in the beginning when a lot of construction is going on all around.

I told him I would report to work in two weeks. The deal was made. I flew home and we leased our house in White Rock to a young scientist and his wife from Pennsylvania, who was on loan to the Lab from the Westinghouse Company. Soon after we were on our way for a new adventure.

It was September 1, 1964. It seemed like every time we made a change in work it was September 1st. It was September 1, 1961 when we arrived in Los Alamos and I had crammed a world of experience in the home selling business into the past three years — mostly to young couples in Los Alamos. Now I would have a new experience with older couples in Hueneme Bay. I was up to the challenge as I was only 39 years old, turning 40 in November.

We got settled into our new home and got Andra started in school in the 7th grade. Tim and a friend from Las Cruces, who had been playing music at the Peppermint Lounge (across the street from the Los Alamos Post Office), went to Los Angeles to form a band and joined the musician's union in Hollywood, as Tim is an accomplished trap drummer. He was just 19 on September 17th. He and his buddy got an apartment in L.A. As Tim had not been able to start college in California on such short notice, he took correspondence courses in psychology and calculus from UCLA.

At Hueneme Bay the age rules for our buyers were: one of each couple had to be fifty years old, so there were no young couples with small children and there were only a very few children of any age living there. Certainly no little rug-rats, curtain climbers, or yard apes to disturb our old retired residents. Noise was nil. Each weekend Bolker would place a full-page ad in the Los Angeles Times at a cost of $4,000, which was a lot of money in those days. This is why he was so anxious to get this project off the ground and it hadn't really gotten going yet. Each Sunday night he would call me to see how many sales had been made over the weekend. No matter how many we sold, he was not satisfied.

Wednesday was my day off and I really needed it! As I had my hands full riding herd on 10 old salesmen. They would complain to me that so-and-so had stolen the prospect he had been working with, or some other bitchy problem. So I spent my time counseling these salesmen, etc. Each morning I had several couples lined up at my office door with their punch lists of things that they wanted to have fixed in their condo that needed some little something done or repaired. This was quite distracting to me, but I handled it as gracefully as possible, and I tried to be my usual calm and cheerful self. I think the worst thing was that when Bolker would call me on Sunday night, we would say, "Andy, I have you scheduled to speak at the Kiwanis Clubhouse at Ventura, California on Wednesday at noon on "retirement living." So my day off that I needed was gone, gone, gone. Pretty upsetting.

Then maybe the next Wednesday he would have me take Bonnie with me and go to a big competitor's retirement community at Huntington Beach, California called Leisure World. The purpose was to pose as the children of parents who were trying to help their parents find just the right retirement community. This way we could find out all the information that our competition was offering to their prospects, to try and steal some of their good sales secrets, so another day off was shot. He could justify this but I couldn't because it would happen about three out of four weeks.

We were enjoying the Coutts family in Malibu, and Jack and Chris Tobin who had bought a small house in Reseda, California — that is, when we had time to go see them. I got along well with most of the salesmen and spent a lot of time talking about their prospects. The prospects were coming from all the small towns around Los Angeles, as well as from Los Angeles itself. The ads were drawing a lot of people to look, but it was hard to get them back for the second or third visit. I recalled back to the early days in White Rock when we were trying to get the first few sales. I remembered how we explained to the people to pick a lot out that they liked and put a temporary deposit on it until they made up their mind to buy or not. And if they didn't, they would get their $50 deposit back. I then thought this same idea might work on these condos. If they saw a condo in the location they liked and it was the right size, they could put a $50 returnable deposit on it until they came back up the next time, a week or so later.

I talked to Joe Seedman, the marketing director, about this and explained to him how successful this plan had worked in White Rock and told him I would personally keep track of these people and keep their checks locked in my desk and the company would not have any bookkeeping to do with it. He said he would talk to Bolker about it and let me know. Well, in a couple of days I got the go-ahead and we put this plan into action. This at least got the people back to give the project a second look and gave the salesmen another shot at selling them. Almost immediately it worked like a charm!

Bolker was so pleased he and his wife and the mayor of Los Angeles and his wife decided to take an around-the-world cruise. Bolker and all the salesmen were happy, and of course I was very happy that it had worked just like it had in White Rock.

The project was large and had sidewalks between the front yards and the green golf course and the salesmen had these small electric golf carts to haul the old prospects in so they could cover a lot of places and not have to walk. This was a real plus for these old folks and also the salesmen. The big tall red-headed, good-looking Ruth Clark, who was about 50 years old, could really wheel that golf cart. She would tell them, "Come on children, let me take you for a ride in my merry Oldsmobile," and away they would go. She was a real card and a very good sales gal. We got along really well.

Oh, yes, I had another plan to increase the salesmen's incentive. It was this: all our salesmen wore gray flannel trousers with navy blue blazers, a white shirt and tie — except the ladies and they wore lighter blue knit suits and white blouses. Well my incentive plan was this: if a salesman made a second sale in one week he got a new white shirt. The third sale made by him in one week got him a new pair of gray slacks, and if he had four in one week he also got a new blue blazer. I had a little trouble getting this deal approved, but after I said, "Hell, it doesn't cost anything unless they make extra sales," so they finally okayed it. This worked, too. We were rolling.

I was working my ass off and the smog was terrible. I was allergic to it and my eyes burned all the time. I was not used to the traffic on the freeways, which was constant, even at midnight some California hotrodder would be honking to have you get out of his way. This was such a far cry from the much slower pace of our beloved New Mexico. And we longed for the blue sky and sunshine and great climate of New Mexico and the slower pace of living.

Chuck Coutts would come up to the project once in a while, even though construction had all been finished and he would stop by the sales office to see me. He knew my 40th birthday was coming up on November 17th so he talked to some of the salesmen about them throwing a surprise birthday party for me. What a party it was! They took pictures which I intend to include with this. What a night! Turning 40 years old was the hardest birthday to accept up to then. I thought I was really getting old. We all tied one on that night!

That night I also informed all of the salespeople that since September 1st when I came on board, "You folks have sold 57 new condos." Everyone thought this was great and so did Bolker when he got this news.

About this time, around November 19th, I got a phone call from the family who were leasing our home in White Rock. They were being recalled to Pennsylvania and the husband asked if I wanted him to sub-lease our home or what? I told him I would call him back the next day. Bonnie and I talked it over very seriously from all angles. After a restless night of thinking and talking, we decided that neither of us wanted to spend the rest of our lives in California, and we didn't want our children growing up there either. We longed for the lifestyle that had drawn us to Los Alamos in the first place. I knew I would not be able to keep up the pace that I set at Hueneme Bay, the smog and the traffic wasn't going to get any better, let alone being able to keep Joe Bolker satisfied. After all, I was sales manager #10, so I could see that I could get fired just like the other nine before me when all my ideas and energy was used up. We decided that it was a real blessing that our home in White Rock would be available again. We were going home.

Bolker's ship was due to dock in two days, so we had to really hustle to make sure we were gone before it docked. I didn't want to go through an argument with him since I had already make up my mind to go. We called the movers and they started loading the moving van. Naturally, we had to pay for our own move back, but this was no problem.

Early the next morning after telling all the salesmen what was happening, they told me it was a surprise to them all, but they would miss me and wished me well. For years Ruth Clark corresponded with us. She was sure a card. I asked her one time while I was there if she had ever been to Santa Fe and she said, "Oh, yes, I had a couple of honeymoons there at the La Fonda Hotel on the square." What a character! She had been a nurse at the Camarilla Mental Hospital near Ventura, California and had to handle some of those crazies there. Like giving a wild, crazy, big, old black gal a shot to calm her down that didn't want to take. She was a big, tough redhead. She hated to see us go. She said she knew how tough Bolker was to work with and didn't blame me for leaving.

That afternoon we headed out for New Mexico, Tim in his little green Corvair station wagon and Bonnie, Andra, and I in our car on our way. We spent Thanksgiving 1964 in our home in White Rock with friends and started to think about how I was going to make a living. We didn't get in a hurry trying to decide what I was going to do. We went to see my mother and brother in Dewey, Oklahoma for Christmas and on the way back to Los Alamos I came up with an idea.

Once again I had to make the circumstances I was looking for. I remembered that there were about fourteen scattered vacant lots left in Increment #1 that now belonged to Ed Leslie. Ed's Home Planning Development Co. was going full blast now on Increment #2 and he really had no use for fourteen scattered lots. I approached him about buying those fourteen lots. He was willing so we arrived at a price and I told him we had a deal if the bank would make me a loan for the lots. I had rented a small office for my real estate office and Andy Long Realty was born.

About this time the Los Alamos National Bank was beginning to do really well. A group of business men and the sons of an older Los Alamos top scientist had formed a group and had started a local bank. The only bank that Los Alamos had up to this was the branch bank of the First National Bank of Santa Fe. (Remember I wrote about this bank and its banker, John Helms, back when I first came to Los Alamos selling cookware.)

The bank had leased about a quarter of the first floor of the new Los Alamos Credit Union building, and had hired a president by the name of Reed Chittum. The bank was doing well, so I talked to Mr. Chittum. He was a really good guy and the father of twelve children. I explained what I had in mind was to find a good contractor to build houses on these fourteen lots that I wanted to buy. I said I would furnish the lots to my builder and charge him a 5% commission on these houses he would build. I told Reed I wanted a loan to pay Ed Leslie, who he knew, for the lots and would pay for each lot when I sold each house.

He said, "Andy, this is going to be a $29,000 loan and that is about the limit that the bank can loan any one borrower according to our capitalization." He said he would present it to his board and would let me know. Well, a couple of days passed and Dick Spear came over to my little office to talk to me. He was on the Board of Directors and a big stockholder in the new bank. I told him exactly what I had told Reed Chittum and he thought I had a good idea.

Dick Spear had been in the ladies clothing store business since Los Alamos had been a town. He said, "Andy, I have been watching the work you have done in White Rock and admired you for it." He told me he had started out in one little dime store in Snyder, Oklahoma years ago and now owned a chain of stores. He said, "I still own the buildings and lease them to the store owners. I know how you came here from Oklahoma selling pots and pans and what you have done in White Rock in four years." He said, "Andy, you are going to be a millionaire someday."

I said, "I don't know about that, Mr. Spear, but I do like to sell."

He said, "I've been selling all my life and I do too, and I can tell a good one when I see him."

Then I found out right quick what was on his mind. He said, "You know, our new bank is building our own bank building and I think you need to move out of this little old space you are trying to operate in. We have two more years on our lease where we have the bank now in the Credit Union's building and if you will sub-lease this space from us, I think the bank can make you this loan you need to buy those fourteen lots in White Rock. I will talk with Reed Chittum about this and let you know."

Well, we had some money saved and I could see that I did not need all the space I would be leasing so I began to really get a good idea. I got a floor plan from the Credit Union manager of the bank's space so I could see what I would have to work with. I had been using a title company that had just gone into business that was owned by a local lawyer, Sterling Black, the son of former United State Supreme Court Justice Hugo Black. They had a little one room office upstairs in the Credit Union Building at that time. I knew I was going to need a lawyer in my business, so I approached Sterling Black I told him I was thinking of leasing the bank's space when they moved into their new building. I told Sterling that I thought I would partition off some small offices within the large space for his title company. If he would move into our space I would see to it that he would get all of our title business on the houses I would sell. He liked this and said, "I think we can work this out. We'll see."

Then I contacted an insurance guy from Española who was planning to open a branch insurance office in Los Alamos, and offered him the same deal as the title company. He was eager to make a deal. His name was Gene Kelly, the same as the famous dancer and actor of that day. He was pleased to join us in our little complex. Also a stock broker from Taos wanted to have an office in Los Alamos and he joined us too.

During the summer of 1965, a group of Los Alamos business men wanted to form a local Chamber of Commerce and Peggy Corbett was the ideal choice to be the executive director of it. They needed a place to have an office and I saw an opportunity and "seized the moment," as Lyndon Johnson had said was the thing to do. I offered to give the Chamber of Commerce free rent for her and Marilyn Bond, her right-hand gal Friday, to have an office if she would act as our receptionist for our complex. This was welcomed by all of my new tenants, so we named our complex The Los Alamos Business Center and got permission from the Credit Union to have a sign at the side street entrance in full view of people driving or walking on the sidewalk.

It took about a week to have a good carpenter make partitions with walnut paneling and glass to give each office privacy and easy access in a first class style. When the bank moved out they took their big expensive vault door to be used for the vault in the new bank building. I had a big four foot solid core door built to fit the door frame, so that each of my tenants could use this big 8'x10' fire-proof vault for their locking file cabinets, giving each a key to the door to the vault. Naturally, we had a nice bathroom and the whole place was heated and air conditioned.

The side and front view was of the gorgeous Ashley Pond in the center of the town near the old Lodge that I wrote of earlier, with the huge mountains rising above the pond and town — the best view in the whole town. My office had a very large window facing this view as well as the Chamber's office. Best of all, I had a door installed between my office and the Chamber's office. Usually when new people come to any town they visit the Chamber of Commerce for information.. This way Peggy could introduce them to the best real estate company in town to take care of their real estate needs. This worked out beautifully!

I was a great believer in having a local Chamber of Commerce and as such, I volunteered to take the job of membership chairman. I was always a glutton for work if it would accomplish a good purpose and I truly felt that this would. All the members saw what a good job I had done as membership chairman, so they appointed me for a second year. Like any eager young business man, I accepted for a second year term. They immediately elected me to the Board of Directors, which I was on until I became the sixth president of the Los Alamos Chamber of Commerce.

When I was getting started in 1965 all I had to sell was a very few resales and this is why I needed to buy these fourteen lots from Ed Leslie in White Rock. The A.E.C. was about to begin selling all of the government houses to the present occupants that had been renting them for years and years. These homes all needed to be appraised by government appraisers to establish their prices. The occupants would receive a 25% discount off the appraised value for their purchase price if they waived any and all warranties. This made an excellent deal for people to buy the house they currently occupied. Of course, these homes were not appraised and sold until 1966. So you see, I had to do something to "stay alive in '65, and get our kicks in '66."

With the fourteens lots in my possession, I ran and ad in the Albuquerque paper for a contractor to build houses in Los Alamos and right away I found one. Mr. John McDonald called me and had Bonnie and I come to Albuquerque to look at some houses he had built. He called his building company the American Scene Company.

The homes looked good and he explained that he had been a mortgage broker before getting into the home building business, so he understood financing as well as construction, so this was a plus in us dealing together. He had a young superintendent named Paul Corey. He was a small, young guy and a fast, hard worker. John said the houses he built were prefabricated homes built in Ft. Worth, Texas, named Holiday House.

I told him I had sold this type of house in White Rock and I thought they would fit in okay. He said, "Why don't we both fly to Ft. Worth and go through their factory?" So we did. I was well pleased as they looked better than the National Homes we had sold in White Rock. Paul Corey and a small crew found apartments in Los Alamos and we got started. I arranged financing for these houses locally through the Los Alamos Building and Loan Association and we were rolling.

A large home building company in Santa Fe owned by Allen Stamm made a deal with the A.E.C. to buy about forty acres to build houses. This forty acres was south of the White Rock project where Ed Leslie and Home Planning Co. were building. In fact, it adjoined Ed's property on the south. The subdivision was named La Vista. Stamm was primarily an adobe-style home builder. He built some pitched-roof homes and had sold some houses, but not too many. He was big in Santa Fe and couldn't see why people weren't buying more of his homes.

One day he came into my office in Los Alamos. It was just about the time I was getting started with John McDonald. Allen Stamm said to me, "Mr. Long, do you have any idea why people aren't buying my homes?"

I said, "Mr. Stamm, this is a different type of people here in Los Alamos than your prospective clientele in Santa Fe."

He said, "What do you mean?"

I answered, "People here all come from a different part of the country than the southwest. Also they are young, and are first-time home buyers. Most of them grew up in the home of their parents and they want to buy a home like their mom and dad had back in the east or the mid-west." I continued, "On the other hand, most of your prospects are local people who grew up in homes of the Santa Fe style."

"Oh," he said, "I see what you're saying. I'll start offering more pitched-roof style homes."

I said, "That will help, and something else I might mention, Mr. Stamm. Do your salesmen live in Santa Fe?"

"Yes," he said, "I only have one, and he goes home to Santa Fe every night."

"I have something else I will suggest," I said, "You need someone here to represent you who lives here and can visit people in their homes at night and make sales. It's hard to corner new prospects long enough at open houses to make very many sales."

He got the picture. He then asked, "Could you also handle our sales?"

I said, "Yes, we can." The deal was made. "I have a small builder I'm working with on some lots in White Rock and I would be interested in buying some more lots from you if you want to sell me four or five."

He said, "Yes, I would do that." So I did buy four lots to start with.

John McDonald's boys were doing pretty good and they would go home on weekends. Well, after about three or four months, one night his lead carpenter was driving home and he got a little drunk driving down the mountain and for some reason he didn't make the sharp horseshoe curve, ran off the road and was killed in the wreck. Well, this also killed the deal I had with American Scene Homes and John McDonald. He had about all he could of trying to build houses about 100 miles away from his base in Albuquerque. I was about out of lots anyway, so we parted company on friendly terms.

I was not able to produce many sales with Stamm's outfit at La Vista, but I had gotten acquainted with his subcontractor, Dan Webb. Let me tell you about this man: Dan was about 6'3" or 6'4" tall, but not fat at all. He was born and raised in Tennessee and his mother was a descendent of Daniel Boone, whom he was named after. Anyway, Dan had worked for years in Dallas, Texas for a volume home builder and was the best I had ever seen as far as the quality of his homes. A real "primadonna" however. He knew he was good and he was not bashful about letting you know it, too.

He was working in Dallas at the time that Jack Kennedy was killed. Dan told me that after this happened it was just like Dallas had a "wet blanket" put over the fire of the city. Dallas home building, along with a lot of other businesses, was really hurt. About that time Allan Stamm had placed an ad in the Dallas paper for a superintendent for a new subdivision in Los Alamos, New Mexico. This was La Vista, of course. Anyway, Dan built a home for him and his wife, Pearl, and lived on the La Vista project. He had been there working for Allen Stamm about a year when I met him. He really didn't like the adobe homes that Allan Stamm was famous for, but he didn't have any say in that, and he did an excellent job on both types of houses. Dan told me one day that Allen Stamm had had about all of White Rock, namely La Vista Subdivision, that he wanted and that he might get laid off. Well, old Andy Long got his pea brain to working again.

I had the thought that if I got my state contractor's license, Dan Webb and I could form a home building partnership. Well, I talked to Dan about this and told him I still had a few lots in White Rock and two in La Vista that we could start with. He said, "That sounds good to me and we could probably buy more lots from Stamm if we want." To make a long story short, we went to see my lawyer, Sterling Black, and asked him to work up our partnership contract plan. He suggested after a couple of days to name the company Western States Builders, Inc. Each of us would own 50% of the corporation. I would be president and Dan would be vice president and Bonnie would be secretary/treasurer.

Allen Stamm did approach us to buy a big block of his developed lots. We went down to his office and negotiated a price that was not hardly a bargain, so we told him we would think it over and let him know. In a couple of days we went back down and Allen and his vice president, Lee Brown, a guy about my age, set down with us and the first thing Allen said was, "What do you think, Andy?"

I said, "Dan and I think maybe we can work something out with you. We would like to first buy ten lots and test the water rather than agree to buy all fifty of them."

"Oh," he said, "Andy, in that case we will have to have $1,000 more for these first ten lots. If you don't want to take them all now." Allen had a reputation of being hard to deal with and I was getting my first lesson in this regard.

I turned to Dan and said, "Dan, unless you disagree with me, I think we need to get the hell out of here and go up the mountain and go to work on the lots we have left." I stuffed the papers we had out back in my briefcase and said, "So long, boys, we're going." As I said earlier, all we had to do was be able to do enough to "stay alive in '65" and we would really "get our kicks in '66."

Dan was building a few homes and our arrangement was that he would get paid a salary from Western States Builders of $150 per week and the Andy Long Realty would be paid 3% commission from the sales and do all the bookkeeping and payroll work in connection with the workers and subs. Dan's wife would get paid a little plus her housekeeping, cleaning, etc., of their personal home once a week and she would work with our buyers on picking out their carpet, appliances, paint, brick and tile choices that they wanted, and coordinate this with Dan during construction. Bonnie and Dan would work together on the cost estimates and sub bids and her pay would come out of Long Realty's sales commissions. So all this was settling out to where everyone was satisfied.

I was responsible for all the house plan selection, sales and worked with the draftsman on the plan drawings. The draftsman's name was Joe Dubin and he was really good. His full-time job was as draftsman and artist with the Laboratory, and a big plus was that he lived right across the street from me and I could go over to see how he was coming on the drawings as often as I needed to. Western States Builders would pay for all this and any profits would go back into our account and would be split whenever it was needed to buy anything, like more lots or machinery, vehicles or for the new pickup we bought for Dan to use. This all worked well because we all wanted it to, and we worked hard at it. We knew by this time that we would be in Los Alamos for a long, long time.

Tim was in college in Albuquerque and Andra was in junior high and still being bussed to school in Los Alamos. The A.E.C. was making big plans about getting ready to turn the town over to the county government and the homes that would be sold to the people who had been renting them and the buildings that would be sold to the business people. A new elementary school had been finished in White Rock and a big new junior high had been built in Los Alamos's far east end on Horse Mesa. There would not be a junior high school built in White Rock as the bigger kids would continue to be bussed to Los Alamos.

Work had begun on a massive, beautiful, new County Courthouse of granite stone facing Ashley Pond, right across the Pond from my office window. When spring came the white geese would be put back in the pond and a half dozen of them would be a joy to watch as they would even walk across the street to the sidewalk outside my window. Nice, huh?

It was time we talked to my mom about her and my brother John moving out to Los Alamos. She agreed that this was the thing to do. So she sold our big house for us to Burt and Mozelle Quimby, the parents of Tim's saxman, Vaughn, in his first professional band in Oklahoma (1959-61), as well as the little house of hers that she had been renting out. I was able to finagle a house for her to rent in Los Alamos. I paid for the moving van and I promised her that when they started selling the government houses that she and Bonnie and I would split the cost of a house for her. This was a promise I kept.

We took her with us when we went back on our regular Thanksgiving trip to Galena or Wichita when Bonnie's family had their family reunion.

They have done this for years and years, and they still do. We've spent almost every Thanksgiving with them for the past fifty-seven years. However, we would not have to make any more Christmas trips now that we were all together in Los Alamos.

My brother, John, got a job at the local service station from a friend of mine. He had his own car, so I bought a used car for Mom to drive and she was very happy to be living near her kids and grandkids. Of course, my sister and her family still lived in Wichita and they came out to see us several times over the years. Mom really liked the mountains, just like she did when they lived in Albuquerque in 1949 and 1950. And she liked the small town as she could drive around safely there and to White Rock, but never to Santa Fe — she would go with us or John if she needed to go there. She made friends easily, as I did, and soon she joined the local senior citizens group. She even performed in a little play they put on for the public. She was happy, especially when she moved into the little two-bedroom, single-family home that we bought with her. It backed up to a canyon and the deer would jump the four-foot high fence and eat some of her garden and she would run them off with her broom. She loved it. We got our furniture for our new home because she had been using it in the big house of ours back in Dewey. Now we both had plenty of furniture for both places, hers and ours.

Having met all those people I had sold houses to in White Rock — running the real estate office, running ads in the paper twice a week in the Monitor, a local publication, and radio ads every day, being the membership chairman of the Chamber of Commerce — I had many, many friends and business acquaintances by now. As a guy told me one day, "Andy Long, your name is a household word in this town." I hadn't thought of this in a long time, but I guess it was true.

It was Christmas time by now and we had survived and grown but nothing like we would in the year of 1966, which was just around the corner. I had bought a Jeep from the bank that they had repossessed and we enjoyed it as it was a nice red 4-wheel drive. Bonnie and I drove it up in the mountains with a Christmas tree permit and cut us a nice, big tree and we had a wonderful Christmas that year of 1965.

We were about out of building lots and Dan and I didn't want to buy any more from Allen Stamm. So we decided to talk to Ed Leslie about buying some from him. His Home Planning Company was going great guns by now and he agreed to sell us six lots at a time, and we could pay him each time out of our construction draws as the house progressed, with the final fourth payment when the house sold to our buyers. This was a fair deal for all concerned and it worked well for us.

We lined up a mortgage company in Albuquerque to make the permanent loans and Dan and I had them come up and inspect some of the houses that Dan had built for us. Dan showed them proof of his 102% quality rating that he had as an F.H.A. builder. This rating is exceptional in the business. Soon thereafter the mortgage company extended us a one hundred thousand dollar construction drawing account whereby we could keep four spec houses under construction at a time. This helped us all out as you see building a house for someone that has signed a contract to have it built was really a "pain in the ass."

I had sold many, many houses with Noxon and White Rock Development Co. this way and had to babysit the people and put up with all kinds of questions and phone calls and visits for the three or four months while the houses were being built. Dan was a great builder, but his rapport with people and "bedside manner" was not so hot. This line of credit made it possible to build four at time and not offer them for sale until they were finished.

What I would do when I got a prospect from the model home we had built was show the spec houses we had under construction and if they liked one of them and liked the lot it was on, then I would offer them a first option to purchase it when it was finished — or at least past the point that no structural changes could be made. Then, Mrs. Webb could work with them on their color selections and at this time we would take their $500 first option money and let it apply on their down payment on their purchase contract. This plan was great. It took out most all the babysitting problems and time wasted for the three or four months it took to build the house.

As soon as one of the four houses sold we would immediately start another and this helped us and our subs schedule their work better. By buying our lots from Ed Leslie, he let us use his good subcontractors that came with him from Roswell, and this gave them more work, too. It was good for all concerned.

The government appraisals had finally been completed on all the single-family homes of the same size and floorplan, as well as all the duplexes and four-plex units, and sales were made to the current tenants of each home. The prices ranged from around $4,000 for one-fourth of a 4-plex, and around $6,000 for half of a duplex, a small single-family home from $7,600 -$9,000 and a large single-family home on a well-located lot would appraise from $10,000 -$14,000. Remember, the government gave the tenant a 25% discount off the appraised value if they waved any construction warranties. So this was a real deal, whether they wanted to continue living where they were or, if they wanted to sell the unit they were in and buy one of the larger government houses that someone else was selling, they could do that. It became a so-called "musical chairs" situation in many, many cases. It was not uncommon to have as many as five or six house sales tied together and close all the sales the same day. So the great days that the people had been waiting for had finally arrived.

The title company was real busy closing all these resales that usually were tied together in multiple numbers. Bonnie helped the title company pro-rate the taxes and utilities with each buyer and it was a lot of work but everyone was making money on these deals. The sellers and buyers and the title company and our real estate people. As I said before, we were the only one in the business and it was wild!

We charged 5% on each resale we handled. And on our printed contracts to purchase, we had printed in it that the sellers would provide a clear title at the buyers expense to be provided by the Title Guarantee Insurance Company that was in our complex as our tenant. This gave us complete control of the entire transaction, not bad planning, huh?

By this time we had hired two full-time sales gals and two part-time salesmen. The part-timers were Chester Kazek, Sr. and Chester Kazek, Jr. Junior was a high-powered mathematician at the Lab and his dad was a really good engineer in the weapons division. The son had sold for a short time under Pat Patterson's company when White Rock was getting started, but had quit as a part-time salesman when Pat had his heart attack and I took over in White Rock in the early days.

The older Kazek would soon retire at the Lab and then become a full-time salesman with us. He was a very good one as he had sold Studebaker automobiles in Chicago during the Depression years and really knew how to sell. He was a very friendly gentleman and we hit it off really well. In about six months he went full-time. He looked very distinguished with his little narrow mustache — and he always dressed like a banker. He was with me for a long time and was a top producer.

One of the sales gals was Marion Perkins. She was a housewife and the wife of a group leader at the Lab and she had been selling mutual funds for a stock broker, so she was an experienced sales gal and a real pusher. She was always "charged up," even to the point of me having to slow her and calm her down occasionally. She became a top producer and her sales ran neck-and-neck with Chester Kazek's, both real competitors and I was glad they were both working for me. It took a long time for me to get her trained on how to close a house sale, but when she finally learned how, she was a fireball!

Business was so good that year of 1966 both in resales and new homes that Andy Long Realty sold 100 homes that year! I had initiated a trade-in plan for the sale of our new homes so that business flourished. And I announced in our radio and newspaper ads that Andy Long Realty would not engage in purchasing any of the resales of government houses and thereby not be in competition with anyone wishing to buy a home for their family. We had a fabulous year in 1966 and the government houses continued to be resold as everyone wanted to upgrade their homes as their families continued to grow and the musical chairs of houses continued on and the last ones to be bought in the chain were new homes.

White Rock was really growing under Ed Leslie's Home Planning and Development Co. and Dan and I continued to buy lots from Ed and build Western States Builders' new homes. Our sales crew would hold open-house on weekends, then work their prospects during the following week. Chester Kazek, Sr. and Marian Perkins, were really producing, as well as myself. Chester Kazek, Jr. was selling part-time but not doing well as Real Estate is not a part-time business. So, of all things, Chester Junior decided to study for the Catholic priesthood. He was a good Catholic and had a lot of energy and he needed to do something besides his high-powered mathematician job at the lab. So, I needed to replace him.

A young man came into my office one day looking for a job selling Real Estate, very presentable and about 30 years old. He was broke and didn't have a car and was on his ass, but for some reason or another, I took him under my wing. I saw promise in him as I had hired several men in the cookware business who had been in the same shape. I needed another salesman so I went to Santa Fe with him and we picked out a used car and I let him make payments on it to me until he got started. It wasn't long until he was doing quite well. I trained him well from the start and he never really gave me any trouble that I can remember. He was from Albuquerque and his name was Hershel Young. So, counting myself, we now had a four-person sales crew and all doing well.

Each year, for a long time, our office sold a hundred houses a year. Some years 101, some 102, some 99 but all around 100 sales per year. This was quite an accomplishment in the whole State of New Mexico. I had initiated a trade-in plan for the folks who wanted to buy one of our new homes and didn't want to wait for their present home to be sold, so this helped our sales. Also, if someone was leaving town and their home had not sold, we would buy their equity for 10% less than the sales price. This was a fair deal for them, and we would have 5% more to pay monthly payments on the house loan and for any repairs that were needed — and a little bit left in the event we had to drop the sales price to get it sold. We usually didn't get hurt on this trade-in plan and it did increase our sales overall.

Let me give you a little insight into what the people of the upper half of our state of New Mexico thought about Los Alamos and what was going on up here on this mountain top. Most of them were in awe! Most of them didn't have any dealings with these people in Los Alamos except when our people would go shopping in Santa Fe and Albuquerque for automobiles and other such things. We had an appliance store, hardware, furniture store, 2 or 3 clothing stores and other essential things, so not a lot was known about these people on the mountain.

Some of the lab people lived in Santa Fe such as the ones that wanted to own their own homes and chose not to rent from the government (but it was a 34 mile one-way commute to their job from Santa Fe). So not too many lived off the mountain. Little by little this was all changing as the town was not under government ownership.

The A.E.C. had started the survey and appraisal work on the parcels of land that were going to be sold for housing subdivisions in Los Alamos and some in acreage tracts or 3 to 5-acre lots near White Rock. Also, for the commercial lots and buildings in Los Alamos that could be put up for sale. These parcels and buildings were put up for sealed bids at their appraised value and with government financing available. Especially to the merchants who owned their businesses but were renting their buildings from the A.E.C. They were wanting to buy their own building and were anxious for them to get started.

Our family had become pretty well-known by this time with my constant advertising in the paper and on the radio and by going to church, Kiwanis Club, Elks Club, Masons, Chamber of Commerce meetings, etc. I had been asked to serve on the Los Alamos County Democratic Central Committee and had accepted. It was now 1967 and the Real Estate and building business was going real well and I had been appointed, if I would accept, to serve on the 6-man Hospital Advisory Board of our local Medical Center, which was a fine one, by the way. The board consisted of John Helm, the banker; Darryl Burns, owner of the local K.R.S.N. radio station; George Brenner, owner of the local department store; a well-known architect, I cannot recall his name, that worked for the A.E.C.; and the head man and Director of the whole Los Alamos Laboratory, Dr. Norris Bradbury, who had been the Director of the Lab after Robert Oppenheimer was replaced many years ago; and myself. Quite a prestigious committee and I was proud to have been chosen to serve. I was beginning to get pretty well loaded up on my time and duties.

I was becoming well-known by our two banks by now and if I didn't get what I thought was a good deal from one of them I could go to the other one. I was partial to the new bank of Los Alamos. Their board was composed of all local people; and the old bank, run by John Helms loan committee and board, were all Santa Fe people who I did not know. The local bank knew they had competition and they tried hard to please me, for which I was very grateful.

A strange thing happened one day in 1967. Bonnie and I were in our offices in the Los Alamos Business Center and Peggy said, "Andy, there is a young couple here to see you that are old friends". I looked up and there stood Lloyd and Sue Dunn from Dewey, Oklahoma. Sue had been married to Lloyd by Gene Butts, our old preacher of the First Christian Church of Dewey —and Sue Dunn was the preacher's daughter.

I asked, "Are you folks on a New Mexico vacation?" and Lloyd said, "No, Andy, we have been hired by the First Christian Church of Los

Alamos to be your new preacher." Well, we had a nice visit with the new preacher and Sue. We were glad to hear that her dad and mom were still preaching at the Dewey church and doing okay.

Lloyd said, "Andy, do you think you could find us a place to live?" I said, "I think I can do better than that, Lloyd. I think I can find you a nice little single-family home near the church that you can buy on very favorable terms since you are employed by the church." Oh, they were overjoyed. Lloyd then said, "Andy, my dad never did own a home of his own and I think this would be wonderful. All these government homes were in top shape from being maintained by the government and we did find one real close to the church. They were so happy — and so were Bonnie and I.

The church congregation liked Lloyd and Sue as they were both very personable people and had grown up together in that little Dewey, Oklahoma church. So they did just fine. About 6 months later, Lloyd came in to see me again in my office and asked if I knew a place that they could get a good deal on buying carpet for the church as they really did need to replace it. I said, "Yes, you do need to replace it and I can help. Lloyd, my construction company buys all our carpet for the new homes we build from the House of Carpets in Albuquerque and I get a builder's discount on it. Why don't you and I make a trip to Albuquerque and take a look?" So we did.

On the drive to Albuquerque I said "Lloyd, our company has done very well this year and I want to do something special for the church and you. If you find some carpet you like I will pay for half of it after the discount if you can get the Church board to pay for the other half." He was elated. We found the most beautiful carpet, the color of red wine that we both liked. We said that if the church okayed the deal we would schedule the installation.

So, Lloyd and I returned to Los Alamos happy until the board had their meeting. They thought the deal was great until one old lady said, "Why did you pick red carpet?" Lloyd told her that was the color Andy Long wanted. She said to him, "What is Andy Long trying to do, run the church"?

When Lloyd told me this, it hurt. But after thinking about it I told myself and Bonnie that you just can't please everyone. Everyone else that talked to me loved the beautiful red wine color, which helped mend my feelings.

It wasn't long until Lloyd approached me again and asked if there was any way I could make the same deal on new pews for the church. They really did need to be replaced. So, I agreed to pay half but I told him that I was not going to get involved in picking them out. I had learned my lesson.

I'll jump ahead in time a couple of years right now so I can keep on the subject of Lloyd Dunn, our preacher from Dewey, Oklahoma. A couple of years later Lloyd informed the church that he had accepted a preaching job in Albuquerque and would be leaving. We hated to lose him, but I understood his position and gave him my blessings. It wasn't long until Lloyd called his old friend Andy Long and told me that his congregation wanted to build a new, larger church and if I knew where they could get a large loan to build the new church. I thought for a minute and said, "I think I can help, Lloyd. The young president of our Los Alamos National Bank has gone to work as president of The Republic Bank in Albuquerque, which is brand new and has some Los Alamos stock holders." I told him that I had done a lot of business with Jim Steward at the Los Alamos National Bank and that I would talk to him and then get back in touch.

I did call Jim Steward and he said, "Send your young preacher friend in to talk to me." To make a long story short, Lloyd's new church did get the loan they needed and their new church grew and grew into a large one and the Lloyd Dunn family did too, and it made me feel good — and proud of Lloyd and Sue.

Now, back to the old ranch with Roy and Dale once again.

My personal popularity was continuing to grow and so was our real estate business and our building business — and our demand for loans and mortgage money was great, so I had to find some more places, and companies, to deal with. Right now F.H.A. was handling almost all the resale of government homes and we were using F.H.A. new home construction and buyer loans through the finance company managed by Jim Carnes in Albuquerque. Our conventional loans were being financed by Los Alamos Building and Loan Association in Los Alamos and, of course, I was using both of our banks in Los Alamos.

We needed another conventional loan source, so I heard of First Northern Savings and Loan of Taos, N.M., and they had a branch office in Espanola and were getting ready to open another one in Santa Fe. So, I drove down the mountain, 18 miles to Espanola and met a young man about 30 years old by the name of Bob Morris who was vice-president of First Northern at the Espanola branch.

We visited awhile. He had heard of me and our success in Los Alamos. He was anxious to have us do some business with First Northern for some of our conventional home loan business. We talked for quite a while and he told me he had been out in California for several years working with the F.B.I. in their accounting section — fraud, etc. And that he had been raised in Espanola and had recently been back on vacation and had read in the newspaper that First Northern Savings & Loan was looking for a manager for their branch office. He was homesick for New Mexico anyway, so he applied for the manager's job and they hired him — so he was new. We both understood each other's love for New Mexico over California. It was a mutual friendship so we started doing some conventional home loans with First Northern and we then had about the best source of home loans in the state available for our type of business.

We didn't fully realize our growing popularity in the real estate business as yet, but it was due to our real estate and home building ads in the Santa Fe New Mexican newspaper, because lots of Los Alamos people took the Santa Fe New Mexican in addition to our twice-a-week local Los Alamos Monitor paper.

In the real estate business there are real estate brokers and salesman, and then there are real estate brokers and salesmen that are also Realtors. Not all brokers are Realtors, but it is a state-wide organization and each full-sized town also has a local Realtor's Board. The members are trained to be very ethical, with high standards of trustworthiness. Remember me saying that Lee Skinner was a real estate broker but not a Realtor, and you see in him a good example of what I am talking about here.

Anyway, one day three fellows came to my office. They were from Santa Fe and all Realtors of the Santa Fe Board. They had all heard of our company and asked if I would join the Santa Fe Board of Realtors — which would then take members from not only Santa Fe, but also Espanola and Los Alamos brokers and their salesmen. This way we could all be in the Santa Fe Board of Realtors. For some reason Mary Deal was not asked to join and I didn't mention her either. However, a couple of years later, apparently she had learned more about business ethics and did join the board.

One day I was in my office and I would get the surprise of my life. Our son, Tim, was in his second year of college at the University of New Mexico in Albuquerque and 20 years old. Well, he told me that he was going to get married. What a shocker. It was such a surprise it really didn't sink in at the time, as in those days, I was on the phone almost continually and had a call waiting on the other line. When I finally got a break, I walked into Bonnie's office and said that I had received a call from Tim and he said he was getting married.

"Oh, my God", she said, "what are the details", I said "I don't know. I had several calls waiting at the time so lets call Tim back and find out what is going on". Well, the time is May 1967. So the day was set and Grandma Long, Bonnie, Andra and myself all headed for Albuquerque and a wedding.

We had not met this young girl. Her name was Juanita Busot, a college classmate of Tim's. They had it arranged with a Justice of the Peace. And, the little petite bride and her maid of Honor, Francis, were all prettied up. She was a beautiful young lady.

So, the wedding took place with rice throwing and our cameras clicking, then a short trip to an Albuquerque park for more pictures. We then all went out on East Central to the most beautiful resort motel in Albuquerque at the time. We had a wonderful dinner and dancing and checked the happy couple into the Bridal Suite for the weekend. Then we returned to Los Alamos and home. They moved into an apartment and started married life and more college.

Our business was still going full blast and the A.E.C. had begun selling some commercial buildings and vacant commercial lots and larger parcels of land to be subdivided for housing. Also, I think I mentioned that there were about 3 or 4 acres of vacant land designated as commercial that were to be awarded to the developer of Increment #1 in White Rock when it was built out. All 209 residential lots. Well, this had occurred and Home Planning got the commercial acreage. They were not commercial builders so they wanted to sell this 3 or 4 acres.

A group of Los Alamos guys formed a corporation called White Rock Shopping Center and bought the land from Ed Leslie. The group consisted of Ed Stockley, lawyer; Jack Wallwork, accountant; Roger Corbett (Peggy's husband); Jim Brown, the local Prudential agent; Bob Waterman, who owned a house-moving business and also the local Mayflower moving and storage company; and Benny Moore, who owned the local Mobil gas station and auto garage. All these guys were smart at their individual professions, but I saw an opportunity to be of help — and with my heart and soul in White Rock from the beginning, I waited for my chance to be needed.

I really didn't have time to spend as a Real Estate Agent with all my other activities, but when I found out that the lawyer and the accountant wanted to sell their stock, I bought theirs. Later the Prudential Insurance man, Jim Brown and Roger Corbett wanted to sell their shares, also. So, Bennie Moore and Bob Waterman bought their shares and old Bill Heath, who lost his job with Noxon (remember him?) when Ed Leslie and Home Planning took over the home building in Increment #1. So, old Bill Heath had stayed in Los Alamos and had started doing small construction jobs — mostly remodeling jobs. The White Rock Shopping Center Corporation had shrunk to only four of us: Waterman, Moore, Heath, and Long. We all got along pretty well. I bought all my gas and car repairs from Benny Moore for years and, of course, knew Bill Heath. It didn't take long for Waterman and I to become friends also. Heath then got started on the construction on the little shopping center as I had located a druggist.

Chapter Five

Building The House In Pajarito Acres

Tim at the Village Place Townhouses

Dan Webb built 2' X 2' footings all around the house to hold the heavy weight of the basalt rock walls. Also instead of using brick mortar to lay the rock, they used cement. You can't knock a rock loose with a sledge hammer! And the windows were all aluminum instead of wood so there would be no decaying. The roof was 5-quarter cedar shake shingles or 1-1/2 inches extra thick. Instead of using galvanized sheet metal for the roof valleys, Dan used sheet copper — it will never rust. All the material was the best we could buy and Dan saw to it that the carpenter labor was the best. He watched it like a hawk.

We used the same basalt lava rock for the walls around the house and across the front of the lot and lined the two driveways with the same rock. Tim's crew gathered it from a dirt road near Ancho Canyon. There is a blacktop driveway and also a circular drive in front of the house where I made a rose garden in the center.

I planted a nice garden and orchard and a beautiful blue spruce tree in the front yard that we decorated with lots of lights at Christmas time. Then we built a split rail cedar fence all the way around the 3-1/2 acres.

Inside the house there was a rock water fountain in the quarry-tiled entry. The family room was paneled in black oak, with a rock wall fireplace across the end. The kitchen had beautiful black ebony counter tops and a view from the kitchen window of the Sangre de Cristo mountains. The sunken living room, dining room, guest room and hall was carpeted in a true blue plush carpet. Andra's room was done in a soft lavender carpet and drapes, and our master bedroom suite had plush red carpet throughout, and a large, sunken shower.

Our home in Pajarito Acres was not only the best built home in Los Alamos, but personally I think it was the most beautiful one too. We moved there in October of 1967 and sold our other home on Rover Blvd.

While I'm on the subject I might as well tell you what we did to the new home several years later. After about eight years, I had our crew build a big barn with a hay loft, stables, and the works. Tim had found the plans at the local library and scaled it down to one-half size. It was not for hay storage in the loft, but to store lots of construction materials, such as tools and so on. It had two horse stalls and hay, feed and tack storage and an 8' X 10' fireproof room with double sheetrock plus asbestos hardboard lined walls and door for record storage of plans and valuable papers. Oh yes, and we roofed the barn with shake shingles like the house.

Now back to the "ranch with Roy and Dale…"

In November we had been in the new house about a month when my mother's brother, my dear Uncle Jack Henderson, became quite ill. He and Mom had been very close all their lives. Mom was about two years older than Uncle Jack. She had turned 67 in March of this year. Anyway, she decided to go back and visit him. Aunt Code, his wife, just wasn't the type to make a good nurse, so Bonnie and I drove Mom to Dewey and she stayed and gave him very good care, but he passed away about a month later. About December 1st, 1967 Bonnie and I went back to the funeral and to bring Mom back to Los Alamos and home.

About this time our new little daughter-in-law, Juanita, was getting very near to having her and Tim's new baby. This little gal didn't weigh 100 pounds and she was so big she looked like a half-ton truck with a two-ton load. I took a profile picture of her with my camera and right after that her water broke and away we went to the Los Alamos Medical Center. Lo and behold, she didn't' produce one baby, but TWO beautiful baby girls on December 10th. You can't imagine how proud we all were of them! My mother got to see her great-grandbabies and she was so happy, especially after the recent sadness of her brother Jack's death.

Bonnie and I were elated and the owner of our local radio station, who was my very good friend and the fellow that did all our real estate radio ads, was on the radio so often telling about Andy and Bonnie Long's new twin granddaughters that everyone in the whole county knew about them. Mark McMahon, the owner of our local newspaper also wrote a very nice story about them too. He and Darrel Burns, the radio guy, really liked us and we were the best advertisers they had, so they did it up big. How proud we were!

Thank the Lord my mother got to see our twin girls in the hospital, as on December 20, 1967 she had a heart attack and was rushed to the Los Alamos Medical Center. It was just a few days until Christmas time and Mom hadn't done her shopping yet. She was sure frustrated about this! She had been babysitting her neighbor's two small children when the husband came home for lunch. It had snowed about a foot that day and he got stuck when he started to leave to go back to work. Well, my mother always thought she could do about anything, so she was pushing on his car to help him and she had a heart attack.

Bonnie and I got a phone call from that hospital. Mom's regular doctor, Dr. Noth, was out of town so she was being attended by Dr. Schaefer, who was a very good doctor, but not a heart doctor. When we got to the hospital, she was still alive and we asked to see her and the doctor told us that she was being washed up and putting on a clean gown and would be upstairs in her room in just a few minutes. We waited 15 or so minutes and then Dr. Schaefer came in and said, "Andy, your mother had another heart attack in the elevator on the way up to her room and we could not save her. She passed away. I'm so sorry that I didn't let you see her when you asked me."

I don't think there is anything harder to take than when your mother dies. My dad had told me this in Wichita, Kansas, just a couple of days before he died. He knew he probably would and tried to prepare me for his coming death by telling me about his mother and he knew how hard it was going to be on me when he died. You see, my dad's father died of heat stroke at the age of 36 when Dad was only two years old, so he had no father that he knew, only his mother and he was so close to her all his life until she finally passed away at the age of 93. Dad and I were very close for the 37 years that I had lived at the time of his death.

Well, here we are with twin granddaughters, 10 days old, and five days before Christmas and 650 miles from Dewey, Oklahoma. The first thing we did was call my sister, Marjorie, in Wichita and she caught a plane that evening and Tim met her in Albuquerque and drove her to Los Alamos. We made arrangements with a funeral home in Santa Fe, as there was not one in Los Alamos and they would fly her to Dewey for burial. When we got to my sister's home in Wichita we found out that in Dewey they couldn't open a grave on weekends or Christmas, so we had to wait almost a week for the funeral. We spent a sad Christmas in Wichita.

My Uncle L.D. Henderson still lived in Dewey, so we all gathered there. A very surprising thing happened the evening of the funeral. I got a call the day before from Bob Waterman and Benny Moore, my two partners in the White Rock Shopping Center and Los Alamos Motor Lodge, and from Jim Browne, my friend and Prudential Insurance agent, that they were all three flying in Bob's plane to the funeral. Mom had met all three of these guys and she liked them and Bob Waterman had grown up in Dewey. I had not known him then as he was a few years older than me. I was so happy that these men were coming to show their respects at my mother's funeral. I picked them up at the airport and on a cold winter day two days after Christmas of 1967, we all said our last goodbyes to Annis Marie Henderson Long.

Three or four days before my mother died, we brought Juanita and the little girls home in two feet of snow in Los Alamos. Christmas Eve, Juanita started to hemorrhage, and needed to go back into the hospital. Tim was away at band practice, so Andra called our dear friend Peggy Corbett who called her friends, Tom and Pat McKenna, who lived on the neighboring acreage, to come over in their four-wheel drive Jeep to take Juanita to the hospital in what was then about 34" of snow. Andra, who was 16 years old, and her girl friend, Barbara Rice, who was about the same age, had baby duty. Neither of the girls had ever been around a baby, much less knew how to take care of a baby, and Andra considers it a miracle that the babies survived the night! Barbara had enough after one night; Tim had made it home, so the two of them took shifts to feed and care for the two babies — either one was always awake 24 hours a day. As soon as the funeral was over we headed home, but we had been gone about a week and I think this was the longest week that Andra ever spent in her young life.

Our gratitude to Peggy Corbett, and Tom and Pat McKenna was abundant! Tom McKenna became a very good friend. He and Pat owned two 7-11 Speedway convenience centers in Los Alamos, one in White Rock, and one in Santa Fe.

Juanita stayed in our big house in White Rock with the girls and Tim went back to their apartment in Albuquerque. A few weeks later when Juanita's second semester of her sophomore year started, she joined Tim in Albuquerque in a larger place. A neighbor of theirs, Marliss Kuntz, had studied how to take care of babies and helped her immensely. Juanita only had classes three days a week, so they managed pretty well.

Juanita was a pretty little thing, a mixture of French and Cuban and was raised in a very well-to-do family. Her father owned a chain of jewelry stores in Cuba and was a diamond-cutter. This was all before the Castro days. His wife never had to work or even cook and the children, Juanita and Frank, were driven to school in a limousine, and didn't want for a thing. Well, when Castro took over and during the Bay of Pigs invasion of Cuba, Mr. Busot, Juanita's father, and some others conspired to blow up a power plant and someone had ratted on them and they were thrown into prison. Later with the help of the Catholic Church, the two children were taken to the U.S. and they wound up in Albuquerque. Frank went to California after he graduated in engineering from the University of New Mexico. My knowledge is not too clear, but I think Juanita was in a foster home or two, put into school not able to speak English, but being a very bright child she managed to learn English quickly. She graduated high school in Albuquerque and went on to the University of New Mexico where she met Tim.

I sold Mom's house and distributed the money to Marge and John and stored some of her furniture. Marge took some, and John the rest and he rented an apartment and traded his car in for a nice little Dodge Club Coupe. John had been in the US Marines and had developed quite a drinking problem some time before Mom died and this had added to her stress. Soon after Mom died he got married. His new wife wrecked his car, but we got it fixed. The marriage didn't last too long as one day after school Andra and some of her girlfriends spotted John's wife riding in a car with a couple of other people. The girls followed them up to Horse Mesa, where they stopped in a wooded area and got out — two men, two women, all holding beer cans. Andra stopped and let her know that she knew what she was up and a short time later John and her were divorced.

John got a new job as a busboy at the new Los Alamos Inn which had just been built across the street from the new courthouse and next door to our Trinity Square Professional Plaza.

The commercial land in White Rock, the 23 acres I mentioned earlier, was put up for bid and Benny, Bob and I bid on it, along with some other bids but all bids were turned down, and would be offered again at a later date. When we left Hueneme Bay, California Chuck Coutts had started another project for Joe Bolker called The Villas. They were duplexes but the property lot line runs right between the middle of the duplex, so what a person buys is what they call a "single family villa or townhouse." Each side had three bedrooms and three baths and each had a two-car garage and the three bedrooms were sound protected, of course. They were selling really well, so I had Chuck send me the blueprints of the three bedroom units and the 2 bedroom, 2 bath units.

I mentioned that the B.L.A.W.S. Corporation had bid on, and was awarded, the small piece of land about one block from the Community Center and also the large piece near the Golf Course. Well, old Andy got a bright idea — I offered my one-fifth interest in the Golf Course property to the other four members for the total interest in the small piece near the Community Center. This was discussed and they accepted my offer. This was a fair deal for us all as we would have sold the small piece to someone else anyway. I had it surveyed and drawn into six building sites, which made twelve villas.

I submitted this plan to the planning commission and the bright young planner that the County had hired, Ron Short, was smart but had no experience with this type of project. The problem they faced with my plan was that this would be the very first "planned unit development" in the entire state of New Mexico! I got all kinds of resistance to it, but I was persistent and I kept at it and very nearly drove the young planner nuts. He was just scared to be setting a precedent in the state. Anyway, after weeks of persistence I finally agreed to their demand that I would build a brand new street around one-third of the project, connecting to the other two-thirds which was already paved, curbed and guttered with black-topped streets. The piece of land was oval shaped and we laid out six buildings all the way around, facing the streets and backing up to a vacant area of land filled with large pine trees. The vacant land was about one acre of common area, and with the pine trees it made you feel like you were thirty miles out in the forest instead of living one block from town. On one end of the parcel coming off the new street, I made a curb cut. I then built a grape stake cedar fence all the way around behind the twelve units of six buildings. It had a large double gate at the curb cut so a fire truck or other vehicle would be able to get into the common area behind all the buildings, mostly for fire protection and so on. Between he back of the buildings and the circular fence, each unit had a small fifteen foot back yard with a gate going into the common area. Each unit had a short fence separating the small lots from each other for privacy. Then in the common area we built the following before we even built the first building so I could show what the common area would look like when the prospects looked at it before they bought: 12 picnic tables, 12 barbeque pits, a horse shoe pitching place and a nice deluxe concrete shuffleboard. Dan Webb enjoyed building these things, with Tim installing all the barbeque pits & shuffleboards. It looked super good. We named the project Ponderosa Manor and we had a very attractive information brochure drawn up and printed.

I hadn't done much in the way of real estate loans with John Helm's bank, The First National Bank of Santa Fe, so I went in to see my friend John and showed him the brochures and he liked what he saw. I told him that I wanted to borrow money for the construction loan for the buildings to be built and then I would have the long-term permanent loans handled through the Los Alamos Building and Loan of Espanola. They also had a branch office in Santa Fe by this time. Well, John Helm got the construction loan approved. The six three-bedroom units sold for $29,750 each and the six two-bedroom units sold for $27,950, so John's bank approved a $240,000 construction loan for all twelve units and would be funded in construction draws as the work progressed. This would be paid back from the proceeds of the buyer's permanent mortgage loan. This was a big chunk of money and we already had the land paid off, so the loan was for construction money only. But by this time we had a hell of a good track record so away we went with Ponderosa Manor, the first planned unit development of townhouses in the whole state of New Mexico.

This was going on in 1968, and a lot of others things were happening with me too. The Democratic Party asked if I would consider running for State Representative from Los Alamos County. The incumbent was a Republican named Ed Grilley. He was something of a big-shot with the Lab and they wanted to run a Democrat and try and beat him. He hadn't done much — as he couldn't when the Government owned the whole town until just recently. I was unopposed in the primary and ready to start campaigning.

Now enter Bruce King into my life again. Remember him, the guy I ran across up on that trail at the Valle Grande looking for strays on the ranch he and his two brothers had leased? We had visited with each other for quite a while and I mentioned he reminded me of Will Rogers. Anyway, Bruce had been a Santa Fe County commissioner for three or four years and was well liked and he was running for Governor of the State of New Mexico. Well, one day he showed up at my office and we visited some more and he asked me if I would take him around town and introduce him to the business owners. I said "Sure, Bruce, I know them all through the Chamber of Commerce. Let's go get some votes for you and me." So we did and had a good time in doing so. We seemed to hit it off really well. By the way, this friendship lasted for years and years and still does. We still exchange Christmas cards, letters and birthday wishes. He is nine months older than me. I have never met a better man.

Well, to make a long story short, he won his election for Governor and I lost mine, but we had fun. I found out I really was not cut out to be a politician. While Bruce and I were still running, just before the general election, Bruce called me and said, "Andy, Senator Clinton Anderson, Congressman Tom Morris of Tucumcari and I are coming up to Los Alamos this afternoon to campaign as they are both running for re-election, like you and me. They would like to meet you and have you take them to one of the main laboratory gates when the employees get off work at 5:00 PM this afternoon."

I said, "Sure, Bruce. Stop by my office and we'll get in my car and away we will go." So we did. This was memorable because I stopped the car and opened the back door to let Senator Anderson out and when I closed it, I closed it on my right hand. Oh, how it hurt! I didn't shake anyone's hand that afternoon, but they did and all three of them were elected. Very memorable.

While we're on the subject, when Bruce ran for re-election two years later, he and his wife, Alice, spent his birthday at our house and Bonnie cooked us a real nice dinner. Then we went to a private home in Los Alamos at a Democratic Coffee Party to campaign. I'll take time to tell you a little funny now: When we left our house Andra, our daughter, went with us to the coffee. She was sitting in the front seat between Bruce and me. Bonnie and Alice were in the back seat. Well, I asked if he had heard that Oral Roberts had died. He said, "No." So I said, "Oh, yes, and when he got to the pearly gates and knocked, Saint Peter asked, 'Who's knocking?' Oral said, 'Oral Roberts.' Saint Peter said, 'Come in. We've been waiting for you.' So Oral came in and said, 'I am so anxious to meet God. Can I see him now?' Saint Peter said, 'Oh, yes, you can in a few minutes. First I need to talk to you, Oral, about this hurting I have in my shoulder.'

Well, old Bruce thought this was so funny he raised both his arms up and when he brought them down, his elbow hit Andra in the ribs. She told me later, 'Dad, when I'm in the car with you and Bruce, don't tell him any more jokes. He just about broke my ribs!' We have laughed about this many times over the years. Bruce King is a tee-totaller and a pretty religious man. I'll tell more about him later.

About this time in mid-summer of 1968, I got a call from a man by the name of Stephen Mitchell. I knew who he was, but had never met him. He was the chairman of the First Northern Savings and Loan Association with their main office in Taos, New Mexico. They had made several permanent loans for us on properties: on our new home that we built, as well as our Ponderosa Manor Villas. He said, "Andy, I'm in my son's law offices in Santa Fe today, and I would like to talk with you."

I said, "Will this afternoon be okay, Mr. Mitchell?"

He said, "Yes, at 2:00." I had no idea what he wanted, but I did show up at 2:00. He was a jovial fellow of around sixty years old, with sandy red hair and glasses. Well, he told me about himself when I saw all the autographed pictures on the office wall. He was the former chairman of the National Democratic Party during the Adele Stephenson era and a very high-powered Chicago attorney. I found out later that he was the convention chairman of the up-coming election of the primary of this year's presidential election, to be held in Chicago in the fall. He started out by complimenting me on the good-looking houses that Dan and I had built in White Rock. He said he had seen them and had heard a lot about me from Bob Morris, who was his 'right hand man' that I had been working with for about a year now on our construction loans.

Mr. Mitchell said, "Andy, I think you have the Midas touch."

I said, "I don't know about that but I know I have been working pretty damn hard for a long, long time and I practice what your good friend there on your wall taught me, 'to seize the moment' and I do every chance I get."

Well, he liked what I had just said. And he said, "Well, I have another opportunity for you to consider. I have a ninety-nine year lease on about four acres of land in Taos right next door to Kit Carson Park. I built a drug store and a savings and loan office facing the street with a driveway going all the way to the back part where I built an office building for my law office, along with two nice apartments upstairs. I have enough more land to built about twenty-four nice two-bedroom condominiums and still have enough land for the necessary landscaping. I am looking for a partner to handle the construction and sales for these condos." He said, "I have the land lease and I'll do all the necessary legal documents for the condos. First Northern will do the financing and your Western States Builders will do the construction."

I said, "Mr. Mitchell, do you think I can do this?"

His answer was, "Andy, if I didn't you wouldn't be here."

"Will tomorrow morning be okay for me and my partner to come to Taos and take a look at the property?

"Yes, I'll see you tomorrow."

Well, Dan and I drove up to Taos the next morning and we discussed it all the way up there. It sounded pretty good, but it was a long way for Dan to commute each day — about sixty miles one way. Anyway, we liked what we saw, and a big handshake and lunch sealed the deal. Of course, Dan still had a few houses under construction in White Rock to finish in about a month or so and it took Steve and me about a month to get the drawings and blueprints the way we wanted, working with an architect, a Democratic friend of Steve's. I told Steve I would oversee the sales, but we would have to hire a local broker to do the retail selling in order to have local representatives on a day-to-day sales effort. I talked to three brokers and chose one my the name of Charley Brooks who was just the right type.

On the trip to Taos that first morning with Dan, we were discussing the lonely long road that he and I would be driving in order to complete this project. Dan was a big guy with strong arms — and hard as steel. He said, "I'm not worried, I have a good knife and if anyone gives me trouble, I'll operate on him — and him wide awake." I believed him as he had a short temper and I had seen it on a couple of occasions with some of our sub-contractors.

I said, "Well, if I have any trouble out here on this lonely road, I have a little 25 caliber automatic pistol here in the glove box and I'll be okay." More about this later....

We were feverishly working to finish up on three or four houses in White Rock and wrap up the Ponderosa Manor project, and we didn't buy any more lots from Ed Leslie as we hadn't planned on starting any more houses locally. This would free up Bonnie from all the Los Alamos construction bookkeeping as she was going to be doing the construction bookkeeping on the Taos project, which Steve named "Las Milpas" which means 'cornfields.'

Dan and I would go to Taos about once a week. Sometimes Bonnie would join us since she needed to get better acquainted with Steve Mitchell. This would be a little easier on Bonnie as the payroll on our people who were building the homes for us in White Rock along with the construction bookkeeping on those houses was about to cover her up. She was a hell of a work horse, but it was just too much if we added the Taos bookkeeping on her too, since she was also doing the Andy Long Realty books as well.

Construction got started on the condos and Dan was trying to handle both projects, one in Taos and one in White Rock, but White Rock was coming to an end and Dan was happy as it was stringing him out pretty well trying to take care of both jobs. Election time was getting close and Steve's job as National Democratic Presidential Campaign Chairman at the Convention to be held in Chicago was taking up a lot of his time. He, Dan and I would still have time for necessary meetings on our project, but all of us were very, very busy.

The last one of the houses in White Rock was almost finished except for the final grading of the yard. I came down to take my buyers through the home for their final inspection before closing their deal. They had been in the house the day before and had found a problem. The house was built on a concrete slab, covered with carpet except for tile in the kitchen. The heat ducts were all in the slab before it is poured and in pouring the slab the heat duct in the doorway going from the kitchen to the patio had somehow gotten bumped while the concrete was still wet and it was not at all square with the doorway, being off about two inches. The F.H.A. inspector had not seen this when he had made his final inspection the day before because someone had placed a small piece of carpet over the heat duct to hide it.

Well, the buyer pointed this out to me and I said, "Oh, hell, this has to be fixed and it is going to be one hell of a job."

The buyers said, "We know, but it has to be fixed before we close." I agreed and the buyer's left. I assured them it would be taken care of. Well, I hated to tell Dan that this had to be corrected because he was such a primadonna and could do no wrong. Well, I said, "Dan you have to fix this before I can sell the house."

He said, "Andy, let's get something straight. My job is to build these houses and yours is to sell them. I'm not going to fix it."

I said, "You have to because I can't sell it this way to anyone."

We were standing on the sidewalk in front of the house and he got right up in my face and said, "You and I are going to fist city over this."

I said, "Dan, no we're not!"

He said, "What makes you think so?"

He had his hand in his pocket where he kept his knife, and I had my hand in my right hip pocket and I said, "If you pull your hand out of your pocket I am going to put two little holes in your head — one in and one out." He took his hand out of his pocket, but his hand was empty. He turned and walked away and I'm damn glad he did, because all I had in my hip pocket was a fine-toothed comb. If he had pulled a knife or his fist out of his pocket I would have had to burn a streak down the sidewalk to get away from that big SOB. He did fix that duct and we did sell that house.

I went straight to the office and wrote Dan a letter proposing to buy all his half-interest in Western States Builders Corporation and sell his home for him and not charge any commission. He could keep his job in Taos and Steve Mitchell could pay him his wages and he would be responsible only to Steve and in no way to me. I then went to my new lawyer, Harry Moore, and had him draw up papers with the information I had given him and he went to see Dan Webb to get him to sign off. Harry said it went easier than he had expected. It was time we parted company and I think we both knew it!

The Taos job was half finished and the condos were all sold to date by the Taos broker Charley Brooks, and Steve Mitchell said that he thought that his office in Taos should take over the construction books from Bonnie as the project had not made a dime profit so far. I knew this was a damn lie and put up some pretty good arguments, but I knew I was out-classed in the lying and bull-shitting business with this high-powered politician, so I agreed that Dan would be working for him from now on and he said, "Good, as when Dan is finished here, I want him to build a large three story building in Santa Fe for First Northern Savings and Loan Association. They were moving their main office to Santa Fe has soon as the project was completed. I figured it all out later, that this crooked SOB had figured on doing all of this probably from the beginning. He had taken

Dan to lunch up the street from his office lots of times in the earliest days and had his right arm over Dan's shoulder all the time, spinning him a big yarn. Also, one day before the blow-up, Dan, Tim, and I were in Steve's Taos office in the morning and his secretary said, "Mr. Mitchell, vice president Humphrey is on the phone."

I said, "Come on boys, let's let them talk."

But Steve said, "Keep your seats, boys. You might as well hear this." Steve had been backing George McGovern as his presidential candidate, but he had just been defeated at the National Convention by vice president Humphrey. Well, Steve said, "Hello, Hubert, what can I do for you?" And he turned on his speaker phone so we could hear what was being said.

Hubert Humphrey said, "Steve, yesterday we were political enemies, but today we are both Democrats. So I want you to take over Texas and New Mexico for me and help me win the presidency over Nixon."

Steve said, "Sure, Hubert, you can count on me." (Tim was upset that he switched sympathies so easily as he was a big supporter of McGovern and had chauffeured him around Santa Fe to several breakfasts and dinners for a week, and had recorded his speech for him at the Greer Garson Theater, getting quite close to the senator before driving him to Albuquerque for a radio interview). I have thought about that Democratic convention many times since with all the trouble that happened in Chicago. Remember this is the campaign that Bobby Kennedy was running in against McGovern and Humphrey when he was assassinated in California.

Well, the Taos condos were finished and the big savings and loan building in Santa Fe was finished and not too long after this Steve Mitchell had a heart attack and died. I never knew that he had heart trouble, but the thought did enter my mind that he certainly had some high-powered political enemies that were probably capable of doing old Steve in. We did not make any money on the Taos job, but neither did we lose any. We were grateful for that.

I attended Steve Mitchell's funeral in Taos out of respect for my good friend, Bob Morris, who was now president of First Northern Savings and Loan in their new office in Santa Fe. We continued to do lots of home loans, as well as some very large commercial loans which I will be telling you about down this long road.

Our real estate business was booming! It seemed like everyone in the country was either buying or selling a home and our sales people were performing in great fashion and all of us were making money. My campaign for state representative was humming along and my good friend, John Rogers, a long-time Democrat and lab employee, was writing my speeches for me and the accountant Jack Wallwork, one of the original White Rock Shopping Center group from whom I had bought stock in it, taped some very good campaign ads written by Tim that were played on the radio station quite frequently as well as the taped speeches I made from the ones that John Roger's had written.

John Rogers had run for state senator two years earlier and was elected. I had sent $500 from Hueneme Bay, California when I was working out there and John had not forgotten, so he was a great help to me in my campaign. He had beaten my former lawyer Sterling Black in the primary in 1964 and won the general election later that year.

Jack Wallwork was not only an accountant, he liked to act every chance he got in stage plays in Los Alamos and Santa Fe county. He had a deep baritone voice and did an excellent job in his taped messages on the radio. I would also speak, myself, at the Kiwanis meetings, of which I was a member, and served as chairman of the "Support Our Churches" committee. As I mentioned earlier, I was running against an incumbent Republican by the name of Ed Grilley, a long-time employee at the Lab. He hadn't done anything, but hadn't done anything wrong either.

I thought I had a good chance of winning as I had the backing of the Democratic party including Bruce King, who was also running for Governor, as well as United States Senator Clinton P. Anderson and United States Congressman Tom Morris. Well, I got beat, but not by much, for which I was grateful, but it was a Republican year — Nixon won the presidency over Humphrey and so on. However, Bruce King did win his election and we remained the best of friends as we had campaigned together and I always helped him all I could in his state elections in years to come. Looking back, I never did care for most politicians, and I don't think I would have been happy if I had won but I had tried hard as I always did with everything I tried. I was enjoying what I was doing and things were still going great.

The B.L.A.W.S. Corporation was about to bid on a large tract of land that the government was selling by sealed bids. As I remember it was around 200 or more acres and was zoned for large tract lots for housing, similar to Pajarito Acres which it adjoined. Our lot was three and a half acres. Each lot was 3-5 acres and had horse trails bordering them and they had sold very well. Mary Deal someway got the exclusive sale of those Pajarito lots. I had purchased one that we built our home on from a guy I knew, on a re-sale. So I hadn't had to deal with old Mary Deal. Thank God!

Anyway, B.L.A.W.S. Corp. consisting of Black, Waterman, Agnew, Shreffler, and Long, were the successful bidders and we decided to probably subdivide it into the same type of large lots as Pajarito Acres had done. A short time later we held our victory meeting and I figured that since I had orchestrated the deal and had made the estimate of what our bid should be (and since I was a realtor), that our little group would let our company handle the sale of the lots once we got it ready to sell. A lot of work had to be done in steering it through the planning and zoning commission and drawings, utilities, streets, and all the other things I could be called on to have done, that surely they would let me handle the sales. Well, during the discussion Harold Agnew, the second in command at the Laboratory, and his good friend, Shreffler, another Ph.D., suggested that we let Mary Deal bid on the sales rights of the lots after I did all the work getting them ready to sell. I was stunned, to say the least! I thought you ungrateful egghead SOBs! They hadn't thought about how much work I would have to do in getting the project to the point of being ready to sell. I knew Mary would be waiting to see what I would bid and cut it just enough so she would get it. Then I quickly put two and two together and figured that her husband, Bill Deal, worked for Harold Agnew and since he and Shreffler both knew Bill and Mary Deal that she would definitely beat my bid. So I was MAD, but I did not say anything. I kept my mouth shut. Well, the meeting adjourned and I spent a sleepless night. The next morning I wrote a letter to all the other four members and Bonnie typed it up and I mailed them out. The letter simply said due to the lack of loyalty shown to me last night, of me having to bid for the sales rights of this new project, I am now offering my total twenty percent interest in the B.L.A.W.S. Corporation for sale or trade for money, marbles or chalk, or Los Alamos National Bank stock or Los Alamos Building and Loan stock.

The following day after I sent the letters out, I got a call from lawyer Sterling Black that he wanted to talk to me. Well, no one attempted to get me to change my mind and I think they knew it wouldn't do any good anyway. So I went to see Sterling and he and I made a trade for a large block of building and loan stock he had for several years and he now owned 40% of the B.L.A.W.S. Corporation and I was a big stock holder in the Los Alamos Building and Loan Association. I knew that the other large stock holders and directors did not want a real estate man that made lots of loans from them for his home buyers to have the leverage that owning a large block of stock might provide, so the president, Jim Teere (he and I didn't like each other much) presented me an offer to buy my stock. I think he was representing not only himself, but probably other stockholders too. Anyway I accepted the large chunk of cash very graciously and Bonnie and I were happy as clams.

I was almost finished with partnership deals, having concluded the one with Dan Webb a short time earlier. Then after this one, I had just about had it with partners that had no loyalty. I just didn't need them. Certainly no more of them with people like Steve Mitchell and the Taos condo deal. The only one left now was the one with the boys in the White Rock Shopping Center, Bob Waterman, Benny Moore and Bill Heath. In addition to the four acres in White Rock where we built the White Rock Shopping Center, the government still owned 23 acres of commercial land adjoining the other four acres that had been put up for bid. It ran along State Road #4 all the way south to Sherwood Blvd. which was the other entrance, besides Rover Blvd., to White Rock from State Road #4. This was one very nice piece of land as all along the east side it bordered the back side of homes on Aztec Street in Increment #1 of White Rock, which I had sold five or six years earlier. I had been watching this beautiful piece of land for years as it was ideally located for a large neighborhood shopping center at the proper time.

The White Rock Shopping Center boys and I had bid on this piece two times before over the past year and each time we were the only bidders and both times our bid had been declined! Now it was coming up for the third time and I told the boys we should try again and this time raise our bid a considerable amount and try and get this land. All three of the other guys in our group said "No, we're not interested in raising our bid." They didn't even want to make a bid. They just didn't have the vision and were scared to take on any more debt.

I think it was just the lack of experience that stopped them. "Well, boys," I said, "I'm going to bid on this twenty-three acres so either join me now or not, but if I get it, I'm going to keep it myself. And don't expect me to let you in later. No guts, no glory."

I then went to Ed Leslie of Home Planning and asked Ed if he would like to go in with me and bid it together. He said, "No, I don't think so." So I thought I would play 'lone ranger' and go for it by myself. I raised my bid $4,000 more then the last one we had made and crossed my fingers. It just so happened that a friend of mine saw John Mendius, who was Ed Leslie's surveyor and engineer, in the bank buying a cashier's check that was to accompany the bid for Ed Leslie's Home Planning Company! "Well," I thought, "What a double-cross this was!" I certainly didn't expect this from Ed Leslie! But, there it was.

The bids were opened and I was the high bidder.

The twenty-three acres of land kept me busy for several more years to come. I was tired of getting kicked in the belly every time I turned around, but it wasn't going to get any easier. I told myself that "when the going gets tough, the tough get going" and this was very true. I really couldn't believe that I had purchased this 23 acres that was all that was left undeveloped of commercially zoned land in White Rock, except for a two-acre piece that Ed Leslie owned that fronted on Rover Blvd. and backed up to my land on the south. Some time later I acquired that piece from Ed, so I had all twenty-five acres running from Sherwood Blvd. on the south end to Rover Blvd. on the north. More about this later. Things quieted down with me and my White Rock Shopping Center partners, as it was not time for me to start doing anything with my commercial land in White Rock yet. I would walk over it every Sunday and dream and plan. It was pretty well covered with mature pinon trees and it was so pretty.

My office space in Los Alamos that was leased from the Los Alamos Credit Union was about six months from coming due for renewal. After the first two years when I sub-leased the space from the Bank, I leased the space for another three years directly from the Credit Union. I then began thinking about building my own office building. A local man had bought a very nice piece across Trinity Drive from Ashley Pond and next door to the new Los Alamos Inn. A perfect spot for my office, I thought! He had planned on putting in a little "pitch & putt" golf course there, but the location was just too good for this rinkey-dink thing, so I offered him a nice profit and he took me up on it.

The piece was really too large for his purpose — it ran a hundred yards back from Trinity Drive and this was plenty big enough for a small office park — an ideal location. The Southwestern Bell Telephone Company built a beautiful new telephone building on the south, so everything around this land I bought was new. Ideal! The money I acquired from the sale of the Los Alamos Building and Loan Association stock, that I had traded my interest in the B.L.A.W.S. Corporation for, came in handy to purchase this nice piece of land, and now ol' Andy didn't have any damned ungrateful partners!

Soon after I bought the land, Bonnie and I went to Albuquerque with our camera and started looking at office buildings that would give us an idea of what we wanted to build on the front part of our land on Trinity Drive. We found the best-looking building! It was just the right size to fit the space we had and still leave room for another building next to it. The building was so perfect for our taste that I located the owner and asked if he would sell me the plans. He said, "Sure," when he found out our building would be in Los Alamos, some ninety miles away.

I took the plans to my draftsman and told him to draw it up and partition it into four different offices — one for our real estate office, one for the title company we were using, which would move with us, one for my new lawyer, Harry Moore, who had bought the title company from Sterling Black (my old lawyer and partner in B.L.A.W.S.) and one other office space for an insurance company that would also come with us. The Chamber of Commerce had really out-grown their space where we all were and would be moving into the old Los Alamos Lodge, which was no longer being used as a hotel since the Los Alamos Inn opened.

R. C. Dennis, who was one of Ed Leslie's framing contractors, took a contract with me to build my building and had just gotten started when he came to me with a new plan. He told me he had a friend, who had come to Los Alamos from Colorado that he had known for years, who was a commercial builder. This fellow was looking for a job and R. C. asked me if I would hire him to work for me on salary, replacing R. C. R.C. would then give me back his contract. He figured it would work out well for everyone — the building would be completed sooner as this job would be the only one that his friend worked on. His friend's name was Gene Altoff. He was a huge man, who had done some professional boxing in his younger days and he was plenty tough! We hit it off fine and he took his exam for a New Mexico contractor's license and he passed it.

This was good as there were no partners and no contracts — just a good salary for Gene full-time. He was plenty smart and knew how to cost-estimate commercial jobs really well. The building was finished in fine form within two or three months and Andy Long Realty and Western States Builders, along with their three other tenants were moved in and all doing good business. We had planned our work well — and worked our plan.

A short time before I started building the Trinity Square Complex, the county decided to replace the young county planner. The guy that they hired was from California and in his mid-forties, same as me. Bonnie and I had to always eat out at lunch as it was nine miles down to White Rock to eat at home, so we usually had lunch at the Carriage Inn. Some time before we started those two buildings, we were having lunch and Bonnie said, "Andy, that fellow at the cash register is George Brenner, the new county planner." Marion Perkins had sold them a house. She said to me, "Why don't you go over and introduce yourself to him and his wife and thank him for buying his house from our firm."

I said, "Good idea," and did. He response was shocking when he said, "Well, I wouldn't have except that I had to." I then said, "thank you anyway," and left. This was this "ass-hole's" attitude until he left Los Alamos about three years later. If you asked him how he was, he always said, "Terrible." I guess there are some people like this, but thank God there are not too many of them! It was a real struggle trying to deal with this man until the day he left. Looking back, I think he figured that many of the town's people at the Lab didn't want the town to grow and would rather that it had been left a totally government-owned town.

About the time that Gene finished our building, he said, "Andy, why don't you build another building next to your new building?" He said he could design it using the same type of materials, so it would match and look really good. I said, "Okay," and he came up with a good-looking building — and in another three months I was moving in other office people.

Before we started the building my surveyor and engineer, Wes Trask, and I were going over the plans on the second building and Wes said, "Andy, you may have a problem on the lower floor of your new building you're about to break ground for. As I remember in the early days of Los Alamos, there were buildings on this ground where you are going to build. I remember there was a six-inch water line there that will go through the center of your new building about four feet above the floor. We had better go over to the county and see if they have any old plans available for us to look at to see if that old water line was ever removed, or if it is still there." We gathered up our plans and went. We entered the big double doors and into the lobby and there was the building inspector standing there. He was a good old buy by the name of McDaniels. Everyone called him Mack.

I said, "Hello, Mack. Do you know Wes Trask?"

He said, "Andy, I've known Wes Trask since the early days of Los Alamos. He used to moonlight as county engineer when the government owned everything in Los Alamos." He said, "How are you guys doing?"

Wes said, "Okay. We're here to check on some old water line drawings that the county might still have available." Just about this time the obnoxious county planner came out of his office door and turned to go up the large stairway to the second floor and he saw us and the set of plans under Wes' arm, and said, "Go ahead, Mack, and take their plans so I can turn them down."

I said, "You SOB!" and at the same time I quickly reached into my left hand suit coat pocket and grabbed my black glasses case and whipped it out like it was a pistol. Old George saw it coming and he indeed thought I had pulled a pistol on him! He took the stairs three steps at a time and continued all the way to the mezzanine floor. Old Mack's eyes got big too as he thought at first my glasses case was a pistol also. Years earlier when he was a young man living in Texas he had been a policeman, so he thought I was indeed going to shoot George Brenner, the county planner, for sure! Within a couple of seconds everyone saw I was only holding my glasses case in my hand, and not a pistol, and we all three laughed until we cried.

George Brenner heard the laughter and cautiously came to the mezzanine railing on the second floor and looked over it to see why we were laughing. Anyway, we laughed about this for years and years to come.

We did find out the old water line had been removed and we didn't have the problem we thought we might have had, but this planner gave me trouble almost continuously for three or four years. With the planning commission consisting of nine members, all laymen made up of Laboratory employees with no experience at all with construction, architecture, economics, landscaping, or finance, you can see what a job it was to get approval for a building permit each time I started a project. I used to have the patience of Job, but they finally wore my patience so thin that occasionally I did lose control and indeed blow my top! Several times, when they would meet every two weeks, they would not have a quorum, so they wouldn't even take a vote on a project that you were waiting for approval on. I would have the plans all finished and financing arranged for sometimes $100,000-$200,000 and the interest clock was running at quite a daily expense. One night at the planning meeting I said, "Do you fellows have any idea how much money you are costing me when you delay these meetings like this?"

"Well, Mr. Long," one planner said, "Your money problems are not our consideration.."

I just shook my head and said, "I just wish you understood what I'm talking about." You see most of these committee members were young scientists in their twenties and thirties and even though they had lots of education and knowledge at their jobs at the Laboratory, they lacked the most important thing in life as far as I'm concerned — just plain old common sense.

I even tried a new twist on my presentation. I wrote a detailed description of exactly what I was proposing and made a type-written copy for each of the nine members and the county planner. I explained what I was passing out to them and they started reading it. Well, one of them spoke up and said, "Mr. Long, you have a problem in the second sentence of the second paragraph."

I responded with "What is the problem?"

"Well, you split your infinitive."

I just shook my head and laughed out loud and said, "Oh, gosh, I hope no one got hurt." Most of the others laughed, as most of them saw how ridiculous it was. Split my infinitive!

It got so hard to deal with those people that I started taking my lawyer, Harry Moore, with me to every planning committee meeting to try to keep these young planning commission members from abusing this old guy. It did help a considerable amount. It was expensive, though Harry was as reasonable on his charges as he could be, but the charge was from $50 to $100 per hour in the late '60's, so it would be about $200-$400 an hour now — but it was worth it to me. One time we had an important project to get approval on so Harry Moore had covered the thing from top to bottom with the county attorney. Bonnie, Harry, and I all went to the meeting together. Before we went in the building that evening Harry said to me, "Andy, you don't need to say anything at all tonight and get them shook up. I have everything cleared with their lawyer Ed Stockley and you just keep your mouth shut." I agreed to do just that. Well, the meeting got underway and apparently there was some mix-up between the lawyers and the planners understanding and they were totally at odds with what the lawyer had assured us would happen. This was the first and last time I ever saw Harry Moore really mad! And he dressed all of them down, including their lawyer. Harry said, "Andy, I'll never tell you to keep your mouth shut with these idiots again." We laughed about this many times over the thirty years that Harry Moore has been my trusted lawyer and dear friend.

Much later, when I was preparing plans for a chiropractor's clinic for White Rock, I had the plans all drawn and I took them to George Brenner for his review before I made my formal submittal. So I set down with George and he took his red pencil and started making several changes and marking up my drawings. I said, "Okay, I'll have my draftsman make these changes and I'll bring these plans back for you to review next week." So when I went back I took lawyer Harry Moore with me. George and I sat down at the table and Harry remained standing. George got his red pencil out again and started marking up the new plans I had made which included all of George's original changes.

I was so disturbed I said, "George, it looks like to me that you and I can surely work a little closer together."

His answer to me was, "Andy, you get more help than you deserve."

Well, this set me on fire! I said, "George, you are a shit-head!

Then he said, "It takes one to know one."

I jumped to my feet and said, "I am going to deck your ass, you SOB!"

I cocked my arm back and Harry Moore grabbed my arm and said, "No, No, No, Andy! Not here!" and with that said, George lunged for the door with Harry right behind him and they ran into the county clerk's office and closed the big four foot wide solid core door. Both of them held it shut and I pounded and pushed on that door, but I could not move it with both of them holding it shut. I made the final changes on the red-lined drawings and Harry took them over and got them okayed for a building permit from the building inspector that had already heard about the problem I had with George Brenner. Anyway, it was only a short time before the county commissioners hired a replacement for George and we had a new county planner that we got along with very well and had many years of pleasant meetings with, even though we still had problems with the nine members of the planning commission. We were about the only ones doing any commercial construction to speak of — Home Planning was still building homes, and a few small contractors were building custom homes, one at a time.

When the second building was completed I signed a lease with the Laboratory, as well as the general offices of the Speedway 7-to-11 Convenience stores (not the store, just the office headquarters). Remember my neighbors in Pajarito Acres — Tom and Pat McKenna who took Juanita to the hospital after the twins were born? They owned five stores — two in Los Alamos, one in White Rock, one in Santa Fe, and one in Las Vegas, New Mexico. They were good friends and they made fine tenants. We also had space for a nice beauty shop and there was a large room on the front that I had saved for Western States Builders, Inc., of which we owned 100% of the stock. I figured we needed a place to talk construction away from the real estate office and a few months later, it came in very handy.

We had to talk with our sub-contractors and needed a place to do so, and there was quite a bit of bookkeeping and payroll to be taken care of with our labor crew. Bonnie did not have time to do this as our real estate business kept her busy as a bee. I got a chance to hire an old guy who was retiring at the Laboratory after many years and he asked if he could be of help on my construction bookkeeping and payroll work. His name was

Clark Seay. He was retiring as head of the payroll department at the Lab and had signed all of their checks. It was a very important job. He had been doing it for years and he really knew his business. Well, I jumped at the chance to hire him. Especially after the big debacle in Taos with Steve Mitchell and the condos, which had gotten me a big screwing in the deal. So Clark took over the bookkeeping for Western States Builders in fine fashion.

The two buildings of Trinity Square Complex formed an "L," nearly touching each other at the end of the corner. The real estate office faced east and the new building faced north, sharing the same parking area in front of each. The big building was one story in the front, the same height as the first one, but two stories in the back as the land dropped off at a steep angle. There was plenty of parking on the back side. The beauty shop took up about half of the space on the bottom floor and the rest was office space that was leased to the Laboratory. It was quite a large building.

Both buildings were built of blond brick with porches across the front with built-in planters and blue slate entryways. There were lots of windows and they were very attractive. Gene Altoff and Clark were getting along very well, as each had a lot of respect for the other's abilities.

The year is now 1969 and we are moving into our new building. My mind is spinning in the direction of just how I should proceed with the development of the twenty-three commercial acres in White Rock. I felt that a large discount store was just what Los Alamos and White Rock needed, so I visited the large Gibson store in Albuquerque and met the owner, McAfee, an old fellow that had grown up in Oklahoma. He and I hit it off immediately. His two sons-in-law worked with him and they owned several stores in New Mexico and one in Pueblo, Colorado. One son-in-law took care of their building program and store maintenance and the other one was the general manager, along with Mr. McAfee, in working with their merchandise suppliers, etc. I talked him into coming up to White Rock and looking at our location for a store. He and Mr. King, one of the sons-in-law, came up and were quite impressed with White Rock especially, and I did a first class job of selling them on White Rock, telling them of the history going back to 1961. I explained that there were about a thousand homes here now and room for a couple thousand more to be built, and the only shopping was one supermarket, one dime store and one convenience store on the four acres that my three other partners and I owned in the White Rock Shopping Center. I told the Gibson people we could build a building and lease it to them in the White Rock Shopping Center, or I could sell them three acres of land and they could build a larger building themselves, as I would be developing the remaining 20 acres into a larger shopping center. I gave them their choice as to leasing, or buying land and building.

Mr. McAfee said, "Mr. Long, we never lease our locations. We always buy the land and have our own buildings built to our specifications. I was glad to hear this. I felt an obligation to my three partners in the White Rock Shopping Center — Bob Waterman, Benny Moore and Bill Heath — to make the Gibson's an offer to lease from our group or to sell them land and they could own their own building.

I said, "Mr. McAfee, what would you be willing to pay for three acres of land facing Sherwood Blvd., which would be the future entrance to our future shopping center with the street coming north along the side of your building? You would have a choice corner location."

He said, "The most we could afford to pay for three acres would be $50,000."

I took my time in responding to this and kicked the dirt a little and scratched my head and finally said, "I'm going to let you have it for the $50,000 cash." We shook hands and the deal was made. I never mentioned to anyone in town the amount I got from Gibsons for the three acres. The news traveled fast that Andy Long had brought Gibson Discount Stores to town. This was great news to all the people in White Rock, especially. They were no longer nine miles away from some good shopping.

My superintendent, Gene Althoff, being a sharp guy, suggested to me, "Why don't we try and get the job of doing all the cement work on their new building including all the block work?" I hold him, "Let's make it happen," as he was almost finished with our second building at Trinity Square. This kept Gene and his crew busy for quite a while.

With Gibson's money in hand for the land, I now had enough money to start work on the development of the rest of my commercial land in White Rock. This included all the following: grading, leveling, leaving all the nice pinon trees to help with the landscaping later on, planning of streets, utilities, etc. First though, it was necessary to do the planning and platting on paper, dividing the land into nine additional large lots, such as the one for Gibson's. This is when Wes Trask and I really became close. He was wonderful to work with and so talented.

Let me tell you about Wes now. He had been with the Laboratory for many years as a civil engineer. In fact, he was head of the engineering department in charge of building the new $290,000,000 plutonium facility that the Atomic Energy Commission was building in 1969 in Los Alamos, replacing the old one. He had sixteen draftsmen working under him. He was really good and very well-respected. I was so fortunate to know him and have him work on my jobs moonlighting on nights and weekends. He did all the surveying with me helping him sometimes on weekends. He did all the drawings for the streets, curb and gutter, sewer lines, water lines, electric and gas lines that the various contractors would work from. After the county had checked over the plans he drew them up for their approval.

We even named the streets in the Center, which we called The Village in White Rock. The main artery street he named Longview Drive, and another one Bonnie View Drive. The people in White Rock didn't mind as most all of them knew Bonnie and me and lots of them bought their homes from us. They were so glad to finally get a nice shopping center built!

My twenty-three acres did not go all the way north to connect with Rover Blvd. from Sherwood Blvd. on the south. (You see the two entrance streets to the White Rock subdivision were Rover on the north and Sherwood on the south) Ed Leslie owned about two acres between my land and Rover Blvd. I had to have this additional land in order to connect to the main sewer line for my proposed center. Ed did not do any commercial building at all, only residential, so I offered him a good price for this additional two acres and this gave me not only sewer service to the manhole and the White Rock sewer plant, but we were also able to connect Rover Blvd. on the north end of our land with Sherwood Blvd. on the south with our new arterial street, Longview Drive. We now had State Rd. #4 on the west side, Sherwood on the south and Rover Blvd. on the north.

On the east side of our project, all the way from south to north, were the back of houses that I had sold to the first White Rock buyers in 1961, 1962, and 1963. I knew each and every one of them. In order to keep the good relationship that I had enjoyed, I made a twenty foot wide buffer strip of land all the way from Sherwood Blvd. to Rover Blvd. This buffer strip abutted the backyard fences of the homes that backed up to the property line. I then planted poplar trees and landscaping in the buffer area and then dedicated it, by deed, to the county so that it would always be there. Again, I got a chance to be sort of a hero, not only to these residential neighbors, but also to the new Los Alamos County planner, by the name of Pat Brown and his current planning committee.

It was now still quite some time away before any more construction could begin, and I need to bring you up to date with several other things that were going on in our busy, and sometimes hectic, lives.

I had anticipated that my sale of the three acres to Gibson's would cause problems with my relationship with my three partners in the White Rock Shopping Center. They thought that I should have been able to persuade Mr. McAfee to let them and me build their building and rent it to Gibson's Department Store. I told them that I tried to do this, but Gibson's people, McAfee and his two sons-in-law were adamant about never renting their store buildings and that they always bought their land and owned their own buildings. Anyway, my partners decided to file a lawsuit against me saying that I was their realtor and I should not represent anyone else, even myself. Well, this was illegitimate to begin with because a client or partner does not own a real estate broker exclusively. A Realtor can have an exclusive listing with a client, but a client cannot have an exclusive Realtor unless there is a contract as such, which was not the case here. Even though this was illegitimate, I still had to fight it, and it cost me considerable time and money.

Remember I told them when I bid the land in White Rock for the third time that if I got it they would not be involved later and they still refused to join me in the bidding. Therefore, they had no claim except to bitch. I might add that they never consulted me on any of the decisions they made on other things in connection with what they wanted to do that involved the White Rock Shopping Center. So, I made a big decision after the lawsuit to sell my interest and stock in the White Rock Shopping Center, which also included the interest in the motel that we had bought in Santa Rosa and moved to Los Alamos, rebuilt it, and opened it as the Los Alamos Motor Lodge. They showed no interest in buying my stock in both ventures. Fortunately, I found a buyer for the motel right away. His name was Hugh Lehman, a laboratory employee. We had previously built a house for him and his wife. There was a clause in the agreement with my other partners that stated that if either of the three of us decided to sell, that the remaining partners had the right to match any offer that the selling partner received from a new buyer. So I presented my offer from Mr. Lehman, and Waterman, Moore matched it and paid me off.

One day I was on my way to Taos, New Mexico. The highway runs alongside the Rio Grande River and it is a beautiful sight of swift running water. About halfway to Taos there is a small village named Embudo on the east side of the highway running north the same as the river. There is an old one-way tressle bridge crossing the river to the west side of the highway and a beautiful site with large cottonwood trees and an old vacant building in much disrepair. In investigating this I found that many years ago this was a hunting lodge and an old jail for rustlers and outlaws and such and that it was a stopping place for the old abandoned narrow-gauge railroad.

Explaining further, the Santa Fe Railroad (now Amtrak) that runs from Chicago to California, enters New Mexico near Raton and onto Las Vegas, and then on to Albuquerque and California. It was, and is, the only railroad named Santa Fe that does not go to Santa Fe. Strange, but true. It goes through a small town about sixteen miles east of Santa Fe, named Lamy (after Bishop Lamy) — then on to Albuquerque. In the early days the narrow-gauge train ran from Lamy on to Santa Fe and north along the Rio Grande River to Taos. This narrow gauge train would stop at Embudo and the hunting lodge there would furnish rooms, meals, and guides for the hunters and fishermen, gambling facilities and female companionship if they wanted. The young Spanish and Indian girls were available. What a place! The rumor goes that Al Capone visited here regularly, as well as other Chicago gangsters, to cool off, so to speak.

The train would stop at Lamy in the middle of the night and no one would ever know who got off to catch the narrow gauge to the Lodge at the stop at Embudo. Anyway, this had not operated as such for many years, though the setting was still beautiful.

The reason I have just described this location is that there was a For Sale sign on the vacant land adjoining this property at the south side of the end of the bridge across the Rio Grande. It ran about 100 yards deep and about 800 feet of river frontage south along the west side of the Rio Grande River. The For Sale sign on this property had a Los Alamos phone number on it. I made a phone call and talked to a bachelor of around 40-45 years old by the name of Burt Thamer. I made an appointment to go to his house one evening as he worked at the Laboratory in Los Alamos during the day. He explained that his mother had been a real estate investor over the years and had recently passed away and he wanted to sell or trade the property. Well, he said the magic word when he said "trade." I told him I owned a 25% share of the stock in the White Rock Shopping Center and maybe we could make a deal. We talked for a long time. My stock in the center was a lot more valuable than that eight or so acres of river frontage and he didn't want to come up with any more money. He did say, however, he owned an adobe home that he had for sale on Tano Rd. in Santa Fe on the west side of the highway. Anyway, after several sessions of hard trading, we finally agreed that I would come up with some extra cash and trade my stock in the White Rock Shopping Center to him for the eight acres on the Rio Grande and his nice adobe home in Santa Fe. Once again, I separated and terminated my association with vindictive partners and I would be able to make positive decisions without a lot of backbiting and arguments, etc.

Gene Althoff and his crew were about finished with all the block work on Gibson's new store and he told me he was looking over the Dodge report, which is a statewide publication listing all the large construction jobs coming up for bids. He said, "Andy, why don't we bid this big job that is coming up soon in Raton, New Mexico?" He said, "The City of Raton is going to have a building to be leased to a man that will be moving his equipment and machines for the manufacture of tennis shoes from the Navajo reservation to Raton, thereby creating lots of jobs for the people living in Raton. The man's company was Solomon and Son, and he's a large Jewish man."

Gene said, "They will be offering two different types of bids on the building. One for the structure for the concrete and steel building and a separate one for the installation of the heating and cooling of the building." Gene said, "Let's leave the heating and cooling bid alone and bid only the rest of the building." I agreed and Gene and Clark Seay became very busy in preparing our bid.

The architect for the job was a young man from Albuquerque by the name of Crawford. He grew up in Raton and that is probably why he was chosen as architect for this job. When our bid was complete, Gene and I took it to Raton to be presented at the bid opening by the architect and the mayor of Raton, a Mr. Dwayne Legg, and his city council. To our surprise, and great pleasure, our bid was low by only $287. The closest bid to us was a local Raton Construction Company by the name of LaMesa Builders. They would have beaten us, except that at the last few minutes, before the bids were opened, they had forgotten to add in something and they raised their bid $300 to cover this last minute change. What a break for us!

It didn't take long to say our 'thank yous' and 'goodbyes' and have a few drinks at a nearby bar to celebrate, and take our long drive back to Los Alamos. The first one of many as I would be making this drive many times in the near future to bring payroll over and attend various meetings with the city council, etc. I rented a large old house in Raton for Gene and his concrete and labor crews to live in and we went to work. The time is August 1970 and the summer monsoon season begins right now.

For a building as large as this, it was going to have to have some large and deep concrete pours for the base to support the structural steel. The first problem we incurred on this job was when we dug the large holes for the concrete to be poured into, they would be full of water after the night rains. This caused us considerable delay and expense that we had not anticipated. When we finally got this done, we realized the small ready mix plant in Raton was not sufficiently large enough to handle our job, so we leased a portable concrete batch plant to be moved over from Amarillo, Texas. This way we had plenty of concrete when we needed it and in the amount we needed. Gene was smart and innovative.

The building was huge! I don't recall the square footage, but it was larger than the large super WalMart buildings of the present time period. We had ordered our steel building and it arrived on schedule and we hired a steel erection company owned by a man named Dutch Burgdorff of Clayton, Texas, which is near Amarillo. He was a big, strong guy and really knew his business and had a very good crew. A very nice guy and we had no complaints.

One big problem we had in the beginning was with the inspector that the city council had hired to be on the job to inspect the construction. He was ridiculously stopping progress when we were trying to set the forms for the long concrete pours for the perimeter of the building and other concrete forms. He would require them to be re-done if they were even one-quarter of an inch off in a 100 ft. or more form! We finally decided that this was done by him for the purpose of delaying the job and maybe we would throw in the towel. We did some investigating and found that this inspector was the uncle of the man who owned LaMesa Builders, the company that we beat by only $287 under their bid.

This caused one hell of a stink by Gene, Clark Seay, and myself! And we got ourselves another inspector! He was the man that owned the motel where Clark and I stayed when we first came to Raton. He had built his own motel and knew his business — and he knew that Gene knew what he was doing. (By the way, Gene had built steel buildings in Denver for several years before he came to Los Alamos. In fact, Bonnie and I had gone to Denver on a weekend with Gene to look over some of the work he had done there before we decided to make the bid on the Raton building.) Everything went smoothly after that and we were on schedule.

Gene was having lots of problems with his kidneys and left before the job was finished. He drove to Albuquerque and checked into the Veteran's Hospital. I don't know exactly when he left Albuquerque, but he did go back to Colorado where his father lived and I didn't hear anything from him for about ten years. More about this later.

Tim was working with us after finishing a commercial building project he ran at the office complex across from Ashley Pond. He had recently quit selling commercial real estate for Berger Briggs in Albuquerque to work for the family development company again. He also brought a lead carpenter, Don Powers, from Española that had worked on the commercial project and we hired some local laborers.

Tim and his carpenter's crew finished the project tightening the steel beam supports, forming and pouring the concrete loading docks and the long sidewalks that ran the full length of the building. It was so cold when the sidewalk pour was made that they had to build 26 bonfires along the length — on Tim's 26th birthday! — for the concrete to cure properly.

Mr. Solomon and his people were installing their machines that make the tennis shoes, the mechanical contractors were winding up their contract for the heating and cooling and the city fathers were making preparations for the Grand Opening Evening celebration of the various dignitaries. Our own Chamber of Commerce manager and friend from Los Alamos, Peggy Corbett, began to line up some of the state-wide politicians. She worked with the Chamber manager of Raton and they invited Senator Joseph Montoya, Congressman Manuel Lujan, and Governor Bruce King, my friend. All these fellows were up for re-election and election day is only about a week or so away, so they all welcomed the chance to join in on the accomplishment of the mayor and city council, as well as me and our people, for a very good job well done. Pictures were taken of me and the other politicos, as well as newspaper pictures and a story. The banquet was enjoyed by all and the big, yellow steel building is still in full view on your left on the outskirts of Raton, New Mexico off Interstate 25 as you leave Raton up thru Raton Pass and on the way to Colorado.

The Raton Building was finished and the City of Raton had held back $3,000 of our final payment for two months after completion to cover any problems they might have with roof leaks, etc. When the time period had passed with no problems, Clark Seay and I drove over to Raton to pick up the $3,000 retainer from the Raton city finance manager. He was a short gray-haired man around 50 or 55 years old with a crew-cut hairstyle and he had moved from Boston, Massachusetts and taken this job. He signed all the checks, so we went into his office, which adjoined the city fire department. I had met him before so he knew who we were.

He said, "What brings you fellows to town?" I said, "We are here to pick up the $3,000 retainer you still owe us. Since there were no problems at all, we would like to have our check."

Well, he scratched his chin, and head and said, "Men, we are going to have to extend the time on your retainer for 60 days more." I said, "No, that was not the deal. We had the building erector, Mr. Burgdorff, go over the roof himself personally, and there were no problems and there has not been any since as we checked with Mr. Solomon just a few minutes ago before we came in to pick up our check."

"Well, we are going to hold it for another 60 days anyway." he said.

I then said, "Mr., you are putting your spurs pretty deep in this old boy and you are in trouble." At that moment I got out of my chair and grabbed the front bottom of his desk, picked it up and tipped it up, pinning him between it and the wall behind him. With this happening, he quickly said, "Okay, I'll write your check." I said, "You are making the correct decision. Thank you for your generous courtesy and fuck you very much." This easterner from Boston must have thought all these people out here in the west were a bunch of hay seeds or something, but he found out this is not true with all of us. Old Clark Seay's eyes were as wide as saucers and we laughed about this from time to time.

Old Andy Long was staying busy with other things while the Raton building was being built. Bonnie and the Andy Long Realty sales crew were still doing a first-class job and business was very good, and we were very busy with several different things in our lives.

The election for Governor Bruce King's second two-year term was not over (they later changed this to four years, but presently it was a two-year term and the right to run for a second two-year term). He was running against a young Republican lawyer from Albuquerque named Pete Domenici. The Chamber of Commerce had decided to have a meeting in Clovis, New Mexico for all the state-wide chamber secretaries (the managers as they were called then). The Chamber president of Clovis was in charge of the meeting in Clovis and they were preparing a luncheon banquet for all the Chamber presidents and secretaries to attend, to be held at the Clovis Holiday Inn. The two gubernatorial candidates were to speak at the luncheon.

I was president of our Los Alamos Chamber of Commerce and Peggy, our secretary, and her right-hand assistant, Marilyn Bond, all drove over to attend this meeting. Of course, this was the last week or two before the election, and both candidates were coming down the stretch "neck-and-neck." I had been campaigning for Bruce in Raton, as well as Los Alamos, all the time that we had been building in Raton. I had put the arm on the local building supply owner as well as Solomon, who was the big tenant in the tennis shoe factory. I had gotten $500 from each of them and had given it to Bruce one evening when he held a campaign rally in Raton at the local courthouse. He was so grateful for my work and our friendship.

Anyway, all the presidents and managers there had held a meeting that morning before the luncheon. They were interested in finding out the best they could which one of the two candidates for governor was interested in economic development for the state and what kind of person they would choose to become head of the state economic development department, regardless of which political party the best person belonged to — and which one would be best to hold the job as head of the Department of Development. In other words, taking politics completely out of the picture.

We all had decided that we would pose this question to each candidate and whichever one said that he would indeed choose the best man for the job, regardless of his personal politics would be the man they would support. And with this information all statewide Chambers of Commerce presidents and managers would go back to their own towns all over the state and spread the word which candidate would be the best to elect for the economic development of their towns and state.

The stage was set. I happened to know that Bruce would be arriving by plane for the luncheon. I stationed myself outside so that when the car that had picked him up at the airport arrived at the motel, I would catch him. I said, "Bruce, I have something very interesting to tell you. How would you like to hit a grand slam home-run, cowboy, " as I called him in those days.

He responded, "What do I have to do?" I then explained in detail what all of these Chamber of Commerce people had decided at our meeting that morning and I told him that he and Pete would be asked the big question which I described.

I said, "Don't hesitate. Be sure you are first on your feet to answer their question with what they want to hear. If I read this right, Pete will have to take the opposing position and probably say that the job of economic development chief should be at the direction of the Governor."

Bruce and Pete each gave short speeches at the luncheon and then we all retired to the meeting room that had been set up in order to pose the big question about how they would handle this department if they were elected. I positioned myself directly behind Bruce King and the Clovis Chamber President started the meeting. It didn't take long until he laid the big question on the two candidates. The second he finished his question, I jabbed Bruce in the back and he jumped to his feet and used a quote from our past president, J. F. Kennedy, saying "I would like to say this about that." He said exactly what they wanted to hear.

Bruce was fully prepared because of my information to him and it had caught Pete Dominici totally by surprise. He did take the opposing position on this as I thought he would, but the state-wide Chamber membership at the meeting had already heard what they wanted to hear. Each and every one went back to their local newspapers and spread the latest new political information that they had heard. Shortly afterward, Bruce King was elected for his second term as Governor of the State of New Mexico.

Within a few days I received a letter from Bruce King which said among other things, "Andy, I could not have done it without you." He didn't go into any details, which was wise, I think. Our friendship became even closer than it had been, and his office was open and available to me anytime I wanted to call him or to go in for a visit, business or otherwise. I had met the gal that became his receptionist and right hand for him during the campaigns, so all I had to say when I called or dropped by the capital was, "Emelda, I need to talk to the man" or "I need to see the man." She was the girlfriend of the man who was the strongest political force in Rio Arriba County in those days, Emelio Naranjo.

I had never asked Bruce for anything or any favors, but one day shortly after the election I saw his right-hand gal, Emelda Salazar, in a restaurant in Santa Fe. She said, "Andy, Bruce wants you to send us a resume of your real estate and building career."

I said, "What is this for?"

Emelda said, "He is thinking of appointing you to the New Mexico Real Estate Commission."

I said, "This is news to me — I'll get it to you right away." The Real Estate Commission consists of a five member board, appointed by the Governor of the state, to run for five years each. Their terms of office are staggered in order that there is only one new member each year. They change each time the Governor is elected from Democrat to Republican, and so on. It's a "thankless" job, but I enjoyed it very much as I served with some very good people and became good friends with all of them and we grew very close. The five members were located throughout the state so all areas can be assured of equal representation. We hired an executive secretary who managed the office and hired the people who worked in the office in Albuquerque.

We all met once a month for our meetings, most of which were held in Albuquerque because of the greater number of real estate people being located there. Once in a while we would go to other towns, especially if we had a public hearing involving irregularities with the actions of some salesmen or broker, who might, or might not, be in trouble.

Each state has a five member board such as ours that has a national meeting once a year and sometimes a district meeting once or twice a year that might involve changes in the law or other news that effects the real estate trade.

I not only served the five year term, but later when Jerry Apodoca was elected Governor, he appointed me to a second five-year term. I attended lots of national meetings over the ten years, speaking at a few of them occasionally. For example, I attended national meetings in Miami, New Orleans, Milwaukee, Washington D. C., Duluth and others. We usually went in pairs, so that all of us didn't have to go each time there was a national convention. My stature in the business grew considerably, to say the least!

There were over 4,000 real estate licensees throughout the State of New Mexico and we had a monthly publication sent to each licensee to inform them of what was going on in the business state-wide, and of new laws and changes that were occurring as well as the results of any hearings we had that involved revoking any of the licensees licenses or any admonishments for a lesser penalty, etc. All of our pictures were in the monthly publications, prepared by the Albuquerque staff. So, I became very well known over the years I served. The Chairman of the five-member board was elected each year by the five members and it usually rotated so as to give each member his turn at the wheel. I served as chairman twice, once at each five year term.

During this time period, I served as president of the tri-county Realtor board, consisting of Rio Arriba, Santa Fe, and Los Alamos counties. We only had enough Realtors for one board and called it the Santa Fe Board of Realtors. I was also elected by this tri-county board for the cherished award of Realtor of the Year in 1974. I was also elected to the board of directors of the New Mexico State Board of Realtors and served one year as vice president of that association. We would hold a state-wide convention each year and elect officers for the coming year. This is separate from the New Mexico Real Estate Commission board of commissioners. I was due to become the president of the New Mexico Realtor's Association the year following my term as vice president, but I turned it down as it was going to be during the same year I was to serve as president and chairman of the Real Estate Commission. I knew I couldn't handle both jobs at the same time for an entire year and still run a successful business without going broke. My plate was full and "running over" so to speak. Time after time many of the important Realtors around the state asked me to please reconsider being their new president, but I "stuck to my guns" on this matter as one of my friends, Reyes Padilla of Santa Fe, held both jobs the same year and damn near lost his business. Both jobs required a lot of meetings state-wide and a lot of travel time away from the office, constant phone calls and correspondence, etc., as well as handling lots of problems.

Anyway, one reason they wanted me to head up the New Mexico Realtors presidency was that the first woman to run for the office was right behind me in line for the job — and they couldn't get used to a woman serving as president. But Jean Beetcher from Albuquerque did become the president and did a very good job. She was a selling broker working for Sam Brown Realty in Albuquerque. Sam was a very well-known broker and sold a lot of large properties and a lot of ranches. He was licensed in several states — New Mexico, Arizona, Colorado, Wyoming and Texas. He had an airplane that held five passengers besides himself and he was also liaison officer for the New Mexico State Realtors Association and he would attend all the Real Estate Commission meetings and cover them and report to the Realtors what was going on currently such as new laws we were working on that were important to the Realtors membership. Often when the R.E. Commission had a meeting a long distance from Albuquerque, he would fly us to the out-of-town meetings. Sometime we would fly in the New Mexico State plane if it wasn't busy. For example, Hobbs, New Mexico is a hell of a long way to drive for a meeting, so this helped a lot. Sam was a good guy and a very good friend of mine for years. He gave me a lot of good advice, as he did to lots of other young Realtors.

When the Hot Air Balloon Festival first got started in Albuquerque, Jean Beetcher was the one that got it started and remained the head of it for many, many years and was and is still known for her hard work in making it the success it is today. She made the State Realtors Association a very good president that year and opened it up to several other women to be president in the years to follow.

Meanwhile, Tim and his wife, Juanita, had decided to get a divorce. Tim and Juanita just couldn't get along. It was like trying to mix oil and water. It just wouldn't work and they both realized it. She was living in Albuquerque with the twin girls and since we had all the visiting rights we wanted, we drove to Albuquerque each Friday evening, 93 miles, and kept the girls each and every weekend. Juanita didn't mind this as it gave her a chance to be away from them on weekends. We had a good working relationship with Juanita and this was good for all concerned. Once in a while she would meet us in Santa Fe, so this cut the driving time in half. The girls loved to come to Grandma and Grandpa's house as we enjoyed them so much, especially when we would take them in the car and to restaurants. Juanita married again to Danny Valdez. This marriage lasted only a year or two, and they divorced. Danny was not good to the girls and mistreated Juanita, so we were happy when they divorced.

The girls were not identical twins —they were opposites but both smart as a whip. This was not only in looks, but in every way. When Bonnie would take them shopping at the grocery store, Kathy would grab things and put them in the grocery cart and Taña would grab them and put them back on the shelf. When they had little candies, Kathy would eat hers right away, but Taña would eat a little of hers and hide some in the back door ash trays of the car so she would have some later on. She reminded me so much of Bonnie that I called her my "little Bonnie." She would laugh at this — she loved her grandmother so much, as did Kathy.

They had twin beds in the bedroom, but some time during the night they would get out of their beds and come and get in bed with us. Every morning they were in between Bonnie and me in our big, king-sized bed. We enjoyed those girls so much it is hard to describe.

For Christmas we would get in my little red Jeep that I used for hunting and we would go up into the nearby mountains and cut us a large Christmas tree — and we had a great time decorating it together. Christmas was very big at our house, with lots of presents for everyone. All kinds of toys and dolls, tricycles, and later bicycles, and skis. I bought Bonnie a Mercedes Coupe the Christmas of 1971. Candy Apple Red with black leather upholstery. It had a removable hard-top as well as a regular convertible top and Bonnie really enjoyed this little car. She could really wheel it, and the twins had fun when she had them with her. It had a small area just behind the seats in front and one could ride there and one in the front passenger seat. So they would fight and fuss over who would get to ride "shotgun" as they called it.

That same year I bought Juanita a little blue Volkswagen (before they divorced) for Christmas. Tim and Andra each had their own cars. Andra's was a little Carmen Ghia, a cute little Italian sports car and she loved it also. No shortage of cars around our place in those days. I always drove a Lincoln Towncar and, of course, I had a pickup with a camper shell for hunting and camping. I hitched the Jeep up behind it when camping overnight in the mountains. This old country boy had come a long way from the farm boy he once was before he joined the Merchant Marine to see the world!

Our wonderful little twin granddaughters came to live with us in the summer after they got out of the 2nd grade. They stayed with us that summer and all during their 3rd grade and the summer before they started into the 4th grade. They would catch the school bus right at our driveway.

The barn we built at our home had two horse stalls, so we bought two little black Shetland ponies with bridles and saddles for Taña and Kathy, and they named them Mr. and Mrs. Blackie. They loved these ponies and took care of them pretty well, keeping them fed, watered and hayed every day.

It got cold during the winter in White Rock and Los Alamos, so I had a freeze-proof water faucet installed near the barn, so it was easy to keep them watered and we had plenty of room for hay storage. When the snow got one or two feet deep occasionally, they would say to me, "Would you feed and water the ponies for us Gramps, the snow is too deep for us to walk out to the barn," and, of course, I would. Otherwise, they took care of their ponies themselves.

Everyone in Pajarito Acres owned three to five acres, so the houses were not too close together, but close enough so the kids could visit with their friends. The Stafford family lived across the cedar rail fence that we had built around our place. The Stafford's had three little boys, two of which were about the girl's age. They all enjoyed playing with the ponies and were great friends.

Our daughter, Andra, was about twenty-five when the girls were in 3rd grade, and they loved their "Auntie" and she loved them.

Chapter Six

J and L Products

Taña, Katae and Tim

ONE DAY IN 1970 A fellow came into my office to see me. His name was Reggie Jones, a man around fifty or fifty-five years old and a pleasant little guy. He was a Laboratory employee in the capacity of an inventor, as well as a very good mechanical draftsman. He could invent things and also make detailed drawings of his inventions so they could be manufactured. He said, "Andy, I have a lot of ideas that I would like you to look at, and I have the drawings with me."

I said, "Reggie, why do you want me to look at them?"

He said, "I need your financial backing in promoting them if you see something that you think would sell. We could become partners, get the patents and make a lot of money. I have watched your success in business here for the last several years and am convinced you are an honest, hard-working guy and I would like for you to become my partner." He aroused my curiosity and I asked him what was his favorite — that in his opinion would be the best one to start on. He said, "It's an educational toy that can teach children to spell and read. The reason kids can't read is they can't spell."

I said, "Yes, you're right, Reggie. What would you call it?"

"Spin and Spell," he said.

"Have you got a drawing with you?"

"Yes, I have." Well, it consisted of a frame with twenty-six discs about five or six inches in diameter and about one-half inch wide. The discs each had all twenty-six letters in the alphabet and numbers 0 to 9 all the way around the edges of the discs, in little raised letters. A bar across the top displayed the word a child would spell. (Tim later designed a slit in it to hold flash cards with an animal's picture on it, like a cat, dog, horse, etc., with the spelling of the name right below the picture on the card.)

I said, "Wow! Reggie, if you have time to go with me to see my lawyer we will talk about forming a partnership and a corporation. How would you like the name of the corporation to be "J. & L. Products, Inc.?" At the direction of my attorney, Harry Moore, we also made an appointment to see a patent attorney that worked at the Los Alamos Scientific Laboratory to help us get our product patented without the Lab being involved.

This visit was taken care of a few days later and he assured us the Laboratory would not have to be involved. This was good to know since Reggie was an employee of the Lab and we didn't want this to be a problem to us in the future. The patent attorney said that as soon as we got a working model he would begin his patent search on his moonlighting time and there would be no Lab involvement. Plastic was to be the material and there was a company in Albuquerque that did injection molding so we went to see them with Reggie's drawings. My son, Tim, went with us as he was very involved in the development of this educational toy called Spin & Spell. Well, it took quite a bit of money just to get the tools and dies made to be used to produce the necessary parts for this thing. As I remember the up-front cost for the dies was $4,500. This was quite a bit of money in 1970! But it had a lot of promise, so we put up the cash and work began. Finally, we had produced a working model and the patent pending work began with more legal expenses.

Tim became an important part of our team designing a full-color 8 1/2" x 11" multiple page promotional brochure with his twins' picture on the front as well as an instruction booklet. In January 1971 we were ready for Reggie, Bonnie and I to take our new educational toy to the International Toy Show at the New York Hilton Hotel in New York City. Plane tickets, hotel and travel expenses for the three of us were provided by ol' Andy Long and we were under way. Of course, I had been in New York City many times years ago when my home port was there. It had changed some in the last twenty-five years, but not really that much. It was quite an experience for the three of us to go to the big city!

The International Toy Show is held in NYC once a year and you can't imagine how big it is, how many toys and how many different countries are represented! Ours was well-received and the only thing like it there. The Japanese and Chinese folks with their cameras were taking pictures of everything at the show. This was Bonnie's and Reggie's first trip to New York City so we all took in the sites. Bonnie and I would go, then Reggie by himself most of the time as someone always had to man our booth. We visited the Empire State Building, Statue of Liberty, Times Square, etc.

My friend Roy Walker from New Mexico was living there at the time. Roy had been the State Director of the Federal Housing Administration (FHA) up until the election of Richard Nixon in 1968, the year I had run for State Representative and lost and Bruce King was first elected as Governor of NM. Well, when Nixon was elected, the Republican administration decided that they wanted a Republican to be the director of the New Mexico FHA in Albuquerque, so they gave Roy Walker his choice of either quitting and losing his retirement or accepting a job with the FHA in New York City. They thought old Roy would quit, but he was hard-headed enough to take the transfer to New York so he could have his retirement pension in just a few more years. I had gotten pretty well acquainted with Roy when we were building FHA houses in White Rock so when we got to New York I called him and told him we were in town and he was so glad to hear from a friend from New Mexico! He and his wife invited us to go to dinner with them. He took us to a famous Italian restaurant in Times Square by the name of Mama Leone's. We had a great visit with interesting stories of his experiences in New York. For one thing, he said the building projects went on twenty-four hours a day. He said if they shut down at night they would be stolen blind by the next morning! He also took us to their apartment right in the heart of the city. He longed for the day that he could finally retire and he eventually did, to his home in Clovis, New Mexico where he had spent most of his life before going to Albuquerque in the 1960's. We were having a wonderful time and were very much excited about our chances of being able to make some kind of deal with someone on Spin and Spell.

Back in Los Alamos, New Mexico, Marion Perkins, Chester Kazek, Sr. and Clark Seay were holding the fort down at Andy Long Realty Company. We got some terrible news one morning that Marion's husband, Ralph Perkins, whom we knew very well, had committed suicide. It was totally unexpected by everyone, so there was nothing to do but to get the first flight home and close our booth at the International Toy Show. It was about half over — we had expected to stay in New York for the whole week. Anyway, we flew back to Albuquerque and just in time to get to Ralph's funeral. What a sad thing that was! They had two young daughters that were in junior high school.

Ralph was a group leader in one of the weapon's departments that was to be revamped to make some big changes in their method of designing, and it was going to be necessary for Ralph to go to California back to school for some new training for a couple of years. Marion was very adamant about not leaving Los Alamos and their family was pretty upset over the fact of him having to leave town. Apparently, it couldn't be avoided and Ralph was in great distress over it. He went to the local shooting range where everyone that hunted practiced shooting and during his noon hour shot himself then and there. The awful part of all this was that during the noon hour where he worked, his boss had taken him a letter and left it on his desk. They had found another job that he would be able to transfer to so that he would not have to go to California after all. So sad.

We all were very sad for Marion and pitched in and helped in every way we could. She had been with Andy Long Realty since 1965, just about six years, and had become an excellent real estate sales gal. Their family and ours had been very close for several years and had spent lots of good times at each other's homes as well as on various real estate meetings out of town and out of state.

Bonnie and I had made lots of trips to California to visit our good friends from the old White Rock days, Chuck and Pat Coutts, who still lived in Malibu, California. We decided to take a long weekend trip in February or March of 1971. Chuck was in a motorcycle race while we were there and we went with them to watch The race was at a track named Bay Mare north of Los Angeles and they all were racing these big dirt bikes up and down these big humps and mounds. Wild as the wind and dangerous — and Chuck Coutts fit right into this mold. He was good and he really enjoyed it as well as his two sons who were teenagers. The boys were not old enough to race but they loved to go and help their dad and cheer him on, as well as Pat. After the race we all went out (the adults that is) eating, dancing and Chuck and I drinking and had a wild time. It had been quite a while since we had seen them and we were all enjoying each other.

Well, the next morning Chuck and I were pretty hung over, so he had a big wash tub filled with ice and dumped a case of the little cans of Coors beer in the iced tub and we all laid around the side of their swimming pool in their beautiful back yard. Big sycamore trees made it look like a picture post card. Well, about 3:00 PM we were feeling no pain, being sufficiently full of Coors beer. Chuck decided that he should teach me to ride his big dirt bike, so I get on behind him and we ride around the block a couple of times while he instructed me what to do.

He said, "Now, you take it around by yourself. Okay, I'll start it and you get on but don't pop the clutch when you take off."

I said, "Hell, I'm not going to pop the clutch. I've been around the block twice. I'm an expert." Well, I revved it up and promptly popped the clutch and the bike reared up on it's back wheel and down we went with me still holding the throttle open, not having the good sense to turn it off, and the bike had me down spinning around on the ground. Well, Chuck finally got it shut off and my left leg was pretty tore up. My left tennis shoe was torn up and my leg badly bruised but not much blood, so there was no panic about getting any medical treatment and so on.

Well, Monday morning saw us back on a jet plane for Albuquerque and on home to Los Alamos. My leg was very sore but no indication that it was going to be any serious injury. Well, I hobbled around and went to work as usual for the rest of the week and week-end.

Monday morning I woke up in such pain with my left leg, I could not touch it to the floor sitting on the edge of the bed. I managed to hobble into the bathroom, draw a big tub full of water, get in the tub and started massaging my leg. Well, it continued to swell and I told Bonnie that I was not going into work that day and that I would just sit there in my big lounge chair with my legs up and use the telephone. I expected a land man with the Phillips Petroleum Co. to meet me at 10:00 AM this morning to look at a site for a Phillips service station location that I was to show him on the corner of Sherwood Blvd. and State Road #4.

I told Bonnie I was not going to miss selling this site next door to the Gibsons store and would be able to show him the location I had previously told him about and I had made the appointment for him to come up today. Well, Bonnie said, "Okay. I'm going in a little early today as I have an appointment to have May Ann fix my hair." She was one of our tenants in the building at Trinity Square in Los Alamos. Well, it wasn't long until I got a phone call from Bonnie that May Ann had told her that I surely had a blood clot in that leg as she had had a similar experience and she told Bonnie to get me to a doctor as soon as she could or it could kill me. Then Bonnie said, "I'm coming straight home."

I said, "I'm not going to see a doctor until the Phillips man leaves here. I want to sell them this corner." She got back to our house and the phone rang again and it was the Phillips man calling. He was very apologetic that he would have to postpone his appointment with me for this morning and would reschedule it later.

Well, my left leg was hurting real bad by now so I placed a call to my doctor at the Loveless clinic and hospital in Albuquerque and told him what had happened and the condition of my leg. I had been going to Dr. Charlie Weed for a couple of years now and we had become friends. Mostly for the purpose of physical exams for insurance companies. Each time I would make an extra large loan at the bank, they would require that I buy life insurance coverage in the amount of the loan in favor of the bank. They would always say, "Andy, we know you will repay it okay if you live, but we don't know if we would get the loan paid if you die. So, get us a life insurance policy and we will make you another big loan." That made sense to me, so I had no objection.

Anyway Charlie listened to my story and said "Get down here just as soon as you can. I will stay here over my lunch hour as it will be noon before you can make it, and we will meet you at the side door with a wheel chair."

I said, "We're on our way." Well, old Bonnie really put her foot in the carburetor on the T-bird we were driving at the time, and with me in the back seat with my left leg stretched out on a pillow with the arm rests turned down between the front seats for my left leg to stretch out on, we headed down the mountain to Santa Fe. And when we left Santa Fe, on the flat stretch to Albuquerque, she really opened it up. She would be hitting 90 miles per hour, and I would say, "Slow this thing down," and the leg would start hurting again and I'd say, "Bonnie, kick this thing in the ass and let's go," so back to 90 miles per hour again. We made the fastest trip to Albuquerque we had ever made —130 miles in one hour and 15 minutes. Whew!!

When we arrived, the wheel chair was waiting and just inside the large lobby was one of these one-man flat tables with wheels and I got on it and laid down. Charlie was there with two other doctors and a nurse with her blood pressure machine. One of the other doctors was a heart specialist and the other a surgeon. The nurse was standing just behind my stretcher on wheels and she was taking my blood pressure. Charlie Weed was standing at the other end of my stretcher talking to me and looking at the nurse and me. When she said to me, "What are you doing, trying to have a heart attack on me?" At that instant I saw Charlie look at her like he was mad as hell and shaking his head at her to shut up.

I think this is when it began to soak in to me that I am in plenty damn bad shape. Well, Charlie and the other two doctors were huddling over in the corner of this big lobby room out of ear shot of me and after a few minutes Charlie came over to me and said, "Andy, we think you are going to have to have that leg amputated."

I said, "Hell no, I'm not going to have my leg cut off and be a cripple the rest of my life, Charlie."

He said, "If we don't operate you may die."

I said, "Doc, I will just have to die. I'm not going to be a one-legged man. Forget the amputation. Let's try something else."

He said, "Okay, we will try the only other thing we can do and that is take you up stairs to your room and start a strong intravenous blood thinner called cumodun and try and save your life and leg."

I said, "Okay." Well, in a little while I was hooked up to a bottle of this blood thinner on a tripod with a permanent needle in my wrist. They also started me on some blood thinner pills, and got me hooked up to a catheter so I wouldn't have to move, and told me to stay as motionless as possible. I got excellent care and they kept me doped up so I wasn't in much pain, thank goodness, and checked on me through the day and that night. I think they were all surprised that I was still alive by morning.

I realized I was in a double room and my room-mate was a younger guy than me. I'd say around 30 years old by the name of Pete Brady. He was a forest ranger that lived in Sacramento, N.M. near Cloudcroft. He had just had an operation for hemorrhoids. I understand this is a very painful operation and he was in great pain. Neither of us felt like talking for a couple of days. Before it was time for another pain shot, the pain was so bad he was really hurting. Well, he suffered pretty badly and he was a big strong guy. By this time, word had got out about how seriously hurt I was and lots of Los Alamos and White Rock folks sent flowers to my room. A lot of them thought old Andy was going to croak. It was touch-and-go but I was thinking I was just too damn young to die. I was only 47 years old, and right in my natural prime, so to speak.

Both Pete and I were doped up half out of our minds and we got to putting two and two together and getting 6 or 7 instead of 4. I said, "I think these orderlies and maybe a nurse or two are in some sort of dope ring and are substituting your pain shots with water and probably selling the dope shots they should be giving you." He was doped up enough that this sounded logical to him.

He asked, "What can we do?"

I said, "I have an idea. You see all those flower vases and pots on that window ledge on the other side of your bed?"

He said, "Yeah."

I said," You get hold of that drapery cord and flip it until you get it behind all of the flower pots and vases. I will take this stainless steel pitcher that my water is in and when I count three you pull that drapery cord behind those pots and I'll throw this pitcher through the picture tube of that television set on the wall. We'll shake this place up and we'll find out what they are doing with the pain shots you are supposed to be getting."

Pete said, "Good idea." Well we got everything set and I started counting.

I said, "One, two..."

About this time the door to the hall opened and the big old gal that was superintendent of nurses asked, "What is going on here?" She was close to 6 foot tall and weighed at least 230 pounds. She was Italian and with black hair and dark hair on her upper lip similar to a mustache. She stood at the foot of my bed with her hands on her hips and asked "What's gotten into you guys?"

I said "It was time we shook you folks up around here. My partner is suffering so much that we figure someone is selling the dope he is supposed to be getting and he is not getting it."

She said, "That is crazy and certainly not true and I'll look into how much pain killer he is supposed to be getting." Well, in about 30 minutes they wheeled in one of those one-man tables with wheels and wheeled me out and, I asked, "Where are we going?" She said, "We have a nice private room for you up on the next floor."

Well, I did rest much easier because Pete's moaning and groaning was not good for me in my condition. So, it worked out okay. After this the big old superintendent of nurses and I became friends and indeed she was Italian and had been raised in Raton, N.M. There is quite a lot of coal mining going on in Raton and her Dad worked in the coal mines there. On further up country, in Trinidad, Colorado, there was also a lot of coal mining going on there for many years, and they have always had a heavy population of Italians. It was reputed that there were quite a lot of mafia types there — and perhaps still are. Anyway, the big old head of nurses and I got along real good during the long stay I had at Loveless Hospital.

I had a telephone in my room and I treated my room just like it was my office and made and received many, many phone calls. I was there for a month. My bed would crank up to about any position and they did their best to make me comfortable. I still had this blood thinner tube in my arm. I had to lay on my back, not on my sides or stomach and they would wrap my leg with wet towels and put heating pads around it, then put a large plastic bag around my complete leg to keep the moisture off the bedding.

In order to keep myself occupied, I had my draftsman and artist, Joe Duben, who I mentioned earlier, come to my room as he was now living in Albuquerque and was working in a building just down the street from my hospital.

Behind the two office buildings we had built at Trinity Square before Gene Altoff went to Raton to build the large building for the tennis shoe factory (Gene was no longer with us and had moved back to Colorado about a year ago), I still had enough land to build three more office buildings that had an unobstructed view of the Sangre de Cristo mountains to the East around Santa Fe. They were majestic mountains and snow-capped a good part of the time. The location was excellent with plenty of parking and with good access off Trinity Drive. They would back up to the long row of two story motel rooms at the Los Alamos Inn.

I had Joe design the most beautiful three office buildings anywhere. They were end-to-end and extended south clear to the canyon rim. We set railroad ties as posts about 30 inches tall and ran heavy cable through them to make sure no cars would wind up in the canyon. Each of the three buildings were about 30 to 40 feet wide with two of them having a breeze-way in between them for a shaded patio and each had about six different office spaces. The Los Alamos Laboratory quickly leased these two buildings. The other one had 4 offices and my lawyer took one of them for his office and one for his wife, Kaye to open a gift shop in. Then the E.G.& G. corporation, a scientific sub-contractor for the Los Alamos Laboratory took one and a promising young dentist took the other one on the end. There was no problem at all getting them leased after they were almost completed.

The construction was white concrete slump block (sometimes called mission stone) — a very attractive block material — and each office had half round arching, very large windows on the front walls running from the floor to almost ceiling high. Very, very attractive. The buildings all had mansard roof decorations out of red half-round clay tiles. Nothing had been built in Los Alamos that was as attractive as these offices. Joe Duben made numerous trips up to my room in the hospital so we could get the drawings just right, and we did.

I had been in Loveless Hospital for a month or so and it had finally got to the point that I was about to see if this treatment was a success or not. One day Charlie Weed and the heart doctor came in to tell me they were going to insert some blue dye in my veins and then x-ray me to see if there was any blockage of any consequence. I don't remember the details of the results of this except in a day or two the doctors came back into my room together. Charlie had been checking on me every day that I had been there. Anyway, they said, "Today is the real test day. We want you to raise up and put your feet over the edge of the bed and try and walk about 4 or 5 feet to the bathroom."

This was the first time I had been on my feet in the month I had been there. Well, I did it, though it was very difficult to just stand up, let alone walk with one of them on each side of me. I slowly made it to the bathroom door. Well, it was jubilation time and the doctors and nurse cheered.

I said, "Why all the cheering?"

They said, "Andy, this was the supreme test. When you put your feet over the bed and put your weight on them, you were either going to die or live. We did not want to tell you this until we actually had you do it because it could have been all over in a flash and we didn't want you to know that it might happen."

I said, "Well, folks, congratulations are in order." For the next week I was told to walk up and down the hall of the hospital. I did this, but I overdid it, just like I do everything else in my life.

After I had been there for a total of six weeks, it was time to go home. All the time I had been in the hospital my good wife, Bonnie, would drive down to Albuquerque after working all day. She would drive down from Los Alamos every two or three evenings, then drive home again. The twin granddaughters were about four years old then and were living in Albuquerque, and Bonnie would bring them to see grandpa quite often.

Of course, Tim and Andra also visited me frequently — since they were both living in Albuquerque attending UNM — as well as several of our dear friends. They were all glad old Andy had cheated death one more time. Neither them nor I realized that this was the 14th time I had a near-death experience, as I had mentioned much earlier in these writings. When the doctor released me to go home, he said "Andy you won't be able to use your left leg to push in the clutch on your jeep and camper pickup to shift gears. You will have to use only an automatic shift car."

So I sold my pick-up and gave the jeep to my son, Tim. The doctor also told me to use crutches to do most of my walking for quite a while. He said, "I want you to get a one-legged Jobst elastic stocking for that left leg. It will be for the left leg only, but will extend up above your waist." To watch me get into this thing was like watching Red Skelton put on his act when he would pretend he was a fat woman putting on her girdle.

The doctor said, "Andy you are going to be retired now. No more work."

I said, "Hell, Doc, I can't quit. I'm only 47 years old and have a business to run."

He said, "Well, work only half days."

I said, "I'm in the real estate business — that is impossible. One person may want to see a house or property in the morning and another person may want to see one in the afternoon or night. I know, I'll have to cut back a great deal, so I will just have to work it out."

This was something I had not thought about, so, while I was recuperating at home I decided to put a new lawn in the back yard. I had my right hand man, Pete Chavez come down and roto-till and plant the new lawn. Our family room was just inside the large sliding door inside from the patio so every few hours or so I would get up on my crutches and move the water sprinkler around. This gave me the time I needed to plan how I could change my work style to accommodate my new problems.

I decided it was now time to think about getting started on the new office building that Joe Duben had designed for me. Let me digress somewhat at this point and tell you what I had done during the time period after we finished the Raton building and before the motor cycle accident.

310

Up to that point I had had to depend on a superintendent that had a N.M. State contractors license to handle our construction jobs, like Dan Webb and Gene Altoff. I was at the mercy of this situation so I arranged to take the commercial contractors exam which was much more difficult that just a residential license for housing. I happened to know the man that was in charge of giving the written examinations and issuing the licenses for the State of New Mexico. Some ten years before, he worked for the Noxon Construction Company when they were building the first homes in White Rock in 1961, when I was sales manager for the Noxon Company.

Well, I went to the State Contractors License Board office in Santa Fe and was surprised to see my old acquaintance Bob Bornstein was in charge. I told him I wanted to get a commercial contractors license myself so I wouldn't have to depend on someone else just because they had a license. He said, "Andy, that's what you need to do. I'll give you some books to study and some old examination tests with the answers. Go somewhere you can have some peace and quiet and cram for 3 or 4 days, then come in and take the exam and I'll bet you will pass it."

I said, "This sounds good, Bob. Give me the books and papers I need to study and I'll see you in a few days." Well, it so happened that I needed to go to Ruidoso, N.M. to look at a piece of land that Clark Seay and I had seen before and we thought this would be the perfect location to build a Holiday Inn Motel and lease it to the Holiday Inn Company. The land was located right in the heart of Ruidoso on the one main street that runs about one and a half miles long with shops, restaurants, and businesses on both sides of the street. It was a good size piece of property scattered with large pine trees and it was called the Tall Pine Lodge. The small structures on it were pretty dilapidated and in disrepair. So, I decided to have the property appraised while I was there and to see if it would be suitable for a Holiday Inn location.

I packed my suitcase with four days of clothes and headed to Ruidoso. I checked into a motel that had a restaurant in it and started studying. I would set the alarm for 6:00 AM, study until around 9:00 AM, go to breakfast while the maid would make up my room, then I would study until lunchtime, eat lunch, then come back to the room after lunch and study until supper time, then knock off for the day. This went on for four days and I was crammed full of instant knowledge on construction, and what I had already learned in the contracting business. I passed with flying colors.

The land I was looking at for a motel site was not located where it could tie onto the Ruidoso sewer system and was not enough land to build a septic system that would handle the amount of sewage that the motel would generate. This was probably why the land had not been developed already. But, I tried! This all happened before I had the accident on Chuck Coutts motor cycle so it was probably a blessing that I didn't start a motel project in Ruidoso, N.M.

During my stay in the hospital, I had planned the new office complex so this fit right into my plans and I just wasn't up to starting another big job two or three hundred miles from my home base.

I had also leased a large piece of land from some real estate friends in Ruidoso. Their names were Ruben and Betty Larson. I leased it for 99 years and planned on building a lot of condominiums. The land was a large apple orchard and most of the apple trees could be saved and would have a beautiful natural setting for a large condo project. It was located on Highway 70 and fairly near the Ruidoso Downs race track.

Again, the accident on that damn motorcycle blew this deal up too. It was a long way from my home base, so while I was holed up in Ruidoso studying for my contractors license, I called another good friend of mine who was a big Realtor and builder there and I showed Jim Wimberley the land and he was happy to assume my lease on this 20 acre apple orchard. He didn't build condos on it, he built a large mobile home park leaving the apple trees. It was a natural and turned out great. He ran it for a number of years and finally sold it to Johnny Carson, the late night show comedian.

My plate was pretty full anyway with Andy Long Realty going great — and the 23 acres of commercial land in White Rock that I had acquired and needed to get started on. Well, if I had tried to build a motel or a big condo project in Ruidoso, my plate would surely have run over. It was a blessing that these two out-of-town projects did not pan out. I surely would have been spread too thin. In my present physical condition and the doctor telling me to work only half days, the office project I had planned in the hospital was just about the right size I needed to keep busy.

As I said earlier, I spent my time in my big chair, watering my newly seeded lawn —and thinking. I called a friend of mine and a contractor who had done some sub-contracting for us on new housing a couple of years back. His name was Paul Franklin. He had just finished a large addition to the Los Alamos Medical Center Hospital. I asked Paul if he knew anyone who I could hire as a superintendent for an office project I was about ready to start.

Paul said, "I sure do, Andy, and he is a good one. He was my superintendent on the hospital we just finished. His name is Kermit Price. He is an older guy around 54, but he really knows his business. However, I think he is getting ready to move to Dillon, Colorado. He lives in a forty foot trailer that he and his wife own, the largest one you can pull on the highway with a car or pickup, and he may have already left for Dillon. If not, I'll have him call you."

I said, "I think he is just the man I am looking to hire for this job coming up."

Kermit Price did call me and we sat down on the patio at my home and I showed him the plans Joe Duben had completed and he looked them over and said, "I can build your buildings, Mr. Long. When can I get started?"

I said, "Mr. Price, I'm going to give you a try and if you do a good job, I have a lot of other work that will keep us busy for some time."

He said, "I do not have a N.M. contractor's license, but I have a Colorado license."

I said, "Don't worry about a N.M. license, I have a commercial license myself and it also covers residential. Can you start work in about a week?"

He said, "Yes, I have to go up to Dillon, Colorado and pull my trailer house back as I took it up just last week." We were both happy and I will add that this was a relationship that lasted for the next nine years.

The time period was early spring of 1971. I was trying to go to work in my real estate office but about all I could do was lean my big desk chair back and put my left leg up on the desktop on a pillow to keep my leg elevated and not do much walking.

Marion Perkins and Chester Kazek had become accomplished salesman and doing a very good job. In fact, both of them earned $15,000 during the year of 1970 and were off to a good start in 1971. At that time, the average salary of Los Alamos Scientific Laboratory employees was $12,000 per year. Marion was still having trouble coping with being a widow but it was good that she was very busy selling. We were proud of both of our sales people and I had deeply instilled in them the importance of business ethics and honesty in all their dealings. I simply would not tolerate anything else and they knew it.

Bonnie was overloaded with work as she had so very much to do. If we went on a trip, or out-of-town, she would always be working on her books in order to keep up. I had just got into Spin and Spell and that made extra work for her. The correspondence and bookkeeping work was also becoming a burden. She rarely complained but she was very tired. Andra was in college but often helped her mother around the house when we had her and the twins up from Albuquerque for the weekends and the summer. Tim was in college and doing very well, and doing J & L Products' development of the Spin & Spell educational toy.

I was about ready to start the new project of white office buildings in Los Alamos and Marion Perkins told Bonnie that she and Bonnie could run the real estate business — and why didn't we sell her half interest in it. Bonnie told me what Marion said and this got some wheels in motion. We had just had our annual session with Joe Sisneros, our accountant in Santa Fe. It was tax time and he had been doing our taxes for 10 years and had set up Bonnie's bookkeeping system for her so she could keep the records of our various projects separated. This got the wheels turning real good in old Andy's head.

Joe had told us, when we met to sign our income tax papers for the previous year a couple of weeks before, that we were making more money with our building business and land deals than we were making in our real estate business. He was wondering how I was going to handle everything like I had been doing with my new handicap.

So I told Bonnie "Lets take several file boxes of records of everything and go to Albuquerque for the weekend." Well we did, just the two of us, and checked into the Winrock Hotel at the Winrock Shopping Center and started analyzing just how much and where our income was coming from. Sure enough, Joe was right in the advice he was giving me.

So Bonnie and I decided to tell Marion Perkins that we would sell her the total real estate residential business in Los Alamos County and not compete with her for three years. This would include the office furniture, desks, file cabinets and complete equipment. I would be free to sell real estate outside of Los Alamos County — mostly large properties, farms, ranches and other commercial properties.

I would do this for only $12,000 provided she would buy the two office buildings that we were in and had rented to others in Trinity Square. I put a very good price on these two Buildings — for both me and her, and she knew it. I don't know how much insurance money she received when her husband, Ralph died, but it was a bundle. Bonnie and I felt good about this as it would be a good long term investment for her while she got her daughters educated.

Well, she decided to take the deal, and it didn't take her long to pass the Brokers exam that she would have to have to operate her own office. I changed my license to read Andrew E. Long, Commercial Realtor and moved my office into our big two car garage in our home in Pajarito Acres in White Rock. This arrangement never caused either of us any problems at all. We put the announcement in the local paper and on the local radio and asked the people to continue using Marion just like they had us and actually she would keep the same name of "Andy Long Realty, Marion Perkins, Broker" for some time to come. Later she did change the name to "Tri-Square Realty," which was okay.

This really took a load off of Bonnie's shoulders and before long we both were busy as we could be again with Spin & Spell, and the large piece of land in White Rock which I had named Sherwood Village Commercial Subdivision. I still had my Realtor meetings and Real Estate Commission work meetings, serving on the Chamber of Commerce Board, and the Hospital Advisory Board and in getting ready to start construction of the three office buildings that Kermit Price would be building for me. So, I had plenty to do in my condition.

The first thing was to line up the construction loan money, so I had to separate the land for the two buildings I had agreed to sell Marion from the land where the three new buildings would be built. I had about two thirds of the land left to build on, including parking. Marion was paying cash for the two buildings and land I was selling her, so I was able to pay off the loan I had on them. So, all I had to do was borrow part of the money I needed from the Los Alamos National Bank, who considered us their most valued customer and borrower.

I had to split off this new building site from the legal description and in order to do so, my attorney, Harry Moore's advice was to form a new corporation. We all tried to think of a good name. In those days I had been doing some personal thinking about my future health — not knowing how this circulation problem would turn out and having to wear this damn elastic stocking and elevate my left leg to keep it from hurting. My mind turned to what my family would do if suddenly my lights went out. So, I suggested that the name for the new corporation for the three new office buildings and land should be called "The Bonnie Jeanne Corporation."

Harry agreed and I think Bonnie liked it too. So, The Bonnie Jeanne Corp. was born and the bank laughed and gladly made me the construction loan and later, when they were finished and leased, made the long-term permanent loan which paid off the short term construction loan that we used to build the buildings.

Kermit got started on schedule and he and Wes Trask (remember my old friend and surveyor-engineer) surveyed and staked out the buildings. Naturally they were built one at a time up to the point of finish work and paving. I was well satisfied with Kermit C. Price and I started calling him K.C. for short.

Soon the buildings were coming along very well and relations were much better with the planning commission because the new county planner was feeling more comfortable in his job and all this made me feel more pleasant and easier to deal with.

Marion's business was doing just fine. She had hired two women sales ladies to work with her — and Chester Kazek had decided to retire. His wife had had emphysema for years and he took good care of her, going home several times during the day to check on her to change her oxygen bottles. She was such a disagreeable old woman and Chester had lots of patience with her, but she would not quit smoking and finally she died. Later on he married the old lady that lived across the street from them that had become a widow, and this was good for both of them. Shortly afterwards he and his new wife moved to Florida so they could live close to his brother and his wife. This was really good for my old friend and salesman, Chester. It was good for him to get away from these long cold winters of Los Alamos where he had lived for many years. Several years later we heard from his son Chester, Jr. (who had also sold for us for a while), that his dad had passed away, at the age of 83.

Let me take a minute to introduce four young men who were all nephews of ours. Two of them were Bonnie's nephews (and were brothers). The two others were my nephews and were also brothers. Bonnie's nephews were Tom and Ron Sawin, but their names changed when Bonnie's sister, Dorothy, divorced Garnet Sawin when the children were young and they became Tom and Ron Johnson. These boys served in the Vietnam war and went on for a 20 year career and both retired. Tom served in the Air Force in the rescue helicopter division, which was a very dangerous job. When the helicopter would land to pick up a downed pilot or some wounded soldiers, Tom was the first man to get out on the ground when they landed and to use his automatic shotgun to take care of any gooks while the wounded would be put aboard the rescue helicopter. It was very dangerous work. Tom was a big, tall man and gung ho.

Ron was a year younger than Tom. Growing up in high school he would go to an airport close by and make parachute jumps when he was only 17 years old. He was a gutsy and fearless type guy. The boys' dad, Garnet had been in the army during World War II so I guess they wanted to be like their dad. When Ron was real little all he wanted to do was play with his little toy soldiers.

It wasn't long after he graduated high school that he joined the Army. Shortly after he went in they put him in the Green Berets. He served two hitches in Vietnam and after his first hitch, he came to our house on his leave. He had already had some terrible experiences resulting in PTSD. We hit it off great, did a little drinking together and when we were building the Raton building, he would make the trip with me when I would take the payroll over to our men. I would let him drive my T-Bird and sometimes we would kick it up to around 90 miles per hour. Just two wild guys, you might say. One time when we left Raton instead of going straight back to Los Alamos we decided to go to Ruidoso. We spent the night in a good motel, had plenty of drinks that night and spent most of the next day sightseeing. I remember he bought a pistol in a gun shop there that he carried as his personal weapon all through the rest of his 20 year hitch.

Ron would have nightmares sometimes, and it was better not to stand too close to him when you would wake him up in the morning. Having gone through some terrible times, he would relate some of them to me. I introduced him around to some of my friends in Los Alamos as he stuck to me like glue. I introduced him to my friend Mona Williams who used to run the title company and she now was the current president of The Los Alamos Bank. He opened an account at the bank, and on his next leave he and I picked him out a good used car in Santa Fe that he bought.

Sometime later he met a Santa Fe girl at a party at Tim and Juanita's home in Santa Fe and married her. Later he was transferred to Germany to serve in the special forces, and he and his wife had their first child in Germany.

His brother Tom was stationed in Alamogordo, N.M. in his early days for his helicopter training. So, I was taking an educational course in real estate to earn a real estate designation of G.R.I., for "Graduate, Realty Institute" in Las Cruces, N.M. which was about 60 miles from Alamogordo where he was taking his training at the base there. One evening while I was there I called Tom and said, "How would you like for me to pick you up and the two of us go to El Paso, Texas, cross the border to Juarez, Mexico for the evening and have a good time, see some shows and have a good steak dinner?" Tom had the time of his life! We returned to Las Cruces and he shared my motel room and I took him back to his base early the next morning so he could go to work and I then drove back to Las Cruces in time for my class to start at 9:00 AM. Tom never forgot about the good time we had.

Later, he drove to Los Alamos with three of his buddies and I took the four of them deer hunting in the mountains there.

My two nephews were my sister's boys. The oldest was Mitchel Stanfield and his brother was Michael. They were about a year apart and very close. The oldest was a real brain. He went to college instead of the armed service. He won a scholarship in debating and was very good at it too. He went on to great things and great jobs as he grew up and older. I will talk more about him later.

His brother, Mike did not attend college nor did his sister Marla. They were also very sharp individuals. Their dad, Dwight Stanfield, was my best man at our wedding and their mother, my sister, was Bonnie's bride's maid. We were a very close family during the war years as my mom and dad also lived in Wichita, Kansas during that time.

Mike worked after school and on Saturdays at a service station and mechanic's garage near his home and he became a good mechanic while he was still a teenager. He was very sharp and a hard worker and had a winning personality. We loved all three of Dwight and Marge's kids and they had visited us in Los Alamos several times.

Mike told me if I would send him some real estate books he would study them while he was in Vietnam and that he would like to go to work with me in real estate when he got home from his four year tour of duty in Vietnam. He had married his girlfriend, Debbie, before he went to Vietnam and a little baby girl who was born while he was gone. I sent Mike several real estate books and things to study while he was in Vietnam. He was a rifleman and was right out in the bush most of the time, and was very lucky to have survived, but he did and when he was discharged, Debbie became pregnant again shortly thereafter.

One day Mike and Debbie and their little girl showed up in Los Alamos and Mike was ready to go to work. The problem was that I had just sold my real estate business to Marion Perkins. So, I told Mike, "I can give you a job with Western States Builders as I am just ready to start construction on three office buildings and we will teach you the building business."

Mike agreed and Kermit put him to work as a laborer, along with several other guys and work began on the buildings. He made a really good hand and learned fast. Kermit liked Mike and this helped. He was a cut above the others in the labor crew. It wasn't long until he had learned to lay blocks and to paint and to weld. He needed a place to live and I could see that he was in Los Alamos for probably a long time, so Uncle Andy and Aunt Bonnie bought a resale house in White Rock, paid about $2,000 down and assumed an existing loan on it and rented it to Mike and Debbie for just enough to cover the mortgage payment on it. The house was practically new so they were happy as clams.

Later on when work got under way on a much larger scale, Mike being an apprentice mechanic at his job during high school made him a more valuable employee to us than a laborer. By this time we had bought a small tractor, a bulldozer, a dump truck with a removable snow blade and a couple of pickups. Mike was taught to use all of these and to do light mechanical work to keep them all running. Soon their second baby girl was born. His mother and dad came out to Los Alamos to visit with us and to see his two young daughters, their first grandchildren. We all had a good visit.

I haven't said much about my brother, John for some time. He worked at several places around town; filling station jobs, working as a busboy in the restaurant at the Los Alamos Inn and as a security guard for Ed Leslie's Home Planning Development Co. in White Rock at night; all the while spending a great deal of his time at the VFW bar and others in Los Alamos. He had been in the Marine Corps after the Korean War and before the Vietnamese War, so he missed being in the thick of the fighting in both of these wars. He got married shortly after he came out to Los Alamos with our mother and he stayed here after she died. He never held a real good job while in Los Alamos, but he worked at something most all the time.

I kept him in cars for many years. After all he was my only brother and he was the youngest of us three kids. He loved all his nieces and nephews dearly as well as our little twin grandchildren. Christmas time was a very special time for all of us and we would all get together every year.

When John was in the first grade, he got hit by a car. It didn't seem to hurt him much but it knocked him out and injured his head. There seemed to be no ill effects until we noticed that it did affect his concentration and he never did very well in school. However, he did graduate from high school before he joined the Marines.

He always looked up to his big brother. When I came home on my first leave from the Merchant Marines, he was in the first grade and he wanted a uniform just like mine. So, my mother, who always babied him all his life until she died, made him a little uniform just like mine, including the hat. She was a very good seamstress and he was so happy with this. If I can find a picture of him and me in our uniforms it will be included here.

Getting back to the white office buildings -- Trinity Square Plaza, behind the original Trinity Square Complex next to the Los Alamos Inn across from Ashley Pond -- were coming along very well and relations were much better with the Planning Commission and our new county planner. As he was feeling more comfortable in his job, this all made me feel more pleasant and easier to deal with as the buildings were nearing completion, putting the black top parking in and the landscaping around the buildings, Kermit suggested we build a large sun dial in front of the covered patio between the two largest buildings where we had made a large planter. I immediately agreed that it was a good idea and Tim designed one which Kermit built.

I called on my son and brain child, who was a college graduate and very good at science and math, to see if he and Kermit could build it to be extremely accurate. I told Tim, "It has to be accurate, son, or it will be worthless." Due to the hard and dedicated work of Tim Long and Kermit Price, it was very accurate and a great success, with the sundial's style cut in the shape of a unicorn head, and the base built of concrete. It is still there to this day.

We finished the buildings in fine style and had no trouble leasing them to the Los Alamos Laboratory as well as to other tenants such as E.G.& G., Harry Moore and his wife in her gift shop, and a promising young dentist. All with the best view of the mountains in Los Alamos County. The new Bonnie Jeanne Corp. had its first tenants and very good ones, I must say.

About the time we finished the three office buildings, Clark Seay said, "Andy, I don't think you have much for me to do now, so my wife and I are going to sell our home in Pajarito Acres and move to Belen, N.M. It's a small town south of Albuquerque, but close enough to a big city, and much warmer climate. This ended the good accounting work Clark had done for us and it worked out fine as Bonnie now how time to handle it since we had sold the real estate company to Marion.

While Tim, Kermit and the men were building the Bonnie Jeanne Corporation buildings in Los Alamos, I had a lot of time to think about just how I would develop my twenty-three acres in White Rock. Gibsons was doing a good business, so it was now time to do the planning on this project.

Wes Trask had about finished his drawings and paperwork required for the twenty acres that I had plus the two and-a-half acres I had purchased from Ed Leslie that fronted on Rover Blvd. and backed up to my remaining twenty acres on the south to Sherwood Blvd. We came up with nine large pieces of land numbered into nine lots. He and I both knew I was not large enough financially to handle it all in one huge shopping center, all at once, nor could I convince any lender to make a large enough loan to me to build it all at once. By putting it into nine separate lots, each of which fronted on a main arterial street, Longview Drive, I could build on one or two of these smaller lots at a time and be able to finance each project separately.

So this was the challenge. I tackled it this way: I told Bonnie to address an envelope to each and every family in White Rock and Pajarito Acres and also to enclose a stamped envelope addressed back to us. "Bonnie, I am going to survey all the people in White Rock and find out what kind of shops and stores they would like for me to include in my planning of the new neighborhood shopping center." We listed everything we could think of that we should include in it — a supermarket, drug store, department store of men's, women's and children's clothing and shoes, post office, savings and loan, bakery, fabric shop, toy store, cleaners, photo shop, café, beauty shop, barber shop, and so on.

When we received the answers back from the mailing, Andra and Tim sorted and categorized all the responses. The people of White Rock were fabulously in favor of all of the things that I had listed, plus they added some more. Of course, they already had a Gibson's store, so we didn't want another large discount store. When the people in White Rock learned I had sold my real estate business, they fully expected me to start the shopping center so it did not surprise them that I was planning something special.

It was obvious to me that I needed to educate myself on how to go about building something of this magnitude. I might have talked like an "Okie" and acted like an Okie, but I knew how to think and I knew how to sell myself and how to sell to others in order to acquire the necessary financing to make my dream come true. Now it was time for me to acquire the necessary education I needed to be able to put this plan into action.

After I had acquired my commercial contractor's license, I joined the National Home Builders Association so I received a lot of their publications on all kinds of construction. I read in one of them about a seminar to be held in Scottsdale, Arizona on how to build small shopping centers and small office building projects. This was exactly what I was looking for. It was a four day affair and the fee was $400. I made plans and was there when it got under way. Guys were there from all over the country, all interested in the same thing I was. It was almost a miracle — the timing was exactly what I needed when I needed it.

One of the lectures was done by a fairly young architect from San Francisco by the name of Robert W. Hayes. He had slides and all and made an excellent presentation. I tried to absorb it all. I made an appointment to talk with him that evening and showed him my land layout and agreed to pay his travel expenses for him to fly out to see the location and lay of the land for my proposed project. He agreed to come the next week. I met him at the Albuquerque airport and he spent a couple of days at our house and we really hit it off well.

Robert Hayes took our drawings back to San Francisco to work on preliminary drawings for us and said that if I approved them on his return trip to White Rock he would do the whole thing for $4,000. At today's prices this would be about $12,000 - $15,000 for the whole package. About two weeks later he showed up for another two days. I did approve the preliminary drawings and signed the contract and he went to work. While he was in White Rock we went to a planning commission meeting so he could get acquainted with the commissioners and this was time well spent. They were very impressed with his preliminaries and they were glad that old Andy Long was using a real professional. They were all anxious to see the final plans and drawings, as was I. They would be in full color with details on landscaping, etc.

He planned the shopping center on two of the lots — one on each side of Longview Drive, right in the center of the whole piece of land, including the professional office building on the land I bought from Ed Leslie. He also designed a large lot for apartments and another lot for a large motel fronting on State Road 4. No drawings on those two projects at this time. These projects would come along later.

Tim and I made a trip to San Francisco just to look over his office and similar projects that he had done in Sausalito and Mill Valley, California. It looked very good to us and we told him so. It was sort of a rambling style with portal covered walkways with planters and arbors. I told Bob to make ours similar to this and that pleased him. Tim and I checked into the Holiday Inn and it was fairly close to China Town, so we went there that night, had a nice Chinese dinner and a great time walking through the shops and shows.

Bob Hayes was divorced, but he also had visiting privileges for his pre-teen son. He had promised to take him on a chartered deep sea fishing trip out of Sausalito the next morning, so he asked Tim and me if we wanted to go along too. We agreed, paying our own way, of course, on the boat which held about ten to twelve people. We had a great time. We caught several nice fish, about 20 pounds, so we had them cleaned and frozen and wrapped up good and took them home on the plane with our luggage. We flew back to Albuquerque that night and had only been gone two days and one night.

A couple of weeks later, Bob Hayes, our architect, was back in Los Alamos with our drawings. They looked even better than I had expected, drawn on very heavy paper and in color for the exterior drawings. He had also designed and had the full plans for four professional buildings of about 3,000 square feet each. I remember the total was 13,712 sq. ft. in all, using the same type of material, which was light brown slump block and heavy rough-sawn timbers to support the portals. The four buildings faced each other set in a square configuration with parking at each end of two of the buildings.

I liked the drawings very much and so did the planning commission. We were close to getting started and they had approved the total project, when I started by having the office buildings appraised for loan purposes. I named the project The Village Professional Plaza.

With my appraisal in hand and the estimates that Kermit and I had made for our complete construction cost — all in a nicely typed proposal, I went to New Mexico Savings & Loan Association in Albuquerque to request a loan.

New Mexico Savings & Loan had originally started business in Roswell, N.M. and Ed Leslie's wife's family were the largest and main stockholders. Somewhere along the line the main manager of the entire savings and loan and the president had made some very large loans to some big builders in Clear Lake, Texas near the Houston Space Center, and they were in very bad trouble with those loans. The board fired the individual that had made the loans that had gone bad, and being the son-in-law of the big investors, the job of bailing out the savings and loan association fell on old Ed Leslie's shoulders.

This was a new experience for Ed as he was a large project home builder and a very hard worker. He also drank a lot and he had a quick temper. Ed and I were the same age, around 50 years old in 1973. Ed's Home Planning had a lot of homes under construction at the time, so he would get up about 3:00 AM and go through the houses that were under construction with a flash light and make a punch list for his workmen, then drive 93 miles to Albuquerque and tackle the problems of the savings and loan, then drive 93 miles back home in White Rock. Then he would get up the next morning at 3:00 AM and start the same thing all over again.

We were about half finished with the professional office project they had the loan on and were ready for our third, and next to last, draw on our construction money. Ed had his superintendent in White Rock make the inspections, and he did make the third draw. He didn't contact me at all when he made his inspection, if he even made it, but when I went down to their office, Ed was out of town, maybe in Houston, and the girl in charge of the draws said, "Mr. Long, Ed said not to make any more draws to Mr. Long. My superintendent said he was not going to be able to finish the project with the money he has left to draw." This guy that had made the inspection for Ed had never built anything except houses and I don't know even to this day if it was inability on his part or not, or if it was Ed Leslie's instructions to him to stop the funding because the savings and loan was in such a financial bind, or even if it was professional jealousy since I had bought the piece of land from Ed, right after I had bought the twenty-three acres that adjoined it, to build this project. This could have been his way of stealing a project that was almost complete so the savings and loan would acquire it. What a nice plum he was about to pick off old Andy Long.

Anyway, it was about panic time for Bonnie and I. On our way home we stopped by the First National Bank of Santa Fe and went in to see their top loan man, John Meyer. He is the one who handled all the large loans that John Helms, the manager of their branch in Los Alamos, brought in. I had done lots of work with John Helms over the years. John Meyer knew us pretty well, and our track record, though I had not dealt with him face-to-face before.

Anyway, I explained the problem I was having with Ed Leslie and the New Mexico Savings & Loan Association. He had heard the news that they were having big problems, so he listened to what I wanted to do. He said, "Andy, I think our bank can make you the rest of the construction loan, but the bank cannot make the long-term permanent loan that you will need when the buildings are finished."

I said, "Thanks, John, but I need the permanent loan also," and he said he was sorry. I left his office and got into the car and told my nervous wife that I didn't' get the loan from the bank.

I told her the details and she said, "Look, it will take you a month to finish the buildings, so you have a month to place the permanent loan with someone else. Go back in there and take what he offered you and pay off that damn Ed Leslie before he decides to foreclose on us." Boy, she earned her keep that day! I did just that and a month later we paid off the First National Bank of Santa Fe with a permanent loan that I was able to get from a brand new source. Let me explain:

When I was building the Ponderosa Manor Villas, I had made two or three loans from First Northern Savings & Loan Association through their newly formed Santa Fe branch. At that time First Northern had hired a branch manager by the name of Bob Boardman, who had previously worked for a savings and loan in Las Cruces. Steve Mitchell, the head man of First Northern who lived in Taos, hired Bob Boardman to run the little Santa Fe branch office (later they built a large building and moved their main office from Taos to Santa Fe), but Steve and Bob Boardman had not hit it off very well and Bob and his wife had both gotten other jobs. Bob became the president, and his wife the office manager, of Southwest Savings and Loan in Santa Fe.

Bob was glad to see me and I him. He was a real good guy and plenty knowledgeable. This friendship lasted for a long, long time. Anyway, he made the permanent loan we needed and we finished the building right on schedule. The only thing that happened was we had just started our parking lots, one at each end of the buildings. We had the base course down and were just ready to lay the hot mix asphalt surface to finish when we got a freezing rain that night and we could not lay any more blacktop in the freezing weather. We never got to do the final surface until spring. That didn't stop us, however, as we just parked on the base course and it actually helped to pack it down. We got a really good surface job in the spring.

A fellow by the name of Danny McReynolds of Espanola, N.M. (who owned McReynolds Construction Company, a pretty big company that did highway construction, street and sewer lines and manholes, as well as curb and gutter) had just finished Long View Drive from Rover Blvd. to

Sherwood Blvd. He did an excellent job so the street was complete, as well as the parking around our proposed Village Shopping Center.

I had started leasing the professional plaza while Kermit was finishing it up. I was badly in need of an office for our construction company where Kermit and I could go over plans and work with our subs, so we moved into one of the buildings and also leased part of it to an optometrist named Carl Zimmerman, a young lawyer and his lawyer wife for their offices, and one to a health club for a White Rock branch of one they ran in Santa Fe. A young man who owned a furniture store in Espanola opened a branch furniture store, taking one whole building, and Marion Perkins put in a White Rock branch of her real estate business, which one of her sales ladies ran for her.

Remember, Peggy Corbett, my long-time friend and Chamber of Commerce manager in Los Alamos? She came into my office one day and said, "Andy, I am so tired of trying to please all of the business owners and Laboratory heads. Why don't you let me work with you? You need someone to help you with your tenants when you really get started leasing the shopping center."

I told her, "Peggy, I don't want to get all the business people mad at me for hiring you away from the Chamber, but why don't we do this. You go ahead and give the Chamber of Commerce your resignation, then take a two week vacation, which you need. Then, ask me for a job and you will have it."

"That's good. I will do just that, she said, "Marilyn Bond has been my assistant long enough that she can handle my job well enough when she hires an assistant." So the deal was made. She lived in White Rock, only a few blocks away from the shopping center site. Her job lasted a long time — she was just the person I needed to make things come together and stay together. She ran the office where Kermit and I went in and out and answered all our phone calls and took messages when we were out on the job.

As we were winding down on the Village Professional Plaza, I was getting geared up to start the Village Apartments. I hired a local architect to design them and the plans were almost complete. At the same time I also hired Danny McReynolds to design and build a $20,000 concrete bridge over a large arroyo, as required by county specifications, from

Long View Dr. to the apartment site. There was plenty of room to build sixteen units: four buildings with four apartments in each. There were eight 2-bedroom/2-bath units and eight 3-bedroom/2-bath units, plenty of parking and room for a swimming pool and a shuffle board court and a small putting green. When they were finished they looked like a picture postcard.

My Bonnie Jeanne really did a good job coordinating the interior color schemes, choosing all of the carpet, plumbing fixtures, paint, drapes, refrigerator and built-in range and oven, dishwasher and combination over/ under washer & dryers colors. She did her "usual good job" and stayed busy doing the payroll and the sub-contractor's bids and payments to them.

Ed Leslie's sales manager, Dick Bock, who we had gotten to know pretty well over the years (along with his wife, Joan, and their children), came to my office one day while we were building the Professional Plaza and said, "Andy, do you know anyone who I could hire as a salesman? My top man is retiring and moving to Albuquerque and I need one real bad."

I thought about my nephew, Mike Stanfield, who I had sent the real estate books to while he was in Viet Nam and I thought, "This could be his chance." I said, "Yes, Dick, I do have a young man who was ready to take the salesman's exam to get his license when I sold my real estate business to Marion Perkins and he has been working for us in construction for about a year. He has made us a good hand and he lives in a house just a few blocks from your sales office."

Dick said, "Can I meet him?"

I said, "Yeah, it's lunch time. I'll take you and Mike to lunch at the Pub right now."

"Okay," he said, "Let's go."

Well, I explained to Mike this might be his opportunity to get started in real estate. I could tell he was quite excited. He had a great personality and Dick liked him, I could tell. He then asked Mike if he would mind cutting his hair.

"How short do you want it, Mr. Bock?" he said. They agreed to meet for several nights so Dick could tutor him for his real estate exam and in a couple of weeks Mike was starting his real estate career and was as happy as a clam. Their third child was on the way so the timing couldn't have been better. Everyone at Home Planning liked Mike after he was there a little while, so he was off to a good start. He worked tirelessly and he really "set the woods on fire," so to speak, during his first six months and then kept on going up and up and was becoming a top-notch producer.

About this time, Andra, who had decided that she wanted to become a Montessori school teacher, was ready to leave to start school in California. There was a graduate school in Los Angeles where she had been accepted, so Bonnie and I took off work for a few days and helped her drive to California and get settled. Bonnie had just bought her a brand-new Datsun station wagon, which we loaded from top to bottom with everything in the world that she might need. We found her a nice studio apartment in a rather small apartment complex a few blocks from the school (just across the street from Universal Studios in L.A.). I introduced myself to the manager and he promised to look out for her. Chris and Jack Tobin lived about fifty miles and several freeways away, and she visited with them as often as she could.

The apartment job was going really well so we decided to think about getting started on the main shopping center.

Bob Hayes had designed the center section first, consisting of six buildings, three on each side of Longview Drive, with walkways between each building and entrances at each end of each building. There were portal-covered walkways front and back with shake shingle covered roofs under portals supported with 10"x10" rough sawn timber support posts and several 3'x 3' square planters on the walkways made of redwood, which does not decay. It was a very attractive layout, and so functional with parking at the front and back of each building.

Kermit had his hands full winding up the apartments, sixteen in all, so I decided to hire a large construction company in Albuquerque to do these first six buildings: Bradbury and Stamm. The Stamm partner was the brother of Allen Stamm, a home builder who we had dealt with earlier on lots and houses in White Rock. The brother did not do homes at all, only large commercial jobs. They did everything except the electrical and plumbing and floor covering. We had our own plumbing and electrical company that we had used for a long time, so we bought the material and they did the labor. That gave me more quality control, with Kermit providing the inspections over this part. This way nothing was over-looked and it went as planned. We had all underground electrical and plumbing.

No utility poles of any kind. This kept all the environmental "Willie Nillies" happy, which was also good for our image as well as making a good appearance.

I wanted this to be the prettiest project in the county and it was. When we finished the Professional Plaza, I volunteered to resign my board position on the advisory board of the Los Alamos Medical Center. They felt that I would be competing with the Medical Center by renting medical offices while the Medical Center had offices for rent in their new addition that they had just finished. I wanted any doctor to be able to use the Medical Center Hospital should the need arise, so I volunteered to resign my board membership. They accepted it reluctantly, but I had gladly fulfilled this volunteer job for eight to ten years and I was getting way too busy with my various activities anyway. So I made it happen.

My wheels were always turning with new ideas, so one day before we started construction on the Professional Plaza, I said to Kermit that I had Joe Dubin design me a small building with one-bedroom, one-bath, living room, a very small kitchen and a free-standing fireplace. It had a pitched roof of shake shingles and a very large front deck. It was designed for a small guest house or mountain cabin and the whole thing could be loaded onto a big lowboy trailer and hauled to the mountains or lake for a vacation cabin. It was a pretty little thing and my draftsman and artist, Joe Dubin, had named it "Half Pint Haven." I thought I might set up a place someday, say in Santa Fe, for a production line and produce lots of these for sale. (By the way, Joe later did the graphics for Tim's patent application for Photon Structure.)

I had Kermit build one of the cabins and it turned out beautifully. The only thing wrong was that it was going to be too expensive to produce in any kind of volume to make it a worthwhile business. Also, I just had too many things going on at the time. We had the one built, so I figured out the ideal use for it while we were building The Village Shopping Center. We moved it across the street from where we were building the Center and Peggy and Kermit and I had an office so we could all three be right on top of what was going on. Tim also used the drafting table for preliminary lot layouts for the Joplin, Missouri subdivision we were developing at the time.

I gave Peggy the title of Village Coordinator and she took care of public relations and was the "go-between" between me and the tenants when we started leasing the various spaces within the Center. Peggy was very good at this sort of thing and she and I had complete trust in each other. She and Kermit didn't see "eye-to-eye" all the time, but they managed to get the job done. She called him, "Kermit the Frog," and he called her "Miss Piggy" after the muppet on the Sesame Street children's program at the time.

One day I decided to look into the possibility of getting a major supermarket to locate in our Village. So, I found the main guy that ran things for all of New Mexico and West Texas for Safeway in El Paso. I put all the papers of the results of the survey that we took of the White Rock resident's choices of what businesses they would like to have in The Village, put them in my briefcase and flew from Albuquerque to El Paso unannounced. I rented a car at the airport and drove to Gordon Richie's office. When the girl ushered me into his office, the first thing I did was to open my briefcase and dump the contents on his big desk.

He said, "What is this all about?"

I said, "Mr. Richie, my name is Andy Long and this is the result of a recent survey I took of all the people who live in White Rock, New Mexico. I am building a new shopping center there right now and all of these people want you to open a Safeway market in our Center. We know you have a store in Los Alamos already, but it is nine miles away and a second store would be great for White Rock. This had shocked him, but we were soon on common ground and he made arrangements for his young land man and his wife to drive to White Rock to size up the situation.

The outcome of this was that they felt that a second store would take business away from their store in Los Alamos, so Safeway backed out after they considered all the pros and cons. I continued looking and asked the Piggly Wiggly grocery chain with headquarters in Ft. Worth, Texas come up, so a fellow named Worth Marshall and his land man came to see me and they seemed very interested. At the time we were talking to them, their whole nationwide chain was having big union problems. I don't know the details, but both Worth Marshall and I were very disappointed that they would not be locating a store in White Rock.

Well, I'm pretty hard-headed, so I put the supermarket on hold after about a year had passed. Meanwhile, I had been leasing a bunch of other tenants for our brand new center, and some of the buildings had two to three businesses each in them already.

I should explain now how I financed The Village. I mentioned earlier about the new president of Southwest Savings & Loan, Bob Boardman, in Santa Fe who had financed the permanent loan on The Village Professional Plaza and had also financed the sixteen Village Apartments. Bob decided to talk to me about how his savings and loan and First Northern Savings and Loan (who now had finished their new three-story office building in Santa Fe) would each finance the shopping center together. As Southwest was making me too many big loans for their regulators, they had to share The Village Shopping Center financing with First Northern. Steve Mitchell has since passed away and his lawyer son, Tony Mitchell, was now chairman of the board, and my good friend, Bob Morris, from our new home construction days was now the president. These two men got along well together, so this was a big plus for Andy Long. I was riding high!

First Northern was so gung-ho on White Rock that Bob Morris opened a branch savings and loan in our Center. Leasing was very good and in no time at all I had all the space leased in the Professional Plaza, the Village Apartments and the Village Shopping Center. Kermit had done an excellent job of finishing up these three projects after Bradbury & Stamm had completed their part as agreed. Kermit took over the finishing touches on it and all the landscaping on all three projects as well.

We were all very busy helping get the various tenants situated in their businesses and preparing for our Grand Opening in a month or so. I'll name my first tenants to give you an idea how many there were to start with and who they were: First Northern Savings & Loan took 2,400 sq. ft., The Carousel, a ladies & children's clothing and store took 3,600 sq. ft., A western wear store, The Hitching Post, took 2,400 sq. ft, Radio Shack took 1,200 sq. ft., and art shop and cleaners pickup location owned by Roger Corbett, Peggy's husband (he had their main shop in Los Alamos for many, many years), a 2,400 sq. ft. fabric shop, The Village Bakery had 2,400 sq. ft., a beauty shop, a barber shop, The Ice Cream Saloon, a Christian book store, and a kitchenware shop.

I had also built a combination drugstore and branch post office together across the back parking area from the Village and I had made a land-only lease and the couple built their own flower shop and nursery on the land lease next door to the drugstore. We had a pretty good selection of stores and they were all doing well.

Two of my tenants rented two spaces each. A young veterinarian and his wife, fresh out of Texas A&M, rented space in The Village Professional Plaza as well as an apartment from us in the Village Apartments. Another couple rented an apartment and opened the large ladies and children's clothing store, the largest store in the Village at 3,600 sq. ft. To give you an idea of how big 3,600 sq. ft. is, it is 40 feet wide, by 90 feet long. The 1,200 sq. ft. spaces were all 40 feet wide and 60 feet long. Each had plenty of room.

I mentioned earlier that there were mature pine trees on the 23 acres so we dug large holes and a big Michigan front-end loader transported these trees to be planted in front of the stores on each side of the Village for shade and we decorated them with Christmas lights every year.

I must make time to tell you about my Mexican pal and right-hand man, Pete Chavez, that had run our labor crews for years since I had started building homes in 1965 and had been continually employed ever since. He took care of keeping the Center grounds clean, watered the landscaping, did the maintenance on the Village and took care of any problems the tenants had with their spaces, etc. Also he did all of the Christmas decorating outside for the tenants and stringing the lights in the trees, etc. It was really a beautiful scene at Christmas with the outside speakers playing Christmas carols and other music.

Chapter Seven

The Joplin Project

Bonnie Scott, Salutatorian of her 1943 graduating class

I MUST GO BACK NOW to 1973. I had mentioned much earlier in this long story that Bonnie's family was large, ten children in all, two boys and eight girls. Well, the youngest boy, J.R. Scott, who was just younger than Bonnie and the fourth child, was diagnosed with inoperable cancer of the esophagus. This was devastating to us all as he was a great guy and had a wife and two boys. A short time later he died and as it took two or three days for all of the family to get together for J.R.'s funeral, I drove around the area just to look around. Galena, Kansas, where Jay (as we called J.R.) lived was only a half mile to the Missouri state line. I drove another half mile inside Missouri and there it was — a stone building where I used to buy whiskey from a bootlegger in Missouri to take back to Wichita to sell to the men that were building the houses that my father-in-law and I were working on laying bricks and mixing mud. I wrote about this earlier in this story, just before I started selling Lifetime Stainless Steel Cookware.

Well, the building was vacant. Kansas and Oklahoma had long since dropped the laws making them dry states and now had liquor stores just like Missouri, so this had put the bootleggers out of business, of course. Next door to this stone building was a large block building with a metal roof, and a big sign in front of it said "Club 66." For years and years U. S. Rt. 66 came right through Joplin, Missouri and then right on past these buildings to the Kansas state line and on to Galena, Kansas. Galena, Kansas and Joplin, Missouri are only about six or seven miles apart, though Galena is much smaller than Joplin. The people in Galena do most of their shopping in Joplin, it being a much larger town. Club 66 had been a nightclub bar & lounge for many years. In fact, it had the largest dance floor in Jasper County, Missouri — quite a place.

Old Rt. 66 was not used for cross-country traveling any more since the interstate highways were built. The new interstate had by-passed Galena and now went around it. Rt. 66 became Joplin's "7th Street." About a block east towards Joplin on 7th Street was the cross street Malang Rd. and on the corner of 7th & Malang was a large beautiful old brick home with very large two-foot-thick oak trees all over the yard and surrounding grounds. In the olden days when the bootlegging was going on and Oklahoma and Kansas were making bootlegging a very profitable business, the couple that lived in this house ran the bootleg business and Club 66. Their names were George and Fran Downing. The basement under the home was large and it was used for gambling of all kinds — craps, slots, poker and the like. In fact, George Downing had the largest gambling place in southwest Missouri. In addition to this, they had five small rental houses that Fran took care of by cleaning and looking after the girls, as well as fixing food and drinks for the gamblers who used them for a price. Again, I'll say, quite a place —though I did not know about anything other than the little stone liquor building back when I would buy whiskey to take back to Wichita. I found out about the other after we came back for Jay's funeral.

Well, I drove on down Malang Rd. south to 21st Street, which was about a half-mile or so from 7th, and about half-way down Malang there was a sign, "50 acres for sale." All fifty were covered pretty much with large oaks, hickory nut and walnut trees. Absolutely beautiful, with a creek running through it north to south. I guess I've been like my grandfather's friend and sidekick, the famous Will Rogers, who said he never saw a man he didn't like. Old Andy Long was also like Will Rogers in that he never saw a beautiful piece of land he didn't like. I liked this piece of land! The sign said to inquire at the house at 7th & Malang. I did and was greeted by a lady in her 60's, Fran Downing. She said, "Come in Mr. Long for a cup of coffee or maybe a drink." So I did.

Fran told me her husband had died several years before and she was trying to take care of the place by renting the Club 66 and the five houses and the pasture land to a guy that had cattle on it. There was a huge hay barn behind the rent houses. She said, "I want to sell this 50 acres and keep my rental houses and the Club 66 rental."

I asked, "How much land is in the entire property?" She said it was an original eighty acres but the highway curves and they bought five acres across the back corner. So I have 75 acres in all. I told her, "Let me think about this. I'll be in town a couple more days for a funeral and I'll be in touch. How much do you want for the fifty acres?"

"$50,000" she said, "$1,000 per acre." I drove back to Galena and got Bonnie and we both went back to see this beautiful piece of property. I let the old gal sweat a couple of days and after Jay's funeral I went back and saw Fran Downing.

I said, "I like your property. Why don't you survey out ten acres of land which would include all of your rental property, your big house and barn and your five rent houses and I'll give you $50,000. for the rest of the property. I don't need the buildings, rental property or your house. I'll pay you 10 percent down and 10% each year annually and pay 10% interest on the balance." To make a long story short, Fran and Andy made a deal.

This was in the spring of 1973 and as you have seen, I had a hell of a lot going on, but with her carrying the mortgage, I didn't have any immediate problem of financing. I returned to Los Alamos and I was anxious to tell my old pal Wes Trask about buying fifty acres in Joplin, Missouri. I asked him to go back with me in a few days and get his ideas about how to develop it. He was anxious to go and we met Fran and her young friend, a fellow about 34 or 35 years old. We met at her house and all four of us started walking over the land.

After a while Fran said, "Andy, I'm getting tired, let's you and I go back to the house and I'll pour you a drink. I have a half gallon of Beams Choice. You look like you could use one." She said, "Gary, can show Wes the rest of the land." So I said, okay.

I didn't know what she had in mind, but would soon find out. We passed her two-car garage and I looked in and there were two Lincoln Mark IV's, side-by-side. I said, "How come you've got two Lincolns, Fran?"

"One of them is Gary's." She said.

I said, "Oh?"

"Yeah, I bought it for him." She said. She told me he used to be a surveyor's helper, but I got him a job selling hospitalization insurance and he is doing well and he needed a good car." We went into the house and she poured us a drink and started showing me the house. It was very nice and very well built.

When we got to the master bedroom, I said, "Where does Gary sleep, Fran?"

"Under the bed, Andy." She said. We both laughed and nothing more was said about it.

We sat down in the living room and she said, "Andy, I've been thinking about asking you to buy the rest of my property. You might as well have it all and I'll finance it for you like we did on the fifty acres, 10% down and 10 years on the balance at 10%."

"Well," I said, "I'll give it a thought. How much would you have to have for the ten acres and all of the buildings, house, barns, and rent houses?"

"$208,000," she said.

I said, "Fran, why don't Wes and I take you and Gary to dinner this evening and talk about this some more." We did. In the meantime, Wes and I contacted an engineering firm in Joplin by the name of Stewart Engineering. I asked him to survey the land I had bought earlier and make me a plat and stake the corners and calculate the acreage. I also asked him to make arrangements for it to be aerial surveyed at Wes's suggestion. This did turn out very well. It showed the trees, the creek running through it and a small pond.

I took us all out to dinner at the best steak house in Joplin and things went well. I had told West that there would be room for 100 homes on the 50 acres and that I got to thinking that I could build a shopping center off of old 66 Highway (7th Street), which could serve all of Galena as well as the homes on our acreage. He got pretty excited about this. Negotiations started while we were having dinner. She had said that she wanted $208,000, so I said, "Fran, I'll make you an offer of $180,000 for it all, and at the end of five years I'll pay it all off. 10% down, at 10% interest, on a 10 year term, all due at the end of the fifth year." The figure I had in mind was $200,000 when I offered the $180,000.

Fran said, "Andy, I like the five year payoff real well at my age, but the least I'll take is $200,000."

This was the answer I was waiting to hear.

So I said, "Would you like to shake hands on that amount and these terms?'

"Yes," she said. "Let's shake on the deal."

I told Fran to have her old lawyer draw up the papers and I would be back with my wife in one week to close the deal, "Have a copy of the lease on the Club 66 for me when I get back." Wes and I went by my mother-in-law's house in Galena, waited for her to pack her little suitcase and I said, "Mom Scott, we are taking you on a week's vacation to Los Alamos to see your daughter, Tim, Andra, and our twin granddaughters." She was an elementary school principle school in Galena, but it was summer and she was off for the summer.

Viola's world was small in those days. I think she had only been in four states in her whole life: Missouri, Kansas, Oklahoma and Arkansas. She had never seen any large mountains in her life. She really enjoyed this vacation. Bonnie and I drove her up into the Jemez Mountains and along the little mountain streams and she would have me stop so she could pick wild flowers. She got altitude sickness and would have to stop and throw up once in a while and wash her false teeth in the mountain stream and then she'd pick some more wild flowers. She enjoyed her vacation very much, and seeing our new home, our new shopping center and other buildings we had built. She was so happy for us and proud of us to have done all of this with a high school education.

Bonnie explained to her that I had taken all kinds of real estate courses, sales courses, appraisal courses, construction courses, and seminars. She told her mother, "Andy always says he didn't need a high-powered degree, that he could hire all of the experts he needed and all he needed was sixth grade arithmetic: adding, subtracting, multiplying and dividing." I always thought I was her favorite son-in-law, but she loved us all, and we all loved her.

She had a beautiful voice and she would sing and we would all join in. Bonnie said that with ten kids and only a radio for entertainment, she taught all her children, especially the girls to sing and this was their entertainment while they were growing up. When her youngest daughter, Beverly, started school in the first grade, they were living in Wichita and Mom Scott entered Friend's University Bible College there and got her teaching degree. A little later she started teaching school in the Galena, Kansas school system. The oldest son, Robert Scott, served forty years on the Galena School Board there. This helped. But she was exceptional. Later, she attended summer classes at the university in Pittsburgh, Kansas and got her master's degree. All this after raising ten children and then she became a teaching principal for many years. She is listed in "Personalities of the West and Midwest," as described elsewhere in this story. She taught up until about a year before her death at age 74. What a woman!

Anyway, we took Mom home the next week and Bonnie and I met Fran at her lawyer's house, as he was old and didn't keep an office anymore just to serve his old long-standing clients. We signed the papers and Fran said, "Andy, Gary and I have bought a house in Joplin and will be moving out of my big house soon." She said she had someone who wants to rent the big house if I wanted to rent it.

I said, "Yes, who is he?"

Fran said, "The First National Bank of Joplin has hired a new vice president and he is looking for a nice home to rent. I think he will be a good renter." The banker did rent the home and he and I hit it off well. Fran introduced us to the other five renters in the small houses and I explained that my brother-in-law in Galena would be collecting the rent and if they had any problems he would take care of them. Fran said she would have the guy that ran the Club 66 call Bob Scott in Galena who would be collecting the rent. All of this was taken care of without any problems.

A couple of days later Bonnie and I headed back to Los Alamos. On the long trip home down Interstate I-40 I had Bonnie read me the lease that Fran had given me on Club 66. Well, this was a shock! She read that our Club 66 tenant not only had a three-year lease with two years left, but also had five more 3-year options as well. I had failed to ask about any options and Fran had not told me — only that he had a three year lease. Well, this was going to play hell with me developing a shopping center on the land. It could be a seventeen year problem! Oh, I was so upset! I called Fran the next day and raised me some hell. She said, "Andy, don't worry about this guy. I've had several tenants in that old building over the years and in that type business they don't usually stay very long. I don't think he will be there very long either." Well, it still worried me pretty bad, but I realized that I had been had.

Meanwhile, back at the ranch with Roy & Dale, so to speak, the Village Shopping Center had been leased. Us and Kermit, Peggy and Pete were all working their tails off getting ready for our Grand Opening. Tragedy was about to happen.

Robert W. Hayes and his girlfriend had planned to attend our Grand Opening and we were looking forward to seeing them both again. They both had been out to see us about her laying out on paper various signs for each of our businesses in both the Professional Plaza and the Village Shopping Center. We had enjoyed meeting her and she and Bob stayed at our home. She was a pretty thing, tall and lean and she had the longest legs I had ever seen on a woman.

The funniest thing happened at breakfast that morning. We sat down to our big table. Tim, Andra, Bonnie and I and the two of them, six in all. Bob remarked, "Bonnie, what a beautiful breakfast!"

Bonnie responded graciously, "These eggs are fresh layed." It got very quiet and Bob and his girlfriend looked at each other and both began laughing at what Bonnie said. They didn't ever think about chickens laying eggs. They probably thought of eggs coming from the grocery store, period. Fresh layed meant something else to them. Well, we all had a good laugh all through breakfast.

Bob Hayes was really proud of The Village and the next day they returned to San Francisco. I told Bob I would think about the signs and let him know.

Peggy was busy with the tenants getting all of their publicity lined up with the local paper and the radio station. I had agreed that all the advertising for the Grand Opening would be paid by me. After that Peggy would work with them and pro-rate the cost to each business and they would have a breakfast meeting at the ice cream saloon once a month and Peggy would work with them on the advertising for the month ahead. Sort of like having our own little Chamber of Commerce within The Village. She would write the script and work with Rick, the radio announcer for the radio spots. Darrell Burns, the owner of the radio station, had become such a good friend that we subscribed to Muzak, which is a medley of instrumental music played several times a day throughout The Village. The tenants also had radio spots that they paid for individually. Peggy would collect all the rent checks from the tenants except for the apartments and turn them over to Bonnie.

The Grand Opening was about a week away. Early one morning the phone rang and I received a call from Galena, Kansas. It was my brother-in-law, Bob Scott. He said, "Andy, Joplin has gotten hit hard by a tornado about an hour ago and you have had some damage." The roof of Club 66 had lost a lot of its metal roof, and about fifteen of the large oak trees surrounding the big house have been uprooted and laid over. The big barn has had some of its roof blown off and one small house has lost its carport and another has a small amount of roof damage. The big house escaped any serious damage as far as he could tell.

Well, what bad news coming when it did, just before our Grand Opening! It was still a few days away, so I said, "Bonnie and I will leave right away. Did anyone get hurt?" He said, "No, none of your tenants were injured but a little girl was killed about a half mile north of Highway 66, and believe it or not, her name is "Tanya Long", the same as one of your granddaughters, Tañia, when their mobile home was destroyed, and her folks are injured." Joplin took quite a bit of damage, but there were no other deaths, thank God.

I told Kermit and Peggy to keep the schedule of our Grand Opening as planned, that I would be gone only a couple or three days. Joplin was about 700 miles from Los Alamos, so we drove in there about midnight that night and I was out there early and met Fran and Bob Scott and examined the damage. About two-thirds of our large oak trees were gone and the yard was in one hell of a mess. The barn roof damage was covered by insurance and also the small house carport and screen door were covered. So all-in-all, we were not hurt too bad.

Bob got in touch with a friend who had a dump truck and backhoe and we made a deal for him to take care of the tree damage. He cut the big trees off of the big root balls, which were about six feet in diameter, and he hauled them down to the dump. He could get only one at a time in his truck, so it was quite a job. I told him he could have the large tree trunks, all two-foot thick and long, to take them to the sawmill. He also hauled all the brush away and did a real cleanup job. His name was Lloyd Kitch. He and Bonnie were in the same high school graduation class and Bob Scott had known Lloyd for years. So the job went as smoothly as possible and Bob arranged for having the repair work done on the little house and the barn. The insurance covered this, but the tree damage was my expense.

I asked Fran if there was any insurance on the Club 66 and she said, "No, Andy, it was a concrete block building with a metal roof, so it was really not worth insuring as beer joints and dance halls carry a large insurance premium because of their very nature. They often get burned down for some reason or another, so I didn't bother insuring this one." Fran said, "The tenant called me yesterday and I told him you would be here, so you need to talk to him. The rain has done some damage to the hardwood dance floor and some of his fixtures."

Well, that afternoon I saw the tenant there so I walked across the back yard and up to the fence which was a four foot high chain link fence around the big house and the five rent houses. Let me back up a little bit now. As Bonnie and I drove to Joplin that day we got the lease out and she read it to me again. In the lease it so stated that should the building become damaged in any way to the extent that the damage was not economically feasible to repair, in the opinion of the owner, that he would not be obligated to repair or replace the building.

So I told Bonnie that day that this was a blessing in disguise. This was our chance to cancel the lease and all the five other options on it. This would let us get rid of the building and go ahead if we indeed did decide to build a shopping center on the site. The building only rented for $300 per month and the lease so stated that if it was not economical for the owner to repair it, that the lease became null and void. So I said, "Bonnie, this may turn out okay after all." We decided that this would let us cancel the lease and we could proceed with our long term plans.

So, now, I walked up to the fence and met the tenant for the first time. I had put my little 25 caliber automatic heater in my hip pocket for any serious emergency when I met the guy. He was of medium height and weight, about my size or maybe a little smaller and about the same age. The first thing he said was, "Are you going to put my roof back on the building right away?"

"I don't intend to replace the roof or anything else. The lease states I don't have to."

Well, he got real red faced and said, Mister, you are damn sure going to replace this roof damage or we are going to have trouble."

I said, "Let me now tell you something very important, you SOB. You may think you are bad, but you just smell bad."

"I'm going to see a lawyer." He said.

"You see all the lawyers you want to, but I'm not putting a roof on that building." So we parted. Well, in a few days I heard that he had someone putting the roof back on Club 66. And he opened up again for business.

Bonnie and I had returned to Los Alamos and Peggy, Kermit and Pete had everything ready to go. About noon that next day we got a phone call from San Francisco, thinking it was Bob Hayes. But it was his partner calling, saying that he had some real bad news to tell us. I got Peggy on the other phone and his partner said, "Folks, Bob and his new wife were killed yesterday. Bob had been working with a new client in northern California and had taken the afternoon off to spend with his new bride who was with him and they were on the beach playing in the tidal pools and a huge tidal wave came in and washed them off the beach. Well, Bob was able to get back, but his wife was not and was struggling and Bob jumped back in to save her and both of them drowned. It was a freak tidal wave. Several small boats were sunk in the same tidal wave. It must have been a huge one."

All of us took this so sadly. It was just hard to believe. He had been paid for all of his work and I was glad about that. His partner sent me a newspaper clipping about the accident a few days later. This tragedy along with the other one with the tornado in Joplin sure took its toll on Bonnie and me. But we survived, as usual.

The opening was a great success. Enjoyed by all. The weather was very nice. Peggy had arranged for a parade and Tim's band, "Stream," including Hugh Felt (Peggy Corbett's son) and Steve DeRuby (a soloist at the Inn at Loretta in Santa Fe for many years), played on the bandstand.

Peggy had arranged for Indian dances by the Pueblo Indians of the Española valley who performed all of their very colorful dances and this was enjoyed by everyone. I think almost all of the people who lived in White Rock were in The Village that day as well as hundreds from Los Alamos, too. The opening was a real success. Peggy's Chamber of Commerce experience sure came in handy!

My very, very good friend, Jim Brown's wife, Margaret, led the parade in her light blue Chrysler Imperial convertible, as usual. Jim and Margaret had been our friends for many years. He was my Prudential Insurance man and I had bought a lot of his life insurance policies to satisfy the banks, from whom I had borrowed a lot of money. (The banks all knew that if I lived I would pay them back, but if I died Bonnie would have the money to pay them.) The two couples of us took many trips together — Denver, Colorado Springs, Reno, El Paso, and Juarez, Mexico. I have a real good story to tell you about a trip the four of us took to Juarez and Mexico later on.

Margaret and Jim spent every Christmas with us and our family in our big house in White Rock. They didn't have any children and they enjoyed all of ours including the twins, very much. Jim knew as many jokes and stories as I did and we sure enjoyed the two of them. Jim was about my height, but a real "round" man. He did not have a hair on his head and hadn't since he was a child. He reminded me of the television character of the day: Mr. Clean. His wife Maggie, as we called her, had been a physical education teacher for many years and had taken a job later as secretary to the superintendent of schools for Los Alamos. Both of them were thought of very highly by the community.

Once a week in the summer Peggy arranged for the Los Alamos High School Band and Orchestra to play and perform in the cool summer evenings. People would bring their folding chairs and we would block off the ends of the street between the buildings of the shopping center and the band would set up under a gazebo facing the street.

Christmas was also very nice. Pete would have all the portals and trees strung with Christmas lights and another one of our great friends, Fred Roach, would put on his Santa Claus suit and he enjoyed all of the little town children, including our twins, sitting on his lap and telling him what they wanted for Christmas. Fred did this every year for years and also in Los Alamos. He loved it and the community loved Freddie Roach. He also loved his Scotch Whiskey, so old Andy always took good care of Fred.

I must tell you the story about the Christmas party that Bonnie had for the adults that had all rented apartments in the new Village Apartments that had recently been completed. A couple of my favorite friends, and both real Irish characters that lived there, were Bun Ryan and his wife, Jean. Remember, I wrote about them when they had the New Year's Eve Party at the Carriage Inn the first year we came to Los Alamos in 1961. This is now 1977. Bun was still working at the Los Alamos Laboratory, but had not run his part-time lounge business for several years. In fact, he had joined Alcoholics Anonymous and was a tee-totaler. Still a fun-loving guy and a real friend.

Another one of our friends had just recently come to Los Alamos and he also was a big Irishman, Elmer Kelly, and his wife Rosalie. Elmer was in the construction business as he and his partner had landed a very big construction job for the Lab. He was a huge man — 6'7" tall and around 300 lbs. When he put on his cowboy boots and 10-gallon hat, he looked bigger than God! He was just as fun-loving as Bun, so the pair of them had become instant buddies, as had their wives. Bonnie and I loved all four of them. Elmer was looking for a place for himself and his wife to rent when I first met them. We had just finished the apartments and they settled in. We hit it off almost instantly with Kelly, as we called him, and Rosalie.

Our friendship has now lasted for 31 years. He had planned on only being in Los Alamos several months but they liked it so much that he made the Village Apartments his home headquarters for several years and worked his away jobs from there. We still see each other at least a couple of times a year and have for years, and Elmer phones us every week, the same with the Ryans. This is what you call <u>real friendship</u>.

Elmer and Bud both liked Western Cowboy and Indian art. Every weekend in their earlier days as friends they would travel all around New Mexico, especially Taos and Santa Fe, and look for paintings to purchase. Kelly has a huge collection.

Young Marley and Ann Delaney, the veterinarians, also lived in the Village Apartments along with a single lady who had just retired from teaching school. Another tenant, a young female astrophysicist, had just started working at the Laboratory and lived next door to the Kellys. She was a real brain! Her mother was a high-powered lawyer in New York City. She wasn't real good-looking, but she was really smart, as were a lot of people living in Los Alamos.

Tim was at the party and he and the astrophysicist were deep in conversation about space — trying to impress each other, I think. They were seated on the couch at the end of the living room near the waterfall and fish pond between the living room and entry. Kelly and Bun came out of the bathroom together laughing and I felt that maybe everyone was about to get a surprise. Indeed, I was right! Ann and Marley Delaney were just arriving. I let them in and took their coats and everyone greeted them and all our guests had arrived. Well, Marley and I and Bun and Kelly were all standing in the entry and Marley had on his new cowboy boots. He had put one foot on the rock wall of the fish pond and we were all talking when Kelly had his pants fly open and his hand inside his waistband and low and behold, he stuck the biggest dingus we had ever seen out and started pissing on Marley's new boot!

Tim and the physicist were the first ones to see it besides Marley and me. The astrophysicist had never seen anything like this before, I'm sure! Her eyes were as big as saucers and Tim was shocked in amazement as well as the little old maid school teacher and all the rest. Well, Marley looked up at Kelley and I'm sure he wanted to smack him good, but Kelly was so damn big, he didn't try. By this time Bun and I were laughing so hard and Kelly pulled out the big rubber dong with the rubber tube and bulb attached to it so that everyone could see it was not real. That certainly got the party off to a good start and we all had a good time.

To give you a little more about the big jobs that Kelley ran, for example, he was working for the big construction company Morris-Knutson out of Boise, Idaho and was superintendent on a huge dam they were building on a big river in Oregon. Bonnie and I went on a trip to Seattle, Washington some time later on and stopped to visit them in Boise; and Kelley and I and the company pilot flew the company plane up to Oregon to inspect the huge dam with some high powered investment bankers from New York City. It was the biggest construction job I had ever seen. Kelley was in charge of the entire construction project. The big turbine engines inside the dam that generated electric power were built in Japan. So, this big man really knew his construction and he knew how to handle all kinds of men. He told me that when he was ready to start a project he would call a meeting with everyone there and would say, "Boys, there are two ways that this job is going to be run. My way or the highway. I want to let you know this from the very start so that you really understand this." He was big enough to make it stick!

The job he was on when he came to Los Alamos in 1974 was several years earlier than the big dam in Oregon I have just described. The 1974 Los Alamos job was for the Atomic Energy Commission, now the Department of Energy. It was called "The Meson Facility." It was all constructed of steel and it had to be perfectly level for one-half mile, necessary for its experimental accelerator. He took me with him one day while it was being built. They were placing all the steel reinforcing bars in it — all about one inch thick. I had never seen a job of this magnitude in all of my life. When it became time to begin pouring, and it had to be continuous, the number of ready-mix trucks numbered in the hundreds. They were from all over New Mexico, all coming up that mountain road one after another. Just like a long string of ants, only much larger.

I did admire Elmer Kelley and I still do to this day. You might say we have had a mutual admiration society going for a long, long time. Him for the size and importance of handling his huge jobs and for me to go it completely alone, from an idea to the completion without any partners, so to speak, and to accept the complete responsibility of success or failure. He would say, "Andy, I could never take the kinds of risk you do. You have balls, son. You are a true gambler and I admire what you have done." We have total respect for each other and our abilities — true friends.

Kelly later was in charge of a huge section of the Alaskan pipeline. I have seen lots of video film of these experiences and the big game he hunted and killed while in Alaska. He has built big bank buildings in Nairobi, Africa and hospitals in Brazil and a number of other places. He is about seven or eight years younger than me and is essentially retired now, but once in a while he takes on a two or three month consulting and estimating job with some big companies.

They still live in their big rambling home on Eagle Mountain Lake near Fort Worth, Texas. He said, "Andy, I've lived there longer than any other place I've lived: 27 years." He has a terrific art collection and a large rifle and shotgun collection. He and his sweet wife, Rosalie, are some of our most memorable friends. We see each other a few times for several days each year, regardless of where we live, and have a great time playing Dominoes and telling stories. He knows more jokes than I do and this is saying a lot! And he does a good job of telling them, too.

Now something about Bun Ryan and his wife, Jean. They met Kelley and Rosalie when they all lived in The Village Apartments, and later they bought one of the town homes that we built that I haven't talked about much yet. They are both retired now. In the early days Bun not only worked at the Laboratory, but he managed and pitched the only five man softball team in New Mexico. They could out-play and beat any of the nine men teams in the state! Mostly, the reason was that Bun could throw that softball harder, faster, and more accurately than any other pitcher in the state. They were very, very good! All of the five men lived and worked in Los Alamos.

Bun also ran The Carriage Inn Bar & Lounge that I wrote about earlier, also while working at the Laboratory. In his later working years he had a job with the Lab where he would work with any of the Lab employees that had a serious drinking problem, men or women. You might say a company-owned "alcoholics anonymous." Bun would visit with them and work on their problem with them and he did a very good job and was a great help to the individuals, as well as to the Laboratory. Bun is a wonderful guy, is liked by everyone and has a great personality. He loves the Colorado Rockies baseball team, as well as the Broncos football team and he and Jean go to Denver quite often for the games.

The time period now is late summer of 1974. The Club 66 has re-opened for business and my hopes of building a shopping center seemed out of the question now. Bob Scott was doing a good job as my property manager there part-time as he had a full-time job for many years as superintendent at the local smelter. I paid him 10% of the rent he collected and we both were happy.

He called one day and said, "Andy, the Joplin Gas Company tells me that they will lay a big gas line from 21st Street for a half-mile up to 7th Street, or old 66 Highway." This would enable us to put all of the six houses and Club 66 on natural gas instead of propane tanks. And it would take care of all the homes that would be built on our fifty acres of land in the future. This was great news! We had a 1,000 gallon propane tank that took care of all six of the houses I bought from Fran. Bob said, "I have a buyer for the 1,000 gallon tank for you, too." He said, "My son, David, will buy the tank. He's offered $200 for it." I said, "He has a deal!" It was worth about a thousand dollars but since he was my nephew and one-hell-of-a-good-guy, I said, "It's his if he will move it." The Gas Company said our share of the one-half mile long line would be $4,000. I though this could be great for all the future houses and the shopping center too.

About a month later tragedy number two was about to happen. Bob Scott called me in the middle of the night and said that the Club 66 had burned to the ground. Bob was on the Galena Volunteer Fire Department and had been for years. Galena, Kansas was only a half-mile from the Club 66. Well, when morning came, Bonnie and I were on our way again, back to our Joplin property.

It was dark when we arrived at the Club 66 with Bob. He said, "Andy, this was a strange fire." He said, "Usually a block building sort of collapses and the block walls fall to the inside, but on this one the block walls were bulged out and some fell to the outside. About the time we thought we had it under control, another explosion would occur and it was roaring again!" It sure was a total mess, to say the least.

Bob told me the Galena Fire Marshall wanted to talk to me, so I said, "Okay, let's go see him."

He said, "Mr. Long, where were you when this building caught fire?"

I promptly answered, "Marshall, I was in bed with the Los Alamos, New Mexico County Sheriff's wife." He didn't say a word to this. He just looked very sternly at me. I said, "You and I both know that was a damn lie, so let me tell you something. I did not have a dime's worth of insurance on that building, but if I knew it was going to burn I damn sure would have it insured. I didn't have anything to do with this fire and I don't know who in the hell did." I never heard another word about this.

I talked to Fran and she said she didn't know anything about it either. She said, "It's a mystery." Well, this did solve the problem I was having with the tenant of the Club 66 and it looked like we could proceed with our plans. I made arrangements with Lloyd Kitsch again to clean up another mess. He had done such a good job with the tornado tree damage clean up and he did the same kind of good job with the Club 66.

A couple of weeks later we received word that we were being sued by the tenant to recover the $4,000 that he paid to put the roof back on the building after the tornado damage. I had my young lawyer take some big glossy pictures of the fire damaged building right after it burned just in case we would need them. Here we go again — back to Joplin when the trial started, a jury trial. Fran, my lawyer, Bonnie and I didn't think we would have any problem as the lease had clearly spelled out that in the event the building was damaged for any reason that the landlord would not have to replace it if the cost would exceed the amount that could be recovered by the rental income. We felt safe enough. Well, we soon found out about local politics.

Their lawyer was a short pudgy individual and was a good friend of the judge. The judge was a pompous S.O.B. and during a recess the two of them would huddle behind a screen and we could hear them laughing and joking. We were about to be had. Naturally, Bonnie and I were dressed up nice, as was Fran. The lawyer portrayed me as a big out-of-town developer and I was taking advantage of this couple who were the tenants. This really had an effect on the jury as I never saw such a bunch of hay-seeds in my life; some of them were as dumb as dirt. One of them was a beauty operator, one ran a little old service station, and the rest the same types. None had experience of any kind involving leases and the like at all. My lawyer tried to explain the clause that let me have the option of canceling the lease, and so on but it just didn't penetrate the closed minds of the jurors. Especially when their lawyer asked the woman who had put up the money for the repairs where she got the money to put the roof back on and she said, "I had to get a loan on my furniture and sell my dead husband's guns." She and the guy that ran Club 66 were not even married. They were just shacking up. That didn't come up in the trial, of course.

Anyway, this had a great effect on the jury and the outcome of the trial against this big out-of-town developer. I started talking and I tried to show the pictures of the burned building but I was reprimanded by the judge several times about this and finally he said, "Mr. Long, I've told you several times to keep your mouth shut. Now if you say another word during this trial, I'm going to sentence you to 30 days in the Jasper County Jail. Do you understand this?"

I said, "Yes, judge, I do understand." So I shut up and shortly thereafter the jury ruled in favor of the tenants. Anyway, they filed the papers for me to pay the $4,000 in damages. However, the dumb clods filed it in the name of Andy Long. My lawyer called me in New Mexico and said, "Andy, they misfiled the paperwork. It should have been filled out in the names of Andrew E. and Bonnie J. Long, so you are home-free, hooray, hooray!"

Nothing more was heard about this whole deal for a year or so. Then we got notice that there would be a re-trial. Well, the advice of my good friend and brilliant lawyer in Los Alamos, Harry Moore, was, "Andy, I think you would be way ahead to pay them the $4,000. If they re-try it again you would still probably lose and also have the same worry and expense of it all over again." So that is what we did.

Winter is approaching in Los Alamos and White Rock. It's fall of 1974. Trying to build in the winter in Los Alamos is difficult, but not impossible. However, I had bought a piece of land in Los Lunas, New Mexico, about sixteen miles south of Albuquerque. It's a small town and a very old town with lots of Spanish-speaking people, some Indians, and some Anglos. The land I bought was on the site of the famous cottonwood hanging tree that had been used many times during the old wild west days.

I bought the land through a Realtor friend of mine, Lola Scotchtapole. The lot was directly across the street from City Hall, an ideal location for most anything we wanted to build. Lola knew a young chiropractor who was looking for a building he could rent for his office, so we started negotiations. For some reason he got cold feet so, I had Joe Dubin redesign the interior into four separate sections. The lot was large and the building was about 100 feet long by 40 feet wide. Separate doors and separate bathrooms, suitable for about anything. I thought of a doctor's office for one, a dentist and eye doctor for two more, with one left for something else.

I told Kermit we could build all winter long in Los Lunas and he would have a job, as well as a couple of his best men that were single, and they could move to Los Lunas for the winter. He said, "Great! Frieda, my wife, and I will live in our large pickup camper shell and go to Los Alamos on the weekends. We can park the pickup right on the jobsite." Kermit loved to fish and each evening after work he and Frieda would drive a short distance to various places to fish in the Bosque on the lower Rio Grande. This worked out very well. Again, we used white slump block with a mansard roof of red clay tile. A very nice looking building. Things went well and we finished on schedule and everyone was happy.

It just so happened that there was a large building supply business in Los Lunas that handled everything we needed to build the building. I can't remember the fellow's name that owned the business, but he was a Spanish guy of good character and a close personal friend of the upcoming candidate for the election of Governor Jerry Apodoca. (Bruce King had finished his second term, and could not run again in this election.) Jerry Apodoca was from Las Cruces. One of my Realtor friends in Albuquerque was a fellow by the name of George Koury and George was beating the drum for Jerry Apodoca just like I had done for Bruce King when he was running.

George came to me and said, "Andy, the guy you are buying all of the material from for your Los Lunas building is having a big political party barbeque for Jerry Apodoca and I am invited. I want you to go with me because when Jerry is elected, he is going to appoint me to the Real Estate Commission and if you want to be re-appointed to the Real Estate Commission for another five-year term, come with me to this party and I'll do my best to get Jerry to re-appoint you. I know you have done a good job on your first five-year term and I would like to work with you if Jerry gets elected."

I agreed to go with George Koury, as well as two other men, Jack Daily, another well-known Realtor from Albuquerque who I also knew, and Ben Abruzzo. Ben was the builder and owner of the Sandia Peak Ski

Area, and the Sandia Peak Tram, the cable car that goes up the Sandia Mountain from the west side, to the ski lodge and overlook. He was a good guy and well thought of in Albuquerque. So, the four of us went to the "get acquainted party" for our new prospective governor. We had a good time and on the way home George Koury said, "Why don't all four of us write a check to Jerry for a political contribution for his campaign expenses? I'm sure he would be very appreciative."

Well, we did and George delivered a check from Bonnie and I for $2,000. I also asked John Rogers to help me with a word to our new potential governor to consider re-appointing me to the Real Estate Commission. John had written my political speeches when I ran for state representative in 1968, and he had recently been elected to state senator himself. I had also given him a nice contribution for his campaign. Jerry Apodoca was elected governor, and George indeed did get me re-appointed on the Real Estate Commission. I served another five years right beside George Koury.

George and I became partners in a pretty big joint venture in Albuquerque, along with one other fellow, Dick Bock, who had been Ed Leslie's sales manager in Los Alamos years earlier, which I will get into a little later on.

Now back to the new building in Los Lunas. There were no medical services at all in Los Lunas and it was sixteen miles to travel to Albuquerque for medical care. The State Medical Board was looking for a location for a clinic in Los Lunas with the help of our U. S. Senator Joseph Montoya, who I became acquainted with at the grand opening of the tennis shoe factory we had built in Raton. Senator Montoya did manage to get the funding for a clinic to be located in the building we had just finished in Los Lunas. They took a lease on the whole building which had an option to purchase included, and in about three months they exercised the option. We were all happy and had a big celebration at the Los Lunas High School football field. Old Senator Montoya got a lot of political mileage out of it, and we enjoyed it too. Kermit and I had met quite a few people in Los Lunas by now ourselves.

At this time of my life in New Mexico, if I had had any ambition to run for political office, I could have won an election pretty easily. However, I did not have a single ounce of political ambition at all. I was having a ball at what I was doing and I was making a lot of money too. Talk about busy! Most people don't know what busy is.

Whenever you would see Andy Long, he had a yellow tablet in his hand or in his car. I kept it with me all of the time. It is the only way that I could stay in touch with everything that I had going at the same time without forgetting something or other. Each night before going to bed I would empty my mind out on the yellow tablet with all the things I had to do for the next day. That way I wouldn't lay awake half the night worrying about them. It worked out well, except in some cases, when I had a big important job to get ready for, I might occasionally have trouble sleeping.

It was time to open up another street coming into The Village Shopping Center, off of State Road #4, so we put this together, along with a $20,000 bridge across the large arroyo running through our commercial land. Wes Trask had laid it out and he named the new street Bonnie View Drive. So we now had a Bonnie View Drive and a Long View Drive. This would open the whole Village with a street directly off of the highway.

There were quite a few large lots laid out originally on this land. One large piece of land on the east side of the State Road #4 and the south side corner of Bonnie View Dr. which we had shown on the master plan as a motel site. Another lot was east of the motel site, which I sold to Marley Delancy for his veterinary clinic, and on the north side of Bonnie View there were two more lots. Tim negotiated a sale of one on the north side of Bonnie View that we sold to the Pizza Hut company and they built a nice building which was a welcomed addition to The Village. That left one more building site between the Pizza Hut and the arroyo on the north side of Bonnie View Drive. I decided to build a duplicate of the one we had just finished in Los Lunas and I did. I sold it to our local chiropractor who had outgrown his present facility. It was also welcomed by the White Rock residents.

The time period is now August 1975 and Tim's ex-wife had remarried for the third time to a good guy by the name of Neil Morgan. So our granddaughters now had a good step-daddy and they were ready to start the fourth grade in school. This new husband and step dad had a good job as an industrial engineer with the Levi Strauss Jeans Company in Albuquerque.

Neil's folks lived in Albuquerque and we all got well acquainted with each other. They were about ten years older than Bonnie and I and were great folks. It was good for our granddaughters to have another set of grandparents. Their names were Mickey and Ellen Morgan. They had lived in Albuquerque for many, many years. Mickey was retired from the railroad and was a good Irish guy who always wore red suspenders.

One day Neil and Juanita informed Tim, Bonnie and I, as well as Neil's folks, that Neil had accepted a really good job in San Salvador, the capital of El Salvador, in Central America. Neil Morgan had been hired by Levi Strauss to oversee the construction of a brand new factory building to replace an old existing one. He had not only had to oversee the building, but also had to select the machinery they would use, and to train all the help to get the new factory going. Quite a responsible job.

So Neil, Juanita and the twins moved to El Salvador and set up their home together. At Christmas the four of them came back to New Mexico for the holidays. The twins stayed afterwards with Tim and us, and then Bonnie and I flew them back to El Salvador. It was quite an exciting trip for us. We went through Mexico City and had to change planes there. We waited and waited for about six hours and finally I found someone I could talk to and asked what the delay was. The only answer I could get was that there was a problem with the "machine," meaning the airplane we were waiting to fly to San Salvador. Finally we boarded and started taxiing for take-off. Well, we went on and on and on and I just knew we were going to run out of runway, but finally we were air bound — and what a sigh of relief.! I think the Mexican Airlines bought old 'half worn out' U. S. planes for their airliners! Later I found out that the elevation at the Mexico City Airport is 7,500 feet, so this is why it takes a long time to lift off, because of the thin air.

We arrived safely and had a great time. On the weekend Neil drove us all to the country of Guatemala and we did a considerable amount of shopping, even in the remote Indian villages. We stayed all night in a nice hotel and saw the aftermath of a serious earthquake they had experienced several months earlier. It was beautiful scenery and we all had a good time. With Juanita speaking fluent Spanish we made out okay.

Neil's boss was a real nice fellow and he had found a home for them to rent, with a large walled yard and a locked gate, in a good neighborhood.

His boss lived in a huge home in an exclusive area and we were invited to dinner with his family and a lot of other big shot folks one evening. Something very exciting happened just before we were ready to eat. We heard loud gunshots and most of his guests half-panicked because of all the unrest that was going on in El Salvador at the time. It turned out, though, not to be gunshots at all; someone next door had set off a long string of firecrackers! Things settled down and we had a very nice evening after all. On the way home we did run into some large protest rallies downtown and we had to make some detours to get back to Neil and Juanita's house.

Neil's boss had a great beach house with a swimming pool, and a gardener, maid and cook, so we all spent the weekend up there and enjoyed it very much. He drove us in his Mercedes sedan, in which he kept a short-barreled automatic shotgun right between him and the door on the driver's side, just in case it was needed.

Let me now tell you another reason we took this trip. I had gotten acquainted with a fellow in Santa Fe that was a collector and trader of Central American Indian art, artifacts, jewelry and such. He even published a catalog for such things. His name was Rex Arrowsmith and he lived in the art colony section of Santa Fe on upper Canyon Road. He was very likeable and in our conversations I mentioned I had been reading a lot about Costa Rica. He said, "Andy, I own a place in Costa Rica and I happen to know of a large piece of land near where I live when we are down there on buying trips. It's near the little town of Golfito on the Gulf of Dulcie, very close to the Costa Rico and Panama border." I asked about the land that was for sale and he said, "A man by the name of Al Monte, a Canadian, owns it."

Rex said he had seen the piece of land and he said it was a sloping 500 acre piece, going up a mountain side with a three-quarter mile beach front of beautiful black sand. He said there was no road to it yet, but there was talk of a road that was going to cut across the upper corner of it when they extended the Pan American Highway across Costa Rico to Panama. It had thousands of dollars worth of large hardwood trees that could be harvested there later and it had a swift-flowing stream down it. This all sounded very good to me. The only problem was that the only way that you could get to it was by boat, and that took about 45 minutes from Golfito. Golfito had a small airstrip that split their local golf course. Anyway, I asked how much they wanted for it and he said he thought $35,000. Today, it would be about three times that price.

I had decided that when we took the girls back home to El Salvador we would fly from there to Costa Rica and pay Mr. Al Monte a visit. So we did. Juanita accompanied us on the rest of our vacation and was our interpreter. This worked out very well. We checked in at the Balmorals Hotel in San Jose and gave Mr. Al Monte a call. Being a Canadian, he spoke English, which was a plus.

Bright and early the next morning and after paying $350 rent on a plane and pilot, we took off. Bonnie, Juanita and I boarded a little twin engine Cessna airplane with the pilot and a lawyer that represented the owners. (There were no real estate agents in Costa Rica. They only use lawyers on land transactions there.) We flew for about an hour south over beautiful forests and there was Golfito. We circled the town and the Gulf of Dulce and headed up the Pacific coastline with our camera taking pictures. I had a small motion picture camera and I would have the pilot zoom in on the beach and I got some really good shots.

Juanita was holding Bonnie's hand so tight and said, "Bonnie I am so worried. If we should crash and be killed, what would happen to our little girls?" Well, we calmed her down and headed back up the west coast of Costa Rica. We landed at the town and beach resort of Placitas on the coast, had a nice lunch and then returned to San Jose later that afternoon. I called Al Monte and said that I would have to think about it. I wanted to wait a while until we could find out more information about the road that was supposed to cut across the top corner of the property. With no road to it I couldn't see any way that I would be interested in it.

The next morning we decided to take the train that ran east from San Jose across three fourths of the country to the town of Limon on the east coast of Costa Rica, on the Caribbean. This was an unforgettable experience! The train was old, from about the Jesse James era, and we made about 67 stops. We stopped at every little village across Costa Rica! There was no highway and the train was the only way the people had to cross this jungle of coffee bushes, banana trees, coconut trees and forests. At every little place we stopped people were getting on and off with their chickens and goats and pigs and things. The people at the small villages would come to the train with their small handmade crafts and food items (hard-boiled eggs were the only thing we bought). This was as unique to us as it was smelly. We would cross small, swift rivers and large streams and they were very picturesque.

Almost all the people who lived along this train track in the small villages were black. Later we found out that the train track had been built by black natives from other countries and islands around the Caribbean with the promise that when it was finished they would leave. But this hadn't happened, so most of them stayed to live there. Their little houses were along the tracks and were very colorful with front porches on them. We talked to one young man from the United States who told us he was an American and was there with the Peace Corps, teaching the people how to farm. What do you think of this for a job?

We got into Limon about dusk and got a cab to a hotel; small, but clean, two stories and quite satisfactory. It had a discotheque with a dance floor that was made of glass blocks with lights under them — quite unique. We hired a cab after dinner and toured around the little town and found out about a small airport along the beach. The next morning we got tickets to fly back to San Jose, about a one hour flight in and old twin engine C-47, the ones used as the workhorses flying over the hump in Indo-China during World War II. That evening we visited the most elegant and beautiful opera house in all of Central America. People come from all over to see performances held there. Nothing was going on at the time, but we enjoyed seeing it.

One thing that got my attention about Costa Rica was that the country had no standing army. Their police took care of any problems that they had. I was impressed with the thought of this, especially with the things that the rest of the world was doing and what had been going on in Viet Nam for the last few years. I thought how nice it was just to live, love and work in a country like this. However, I figured, to suit our lifestyle and not get bored to death, why not just have a place to come to on the Gulf of Dulce with access to the San Jose airport and back to the States. This is why I was so interested in the 500 acres that we had looked at.

The next day we were winging our way back to El Salvador and decided to go with Juanita for a tour of town, shopping and to have lunch at a famous hotel where they had the Miss Universe competition about a month before we were there. Absolutely beautiful surroundings! Tables and chairs for drinking and dining all the way around a very large swimming pool. I could imagine the show that took place at the Miss Universe contest.

Our two week vacation was about over and the next day we caught a plane home to Florida, had a nice evening and spent the night there, and on to Albuquerque the following morning. We enjoyed our vacation and our world had grown a little larger and more interesting. I will have more to tell you about our second trip to Costa Rica later on in this "long story."

It is now early 1976. I was planning three additional buildings in The Village, one fairly large office building and a smaller one, and in between them, a building for a drugstore and a branch post office for White Rock. It would soon be warm enough to get started on them. I decided to turn my attention back to "Spin & Spell." Reggie Jones, my partner in J & L Products, had found out about the Mead Company, the largest company in the educational toy business which was located in Atlanta, Georgia. So we decided to pay them a visit. We made our appointment and after a long plane ride we arrived in Atlanta the afternoon before our appointment the next morning. We told the cab driver to take us to a small hotel and he did. It was an older hotel of white stucco, but very nice. It turned out to be famous as the one Al Capone stayed at when they would let him take short leaves from his internment in the Atlanta Federal Prison. They would let him take a few days or week from the prison and stay at the hotel where he could have visitors and female companionship. This was not public information, but true. He had been dead many, many years before we stayed there.

Atlanta was a very nice, clean city and we enjoyed touring it. The following morning we kept our appointment and met the young manager of the Mead Company, a fellow named Bill Ceroni. Bill was very personable and we hit it off right away and he liked our product, Spin & Spell. He said, "Fellows, leave me one and I will send it to one of our teachers that will analyze it for us and give us her recommendation." We thought this was great and that we might be on our way at last. We had made another trip to the International Toy Show in New York City a year after the one that was cut short by Marion Perkin's husband's death when we had to return home early from the second show, also unsuccessfully. We had high hopes after our visit with Bill Ceroni of Mead Company.

About two weeks later we got a letter from Bill that dropped us from the pinnacle of enthusiasm to the very depths of despair. We read that the teacher had given a very negative opinion of Spin & Spell and this is what their company would be abiding by and they could not consider it further. How heartbroken we were! A little later on, I learned of a sales company in Costa Mesa, California that had heard of our toy and would like to talk to us. This time I decided to take my attorney of long-standing, Harry Moore with me. Harry, Tim and I flew to California and we met with them, and by verbal agreement it was decided that we ship one dozen cases of Spin & Spells and they would test them out and let us know. So we visited the two fairly young ladies who would be trying to sell them and returned home. About a month later Bonnie and I decided to go to Malibu, California to visit our friends Chuck and Pat Coutts, so I drove up to the house where these gals lived. Unfortunately, they had not sold any.

I went to see the people that had hooked me up with the two gals and they apologized and said, "Mr. Long we have another plan. There is a manufacturing company that would like to produce them out here, but they will need the dies to do so." Well, I agreed to lease the dies to them, but we would retain ownership. Back to Albuquerque and inform Gordon Thompson, the fellow who had made the dies and the first 400 of these toys for us and tell him of my deal in California. He was glad to get the dies off of his hands and wished us luck.

Tim and his artist friend, Jeri Osterhaut, had his econoline van and they thought this would be a nice vacation for them — to take the dies to California and then travel up the coast before returning to New Mexico. This was after Tim's divorce from Juanita, so away they went to deliver the dies. These dies were tremendously heavy and the load in the van was really too much, but somehow or other they made it.

Time passed and nothing happened and there was no word heard by mail or phone. Bonnie and I decided it was time to drive out to California and see what in the hell was going on. We got to their building and it was closed and locked up. There was a telephone number on the door so I called and the person on the other end said that he was the owner of the building and the people I wanted to see had taken bankruptcy. Oh, my! I explained that I was here to pick up my dies that I had leased to them. I had a copy of my lease with me in my briefcase and after a while he thought it would be okay to let me take the dies. We drove to a welding shop and had a very strong trailer hitch made to attach to my big Lincoln Towncar to pull a trailer, the dies, and the Spin & Spells that I was picking up from the two ladies that had not sold any of them. The big dies were not large in size, but were very heavy -- probably about 2,000 pounds of steel, 4 feet square and about 2 feet thick. We rented a small, strong little trailer from U-Haul, loaded everything up, and Tim and I headed for White Rock.

Upon our return home there was a registered letter from the Parker Brothers Toy Company threatening J & L Products with a law suit because they had a toy on the market called "Spill & Spell." A lot of small chips of wood with a letter printed on them that you simply spilled out on the table and spelled a word with. They said our product was infringing upon their product's name and that they would sue if we did not cease the production and sale of Spin & Spell. This did upset us because the products were not similar in our opinion, but as the old saying goes, "The golden rule in business is that the one with the gold makes the rules," so Parker Brothers would have caused us to spend a lot more money to fight a lawsuit, so we decided to cease and desist the production and sales of Spin & Spell. I contacted my accountant of long-standing, Joe Sisneros, who handled our taxes on everything and had done so for years, and he came up with a winner for us. He said, "Andy, if you can sell those dies for Spin & Spell to someone, for any amount of money, you can deduct your loss of $40,000 that you have spent on product development, promotional trips, etc., from the amount of income tax you will have to pay on your taxes when you sell a large piece of property. This was the silver lining for us.

One of our fine, young neighbors had started up his own construction business. I will not mention his name here, but his main business was dirt work with his backhoe, grader and dump truck, etc. We had used him on our jobs and he was such a good guy. He would always plow our driveway when it came a hard snow and never charge me. They had a daughter the same age as our two granddaughters and we were all good friends. His wife later started her own real estate business and I helped her get everything set up in her business. Anyway, I had him come by the house and said, "I want you to buy something from me, and here are five one-hundred dollar bills to buy it with. You deposit the cash in your bank account and write me a check for $500 and mark it payment in full for Spin & Spell dies.

You have your dump truck to load the dies on with your backhoe and you can sell them for scrap metal whenever you want to. This will not get you in any trouble, or me either, but it will help me take some of the loss I have had." Deal made. What a blessing! Once again, like I've said before, if you don't find the circumstances you want, make them. To give our promising venture of Spin & Spell a happy ending, I did indeed take this $40,000 loss off my taxes later on. This old boy stored the dies out behind his barn for several years just in case I would need them later or if there were any problems. What a friend!

Now, back to The Village Shopping Center. Tim designed a large sign on a strong and tall base for the corner of Bonnie View Drive and State Highway #4 to direct traffic to the shopping center. It would light up at dusk and was much needed. It cost about $4,000.

We finished the two office buildings, the drugstore and the branch Post Office building that summer and the tenants' businesses were all doing well. The Los Alamos Laboratory wanted to lease both office buildings, so some of their employees that lived in White Rock would be close to work. These two buildings would hold about 30 or 40 office workers, and this, added to the ones occupying the Bonnie Jean Corporation buildings in Los Alamos, about 30 more offices plus the four tenants in the other building in the Bonnie Jean Corp. complex, totaled about 60 workers in Lab offices plus the other four tenants in the third building, my lawyer, his wife's gift shop, a dentist's office and the E.G.&G. office. So, counting everything at the Lab, plus all the others in the Shopping Center and The Village Professional Plaza and the sixteen apartment tenants, we must have had about eighty or ninety tenants. Along with all of this going on, I had never stopped trying to attract a supermarket chain for The Village.

I made contact with two brothers who owned and operated an I.G.A. market in Monument, Colorado. Their names were Ed and Bob Longfield. They invited Bonnie and me to come to Monument, Colorado and see their store. Well, we did and were impressed by the cleanliness and size, etc. of their store. They said it was time for them to add another market, so each would have a store of their own. They were young and anxious to succeed and were off to a good start.

With the blessing of the main headquarters, permission was granted for the brothers to work with the fine architect that designed all their various stores. The architect came down and met with Kermit Price and me and we wound up with a 12,600 sq. ft. building that was 100 ft. wide and 120 ft. deep. All this was taking place in the summer of 1976 and a lot of time was spent in getting all of our cost estimates together. We employed the help of a fine engineer by the name of Floyd Zimmerman, who lived in White Rock. I knew him well and he was a long-time employee of the Laboratory.

My good friend Wes Trask had recently retired from the Laboratory, moved to Albuquerque and gone to work with the Albuquerque City engineers group office. He had a great job with lots of responsibility laying out all the street drainage coming off the Sandia Mountains in the northeast heights of Albuquerque. He had a crew of young draftsmen working under him like he had done at the Los Alamos Laboratory. We were fortunate in having Floyd working with us. He got along well with Kermit as Kermit respected his knowledge and experience. The Laboratory hired only the best qualified people to work there, so it was good to be able to use some of their people who moonlighted, of course. One thing I mentioned to Floyd was that we would need to somehow muffle the noise the large compressors would make that were used for all the frozen foods that a market sells. So Floyd had us hire a friend engineer who knew how to handle problems like this. The compressors would be only fifty feet away from the backyard fences of the homes that were backing up to the Village property line. A driveway also had to go by the back of the store for unloading the big grocery trucks. We got this problem well taken care of to the satisfaction of everyone, including the neighbors and customers. Every one was real happy that we were finally getting a market in The Village.

Our own construction company, Western States Builders, Inc., was doing the whole job and hiring the subs we usually used for the concrete slab, electrical and plumbing which all had to be installed under the slab except for the lighting, heating and ceiling units. We handled all the purchasing of the structural steel from a steel company in Albuquerque. We leased a huge crane at $75 per day to do the steel erection to support the roof and our own men bolted it all together. This was a fairly hazardous job, but we got it done without any serious accidents or injuries. Kermit watched every move they made. This was the largest of our buildings, except for the tennis shoe factory in Raton, but we subbed out the steel for it like we did there.

The side, front and back were all twelve inch wide concrete blocks filled with pumice for insulation and high off the ground, so it was quite a task in getting this done. The store front glass and doors were subbed out, but we did all the rest with our regular subcontractors and employees. By the time we got all the cost estimates together, and the final drawings agreed to by us, I.G.A. and our Longfield brothers, and the contract signed as well as a loan package sent to the appraiser to be submitted to a lender, it was late November — not a good time to start construction.

The piece of land that would be for the building and parking was a full one acre in size, Lot #2 of The Village. Lot #1 was two acres in size and was between the south side of Lot #2 and, running south, to Sherwood Blvd. Both lots were across Longview Dr. from Gibson's discount Center. It was an ideal location for the market and across from the parking for The Village. The savings and loan branch of First Northern was right across the street.

We got the loan approved from Southwest Savings and Loan of Santa Fe. They were also a joint venture lender with First Northern Savings and Loan for the rest of the center. Well, about a week before our start date, there came a big snow storm, leaving snow about two feet deep! It was the day after Thanksgiving 1976 and we all gathered for the groundbreaking ceremony with the radio station and our local newspaper, the savings and loan branch manager, Floyd Zimmerman, Kermit Price, Peggy Corbett and myself for pictures. We had a big road grader come in and plow the snow back for the groundbreaking to take place. The ceremony went well and as soon as it was over the savings and loan manager went back to his office and called Bob Morris, my friend and president of First Northern Savings and Loan, and said to him, "You won't believe what that Andy Long is doing now. He's starting the supermarket in two feet of snow. How about that!" The only reason we had considered starting the building in late November was that we had signed a contract stating that the Longfield brothers could have their grand opening on April 1st. Well, to wind this up, we did have the grand opening on schedule, all except the blacktopped surface on the parking lot. We had the base course down, so it was okay to park and not have mud, but it had to be warmer weather in order to lay down the hot mix blacktop finish (that was done by April 15th). What a nice opening!

One little funny thing that I will now tell you about took place during the construction. Kermit, me, Kermit's lead man and Peggy were all in our Half Pint Haven, as we called it, situated right at the west edge of the lot and Longview Dr. We could look out and see all that was going on with the market job and The Village. We were studying the plans and a pickup drove up and parked near the market building. Two long-haired young guys got out and were walking up to the building. Kermit told the young lead man to go out and tell them we didn't need any more help. "Couldn't we use some more help, Kermit?" asked the lead man. Peggy was close by at her desk and phone and was overhearing the conversation. She and Kermit usually had their own "tit for tat" running and Kermit loved to set her hair when he had the chance. Well, he said to the lead man, "Tell them our workman's comp insurance doesn't have any maternity benefits." Well, the lead man and Peggy both responded at the same time and me, too, with "What are you saying?" Kermit said, "One of our tough carpenters might grab one of those longhairs and get him pregnant and then where would we be." Well, this being said, Peggy grabbed her purse and said, "I'm going to lunch, Andy." He really got her goat this time, and the three of us laughed until we cried after she left.

While I'm in a story telling mood, I'll tell you another one. Sometime later, after the market was opened, Kermit and I were discussing another project we were planning and the phone rang and Peggy said, "It's for you, Andy."

I said, "Who is it?"

"I don't know," Peggy said.

I said, "If I have one more climax this morning I am going to explode!" It had been one of those mornings.

Peggy laughed and said, "I keep telling you, Andy, it's not climax, it's crisis."

I said, "Yes, Peggy, I'm going to have to remember that."

And she said, "Yes, you should."

Well, I said, "Hello." and the voice on the other end said, "This is Mr. Martinez with the I.R.S."

I said, "What the hell do you want to talk to me about? Joe Sisneros does our taxes and has for years. You people have checked us before and have never found anything wrong that needed to be changed. You check with Joe."

"No," he said, "I have to talk with you."

I said, "You are not coming to my office or home you revenuing S.O.B. I don't have any information that would help you. Joe does it all," and I hung up on him. The reason I had gotten so rough with him was that a couple of years earlier they had called Bonnie at the house and she agreed to let the guy come to our home. Well, he came every day for a week and went through everything and never found where we had done anything wrong. Joe had handled it perfectly as he always did and our bill to him in those days was usually about $4,000 and involved a two-hour conference with him before he started and the same when he finished — and we signed all the forms he submitted. I guess I just happened to draw a hard-headed S.O.B. who caught me at the wrong time, and I gave him two ears full.

Well, he did make an appointment with Joe, and later Joe said to me, "Andy, please don't cuss them out any more. It makes it hard for me to talk to them."

There were several women artists in Los Alamos County and most of them were pretty good and, with the local garden club, they did a lot of good work for the community. One day the wife of the newspaper owner and publisher came to Peggy and asked if I would let them paint some Indian art across the front of the supermarket above the windows all the way up to the roofline. We all agreed that this would be very nice and Kermit, being an artist himself, rigged them up some nice metal scaffolding that we used to build tall building walls. It was pretty safe and high off the ground, but they got the job done and it was beautiful.

The Village Shopping Center was certainly the most beautiful one in the state. Everyone was proud of it and we got lots of compliments which helped make it all worthwhile. I had taken on a lot more debt with the addition of the supermarket. The land value of our property had increased immensely after the center was built and doing well and the value of most of the vacant land that was left was appraised at around $4 per sq. ft. There are 43,560 sq. feet in an acre and the market, including the parking lot, totaled one acre, so that land alone was valued at $170,240. The building and land was appraised at $650,000. The land value was almost 20% and Southwest Savings and Loan loaned me $402,000, so I didn't have to come up with very much cash out-of-pocket — approximately $50,000 was all. The twenty-year lease would bring in $4,500 per month, so the loan was secured for the twenty year term.

We were growing pretty big, pretty fast. Looking back now, I guess we were about the biggest independent business in the County of Los Alamos at this time. I didn't think of it in this vein then, but looking back at it now, it was true. I came to town about fifteen years before selling pots and pans and look at old Andy Long now. Wow! My trademark always was honesty, loyalty, and being personable, and I was about to take on a couple of more now: calm and cheerful. These things certainly contributed to our success and, adding a lot of very dedicated hard work, were making it all come true.

The previous fifteen years of selling stainless steel cookware contributed more to our successful ability than anything else, I think. I have often said it was like having two Ph.D.'s in salesmanship. I truly believe that — meeting and dealing with people. And, we weren't done yet.

The parking lot for the market was really more than they needed. So, we had room for another nice office building for Peggy, Kermit, Tim and I. Quite a plush one at the upper end of the parking from the market on Longview Drive facing the end of The Village. We could see the whole thing, as well as the market front. We called it The Triangle Building, and it was very attractive.

Bonnie and I decided that we should have a swimming pool at our house. We then started designing one. The season for outside pools was short in Los Alamos County, so we decided to build an enclosed pool, attaching it to the backside of our house and opening from our master bedroom through an eight-foot sliding door from the den area. We could step right out the door and down three steps into the shallow end of the pool. It was sixteen feet wide and thirty-six feet long — heated with gas and also solar heat. It was all enclosed with glass mall sliding doors with an eight-foot concrete area around the other three sides of the pool, with large cutouts for planting. It looked like an Hawaiian garden, lots of moisture for the plants and they were gorgeous. An exhaust fan was at the upper end as well as a circulating gas heater at the other end so that we could swim year-round. In one corner we had a hot water jacuzzi which was also great. One of the sides opened out with the sliding mall doors adjoining the back patio of our home. So we had a very large entertainment and play area all shaded by late afternoon and evening.

When we finished the triangle building we did not need the little Half Pint Haven that we used while building the supermarket, so we had it moved about thirty feet from the end of our house by the side of the enclosed pool. It was an excellent location for a little guest house. It became very useful after our daughter, Andra, got her divorce and moved into it. It was just the right size for her. One bedroom, small kitchen, bath and large living room with a large open porch that faced the mountains to the west — just a little doll house. Andra Morehead was about to become Andra Long again, and just in time to become a very important member of our staff in the near future. Stay tuned.

Now back for a short time involving me and my chairmanship on the Real Estate Commission. We had a meeting in Deming, New Mexico, so I left Los Alamos one evening and spent the night at the Elephant Butte Lodge, near Truth or Consequences, New Mexico. The next morning in the lobby I ran into G. Y. Fails, the director of the Albuquerque Chamber of Commerce. I hadn't seen him since our big meeting in Clovis where we met with all the other Chamber managers and presidents about Bruce King running for Governor against Pete Dominici. G.Y. recognized me and he said, "Andy, where are you headed?"

I told him I was going to Deming for a Real Estate Commission meeting. He said, "I have a lead for you. A good friend of mine has a widowed mother that was left with a large mobile home park in Española, New Mexico, up in your neck of the woods. She needs to sell it. Her name is Ruby Alexander. You tell her that I sent you to see her and you should get you a real good real estate listing." Well, I thanked him. I did follow up and I did get the listing. It was called The Enchanted Mesa Mobile Home Park. Ruby was a really nice lady and we hit it off.

In due time I found a buyer by the name of Quinn Cramer. Quinn was a young Los Alamos plumber that had done quite well in Los Alamos and wanted to make an investment. I told him, "Quinn, you are lucky! Ruby and her husband had financed the park with a big insurance company and you cannot assume the loan, but they will allow you to buy it from Mrs. Alexander on a real estate contract." Quinn agreed and we wrote it up as such.

Quinn said, "I'll have to take this to a lawyer for advice before I sign it, Andy, so I will let you know in a few days." I said okay, and told Ruby I thought we had a sale.

She said, "Mr. Long, my daughter is a teacher and she has to go back to school the first week of September. She wants to take me on a trip to Hawaii before school starts right away. I hate to leave before the contract is signed, so I guess I'll miss my trip to Hawaii."

I said, "That's a shame, Ruby. I'll tell you what. If Mr. Cramer does not sign that contract, I'll buy your mobile home park. You go ahead and take that trip with your daughter." So she did. Well, what I didn't count on was the lawyer that Quinn chose had just moved to New Mexico from Texas, and in Texas real estate contracts are illegal and he advised Quinn Cramer not to buy this on a real estate contract. So, old Andy Long got hooked on this one. When Ruby got home from her trip, I had a contract signed with Bonnie and my signatures and told Ruby we were buying her park like I promised I would.

It just so happened that, included with the Park, Ruby owned two trailers there that were part of the deal, so I bought them too. One was a real nice big one, very nicely furnished. The other was just average, but nice. I was telling Kermit about these two trailers as he and his wife were living in one in Los Alamos and had done so for years and they loved their trailer — it was about forty feet long by eight feet wide — one you could pull from town to town and with Kermit being in construction, he had moved a lot before he met me. Kermit said, "Could I look at the big trailer?" And I thought, "I have me a good prospect," and he had a trailer just the right size that we could use as a portable construction office. I made him one hell of a deal on the big trailer and the bank helped him buy it and I bought his trailer for a construction office and parked it out behind my barn temporarily. We would soon be using it. Anyway we had a big mobile home park to run.

I hooked old Bonnie-girl up and we went down to meet all the renters, and low and behold one of them we knew real well and had worked with him with the Noxon Construction Company in 1961-1963. He was their fireplace subcontractor on all the homes we sold back in the early days of White Rock. His name was Joe Baldonado, a huge man, big and fat, a real good guy. Spanish, of course. Joe became our Park manager; he lived at the Park in his trailer, so he got along with all of the other renters. He collected the rents and Bonnie did the bookkeeping and it worked out beautifully. Joe got free rent, Kermit had a nice new mobile home and he and his wife were both happy and all I had to do was find another buyer to take me off the hook. Oh, yes, one of the renters in the Park was a State Police officer, so we didn't have any trouble with any of the other tenants that he and Joe couldn't handle. I had a soft spot in my heart for Joe Baldonado as he had been taken prisoner on Corrigedor and had been in the Bataan Death March like my lifelong friend Bobby Jones of Altus, Oklahoma.

Within a few months I had a buyer, and good ones at that. One was Danny McReynolds and a lifelong friend of his whose name I can't remember, but a former mayor of Espanola. Danny was the man that owned McReynolds Construction Company who did all of our street, sewer and blacktop work as well as the two bridges that we had to build in The Village. I had paid him thousands of dollars and we were very good friends. He and his buddy both lived in Espanola and they got a big bank loan and paid off the insurance company that had financed it for the Alexanders in the beginning. It had taken up a little more time, but it worked out well for a lot of folks along the way. We were all happy, even a young, single gal that worked in Governor Jerry Apodoca's office in Santa Fe, who I rented the second trailer to that I had to buy from Ruby. I made her a real good deal and got her a loan through a bank in Espanola so she could buy it from me. It wasn't long until she sent Bonnie and me an "Aide-de-camp" certificate, just like Bruce King had sent to Bonnie and I for all the good work we did for him, as well as our advice and true friendship. I think she had told Governor Apodoca about the trailer she had bought from us and he must have decided I was an alright guy. Of course, I had been serving almost five years on the Real Estate Commission under his term as Governor, so he knew me quite well. He had spent his fortieth birthday at our home in White Rock, just like Bruce King had spent his fiftieth birthday there.

Remember the couple who opened the ladies and children's clothing store in The Village called Ira's? Their names were Ira and Fern Clark. He also ran another store in Santa Fe. Fern ran the one in The Village. They, along with their two young sons, also rented one of our Village apartments. Anyway, I had co-signed his note at a bank in Santa Fe for $82,000. I had questioned him well before I did so, as I had to put up as collateral two or three acres of land at the north end of The Village and south end of The Village Professional Plaza offices. The land was right between these two projects and right across Longview Drive from The Village Apartments. It was destined to be a retirement village of town homes. Well, remember, I had asked Ira if he and Fern had any family problems along with other questions, of course, and he laughed and said, "I'm getting along real well with my wife and my mistress this week." This was about a year after he opened his Santa Fe store just before our Grand Opening of The Village Shopping Center. It turned out that his mistress was a cute little Spanish girl that worked in his Santa Fe store. His wife caught them one day and divorce followed quickly thereafter. What a blow! We not only lost a store tenant, but also an apartment tenant, and by signing Ira's note at the bank in Santa Fe, we had to pay the bank $71,000 that was left to pay on the note. Bonnie and I wound up with a store full of clothing and fixtures that we really didn't need, but there it was.

I made a trip to the Los Alamos National Bank and talked to the young new president there, Bill Enloe. He was a bright young man and his father was a well-known leader in the local Democratic Party and a friend of mine, although that didn't have anything to do with my banking business. Anyway, I said, "You may have heard the news about Ira Clark" (who was about his age), and he said, "Yes." "Well," I said, "Bill, I had signed Ira's note at the Santa Fe National Bank and it is up to me to pay it off. To make a long story short, Bill, I want to borrow $71,000 on a large lot in The Village that I plan to build a retirement village on soon."

I had not done any business with Bill since he had become president, but he had been vice president for quite a while, so he was pretty well acquainted with my performance. He leaned back in his chair and said, "Well, you may have to come up with more collateral, Andy."

I was sitting right across the desk from him and I said, "Either that or see another bank."

He turned red-faced and said, "I'm going to pretend I didn't hear that, Andy."

And I said, "I don't give a damn, Bill, I don't have any holes in my shoes or pants. You had better get my file out and take a look at the collateral you already have."

I just sat there and he did get my file, looked at it and said, "Andy, I'm sorry that I didn't look at your file before I told you what I did. I think the board will go along with you, okay?" Well, I thanked him, wished him luck in his new job as president and he learned a lot more about Andy Long than he knew before. I had to take this all in my stride as after all, he was young. In fact, the same age as my son Tim. We had had several new presidents at that bank up to now, and all were pretty good, but they didn't stay too long and would leave to take better banking jobs in other towns. The Los Alamos people were too difficult to deal with in business for them to put up with. Bill was the first home-grown banker, so-to-speak, that we had had and I understand that he is still at the same bank to this day in 2002. He became president in 1978, so his string has run for twenty-four years and he is well known throughout the state and has won several awards in the banking business.

So now Bonnie was in the business of running a clothing store, without any experience, except general business experience. The first thing we did was change the name from Ira's to The Carousel in The Village and to the fine lines of ladies clothes we added men's and children's clothes and shoes. Bonnie had always dressed nicely and had bought good clothes and I had a couple of years experience in selling men's clothing when we were in Bartlesville. I didn't have time to work in the store, but I did advise her on men's clothing and would go to market with Bonnie and her manager, a very enthusiastic gal by the name of Gladys Smith, whose husband worked at the Laboratory. We would go to the Denver Market and also to the Dallas Market, twice a year — to buy for Spring and for Fall. What an experience! Like I've said before, "If you don't have the circumstances you want, then go to work and change them." We didn't have much of a choice. We simply had to make it work, and we did.

Our darling daughter, Andra, was put into full swing. She took over for Bonnie in all that she had been doing with the bookkeeping and payroll with Western States Builders and all the receivables and payables involving the various projects and all the tenants — with Bonnie's help. The latest building we had just finished was the plush office building, The

Triangle Building. It was well located in The Village for me, Peggy, Kermit, Pete Chavez, Tim and Andra, and was just down from The Carousel and Bonnie. We were in the planning stages of our newest project, the retirement town homes to be built on the large lot at the north end of the shopping center, just across the street and along Longview Drive. Due to the unexpected problem with the clothing store, we decided to accelerate the next project. We got busy in a hurry.

Several things had happened at about this time. Ed Leslie had died at age 50. He and I were the same age. He had been dead about two or three years and White Rock had about been built out for two or three years, and Home Planning had been doing a lot of building in Albuquerque. My old friend Dick Bock, who had been one of Ed's top managers wasn't doing much, so I hired him to help me with the planning and estimating on our proposed town house project that we call "Village Place." Dick suggested that we use a young architect in Albuquerque who he knew was very good, so we did.

With the lay of the land, we came up with a horseshoe shaped design with the opening coming in off of Longview Drive, across the bridge to The Village Apartments. Both residential projects would be fairly close to one another and flanked on each end by the Professional Office Plaza on the north and by The Village Shopping Center on the south, with the White Rock homes on the east. The town houses would be built all around the outside of the horse-shoe design with the cul-de-sac street around the inside of the horseshoe, and a landscaped center area. The curve of the horseshoe shaped street was just wide enough for a fire truck or garbage truck to drive around easily. All the units would be attached to each other with a one-inch gap between the outer walls of each townhome, but stuccoed over, and would go all the way around the horseshoe opening, except for one eight-foot wide walkway through a wrought iron gate with a combination lock, so all the owners would have private access to The Village Shopping Center — very convenient. This was a tedious job for the draftsman to design each townhouse floorplan to be usable and attractive to our buyers. We put in lots of hours of hard work and sound-proofing of the attached party walls of each unit. There are various sizes: two and three bedroom units, with several being two-story homes.

We got underway in the early spring of 1978, fitting into this time period our twin granddaughters and their mother and stepfather, Neil Morgan, who were on their way back from El Salvador. The new factory had been completed and was running well, but there was a lot of political unrest in El Salvador, as well as in Honduras and Nicaragua. Remember the Contras, etc., during these years. Well, Neil's boss, Kiekee's brother-in-law, who was his bookkeeper, had been kidnapped and Kiekee and his family were considering shutting down the factory and moving to Miami, Florida. It was high time that Neil brought his family back to the United States. We were very relieved with this news. Tim and his wife Dottie drove to San Diego to pick them up at the airport, and took the twins and her three boys to Disneyland. Unfortunately, the La Mesa fire was burning in the Los Alamos area at the time and almost burned their home and ours while they were gone. Soaking the roofs was the only thing that saved them. Fires were also burning in Flagstaff and Ft. Huachuca (where Ron Johnson and family were stationed at the time) — all along their trip out to California and back.

The twins started school with us in the 6th grade and stayed with Tim and us in our big house during the summer and 6th and 7th grades. They enjoyed the new White Rock school and would catch the school bus right at our driveway. They would ride their ponies and swim in our big enclosed pool with their friends and our family. With this change, and with Bonnie very busy with The Carousel and her other work, Andra and I needed to have a place to watch out for our precious twins and also do our work on planning and building Village Place. I decided to turn our big double-car garage into an office. It didn't take much, just replacing the garage door with a big sliding wall of glass doors, hanging drapes, paneling the walls, laying carpet, adding more lighting and extending the heating. We were in business!

Kermit was superintendent and Tim, who was project manager and doing the purchases for the project, needed to be closer to their new project with their office. We decided to move Kermit's old trailer that I had taken in trade when he bought the new one from the Enchanted Mesa deal, over next door to the new project. It was in very good condition with a bathroom, refrigerator and stove, good heating and lighting. Kermit's legs were not in good shape at all; they had been broken when he had fallen off a roof many years before and he had to wear steel braces on both legs. This cut out a lot of walking for him. He had a phone for ordering all his sub-contractor work and materials. Tim was a great help to him and worked hard, but Kermit was not the easiest person to get along with. I had to explain to him that the easier he was on Tim, the easier I would be with him and vice-versa.

Can you just imagine building nineteen town houses all at one time? This took one hell of a lot of careful planning. We started out on the first ten with the ten footings, then the plumbing and hot water heating pipes all under the slabs. Then all the framing next, and so on and on. Lots of material had to be ordered and this is where Tim came in very well. We had gotten off to a rather late start in the summer of 1978, but we did get the ten closed in by winter and had a lot of framing and finish work going on, but it is slow going in the winter on that mountain.

We had been so happy with the hot water circulating heating that our old friend Jasper Connor and his plumbing and heating company A.B.C. Mechanical had done for us on our big house that we decided to use his system in our new town houses. I told Jasper to give me one bid on all the nineteen homes for all the plumbing and heating, so he took the plans and in a week or so came to me and said, "Andy, the total cost on all nineteen units is $78,000."

I said, "Jasper I will write you a contract right now for a complete package and pay you in progress payments as you complete each unit." I took my yellow tablet and made two copies — one for him and one for myself that said, "A.B.C. Mechanical will furnish all labor and material for plumbing and heating for nineteen town homes on The Village Place project for the total of $78,000." Signed, Jasper Conner for A.B.C. Mechanical and Signed, Andrew E. Long, for Western States Builders. Jasper told me later he thumb-tacked this yellow tablet sheet contract on his office wall in Albuquerque and when he got a real picky customer when signing a contract, he would take them over to the yellow sheet tacked to the wall and show then how a long-standing customer and friend trusted him and the good work that he had done for him for years. This is how real gentlemen treat each other when there is mutual trust and respect. He said it sure took a lot of haggling out of getting contracts signed after that. I thought that was great!

People used to say to me, "Andy, you are the luckiest guy I know." I would say to them, "Yeah, I am. You know, the harder I work, the luckier I get."

Well, this project was the largest one I had tackled since the shopping center and interest rates were climbing, but at the time I started, right after Ira's "screw up" as I called it, I had no choice but to proceed and try to recover.

For financing I went to First Northern's branch right in our Village center and laid out my proposal to their manager. I told him I would need to borrow $1,600,000. "Wow," he said, "How do you propose to pay the loan back?"

I said, "When I sell each town home I will pay off the construction loan with a permanent loan your savings and loan company will make to the buyers of the town home. This way you will be making the interest on the construction loan from me and on the permanent loans that you make to the buyers." This sounded real good to the branch manager, so he said he would submit it to Bob Morris and the loan committee, along with the appraisal that they would have to make at my expense. I said, "Okay." Well, this all happened before I started, and in a week or so I got the loan approval from them with some terms and conditions, of course.

First of all, the branch manager said, "Andy, they will lock in the permanent loans to your buyers at 9 1/2%, which at the time was good. "Then," he said, your construction loan of $1,600,000 will start out at prime plus 2% and every three months it will be adjusted to prime plus two percent, whatever it is. This will be renewable and payable every six months." Well, that didn't sound too bad, and we were ready to go, so we agreed.

As we finished each one of the first ten, we would start the next one of the second nine units. We were beginning to come out of the winter months, but our projected finish date was dragging because of the winter weather. We had planned on having them ready to sell in the spring of 1979 in order to sell in the summer months, but this didn't happen. It was late summer and we were behind in sales.

Also, interest rates were still climbing and the famous rate increases during the late Jimmy Carter presidential years were killing us financially. The problem nationally with Iran and the hostage situation were big headlines and interest rates climbed rapidly. We were locked in okay on the permanent loans for our buyers, but most of them had to sell their present home before they could buy our new home and therein was the big problem.

Interest rates were still climbing — 16, 18 and even 20% on all home loans — and it became nearly impossible for people to sell their homes. Our lock-in of 9 1/2% on our permanent loans that First Northern had agreed to was great, but if the people couldn't sell their homes, they couldn't buy ours. On top of the interest problem was a hiring freeze at the national laboratory. With Los Alamos being a one-industry town, this really hurt us. Every night when I laid down to sleep, interest rates went on. Our construction rate had cost me $360 every day with no way to shut it off, month after month.

I managed to sell ten of the first town homes by trading for people's property — I had even taken two lots in Deer Park, Texas and Conway, Texas from the parents of two young couples that had recently gone to work at the Laboratory and I had also sold one to Andra and one to Tim; each of these were two-bedroom units. They were locked in at 9 1/2% interest loans, so this was good for them and good for us. It took me a long, long time to sell the two lots in Texas, but it finally came to pass after several years. This problem went on for about nine months and was just eating me alive.

I had even made a sales office in one of the garages and put Andra in charge there, but the market was just not good enough to hardly make any sales. She worked very hard at it and it was also good for us to have a place for her to be close when the units were in the final stages of finishing. She had done all the color selections for the paint, floor coverings, bathroom tile, appliances, carpet and cabinets. She did a fabulous job in working with the subs. It was very good experience for her and they turned out beautifully.

Dick Bock's wife, Joan, was a good interior decorator and had done all of Home Planning's model homes in the past. She told Bonnie that Shirley Leslie had lots of model home furniture stored in their warehouse, so we bought some and Joan furnished one of our homes for a model.

In the fall of 1979 Ronald Reagan defeated the peanut farmer from Plains, Georgia, but the election didn't have time to affect the national interest rate problem for people like me. Fortunately, I had decided to sell The Village Apartments a year or so earlier to an investment group, and I had also sold the Village Professional Office Plaza to the local Los Alamos Laboratory Federal Credit Union. I had invested the money in the other buildings I had built to finish the Village Shopping Center and had planned on making the town house project my last project. I just knew that when I sold all nineteen of them I would have made two to three hundred thousand dollars on it — and in those days that was a lot of money. But it sure didn't look very promising right now.

I was pushing Kermit and Tim pretty hard to get finished and they were working on the last eight units, of 19, with the inside finish work. Kermit was riding Tim pretty hard and the stress was affecting all of us. One day I told Bonnie that we needed to get away for a couple or three days so I could think things out. We caught a plane to Las Vegas. It was the only place I could go that would take my mind off my business. One our way home on the plane I told Bonnie I had to lay Kermit off.

She said, "Why?" I said, "His legs are really bothering him and he has so much walking to do to keep up with the finish work on all the different homes and it is getting very hard for Tim and the other men to get along with him. I think he wants me to lay him off so he can draw his unemployment, and he is now 65 or 66 years old and he can retire and draw his social security. He knows he is not able to do the job, but does not want to quit me in the middle of a job."

Bonnie said, "What are you going to do for a superintendent?"

I said, "I just don't know."

Well, it was the hardest decision I had had to make in years, but I knew I had to do it. I went to my office in the triangle building in the Village and Peggy was already there and she said, "Andy, I have some bad news for you. Kermit came to me at quitting time for his check and handed me all of his keys. He told me he was leaving without any explanation and then he was gone."

I said, "Peggy, that's not bad news at all. It is good news."

Peggy said, "What do you mean?" I told her that on the way home from Vegas I had made the very difficult decision to lay him off. I talked to Tim and he said, "Dad, as project manager and purchasing agent I've been the one working with the carpenters and subs anyway, so I can handle the job for you myself." The project was about half done with only the interior finish work and patios on all nineteen homes, roofing on the last 10 units, exterior stucco and landscaping on all the front yards and the center area of the street still to be completed. I said, "Good man."

We then hired one of our workmen, Kevin Leveque, who had done some landscaping work before, to work up the landscaping plans. I told Kevin, "Well, young man, you've got the job and I'll go to Albuquerque and get you whatever you need in trees and shrubs. We'll get the gravel locally and you will be in charge of the landscaping." So, we turned a big minus into a plus once again.

We still had the problem of selling the final nine homes to stop the bleeding, so to speak, at 20% interest. One morning Andra told me that my good friend and Realtor-builder Jim Wimberley in Ruidoso, New Mexico called and wanted to talk to me. I called Jim back and he said, "Andy, I have an idea and have been thinking about it for some time and I want you in on it with me."

Jim was the fellow that I had assigned the long-term land lease in Ruidoso several years ago that I wrote about when I was going to build a lot of condos but changed my mind when I decided that it was too far from Los Alamos. Jim took the lease on the land from me and put a large mobile home park on it. He later sold it to Johnny Carson, the late night talkshow host and comedian. Anyway, Jim and I get along real well as we respected each other and our abilities. I still see him frequently and have stayed in touch over the years.

Jim said, "Andy, you have been to my swimming and racquet club that I have near the little Ruidoso airport. I'm thinking of forming a limited partnership and I want you to be one of the general partners along with two pretty strong oil men from Roswell. What I want to do," he said, "is build a hotel and lease it to the Hilton Hotel people. I have two guys coming in from Salt Lake City that are specialists in setting up limited partnerships. They are coming to Ruidoso the day after tomorrow and so is Eric Hilton, one of the two brothers that run the Hilton Hotel chain. Eric takes care of all the hotels in the USA and his brother takes care of all the hotels outside of the USA." Jim continued, "He will also be here for our meeting day after tomorrow."

Well, I told Jim that my daughter and I would be there. He said, "Drive down tomorrow, Andy. I have just finished a condo project and I'll put you up for the night at no charge." The following day we drove down and everyone gathered at the Alpine Swim and Racquet Club. Eric Hilton had flown into El Paso from his office in Houston and rented a car and driven up to Ruidoso that morning. The meeting started about 9:00 AM with all present including the two oil men and their wives from Roswell. The two limited partnership experts from Utah started telling us all about how it worked; in those days limited partnerships were fairly new. This was pretty dry stuff to the two Roswell wives and Andra, so they suggested that the ladies go shopping.

The two gals didn't know Andra and my relationship, and when Andra said, "Daddy, could I have some money to shop with?" And I said, "Yes, honey." and handed her a one hundred dollar bill. Well, they thought Andra was my girlfriend and didn't know she was my daughter and their mouths dropped open and they left without her. I think all of them except Jim thought the same thing.

So, Andra stayed at the meeting and we listened to these guys for a couple of hours and took a break. Eric and I went to the rest room and he said, "Mr. Long, I have heard all I need to about the monkey screwing the dog from these two boys from Salt Lake City. I am not the least bit interested in any limited partnership deals. If you other fellows want to build a hotel, Hilton will lease it from you and I'll tell you how to get the money to build it." He went on to say that the state economic development committee would help for towns the size of Ruidoso where there is little or no industry and a lot of people could work in a hotel such as cooks, waiters, maintenance, cleaning people, maids, etc. "Our hotel would employ a lot of these type people and the state knows that and will probably make you a loan to build the hotel. I think we can make a deal, I'm pretty sure."

Well, I immediately got excited when we broke for lunch. I told Jim Wimberley about this and he got equally excited. He told the two oil men about it and we decided to tell the Utah hot shots that we would let them know if we wanted to go the limited partnership route or not. The four of us then got together to discuss the new idea that Eric Hilton told me about. Bruce King was getting ready to run for re-election as governor and, of course, the oil men and Jim were Republicans as well as Ruidoso,

New Mexico being a Republican stronghold area, so Andy Long was the one to talk to Bruce about a state sponsored loan. I suggested that each of them write out a $500 check for Bruce's upcoming campaign and Jim and I would make a trip to Santa Fe and present our plan to Governor Bruce King.

It was agreed and Bruce met with Jim and me and introduced us to his bright young nephew, David King, who was the head of that particular loan program, administrating the loans. We all four agreed to supply him with our personal financial statements. Our hopes were high that everyone would benefit from this project: the town, the people, our joint venture, the Democratic party and Governor Bruce King.

It wasn't long before we got the news. The loan had been approved subject to all four of us signing the note and mortgage personally, which meant any one of us or all of us would be responsible for the whole debt. Well, this blew the hell out of the deal as none of us had suspected this and none of us wanted to go along with it. The deal died right there.

Bruce did appreciate the campaign contribution and his and my relationship grew a little stronger, if that was possible. To this day our friendship has been rock solid. He is one of the best men I have ever known. He loves New Mexico. We still exchange Christmas cards and birthday wishes every year. He is nine months older than me, his birthday is in April and mine in November. I will have some copies of letters we received from each other over the past forty years later in the book.

This particular deal could have set me up for the rest of my life if it had worked out, but it didn't and we still survived. The important thing is, at least, we tried. The amount of money the State approved for the loan was $4,500,000 and this is why we spooked when they wanted each of us to sign personally for the entire amount. Most of the deals I was involved in worked out well and some didn't. However, it takes pure grit to even try and we had plenty of that in this life.

Now before I go back to the story and Village Place, I want to tell you about some other things that have been happening in our private lives with relatives and friends and then we will tell you the rest of the story about Village Place.

My good friends, Bob and Mary Boardman, who both worked for Southwest Savings and Loan in Santa Fe, had both accepted jobs with a savings and loan in Eldorado, Arkansas and had been replaced by a fellow by the name of Wayne Miller. He was a great guy to work with and he had just made the big loan of $402,000 on our supermarket and we had very good relations.

Anyway, I got a phone call from Bob Boardman from Arkansas and he told me that he was working with a small home-builder who had a piece of land, and that he wanted to talk to someone on a consultant basis about how he would go about building a small shopping center on the land he had. Bob told him that Andy Long was the only guy that he knew that could advise him on how to go about it. I said, "Bob, I'm getting ready to drive my wife and her store manager to market in Dallas in a few days and I could then drive myself on over to Eldorado and visit with you and Mary and talk to your friend about his project."

Bob said, "This is great. I'll tell him you will see him in a few days." Well, when Bonnie, Gladys and I got to Dallas, I stayed with the girls for a day. When they came back to the rooms in the hotel where the market was being held, they told me what a good deal they had made with the nicest man on buying men's suits for the fall and winter market. They said the nice man told them they really did not need to buy suits in shorts, medium and longs for short men, average sized men, and tall men. He told them to just buy all longs and this way all they would need to do was to cut off the length of the pant legs and coat sleeves for the regulars and short suits. When they told me this I laughed and laughed and laughed. They asked, "What's so funny?"

I said, "Do you think you could buy one size brassiere and all you would have to do was lengthen or shorten the straps?"

They said, "Oh, no. That would not work."

I said, "What makes you think this would work on men's suits? The length of the tall men's suit coat would reach almost to the short man's knees if you only cut off the sleeves, and so on. The crotch and waist area would be much too long also. You girls have been had and taken for big suckers. How much money did you sign the bill for?"

They said, "About $3,000."

I said, "You see this guy the first thing in the morning and tell him that your husband used to sell men's fine clothing and either he cancels the order or he is going to the Dallas Police Department with this scam at the Dallas Market." Well, they said they would and they were sufficiently mad enough at that guy that they made their story stick and the problem got solved.

I left Dallas for Arkansas early that morning and met with the builder there. We talked all day and half the night and we came up with a great design and he said, "Mr. Long, I will cut you in for 15% of the project if you will work with me on a continuing consultant basis."

I said, "Well, I will give it some thought." At the time I just couldn't imagine how I would have time to do this as busy as I was. Anyway, I drove back to Dallas and the girl's were wrapping up that buying session and said, "Andy, we got a call from Andra with some bad news." My Uncle Walter Long had died and his American Indian wife just didn't know what to do. They lived in Marlow, Oklahoma about 150 miles north of Dallas, so we all got in my big Lincoln and headed for Marlow.

I called the funeral home in Marlow and they told me, "Mr. Long, your uncle was a member of the local American Legion and they will take care of the expenses and they have made arrangements with a church for his funeral for tomorrow." I told them we would pay for him to be transported to Bartlesville, Oklahoma for burial in White Rose Cemetery, where his mother and father and two brothers were already buried. We drove as far as Lawton, Oklahoma that afternoon, stayed overnight and went directly to the church at 10:00 AM that next morning, said goodbye to his widow and we followed the hearse all the way to the cemetery in Bartlesville. We met my cousins who lived there for a 3:00 PM burial ceremony. Uncle Walt was a World War I veteran like my Dad was, and he was two years younger than Dad. However, he was 83 or 84 when he died and my Dad had died at age 72.

We had stopped by their home in Marlow two or three different times before on our trips to Wichita for Bonnie's annual Scott family Thanksgiving reunion. Bonnie would go to the Marlow supermarket and buy three or four big sacks of groceries to take to Uncle Walt and his wife Mary, as they were pretty poor and he really appreciated this. We would stay for a two or three hour visit and then drive on to Wichita. Uncle Walt had worked with all kinds of explosives all of his life until he got too old. He was quite a site on his front porch with a corncob pipe and straw hat, rocking in his rocking chair with his wife nearby.

Remember I wrote about Dad and him driving nitroglycerine trucks back in the early oil field days in Bartlesville? During World War II and some before and after, he had worked in a munitions factory in McCallister, Oklahoma. I asked him one day how he had lived so long and he said, "By being careful, Andrew, by being careful." I have never forgotten that since then and I haven't had any more near death experiences since then either.

He was an excellent mule skinner back in the oil field days hauling wagon loads of big oil field pipe all over the northeastern part of Oklahoma. He never did learn to read or write, but he made up for it in being able to communicate common sense very well.

This was just the beginning of the list of several deaths among family members in both mine and Bonnie's family. It was long trips each time, but we made them all.

The next trip I made to Eldorado, Arkansas I flew all the way from Albuquerque. There was a small commercial airport in Eldorado serviced by only one airline where the builder I went to see had a part-time job as manager and night clerk. We did some more work on what I told him he would need to do and he got it down pretty well. I still hadn't made up my mind whether I was going to have the necessary time to be of much help to him or not, being so far away from my home in New Mexico, however, he was insistent that he needed me. I had been there two days when Bonnie phoned me that my sister, Marge, in Wichita was in very serious condition.

Marge and Dwight Stanfield had three children: Mitchel, Michael, and Marla, plus Michael's four beautiful young daughters. They had finally discovered what was wrong with Marge a few weeks before she died and it was cancer in her back and lungs. She had smoked cigarettes all her life from the time she was a teenager and simply would not quit. The doctor told the family the cause of her death was just excessive cigarette smoking. I had quit smoking when I was 33 years old, but I couldn't get her to quit, so it finally got to her. So sad because she was only 48 years old.

Bonnie had told my nephew Mike where I was and he called me that day while I was having lunch with the Boardman's and said, "Uncle Andy, Mom just passed away." It was Easter Sunday. Well, I said I would fly to Wichita and Bonnie would fly from Albuquerque to Wichita and we would both be there by that evening to be with them. I went to the airport to fly out of Eldorado and because it was Sunday, my new builder friend there was on duty, so he booked my flight. This had all made up my mind that I had to tell my friend that I was not going to be a part of his project. I explained that this was just an example of being too busy. I said I should have been in Wichita with my sister these past few days instead of running all over the country. I was so upset with myself and at what had just happened.

It was an hour or so before my plane left and for every minute I sat there this guy simply begged me to get involved with him on his project. Anyway, I did leave and told him if I could help him with any of his questions to just call me. Well, I flew away and you know, I have never heard a word from him again. I had just learned a good lesson and that was that I was just too busy and had too many things going at the same time.

Anyway, my favorite Uncle L D Henderson and his wife Cora drove up from Bartlesville to attend Marge's funeral in Wichita and I sure enjoyed seeing him. When they left I said, "Uncle, take care of yourself. We just don't need any more of these type meetings."

He said, "I really agree. I will take care." and they drove off for home. It was only a few months when we got word that L D had another heart attack at their home playing cards with his wife and their daughter Carolyn and her husband, Ralph Young. He died almost instantly before the ambulance arrived. He had a previous heart attack a year or so earlier after putting on a lot of excess weight, but still worked very hard,as he always did in his welding shop. One day in the middle of a hot Oklahoma summer he had a job out on an oil well pump jack and was out there by himself and had to do some very heavy lifting which caused the first heart attack. After the first attack he took pretty good care of himself and had lost a lot of the weight, but the second heart attack got him. He was only 59 years old.

My mother, his sister Belle, and his brother Jack had all died of heart attacks: Jack at 64, Belle at 69 and my mom at 67.

Anyway, this was the third death so far this year and within a few weeks Bonnie's favorite Uncle from Wellington, Kansas died. Her Uncle "Lew," Louis Gwinup, was in his middle eighties. That made four and there were more to come.

The next to die was my dear cousin Annabelle Shattack's husband, Bruce and two second cousins — Bill Nelson who was my age, and Dorothy Jean Squire — and her dad, Earl Squire, a favorite cousin's husband. All of these were within one year. Talk about being physically as well as emotionally drained! Well, Bonnie and I both certainly were, as we had attended all eight of those funerals, all were around 700 miles from Los Alamos, New Mexico. Thank God I had decided to not take on the extra work where I would have had to make trips to Eldorado, Arkansas! It was the first time I had said, "no" to anyone offering another job opportunity, but I was very glad that I had.

Enough of all this sad stuff! I want to tell you about some of the trips I made on behalf of the New Mexico Real Estate Commission. One of my favorite commission members, while I served, was George McKim. He and I were always together when we attended most national conventions of the National Real Estate License Law Officials. One time, we were the two chosen to go to Washington, D.C. for a national convention. I was to speak at the opening breakfast meeting. Well, the exciting part of this was my luggage got lost on the plane trip and, thankfully, it was found and gotten to me about 30 minutes before I was to speak. That really shook me up, as I could not shave, change clothes, or anything! The airlines delivered it to our hotel just in time.

George McKim was several years older than me and a very, very dedicated Republican, even more so than I was a Democrat. In Albuquerque he was called, "Mr. Republican of Albuquerque." He was the one that met the Republican presidential candidates at the airport and squired them around. He had been the real driving force of the successful elections of both the recent senatorial and congressional candidates, Pete Dominici to the senate and Manuel Lujan to congress for the northern district. New Mexico has two representatives as well as two senators. I had helped both Democrats get elected to congress. One was Jeff Bingaman for the senate and Harold Runnels (who was my friend) from Lovington, N.M. — two for each end of the state. So, it was only fitting that we visit them in Washington D.C. on our trip.

The day George and I arrived we met Congressman Lujan, who I had donated a large check to for his recent campaign as George had put a big arm on me to do so, and I knew he was a very good man. He was also the brother-in-law of Reyes Padilla of Santa Fe, my very good friend with whom I had served during my first two years on the Real Estate Commission. Manuel took us on a walking tour of the Capital Building and White House that first evening we were in town, after we had a nice dinner together. He showed us what a remarkable job Jackie Kennedy had done on redecorating the White House. It was gorgeous! Manuel was a very dedicated congressman.

The next morning we met him, as well as my Democratic congressman Harold Runnells, in the famous Senate Dining Room for breakfast. I enjoyed this very much. They introduced me to the Secretary of State, whose name escapes me. George had already met him before. We had a wonderful time on this trip! I had helped both Jeff Bingaman and Runnels with their campaigns financially. I just didn't have time to do it physically, however. They were both very grateful and showed it.

For lunch that day we both met Senator Dominici and Congressman Lujan for lunch again in the Senate Dining Room and had a nice lunch, as well as the famous bean soup, there. Pete Domenici seemed rather cool to me. I think he remembered me from the meeting in Clovis, New Mexico when all of the Chamber of Commerce managers and presidents met to see which one of the candidates for Governor we would support. Remember, Pete was running against Bruce King and I had tipped Bruce off to what all of the Chamber people there were looking for in a candidate. I think Pete remembered this day well and I think he knew this is where he lost the election for governor. However, in the long run it all worked out for his betterment as he later ran for U. S. senator and was elected and now he has served as a senator for New Mexico for many, many years. But I must say, he and I have never hit it off very well and I'm sure that doesn't bother either of us at all.

George McKim and I also made a trip to Miami, Florida for a national convention and meeting of the real estate license law officials and also had a great time there. I remember the beautiful view of the beach and Atlantic Ocean from our room, high above the beach. The Bunny Club was part of the hotel and they had a party for us all the first night with the cute little bunnies running around serving drinks. It was quite entertaining. I recall George got a little too much to drink and as one bunny walked by he reached out and squeezed her bunny tail and said, "Ah-oogga" and this just about got us thrown out. The meeting went well. I had rented a car, so we had a great time touring around Miami during our off hours. It was a long flight home, however, from Florida to New Mexico.

Another meeting that George and I took together for the Real Estate Commission took us to Milwaukee, Wisconsin. George McKim gave such a great speech that when it was over everyone there wanted a copy of it! Ken Miller, our executive secretary and manager of the commission office in Albuquerque, had written a speech for George, but when he started his speech by reading it, he just stopped and laid it aside. Well, he started out, right off the cuff, and did so well because it was a subject he was very passionate about.

I'll explain. Some of the cities and states around the country, especially back east, were complaining about the sales tactics of AMREP, the big development company that had bought a large ranch on the west side of the Rio Grande River in Albuqueqrue. The ranch had belonged to the King Brothers of which Bruce was one. There were three of the brothers, and they owned several big ranches in New Mexico. One of Bruce's brothers managed the ranch operations. His name was Sam King. His other brother was a real cowboy type and they all lived on the ranch headquarters in Stanley, New Mexico near Moriarty, in separate houses, of course.

Anyway, the large ranch west of the river was ideal for the continuing growth of Albuquerque because the Sandia mountain on the east had stopped the growth essentially in that direction. The land on the north, as well as the south, was Indian land so the only way Albuquerque could grow was across the river and on west for miles, if necessary. AMREP had a large organization and operated in the big cities back east using what, today, we call "telemarketing." They even had airplanes and would fly in plane loads of easterners to the big sales building, model homes, and motels for people to stay in while visiting what they named: "Rio Rancho."

Well, the local real estate people, and others back east, didn't like this at all, so there was an effort to try and knock out the Albuquerque AMREP operation and activities. They had speakers at our meeting that were saying that it was all a big scam and that they were selling people worthless land and that they would lose their savings by buying desert land, etc. George McKim laid his prepared speech aside, and talked from the cuff. He said, (approximately) "People, you have to have a vision of the future. The big cities back east have about run out of land where people can build a home and have a nice yard and lawn to raise their families, and have turned to thousands of high-rise apartments that they have to rent. It's not real living for families, it's just like filing cabinets for people. Lots of smog, crime, traffic, and congestion, and when they get ready to retire, there is no way out except to be stuck in the same situation. All AMREP is doing is offering a piece of land to these people, as large as one-half acre to one full acre, at very reasonable prices and on very reasonable terms. Now, this is a great place to retire and have a nice flower or vegetable garden and plenty of elbow room in a climate that is filled with clean, fresh air to breathe. Nice golf courses available as well as fishing and boating on the Rio Grande River and hunting in the nearby mountains. It is a wonderful opportunity for many, many people to enjoy their retirement. You shouldn't try to stop growth, when it involves happiness for people, because when you stop growth, decay sets in. In the big cities it is very obvious decay has already set in and the future does not look good." When George finished his speech there was a thunderous roar of applause as all states were represented at this meeting and most of them knew that what he had said was true.

They all wanted copies of his talk and he said, "I'm very sorry folks but I didn't have anything written down. It all came from my heart." Then there was another round of applause. That afternoon the Milwaukee Real Estate Commission office gave us all tickets to attend a big league baseball game there between the Brewers and the Chicago Cubs. It was the first big league baseball game I had ever attended. We had a great time. Then they took us by bus to the Schlitz Brewery and gave us all the ice cold Schlitz we could drink.

George's speech really opened the door for AMREP and today, years later, there are almost as many people living west of the river as there are east of the river, as far as you can see, and still growing.

The meeting was a great success and the big effort put forth by the anti-growth people had failed and free enterprise flourished again. My respect for George McKim continued to grow. We remained good friends until he died in 1987. I felt honored to be one of the four pall bearers at his funeral. They were: me, Glen Giles (another of his close friends), Manuel Lujan and Senator Pete Dominici. He was buried in the beautiful national cemetery in Santa Fe, New Mexico. His funeral was quite lavish, if that is the right word — maybe not, but there was a very large attendance. Even a band, and the last piece they played, much louder that the others, was the Battle Hymn of the Republic. I will never forget that!

Upon leaving Milwaukee, Wisconsin I had to catch a plane to Denver, change there for Los Angeles to meet Bonnie, and our twin granddaughters. They had driven out there so we could pick up the dies for the Spin & Spell toy I told you about earlier, and returned to Los Alamos.

The plane I caught in Denver was a large DC-10 and I had one of the three seats near the window. The window seat was occupied by a well-dressed guy of about 45 years old. I was in the aisle seat and we had a vacant seat between us. This guy didn't want to talk at all. He acted like he was just too important. Personally, I think he was queer, but I didn't know for sure. Anyway, he was very impolite to the pretty little stewardess that was taking care of us. He ordered some fancy kind of drink and it didn't please him, so he jumped all over her, but she replaced it very politely and it still didn't suit him, but he drank it anyway. Then, she took our lunch order and he really showed his displeasure and the coffee didn't suit him. In fact, she couldn't please him in any way. She was almost in tears. She was young and I began to feel very sorry for her.

Finally, I had all I could stand, so I said to her, "Little lady, don't let this man upset you anymore. You see he works for the airline and he is just testing you and purposely trying to get your goat and trying to see just how much of this kind of abuse you can take before you blow up. I know this because there is no real human being that would be as mean and ornery to you unless his job with the airline required him to do this to you."

Well, this ornery S.O.B. didn't say a word to me or her and was as quiet as a mouse the rest of the trip and stared out the window.

"Oh," she said, "thank you, mister. I had just about all I could take from him." If this had not taken place on an airliner, I would have slapped the hell out of him and I think he was well aware of it. I felt good about helping this poor girl.

One other story about a trip for the real estate commission: This one was several years later and we had a new office manager and executive secretary for the Albuquerque office. His name was Mike Larkey and he was a big, young guy, very personable and a former Realtor. A good guy. He and I were going to the meeting in New Orleans, La. Along with us on this trip was our newest member of the commission. It had been decided by the New Mexico legislature that since the five member board of the commission was there to protect the public's interest, if all of them were real estate people, it was like the coyotes watching the chickens. So we had a new, non-realtor member appointed by the governor. Her name was Sharon Janecka from Lovington, New Mexico. Her job was running congressman Harold Runnel's home office as his secretary and office manager — a real nice gal, very personable and dependable.

Harold Runnels knew I was on the commission and he agreed to let her serve and go to our meetings once a month. Anyway, she attended the New Orleans meeting and the three of us did quite a bit of sight-seeing at night, like Bourbon St., and went to the world famous clarinet player, Pete Fountain's nightclub where he performed every night. We were having our big meeting at the Fairmont Hotel, one of the oldest hotels and fanciest in all of New Orleans. It used to be named the Roosevelt Hotel in the earlier days and was where Sammy Kay's band, "Swing and Sway with Sammy Kay" broadcast every Saturday night for years. A very famous place. They have a restaurant there, and a buffet that was simply out of this world!

Anyway, we had agreed when we all came in from our night on the town, to meet in the morning for breakfast so Mike and I went into the dining room and got a table and were having our coffee. Well, Sharon didn't show and we had been waiting about 30 minutes, so I went to the lobby and there I saw her getting her phone messages, so I went back to our table to wait with Mike until she was finished at the front desk. Well, here she came just laughing her ass off and we asked, "What's so funny?"

Well, she said she met a Realtor from South Carolina at the front desk and the Realtor asked her if she was a Realtor. Sharon told her, "no" that she was a layperson for the New Mexico Real Estate Commission. Well, this big South Carolina Realtor said to her, "I sure wish our commission had one of those. It's has been so long since I've been layed." With this we all three broke out in laughter and everyone around us laughed at us laughing — some fun. We left for home later that day and that was the only trip that Sharon had gotten to go on with the commission. Later on she was replaced by her father who was an old rancher form the Clovis, New Mexico area. He was a real hard-head and we all liked Sharon much more than we did her dad.

While all these other things were going on I got involved in a Santa Fe Corporation called Guadalupe Resources, Inc. It was a corporation that had been around for some time and owned some silver mining claims around Creed, Colorado and Silver City, New Mexico. Several laboratory employees owned stock in it as well as several Santa Fe residents. To name a few, George Glass, a lawyer, Charles Hagerman, a mining engineer, Richard Halford, an architect, and our corporation president was Jack Flynn. I was vice president and had served on the board of directors also prior to that. Other stockholders were Andra Long, Roger Corbett, Gerald Ohlson, Marvin Tinkle, a fellow named Ken Mitchell, another whose name I can't remember, and another that owned a hotel in Santa Fe.

Jack Flynn was quite a character — very personable. He was a cross between a Catholic priest (which he was) and a con man. His main way of making a living was a company called Capital Government Reports. He was on the Santa Fe radio station five days a week with a talk show giving all the various political happenings in and around the capital as well as throughout the state of New Mexico.

He used to brag that he could get an audience with the governor of the state no matter who he was, quicker than any other person. I believed him. We became close friends for fifteen years.

In the spring of 1978 we decided to make another trip to Costa Rica. I still had fond memories of the place and the 500 acres on the mountain side. We decided to take Bonnie's sister, Juanita, and her husband, Cliff Johnson, of Wichita, Kansas with us. They had never been anywhere outside the U.S.A. and we thought this would be a real nice vacation for them and for us.

We all four met at the Houston, Texas airport and flew to San Jose, Costa Rico, checked into the Blamable Hotel, the same one that we had stayed in on our previous trip. The first thing I did was to call Al Monte, the Canadian that lived there and he told me the land was still available, but the price had risen from $35,000 to $50,000. He said, "Andy, you can make that much off the hardwood timber logs that you can sell the first year."

I said, "I have got some other decisions to make with our business back in New Mexico before I can do anything, so I will have to wait for some time later on." The four of us, Cliff, Juanita, Bonnie and I decided to take the train we had taken before to Limon, Costa Rico, on the east coast and fly back just like we had done before. Well, almost the same except for one big difference.

We enjoyed the trip on the train as much as the first time and the same hotel in Limon and dancing, etc. The next morning we went to the little airport and boarded the same old C-47. A couple of mechanics had one of the engine metal covers open and were working on the engine. Well, they finished and one of them hammered the latch shut with the flat end of a hatchet, while standing on a step ladder. Cliff was working for Boeing Aircraft in Wichita at the time and I said, "What do you think about that, Cliff?" He just shook his head.

Just before we took off, here came an ambulance with a guy on a stretcher. He was unconscious and bleeding. He had been in an automobile accident and they were sending him to the hospital in San Jose. The only place they had for the stretcher was to lay him down in the aisle between the seats. It was about an hour flight to San Jose and we took off. We were into our trip about 30 minutes when I thought I would shake up my young brother-in-law a little bit. So I started making a sound with my mouth like a sputtering engine. He just looked at me, didn't say a word and pointed to the engine to my left out the window. Well, to my great surprise, the four blades on the left engine had stopped turning and were dead. Then he said, "They have been that way for five or ten minutes." Well, I was shook! I looked out the window and down — and nothing but jungle!

Cliff was a cool customer and a tough little guy. He looked just like Charles Bronson, the actor, enough to be his twin — from the mustache and whiskers he wore, and he was about the same age and size. We continued on to San Jose and circled the airport and did not try to land, but headed back to Limon on one engine. This was about more than I could take! I talked to the stewardess and said, "Why didn't the pilot land the plane?

The stewardess answered, "The airport lies in an area circled by mountains and it is cloudy. If the pilot should fail to be able to land on his first try, he won't have enough power with only one engine to pull up and turn around for another attempt to land. The pilot has made the decision to return to Limon on the one engine on the right side of the airplane." If I had that decision to make, I think at that particular time, I would have chosen to try to land. I don't know if this was another one of my long list of "near death experiences" or not, but it was certainly plenty close enough! It was a happy ending when we did land on the blacktop strip along the edge of the ocean. When the wheels touched down and made the squeak, squeak sound, that was a wonderful sound to all of us, except the poor bastard that was going to the hospital on the stretcher! I think he died on the trip.

They told us we could catch the plane again in the morning but we had had enough and went into town and managed to get on a rickety old bus. The mountain road that it traveled back to San Jose on was still under construction and was not paved at all. You can't imagine the mix of passengers on this bus! Chickens, goats, pigs, babies and people with their knee socks. I looked at my three weary traveling companions and said, "Are you all having lots of fun?" We arrived about sundown, had a few drinks and a nice dinner and truly felt it was great just to still be alive!

The next morning we went to a really nice motel at the edge of town near the airport and they had a group ready to board a small bus that would hold about 20 people that were going to travel to a seaside resort called Jaco Beach for one week. We all decided this is what we needed to do also. It was about 45 minutes to one hours drive in the little bus with a very polite black driver. He made one stop for a cold drink and pottie break and on to Jaco Beach. Lots of beautiful scenery and a very enjoyable and comfortable trip.

When we arrived, there was a large pavilion-type structure used for serving food and drinks, with a thatched roof, completely open and supported by long poles; another regular building housed their office facilities. All the rooms were separate and all on large poles with the floor about eight feet off the ground with a stairway up to our open-air rooms. All were for one or two couples — so shady and cool with an ocean breeze. There was at least a mile of beach to walk and enjoy and an occasional place to get snacks and drinks and small gifts. There was also a large oval-shaped swimming pool about four feet deep for all to enjoy, ringed by tall palm and coconut trees filled with all kinds of tropical birds and a few monkeys. We had a wonderful week there — very restful.

Bright and early one day we started our ride back on the little bus. When we got to our halfway place for our pottie break and drinks, Cliff and I decided to get a beer and were sitting at the very small bar when a short, fat, bald-headed hospital supply guy from California walked up with his companion, a very tall blonde gal that looked like Glory when she walked away from you, but her face was not nearly as attractive as the rest of her. Anyway, the bar was L-shaped and this little ratchet-jawed

California guy looked across the corner of the bar where he was drinking his beer and all of a sudden he looked at Cliff and said, "My God! Charlie Bronson!" At this I said, "Be quiet, he doesn't want anyone to recognize him, damn it!"

He quickly drank his beer and went out to get back into the bus. Cliff and I followed in five minutes or so and by the time we boarded the little bus, the little fat fart had told everyone on the bus that Charlie Bronson was with us and had been around all of us all week and they had not noticed it. We didn't let anyone know any different and in about an hour we were getting ready to board our plane for Florida and the good old U.S.A.

Cliff and Juanita had a real nice vacation, as well as Bonnie and me. We all flew to Houston, Texas, then Cliff and Juanita caught a plane to Wichita. Bonnie and I took a cab to my cousin Jack Henderson's house to visit with him and his wife. We decided to take them out to dinner, but Jack's wife couldn't go, so the three of us went to a Greek place on the waterfront. A great place. Those Greeks know how to entertain! It was not only a restaurant, but also a dance floor with music and belly dancers and entertainment. We had a wonderful time. The next morning when Jack went to work at his used car lot and garage, we went with him.

I spotted a robin's egg blue colored T-Bird. I wanted to do something for my younger brother, John Long, and I knew he would simply love to have this car instead of his little yellow Volkswagen Bug that he had in Wichita. I bought this pretty little car from Jack and cancelled my plane reservations back to Albuquerque. We decided to drive to Los Alamos. Well, we drove to Roswell, New Mexico from Houston, then to Albuquerque the next day to pick up our car that we had left at the airport. Bonnie drove it and I drove the T-Bird home to Los Alamos. My son, Tim, delivered the T-Bird to John in Wichita. Needless to say, my brother was very, very happy with this pretty T-Bird with wire wheels and leather seats!

Playtime was over and back to work on the several balls we had up in the air. Tim, Andra, and Peggy had done very well while we were gone for those two weeks. Andra told me that Gerald Ohlson had contacted her and had an interest in buying the Village Shopping Center. He had put together a group of investors who worked with him at the Laboratory in Los Alamos. He was the general partner and the others were all limited partners; in other words, he was the responsible party and they were only investors who would share in things like the depreciation benefits, which were plenty as they were all making good money at the Lab.

Remember, I was in big trouble with my townhouse project, Village Place, and I didn't have any way to turn it around and it was about "crisis time." Ohlson made an offer on the Village verbally to Andra as I had told her to handle the initial negotiations with him. I told Andra if we could pull off this deal she would become $10,000 dollars richer than she was now. So the smart little daughter of mine went to work on Gerald Ohlson! Remember, we had sold ten of the nineteen townhouses and still had nine unsold. I had turned down his offer to purchase the shopping center as it was too low. Andra asked, "Dad, do you have any one else that could buy it?"

I said, "No."

She said, "You had better start thinking." Well, I did!

The next day I had an idea for her to try out on Mr. Gerald Ohlson. I told her, "We have three of our largest lots that are still vacant and the price per square foot has appreciated tremendously. If we could negotiate a good price for this vacant land with Ohlson and get him to assume the construction loans with First Northern Savings and Loan Association on all nine of the unsold townhouses, I just might be willing to accept his low offer."

Andra said, "Dad, you are a genius! I believe I can get Jerry (as she called him now) to make a deal." I told her we would put this all in a loose fashion that would outline the intent of the parties and make it subject to the savings and loan accepting Gerald Ohlson's new company assuming all our existing loans on The Village Shopping Center, office buildings in The Village, and the supermarket. He would have to come up with our equities in all of these projects. We would accept one-half of the total equity amount as his down payment to us and we would accept his note for the other half of our equity in monthly payments for a time period of five years, at around $3,000 a month with the balance payable at the end of the five year term.

Andra had a great deal more patience in those days than I did, so she was able to get a verbal agreement in general terms with Ohlson with the understanding that the final agreement and contract would have to be

397

worked out between him, me and my attorney and great friend, Harry Moore. Well, I'll just say this about that: Gerald Ohlson was the most difficult man to work with and firm up an agreement with that I had ever seen. It was like trying to mold mercury. Finally, after many knit-pickin' changes, we came up with a contract that we could live with. One thing I insisted on but failed to put in writing on the contract was that he keep Peggy and Pete on the payroll, for two reasons. Peggy held all the tenants together and helped them a lot with promotions and their advertising and this was the secret to our success in The Village. Pete took care of all the clean-up and kept the place spic and span, as well as all the day-to-day maintenance. Ohlson agreed verbally to do this.

Also, Ohlson asked me, "Would you and Bonnie sell The Carousel?" He said one of his partners and his wife would like to buy it. I said, "Yes, I think we would." Well, it came to more money than they had to pay for it and I was not about to sell it on time payment. Neither of them had any experience in any kind of business, let alone in a dress shop and clothing store. This fellow's name was Kenneth Mitchel and I remember that he owned some Guadalupe Resources stock, so I said if he has $50,000 worth of stock in Guadalupe Resources, and the rest in cash we can make a deal. Well, Ohlson sold him some of his stock in Guadalupe on time payment and he managed to trade me enough stock to buy the store. I had been buying Guadalupe stock from some of the Santa Fe investors whenever the opportunity arose and had accumulated a pretty large amount of shares. With the addition of 50,000 more from Mitchell, I now owned 128,250 shares of Guadalupe Resources stock and Andra also had 12,500 shares. I was the second largest stock holder — Jack Flynn had the most stock. So they decided that I should be vice president.

Well, we finally got a contract we could live with on The Village including the rest of the vacant land, and the remaining townhouses in Village Place, and also cash and Guadalupe Resources stock from Mitchell on the clothing store. Old Bonnie was "out of jail," so to speak, what a relief! And you can imagine how relieved I was to not have all the pressure I had been living with the past ten years or so when we started the first buildings on the 23 acres of commercial land in White Rock. First Northern went along with the transfer of the mortgages they held on The Village and so did Southwest Savings on the supermarket mortgage. I was sold out of everything in Los Alamos County except the beautiful office buildings that the Bonnie Jeanne Corporation owned in Los Alamos across from Ashley Pond, and our big home in Pajarito Acres. We wrapped it all up in November 1980.

I was still on the Real Estate Commission and George Koury and I had become good friends and we decided to buy a piece of land on Eubank Blvd. in Albuquerque, enough to build about 20 homes plus about four acres of commercial frontage on Eubank Blvd. Shirley Leslie, Ed's widow, was now running Home Planning & Development Company in Albuquerque. She was the one that owned the land on Eubank. My friend, Dick Bock, lived in Albuquerque also and had been a faithful employee of the Leslies. So Dick, George and I formed a joint venture and bought the land, about sixteen acres or so.

We bought the land for $89,000. George and I paid $37,000 each and Dick Bock paid $15,000. We named the joint venture K.L.B., which stood for Koury, Long and Bock. Dick had never made any investments like this before and it didn't take long for him and his wife to spook. I had written the original joint venture agreement with the thought that something like this might happen, so I wrote in a clause stating that at any time one of us wanted out of the joint venture we could do so without argument and get our entire original investment back; the remaining partners would equally pay off the guy that wanted out. George and I bought out Dick's interest, each of us now having $44,500 invested. It wasn't long until George decided that he wanted to buy my interest in the residential land, as he wanted to plat it into individual lots and build houses on it. I was not interested in building houses and he really didn't want a partner as he was bringing in his brother with him to build the homes. I can't remember what he paid me, but it was a satisfactory amount at the time. We mutually agreed and we still had about four acres of prime commercial land on Eubank Blvd. to sell. We held it for a couple of years or so and later George called me and asked me and Bonnie to have lunch with him and his girlfriend, Lou Newton, who was recently divorced from her husband who owned the Santa Fe Race Track and formerly owned the race track in Ruidoso, New Mexico. Pretty high-powered people. We agreed to meet them for lunch and he showed me a signed sales contract for our commercial land, if I agreed.

He said after he paid his real estate company a commission on the sale we would each get $200,000 from our land. I quickly said, "George, buddy, you are certainly entitled to your sales commission, where do we sign?" We had owned the land about three or four years. Now there is a big, beautiful church built on one end of the property and a large private school on the other end. So, old Andy Long was still wheeling and dealing without a lot of continuous pressure.

One day about this time I got a call from my old friend, Raes Padilla, who I had served with on my first five year term on the Real Estate Commission. He was a big Realtor in Santa Fe and also on the board of Capital Savings and Loan Association in Santa Fe. He was very well respected and had a lot of Spanish-speaking folks as clients there. He asked me to meet him in Santa Fe the next day for lunch at the Green Onion Restaurant and Lounge at noon. I agreed and for some reason I got delayed and didn't get there until almost 1:00 PM. Raes had finished his lunch and was sipping a scotch and water. I apologized and told the waitress to just bring me a scotch and water also and I would skip lunch. Raes told me that a group of Santa Fe Spanish families had asked him to sell 400 acres of prime residential land. Twelve families owned the land and it was absolutely prime. It extended down the mountainside to just above the town square in Santa Fe, starting right behind where they burn Old Man Gloom, Zozobara, during the Santa Fe Fiesta each September. Well, Raes and I sat there sipping one scotch and water after another talking about different deals that might be made involving this land. I told him I had a couple of guys in mind that I wanted to talk to about it. One being George Koury, who Raes knew, and Jasper Conner, my friend and plumbing company owner that had done all our plumbing on my projects for years. Both of these guys were heavyweight enough that the three of us could make it work.

Well, we talked and talked and Raes looked at his watch and said, "Andy, it's 4:30 and it's Friday. I have to go by my office to see if I have any phone calls to make before I go home."

I said, "Okay, I'll go with you and then I'll buy one for us for the road. Shall we go to the Palace? It's on my way home."

He said, "The State Legislators are all in town this week and all the action is at the Bull Ring Lounge near the Capital. That's where the action is."

"The Bull Ring is fine with me." Well, Raes didn't have to return any phone calls, so we were on our way. We got there and happy hour was just beginning, so instead of half price drinks, they charged full price, but they served you two of them at a time. And they were large ones. We were off to a good start. After the first two big drinks, each scotch and water, some of our good friends came in and ordered drinks. One was a very well known Santa Fe realtor by the name of Walter Keesing and a good friend of both Raes and me. The other was Wayne Miller, president of Southwest Savings and Loan, a great friend of mine, who had made me the huge loan on our supermarket in The Village as well as lots of other loans.

The four of us decided to get a large table near the dance floor and the bank that was playing. People were dancing and having a good time. The table was large and made of real heavy lumber, Santa Fe style, with heavy chairs with short carved backs. Two of us were sitting on each side of the large table and there was once vacant chair at each end. The three other guys, Raes, Wayne and Walter, were up dancing or visiting with other friends and we were all having a great time. I was feeling no pain as I had been drinking all afternoon with Raes and then several more here at the Bull Ring and had not had lunch or dinner as yet. I got up to go to the rest room and when I returned a guy I didn't know was sitting on my left at the end of the table in one of the vacant chairs. He and I were the only ones at the table at that time. I assumed he was a friend of the other fellows in our party, maybe even a brother, a cousin or just an acquaintance. I introduced myself and he told me his name which I didn't remember. Anyway we talked and I asked him where he was from and what he did. He said he lived in New York and was a writer and was in Santa Fe to write a book about New Mexico. He asked me if I knew much about New Mexico. Of course, I told him, I knew all about New Mexico and loved. It. "I know the politics, climate, and the people. I am even a close friend of our cowboy Governor."

With this he said, "I sure like the climate, but from what I have seen of the people I think they're all a bunch of hayseeds. As far as the Governor is concerned, he looks like a queer cowboy to me."

This shocked me! I got real quiet and looked this guy straight in the eyes. He had a black short cropped beard and medium length bushy black hair. The thought came to me that I should beat the hell out of this guy for saying that about the people and especially about what he said about my good friend, Governor Bruce King. The next thought I had was, "Andy Long, you should beat the shit out of this guy. Why don't you stop being a nice milk toast guy and go ahead and do it?"

This thought lasted less than a quarter of a minute and I grabbed this S.O.B. with my left hand and grabbed a hand full of his bushy hair and hit him so hard, square in the face, that he fell backwards in his heavy chair with me right on top of him. He couldn't get loose from my hand-full of his hair holding it right against his head and I just started hammering him like a trip hammer at least 12 or 15 times.

By this time several people had gathered and the big black bartender and bouncer came over and Wayne Miller said, 'Andy, stop hitting him. You are going to kill this guy."

I said, "I'm not going to kill the S.O.B. but I am going to put a hell of a hurt on him for saying what he did." I turned him loose and Wayne said to the bartender, "I know this guy, I'll get him out of here." Wayne said, "Andy, let's run out of the back door through the kitchen. Are you parked in the back?"

I said, "Yes," and he poured me in my big, black Lincoln and, as I drove around the left side of the Bull Ring to the street and turned right to go around the Capital Building, a whole carload of cops pulled into the driveway on the right side of the building and went inside. None of my friends who were there knew what the guy's name was who beat this guy up, or why. Well, I drove very carefully for the thirty-four miles to my home in White Rock thinking, "What in the hell have I done?" and wondering if I might be in real bad trouble. I kept waiting for the other shoe to fall, so to speak, but nothing ever happened. The word did get out to several of my friends in Santa Fe about it and they were amazed at how that good natured, friendly Andy Long was really a tough guy.

That next morning when I awoke with a hangover, I called my three good friends that were there with me. None of them knew this guy and they said that guy was just mooching drinks and I had done good. I was so relieved that he was not a relative or friend of any of them. For several months when I would be driving in Santa Fe and stop at a red light, I would look at the driver in the car next to me, especially if he had a black beard, but I didn't spot the guy.

One evening several months later, I was home and had the ABC Evening News on and a news bulletin came on and they marched a guy across a room with handcuffs behind his back and they said that today the FBI had caught one of the men that was on the top ten of the FBI's "Most Wanted List." His name was Abbie Hoffman. He was captured in upstate New York. They also said that he had been hiding out in Santa Fe, New Mexico and had a job washing dishes in the El Toro Bar and Restaurant across town from the Bull Ring where I had given him a good lickin.' Oh, how good this news was to me, knowing that I had done a good deed instead of a bad one. All my friends were happy also and I got lots of compliments and good wishes. I suffered a fractured knuckle on my ring finger on my right hand, but in time it healed up okay.

A short time later the news was that he had committed suicide. I didn't believe that story. My thinking was that the FBI and/or the CIA had probably decided that it was time for Abbie to go to 'never never land.'

Now for the rest of the story about the 400 acres of land. A few days after the ruckus at the Bull Ring Lounge and the stranger, I saw George Koury and Jasper Conner and we discussed the deal. Japer Conner was just starting a large mobile home park in Las Vegas, New Mexico and didn't want to spread himself any thinner right then. George Koury had started a townhouse project in Albuquerque and his hands were full also. The Santa Fe project was just too big for me to tackle by myself, so I thanked my friend Raes Padilla and later he did put some Santa Fe builders together for his client's land. So it all worked out for him.

The time period was now in the winter in early 1981. We had finalized the sale of most of our property except the office buildings in Los Alamos and our beautiful big house in Pajarito Acres in White Rock. I was like a fish out of water. I had been going at top speed for years and now I didn't have much to do. I was getting restless and upset with Ohlson and the way that he was maintaining The Village. It wasn't being kept clean, and he didn't keep the weeds cut or patch the holes in the parking lots. He had failed to keep his promise about retain-ing Peggy and Pete on the payroll. Instead he put his daughter in charge of doing what Peggy was doing and she didn't know how to go about it, throwing her weight around with the tenants, and so on. He hired her husband, his son-in-law, to do Pete's job and he didn't know how to do that type of work. He just wanted to put them on the payroll, I think. This bugged me terribly and it was getting to me.

A big change was about the take place in the lives of the Long family, but I didn't know what. I had sold, or actually traded, the big house and barn and five rental houses in Joplin to a fellow and his wife, Randy and Becky Harris for their property in Estes Park, Colorado. I had been renting the big house and I got a call from this young couple who were visiting their home town of Joplin and they saw a 'for sale' sign on my property there. They wanted to move back to Joplin so Bonnie and I agreed to go to Estes Park, Colorado and meet them and look at their property there. I will describe the property, the area and little town:

Estes Park looked like something out of a story-book, high in the mountains and the scenery was out of this world! At an altitude of about 8,000 feet, it looked like a Swiss Village. Long's Peak loomed in the background over the town with beauty everywhere you looked. You drive around a large mountain lake as you enter the town and it is a gorgeous setting. Well, to make a long story short, he had a small loan on the property and a large equity and I had put a large loan on the Joplin property previously and had a small equity in it. Well, the equities are about the same so we simply traded equities. Since I completely understood how to do this, being a real estate man, we made it happen. He was getting a big place and simply assumed a big loan on it. I was taking over a small loan and his big equity on his property was enough to pay my equity. What attracted us about this place was someday I was looking to retire and I figured we could enjoy this as a nice place in the cool mountains in the summer and we could also have another home in a warm climate in the winter time. In the meantime, I rented the place to a nice single school teacher in Estes Park and it was just like putting it in storage until the time was right to move into it for a summer place later on in our lives. That would free me up from all the problems I was having with the big property in Joplin. I still had about 10 of the large lots there for sale. I just did not have time to properly work at selling them, but I would have more time now that I had sold most everything out in Los Alamos County.

The property in Estes Park was three bedrooms with a large double car garage and a small one-bedroom little rent house, rented to a young lady. The setting was on three acres of land. A beautiful setting. I fell in love with it immediately. Across the street north was a mountain range and just to the right and east a couple of blocks was a very old, large lodge in good repair, painted white. A gorgeous big building. I can't remember the name of it, but it was the main location of the movie made about 15 years ago called "The Shining" featuring Jack Nicholson as the leading actor. Some of you may remember it; it was very scary.

The house was only three blocks down to the main part of town. As I said before, it looked like something out of a little Swiss Village, filled with shops of all kinds. It was a fair-sized town and had a Holiday Inn motel as well as others. I could see it as an ideal place to spend our summers. To those not familiar with where Estes Park is, it is north and west of Denver and Boulder, Colorado. Lots of retired people and is a famous winter and summer resort. Tourism is their main industry.

Randy Harris was a carpenter by trade and his wife was a school teacher, so Randy could easily take care of the five rent houses in Joplin. I sold him a few more acres so he would have some pasture for some calves and the big barn was very useful now for the animals and hay storage. He built a metal building and started building cabinets and unfinished furniture on the location where the old Club 66 was located before it burned down. Everyone was happy with the trade that we had made.

Now it is a good time to go back to the ranch with Roy and Dale and talk about developments in Las Vegas, Nevada and our friend Fran Downing, from whom we had obtained the Joplin property, and her live-in young friend Gary Pendergraft. Bonnie and her manager of The Carousel before we sold The Village were in Dallas for a buying trip. I was home alone and early one morning a phone call came from Gary in Vegas. He was very shook up. Fran had just died. She had gone out to get the morning paper off the front porch and dropped dead. He said, "Andy, I don't know anyone out here except the lady who sold us this house."

I told him, "Try and calm down, Gary. I will catch a plane as soon as I can drive to Albuquerque and come out and help you. Bonnie is in Dallas and I will call her and have her fly out from Dallas today, also." This relieved him some and I called Bonnie at the hotel in Dallas with the bad news about Fran and she said they were wrapping up the buying trip this morning, so she would have Carol Homuth drive her to the airport and then Carol would drive our car on back to Los Alamos. Gary was so grateful that we were there.

We had been out to see him and Fran several times and had stayed at their house while there. We were even closer to Gary than we had been before. Anyway, the funeral went well, and sure enough, the only ones there were Bonnie, me, Gary, the real estate lady and the funeral director. Gary was really lost for a while and he called us for advice quite often. I told him the best advice I could offer was for him to get a good attorney to help him with everything — and he did.

Fran apparently left him a lot of money. I never asked him how much as I was sure this was personal. We continued to visit him and he really went to work building up his hospitalization insurance business. He wanted to buy a little office complex of three or four offices, fairly near the strip, and I went with him and made sure he had his lawyer working with him. I helped him decide about paint and carpet, landscaping, etc., and he really appreciated my help. Well, in a couple of years he met a blonde girl about his age, 36 or 38, and they got married. She was a librarian at the high school and was divorced from an air force man. Strange as it was, her home town had been Joplin, Missouri, and that helped cement their relationship. Her father was still the owner of a shoe store in downtown Joplin. She and Gary sold his house and bought a larger one and he again got my advice about what to do to improve its looks and value. Gary didn't mind the work, especially the painting, and did a good job. He had kind of adopted me and Bonnie and we also didn't mind advising him, as it was appreciated.

It wasn't long before along came a baby boy. Well, we were now godparents. Gary simply lived for this little boy and when we visited them we had to stay at their house. In a couple of years he and Bobbie, his wife, bought an even larger home on the golf course in a better part of Las Vegas. They visited us several times over the years in Los Alamos, and later on when we moved to Texas. Every year at Christmas and birthdays little Preston Pendergraft would receive some nice gifts. We were close. More about this saga later.

Now back to what was happening after we sold out most of our holdings in White Rock. I had been going at about full throttle for almost 20 years since 1961 and it was now 1981, and I had gone from wide open to almost stop and was getting restless. Tim had his real estate company in Santa Fe and he came up often and stayed in touch. One day he said one of his friends in Austin, Texas that he had gone to school with in Los Alamos knew of a large piece of land near Austin, at a smaller town north, named Round Rock, sort of a nearby suburb of Austin. Well, Austin was simply exploding with computer manufacturing companies, such as Texas Instruments and Dell, and the area was booming.

Tim said, "Dad, I talked to a young Realtor in Round Rock, Texas and he has a listing on a large piece of land north of Round Rock that is 1,200 acres and is ideal for a large industrial and commercial development and still have plenty of land left for residential development for a very large subdivision for homes for the employees to buy and live in that would work in those businesses. Dad, we need to go to Austin and take a look."

Well, I knew I would have to have more help from a partner, so I called my good friend George Koury in Albuquerque. He and I had not yet sold the land on Eubank Blvd. as yet. I showed George the plat of the land that Tim had and the three of us took off from Albuquerque to Austin by plane. It was in January or February and the runway in Albuquerque was covered in snow and when we got to Dallas we had to land and take off on ice. Kind of spooky, but when we got to Austin, it was very nice weather and not cold at all. We had a pleasant day looking at the property with the young Realtor, Bill Nations. Bill's dad was also a Realtor for years and Bill had grown up in the business. He was a natural! Very personable and smart. He had a handicap that made you remember him. He had one eye that was crossed. One eye looking at Dallas and the other at Ft. Worth, as I used to say. He didn't let it bother him at all and soon you didn't' seem to notice it either.

We did get excited about the land. It was at the north edge of Round Rock about a mile from the center of the town and it ran a mile north on Interstate 35. Across the interstate highway was a huge Westinghouse plant and on the south corner across the side street was a large 3-M building. The side street ran east for about 2 miles to the section line road, so the piece of land we were looking at was a mile wide along I-35 and two miles deep. The back section could be developed into housing and the front section into large commercial tracks. Mostly in grass land and small trees. Burrows Business Machines had an option with the present owners on the property across the side street and on the corner from the new 3-M building. So it looked like a real jewel to us with Westinghouse, 3-M and an option from Burrows. It seemed like it was set to go big.

The property was presently owned by the widow of the Austin Chevrolet dealership. She had just recently returned from China with her husband's body. He had a heart attack while they were on vacation.

That evening Bill and his wife, Lynn, took us to dinner to a very nice restaurant in Austin overlooking the Colorado River that runs through downtown. We had a magnificent evening! Lynn was a very charming young lady and very capable in running the bookkeeping part of their real estate office. It was the second marriage for them both. Bill had three young boys and Lynn had one. They were both in their late 20's or early 30's, so Tim was right at home, so to speak.

I think I was falling in love with Austin, Texas and when we started driving back to Round Rock to our motel we passed a bank that had a large sign with the time and temperature. It read 65 degrees at 10:00 PM. I said, "My God, boys, look at that and remember this morning at Albuquerque and Dallas covered with snow and ice! Isn't this wonderful!"

Anyway, the next morning Bill made an appointment with the widow's lawyer and we went to his office and a long conversation with him as he would be handling all the negotiations with Bill and us. The asking price as I remember was eight million dollars—$8,000,000. The lawyer asked that George and I submit, with any offer that we made, a resume and a current financial statement each. Well, we agreed to do this. We then went to visit Bill's dad at his home and had a good visit. He and I hit if off immediately as he was in WWII just like I was. He was about six or eight years older than me and most of his real estate business was selling and buying ranches. He was a typical Texan. I will mention here now that Jim Nations and Andy Long became the best of friends and are still going strong after many years to this day.

Anyway, George and I, as well as Tim, were very excited about this deal. George said, "Andy, this is too big a deal for just the two of us. We need a third partner and what do you think about asking Roger Cox to join us?"

I knew Roger, but not nearly as well as George did, as he was also a big Realtor in Albuquerque. He was a past president of the State Board of Realtors and a very well-respected Realtor and business man. He was a "good Mormon boy," or man, I should say. He ran a very good business office and was also an investor like George and I were, only bigger.

One big high-rise office building in downtown Albuquerque was built and owned by Roger Cox. He was about our age also, which was 56 or 57 years old at the time. I agreed that we needed him for his experience as well as his financial help. This would be perfect. He told us he didn't need to look at the property in Austin, but would also provide us with his resume and financial material. George said he and Roger would prepare an offer to purchase and the three of us would go over it before mailing it to Bill Nations.

The offer was made and not for $8,000,000, but for $6,000,000 and it was sent to Bill Nations to take to the widow's lawyer. Well, the next thing we heard was from Bill and he said the offer was turned down. We asked if they came back with a counter offer and he said, "No." Well, this surprised us, as they were sticking with the $8,000,000 asking price. Bill said that the lady's lawyer told him that her brother-in-law in Lubbock, Texas, who was a half-baked small Realtor there and only sold houses and didn't deal in large property, had advised her not to accept the deal, just to stick with her price.

This was disappointing news to George and I as well as Bill Nations. We tried to get Roger Cox to consider a larger offer, but he said, "Boys, I'm not going to make a larger offer. You two go ahead on your own if you want to, but leave me out." Well, we both respected Roger's advice and experience, so the deal died.

Even though we didn't make this deal, I was so inspired with the beauty of Austin, Texas as well as the weather, the Colorado River, the beautiful Capital of Texas building and the University of Texas that, in fact, I fell in love with Austin, Texas. Tim liked what he saw also. As time went on and I didn't have much going on business-wise so I thought about relocating our home to Austin. After twenty years on this mountaintop and long, long winters, I had climbed all the business and personal mountains that I was interested in climbing. I had plenty of money and also a good income and still had the Joplin lots to play with. I was really ready to retire and do some fishing in beautiful Austin, Texas. These ideas were not done in haste, as it was not in my nature to do anything before thinking it through, however, we had done about everything I wanted to do in Los Alamos County.

We had moved to Los Alamos in September of 1961 and it was now the spring of 1981. Almost twenty years of constant hard work, sound thinking, taking big chances and gambling on our ability to think, plan and dream. We had become one of the most popular and successful families in Los Alamos and certainly in White Rock which had grown from four model homes on unpaved streets to over 3,000 homes and around 12,000 people along with plenty of shopping facilities, to make it one of the most modern and beautiful little towns in all of New Mexico. A fellow told me one day, "Andy, you can't leave Los Alamos. Your name is a household word here." I hadn't thought of it this way before, but I now know he was right. I now had time to reflect back on all this and it made me tired just to think about it.

I had been the first successful real estate man in the county and had built lots of new homes and apartments, office buildings and even a beautiful new shopping center; and developed and built the first planned-unit development in the state of New Mexico, Ponderosa Manor. I had been elected president of the Santa Fe Board of Realtors when Los Alamos County, Rio Arriba County and Santa Fe County were all one board. I was Realtor of the Year of this Board in 1974 and also president and Realtor of the Year of the Los Alamos Board when we got our own board in 1979. I was one of the men who organized the first Chamber of Commerce in Los Alamos and the membership chairman for the first two years to get it started. I served on the Board of Directors for years locally and knew personally several of the presidents of the Chamber of Commerce of various cities of the state. I was also personally acquainted with Governors Cargo, King, and Apodaca. I was appointed to the State of New Mexico Real Estate Commission for a five year term by Governor Bruce King and re-appointed for another five year term by Governor Apodaca. I had served as president of this organization for one of the five years of King and also president for one of the years of Apodaca's term.

I also was a personal friend of Jeff Bingaman of Silver City and had helped get him re-elected to attorney general and later to the U.S. Senate. I was also a friend of Congressman Manuel Lujan and Harold Runnells, and also knew Congressman Tom Morris and Senator Clinton P. Anderson.

410

This was the nice thing about New Mexico. It was a small state, population-wise, but large in area. In size it was 6th in the nation, but in population it was 36th. So, it was fairly important for those politicians to get acquainted with the leaders of the various towns and communities throughout the state. I did enjoy meeting and knowing all of these men. I also knew Senator Dominici, but we never did get well-acquainted.

Just to mention a few other things and people, I served on the local board of advisors to the Los Alamos Medical Center for several years I was elected to serve on the State Board of Realtors board of directors and rose to vice-president. This gave me the opportunity to meet anyone and everyone that were real "movers and shakers" in the real estate business all over the state. Those relationships were priceless to me. I couldn't get over how amazed those people felt about my ability to get along with and deal with all of the scientific types in Los Alamos County. I think my ability to deal with these people came from the thirteen years of selling and training experience in dealing with all kinds of people while I was selling and training salesmen in the cookware business. I did get along well with most of those scientific-types, except in a few rare cases. I have had a lot of time to reflect back on those years we spent in Los Alamos. We were privileged to be there and have a chance to make a real difference in our lives and to help provide homes and businesses in our community and to be accepted as we were — the whole family.

I really need to give a tribute to all those brilliant people. Nowhere else in the world were there more brilliant minds in one small place than in Los Alamos County. I knew two of the directors of the laboratory very well. One was Norris Bradbury, who replaced Oppenheimer way back in the late 40's. I served with him on the hospital advisory board for several years. During that length of time you get to know how people think. He did a wonderful job as the director for many years. He was very dedicated — the laboratory was his life. There was no time for nonsense or commercial business. He didn't even want the laboratory to become a member of the Chamber of Commerce. So he and I really didn't have much in common or to talk about. However, his wife was a nice old lady and one day she said to me, "Andy, I wish Norris had gotten involved in business like you did when he was young." I was flabbergasted at what she had just said. I said, "Mrs. Bradbury, your husband has done a fabulous job running this laboratory for many years and I consider him a brilliant man. There are different strokes for different folks, you know." He served as director until the mid 1970's when he retired and was replaced by Harold Agnew.

I had gotten to know Harold quite well and, remember, he was a member of the BLAWS Corporation that lawyer Sterling Black and I put together during the sale of the government land in Los Alamos. Harold was not as anti-business as Norris Bradbury was, which helped the laboratory's relationship with the business community. When he would throw a party for dignitaries or open an occasional meeting, he would invite several of us business people to attend, and I appreciated this.

Harold Agnew was a young top scientist that was aboard the Enola Gay, the bomber that dropped the bombs on the two Japanese cities to end World War II in the Pacific. He directed the lab in Los Alamos until the late 1970's and left Los Alamos to take a consulting job with some company on the west coast.

Everyone in town knew of our family and the older ones all remembered when we moved to Los Alamos in 1961. Not too many of them knew about me selling cookware part-time for the first three months there while I was trying to decide if I was going to go to work as sales manager with the Noxon Construction Company which was building the first houses in White Rock.

Well, when we sold out most of our property and were getting ready to leave Los Alamos and White Rock, the word got around that "Did you know old Andy Long came to town twenty years ago selling pots and pans out of the trunk of his car and now he is putting millions in a sack and is leaving town?" Well, some of them thought of this as a compliment and others thought it was resentment and jealousy. I don't know how many of each kind heard this, but it gives you and idea as to how the scientific mind works. Most of them brilliant in what their specialty was, but lacking in the broader experience necessary for a well-rounded person.

I guess I still have two thoughts on this subject. One is I am very grateful that we have a town of these kind of people that we can depend on, with their dedication to their work. The other thought is that the majority of them were so very hard to work with, especially the ones that didn't want the town to grow and wished the government still ran the whole show. I still resent the thought of "my sack full of millions that I left with." Their mind-set never considers the cost of all the material and labor and all the borrowed money it took to complete each and every project, to say nothing of the risk of loss that was always present, and sometimes loss itself. Not to mention the years of hard work and stress and strain involved in making it all happen in twenty years.

So we prepared to leave Los Alamos for part-time retirement and were still young enough at age 57 to keep our eyes open to some possible future opportunities.

Chapter Eight

Retiring In Texas

Bonnie and Andy

I CALLED BILL NATIONS AND told him to start looking for a fairly large home on the river or one of the lakes in the area for us. So he did.

Bonnie, Andra and myself all drove down and we spent a couple of days looking over the whole area, as far as seventy miles in all directions, and loved it. Lake Buchanan is the largest lake and the farthest one west. It is the large reservoir that keeps the other lakes at a constant level. All of them vary less than one foot in depth. Below Buchanan is Inks Lake, then Lake L.B.J., then Lake Marble Falls, then Lake Travis, then Lake Austin and Town Lake that runs right through the city of Austin.

Town Lake is gorgeous with manicured grassy banks and concrete walkways, parks and such, with jogging, boating and canoeing and other recreation — ideal for the huge number of college students at Texas University nearby, as well as the other people in the area.

The way the level of these lakes is controlled with dams is an engineering marvel. They serve four important purposes. The huge Lake Buchanan with a big dam generates a lot of electrical power, also they are used for flood control and irrigation, as well as a tremendous amount of recreation. Lake Travis is known far and wide for its fishing and marvelous subdivisions of beautiful homes and vacation resorts. Lake L.B.J. also provides the same things.

Let me recite a little history to you lovely folks that read this, especially the younger ones:

After the Great Depression that you have all heard about (and a few of us who were involved as living participants), our country was in great need of many, many things. Electric power for example was very scarce, especially to rural families, also good roads were scarce in large rural areas. There were some men in Washington D. C. with a great vision for our future. Out of this great need came five great men who were elected to the United State Senate. They took the reins to make things happen for the good of the people of their states. The time was right for some good things to happen, which would also provide much needed jobs. These men were from the four states of our area. They were Bob Kerr of Oklahoma, Orville Fulbright of Arkansas, Russell Long of Louisiana, and Sam Rayburn and Lyndon Johnson, both of Texas.

This was a gigantic undertaking in Texas. Four huge dams were built on the Colorado River to providing electrical power and flood control to several cities, and especially to thousands of farmers and rural people. This alone made L.B.J. a real hero, especially to the rural people. Then lots of good roads became a reality, followed by lots of good jobs.

What happened in Texas also happened in the other states. These five men, that I mentioned above, rose to the occasion and working closely together, made things happen and helped hundreds of thousands of good people. They were all great men of stature who were revered, appreciated and loved. It all seems a far cry from what we see from our politicians in Washington D. C. these days.

Just think of the great vision it took to construct a waterway for barge transportation of goods, starting at the inland port of Catoosa, Oklahoma, near Claremore, then to Arkansas and on and on. Senator Bob Kerr was the great "mover and shaker" who had the vision for this and the ability to make it happen. How great! And the many jobs it provided to many, many hardworking people.

Well, now "back to the ranch with Roy and Dale" and Andy, Bonnie and Andra in Austin, Texas:

We found a great place that we all three liked very much. It was an older home of rambling ranch style on an acre and a half in a beautiful setting with a large creek, called Ennis Creek. The house was about two blocks from where the creek ran into Lake Austin. It was just outside the west edge of Austin on River Hills Road, a curving road winding down from Bee Caves Road, the highway going back east into Austin and west into the Hill Country and Marble Falls, Texas. It couldn't have been any more perfect for us. The creek was wide and deep enough for a good sized boat to navigate two blocks to the lake. Across the creek we looked out onto a jungle of large trees that ran from the creek to the lake.

The trees were magnificent to say the least! There was a very large elm tree in the front yard, at least sixty feet tall and at least three feet thick. The shade covered about a 100 foot diameter. At the right side of the house was a large kidney-shaped swimming pool and the back yard was filled with about six large two-foot thick pecan trees which completely shaded the entire backyard, except for one large magnolia tree and the largest willow tree I had ever seen; it was four feet thick and a hundred feet tall. It was near the rock wall that ran along the creek which had a cutout with a rock slip for a good-sized boat.

I thought I had died and gone to heaven! A place all of us liked and in less than five minutes I could be fishing from my boat on Lake Austin. Well, I told Bill Nations to write up an offer to purchase the place subject to our selling our home in White Rock, New Mexico. He did and called us in White Rock to let us know that the offer had been accepted. We got busy in a hurry to get our place polished and ready to sell.

A very important phone call came in one morning from my good friend in California, Chuck Coutts. Remember him? He was the guy I worked with in White Rock when it was just getting started and the one that helped me put the horse in the El Nido Club. Almost twenty years had passed since we had first met the Coutts family. We had stayed in touch with them and visited them many times in California and they had come back to Los Alamos to see us many times. We were really good friends and when he told me something, I listened.

Chuck had grown up in the construction business — always working for someone else on bigger and bigger jobs. His present job was as General Construction Manager for a big construction company in Los Angeles. They would have several projects going at the same time, each having several hundred homes or apartments in different stages of construction. He was in charge of 7,000 units per year. He spent most of his time in a high-rise office building in L.A. working several computers with his office team helping him. Some of the jobs would be just in the design stage and other ones in the lots, street and utility installation stage, others in the home construction stage and others completed and in the selling stage. Of course, he made all the contracts for buying the construction materials and worked with all the sub-contractors. This gave him a very close relationship with the suppliers and subs, etc.

Well, what he called me about was that he had worked out a plan with several of his material suppliers such as the ones who supplied all the windows and doors, the plumbing material, roofing material, appliances, carpeting and so on. The jist of all this follows:

They would form a corporation and Chuck would be completely in charge and set up a company that would provide production homes on a large scale for the first time in Hawaii. He had thought it through pretty well, even to the point of hiring the various carpenters, plumbers, painters and other labor skills. They would be flown out from the States and if they stayed on the job for six months he would pay their plane fare home. If not, they would have to pay for their own flight home. They would be housed in tents just like in the Army and hire cooks, etc. Up to this time, home building in Hawaii was done one-at-a-time, so to speak. So you see what a big endeavor this would be. He said he told the suppliers that as soon as they deposited $50,000 into his account he would get things in motion. He said, "Andy, I want you to go to Hawaii with me next week as you are going to be in charge of all sales and setting up a model complex just like we do here in the States. You will be in complete charge of the whole sales and financing end of the operation."

"I have called a lawyer there to meet us and help make deals on land for our first subdivision since all land deals in Hawaii are handled by lawyers, not real estate people." Chuck continued, "This would be a great adventure for both of us as we have complete faith in each other's abilities. Since you have sold out in Los Alamos, it would give you another mountain to climb."

I said, "Chuck, when do we leave?"

"We will leave L.A. on Friday evening when I get off work and come back Sunday night so I can be at work Monday morning — and no one here at my office will even know about this. I hate to quit this job as it is a good one, and the Jewish owner is a pretty good guy — and wealthy." Chuck went on, "If this deal works out, it will be the opportunity of a lifetime and I know it will not be any more stressful than what I am doing now. I'll meet you at the L.A. airport Friday evening." He had made reservations at the Halekii Condo Hotel for us in Honolulu. It was a beautiful high-rise of one bedroom condos that were very nice.

We met the lawyer and three other men for breakfast and two of them were Hawaiian and the other was Chinese. One was the owner of the Fairmont Milk Company there and one was the owner of the Buick and Chevrolet dealerships. I don't know that the Chinese guy owned, but it was something big. Well, they had a large piece of land that they would sell and this was rare as it is hard to buy land in Hawaii. Most of the land there is for lease only — long term, of course. Anyway, we got the directions to the land with maps and pictures, etc., and the lawyer, Chuck and I took off after breakfast. The land was on a mountainside that sloped gently to the ocean on the north side of the island. That is the windward side and the side that gets most of the rain. It was covered with trees and jungle. It was beautiful, but it would be fairly difficult to develop.

We were concerned about whether or not it was in the flood plain, which we supposed it would be. This is the only piece that we found for sale that day. I could see that this Chinaman was going to be hard to deal with. Anyway, we drove around the island and enjoyed it and discovered that Del Webb Corporation was starting to develop a large piece of land for a Sun City Honolulu. This was interesting to us as we had not known of this. However, it might help to have some competition. Chuck was familiar with competition as L.A. had lots of it, of course.

That evening we had an appointment for dinner with the lawyer and a businessman from New Zealand who was in the lumber business and was interested in supplying us with lumber on a large scale — most of it being mahogany. It was a very interesting conversation and we enjoyed the meeting very much. We settled in on the beautiful hotel patio for a few drinks and at the large table next to ours was Elvis Presley and three or four of his buddies, probably his band members and several beautiful gals. Chuck and I had a short conversation with Elvis, who was as nice a fellow as you could meet. Chuck asked him if he could give him his autograph for his teenage daughter, Kathy. Chuck handed him a bar napkin and Elvis wrote a short little note to Kathy and signed it. Chuck was happy! We didn't want to bother him so we said our "goodbyes" and left to take the outside elevator to the top floor of the hotel. I have often said that the most beautiful site I had ever seen was Diamond Head all lit up in the distance. It had just turned dark and it was beautiful.

We took a stroll around town and saw a small lake and Chuck said, "Let's take a swim." I said, "I don't think so." "You just watch me then." said Chuck. And I said, "Okay." He had on boxer shorts, so that was his bathing suit. He decided to swim across to the other side of the lake, probably about 75 or 100 yards across. It went okay, but he wasn't used to swimming that far in his backyard pool at home. He was very tired and said that it hadn't been a very good idea after all. After that, we walked back to the hotel and retired for the night.

The next day was Sunday and we met again with the three men who owned the land we looked at and we told them that we would be in touch later. We then did some shopping and more sight-seeing, then that evening flew all night and arrived at the Los Angeles Airport. I stayed at the airport and in a couple of hours, caught a plane to Albuquerque and then home. Chuck had just time enough to shave in his office bathroom and change clothes before work. No one there had any idea that he had been to Hawaii for the weekend.

On the flight home my mind was spinning a mile a minute and I thought I had better not get too anxious to move from our home in White Rock just yet until we had time to analyze our coming venture in Hawaii. I explained to Bonnie all about our trip and she didn't know what to think either, so I said, "Let's just give it time to see what happens. It would be quite an adventure." She agreed.

That afternoon we got a very disturbing phone call from Chuck's wife, Pat. She said that Chuck had fainted at work and they rushed him to the hospital and discovered that he had a ruptured appendix. I thought for sure it must have been caused by his swim across and back on that lake the night before. Anyway, he was very critical for several days and finally he showed signs of improving. What a relief to all of us!

The next call in a few days was from Chuck himself and he said, "Andy we are not going to do the deal in Hawaii."

I said, "Why not?"

He said his boss (I can't remember his name) was very good to him and Pat through his health crisis. "He stayed right beside my bed with Pat in the hospital. I just can't leave him now."

I said, "I understand, Chuck, and that is okay with me as we are on the verge of moving to Austin, Texas to retire anyway. I think that this was an omen to both of us. I'm just like the man that said, 'I'm not superstitious, but I believe in signs.' This is a sign that we should adhere to." Chuck said, "I believe you." What could have been, by bringing production housing to Hawaii, we'll never know.

I was 57 years old and ready to retire anyway, so I wasn't too disappointed. Chuck was about 48 and still had several really good years left and he had always had important jobs in the construction business, but had always worked for someone else. He continued to do this for several more years. They both loved their beautiful home in Malibu and their three teenage children in those days, and now their grandchildren, as well as their visits to come see us and our trips to California to see them many times. Really good friends.

He admired us in our various investments of our own in real estate and construction, and after seeing our shopping center and other projects — one year on their way home, they drove up to Jackson Hole, Wyoming and found twenty acres with a stream running through it, about twenty miles or so west of Jackson Hole, just east of the Idaho border and near a small town in Idaho, close to the Grand Tetons and a fabulous ski resort. He built a huge two-story mountain home on one of the four-acre lots that he subdivided the twenty acres into, overlooking the valley. It is one of the most beautiful places on earth. He sold one of the lots for $200,000 (I didn't believe him so he showed me the closing papers of the sale) to an eye doctor from Texas. We visited them for a week about five years ago. We had a great time trout fishing and relaxing and sight-seeing, and had a great time visiting about old times and our escapades.

Chuck was an athlete and still is. His specialty is throwing the javelin, as he did in college, and his love for motorcycle races. He no longer rides in the races as his present age, but he still throws the javelin and holds the senior citizen championship record. He always was a gung-ho guy. I would say the typical "piss-and-vinegar" type, is the best way to describe Chuck Coutts. His wife Pat's specialties are shopping and eating out at restaurants.

Now it was time to sell our home in White Rock and get ready for the huge move ahead of us. I put my For Sale sign up and several calls came in but I had only one showing, which is all it takes if the price is right and the buyer is qualified. He was. Not many people in Los Alamos could or would buy a home as expensive as this one. I priced it so that anyone could see that it was well worth what I was asking, at $230,000 (it's worth about a million dollars now). I knew this young couple that wanted to look at our home very well. They were Tom and Janette Metzger. She was the daughter of the Los Alamos County finance manager and her mother worked for Sterling Black's title company that had their office in our Los Alamos Business Center and had done the closings on all the homes we sold. We also knew her parents, Pat and Roy Starkey, very well. In fact, I bought my first pickup with a camper shell from them. Anyway, Janette had married Tom Metzger, who was quite a young, big-wheel in town. His dad had owned a Texaco service station and Metzger's hardware store in

Los Alamos for many years and also put one of each in the White Rock Shopping Center when it got started. Lee Metzger never ran the stores himself but had very good and loyal managers for years until Tom got old enough to take over the Los Alamos Hardware Store. So, young Tom was well qualified to buy Andy and Bonnie Long's house. Janette Metzger was the younger of the two Starkey sisters and was more than a little bit spoiled. So you can see I had me a very, very good prospect.

This being the case, I stuck to my price and got it. I did, however, throw in some goodies that they liked. The one thing he liked most, as I remember, was the big oversized walnut desk in my study just off of the master bedroom and indoor pool. The little "Half-pint Haven" guest house became Daddy Lee Metzger's place to stay in when he made his frequent visits to Los Alamos and White Rock from California.

We closed both home loans essentially at the same time. The one we were selling and the one we were buying in Austin. I rented a big U-Haul truck and my good friends and neighbors that were young and had just started in both the construction business and the real estate business, Jack and Gwen Tucker, provided the help I needed in loading all the things I wanted to keep that were stored in my big barn. I had lots of concrete tools and other big tools that I would never need again, so I gave them to him for his help in loading the things in the barn that I did want to keep. He got a lot of good stuff, so he brought three of his laborers and we filled that truck.

Remember the trailer that was Kermit's trade-in to me when I sold him the real nice big trailer I got when I bought the mobile home park from Ruby Alexander in Espanola? We had used it for a construction office and I still had it parked behind my barn, so I made Jack a hell of a good deal on it and he was very happy.

The Tuckers had a young daughter, Tracy, the same age as Taña and Kathy and they were all good friends.

The next morning we took off. Tim driving the U-Haul semi truck, me in our car, and Bonnie's nephew, the Green Beret, Ron Johnson in my Ranchero pickup. Ron had driven his motor cycle to Los Alamos from his Army base in Ft. Hood, Texas to help us move. He loaded the motorcycle in the back of the pickup, and drove it to Bill Nation's house in Round Rock where he unloaded his cycle, left the truck, and drove back to his base.

Tim and I drove to our new home on River Hills Road and Bill Nations showed up with some strong young guys to help us unload the truck. We drove the U-Haul truck to Round Rock to return it, got in our Ranchero pickup and drove back to the house, parked my car in the garage, locked it up and we started back to White Rock.

The following day we rented two more U-Haul trucks and called our local sheriff, Louie Rojas, who moved furniture as a part-time job. He had the sheriff's job as another part-time job, and he worked full-time as an iron worker with the Laboratory in Los Alamos. He was of Spanish and Indian heritage and one of the nicest guys you would want to meet — and also one of the strongest. He and his crew worked like beavers and got us loaded and after we cleaned the house really well for Janette and Tom Metzger, we left them the keys.. Andra left in her car to El Paso to spend a few days there while the twins finished school. It was exactly 650 miles to Austin. Lubbock, Texas was 325 miles, exactly half-way, so we drove to Lubbock and stayed all night. That next morning Bonnie and Andra's three young kittens in the Ranchero and Tim and I each in our two U-Haul trucks took off for Lubbock, spent the night, and went on to Austin the next day.

To give you an idea how rough and long the winters were in northern New Mexico, the morning we left I looked into the bed of the Ranchero and there was a little skim of ice on some frozen water in the bed. This may not seem that unusual, but this was the 30th day of May — and it usually started snowing in September. So you can see how anxious we were to start our new life in Austin, Texas!

We got into Austin and to our new home in the late afternoon that second day. Bill Nations, his family, and his mother and dad showed up as he knew when we were coming and we all started moving our furniture and things into the house. Just as we got everything piled into the house, with nothing straightened up at all, it started raining and getting dark. So Bill said, "Andy, you folks are going to spend the night at our house tonight. Let's go."

I said, "Let's stop at a good restaurant and we'll all have supper on Andy Long." So, we did. By the time we got to Round Rock it was raining so hard we could hardly see to drive. Well, this was the start of the big flood that hit Austin, Texas Memorial Day Weekend in 1981. It devastated

Austin. Several people drowned in their cars and hundreds of cars on the car lots were washed away and damaged by high water. The rain measured 19 inches. None of us had ever seen any rain like this in New Mexico or Texas. It rained, and lightening was constantly hitting all night long, totally filling the sky.

The next day we went to examine the house to see if there was any damage. The swimming pool was running over and Ennis Creek was out of its banks and at least six inches of mud and silt was over our backyard. But the house was not damaged at all because it was about ten rock stair steps up from the yard to the patio and back of the house. I had bought a small 12 ft. green plastic fishing boat from Kermit several months before we moved and brought it down in the bed of the Ranchero. I had tied it to the big willow tree next to the boat slip in the back yard with a piece of drapery cord. We weren't expecting a flood like that so I thought it would be okay, but it was long gone and we never saw it after that.

I just knew our lovely yard was ruined, but oh, no — the rich silt just fertilized it and the grass grew back richer than ever.

In a few days Bonnie and I settled in and made this beautiful old house a real home. One morning after the top soil had dried out, I thought I would see if I could catch a fish in the creek. I didn't have any bait, so I cut a little piece of block cheese about the size of a sugar cube, put it on a hook and line and tossed it into the creek. It no sooner hit the water when something grabbed it and the cork went way under and I caught a catfish that was 14" or 15" long. Boy was I excited! This was going to be better than I thought it would be!

In a few days Bill Nations told me his neighbors across the street from him had a deck boat for sale. We went up to look at it and wound up buying it, boat, trailer, skis, life jackets, ski rope and the works, for $4,500. It was in very good shape and had a 100 horsepower Mercury motor. It would hold a maximum of twelve people, so it was plenty large enough and it fit the slip just fine. It had a top speed of 40 mph — more about this later.

I must now tell you a good story. I mentioned before about a high school student that worked for us when we were building The Village Apartments back in 1973, Gary Harbour. His folks were Jack and Nadine Harbour. Gary was a very nice boy and a good worker and he went to college and got some kind of degree in management and went to work with one of the big pharmaceutical companies. Within a few years he excelled and went right to the top. He is still with the same company and he and his family lived in Sweden for several years. He has gotten promotion after promotion and now makes several hundred thousand dollars per year. The company now has him and his family living in a villa in Italy. His folks just returned from a vacation to visit them.

Well, anyway, Jack and Nadine Harbour had worked for the Laboratory for many years. They were not the average run-of-the-mill scientific types. She was a division secretary and jack was a very good electrical engineer. They first met in Borger, Texas as Jack was a Texas boy and Nadine was from southwestern Oklahoma. Jack had gotten his degree at Texas University in Austin. They appreciated us giving Gary his first job, and for the fact that we were Bartlesville, Oklahoma folks mostly. They were both working for Phillips Petroleum Co. in Borger and had also worked in Bartlesville several years when they were young. There was a saying in those days by the people working for Phillips in the oil fields in west Texas that when they died, instead of Heaven, they would get to go to Bartlesville.

One day Jack asked me if I had any way that he could make some extra money by investing in my company. I said, "Jack, it so happens that I do. I have a couple of other good guys that invested $10,000 — $20,000 with me in promissory notes. I pay 10% interest payable every six months." Jack said, "That sound great."

I told him, "I have one family that has been with me for several years and they draw $500 interest money every six months each year. They take $500 for their summer vacation and the other $500 they use to buy Christmas presents for their family." I asked Jack if he knew Silvio Balestrini and he said he did. "Call Silvio and ask him if he likes to deal with Andy Long."

Well, he did and Jack said, "Andy, I want to do mine the same way." So this went on for several years, and we became good friends. When we got ready to move to Texas, Bonnie went to the service station that handled the U-Haul rentals in Los Alamos to reserve a couple of trucks. Well, low and behold, whose name was on the list to reserve a truck, also going to Austin, but Jack Harbour! What a coincidence! We all got to Austin, Texas about the same time and started a really long-lasting friendship and had many, many domino games over the years. Jack was a hell of an engineer and plenty smart and so was Nadine, so the four of us hit it off as each of us respected all the others.

I decided to build a cover over my boat slip to keep it out of the weather, so I hired Jack to help me and it turned out really nice. The Harbours had rented a house for a while, then decided to build one themselves. Jack did almost all of the work himself and it turned out beautifully. His daughter was young, but old enough to get married, so she did and the young man was a dandy and he decided to build them a house — a big one near Waco, Texas. Jack and Nadine helped them some and later the young husband became a professor at Baylor University. So Jack and Nadine moved to Waco to be near them and their grandchildren.

So both Kelly and Gary turned out real well and Jack and Nadine had a really loving family for years now as well as their good friends Andy and Bonnie Long.

Now back to 1981 and the Long family in their home on River Hills Road. That summer was unforgettable. I had to make a trip to Santa Fe for a board meeting of Guadalupe Resources Corp. and when I returned, I brought our twin's friends Tracy Tucker and Belle Balibrera with me. Now I had four young 14 year olds to teach how to water ski. My new friend Jim Nations had taught all of his kids to water ski as well as some of his grandkids, so he helped me teach them and we all had a ball. The girls were all there for about a month and they just about wore me out! I was also finding out where to catch fish on Lake Austin and we had lots of fish to eat and enjoy every night.

We also had lots of company that first year! To name a few, my dear old friend and boss, Bill Sontag and his wife, Maxine from Wichita. Also, my old friend Lloyd Howard from El Reno, Oklahoma. Bobby and Myrtle Jones from Altus, Oklahoma, Elmer and Rosalie Kelly from Ft. Worth, Cliff and Juanita Johnson from Wichita, Jack and Krista Tobin from our early house-selling days in White Rock in 1961-1963, visited from Reseda, California, Bonnie's aunt and uncle from Wichita, and our good friends from White Rock, Roger and Peggy Corbett.

Later that year we had a family reunion of my relatives from Corpus Christie, San Antonio, and Austin. There was the son of my uncle Pat Long who was the famous world champion bulldogger that I wrote about earlier. I had not seen this cousin, Bob Long, since we were small children. I found out that he lived in Austin after we moved there. His job was the head of all the uniformed bank guards in Austin's biggest bank and branches in Austin. He was a retired air force veteran who flew the huge B-36 bombers during the Cold War. He was 6 ft. tall and 250 lbs. and not fat. He said, "I am bigger than my dad was, but not as strong." Anyway, we were glad to see him and get to know him and his family. They later moved to Ft. Worth. About the time one bunch would leave, another would show up. That was the busiest summer we had ever had with house guests. It was a good thing that Andra was there to help Bonnie. We had a wonderful summer. The swimming pool and deck boat really got a work-out and were enjoyed by all.

About the last week of August our good friends Tony and Wanda Bowline from Broken Arrow showed up for a visit. We always enjoyed them very much. Tony would still get pretty drunk, as always. Here's a funny story: Tony and I had been fishing the day before and drinking. Well, we went to bed and the next morning Tony told Bonnie, "I hope you don't mind me getting in your refrigerator last night for a snack, Bonnie"

She said, "What did you find to snack on, Tony?"

"Oh," he said," There was some stuff in a jar. Some little squares of cheese and something else in it and I ate it all up."

Bonnie thought for a minute or two and said, "Tony, you ate Andy's old catfish bait. That was a mixture of cheese and liver in chunks and he uses it for days at a time in the hot sun. Did you eat that?"

He said, "Yes, I ate it all." Well, you can imagine how we all laughed at this! He was always doing something like this when he was drinking. He also said, "I was going to take a boat ride in Andy's boat early this morning before you all got up but I couldn't get it started." We all gasped with relief! God knows what would have happened if he had gotten it started!

Well, that evening I said, "I'm going to take us all out for a boat ride and go to the best barbeque place in Texas. It's called the County Line and you can get to it by car or boat. It has boat parking right at the side entrance. You have drinks on the patio overlooking the boats while you wait for your table for dinner." This is a very lovely place, especially with a full moon and running lights on your boat. I never had any drinks when I was in the boat, so we had a safe trip. Of course, they did and he slept all the way back to the house. It was a four mile trip down the lake and we were enjoying this boat and our home very much.

During the night there was a terrific rain storm. The wind was something fierce and it blew down one of our big pecan trees. The next morning Tony and I got on our bathing suits for a swim in the pool and afterwards I decided I just had to do something with that pecan tree. I got out my chain saw and started cutting up the trunk. Bonnie was looking out the window and thinking to herself, "He's out there barefoot with that chain saw!" No sooner had this thought entered her mind, when I cut my foot with that chain saw and started bleeding like a stuck pig!

The only ones dressed in the house were Wanda and Andra. Andra, being pregnant, was too big to drive me to the emergency center, so Wanda had to drive, with Andra giving her directions. It was about ten miles up to Ben White Boulevard where the emergency center was and it seemed to take forever. But, they got me there. Andra stayed with me and Wanda went on back to the house. It was time for the Bowline's to head back to Tulsa and Broken Arrow anyway. Bonnie dressed quickly and was soon at the emergency center to meet up with Andra. They then sent me over to the hospital to have surgery on my foot.

While I was still in the hospital, the good Lord blessed us with a beautiful little baby girl. Andra gave her three names: Tiffany Jeanne Marie. The Jeanne is Bonnie's middle name, and the Marie was my mother's name. Unfortunately, Andra and Tiffany were at a different hospital and so for several days Bonnie went back and forth visiting all of us.

Tim was still in Los Alamos and Santa Fe working in real estate and taking courses in laser electronics, optics and philosophy of science at the UNM-LA Graduate Center. Andra got a very good job working at an advertising company, GSD&M, whose offices were on our side of town, so it was an easy drive for her and she learned a lot there, which would become very important as this long story progresses.

We continued enjoying both the Nation's families: Bill's family, and Jim and his wife. Bill's boys would come up for the day and liked playing with Taña and Kathy, and going fishing with their grandfather and me. Jim owned two thirty-acre tracks of Hill Country land with a hunting cabin on one of them and the other piece just across the road. He took me deer hunting Texas style. This Texas Hill Country has lots of brushy land and not too many big trees, so instead of walking through the big trees like we did in the New Mexico mountains, we would get in a deer blind about the size of an outdoor privy, and scatter shelled corn out on the ground or in a deer feeder hanging from a tree limb about 50 yards away from the deer blind. You would just wait until the deer would show up to eat the corn, then shoot them. This was not the way we did it in New Mexico, but it was the only way they did it in Texas. The reason was that the country was so brushy and filled with small cedar trees, there was no way you could slip up on these little deer. They were not like the big mule deer we hunted in New Mexico. Jim and I hunted and fished together quite a bit and talked about the many years that we had both spent in the real estate business.

We had three nearby neighbors. One young couple on one side that were nice, and both worked. He was a judge and she was a lawyer. They pretty much kept to themselves. On the other side of us was a couple that was a little younger than us, but not much younger. He worked but she was home most of the time and was an artist. He and his buddy were building a small home-built airplane and planned on flying it. We visited with them some but not much. I did find me one good friend who lived up and across the street and he and I fished a lot together. He was a good fisherman, but he did not have any waterfront on his property, so he enjoyed going with me. His name was McGlamery, and I called him "Irish." He was a little skinny guy, older than me and a widower. He had a huge Irish nose, a real outdoorsman. Tim was impressed that the famous physicist John Wheeler lived a few doors down the street. We also had a neighborhood fire dept. with one fire truck and entirely made up of just the local homeowners. We met once a month to practice a little and visit. I enjoyed that.

I bought the first riding lawn mower that I had ever owned as Pete Chavez had always taken care of our yard work in Pajarito Acres in White Rock. That is about all I had to do other than fish and watch ball games on television.

Mid-August we got a call from the Hemperlys, friends of Juanita and Neil Morgan from El Paso. Mrs. Hemperly had been the twin's 7th grade teacher. The girls were very close friends with their daughter, Dottie, who was the same age. The Hemperlys had been on vacation in Alabama with relatives and were returning home when they got to Austin, Texas to spend the night. Well, it so happened that the Texas legislature was in town and they couldn't find a motel room anywhere that had a vacancy.

They had planned to stop at our house to take the twins back to El Paso for Juanita. When they called to tell us their plight, naturally we invited them out. We had never met. So they found our place and we invited them in. I said, "Bob and Carrie, how about a cup of coffee?" They had already had supper. Bob said, "No thanks." So I said, "Well, how about a coke or something else to drink?"

Bob then said, "Andy, I have been driving all day with three kids and a wife in the car and I am beat. If you don't mind, I have a quart of scotch whiskey in my car. Would you like to have a drink with me? I really need one!"

Well, I replied, "Bob, you have the best ideas. I didn't know if you drank or not, so I didn't ask you. You bet I'll have one or even two with you."

He said, "I'm an ex-Marine and an insurance salesman and I do like a drink now and then. I got the impression from Juanita that you folks were pretty religious. Maybe I misunderstood her."

"Maybe so," I said. Shortly after our drinks we all bedded down and woke to a big breakfast Miss Bonnie and Andra fixed for us. The night before broke the ice with these folks. We hit it off so well, not only the four of us adults, but we all enjoyed all the kids and this one night stand wound up lasting for five days filled with water skiing and fishing, cleaning fish, cooking and drinking a little and, of course, swimming in our pool.

One of the days Bob and Carrie went to town and bought a great big basket of shrimp. They told Bonnie this was their treat, so they cleaned shrimp for a long time and then cooked them and we had the dandiest shrimp dinner I had ever seen. They really knew how to do it and the shrimp were just delicious. This was their way of really saying "thank you." As the years passed by, the Morgans and Hemperlys stayed in touch, especially the kids and our twins.

Many years later after the girls had left home, Neil and Juanita moved back to El Paso as Neil was still in the garment business, primarily jeans, and Mexico's factories produce a lot of jeans. Neil is a broker and does a very good business at it and has done very well. They are still good friends with the Hemperlys as Juanita is teaching school in El Paso now and has done so for years. She will retire in a couple of more years. Carrie Hemperly has already retired from teaching. We all attended Dottie's wedding a few years ago.

We continued to have relatives and friends come visit us. Bonnie's brother, Bob Scott and his wife came from Galena, Kansas and we had a great time fishing and sightseeing. Two of the favorite places that we took all of our visitors to was the beautiful state capital building in Austin and the Lyndon Johnson Presidential Library near the beautiful University of Texas. I think we visited them nine different times that first year.

Remember the hard times that the Los Alamos County Planning Commission gave me all through the first ten years, especially that county planner? Well, they finally hired one that I could get along with that believed in growth of the community instead of trying to stop growth as the others had been trying to do. Anyway, his name was Pat Brown. He had some good experience and also have served twenty years in the Navy and had retired from it. So we hit it off pretty well after the first year or so. So about the time I started The Village in White Rock, the planner and building inspector were really helping us and not trying to stop us. What a pleasant change.

The old building inspector, remember the old ex-cop from Amarillo that had been shot by a criminal years ago? Well, he told me one time he just didn't have any trouble at all with what Kermit and I were building because we always followed the plans exactly and did a damn good job. The reason I mention all this is to show you how well our relationship had been cemented. One day I got a call from the old building inspector and his wife and they said that they were at Lake Travis and would like to visit Bonnie and I. I said, "Come on down." So they did and stayed with us for three days and three nights and we had a great visit and lots of fishing.

About a month later, a call came from Pat Brown, the county planner. He said, "Andy, I would like to come visit you on my vacation." I was delighted as we had become friends. So he did. He was single at the time so we also had a great time fishing, boating to the County Line for dinner in our deck boat, and he and I also took in a little night life in Austin. We enjoyed these kinds friends.

Another visitor was Joann Barnes. She and her husband Jack had bought three homes from me in Los Alamos County. The last one was one of the townhouses next to The Village. Jack worked at the Laboratory as a super mathematician and had just retired, so she sold her toy store that she had in The Village Shopping Center. They had two boys and I gave the oldest one his first job as a laborer the summer he graduated. Now he had just graduated from college at Las Cruces, New Mexico and had gotten a job as a management trainee with Dillards Department Stores in San Antonio, Texas. Joann went to work for the Chamber of Commerce. She said The Village was not being run the way Peggy and I had run it.

We knew this family very well. She was pregnant with their second son and had the first baby boy in a carrier on her back when I sold her and Jack their first house in White Rock in 1962. We were close. Anyway, she and son #2 had some to San Antonio to visit son #1 when they decided to drive over and visit with us. We were very glad to see them and I took her and the boys fishing and we caught a nice mess of fish and enjoyed a fish dinner that evening for supper.

Juanita and Neil, the twin's mother and stepfather had moved to Seattle, Washington. He had gotten a really good job there and they all liked Seattle. It would be the first Christmas that the twins would have without being with Grandma and Grandpa. So, Tim, Andra, Bonnie and baby Tiffany and I had an enjoyable time without a lot of snow and ice for the first time in years.

Tim was living in New Mexico and Andra was enjoying her job at the advertising agency in Austin. The spring of 1982 had sprung and we were still enjoying Austin. We were lonesome for the twins, and they wanted to see little Tiffany for the first time. They were now 15 years old and they missed us too. We decided that Gram, Gramps and Tiffany Jeanne Marie would drive to Seattle, Washington to see the Morgan family. Tif was about nine months old, and we took off in my red & white diesel Cadillac for Seattle.

The second evening we arrived in Boise, Idaho where our old friends Elmer and Rosalie Kelly were now living and working at the world headquarters of Morris Knutson Construction Co. Anyway, they had even rented a baby bed for our new grandchild and were ready for us. The next morning Kelly told me that he and I were going to take a ride in the company plane with a couple of financial big shots from New York City on an inspection trip to see the huge dam that Kelly was in charge of building in Oregon that I told you about earlier. We enjoyed our visit with the Kellys, as always, and in a day or two went on to Seattle.

Juanita, Neil, and the girls liked Seattle very much and they had rented a nice place with large pine trees around the yard near a big park with large pines, like a forest. We decided to take a cruise on a ship from Seattle to Vancouver, Canada. Taña did not want to go so Kathy and Bonnie and I and Tiffany got aboard early in the morning and settled in our private cabin. Again, Tif was about nine months old. The trip went exceptionally well and when we got to Vancouver we docked and went ashore and took a tour bus that toured the entire city for about two hours. The city and all the grounds were absolutely gorgeous. So beautiful and clean. We had a fabulous lunch at one of the large hotels, then back to the ship for our return voyage to Seattle. Tif got along really well — no trouble at all — and it was a very enjoyable trip for all of us.

It was mid-June 1982 and the school year was over for our 15 year old grandchildren, so the five of us took off after a day or two so the twins could spend the summer with us. First into Oregon state and down the beautiful coastline we traveled. It was the first time any of us had been in Washington and Oregon. Then on to the Redwood National Park in northern California, and we got into San Francisco about dusk. We spent a couple of hours touring and seeing the lights of Alcatraz Prison. The 15-1/2 year old girls would spot a young guy or two and one would say, "Oh, look at that fox, Taña", then a little bit later the other one would say, "Oh, Kathy, look at those two foxes." This is the first time Bonnie and I realized that our precious twin grandaughters had discovered boys. Bonnie and I enjoyed listening to this.

The next morning we traveled on to see our dear friends Krista and Jack Tobin. Their daughter, that Bonnie had babysat for, had just gotten married. Their son was now 16 or 17 so he and his buddy took our precious twins for a car ride. Well, we hadn't heard how fast they drove that night until just a few years ago when Taña said, "Gramps, that boy drove 100 miles per hour in that car." I shook with fright and anger when I heard that. Then I realized this sort of thing happens all too often when these young boys are at this age, with shit for brains, and full of piss and vinegar.

After a day or two of enjoying the Tobins and their nice pool and Krista's delicious meals, my diesel Cadillac was giving me trouble, so Jack said, "Andy, there's a Cadillac dealer near here so let's take it down there and let them tell us what is wrong."

Well, we did and it was some bad news — about $2,300 worth. So Jack said, "You have to do this Andy to get home, so borrow our second car while you visit Chuck and Pat Coutts in Malibu for a few days." This is what we did. We had a wonderful visit, got the Cadillac out of hock, so-to-speak, and started home. When we got to Gallup, New Mexico just inside the New Mexico border, it was time to spend the night. We picked a motel close to a convenience store and stopped to get some milk for the baby girl. When I parked, I over-steered or something and the line to the power steering pump broke. It spewed power steering fluid making the car very hard to drive. I asked the lady at the motel if there was a Cadillac dealer in town. She said, "We used to have one but they went broke, but there is a Lincoln place." I figured I would take the car there in the morning, which was Saturday, the 3rd day of July.

After worrying all night about this I took it to the Lincoln dealer and they explained the problem and said, "We don't have anything that will fit. Sorry, but we can't help, and since it is the holiday we'll be closing at noon." I placed a call to the Cadillac dealership in Santa Fe where I had special-ordered this lemon from my old friend and sales manager there. I had bought several cars from Pete Rowsacker. He had an Indian name and was about one-fourth Indian. We were very good friends.

Pete said, "Andy, I am going to be open today until noon and if you start right away you can make these 200 miles by then and I now have four new 1982 model Cadillacs for you to choose from, all four-door Fleetwoods. I will make you an extra good deal and trade-in that damn lemon diesel. They have proven not to be good cars. All these 1982 models have gasoline engines." He continued, "From Gallup to Albuquerque I-40 is as straight as an arrow. Then you have a long sweeping curve at the Big-I in Albuquerque to I-25 to Santa Fe with only two more turns into our dealership's parking lot. If you are careful and don't drive too fast you will be okay, and I will stay here and wait for you."

Well, we did just that. Traffic was brisk to say the least because of it being the day before July 4th, but we were careful and did make it without much difficulty. The car we picked out was a beauty: White with blue velour upholstery. We all liked it so it didn't take long to make the deal.

Pete was the only employee there at the time, so we started to leave. I, being a thoughtful guy, looked down where I had parked the diesel and it was one space over from the big overhead door of the mechanic shop at the end of the building. I stopped and went back to talk to Pete and said, "Pete, it's none of my business but don't you think we should put my diesel inside your shop? You know, this is the long 4th of July weekend and this car could be vandalized over the weekend."

He said, "That's a good idea, Andy, I'll open the bay door and you drive it in." Well, when he opened the big door, just inside was an old pickup. Pete said, "I'll have to pull this pickup ahead so you can drive in." He got in and tried to start it. He had not noticed that gasoline was dripping out of the engine and it sparked when he started it and caught on fire. So Pete jumped out to see if we could push it out the door. Well, we did as it was on a slope, and he said, "Bonnie, call the fire department and I'll get the fire extinguisher and maybe we can put it out.'

We raised the hood of the truck and the fire was roaring. I said, "I've never used a fire extinguisher before, have you Pete?" He said, "No."

Taña said, "I know how, Grandpa. I learned how in the 4th grade when I rode the school bus." She said, "You pull that thing there," and pointed to it. So I grabbed that ring and did not have a firm grip on the hose and it blew out of my hand and the contents came out under a lot of pressure and hit me in my left eye so hard I thought it knocked my eye out. It went all over my head and face, inside my shirt and that eye really hurt. By this time, Pete started using the extinguisher and the fire truck had arrived with the ambulance that always comes to a fire.

The driver of the ambulance looked at my eye and he said, "I can't do anything about your eye, but I'll take you to the hospital so you can be treated."

I said, "Give me a minute to go inside and shake out my clothes and wash up and we'll see." So I did and inside my shirt and undershirt was that white powder. I shook out my clothes, washed up and said to the ambulance driver, "I think I'll pass up the hospital as I have a long way to drive yet today, and I'll then drive on in to Austin, Texas tomorrow."

He said, "Okay, but I think you should have that eye looked at." Anyway, Pete drove the Cadillac inside the garage and left the old pickup outside for the weekend and we said our goodbyes.

Tim had an apartment in Los Alamos then and he was going to go to Austin with us and his girls for a week so we drove 34 miles up the mountain to Los Alamos, picked up Tim and the six of us started to Texas. By the time we got to Santa Rosa, it was almost dark so I said, "We'll stay here for the night." Every motel we stopped at had "No Vacancy" signs up so we kept looking and I spotted a Holiday Inn and didn't see any "No Vacancy" sign. So I said, "I know it will cost a small fortune for all six of us to stay here, but we will have to, I guess." So I pulled up and went inside.

The desk clerk was an ugly, skinny old gal and I said, "My family needs a room for tonight." She said, "Do you have reservations?" I said, "Pray tell me, why I would want to make reservations in Santa Rosa, New Mexico?" She said, "No reservations, no room." I said, "You don't have a sign outside saying 'No Vacancy,' so I had to walk all this way in to find this out." "Well," she said, "No reservations, no room." I said, "When you and I both die and you come flying into my motel on your broom, you witch, I'll say to you, 'no reservations, no room.'" She stood there with her mouth open and I whirled around and walked out.

When I got back in the car one of the twins said, "Grandpa, what were you telling that lady and why were you waving your arms around?" When I explained to them all about what I had said to the old witch, they were amazed at Gramps — then they started laughing. If my eye hadn't been hurting I probably would not have said what I did, but she deserved it anyway.

Well, it was dark by now and we were 40 or 50 miles from Ft. Sumner, so we drove on and stopped at the first motel we came to. It didn't look too good, but they had a big room with two beds and a roll-away bed for Tim, all for only $36. A real bargain, under the circumstances. I put an ice pack on my eye and in the morning it was better. We drove all day and reached our home on River Hills Road that night in our brand new white 1982 Cadillac. Andra was glad to see her family and her little baby girl. We had been gone for over two weeks and we were all glad to be back in Texas.

The summer of 1982 was unusually hot and we really had enjoyed that pool and the shade from the pecan trees. The house was large, as I said before, and even had a big full-size pool table in the family room that all of us enjoyed. Our home was cooled with refrigerated air conditioning as the humidity in south Texas is bad and water coolers are useless. The house was well built, but that was before homes were insulated so cooling this big house with refrigerated air became very, very expensive. We had $350 per month in electric bills, so we began to re-think our long-term plans.

Tim was living in Tesuque and Andra was getting homesick for Albuquerque. They came up with the idea of renting a house together in Albuquerque so they could share the expenses.

We were down in Austin 650 miles away — too far for them to drive down and back on a weekend. It was a 13-1/2 hour drive one way. I had already made several trips back to Santa Fe involving Guadalupe Resources, so I told Bonnie if we moved to Estes Park into the house we had there we would only be about 350 miles to Albuquerque and that the flight from Seattle to Denver was half as far as to Austin for the twins to fly back and forth. To make a long story short, I raised the price we paid for the house in Austin about $40,000 and ran an ad. We had lots of calls and a few lookers and then one day I hit pay dirt.

A young guy and his girlfriend came to look. They were a nice-looking couple and quality folks. They were planning on getting married soon. She was in the business of furnishing plants and so on to big office buildings and banks in the Austin area. She really knew her business and was doing very well at it. She would change the plants and small trees out every so often, etc. He had just sold a factory he started back east which manufactured ceiling fans. At that time the things had not been on the market for too many years, but now they were going great guns. He had served in the Viet Nam War and had gotten the idea of manufacturing these fans while he was in Viet Nam, so when he got out he made it happen. He was a young entrepreneur for sure. Anyway, they were real good prospects. He also had a beach house on the Galveston, Texas beach.

They liked the place very much and he said he was going to build his bride a green- house on the property, if he bought it, so she would be able to grow a lot of her plants there. It was a good idea, and there was an ideal location for one as the lot was an acre and a half — plenty of room. He said, "Do you think I can get a loan on the place?"

I said, "If the price is agreeable, I think the bank will let you assume my loan and I'll make you a $40,000 second mortgage for the balance after you make a down payment of $20,000."

He said, "Let's go to the bank." We did and the bank agreed after checking him out. We had a deal. I was so happy to get my price plus a $40,000 second mortgage that I said, "I'm going to make you a gift of my deck boat." Well, this cemented the deal and everyone was very happy.

This was September 1982. We had been in Austin about a year and four months and enjoyed two full summers there. I gave notice to my renter in the house in Estes Park that we planned to make the move in October. I rented a large 24 foot U-Haul and loaded it with most of the things we had stored in the garage, such as tools, shelving and file boxes. The free-standing garage in Estes Park had a large shop space and storage in addition to space for two cars. So the first load was things like that.

Bonnie followed me in our car and the first day we made it to Dalhart, Texas and stayed all night, then on into New Mexico near Raton where we hit I-25 north to Denver and on to Estes Park before dark. Old Bonnie stuck to my back bumper all through that Denver traffic and we made it okay. We unloaded all of the first load in the garage as we wanted to clean the house good before putting anything in it. Most of the things we had on this first load were for storage anyway. We got out of Estes Park about noon and made it back to Austin by mid-day the next day. No big problems, just hard work. We had returned the U-Haul back in Boulder, Colorado, and went back down the mountain so the trip in our Cadillac was quite pleasant. Well, in a couple more days we had rested a little and took two days to load up the house with the help of my Irish friend and neighbor, who I hired to help me.

This time it took longer to load as we had to wrap a lot of our good furniture, piano, dishes and things but we finally got it all loaded, said our 'goodbyes' to everyone and my good Irish friend, Jack, said, "I've got a bed for you and Bonnie to stay all night with me, so you can get a good early start. We did and by nightfall we stayed in Dalhart, Texas again in the panhandle of north Texas. When we hit the New Mexico state line and headed west to Raton. The highway was flat and straight with very little traffic and we were making good time, at about 60 miles an hour with Bonnie trailing in our car.

I had a thermos of coffee in the seat beside me, but the plastic coffee cup had fallen from the seat onto the floor in front of the seat. I didn't want to take time to stop to get the cup off the floor so I just leaned way over with my out-stretched right hand to reach the cup with my left hand on the steering wheel. I took my eyes off the road for a few seconds and all of a sudden I was riding on the rough sloping shoulder of the highway. The shoulder had a pretty good slope to it and it was certainly "crisis time." I believe the left front and back wheels of the truck actually were in the air as I was traveling at 60 miles per hour in the sloping bar ditch which, fortunately, was wide and not real rough. I've never experienced anything like it! Talk about "power" steering — I put all the power I had on that steering wheel to get this big truck back up onto the black top and the wheels back on the road.

Bonnie was following me in the car and saw what was happening — and so did a lady and her dog that were behind Bonnie in a four-wheel drive Jeep station wagon. When I got to a smooth place to pull off the blacktop I stopped. I was shook! So was Bonnie and the other lady — they just knew that truck was going over on its side. The lady came up and got out of her car (as did Bonnie) and asked, "Would you like a cup of coffee to calm down?"

I said, "No, thank you, but I don't need anything to pep me up — I need something to calm me down. I have a bottle of whiskey in the truck of our car. I'm going to have myself a big drink of whiskey!" I don't know if this can be counted as my fifteenth "near death experience," but it sure as hell came very close! It would have torn me up good, not to mention the loss of all our furniture — way out on the open prairie, a long way from a hospital and the town of Raton.

By late afternoon we had made it into Estes Park. We parked the U-Haul at the house and drove to the Holiday Inn and went to bed early for a good night's sleep. After breakfast we found the unemployment bureau in town and hired a couple of big strong young men to help us unload.

Now for the surprise — the renter and the gas company read the meter for her final bill and had left on the heat. The house was warm from being closed up but when you went in, there was the damnedest odor! I have never smelled anything like it before! We finally figured out that it was cat urine! The school teacher renter had two cats and she had apparently left them in the house all the time since it was cool or cold nearly all the time in the mountains at Estes Park. These cats had a favorite place to go to pottie, I guess, because it was mostly in the dining room at the end of the living room. We lifted up the carpet and the smell would knock you down.

Well, we went ahead and unloaded everything, but simply put the dining room furniture and piano stacked in the living room. We took the carpet up and decided not to try to clean it, but to replace it. The carpet people suggested that we go to the paint store and talk to them about some kind of sealer to paint the wood floor to keep the odor from coming up through the new carpet. After cleaning it good with soap and water and letting it dry, a painter applied two coats of sealer and with new carpet we were back in business.

During all this, in a couple of days, to top things off, it started snowing! It was mid-October. I told Bonnie this is like the weather we had in Los Alamos where winter lasted from mid-September to mid-April. We settled into Estes Park and my left leg began to bother me some. I had been wearing the elastic stocking for about 10 years now after that wild ride on Chuck Coutts' motorcycle.

When my leg started bothering me, I remembered the appraiser, Bonnaman, from Harlingen, Texas that had told me all about chelation and the Chinese doctor in San Francisco who had treated him with chelation therapy and made a new man out of him. He had said, "Andy, you need chelation for that leg." I called him long-distance one day and asked him how to get hold of this Chinese doctor. He said, "He has moved his clinic to Reno, Nevada from San Francisco. He calls it Century Clinic." Well, I called and made an appointment and Bonnie and I drove to Reno to start my treatment.

We checked into a nice motel a few blocks from the clinic for a week. The motel rooms were in strips of two, two-story buildings. The strangest thing was about to happen. We were in a room on the second floor and each room had a little porch just outside the sliding glass doors. I looked out my sliding door and said, "Bonnie, come over here and look who is sitting out on his little porch reading a newspaper on the room straight across from ours."

She said, "Is that Gary Pendergraft?"

I said, "Yes, it is!" Well, I stepped back and called the motel office and said, "Would you ring Gary Pendergraft's room?"

They did and Gary answered. I said, "Mr. Pendergraft, would you put your phone down a minute and step back onto your porch. I want to tell you something." He had no idea who I was, so he stepped back out on his porch and I said, "What the hell are you doing in Reno, Gary?

He said, "What the hell are you doing in Reno, Andy Long?" Neither of us could believe it! "I'm up here trying to hire a Reno salesman for my insurance company. I'm spreading out some and selling lots of hospitalization insurance to older people and am doing a really good business, so I'm trying to expand to this area."

I told him, "I'm in room number (something). Come on over." We had a really good visit and breakfast together the next morning.

Gary told us, "Andy, it's been about a year since Bobbie and I visited you and Bonnie in Austin, are you still living there?"

"No," I said, "We sold out and are now living in Estes Park, Colorado."

Gary said, "Andy, I have a real good idea. Bobbie and I are going to take a vacation in Hawaii in January in about a month from now. Why don't you and Bonnie join us in Vegas and we'll fly out to Hawaii together."

Well, Bonnie and I thought about it for about 5 minutes and said, "Okay." His wife never did completely believe this coincidence! She was very jealous of Gary and a suspicious person. But we had a great time on our vacation for a week and visited all the sights and enjoyed the fabulous hotels and beaches, the sunken battleship Arizona, and so on.

The chelation treatments went well. The first thing they did to me was put me on a machine they called "Ralph." The nurse hooked me up to it like an electrocardiogram, except all over my body. It gave a printout and the doctor and I looked it over together and he explained it to me. For the left side of my entire body from my head to my toes, the graph was almost flat. Just a little bit wavy. He told me, "Both sides should be like your right side. You have very poor circulation in the left side of your brain and your whole body. We will give you two different treatments."

The chelation treatments consisted of injecting an I. V. into my right wrist, hooked up to a tube and quart bottle on a metal stand with wheels so I could roll it into the rest room when needed. I was in a large room about 40 ft. square with one male nurse and one female nurse. Three sides of this large room were lined with leather Lazy-Boy reclining chairs, side-by-side. The chelation was administered very slowly and it took four hours to complete the treatment. They gave us each a plastic jug like a gallon milk jug to take with us to pee in and bring back the next day to test. The doctor explained that the chelation was pulling all the plaque and poison out of my body and blood and he said it all comes out of the body in your urine, saliva, and perspiration. All three had an odor. While we were getting this chelation treatment we would visit with each other and exchange stories and jokes, and the time passed fairly quickly. The men were on one side of the room and the women were on the other side.

The other treatment he gave me was totally different. It is called the "Hyperbaric" treatment. I got into a big iron lung type thing that looked like a coffin with a Plexiglas hinged top that is sealed, called a hyperbaric chamber. They would pump pure oxygen into it under twenty pounds of pressure, for me to breath. I could look out and the attendant could see in. We could talk to each other through a microphone during the treatment that took about 30 minutes every other day. This would enable the chelation to reach into the brain. Very expensive. A week of both of these treatments ran about $3,000. I took two weeks of these treatments for each process, about one month apart.

When it was time to go out for the second treatment, I got the bright idea to call our dear friends the Bowlines in Broken Arrow, Oklahoma, who loved to gamble. We had made several trips to Las Vegas with them before. Neither family had ever been to Tahoe, so we decided to drive to Reno and they would fly to Reno from Tulsa and we would meet in Tahoe. We all checked into the same hotel, and being wintertime and high in the mountains, it was cold. The altitude was hard on Tony Bowline's heart, so we left the next day for Reno down the mountain. We stopped to take pictures as we usually did when we got together. Anyway, we got snugly in our hotel and I started my chelation treatments.

Tony told me that day while we were at the crap table gambling, "Andy, you are dull as a hoe, son. What's the matter with you?"

I said to him, "Tony, that's why I'm out here taking these treatments. The doctor told me that it's my circulation."

Dr. Tang had asked me where I lived and I told him Estes Park, Colorado. "What is the elevation there?" I said 8,000 feet. "Oh," he said, "you have got to get out of there to a lower elevation or you're going to have a stroke!"

I asked, "What about Albuquerque? My kids live there and I want to be close to them."

"Well, that's still a mile high. But, it's better there than where you are living now. You are improving, however. We will check you again on the machine before you go home this time." He did and the test showed some improvement.

I tried to tell Tony about this but he said his doctor didn't approve of chelation and told Tony it wouldn't do any good for him. He might as well light a match to the hundred dollar bills and watch them burn as to take these treatments. I had heard that the American Medical Association didn't approve of chelation, so all the doctors felt the same way. Those people I know that had taken the treatments all praised it and were greatly improved including the ones at the clinic. So I told Tony, "I've seen proof enough." I couldn't convince this hard-head, so I quit trying.

Anyway, we had a wonderful time with our dear old friends. One day Tony and I were shooting craps and he was standing at the end of the crap table throwing the dice for his point. He threw the dice and looked up at the ceiling and said in his loud booming voice, "Give me a four, Lord, give me a four." Well, we all looked at the dice when they stopped rolling, sure enough there were two deuces. Tony said, "Thank you, Lord." and the stick man said, "You're welcome." Everyone at the table roared with laughter!

The last day I wasn't doing any good at craps at all, so I decided to try the slot machine. I bought four $10 rolls of quarters and picked out a quarter machine and started playing. I had never played the slots much but I played six quarters at a time in this one and had about a roll and a half of quarters when the machine started flashing and it wouldn't take my quarters. They were just falling straight through. So one of the young attendants was walking by and I said, "Buddy, something is wrong with this machine, it won't take my money."

He said, "Have you been playing this?" I said, "Yes." and he said, "Don't touch it anymore. You have just hit the jackpot. That is a progressive machine and you have just won $2,357."

I said, "Oh, my God! Here son, this roll of quarters is for you for your help." About that time a guard came by and they were paying me off with twenty three one-hundred dollar bills and change, and said, "Come with me to the office and they will put your money in a safety deposit box and you can get it when you leave. You never know when someone is standing around and watching you and waiting for you to leave and knock you on the head."

I said, "Thank you very much and here is a roll of quarters for you, sir. That's the most I have ever won on a slot machine." This one lick damned near paid for my chelation and Hyperbaric treatments this trip. Lucky, huh?

Wanda Boline's sister and her boyfriend Johnny decided to get married in Reno while we were there, which is not unusual in Reno or Las Vegas. We all enjoyed this too. When it came time to go home the two newlyweds flew back to Tulsa, and Tony and Wanda rode back to Estes Park with us to see our place there and to visit with Wanda's niece and her husband who lived in Denver. Then, in a few more days they flew home to Tulsa and Broken Arrow from the old Denver airport.

It was January 1982 and the weather was cold and there was lots of snow on the ground, so we decided not to try and make any more moves until Spring. In the meantime, I got a call from my nephew, Mike Stanfield, in Tulsa. Several years before he and his wife Debbie had four daughters and had moved to Florida from Los Alamos where he had done so very well. Debbie's mother and step-father lived in Florida and she wanted to be closer to them. It didn't take long for Mike to realize that the Florida market was a hell of a lot different than the captive market, so-to-speak, that we had in Los Alamos County. They moved back to Tulsa to lick their wounds and after several more years in real estate there, they were hurting financially and not getting along very well either.

They decided to separate and Debbie's sister in Tulsa was taking the oldest and youngest girls to live with her for a while, and Mike asked us to take the middle two girls for a few months in Estes Park. We agreed to do this as Mike was one of our favorite nephews. So the two of us and the two girls fit in the little mountain house very well. One was in the 4th grade and the other was in the 6th grade. They were Melissa and Mary Ann Stanfield.

Melissa wanted to be in the school band, so we rented a saxophone and she did very well. They were very bright girls and we enjoyed them very much and were willing to do anything for Mike in this hour of need. By April, Mike and Deb patched up their differences. Mike opened his own real estate business in Tulsa and they got all four girls back with them.

We were glad to be of help and Melissa and Mary Ann enjoyed their stay with us and still talk about the good times we had playing in the snow and sight-seeing trips we took around the mountains. Melissa loved hot dogs and Bonnie would fix them so often for her that I called her "Hot Dog." Mary Ann I called "Lucky," as at a class drawing she had the winning number and won a cake that she shared with all of us when she got home that afternoon. So it was Hot Dog and Lucky. They are grown now, but haven't forgotten their stay with Aunt Bonnie and Uncle Andy in Estes Park.

By April spring was just around the corner, so we thought it was time we moved to a lower altitude like Dr. Y. Y. Tang advised me to do. One day I called Jim Bennett in Austin. He had bought our house there and I had taken a second mortgage from him for $40,000. I told him in case he ever wanted to pay it off I would discount it ten percent. He said, "Andy, I have a buyer for my beach house on the gulf at Galveston, and I just might want to take you up on your offer." He did and we had enough money to make a nice down payment on a place in Albuquerque. This was a lucky stroke. I have always said, "Good things happen to good people." You can believe this as it has happened to us time and time again.

We were very fortunate in finding a two-story home on a large corner lot. It was a brick home with four bedrooms, a huge living room and dining room, a large kitchen and laundry room, and a big room with a bar with mirrors, bar stools and an ice maker, just like in the movies. Both the bar and family room opened onto an open outdoor swimming pool and nice back yard, all walled in. I also had a three-car garage, with plenty of storage closets on two walls. The garage even had astroturf on the floor as the guy that owned the house previously was an antique car nut — everything was neat and clean as a pin. Oh, yes, the house also had a covered patio that ran all the way along the big living room looking out on the pool.

The guy that owned the house was a retired Air Force fighter pilot. A real "hot dog" of a major. In other words, a self-admiring sharpie. He told Tim and I that he was smarter than four computers when Tim told him how wonderful computers were. Well, this is about to be recalled — just to see how smart this guy really was.

I knew how to write a good contract, so when we did I told the Realtor to include the items that were not attached, but to be included in the purchase price. They were drapes, curtains, bar stools and four hanging lamps. We both read it carefully and all four of us signed the contract. Well, when we came down to close the deal and inspect the home before closing, the Major was running the vacuum cleaner in the family room. He was so proud that he was leaving it nice and clean for us. Well, so was I and I thanked him for that. Then I said, "I noticed there are only two hanging lamps in the bedrooms and there are supposed to be four, and there are only three bar stools and there are supposed to be four."

He said, "Oh, no, you are mistaken. There were only three stools and two lamps. There never were four of each."

I said, "I know damn well there were four stools and four lamps."

He bristled and got right up in my face and said, "Are you calling me a liar?"

I said, "You can call it anything you choose, but here are the pictures of the stools at the bar and of the four lamps and you know as well as I do pictures don't lie." I said, "As soon as I see the other stool and lamps, we will close the deal, but not until then."

He said, "I'll go to the new house we moved into a couple blocks away and be back in a few minutes." Well, here he came and he said, "You know, my wife gave that bar stool and lamps to our daughter and here they are. I'm sorry about this, Mr. Long."

So I said, "Let's go to the title company and close the deal." And we did. I never saw the lying S.O.B. again.

The house was in a neighborhood of homes ranging in price from $200,000 to $1,000,000 — the finest subdivision in Albuquerque at the time. It was called Four Hills and it was beautiful. As I recall, the purchase price was $220,000 and my offer of $200,000 was accepted. It was well worth the money. I have always said, you make your money on a piece of property when you buy. This is very true. Don't forget it.

This home was big enough for Tim, Andra, Tiffany, Bonnie and me. We all moved in with plenty of room for all of us. Tim was finishing up his master's degree at the time at the University of New Mexico.

The day we moved from Estes Park, it was late April and was spitting snow. God, I was glad to get away from the long winters once again! The Estes Park home was turned over to a real estate agency to rent and later the Realtor decided to buy it from us since we no longer wanted to live there because of the elevation.

This time I decided to hire United Van Lines to load and move our things, and for $4,000 they got it all loaded in one day and unloaded it all in Albuquerque the next day. No more U-Hauls this time.

Andra had gone to work for an advertising agency in Albuquerque as an account executive and Tim had been teaching math and science at St. Pius X High School, a Catholic private school. Tiffany was in nursery school just down the street from the house that they had been renting.

Andra's job entailed a lot of travel all over the country for days at a time and she was having to work a lot of overtime hours and weekends too. Finally she decided she'd had enough and applied for a job as marketing director at the huge property management firm, Cauwels & Davis Management Company that owned thirty-four apartment buildings totalling over 4,000 apartments. Andra's experience in the real estate business with her dad and mom qualified her for this job. It was a very responsible and important job — and paid very well.

One day she needed to go to the dentist, and she had good dental coverage with this new job, so she looked in the phone book and 'lo and behold' here was the name of Doctor Richard Riordan. This was a fellow that she had dated in college, just before he was to go to Kansas City to dental school. He now had a practice in Albuquerque, so she called him for an appointment.

He was still a bachelor and after the dental appointment he had not only cleaned her teeth, but they made a date to have dinner that night. It took some time for this friendship to blossom into romance, but it did. One of the most important things was that Richard simply loved her little baby girl, Tiffany, who was two and a half now. He would play on the floor with her and she really like that.

This went on for almost a year and one day they told Bonnie and I that they had set a wedding date. Richard was a year older than Tim and five years older than Andra. Richard had a nice three bedroom house in the northernmost area of town and a growing dental practice, and he had fallen in love with Andra and her darling little girl.

A few months later we had a big wedding at our house around the patio and pool with several of Andra's friends and Richard's family. His four brothers and their wives and his sister and mother were there. Richard's brother, Bill, was a judge so he performed the marriage ceremony. That was really special. It was a great wedding.

Chapter Nine

Midas Minerals

Midas Oil

Midas Oil Well #1

WHILE ALL OF THIS WAS going on, my old friend and president of Guadalupe Resources, Jack Flynn, called me and said, "Andy, I have something very interesting to talk to you about. Can we have lunch together tomorrow?" I said, "Sure, Jack."

An oil well exploration company was about to be born. It amounted to this: Charles Hagerman, a mining engineer and a good friend of Jack Flynn and a stockholder in Guadalupe Resources, had come to Jack and showed him some old oil well logs that he had obtained from the State involving some land and old abandoned oil wells near the little town of Bernal, New Mexico, close to Starvation Peak, about 15 miles west of Las Vegas, New Mexico.

Charles had a landowner map of the area and had talked with several landowners in the area. He had a Spanish friend who lived in Santa Fe who knew several of these folks and they went together and talked with them. They said that some drilling had taken place back in 1926 and oil had been discovered, but the depression had come along and the price of oil had dropped to 10 cents a barrel and it couldn't be produced for that price, so the hopeful oil field had been abandoned.

Charles and Jack made a deal with the old Spanish man to see if he could get some of these landowners to agree to a mineral lease on their land, and he could have a small share of the production, if and when it came in. So this did happen and the leases were acquired from the landowners who all would get a one-eighth share of the oil that would be produced on their particular piece of land.

I should explain the history of Starvation Peak. Many years ago when the Spaniard Coronado made his march north from Mexico and the Spanish settled the area which is now New Mexico, they set up a capital at Santa Fe and issued land grants to the Spanish families who settled the area. The Indians resented this so violently that they tried to kill all the Spanish settlers in the area. In this particular area there was one hell of a battle and it resulted in the Spanish settlers and soldiers retreating up the tall mountain peak. The Indians simply waited until the Spaniards' water and food ran out — thus the name was given to the mountain: Starvation Peak.

Anyway, what Jack wanted was to tell me this story. He said, "I've known of your sales ability for years now and we want you to raise money to do the exploration drilling on the first well. We are going to form a new corporation called Midas Minerals. The stockholders will be me, you, George Glass (the lawyer), Charles Hagerman and Bob Newberry, as well as the old Spanish man that will help us get the leases. We want you to be president of the corporation and you'll be in charge of selling the percentage interests to raise the money to do the drilling. You will also be in full charge of the drilling and raising the money, paying all the bills and record keeping. We will have five board members when necessary. We'll all have work to do, but it will be you making the day-to-day decisions."

I said, "Jack, I'm interested." I, being a little bit of a damned fool when a challenge was involved, and not being afraid of taking a gamble said, "Let's do it."

Well, I knew I needed to hire someone who really knew the oil drilling business. I called my old friend Vance Rule in Tulsa who I had bought cookware from during my cookware days in 1960 and 1961 before moving to Los Alamos and asked him if he knew anyone that I could hire as a consultant. He said, "Yes, I do."

"Andy," he said, "Do you remember when you, I, Charley Vaughn and John Warner had formed a little company back in the 70's called Jarvac?" (for John, Andy, Vance and Charley).

I said, "Yes, Vance, I remember it but you know I sold out to you guys then and didn't stay in the deal very long."

He said, "Yes, we all sold to the Cypert family of Coweta, Oklahoma." Richard Cypert had three sons: Rick, Stan, and Tony plus his brother, Leon. They all worked in their little company. Vance said, "I wouldn't start any venture without hiring Richard Cypert as a working consultant."

"I remember Richard," I said, "He and I are about the same age. I'll call him." I did and Richard agreed to come to Albuquerque to look over the deal.

Richard said, "Leon and my boys can handle things here and I will go to work for you without a long-term contract for $100 per day plus expenses."

I agreed and said, "In one month I think I'll have enough interests sold to get started. I'll stay in touch." Well, I went to work selling percentage interests. The landowner received, off the top, one-eighth interest, then we sold one-sixteenth interests and one-thirty second interests.

YOUR FRIEND ANDY LONG IS ABOUT TO ENTER INTO A VENTURE THAT COULD WELL BE THE BIGGEST THING TO DATE THAT HE HAS EVER DONE.

I entered into it on a sink or swim basis. In other words, I would not concentrate on anything else but this with every ounce of energy and knowledge that I possessed. I had hired the best consultant that I could find and had complete faith in his judgment.

Our investors had complete faith in me. God bless them all. We all felt that this opportunity was a once-in-a-lifetime chance to all share in wealth that would be much greater than we even could imagine.

If this turned out like we thought it would, it could change the economic wealth of this large area of the state of New Mexico. Unimaginable. I am not over-exaggerating this possibility at all, as you will soon see what I mean when we take our first look at the oil sand that we encountered soon thereafter.

If this venture turns out like it seemingly could, an oil field of great size could change the lives of many people. Untold wealth and employment of many, many poor people that reside in this part of the state for miles around Las Vegas, New Mexico.

I will tell you a little bit about Las Vegas. It is a fairly small town and has been there for many, many years and was the original capital of the state of New Mexico. It was the place where President Teddy Roosevelt recruited his Rough Riders during the Spanish American War.

These men were cowboys and therefore excellent horsemen and their language was Spanish so they were ideal recruits to lead the charge in Cuba up San Juan Hill to success during this war. There is a Rough Rider's Museum still active in Las Vegas right now on I-25 that goes right down Main Street in Las Vegas. It is and always has been a very hard place for the people there to make a good living. A State mental hospital has been located there for many years, also a state college, Hilands University, is there. Amtrak Railroad still runs through town as well as I-25 from Albuquerque, Santa Fe, and on to Raton and Denver to the north.

The country is ranch land and timber. The main things they raise and sell are cattle, Christmas trees, flagstone and marijuana. Not too much, huh. Oh, yes, and cedar fence posts. There are also a lot of welfare recipients. So you see what a blessing it would be for this area to have an oil boom and all the other related businesses that come along with it. This was our dream.

I've been racking my brain as to how I can truly go into enough detail in order to show you the extent of our efforts to make all this happen. It would dwarf any of the other things that I have done in my lifetime by far. I thought, "What a way to cap off my long, hard-working lifetime career." I have many pictures as we proceeded with the drilling which will be interesting and also reports from my consultant and geologists and others, as well as my numerous letters to all our investors, etc.

I will keep it as short as possible but it still may be long and a little boring to some of you, but very interesting to others. So here goes:

The title of the individual in charge of the whole operation in the oil business, the one that is on the job from start to finish is called "the operator." So in this case yours truly is the operator. I had full responsibility and, of course, I also was in close touch with the other officers of the Midas Minerals Corp.

One of our members was Bob Newberry. He was a geologist by training and was employed by the N.M. State Highway Department. He was a knowledgeable individual and a great help in making some intelligent decisions and worked with me and our consultant. He was busy with his job at the highway department but he also found time to come to the drilling site quite often.

The first thing Richard Cypert, my consultant, and I did was to find us a nice motel where we slept and did our paperwork. To give you some idea of how long we worked in Las Vegas, we checked into The Sunshine Motel on September 1st, 1983 and checked out October 21st 1985, except for intervals between wells. I am sure they hated to see us go as we had been the longest running guests they had ever had — we were like family. Richard had a deal with one of the room maids to do his washing and ironing each week. We also had tables set up for our microscope and black light to check the many small bags of sample cuttings that we would take as the wells were being drilled. We had a little lab in our room. Also when

Bob Newberry came over from Santa Fe we would rent a roll-away bed for him. Richard and I had separate beds, of course, and the room was plenty large enough.

We ate all of our meals at the same restaurant about a block down the street as it was the best in town, called The Hilltop Café. The owner even invested in a one-thirty second interest in one of our wells.

At this time I will give a day-by-day progress report:

I was able to raise a total of $60,000 from eleven investors which should be enough to complete Midas Well #1. In the event of an over-run, it would be paid by the Corporation, not the investors. They would not have to pay for any over-runs. Well, when we got all the bills in, we found out, indeed, we had an over-run of $34,450 more than the $60,000 that we had collected from the investors. So we needed to raise this money and it was up to the Corporation to do so. My high-rolling Corporation partners came up with a total of $6,625. We were still short $27,825.

Everyone realized that we had only one source to make a loan for this amount with our collateral, and this was 'good ole Andy Long.' So I did make a loan to Midas Minerals Corporation for $30,000 to be paid back with the first $30,000 earned by the Corporation. This loan would not affect the investors earnings in any way, only the Corporation members. This was agreed to and would be done.

Only striking water, this ended Midas Well #1. Tony Solano asked us to leave it for a water well as it was a very good one for irrigation, so we did. Richard took a plane back to Coweta, Oklahoma to work with his three sons and his brother. He agreed to work with us when we decided to drill Midas Well #2.

This had been a very long year for me, and a very expensive one to boot. First, I had bought a home in Albuquerque in April of 1983, then soon after that started signing up investors for Well #1 and then work, work, work, with lots of problems with the well and lots of expense. Can you imagine how low I felt after almost a year of hard work and worry and not making a dime and spending all this money? I badly needed a good vacation!

It is early Spring 1984. Our good friends Ruben and Betty Larson from Ruidoso, New Mexico moved to El Paso, Texas. They had invested in Well #1 and they had not been to our new home in Albuquerque. So they came up for a visit. They had opened their new real estate business in El Paso and since they already had New Mexico real estate licenses, they took the Texas real estate examination and opened their new offices under the name of Interstate Realty as dual licensees and could work both states. Anyway, we had a great three-day visit with them and in the course of the three days they convinced Bonnie and me to take a trip to Europe with them.

Bonnie had never been to Europe and I hadn't been since 1945, so we agreed to take a two-week vacation with them. We drove from Albuquerque to El Paso and the four of us flew to Dallas an caught an international flight from Dallas all the way to Frankfurt, Germany. The airport lobby was right across the street from the Sheraton Inn Hotel in Frankfurt, so we checked in and spent the next day touring around Frankfurt sight-seeing. What a beautiful city! Ruben and I laughed as that day was some sort of a holiday — he and I saved a lot of money as the shops were closed and the girls weren't able to buy anything.

The next day we split up. Ruben and Betty went to see their son and his wife where she was stationed in the U.S. Navy as a doctor. She had been in the Navy for a long time before they were married. They now had a set of twin boys and Mike at the time was a "house husband" and taking care of the twin babies. Betty and Ruben had not yet seen their grandsons.

Bonnie and I met up with Bonnie's nephew, Ron Johnson, who was stationed in Heidelberg serving in the Army. He had been a Green Beret in Viet Nam when he decided to be a twenty-year man. He was now serving in the Special Forces on one of their nine-man teams. One of their jobs then was to de-bug any building where there was going to be an important meeting. Ron picked us up at our hotel in Frankfurt and drove us back to Heidelberg. We spent a wonderful two days touring this beautiful city. For some reason the Allies had not destroyed these very old and magnificent buildings and Ron enjoyed showing us around.

We got a small hotel right across the street from the Neckar River. There was a walkway and park between the street and the river and a tour boat that held about sixty people stopped there. We caught one of them and took a wonderful three-hour cruise up the river. It was an unforgettable experience. I met a German man about my age who had been in the German Army and was captured by the British Army at Calais,

France, spending the balance of the war as a prisoner of war in Britain. He had learned some English so we conversed in friendly fashion and even exchanged letters off and on for a couple of years. He said the Germans loved Ronald Reagan. He said if it wasn't for him the Russians would have been in Berlin before their tanks ran out of fuel.

We steamed by a beautiful huge old castle. The next day Ron drove us up to it and how interesting it was! It has a great restaurant in it and we had lunch there and looked down and out upon the Neckar River. What a sight. They served us their famous dish of white asparagus, very tasty, as was the rest of the meal. I took lots of pictures on this trip so I will include some of them here.

Bonnie and I went on to Copenhagen and met up with Betty and Ruben at the Holiday Inn and met their son and his family. That evening we decided to take a hydrofoil boat ride for a couple of hours to Stockholm, Sweden, where Ruben's ancestors were from. It was a wonderfully smooth, fast ride as it actually runs right on the top surface of the water after it gets up to speed; and it held approximately 200 passengers. We enjoyed this immensely! We had a delicious steak dinner in a very famous underground steak house. Then, back to Copenhagen to our Holiday Inn and a day of shopping, which the girls enjoyed.

We then went on to Amsterdam and that evening we took a moonlight cruise on a small boat of about 15-20 people and they served us wine and cheese. Very nice.

The next day we bought tickets to Milan, Italy by plane, toured around Milan, then decided to take the train to Venice. What a great ride in a private room! When we arrived in Venice the train stopped almost at the water's edge — it was late afternoon and the boat taxies were there. We talked to a man and said we wanted a medium priced hotel. He said, "I will load your luggage on the boat and I will walk you just a few blocks to your hotel." Well, we walked and we walked, seemingly in circles, and we were wondering if we would ever find our luggage again. I might mention here we were traveling with nine pieces of luggage, quite a load. Two each, plus one. Anyway, we finally arrived at our hotel to check in.

The clerk said, "I need to take your passports and Ruben said to the clerk, "You are not taking my passport."

"Oh, yes," said the clerk. I have to get the information. Ruben said, "You get it right now while I am standing here." So that was that. He said to me, "We just can't take a chance of losing our passports!" I agreed.

We had separate rooms, of course. They were clean but small and very old. The wallpaper was even gone in some places. There was a very narrow stairway up to our rooms. It had a nice view below out our window. You looked out onto the street which was a waterway — fairly narrow. Each building had a small narrow dock as all deliveries to the shops, restaurants, and hotels were made at the little docks. No concrete streets of any kind, all waterways. Even the trash and garbage was picked up at these little docks! Grocery, beer, pop, all the deliveries were this way. Different to say the least, but very interesting to us. We spent two nights and one day in Venice, took a boat taxi to a glass factory where they had hand blown glasswork of all kinds and descriptions. You haven't seen an expert salesman until you experience dealing with a Venetian crystal salesman! "What artists they are!" is the only way an old salesman like me can describe them! Well, we really "blew" our budgets! They knew how to pack this delicate glass to avoid breakage so we paid our bill, which included shipping to our home.

We toured all of Venice in a small boat and under arched walkways, foot bridges, and so on. That night we hired a Gondolier and his Gondola and he took us for a slow and romantic ride in the moonlight listening to him sing Italian songs. Fabulous!

The next morning we said our goodbyes to the hotel people and boarded our boat taxi, with our luggage this time, to the train station. We got to our compartment and were surprised to see that the four of us would be sharing it with another couple. No problem, as it was plenty large with two large windows for viewing. The other couple was a young man and his mother and her little dog. They were large people, very heavy. He looked like a young Peter Ustinov (the actor). Anyway, the son spoke fairly good English, but the mother spoke only French.

I visited with the young man quite a bit. He was a librarian. Anyway, I'll tell you a little story he told me. He said, "The Swiss are strange people and very methodical. You can tell a Swiss a joke on Friday, he remembers it on Saturday, and laughs about it in church on Sunday. Ha, ha."

We saw many, many good sights. Farm land and forest land, beautiful large mountains with waterfalls, beautiful greenery through northern

France and the Swiss Alps. We stayed all night in Basil, Switzerland. The hotel was directly across the street from the train station. It was almost dark so we checked in and went to the dining room for dinner. We were greeted by a very pretty Swiss waitress and ordered drinks, then Ruben called the waitress over and asked if she spoke English. She said, "Yeah."

Ruben said, "Could we see a menu?" The little cute waitress looked puzzled for a second or two and put a finger up to her forehead and said, "Menu, menu."

I looked over at Ruben and said, "Ruben, we are in trouble." Then we all had a good laugh. Ruben said, "We want to order our food."

"Oh," she said, "Yeah, yeah."

Another thing happened while we were waiting on our food. A big, white beautiful Mercedes pulled up at the curb just outside the restaurant window and a well-dressed couple got out of the car and were leading the most beautiful, white Russian wolfhound I had ever seen. Well, little old red-headed Betty Larson got her nose way out of joint and said, "I'm not going to eat with a dog!" They were at a table about ten or twelve feet from our table. Betty could be a pain at times. She had shown herself that day when we had to share our train compartment with the other couple with their little dog.

I had had enough of this crap, so I said gruffly, "Betty, you are not in west Texas, now, dammit. They are not doing anything wrong here, this is traditional in Switzerland." She was still miffed so we all decided to take a walk around that part of the business district of Basil before going to our rooms to sleep.

The next morning after breakfast we looked at our maps and I said, "Folks, if we take this train all the way north across Germany, we will come to Coblenz, Germany right on the north coast where the Rhine River runs into the North Sea. Maybe we can then take a big boat back to Frankfurt. We did and had another day of train travel and beautiful countryside.

We got into Coblenz in time to have a nice dinner out our hotel restaurant, overlooking the beautiful Rhine River. After a nice walk along the landscaped banks of the Rhine, we retired for the night, dreaming of all the sites we had seen that day. After breakfast we boarded a very nice, large boat that held about fifty or so passengers. We loaded our nine bags that we were still lugging around with us from the beginning and had a wonderful ride back to Frankfurt for the night. I got to visiting with some people on the boat when they overheard us speaking English. They introduced themselves and we inquired about where they lived. It so happened that they lived in Lovington, New Mexico! I said, "Do you know Nadine Lovelady?"

They said, "Sure we know her well. She is a great real estate lady in Lovington"

I said, "Yes, I know because I was a Realtor in Los Alamos for many years and I served with her on the N.M. State Board of Realtors for several years." We all thought this was quite a coincidence! "Tell Nadine hello for me when you see her."

Our plane did not leave for home until afternoon, so we called Bonnie's nephew, Ron, in Heidelberg, to come up and visit with us for a few hours before time for our plane to depart.

We had had one hell of a great vacation, but were now really glad to get back safe and sound in the good old U.S. of A. It was early summer of 1984 and now time to think about drilling Midas Minerals Well #2. I was busy talking to some of the investors that had invested in Well #1 as well as some new ones. Richard Cypert told me of a couple of guys from Texas that had previously invested in some wells with Cypert Oil Co. in Coweta, Oklahoma. He told them about us getting ready to drill Midas #2 and they were interested. Several of our previous investors also agreed to invest, too. It wasn't as hard as I thought it might be.

In the meantime, the Larsons, Betty and Ruben, had met a fairly young Mexican entrepreneur in El Paso that wanted them to take on the sales effort in Mazatlan, Mexico for a large condo project he was building. This is when time-share projects were just beginning to get started, pretty much worldwide. They agreed to go down to Mazatlan and look it over. What a job and what a responsibility!

They hired some Anglo salesmen, as well as English-speaking Mexican salesmen and set up a fine sales force. They were capable people in organizing and it didn't take long until sales were being made both from U.S. and Mexican citizens. They told Bonnie and me they wanted us to come down as they had about six couples, counting us, that were coming down together. They had invested in our oil well so we agreed to go — and to make a long story short, all of us bought time shares.

They had the first phase finished as well as the club room, large pool and other nice amenities and since the project was still in the early construction stages, if you bought now you got a two-week time share for the price of a one-week time share. It was a hell of a good deal! This is why we all bought. The price then was $4,300.00 for a two-week share. Today they sell for $10,000 for a one-week share. We had a great time and later when our twin granddaughters had their 16th birthday, we took them and their mother down for a birthday present. I rented a car so we could all go around Mazatlan to sightsee and visit the night spots. The girls learned to dance here as Ruben and I were good teachers, ha, ha. A good time was had by all. We stayed in two units and had plenty of room for Bonnie and me in one, and the three of them in the other.

The project was right on the beach and we had access to over a mile of ocean front to play on and swim. What a place!

When we got home I started getting my investors lined up for Midas Minerals Well #2. Our target date to "spud in" was October 1, 1984. Ruben and Betty, naturally, bought into it.

This year, 1984, like every year before it, Bonnie's Scott family had a reunion. This year they decided to change the date from Thanksgiving Day to Labor Day to give more time for out-of-town people to be able to come without having to ask off work, plus there would be better weather for traveling. The reunion was held in a school cafeteria room in a Wichita school. We brought in our own food since school was out for the holiday. Our New Mexico bunch, Bonnie and I, Tim, Andra, Tiffany, Taña and Kathy all came in our car and had a great time. It did go very well, but it wasn't like having it in a home on Thanksgiving and we didn't do it again on Labor Day.

Time seemed short in those days and it was not uncommon for us to make quick decisions. Betty and Nolan Mize, Bonnie's sister and her husband, lived in Clearwater, Kansas and owned a supermarket and had plenty of help. Nolan and I thought it would be a good idea if we took a trip to New Orleans, where the World's Fair was just getting started. Tim, Andra, and Tiffany (who had just turned three) flew back to Albuquerque, Kathy flew back to Seattle and Bonnie and I, Taña, Betty and Nolan all got in my white Cadillac and headed for the World's Fair. What a time we had! We checked in at the Marriott Hotel right across the large walkway from the famous Super Dome stadium, which we toured. It is the largest in the world and fabulous! We also took in Bourbon Street and other nightspots in New Orleans. Taña was 16 and having a ball with us adults treating her just like another adult.

The highlight of the trip for Taña was while we were at the World's Fair a crowd was gathering so we joined in and they were introducing two new boxers that were going to fight that night. They were Boom Boom Mancini and Bang Bang Bogner. We were all standing right at the edge of the raised platform and the two young boxers were both struck by Taña's beauty. Just as soon as this little news conference was over, here came one of Bang Bang Bogner's young handlers and said that Bang Bang wanted to invite Taña to come to his victory celebration after the fight. He wanted our phone number and name of our hotel. Oh, my! We agreed that she could go if we could also. He said, "Okay." that they would be in touch. Well, a short time later here came one of Boom Boom's handlers also inviting Taña to his victory party. Either way, we would be going to a party that night.

Later that afternoon it was announced on the radio that the fight had been cancelled as the Boxer's Commission doctor said the cut over Boom Boom's left eye was not completely healed and the fight could not take place. When we returned to our hotel there were two messages. One from each fighter that the fight had been cancelled. So that was that. Disappointing for all of us. But we had another great night on Bourbon Street.

We also got to steam up the Mississippi River on a big riverboat, the Mississippi Queen, from New Orleans to see one of the battlefields and forts from the time of the Battle of New Orleans. We were on board with about 50 or 60 others and having a ball. We met a couple from Lynchburg, Virginia by the names of Andy and Ruth Williams. Really nice folks and we were visiting with them about everything and I asked him what business he was in. Well, he said "I'm in the oil business — my company sells heating oil."

"Oh," I said, "I'm in the oil business, too. We're getting ready to start drilling another oil well in a few weeks." He got very curious, so I told him about our operation and that we had high hopes of getting a really good well as we were trying hard to get in a location that would be out of the water that we had hit on Well #1. I said, "You should let me sell you a thirty-second interest in this new well. It's only $3,250."

He said, "Okay, I'll take it. Send me the paperwork and I'll send you a check." This started a friendship that lasted several years. We even went by to visit them later on in Lynchburg, while we were on a trip back east that I will tell you about later. Andy and Ruth were real nice folks.

The World's Fair was wonderful and we spent three days until we took Taña to the airport for her plane ride to Seattle to her home with her sister, mother and stepfather. It was sad for her to leave us, but it was time for school to start. Bonnie, Betty, Nolan and I continued our trip by car northward. Betty Mize was into antiques in a big way and it seemed like we were stopping at every antique shop and yard sale in Louisiana, Arkansas, Missouri, and Kansas on the way home.

Soon it would be time to get started on oil well #2 near Starvation Peak outside of Las Vegas, so we decided to wait to try to sell the house in the early spring and if it didn't sell by then, and if we did hit a good oil well, we probably would put our house on Sagebrush Trail on the market, sell it and move into the large home ourselves (which we did).

Midas Oil Well #2

This time we selected a drilling company in Albuquerque by the name of Sanchez Brothers Drilling Co. They owned a big rig in very good shape and were capable of going to the depth we wanted easily, as they drilled continuously 24 hours a day, which was good. I always like to keep investors fully informed, so on June 25, 1984 I sent a letter to update all the investors in Well #1 and to inform them that we would be drilling Well #2 around the 1st of October, 1984 and to ask them to let me know if they wanted to participate as investors in Well #2.

We selected a site about 400 yards southwest of Well #1 and planned to spud in Well #2 around Oct. 1, 1984. We had sold 13 investors interests in Well #2, and started on time. Some of the investors in Well #1 also invested in Well #2 and we sold several interests in Well #2 to two investors from Texas, one from Oklahoma and two from Missouri.

One of these was my old Merchant Marine buddy that I sailed with on the first three trips I made on the old rust bucket tanker, The Cities

Service Oil Company ship. I hadn't seen Bill Dewald since the end of World War II. What a treat! He also sold an interest to one of his friends for me, and he and his wife, Mary, came out while we drilled the well and we all enjoyed our visit immensely.

My good friend Wes Trask from my Los Alamos days, several locals from Las Vegas, N.M. and Santa Fe also invested. Bonnie and I paid $33,366.19 of the total cost of $90,532.74, a little over one-third of the total. Well, the day-to-day drilling and testing showed very promising tests — just like Well #1 did. We never had any mishaps or accidents as the drillers did a very good job, but the end results were essentially the same as Well #1. By this time I was so tired, both physically and mentally. To be so close, according to the results of our tests, that I was heartsick for ourselves as well as for our loyal investors. I made a trip to Santa Fe to get the forms signed to plug the well and Well #2 was plugged. Now on to Well #3 with reports of actual results as they happened.

Midas Oil Well #3

It is now the dead of winter in northern New Mexico and it does get cold here as the altitude is around 6 or 7,000 feet, but it is time to start on Well #3. I am going to let you see the reports now and they will describe what is happening better than my memory serves me after all these years. The time is January 1985, and we have been at this since September 1983.

In two and a half years of lots of hard work and having spent a lot of money, we haven't yet made a dime in return. We have had lots of highs and lots of lows, but if we can hit it big, it will be worth it for a lot of people. This is what keeps driving us.

An old boy told me once about mining for gold or drilling for oil: "Just a few more feet and you will hit the mother lode or a few more feet and you'll hit a gusher: You live in hope, and die in despair." He said, "It's like the guy in the bar who sits there all evening long buying drinks for the waitress in the hopes he can wind up taking her home for the night, but about five minutes before closing time her husband comes in to take her home.

I wound up carrying about half the cost of this well myself, so I had a lot of money riding on this one. We hired a local water well driller in Las

Vegas to do the drilling. He was a good one and had a good rig. It was an Ingersol-Rand rig and in very good condition and he drilled with air. So we got started. The guy's name was Gordon Hayes. They worked 24 hours a day. Richard Cypert and I were there about 16 hours a day sitting in his pickup drinking coffee and watching the work take place. God, it was cold! Sometimes Richard would fly back to Tulsa and one of his boys would pick him up at the airport and then he would fly back to Albuquerque and I would pick him up. Then sometimes I would catch the Amtrak train in Albuquerque and Bonnie would pick me up for the week or the weekend. One of us would always be at the rig when the other one was gone.

One night we were drilling away when we drilled into uncontrollable water. We had a good fire going at the rig, so the boys could keep warm, but the water would come up as a gusher and put out the fire. Then we would put more diesel fuel on dry wood and build another fire.

I took lots of colored pictures and sent them to all investors, as each of the wells were drilled, in order that they could see what the drilling consisted of, and enclosed a day-to-day progress report. I kept them informed the best I could by phone, mail and pictures.

Midas Oil Well #4

The way Midas Well #4 turned out, it was a death blow for Midas Minerals Corporation. We had all done our very best and all the investors praised me for my efforts. They all realized that if things had turned out differently we would have all been fairly wealthy, as our little corporation would have gotten big and all the investors would have had the opportunity to buy shares in the corporation, but it did not happen.

I think Richard Cypert told it best: He said, "Andy, you can't change the formation down there, and the formation wasn't right and you can't do anything about that." His theory was that the glaciers in the northern New Mexico mountains less than a hundred miles north of our location had been there for centuries and they drain underground and even though the cuttings and sand that we drilled through and examined showed heavy fluorescence as Richard said earlier, even back on Well #1 that it looked like an Arabian oil field, we had discovered that the oil was once there, as we always got oil showings, but simply too much water had apparently washed it down country. Richard explained that the oil zone in our country runs from the northwestern section in a southeasterly direction. Explaining a little farther about this, you know big oil was found in Wyoming, then on into Colorado, then into New Mexico, then Texas and Louisiana and on into the Gulf of Mexico. Of course, southern Kansas and Oklahoma and Louisiana are all in the southeastern area of big oil.

About 200 miles from southeast of Las Vegas, N.M. is the town of Roswell, N.M. That is big oil country, as well as Artesia where a huge refinery is located, then on southeast to Lovington and Hobbs, N.M. with huge oil fields. Most of all the oil field services for this entire area are located in Roswell and Hobbs, employing many people. That is what I was trying to do in our area.

There were a lot of folks watching our efforts while we were working and we even had some knowledge that Philips Petroleum Company was drilling a very deep well north of our area in the mountains. We could not get any real information how they were doing because it was secret. Amoco Oil had a representative working around Las Vegas trying to tie up oil leases. He was a personable young fellow who would stop by our motel and also our drilling sites to see how we were doing.

All we had to do was hit one big one and we would have had a boom on our hands. This is what was driving us, but as Richard Cypert said, "Andy, the formation has got to be right." Our lease on the land ran downhill to the north to I-25 Highway running east and west. Also, the train track ran parallel to the highway so all our wells were uphill to the south, so if we had been able to establish an oil field, all the oil that we produced would simply flow downhill to our large storage tanks, then be pumped into oil tank railroad cars on the railroad spur track and could be shipped by rail about 250 miles to the refinery in Artesia. So simple. Atlantic-Richfield Oil Company, whose chairman had their world headquarters in Roswell, N.M. for many years until it was moved to Pennsylvania, still do a tremendous business in this area of New Mexico. Halliburton, Dresser Atlas, and several other oil well service companies all are headquartered in Roswell and Hobbs. Big, big business.

I just wanted you all to realize what was possible in the event we could have struck oil here. It would have dwarfed anything I had done to date.

All the other corporation members were disheartened and tapped out, so to speak. I remember what an old boy had told me one time, "You can't kick a fart out of a dead horse." I also remember my teachings about never burning your bridges. So, I called a meeting of the other four members of Midas Minerals Corporation and myself and brought along my old trusted friend and lawyer of many years, Harold Moore. I explained, if they all agreed, that I would buy 100% of the corporation with the money I had put up on these wells to cover the overruns, which amounted to around $100,000, and save harmless the other partners from any possible problems that might arise. They all agreed and Harry Moore drew up the papers and I was the sole owner of Midas Minerals Corporation. I explained to them all that they would have an opportunity to get back in if we ever did anything more around Starvation Peak. They all agreed, as they were worried how they would ever manage to pay me back the money I had paid out on their behalf. I knew I was never going to be doing any more drilling on this lease.

The owner of the land where we had drilled all four wells was Antonio Solano and his wife, Toni who had inherited this large acreage from his father and grandfather. He had two very good water wells and the other two wells had been plugged. Tony and his wife lived in Tecolote, N.M., a very small village back towards Las Vegas from their ranch. They were really nice people and we became very good friends over those four years. They had two children, a young boy, and a teenage daughter that was married a few months after we drilled the last well. We were invited to her wedding, which was graciously attended with wedding gift in hand, and Bonnie and I had a good time. We really enjoyed the Spanish wedding, dancing and food and drink.

I had paid $500 to the local title company to bring the abstract up-to-date when we started drilling so we wouldn't have any slipups. I also hired an oil field attorney from Denver, Colorado and flew him to Albuquerque and put him up in our motel for a week to go though all the records in the San Miguel County Courthouse to make sure our backside was well covered. My real estate experience taught me to make damn sure of clear titles when you are dealing with big money projects. So we did have good title on our leases, which could have been very important. I have always believed in keeping the horse before the cart, so to speak. This was expensive, but it could have been disastrous in the event we had hit it big and had a serious flaw in the land titles.

I made many friends of the investors from all over the U.S. Most of them came from the New Mexico area, but some were from Kansas, Missouri, Virginia, Florida, Texas, and Oklahoma. There were not serious hard feelings, as they all knew I had done the best job that could possibly have been done and I had kept them informed with phone calls, reports and pictures. I hope I have not bored you to death with this long story of Midas Minerals Corporation. I always believed that old saying that "nothing ventured, nothing gained" and most of my ventures turned out good, but this one did not. So, I'm not dead yet and I'm not broke yet, and this wild Irishman has operated on the theory that, "When the going gets tough, the tough get going."

Chapter Ten

Back To New Mexico And The Renovation In Four Hills

Andra

A BIG REAL ESTATE OPPORTUNITY is about to begin. The real estate salesman that worked with us when we bought the home from the fighter pilot major that was "smarter than four computers," Corbalee Slusher, was a good salesman, originally from Alabama. In our visits he said he knew George Jones, the country singer, and that he used to be a member of his band. Just thought I would throw this in. (He had the same bushy sideburns as George.)

Anyway, Corbalee came by the house we lived in on Sagebrush Trail in Albuquerque's Four Hills area and said, "Andy, I want to tell you about a deal you can make a lot of money on and it is right down your alley."

I said, "Shoot, Corbalee."

"There is a very large home on Stagecoach Lane right up the street from here in the Four Hills Subdivision. In fact, it was one of the first homes built here by the original developer for his personal home." He said it is a fabulous home and the original owner was a guy by the name of Chisel Smith. He was a wealthy old man of about 82 years of age now but he had been a highway and bridge builder for years. He had contracted the house himself and had put the best of everything in its construction. It sat on an acre and a half of land and backed up to the Four Hills Golf Course. The home was very large with two stories and 5,700 sq. ft. heated space plus a large enclosed patio for a game room plus an indoor swimming pool, all enclosed with sliding glass mall doors. The home was brick construction with a tile roof. The roof decking under the clay tile was 4 ft. x 8 ft. marine plywood, one and a quarter inch thick. This was the best built home I had ever seen.

It had a three-car garage and the driveway would hold another six cars, so you could park nine cars off the street. The home itself was located on about an acre with a half acre of nature walk, garden and shrub area — all under automatic sprinkler.

The acre where the house sat had a decorative 8 ft. high block wall with openings of 8 ft. x 8 ft. sections of wrought iron. There were three heavy wrought iron gates, one directly in front and one opening to the driveway and one going into the garden area. There was a greenhouse and a large fish pond with a filter like on a swimming pool to keep the water clean and it had a pretty waterfall with a wrought iron bridge over part of the fish pond — a real beauty.

The yard, front and back, had about a dozen large pine trees about one to two feet thick and huge rose bushes along the inside of the front yard wall. All kinds of flowering shrubs and several fruit trees. One large apple near the fish pond and greenhouse, and apricot, cherry, peach and plum trees in the back yard.

The back yard was solid block wall, eight feet high and a double wrought iron gate with a strong padlock on it. It opened directly onto the Four Hills Golf Course. Mrs. Smith had had a Japanese gardener for years and when they occupied the home it was a real showplace.

The home had five bathrooms, one right off the pool and part of the maid's quarters, one of the others even had a steam bath (a marvel). The three others served the three bedrooms, library and office. All the closets were cedar lined. This pretty well describes the home when the Smiths owned it. Well, they both grew old and it was too much house for them to keep up with so they moved in with their daughter and traded the home for a big piece of land on the west side of the I-25 right-of-way just at the north edge of Albuquerque, still in the city limits. I don't know how the guy that owned the land that he traded to Chisel Smith for the big home got it, as he was a hustler from Louisiana, but he wound up with this big house. He lived there a year or two and by the time I looked at the home it was in a hell of a shape, inside and out. They had not taken care of the landscaping, plants and shrubs and the inside of the home was in terrible shape too. To give you some idea, here's what it looked like: the kitchen countertop and flooring had burn holes in them, the carpet had had lots of drinks spilled on them and had not been cleaned up, with grease spots where they fed their dogs bones and so on. The closet carpet had shoe polish on it, and the indoor pool was half full of old green stagnant water.

The driveway was cracked all over, the sprinkler system didn't work and the three wrought iron electric gates did not work. The stove and dishwasher didn't work well and lots of the plants were dead and others overgrown.

They hadn't been able to sell the place in its condition and the bank was just about to foreclose on it. The Realtor, Corbalee Slusher, said, "Andy, they are asking $300,000 for the place and you might get it for $280,000 or $290,000." Well, I went to talk to the bank about the foreclosure and they were sick of this guy and were ready to pull the plug on him. I told them I was interested in the place and would be making him an offer to purchase. I told the banker that Bob Morris, the president of New Mexico Savings and Loan, could provide the financing.

I asked Corbalee write up an offer of $230,000. He did and the seller raised hell when he read it. But the bank said you had better take it as we are ready to foreclose, so after some wrangling with the bank he finally accepted. I went immediately to my friend, Bob Morris and told him to come with me to look at the place and he did. I said, "Bob, I know it looks in one hell of a shape, but there is nothing wrong with it except superficial stuff needing a lot of hard work." I told Bob I wanted to make a loan on the place for $300,000. I will pay the owner and bank their $230,000 and I intend to spend $70,000 on it to make it look like a beauty. "When I get through with it, it will be worth $450,000."

Bob said, "Andy, I think it will, too." So I made the offer subject to getting my new loan and the deal was made. Well, the only thing wrong was we were about to get started on Midas Minerals Well #2. I already had a few investors that had been in on Well #1, so I had to get a few more and immediately set to work to get the others that I needed.

I told Corbalee the first thing I was going to do was to get all the outside work done, so I hired a Mexican fellow that had previously done work for Corbalee. I hired him and his wife and two kids to clean and trim the yard and trees. After three solid weeks of work and 30 pickup loads to the dump, I paid them the $3,000 that I had agreed to do. They did a beautiful job.

I had the driveway resurfaced, and then hired a paint contractor from Santa Fe that had done all nineteen townhouses that we built in White Rock and made a $7,000 contract with him to repaint all the inside of the house. I cleaned up the mess in the pool myself and hired a pool maintenance guy to overhaul the pump and filters on the pool and the waterfall on the fish pond.

Then, old Bonnie Jeanne Long became the foreman on the interior work that needed to be done. Over the years, I had bought a hell of a lot of carpet from House of Carpets in Albuquerque, so I went to them and picked out some very expensive carpet, at $24 a sq. yd. to be installed after the painter finished his painting and refinishing all the doors and trim.

Bonnie hired a couple of young carpenters to take care of the kitchen counter tops and install the dishwasher and range and trim the doors, 57 of them, in order for them to clear the thick new carpet. She hired an electrician to change out the light switches to all new toggle switches at quite a cost, $600, and re-work the electric wrought iron gates so we could lock them from the inside of the house before going to bed.

The Smiths had been burglarized right after they finished building the home years before and they think it was the two guys that had installed their burglar alarm system. They think they came in at the corner windows that were over the kitchen sink. They probably fixed it when they installed the system so the alarm didn't work on that window. Anyway, a couple of masked men came in late one night while they were asleep. They wore masks and they terrorized these old folks, but they never told them where their hidden built-in safe was. So they saved most of their valuables but lost some of the other things. Later, Mrs. Smith came by the house and showed us where the safe was and gave us the combination. It was well hidden in the wall behind some book shelves in the little home office. Oh, yes, the home also had a built-in vacuum system; the motor was in the garage and someone had left it on and it had burned out so we had to replace it, too.

All in all, it took six weeks to get everything done with Bonnie's yeoman good job of engineering the scheduling of all these different workmen to get it done.

I took care of getting the large sprinkler system working. Each head had to be taken off and cleaned and replaced; very time consuming, but finally I got the job done. I hired a young fifteen-year-old boy to mow every week and this beauty was ready to sell. I had even bought a full-sized pool table for the glassed-in game room off the family room. I remembered how we had enjoyed the one in the house we had bought on River Hills Road in Austin and figured that it would help sell the place.

We had it appraised at $420,000.00 so the $300,000 loan with New Mexico Savings and Loan was well secured and my friend, Bob Morris, was well pleased when I brought him out to see the place and the appraisal. I put up my "For Sale by Owner" sign and priced it at $475,000.00. I showed it several times, but to no avail. (This was 1983, so the price today, twenty years later, would be in the $1,000,000 range, I'm sure.) When you analyze the people of Albuquerque that could afford a home of this caliber there were not too many of them in town. At close to half a million dollars, the ones that could afford a home at this price would more likely want to have a new one built themselves to their own plans. We were going to have our work cut out for us in getting it sold! It was a beauty and well worth the money, but there were not many people who could afford it then, the same as there are not too many people who could afford a million dollar house today. Of course, it was not furnished, so it didn't show as well as if it had been furnished.

Right now I'm going to go back to the ranch again with Roy and Dale and see how Bonnie is doing with the renovation on the big house on Stagecoach Road in Four Hills Subdivision in Albuquerque. We still had not found a buyer for it yet, so we decided to sell the home we were living in on Sagebrush Trail a few blocks up the street. To make a long story short, we did make this happen and set up the big home on a long-term loan and moved in. What a fabulous house! This all had taken place while I was wrapping up things with Midas Minerals Well #4 and the corporation.

Andra and Richard Riordan had gotten married and Tiffany, who was now almost four years old, and our beautiful twin granddaughters, Kathy and Taña, were graduating from high school. They were 17 years old and wanted to spend the summer with us in Albuquerque, so Bonnie and Tiffany and I drove to Seattle to attend their graduation. We had a great time and no car problems at all this time. The only thing was in going up to Seattle, every time we would go through a town that had a park, Tiffany would spot the swings and say, "Grandpa stop! I want to swing!" It wasn't just a few times, but at least a dozen or more times! The twins got all settled for the summer and Bonnie got them started in driver's education and they both learned to drive. I don't need to tell you what this means to a teenager and they were happy with the pool we had and the beautiful big home. Tim was still in college getting his master's degree and things were beginning to smooth out for old Bonnie and Andy.

Tim was living in Santa Fe now and studying and selling real estate and he had lots of friends there. Several cowboy-types and the movie industry had found Santa Fe and the actor Kenny Rogers was shooting the movie, The Gambler III.

I don't know the details of how it happened but one of Tim's cowboy friends was acting in the movie and he had met Tim's girls and he got some bit parts for them in this movie. They were ecstatic and so were we. They needed transportation to and from the movie set, so I bought a little Plymouth Champ from Richard and Andra as they were buying their first Jeep. It was good, reliable transportation for them. Grandmother Bonnie always fixed their lunch, but the movie people provided their lunch, so the girls ate grandmother's lunch on their way home for dinner. Talk about Hog Heaven! They were in it!

I'll tell you a little funny story about Tiffany. She would stay all night with us quite often and Bonnie would drive her to nursery school each morning. One day she wouldn't stay in her seat belt. We had a C.B. radio in our Lincoln Continental, so Grandma Bonnie picked up the C.B. mic and said, "Is this the police? Oh, it is. Tiffany won't stay in her seat belt. What should I do? You want me to bring her to the police station and put her in jail? Well, okay, if you think it's necessary." Boy, did this get her attention!

Tiffany said, "Call them back, grandma! Call them back! I'll stay in my seat belt!" From then on Grandmother never had any trouble with her staying in the seat belt. We had a ball with this little girl, she was so bright.

When she would stay all night with us she would sleep in the middle of our big, king-sized bed with Bonnie and me. One night we were watching a movie in our bedroom and the movie was called, Amerika. It was about a bunch of Russian tanks and when they were running over a group of peasants, I said to Tiffany, "That is not real, Tif, it's just a movie."

"Grandpa, I know, it's just pretend. I wasn't born yesterday, you know." I couldn't believe this little thing, not yet four years old. I looked at Bonnie and said, "Not yesterday, Bonnie, but I think it was the day before yesterday." And with that we all three had a good laugh.

My good friend, Wes Trask, that I have mentioned several times earlier, and I would go fishing at Cochiti Lake about 50 miles north of Albuquerque in a small boat and trailer that I had bought from Wes' son. We would catch some nice catfish and crappie and one day I caught several small catfish, about 6 inches long, and brought them home to put in the fish pond that we had in the big house. Well, Tif wanted to learn to fish, so Grandpa took a small hook and filed the barb off of it and made her a little fishing pole. She would dig fishing worms in the flower beds and she would also find snails. She had a snail farm and had named all the snails, etc. Anyway, she would catch a little catfish and each and every time she would bring it into the family room where I was watching TV, she would say, "Look, Grandpa, I caught a fish!" I would praise her. We enjoyed her so much.

One time — I remember this so well — we had a half bath off the kitchen and one day I heard her yell and opened the door and she said, "Grandpa, don't you know yet to put the toilet seat down when you leave the bathroom?" When she had gone in to use the toilet, she hadn't turned the light on and had sat down on the toilet with the seat up and she let me know about it. She made a believer out of me! From that day on until now I have never failed to put the toilet seat down when I'm finished.

When summer was over in 1985, the twins, Bonnie and I were sad to have to say goodbye and send them back up to Seattle. Bright and early one morning they left Albuquerque for Seattle in the little tan Plymouth Champ. In a few days Bonnie and I went shopping for another little car, so they could each have one to drive to school. We found one just like it, except that it was black and in very good shape, so we bought it for Taña, as Kathy claimed the tan one. It so happened that the girls step-father, Neil Morgan, had flown to Albuquerque to visit his old parents, so he drove the little black champ back to Seattle for us. They got started in college at Washington State University, each happy with their little cars.

I had told them when they were 15 years old that if they didn't drink, smoke or use dope that when they were 18 years old I would buy them each a new car. They said, "Grandpa, we are not going to do any of those things, and if you buy us a new car it will get banged up in these college parking lots. These little Champs will suit us just fine while we are in college." I was very happy with what they said, and I agreed.

Kathy said, "Gramps, when you buy mine, I want a Porsche." I told her I didn't have that in mind, but something around $8 - 9,000 for each of you. "I was only kidding, Grampa!" Anyway, the little Champs lasted them all through college.

Oh, yes, I forgot to tell you about Kathy winning a Seattle Junior Miss award when she was a senior in high school. She came in 2nd for the whole State of Washington. We were very, very proud of her.

Just in case I didn't mention it earlier the twins were not identical in any way. Taña was strong and Kathy delicate. Taña took after her

Grandmother Long and Kathy after her mother — delicate. Taña knew what she wanted to do and Kathy wanted to do everything.

After college in Seattle, Taña said, "Grandpa and Grandma, I don't want a new car, I want to go on to F.I.T., the Fashion Institute of Technology in New York City, to get my degree." She did this with a lot of sacrifice, working part-time at The Gap in New York to help pay her expenses, earning her associates degree in both women's and men's fashion.

Kathy decided she wanted to go to France to study, and she did. While she was there a young man form California that she had gone to high school with caught up with her in France and they traveled around Europe together. She didn't like the way the French people treated Americans so after a while she returned to California and it wasn't long until they got married. They had a big wedding on Whidbey Island, just off the coast near Seattle where her mother and stepfather lived. It was quite a celebration. Tim, Andra, Richard, and Tiffany drove up from Albuquerque together to attend and Tiffany served as her flower girl. Unfortunately the marriage didn't last, but "Katae" (her name in French which she adopted after returning from Paris) stayed in San Francisco and finished her degree there, working part-time at several jobs to make ends meet until she finished. She soon got a very good job with Joe Boxer, and then Levi Strauss, and she continued to live in San Francisco for many years.

About the time that Katae's marriage ended, Bonnie and I had used our time-share condo in Mazatlan several times and were beginning to tire of it. Since I had given the girls the little used Champs instead of buying them new cars, I decided to give them each $8,000 to cover the difference. Katae still had about $4,000 of it left and when I told her we had decided to sell the time-share, she said she would like to have it instead of the balance of the money she had coming. It was now worth around $10,000. So I asked her, "Katae, if I sell it to you for the $4,000 you still have coming, will you share it willingly with your sister and mother for the rest of the 99 year lease that we have on it?" She said she would, so the deal was made. Not long ago Taña and her husband decided to buy one of the other ones so they could share it with his folks as well. Katae, however, still shares hers with her mother and stepfather. It so happens that on the same date I'm writing this, November 28, 2002, they are all going down to Mazatlan for Thanksgiving, so you see that it all worked out with proper planning.

Back to our story: Bonnie and I are still living in the big house in Albuquerque and enjoying it very much. Sometimes we would have as many as three other couples from Los Alamos or Broken Arrow, Oklahoma, or somewhere else, stay a few days or just overnight. We had plenty of room to sleep them all and it didn't hurt any neighbors if we got a little loud.

It was just about time for Gerald Ohlson to come up with his other half of the down payment that I had been carrying for him on a second mortgage for five years at $3,000 per month. Remember, I had built 19 town homes in that last project and could only sell nine or ten of them because of interest rates going up to 19 and 20% during the Carter administration. Well, old clever Gerald Ohlson decided to rent the ones I hadn't sold so he could make the payments on them and now interest rates were down during the Reagan years, and he was able to sell all the ones he had been renting out. It seems to me that he had about $400,000 due me and he came down to Albuquerque and I discounted it some so he would pay it all and we made a deal. I was completely out of Los Alamos as I had sold the Bonnie Jeanne Corporation office buildings earlier to cover my losses in the Midas Minerals Oil well debacle.

So, I decided to invest in silver bullion to the tune of about $250,000.00 and rented a large safety deposit locker in the bank in downtown Albuquerque, a separate bank from the bank where we did our regular business. Silver was selling for around $6.00 per ounce and I just knew it could go to $10 or $15 per ounce. It had been as high as $30 per ounce just a few years previously when the Hunt Brothers of Dallas, Texas had tried to cover the market. Naturally, I figured it was time for old Andy to get a payback of the money he had lost in the oil business.

Well, it wasn't long until it went up to $7.00 per ounce and I bought more. Then it went to $9.00 per ounce and I bought more. I planned to wait for the $15.00 market and unload. We waited and in the meantime I investigated another oil deal I had heard about in Las Vegas, N.M. This was a five thousand acre ranch owned by an old Spanish widow and her school teacher daughter. I decided to investigate this rumor. It so happened that old 80 year old widow's name was Maria Peña and she was still running a small local bar right on the town square of old Las Vegas.

Her husband had died years earlier and she had the big ranch leased out to cattle pasture. This provided her with an income and the bar was just mostly like a hobby so that she could have something to do and stay in touch with what was going on in town. Her husband had been sheriff for many years in Las Vegas and had to be plenty tough in those days, I'm sure. Her daughter was an old maid of around 40 years old, and didn't care for men.

I went to visit Mrs. Peña and after a couple of visits we hit it off pretty well. She had heard about our oil drilling at the Starvation Peak area, and she was interested when I told her that I would like to hear more about her ranch. She said, "Mr. Long, when the R.E.A. people had dug the deep holes to set the big electric high lines across the ranch, I heard that some oil had shown up in their hole digging."

Well, this got my interest up and I said, "I would like to lease your ranch for possible drilling after I investigate further." She thought about it and I went back to see her again and she told me if I would lease it for $1,800 a year she would lease it to me. I agreed and prepared a one-year lease. The next thing I did was call Richard Cypert in Coweta, Oklahoma and I told him about this.

He said, "Andy, if you will pay for a couple of plane tickets for me and the young geologist we are using here in Oklahoma, we will fly out and spend a day looking your lease over with you." In a few days they flew out and we spent the whole day looking it over. When we were through we didn't really see any positive signs. Richard said, "Andy, it would only be a shot in the dark." I was still hurting from the previous oil venture, so I continued to lease it for a year or two more without any action. Finally, I wrote Mrs. Peña that I couldn't continue to lease her ranch for drilling. I figured if I ever changed my mind that I could probably lease it again, but I never did.

Anyway, while Richard Cypert was there that day, he told me about all the success that his sons and brother had had in Oklahoma while he was out in New Mexico with me. He said, "Andy, you should come in on some of our wells we will be drilling." I agreed to take a look. I knew they had hit some very good wells of around 300 barrels a day the last couple of months we were drilling here in New Mexico.

481

I went back to look into their deal and Bonnie and I had a good visit with Tony and Wanda Bowline and I agreed to take a twenty-five percent interest in a new lease, right next to the one they had hit four wells on, of 300 plus barrels a day. They had gotten "Nigger Rich" as they say in Oakie Land and had bought new homes, pickups and boats and were riding high. I could hardly put up my money fast enough to get in on the deal!

The first well we drilled was dry of oil — a little gas, but no oil. The second well we drilled came in at about 300 barrels a day. Boy, was I happy! My share was around $12,000 a month! I knew I was on my way — finally! Well, I quickly did a little sixth grade arithmetic and said, "Bonnie, that's $144,000 per year on one well." So, we quickly drilled the third well and got a dry hole.

The next month the Cypert boys, who were the operators of the lease I was in on, called and said, "Andy, this big well we hit has gone to two barrels a day. It has lost its gas drive, so it has practically dried up." The well we were talking about was very close to one of the Cypert's wells and I think it must have been hurting their production on their well, and they had control of the pumping, and old Andy was getting the shaft. But I didn't suspect anything at the time and they said they were ready to drill another well on the lease I was on with them. So I went in on it and I spent another $3,700.00 on a dry hole. They said they planned on drilling another well on their lease next to one of the good wells and for $27,000 I could get in on it. After long consideration Bonnie and I did pop for the $27,000. When it came in a dry hole, I began to get suspicious.

I got a lease from another landowner and decided to be the operator on this lease, about 20 acres nearby the Cypert's lease. I said, "Boys, you can get in on my lease if you want to and you can take over the service on my wells if we get some good ones." So, I put together some investors — myself with some of the ones I had in New Mexico, carrying a large amount of it myself. My old friend Wes Trask from Los Alamos and now retired in Albuquerque went in with me and we rented a small apartment in Coweta, so we could be there for longer periods of time at less expense than in motels. We drilled two dry holes right off the bat. The 3rd one was just Wes and I, and the Cyperts had some of it also, but the lease was only in my name. They were doing my service work on the well. Well, we hit a gusher and a big one! I have a picture I will show you when it came in. Wes and I were jumping for joy! This was in the early winter of 1987 and snow and mud on an oil lease was not easy work, but it looked mighty good and I thought that my gambling and perseverance had finally paid off.

Well, one day while I was back in New Mexico, I got a phone call from Richard and he said some other people were drilling in the area on another lease and had set off a powerful Nitro shot in their well and it must have been in the same zone as our well. He said my well was watering out the same as the well that these people had shot. He said, "Andy, your well is ruined. I hate to tell you this, but it is, and me and the boys will buy your lease for $4,000 if you have had enough of the oil business." This was one of the hardest blows I ever had to deal with, but I had spent so much money fooling with oil wells that I told Bonnie that maybe it is time for me to get out of the notion of trying to hit it big in the oil business.

I didn't figure the Cyperts were trying to give me a big screwing at the time, but after many days and nights trying to reflect on all this I have come to the conclusion that this is probably what had happened in Oklahoma: I had trusted Richard completely while in New Mexico, but his oldest son was the one running the company in Coweta and his two younger brothers and his uncle Leon Cypert did what he told them. I think now we got screwed a number of times. This is pretty common in the oil business, I found out later. I took my licking and never had anything more to do with the Cyperts after this. I think they got their just due, though.

While we were first involved with them, I introduced Rick and his wife and the others to Las Vegas, Nevada. I told him how Bonnie and I, and the Bowlines, liked to go to Vegas and he asked me if they could meet us there for a weekend and I agreed to do so. Well, we met them at the airport and Rick weighed at least 250 lbs. and his wife and mother were also at least 250 lbs. each. When they got in the cab with all their luggage, the cab was so loaded the cab driver was not able to get them all in because of the weight. So Rick rode in our cab to the hotel where we were all going to stay.

I took Rick to a crap table and showed him how to shoot craps, then we went to one of the Las Vegas shows and after the show they advertised that they were serving two lb. steaks in the dining room in the Stardust for just $2.95 per steak. Boy, they couldn't wait to get there! Rick, his wife and mother took the lead and Bonnie and I were right behind. Well, Rick's mother was about as wide as she was tall and walking fast — wobbling from side to side. There was some young fellow walking beside Bonnie and me, and he was looking at Mrs. Cypert wobbling and he said to me, while looking at her wobble, "Chucka, chucka, chucka."

'I said, "Hey, fella, that's my wife." Oh, boy, was he embarrassed! He took off immediately and Bonnie and I had a good laugh. We found a nice table and Rick left his baseball cap on his head the whole time we were eating.

We were all staying at the El Morocco Hotel right across the street from the Stardust Hotel and Casino, so the next morning we started walking to the Stardust and some guy stopped us to talk. He said, "I have a diamond ring and an expensive watch I have got to sell. I lost my money gambling and I'll sell them cheap." He cautiously showed them to us and old Rick was a sucker ready to be picked. The guy said, "I'll take $200 for both the ring and watch." Rick couldn't wait to pay him, he wanted them both. He had plenty of oil money and was ripe for picking. That morning the girls were all playing the slots and Momma Cypert laid her purse in between her slot machine and the one next to her. After a while she looked and her purse was gone. She reported it and what had happened was that someone on the other side of these two machines reached through and lifted her purse." She lost a couple hundred dollars and several travelers checks. They went to the Hotel and called the traveler's check company and they covered the checks and issued her new ones as replacements. They found her purse in a trash can behind the Casino and, of course, her cash was gone.

They wound up losing the cash they took with them and learned how to gamble and were hooked on it. It didn't take long for Rick to really get hooked in a big way. I had introduced him to Tony Bowline from Broken Arrow, Oklahoma the day before we went to Vegas with them and told him if he wanted to make some football bets with him that they could. So Rick did just that. Tony was a pretty big bookie by then and Rick would bet $500 to $1,000 a game and also he would bet on race horses with Tony. Even this was not enough for Rick. He even bought a string of race horses himself and was living high. I think he got his just dues as about six or seven years later we were visiting the Bowlines and it was only 10 or 12 miles from Coweta, so I drove down to Coweta and drove by the metal building that the Cyperts had their business located in, as well as their offices. It was vacant and in part of the building was a welding shop. I inquired if the man knew what had happened to the Cyperts. He said, "Yes, they went broke."

I said, "Oh, what a pity." I never checked on them again and tried to forget the good screwing they gave me and a lot of other people.

Oh, yes. I found out about the ring and watch Rick had bought from the guy in Vegas. Rick had thought they were hot when he bought them, and took them to a jeweler in Tulsa to have them appraised. The watch was a cheap one and the diamond ring was fake. So, my introduction of them to Vegas and Tony Bowline probably took care of the Cyperts. Oh, yes, I drove by Rick's house that day when I went to Coweta and the weeds had grown up around it and an old pickup was sitting in the side yard. It was vacant. He must have lost his home too. I was damn glad I had gotten out of the oil business when I did.

About this time the price of oil had dropped so much that many oil fortunes were lost all over Texas and Oklahoma, as well as other states. The Texas economy had really gotten bad. It was a damn good thing that George Koury and Roger Cox from Albuquerque, and I had our offer of six million dollars for the 12,000 acres of land near Austin and Round Rock turned down. The recession that followed would have broken us for sure. We had made the offer in 1981 and the Recession hit in about 1988.

Now back to more pleasant things:

In the fall of 1987 Bonnie and I bought a small motor home. It was called a Dodge Prospector. It was the length of a large van, about 20 feet or so, with a raised up top where you could stand up in it and it also had a double bed that extended over the cab. Just the right size for us and Tif Riordan, having a bed on the couch, to get along really nicely. It had everything in it that the big ones had: a propane furnace and refrigerator, as well as a three burner stove and sink, and a really small bathroom with a shower. A real nice little job with only 12,000 miles on it.

The day I bought it was a cold, windy day in April 1987, spitting a little snow, and dust blowing, and the Chrysler-Dodge Dealership car lot was very quiet. It was not a day with many lookers. And this was to our advantage as they really wanted to make some deals that day. They had priced this little beauty at $19,000. It originally sold for $32,000 new; and with only 12,000 miles on it, it was hardly broken in. We drove it and I liked it. So I went into the office and told them I would make them a first and last offer of $16,500. They hit the ceiling! I said, "Take this offer to your boss. I will give you a check right now for $16,500, but don't come back here with any counter offer."

The salesman said, "Do you want to buy an extended warranty on it?"

"No," I said.

He said, "We can't make any money on you from interest as you are paying cash and you won't buy an extended warranty on it, so I don't know if the boss will take your deal or not."

I said, "Then you had better get into his office and let him decide. I don't think you are going to get many offers on this thing with the weather like it is and at least you will have all the money out of it."

Well, it took a good 30 minutes before the salesman came back to us and said, "Mister, you have got a deal. I don't believe it," he said, "but he took you up on it."

It so happened that I called the guy in Grants, New Mexico who had owned it and had traded it in on a big four door Chrysler. I asked him, "How come you didn't keep this car?"

He said, "I was going to take a job on the road with Snap-on Tools and my wife and I were going to stay in it on the road, but the job didn't pan out so we traded it back in to the dealer."

I had noticed the cook stove had never been used and so on. He said they had just used it as a second car and they had never stayed overnight in it. It was a jewel! We took it on several trips to the mountains with Tif along, like trout fishing at Red River in northern New Mexico. Tif learned to trout fish and loved it.

We decided to take a long trip to a winter resort in south Texas where my brother-in-law Dwight Stanfield and his gal would spend the winters in their large motor home. Then we came back home by way of San Antonio, Texas and visited my cousin Jack Henderson there. We visited with him for a couple of days and then went on north to Austin where we had lived in 1981 and 1982. Then we went about fifty miles to Marble Falls, Texas and about eight miles west was the town of Kingsland and beautiful Lake LBJ.

This was our thinking: the big home we were living in in Albuquerque was much too large for the two of us most of the time and we had originally bought it to fix it up and resell it, so we talked it over and started looking for a lot on Lake LBJ to have a home built when we sold our house in Albuquerque.

We found a beauty! It was about a mile from the small town of Kingsland, Texas where the Colorado River and the Llano River meet and flower into Lake LBJ. A developer had bought about three or four acres which was the site of a famous fishing lodge for many years — an excellent fishing spot. He was preparing fourteen home sites and building four really nice blacktop streets. At that time, they were two blocks long and had about seven lots on each side of the street running parallel to the lakefront. This provided seven waterfront lots on one side of the street and seven off-water lots on the other side of the street. He had already built a seven stall boat dock at the end of the street for the seven off-water lot owners to dock their boats in. A really nice, well-built dock with seven stalls.

I fell in love with Lot 11, which had three large live oak trees on it in the back part of the lot. The location was about a quarter mile off the highway and about a mile to Kingsland to the west and about a mile east to Marble Falls, Texas. The developer had sold two off-water lots, on which one of them had built a home, also two water front lots, #9 and #12, next to #11, which I liked, had homes on them. The price he had on the waterfront lots will give you an idea of just how prime these lots were. They were $100,000 each. The off-water lots were $25,000 each. Well, we bought Lot 11 and paid $10,000 down and agreed to pay the $90,000 balance when we built our home on it. We stayed around there a couple of days before we bought to make sure this was what we wanted to do. We rented a boat and motor and fished one day and thought long and hard if this was where we wanted to live until we were ready for a rest home. I was then 63 and Bonnie was 62. Both of us were still active and I could fish every day if I wanted to. So we made the deal.

We didn't have any other holdings in New Mexico other than the big house we were trying to sell. We went back to Albuquerque with a burning desire to sell this big, high-powered house and got started building on our water-front lot in Kingsland, Texas. As it so happened we had only been back from our trip to Texas a couple of days when a local Realtor in Albuquerque called and asked if she could show our home to one of her prospects. Normally, I would have said, "No, I am a real estate man and am capable of selling my own house," but in this case I said, "Yes, you can and I'll pay a commission to you if you get it sold."

To make a long story short, they bought our home. They had just sold their home in Four Hills, which was only a few blocks away and they liked the location and were ready for a more expensive home. The buyers were about 35 or 40 years old. A strange couple in this way: he was Jewish and she was the daughter of a Methodist minister. They were very difficult to deal with and I'm glad I had this other Realtor to deal with them. They chiseled and chiseled and finally they came up some and I came down some and we had a deal after about a week of haggling. I was not going to come off of my price of $400,000, but finally I did, down to $365,000, then paid the Realtor $25,550.00. I wound up with $339,650. We had $300,000 in the house so we only made $39,650. However, we had lived there three years. At least we didn't lose any money on this deal.

In all my real estate land deals to date, I had never lost any money on any of them. I sure couldn't say this about my oil deals. So I told Bonnie, "From now on Andy Long is my name, and real estate is my game." And after another 20 years have passed since this deal, I still haven't lost a dime. Hooray!

We decided to store a large part of our furniture and move into a two-bedroom apartment in Albuquerque until we could get a home built at Hidden Oaks on Lake LBJ. We did just that and the only thing I had going in real estate was 11 of the 15 three-to-five acre lots in Joplin, Missouri and the lot we planned to build a house on in Texas. The apartment we rented was in a large complex called The White Winrock Apartments, right next to Winrock Shopping Center. About this time Katae drove up in her little Plymouth Champ and said, "Grandma, can I stay with you guys for a while? I want to go back to college and get my degree here at UNM." Of course, she was welcome and she was there when we would be gone a week at a time to Kingsland, Texas while the house was being built.

First we had to select a house plan and have the blue prints drawn as it would be custom built. Of course, I know how to get this done and get the cost estimated. Well, we looked at a lot of homes around the lake and decided on just how we wanted it to look.

The lot was deeper than it was wide, so we wanted the living room and breakfast room and master bedrooms at the back end of the house, overlooking the big oak trees and the lake — the sunsets were absolutely gorgeous. The house turned out to be 2,187 sq. ft. plus a large two-car garage with a large storage room near the garage. It had two full baths plus a half bath off the kitchen, garage and utility room, with a large sink and cabinet for cleaning fish nearby.

I sketched out what I wanted to have a draftsman draw, even down to the kitchen cabinets. It so happens I found a real good draftsman — very experienced. I looked at several homes he had drawn plans for that others had built, and I got him started on ours. I told him to take his time as we were going to go on a vacation in our little van motor home and would be gone about six weeks. I said to him, "Can you have me a complete set of preliminary drawings in three or four weeks?" He said he could. "I'll be in a town somewhere in Massachusetts about the middle of October." It was then around the middle of September. Katae had started school in Albuquerque in September, so he and I selected a small town in Massachusetts and I told him, "When you finish the preliminaries, mail them to me at this town's General Delivery. I will make any changes I want in red pencil and then you can draw the finished plans."

He said, "That will work, Mr. Long. I will get them to you in Massachusetts on October 15th." This worked like a charm. We told Katae we would see her around late November, and said our goodbyes.

Our first stop was Galena, Kansas to visit Bonnie's older brother, Bob Scott, and his wife Inas. Bob was my property manager on the Joplin property and we had a good visit and I told him I had some plans now on how to sell the remaining eleven lots. I made arrangements for him to hire a guy with a tractor and brush hog to mow the whole thing and make it look like a golf course and to make eleven signs of 3/4" plywood, 18" by 24," paint them white and number them with the respective lot numbers and draw an outline of each lot with the acreage amount on the sign. Each sign was to be nailed to a 2" by 4" stake as soon as the surveyor finished staking the corners of each lot and the lots were mowed. I told Bob I planned to have a road contractor come in and re-grade the three streets, which were just gravel, and then blacktop them. I said, "Bob, I'm going to have all eleven of these lots sold by spring."

I stopped by the county road office and signed a contract for $13,000 and left in a hurry when I found out from him that the Cubs were going to play three games with the St. Louis Cardinals starting that evening and on Saturday and Sunday. They were both my favorite baseball teams and I said, "Bonnie, what a way to start our vacation!" It was already 3:30 pm., so I found out just how fast our little van would run. I hit 80 mph several times on the turnpike. I had a CB radio, so I could know where the Smokies were and we made it just as the second inning was starting at the Ball Park in St. Louis. The Cubs won the first game, but lost the next two. We had time to spend between games to look over St. Louis and take a two hour boat ride on the Mississippi River, among other things, including going to the Budweiser Brewery, which we enjoyed.

We stayed at a small RV Park right in town not far from the Stadium. When the Sunday afternoon game was over we hightailed it on east to Anderson, Indiana where our old friend, Grace Riley, lived across the highway from Bonnie and I when our son was born in 1946. She and her husband were great friends to us then and it continued on for many years. They were about twenty years older than us and we visited them two other times and they visited us in Wichita in 1951 when Andra was born. Alva had died of a heart attack years earlier, but Grace and us stayed in touch over the years. Bonnie had sent Grace a round trip ticket to fly out to visit when we were living in the big house in Albuquerque. Grace said, "Andy, you have come a long way since you started your sales career in Anderson selling tea and coffee with the Great American Tea Company! She just couldn't believe that big house! We took her out to several fancy restaurants. She had never been to these kind of places. We loved the old girl and really enjoyed her visit to Albuquerque. Well, when we got there she was living in a little one-bedroom apartment in an assisted living complex. She had a sliding glass door with a patio and a little flower garden space and she said her flower garden won 1st place — she was proud of that. We slept in her bedroom and she slept on her living room couch. It was beginning to get cold weather, so Bonnie took her shopping and bought her a coat and a ceiling fan. She said the maintenance man would hang it for her. She was so glad to see us, we stayed that next day and night, then left early to go to Cleveland, Ohio which is right at the tip end of Lake Erie.

Bonnie's niece, Bonita Kay Ortiz, her husband Charley and their family lived there. He was a store manager for a Walgreen's Drug Company and had been transferred there from Las Vegas, Nevada where they met and married. She fixed a great meal and we spent a delightful evening and night and left the next morning. We drove along the shore of Lake Erie all day and stayed all night on the Lake Shore in our little van, snug as a bug in a rug.

It was nearing the end of September and we continued on northeast, and by nightfall we arrived in Niagara Falls. It was the 26th day of September and our wedding anniversary was the next day. So we spent our anniversary in Niagara Falls. We could drive right up to the river and the falls and it was so spectacular, you can't believe how big and how high. They were offering walking tours and furnishing raincoats and hats to keep you dry and you could walk really close to the falling water. This took about an hour, then back to our van and we drove across the river to the Canadian side and the view of the falls was even more spectacular. We felt really lucky to spend our anniversary in Niagara Falls as this was quite the thing to do.

We had bought three map books of three sections of the country: the east, the central and the western states. These maps show all the historic places and it also shows all of the national park camp sites. So whenever we could, we would spend the night in one of these as we traveled from state to state. The campsite rental price was very low, anywhere from $6 to $10 per night. They would have a place to plug into electric and they had water, toilets and showers so it was very pleasant and the surroundings were beautiful. Deep forests and lake shores, etc.

We then traveled on northeast to the states of Connecticut and Maine. We went through Portland, Maine, the town and sea port where I signed on my first trip on the old Cities-Service Oil Company tanker. We drove by the dock and it brought back some long-ago memories. We had a wonderful seafood lunch at a nice seaside restaurant, one of the highlights of our trip. Then we went on up to Bangor, Maine. This is about as far north as you can get and still be in the U.S.A. By this time we had been through the states of Missouri, Illinois, Indiana, Ohio, Vermont, Connecticut, New Hampshire, Maryland, and Massachusetts. It is now October and fall comes early in these states in the northeast, so the scenery was fabulous. Lots of big timber country, and the leaves were all turning. I burned up the camera, so to speak! I think the thing I liked most were the quaint old towns with their buildings and beautiful farms. Lots of cattle but very little beef cattle — most of these were beautiful milk cows and the largest barns I had ever seen, and so were most of the homes. Most were two story homes with an enclosed walkway that attached the barn to the house. The winters are so long and cold with lots of snow, so the barns had to hold all of the hay and feed for the cattle and horses. They were all very well kept and very pretty. I did not see any ugly farms at all. The towns were quaint, as I said, with lots of shops, and offered a variety of different crafts, jugs of maple syrup and honey — so very good!

Then, the next place we visited was Boston, Massachusetts. We drove all around the city and this also held fond memories as this is the town that I was sent to while waiting for the ship I had been assigned when I finished boot camp at Sheep's Head Bay, Brooklyn, N.Y. At that time I stayed in a huge house with about nineteen other men for about two weeks while we all waited to board that first ship. We would get to have dances and some of the local girls would come to this big house where we were, to entertain the troops, so to speak. We enjoyed the dancing and meeting the young ladies. After all, girls were pretty important to us eighteen and nineteen year old guys. I think they called these girls "U.S.O. girls" if my memory serves me correctly. I remember writing my folks about a beautiful redheaded girl and told my dad I don't think they make them like this in Oklahoma, at least I hadn't seen any like her.

While Bonnie and I were driving around Boston, we spotted a store that sold all kinds of costumes, masks and scary toys, etc., so we stopped in as I was looking to buy another one of those plastic piles of dog poop. I was lucky — I found a dandy! There was no way you could tell it from the real thing. A little later on you will see the fun I had with it.

Next we drove on to Plymouth, Massachusetts where Plymouth Rock is and the place where the first pilgrims landed when they came to America and established a fort and settlement. Plymouth is not far from Boston. Bonnie's nephew, Tom Johnson, her sister Dorothy's boy, was living there with his girlfriend and her son. Tom had recently retired from the Army after putting in his twenty years and he was a big guy — 6 feet tall and around 225 lbs. Very personable and responsible — a leader-type. He had recently been hired as one of the top security people at a nuclear power plant located near Plymouth. A short time later he got a job for his younger brother, Ron, there also. (Ron is the one we visited in Heidelberg,

Germany.) Ron was also recently discharged after twenty years, both brothers having served in Viet Nam, as well as Germany. They were only a year apart in age. Anyway, Ron rented a nice room in the basement of the home that Tom and Beverly had rented. There were magnificent pine trees in the large yard, and their lot backed up to a beautiful lake. A real picture. Anyway, they knew we were going to be there while on our trip, so they were expecting us. We were there a couple or three days and had a really nice visit. We took them out to dinner that first night and Beverly had bought a large goose and planned on serving it for dinner the next evening. Well, low and behold, that morning Bonnie's other sister, Betty, the aunt of the boys, and her husband, Nolan Mize came in from Wichita. They surprised all of us when they showed up unexpectedly.

We, of course, stayed all night in our little van and they stayed in Tom and Bev's guest room. We were having a wonderful time as we were very close to the boys and Betty and Nolan. Beverly was an excellent housekeeper and she had it looking great. We were all having fun as it was Sunday. Tom said, "Let's all go out in the back yard and look at the lake." They had two dogs. One came in and out of the house and the other one they had chained up. He was a big German Shepherd and he hadn't decided whether he liked us strangers yet. Well, I was the last one out of the house as we were going into the back yard. So old Uncle Andy thought this is the time to have some fun. We had never met Beverly before and she was trying so hard to please us all. Anyway, the living room was at the back of the house. Then out through the door to the back yard and about 100 feet farther to the lake shore. About six feet inside the back door I carefully placed the plastic dog crap on the carpet in front of the couch.

Well, in 15 or 20 minutes, Beverly said, "I had better check on the goose I have in the oven." So she started back to the house with the rest of us slowly following and visiting. About this time Beverly opened the glass door and said, "Oh, Tom, come here quick and see what that damn dog has done on the carpet! Tom, here they come! Help me get this up before they see it! Oh, Tom!"

Shock had set in sufficiently, so I said, "Here let me pick it up." So, I did and tossed it over to Tom and all of us realized it was not real and was only plastic.

Beverly said, "Oh, Andy Long! You've got one coming from me! You better watch out!" We all had a great laugh, and Beverly joined in too. The goose dinner was delicious and we had a wonderful visit until late Sunday night.

The next morning they both had to go to work, so the Longs and the Mizes decided to visit the very authentic fort and settlement at Plymouth Rock. It was like a theme park. The people all dressed like they did in 1620 as pilgrims and when you talked to them they answered as they talked back in the 17th century. The little log cabin homes were furnished just as they were back then and so on. One lady was sitting in a homemade chair just outside her front door sewing something and Bonnie asked her what she was sewing. She answered in her 17th century language and said, "I'm making my baby Jonathon some pissin' cloths." So a good laugh followed from Bonnie and me. Workers were busy with a big two-man saw, sawing lengthwise on a long log, making long slabs of wood for slab siding on a cabin they were building. They were shoeing horses and rendering lard and making lye soap with a wood fire and a big iron pot. I remember that, when I was only five or six years old, I watched my Grandmother Henderson make lye soap this same way on the farm back around 1930. How far we have come folks in one long lifetime, huh?

We really enjoyed this morning at the fort. We toured the whole thing and that afternoon we left in both vehicles and a day or so later the Mizes had to leave and get back to work — and Bonnie and I continued on our long vacation. Much more to come…

We were having such a wonderful time. Both of us were feeling great and realizing we were taking the trip of a lifetime. The map book listed all the important places and sights, and Bonnie was really on the ball as our navigator, spotting all of the campsites and historical places to visit on the maps and so on. We journeyed on down the northeastern coastline, visited Martha's Vineyard and tried to stay as close to the coast line as possible in order to enjoy the ocean coastal view. We visited Mystic and saw all the old ships dating back to the whaling days and the ships they used in the maritime business, etc. Very, very interesting.

We crossed New York City at night to avoid most of the heavy traffic as both of us had been to New York City, especially me as it had been my home port during the war years. We got into Atlantic City, New Jersey and did a little gambling in Donald Trump's casinos and walked the boardwalk, etc., sightseeing and we spent the night snuggly in our little RV in one of the safe parking lots. The next day we toured the Annapolis Naval Officers Training Facilities — very beautiful old city. Enjoyed it very much. Then on to Pennsylvania; mostly Philadelphia. We saw the building where our brilliant forefathers wrote and signed the Declaration of Independence, saw the Liberty Bell, crack and all, and several other very interesting sights.

The next stop was Washington, D.C. We visited the Capital Building and the Smithsonian Institution and then took an open view tour bus with various stops of interest such as the Washington Monument and Lincoln Memorial. Lots of beautiful parks with large trees and lots of flowers. Such a very beautiful part of this famous city.

We then went on down the east coast to Virginia and visited the War Museum and the port city of Newport-News, Virginia where my dad boarded the troop transport ship that took the soldiers to France in World War I. Dad had told me about this many times so I was glad to get to visit the city and museum. Then we motored on to Lynchburg, Virginia and visited our friends that we had met on the Mississippi Queen Steamboat, while at the World's Fair in New Orleans. Remember, they invested in my oil well ventures and had told us if we ever got out their way to stop in for a visit. So we surprised Andy and Ruth Williams and stayed a couple of days with them. It was on a weekend so we had time to go to the fabulously beautiful Blue Ridge Mountains, especially beautiful in the fall when the colors turned. They took us to a Floreshine Shoe factory outlet there and Bonnie and I bought some very good shoes.

I must take time to tell you a joke that Andy Williams told me. He said, "An evangelist preacher came to town to hold a big meeting at a local church. Well, he was a very avid golfer, so he decided he had enough time to get in nine holes of golf before he was to start his meeting at the church that evening. He started out and was doing so well that after a while he thought to himself, "If I can continue playing this well, I will break my all-time record." So, he got very serious about it. There were also a couple of lady golfers playing ahead of him rather slowly, so they told him to play on ahead of them, and he did. Well, when he got to the last hole he checked his score and found out that if he made this last putt he would beat his all-time record. So he gripped his putter and was so very careful that he decided the big diamond ring he was wearing was bothering his grip on the putter. He so wanted to make this last shot that he decided to take the ring off and lay it down so he could make this important putt. Well, he did make the putt and was so elated that he had broken his all-time previous record! He looked at his watch and thought, "If I'm going to make my church meeting, I had better get a move on." So he hurried in to take a quick shower and was washing his hands and realized his ring was still on the ground close to the last hole he had shot. He grabbed a towel and put it around himself and started out to get his ring. Well, he looked out and here were the ladies now at the last hole. He thought quickly that they might be at the church meeting tonight and he did not want them to recognize him, so he took the towel from his waist and wrapped it around his head so they couldn't recognize him later. He left a little peep hole and ran out and picked up his ring and ran back into the shower room to get dressed. Well, these two gals looked at each other and one said, "Did you see that?" The other said, "Yes, I did and he is sure not my husband." The first one said, "He's sure not mine either. In fact, I don't think he's even a member of the club!" Well, I think this is one of my all-time favorite jokes that I have ever heard and I remember Andy Williams at Lynchburg, Virginia told it to me in the fall of 1987.

By this time we had been on the road, without mishap one, and were grateful for this and were anxious to think about getting started on our new home to be built on the lot we had bought in Kingsland, Texas on Lake LBJ. We headed home and the plans were almost finished so we started looking for just the right contractor to build it. The draftsman that drew our house plans recommended one so we got with him and toured four or five homes that he had built for others. We were well pleased with his work, so we started negotiations with him and arrived at a price that would cover all the material and labor to build it exactly according to the plans and specifications. I had done so many homes before for others, as well as for ourselves, that I was a hell of a stickler to get everything, and every little detail, on the plans and specs. When we got the final plans and six copies of each page and specs, the contractor, Don Lawrence, and I sat down to go over them very carefully so there would not be any surprises later on for either of us. Finally we got every little detail accounted for and we each signed and dated each page of the plans and specs. I just didn't want any problems to come up later.

This was thoroughly discussed with the contractor and we arrived at a total price of $110,000, not including the lot. It did, however, include the plans and cost of the covered boat dock and storage space for it. I asked Don how long it would take to build and he said, "90 days."

I said, "Very good! This is what I figured it should take." I then said, "Don, I am now living in an apartment in Albuquerque, New Mexico and my lease is up in 120 days. I cannot afford to sign another lease if you don't have the house finished. So, I am going to give you 120 days to finish this house for us which is an extra month just in case you need it. Is that satisfactory with you?"

He said, "Oh, yes, that's fine."

I said, "Well, I have prepared a clause in the contract that so states that if you are not finished where we can move in, in 120 days from the start, you will be charged $100 a day for every day you are late." I had been through this sort of thing before and I knew how talk was cheap. So you should have seen him crawfish!

He said, "Oh, Mr. Long, I have seen it rain for two weeks straight in this country. I don't know."

"Well, you should know," I said, "You said you could build it in 90 days, so this is another 30 days before any penalty begins."

"Oh, I don't know," he said again.

"Well," I said, "I'll tell you what. You keep a calendar and mark off any days that it rains while you are working on the house when you can't work and we can add them to the 120 days. You see, Don, I don't want to worry about you working on other people's homes when you should be working on mine according to our contract. I just intend to keep you honest," I explained. "Another thing you will see in the contract is that I will require lien wavers from all your subs and material suppliers before we close the final deal at the bank. Also, Don, the vice president at the Kingsland National Bank will make the inspections on the home when you are at the required stage of construction, that way it will not hold you up on getting your draw when you should get it."

Well, this satisfied him and we got started on leap year the 29th day of February, 1988 and should be ready to move in by July 1st, 1988. Well, things went well and since we didn't have much else going on, we would drive from Albuquerque to Kingsland, Texas, about 650 miles, every two weeks and stay in a little motel in Kingsland for a few days, then drive back to Albuquerque — another 650 miles, then in two weeks do it again. Due to good planning everything was working well. Bonnie even worked on a handmade bedspread/quilt while in the motel and we also had plenty of time to sightsee all around the beautiful countryside and see the other lakes in the chain of the great Colorado River running through Texas. I had spent so much time getting every little detail just right and included in the plans and specs, these visits every couple of weeks really paid off.

One day Don Lawrence, the contractor, said, "Mr. Long, I'm going to have to charge you extra for all these big floor to ceiling mirrors in the entryway and for the big solid core door going into the garage from the house. I forgot to add these things into the price I quoted you." Well, I knew they were clearly drawn in on the plans and also in the specs. This old Texas boy had a lesson he was about to learn. Contractors try this sort of thing with a lot of buyers. This was why I was so particular to have it included, as I did, and the final plans were signed and dated, as we did.

I said, "Don, did you finish high school?:

He said, "Yes, why?"

I said, "Do you read well."

He said, "Yes, why?"

I said, "Is English your natural language?"

He said, "Of course, why all this Mr. Long?"

I said, "Let's look at your plans and specs and I'll show you why all these questions. Here it is very clearly indicated on the drawings and also included in the specs. I don't owe you a damn thing and I don't appreciate you trying to pull this crap. There are not going to be any extra charges for anything as I am not going to add any extras and that is that."

Well, Bonnie and I came down about three days before the deadline at the end of June and Don had finished the house except hanging three light fixtures in the kitchen and breakfast area and this damn cornpone S.O.B. waited until the last day of the 120 days to hang these three fixtures — just in childish indignation. Anyway, we cooled our heels for three more days and met at the bank and closed the deal. Don was an hour late as he was out getting his last lien waiver signed from the bathroom tile sub-contractor. He then said, "You know, getting these lien waivers signed is a good idea."

I said, "Yes, it is Don. It saves a lot of trouble for us all. You know how important it is to lay your foundation properly when you are starting a house. If it is not square it will cause you problems all the way throughout the job."

He said, "You are right about that."

"The same thing is true about getting all these lien waivers signed and it is just as important to me as a square foundation is to you." Well, we signed off and left for Albuquerque.

We loaded our furniture with the help of Tim and his friend Victor. They drove the two U-Haul semi-trucks loaded from our apartment and the storage where we had the balance of our belongings. We left Albuquerque on July 2nd and went to Lubbock, Texas, about 325 miles, which was half-way, and spent the night. We drove into Kingsland, the next day, July 3rd.

I had made arrangements with the draftsman to line up his son and two of his buddies, big high school age boys, to help Tim, Victor, Bonnie and I unload the trucks on July 4, 1988. We got everything unloaded and turned in the trucks at Marble Falls, about ten miles east of Kingsland. Since our little granddaughter, Tiffany, now about six years old, had come down with us to spend a couple of weeks vacation, we all went to the carnival held in Kingsland over the 4th of July each year.

I remember this distinctly as Tif got bit by a wasp on one of the rides, but she didn't cry much. She was a tough little kid, and said, "Gramps, you shouldn't have killed that wasp. I was the one who sat on it."

I said, "Tif, I had to. It bit my favorite little granddaughter."

The next afternoon Tiffany and Victor were fishing off the boat dock and she caught a 14" bass. Oh, she was so happy! It was the largest fish she had caught to date. She came running up the walk with it and said to Bonnie and me, "Dinner is on me tonight, Gram!" And we all three had a good laugh and a fish dinner. Later that evening we took Tim and Victor to the Austin airport to fly back to Albuquerque where my daughter, Andra, met them and our mission was accomplished.

The draftsman who designed and drew the plans for our home on the lake did a super good job. I have been trying to remember his name since I started telling you about our home and for the life of me, I could not remember it. Today, all of a sudden, it came to me. His name was Cyrus Darnell. He was a really great guy.

Before I change the subject to other matters, I want to give you some good advice, that will be very important to you all of your life: Whenever you are investing a large sum of money on a very important business deal involving important dates, ALWAYS get it in writing. A very good example of this is what could have happened in dealing with the contractor who built this home on the lake. If I hadn't made sure that the expensive mirrors in the entry way of the house had not been detailed on both the plans and specs, I could have been stuck with another $1,000 or more. Also, not getting a firm completion date on the finish of the home could have caused us a lot of trouble and inconvenience. All you have to do to avoid these sorts of things is to put it in writing in your agreement and all parties sign and date it. It is very easy for someone to say, "Oh, I forgot about that."

So, my motto is this: "If you have an agreement in writing you have a prayer. If you don't, you have nothing but air." Remember this, please. They may say, "Don't you trust me?" and the answer to this is: "Sure I trust you, but either of us might forget what we agreed on and if it is in writing, this will tell us exactly what we have agreed to do." This practice has saved me numerous problems in the many, many deals I have been involved in during my lifetime.

I think it evolved in my aforementioned experiences that I have already told you about which I have practiced over the years, planning your work, then working your plan. I have never been a loose cannon, as it just doesn't work successfully over a long period of time. End of lecture!

We had a wonderful summer that year of 1988. I bought another deck boat just like the one I used to have when we lived on Lake Austin in 1981 and 1982. It was almost identical except this one had an inboard motor rather than an outboard motor. It also had a top speed of 40 miles per hour. Just across the lake, about a quarter of a mile, a large creek ran into the lake. This was my favorite place to fish. It took me only five minutes to get there and start fishing. I loved it!

Now, I will tell you two good fishing stories. One of them was in 1959 in Oklahoma when I caught a 36" catfish. It was one of the largest fish I had ever caught. We had three other neighborhood couples coming over for a big fish dinner -- really good food and quite a party. We had put the large catfish in the bathtub to keep it alive while we were cleaning the other fish. Bonnie went in to bathe and let out a loud scream when she saw this gigantic fish in her tub. Needless to say, she was not pleased – to put it mildly.

The other story was around 1990 about my old friend Steve Stoddard. He was a ceramic engineer at the Los Alamos Laboratory and had worked on the shuttle heat tile design; and was also a judge for Los Alamos County. He had only recently been elected to the New Mexico State Senate. He and his wife, Joann, came to visit us. We really enjoyed them and showing them the surrounding countryside, the state capital building and LBJ Presidential Library in Austin. We did a lot of boating and fishing. Well, Steve caught a very large fish on his rod and reel one day. It was a big buffalo fish, about three feet long and had to weight 18-20 pounds. Talk about happy! He and I were in my boat across from my dock and it was quite a thrill for us both. Whenever he writes or calls he still mentions catching this big fish.

We had a lot of friends and relatives visit that first year. I roped off an area at one side of the boat dock about forty feet square for a swimming hole, then spread a large dump truck full of sand on the bottom and we had a great place to swim inside the roped area. I taught Tif to swim that year and she became a pretty good fisherman, too. When the summer was over we put a tag on her and she flew back to Albuquerque to start school again. It was safe as she didn't have to change planes. It did stop at Lubbock, Texas but she did not have to get out of her seat on the plane. We did this several times each year. The stewardesses took very good care of her.

One time she had caught three baby frogs and had them in a small basket with wet grass in a plastic sack. Well, she asked the stewardess if she could guess what she had in the sack. The stewardess could not guess and Tif said, "Three frogs."

The stewardess then said, kidding of course, "I wish you hadn't told me, Tiffany." Tif got a kick out of telling about this. We really had a ball for the next ten years watching her grow up on her visits each summer. When she was sixteen we presented her with a little Ford Escort station wagon and Grandma Bonnie taught her to drive.

We did the same thing for Taña and Katae, and Tif signed the same agreement the twins did, that she wouldn't drink, smoke or use drugs until she was at least 18 years old. I asked her, "Can you do this, Tiffany?"

She replied, "Where do I sign, Gramps?" What a joy she was for us and still is.

She started coming down for the summer when she was about seven years old. Andra would put a note on her, put her on Southwest Airlines and she stayed on the same plane with only one stop in Lubbock, Texas and we would meet her at the airport in Austin. Then we would do the same thing when she returned to Albuquerque.

I not only did a lot of fishing while we lived in our nice big new home on the lake, but I had plenty of time to think about selling the last eleven big 3-5 acres lots on the Joplin property. I now had the three streets paved and the lots all mowed by a guy with a brush hog and it looked like a golf course. I couldn't get any of the Joplin Realtors to do anything for me, they just didn't know how to sell land, so I came up with an idea to do it myself.

I had a surveyor stake off each lot's boundaries, and had my brother in law, Bob Scott, put in the signs we talked about earlier on each lot. Also I had him make a large 4' x 8' sign at Malang Rd. and 21st St. The sign read: Spring Valley Estates, Lots For Sale, Phone Owner Collect, with our phone number in Kingsland, Texas. Picture this. The property looked like a golf course, but with large trees scattered over it. Not thick, but just right. It also had a nice running stream through it, a real picture. Well, I had a lot of prints made of the plat that showed all the lots and each gave the size in acreage and dimensions and the price of each one. I then sat back and waited for the phone to ring and it did.

This really worked. I had plenty of time and was getting a little bored, so when the prospects would call I took lots of time and didn't worry about the collect calls as it was much cheaper than paying a Joplin Realtor's commission. I would mail the prospect a plot with the prices and terms and tell them to go out and take a look, and that no one would bother them. Well, to make a long story short, I sold them all in about a year. One builder bought two lots, moving into the first house he built, then built another one and sold it. I offered the best of terms. Only 10% down and 10% interest and I carried the mortgage myself. I had arrangements with the title company that I used when I bought the land so they prepared all the papers after I wrote the contracts with the people. They would take their signed contract with the down payment into the title company and talk to Cindy Campbell, a young lady lawyer that worked for the Joplin

Land Title Company. She was very good and it all worked like a charm. So old Andy Long once again got a good idea and made it work and had a very nice monthly income of a couple of thousand dollars for several years. It wasn't long before the whole fifty acres was filled with beautiful large homes on big estate lots. One of the prettiest subdivisions in Joplin.

I was completely convinced that real estate was my game and I never got involved in any other businesses or investments of any kind again. I just planned my work and worked my plan. Just like my dear old friend and boss told me when I started out in the Lifetime Stainless Steel Cookware business back in 1947.

During this same time Texas was in one hell of a slump because oil prices had dropped and Texans were suffering financially. The developer of Hidden Oaks in Kingsland, Texas had gone belly-up and the bank had repossessed the remaining six lots in the Hidden Oaks subdivision. The bank contacted Richard Sharp and me. Richard had his house built when we built ours and we were the second and third homes in the area. One other home had been built just before ours. Richard bought two lots and I bought three lots: one water front lot and two off-water lots. The bank carried the notes on these lots for us, so we popped for them. I paid $10,000 each for the off-water lots and $20,000 for the one waterfront lot, $40,000 in all. It was time for us to form a home owner's association in order for us to purchase liability insurance to cover us as the street was private and the Lower Colorado River Authority (L.C.R.A.) required us to have liability insurance to protect them and us against any accidents that might happen with the seven-stall boat dock that was built for the off-water lot owners.

Since I was the only guy that knew anything at all about home owners' associations, it was up to me to get it done. I had Richard Sharp go with me to a real estate lawyer's office in Marble Falls. He and his wife also owned a title insurance company. I made a contract with the wife who ran the title business, which was a good connection and we used them several times later on. We got the association formed and an insurance policy written to satisfy the L.C.R.A. requirement and we let the old blow-hard guy from Lubbock, Texas be the president of Hidden Oaks Home Owners Association. He ate it up. It wasn't long until I ran an ad in the San Antonio paper and sold my two off-water lots — one for cash for $15,000, making

$5,000 profit, and the other for $16,000 with my 10% down, 10% interest, 10 year term plan. So I made $11,000 profit and still have the water front lot. I paid off the bank with the $15,000 cash sale and the money I had invested in the silver bullion that was still in the Albuquerque bank vault. Silver had gone down, down, down, so it was time to sell what was left and pay off the water front lot and the off-water lot I had sold on time payments, which provided us a little more monthly income.

I always joked about my 10-10-10 payment plan. I would always say I liked to keep it simple so if I made a deal while I was drinking I could always remember the deal I made. 10% down payment, 10% interest and a 10 year term. I later sold the $20,000 dollar water front lot for $35,000 to an old boy and his wife from Nebraska who built a very nice home on it. Their names were George and Ruth Russell. This didn't happen overnight, but it turned out quite profitable for me simply using my real estate experience along with an abundance of grit and guts and professional salesmanship.

During this time, the banks all over this part of Texas had made a lot of bad real estate home loans and a huge (Resolution Trust Corp.) auction was formed in Austin, Texas and there were several homes in the Marble Falls area that were to be auctioned off. We got the list and found one house that really tweeked our interest. It was made of a sandstone exterior with cedar trim, which does not ever rot. It had a good 30-year timberline composition roof and a concrete front porch that was covered by the house roof about six feet deep. It had a back porch like a covered patio that was covered by the house roof also. It was about 12 x 16 feet wide and long. The square footage of heated area was 2,180 with three bedrooms, a family room/dining room combination off the nice kitchen and a large living room about 18' x 25', two full bathrooms and a very nice large pantry and utility room about 10' x 14.' The house was locked up and it was Sunday and the auction in Austin started Monday morning. There was no way to get inside to inspect it. The above description with measurements were made later. To sum it up, the house was very well constructed and plenty large enough for us, and then some. It had a 12' x 14' wellhouse and storage and also a 30'x 30' free standing garage. All of this on an acre and a quarter. Best of all there was a clear running creek the entire length of the property and the most beautiful majestic Live Oak tree in the back yard between the house and creek. The house appeared to be eight to ten years old and rock solid. I could immediately see lots of possibilities here. By the way, it was located about seven miles north and west of Marble Falls, Texas in a rural subdivision of around thirty or forty lots of three to five acres each plus several more vacant lots in the subdivision. It had a good gravel road. I found out later that the house had been repossessed by the bank. We couldn't get inside, but we saw that with some hard work and lots of imagination, there were possibilities. The home had been vacant through the winter so there was some worry on our part about whether the under-slab plumbing could have been frozen.

The homes listed in the auction book said "all property is offered in 'As Is' condition without warranty." Well, this gave us some concern but when we looked at the minimum bid that would be accepted, it was only $45,000.00. So I said to Bonnie, "We can at least double our money on this house. Let's bid on it." At 9:00 a.m. the next morning, Monday, we showed up at the Marriott Hotel in Austin. About 200 people were there and the bidding got started. About 30 minutes later the house in Timber Ridge, near Marble Falls, came up. They opened the bidding at $45,000.00. I bid $46,000.00 and no one else bid on it. "Going once, going twice, going three times, sold." the auctioneer said.

We worried, somewhat, whether we had too much guts and not enough brains. I thought, "Did someone else know more about this house than we did?" After all we were not able to get in and look it over before buying it. The Marble Falls bank was offering financing for these homes in our area so I went to the bank to get a key to go inside the house. I met a nice lady that was a loan officer at the bank and we drove out to look the house over inside and out. When I saw the inside I was very relieved! It seemed to be in pretty good shape except that it needed cleaning and painting. I found out that the home was only nine years old and solid as a rock. While the lady from the bank and I were in the yard, a neighbor stopped by and introduced himself to us as retired Air Force Colonel Jack Abercrombie. I asked him about the house and he told me all about it. He was building his home across the creek when the original owner was building this house.

He said, "The guy marched to a different drummer." He told me he was a diesel mechanic, a big guy and his wife even bigger. At least 300 lbs. each. The guy built the house mostly by himself and was a stickler for accuracy and his choice of materials. He turned down half of the lumber the lumberyard brought out on the first load. Then turned down at least one-third of the replacement load. I don't know the details of the family problems, but nine years later the bank repossessed this home.

Jack told us that the well on our property was one of the best wells in the subdivision. It came in at 100 gallons an hour and really good water. I saw the old man later that witched the well and he told me that he found three strong veins of underground water while witching and they drilled where the three veins crossed each other. That is what accounted for such a good well. I had the state test a sample of the water later and it was as pure as could be. We lucked out again!

It worked out great for us. My gambling blood paid off very well this time. We closed the loan and the payment was only $450 per month. Our house payment on the lake was $1,500 per month. Of course, it was for a $210,000 home and waterfront lot. The heated area of the houses were only one square foot apart --- isn't that ironic?

I soon got hold of an old boy that was a one-man construction crew and he could do everything. He worked for $10 an hour. His name was Junior Thurman. He and I went out to this house and made a list of all the things that I wanted to do to the house and of all the materials that would be needed. Then we went to work. About three or four weeks later we had a really good looking place. New paint, inside and out, and we added white shutters and flower boxes to all the windows on the house. It troubled me that the lot size was only 1 1/4 acre and all the other lots in the subdivision were three to five acres, and while investigating this I found that the bank had made a deal with the subdivision developer for him to buy back the property on both sides of the house and reduce their loss. They had sold him an acre and three-quarters on one side and a full acre on the other. I went to the developer who still had several more lots for sale and offered him $5,500 for the two and three-quarter acres and he took it. That gave us a full four acres on the creek, about 600 ft. in all of beautiful clear running water, all slab rock bottom, with one and two foot little waterfalls every 100 feet or so, a real picture with the large trees and all. A little bit of heaven on Backbone Creek, as it was called.

Tim and I cleaned up the land around the house, including the rocks from the garden area, before I purchased the other land from the developer which was across the street. I ran an ad in the local paper but didn't get hardly any calls as the real estate market in Texas was in one hell of a state with the economy and there was a glut on the market. With the $46,000 cost of this house plus the $5,500 cost of the additional acreage and the repairs at $2,500, it all came up to $54,000. Add to this the $210,000 for the lake house and lot and that is a $264,000 investment in personal housing. After a couple of months Bonnie and I decided something had to be done about this.

I said, "Let's advertise both homes and whichever sells first, will be okay." We agreed. I had enjoyed our place on the lake for three years and had about all the fishing I could stand, so we tried diligently. I advertised the lake house all over: Austin, San Antonio, and San Angelo. I had quite a few lookers, but no sales. One day I got a call from a lady in Kingsland that wanted to know if I would consider trading for their small house on a deep creek that ran into the Colorado River area of Lake LBJ. I said, "Why don't we all take a look at both houses?"

Their last name was Dugan. His name was Guy. I asked, "Is this your nickname?" He said, "No, that's my name." He was born and raised in Prior, Oklahoma about fifty miles from my hometown of Bartlesville, so we hit it off right away. He was working for the Dorito company and traveled a lot setting up displays in supermarkets, etc. He covered several states. Quite a salesman. His wife ran a local dress shop in our little town of Kingsland. They fell in love with our big home on the lake and we did indeed make a trade with them. It took some doing, but my real estate experience made it happen. Guy said he could get a better interest rate through his company's credit union, so he paid off my loan which made me happy as this way he didn't have to assume my loan. It relieved me of having any secondary responsibility should he have assumed my loan. The price of our home to the Dugan's was $220,000. We only owed the bank around $150,000, so this gave us $70,000 which was what we were paying for his house. Our equity was large enough to get their house free and clear. We traded our big, beautiful, heavy oak dining room suite for their living room suite and we simply traded our washers and dryer and refrigerator for theirs, so they wouldn't have to move those things. Both families were very congenial and it worked out well. After all, we were all Okies, so what would you expect? We never intended to move into their small house, but this way the trade we made had made it possible to sell the lake house that we hadn't been able to sell outright.

I spruced up this smaller house and kept the lawn manicured and put up my "For Sale" sign and held open house on weekends and in a month or so I found a buyer, took them to the Kingsland Bank, introduced them to the Vice President, Oscar Ricktor, who I had, by this time, become good friends with. He made them a good loan on the house for $87,000. I had $70,000 in it, so I picked up $17,000. I used this money to pay for the extra land and the labor and materials to put our auction home in first class shape. Now we had four acres and a nice home on the creek. Again, just planned my work and worked my plan with confidence.

Now I had not only enough money to do the aforementioned things but also enough to pay the Marble Falls bank loan off, so we had our country place free and clear. No house payments of any kind. What a relief! Just a few months ago we had $1,500 per month payment on the lake house and $400 per month on the country house and now no house payments at all. I think you call it "thinking and planning." We melted into this place, so to speak. I wasn't done yet in fixing it up into a real livable country home.

One day I was driving by Lowe's Hardware and Lumberyard and noticed a stack of 10 foot long 6"x 6" wood posts stacked up by the front door for sale. Lowe's was in the process of replacing their lumber storage racks with new ones. These posts were all in good shape and very well-seasoned. I bought the whole stack for $175, about 150 6"x 6" x 10' posts. What a bargain! Then I drove to the nearby gravel quarry and got a trailer load of sandy gravel. With several sacks of cement, Bonnie and I started work on tearing out, little by little, one and a quarter acres of pasture fence and we replaced it all with two rows of new four-foot stock fencing with 2" x 4" openings in it. We wound up digging over 100 post holes and set my 6" x 6" posts in cement that we mixed in my wheel barrow by hand, carried the water to mix it in 5 gallon buckets and set those nice posts. Then we bought the wire and stretched the fence and painted the posts white. It was a very good looking fence, as fences go. On the corner I had Lowe's deliver me some 10 foot long railroad cross ties, which made excellent corner posts.

On the other side of the house where I bought the other one acre of land, I fenced off about half of it and built a fence around it with the same 10' posts, set two feet deep in cement, but instead of 4 foot fencing, I bought the 5 foot high fencing, then added three stands of smooth wire in order to have a garden fence that was 7 ft. tall that the deer could not jump. They can clear 6 ft., but not 7 ft. and the smooth wire on the top would not hurt them if they tried and failed to clear it. Then I put in a 12 foot gate, 4 feet tall, and made an extension out of one-inch PVC plastic pipe and placed it 3 feet high from gate post to gate post and fixed it so it could be removed easily when I wanted to enter the garden. I painted the steel gate white, just the color of the PVC plastic, so the deer would think the gate was 7 ft. tall just like the fence was. It worked just fine. The deer couldn't get to the Long's new garden plants. I painted all of the 6" x 6" posts white (like the bull's corral) as well as the gate and it was a real pretty picture. The old boy that bought our lake house called me and said, "Andy, I put in a sprinkler system for my lawn and I don't need the irrigation pump you left for me, do you want it?"

I immediately said, 'Yes, I do for my big garden." You see my garden was about 100 feet from the creek and 200 feet from the garage. I bought a 200 foot piece of Romex, a heavy electric cord for my irrigation pump. This gave me an abundant amount of water to irrigate my garden, was well as the eighteen kinds of fruit trees we planted and made into a real orchard. We planted apple, peach, cherry, apricot, plum, persimmon, fig, and pear trees as well as blueberry, blackberry and grape vines. This garden became the envy of the entire subdivision. I simply made myself a job and it sure gave me plenty to do, except in the winter.

I had a really nice neighbor, a young guy that was a surveyor that I used when I bought the extra acreage I spoke of, and he had a small tractor and plow and he plowed my garden for me. His old dad lived in town in Marble Falls and had his garden on his son's place. We visited pretty regularly. I got some good garden tips from the old man. Their names were Bergman. His brother also lived in the subdivision and both had a few head of cattle.

I really enjoyed living here and so did Bonnie, as well as Tiffany. She still came down each summer. Bonnie and her went to the dog pound in town and found the best dog in the world. A medium sized slick haired black and white Australian sheep dog and immediately there was an instant love affair between Tif and her dog, Apache. They were together constantly. As I said before, we had a majestic Live Oak tree between the creek and house and squirrels would play in it and get acorns. I had a little pellet gun, a rifle that shot BB's that could shoot through a coffee can. So Tif learned to shoot. One day I was working away in my garden and here came Tif and Apache with a squirrel by the tail. She said, "Look, gramps, I got him right in the head. He was dead before he hit the ground. But, don't tell Momma. Don't tell Momma."

I said, "I won't tell your Momma, Tif. We are buddies, aren't we?" My thoughts immediately ran back to when I was about her age and lived on my grandparent's farm. I had a little 22 caliber rifle and I did the same thing with it. She literally lived on the creek. It was so pretty and the deepest part was only two to three feet deep, but it ran all the time — clear and cool. The creek ran through a very large ranch of grass land and trees and didn't cross any plowed ground before it got to our subdivision, so this is why it was so clear.

The subdivision was at one time part of a large farm in the old community of Fairland. It had quite a history. The crossroads of Fairland was about a mile from our subdivision and then on about five miles to Marble Falls. So it was no longer a town, but there were still some farms and small ranches around the crossroads and a little church and cemetery. It was near a railroad track and many years ago the people would ship their cattle and sheep from the railroad spur at Fairland. No longer, though. This land was settled right after the Civil War. There were still some big concrete tanks where the sheep were dipped before shipping them out on the railroad.

Now I'll tell you a funny story: Jack Abercrombie, the retired Air Force Colonel, had a little German gal that he married in Europe. She was a school teacher in Marble Falls, teaching German. There are quite a lot of people of German descent living in this part of Texas. Anyway, Jack said to me one day that he and his wife, Rita, had been talking and she wondered where Fairland got its name. He said, "Rita, said maybe they thought of it as a kind of fairy land."

I said, "Jack, I hate to burst Rita's bubble, but I don't think these old settlers that were looking for some good farm land to settle on had that in mind. I think what happened was probably one old farmer said to the other, "Well, boys, it's not good land, but it's not bad land. It's fair land. Why don't we call it Fairland?"

Jack said, "When I tell my little school teacher wife this, it will burst her bubble about fairy land." And we both had a good laugh. Jack told me later that she said, "Tell that Andy Long he's crazy."

Well, after I got my garden plowed I realized I needed a good Rototiller, so I bought one. Then I needed a really good riding lawn mower if I was going to keep this four acres manicured as I intended to do. So, I went to Austin and came home with an $1,800.00 riding lawn mower — a dandy. Tim used it to clear all the scrub brush along the creek which made it more attractive and accessible. I now had about $2,500 more in the place, plus all the fruit trees and fencing, but in time I had the best looking place in the subdivision.

I grew abundant vegetables of all kinds — tomatoes, cucumbers, sweet potatoes, Irish potatoes, green beans, pinto beans, black eyed peas, okra, radishes, onions and sweet corn. This now created a new purchase — a large new pressure canner, at $75. We now had about everything we needed.

I grew at least five barrels of cucumbers! I planted 36 tomato plants, lots and lots of watermelons and cantaloupe and all kinds of squash and zucchini. I never sold any of this bounty, but I gave all the neighbors lots and lots of vegetables of all kinds.

My Bonnie Girl canned hundreds of quart jars of vegetables of all kinds, as well as peaches, pears and plums. It took about four years before the fruit trees started really producing, however.

I not only planted, cultivated and hoed all this, but I helped Bonnie pick and snap green beans and hull peas while I watched my baseball games on television. Oh, yes, I forgot, we had a big satellite dish in the yard so we did have all the TV we could watch.

I watched my ball games and the Tuesday Night fights with my young neighbor, Walt Schultz. He and his pretty young wife, Nancy, were our closest neighbors, about 200 yards west of our house. He was a very bright young man and not afraid of work. He owned Schultz Communications. He had a very good business and I enjoyed telling him about the various real estate deals I had been involved in and he was eager to learn.

There were two pieces of land right across the road from our place and Schultz's property; one five acres track and one seven acre track. I had purchased both of these and one day Walt said, "Andy, would you sell me the five acre piece?"

I said, "Yes, all you have to do is pay me $500 down and $250 per month." Well, he was eager to buy but his little wife was scared to death. Walt did get it closed, however, at the title company, and I got their picture signing the note with her knees knocking. Well, I had made a great deal when I bought the land and by the time Walt bought it from me property values had increased, so by giving him such good terms, I doubled my money. About six months later I made him the same deal on the other seven acres and again doubled my money. I mentioned earlier that you make your money on real estate when you buy and just wait a while. So Walt had twelve acres and Andy Long had $500 per month coming in which was a very nice boost to our income.

Nancy loved horses and Walt bought her a really nice one so this gave them plenty of pasture for not only the horse, but two donkeys and two high-powered registered Limousine heifers. Everyone was happy with our deal.

They were very good young people and good neighbors to us. Walt's birthday was two days after mine, so each year we celebrated by taking our brides out to eat. Walt never missed a payment and had a long-range plan in mind for the land. His brother was a very good young carpenter, and needed some land to build houses on, one at a time. A couple or three years later Walt split off the first of several lots into smaller acreages and sold one at a time to his brother and Walt doubled his money and his brother was happy to be able to buy these lots one at a time. So all of us made money.

I got the idea of buying a couple of Texas long-horn cattle. I saw an ad in the paper for an eighteen-month-old bull. To make a long story short, I wound up buying him and a cow which was already pregnant, so it wasn't long until we had three head of long-horns. Oh, what pets! We loved them. The bull was registered as William something or other, so we named him Billy Boy. In a couple of years his horns were each about three feet long and so were the cow's. Her horns projected up as well as out from her head. They were some picture! The cow and Billy Boy were both calico with blonde and white markings. Along came a little female calf, the same color as her mama and papa.

Here is the fun part: my little pasture was only one and three quarters acre large and I kept it irrigated as well. I bought big round bales of hay from my young neighbor, Philip Bergman. I also fed them cattle pellets. So they prospered and were happy. Real pets. Billy Boy was bored sometimes, so one day a friend of mine, Charley Delancy, who I will tell you more about later, brought me a big, white 50 gallon plastic barrel, one that the local car wash place got their soap in. Both ends were closed with only a two inch screw-in plug on it. He said, "Billy needs a toy to play with."

I then got a huge truck tire, about 8 to 10 inches wide and about 4 foot high, from the local tire repair company where I bought my tires, so now Billy Boy had two toys to play with. It was so much fun to watch him stand them up, the barrel and the tire up on edge, then he would hook them on his horn and toss them into the air. Sometimes even over the fence!

Well, one day Billy Boy was walking the fence all along the road, just back and forth, bellowing and looking across the road at Walt's heifers, who had come into heat and Billy Boy was in love — or lust — or both. He started bothering our long-horned cow and she didn't want to be bothered, as she was already pregnant then, so Billy Boy laid the big white barrel down and started licking it while looking across the road at the heifers and low and behold, he started to try and breed with the barrel! Then he turned his attention to the big truck tire, stood it up on edge and licked on it and started to try and breed with it. Well, this became a regular past-time with Billy Boy! Everyone in the neighborhood that drove by our house on their way to town would watch Billy Boy perform his tricks — and all got a kick out of this!

Well, you may remember where and when I started working selling houses for Noxon Construction Company in White Rock, New Mexico in 1961. Well, thirty or thirty-five years have passed since then and Pat and Chuck Coutts of Malibu, California, still some of our very best friends, decided to come to Texas to visit us for a week. They had never been to Texas so they were enjoying everything and especially feeding the long-horns. One day Billy Boy decided to do his little act with the barrel and big tire and Pat Coutts said, "Oh, look at Billy Boy!" She said, "Andy, I have names for your long-horns that are fitting! Billy Boy is now Bill Clinton and the cow is Hillary Clinton."

I said, "Pat, you are so right! Bill will screw anything and Hillary is just like our blonde cow. She just shakes her head, looks at Bill and thinks how silly he is." So from then on it was Bill and Hillary." Well, by this time our long-horn cow Hillary's little calf is born and so now we had Chelsea added to the little family.

By this time our fruit trees were beginning to bear fruit and each year I grew a bountiful garden and I was enjoying our little four acre place very much. Bonnie had started trying her hand at futures and options trading on the stock market, and doing quite well at it. Also she had been volunteering one day a week at our new hospital at Burnet, Texas. There wasn't one in Marble Falls, so this one served both towns and the areas surrounding them. She enjoyed this as they ran a little gift shop and she met other nice ladies, most of whom were about the same age.

About this time Tiffany was still spending her summers with us and was getting to like horses very much. One of our neighbors had three nieces about Tif's age and she had some horses which they all rode. Anyway, she had this four year old appaloosa (white with black markings) who had been a stallion for too long, and was pretty stubborn. Anyway, Tif fell in love with him and said, "Grampa, would you buy him from Cindy?" So I did. The problem with him was that he had never been broke to have a regular bit in his mouth. He had been used to being ridden with a hackamore bit. When he wanted to go somewhere you didn't want to go, you couldn't get him to do what you wanted him to do. I figured that I could break him to a regular bit. I had paid Cindy $300 for him and I bought a regular bridle with a regular bit and started training him. He didn't like that bit at all! So, the second time I tried to put it in his mouth, he wasn't going to cooperate. I took a halter and snubbed him to a fence post and started to put this bridle and bit in his mouth — I was having one hell of a time!

He reared back and took both front feet off the ground and started pawing at me. Those front hoofs just barely grazing me. If he had come a half inch closer, he could have killed me! I grabbed the halter up close to his head and at the same time I hit him with my right hand fist so hard it was like the actor Mel Brooks did in the movie "Blazing Saddles," with the horse he was having trouble with. When Mel hit that horse, the horse's front legs folded and the horse crumpled over. Well, that was in the movies, and my horse and I weren't, but I hit him so hard in the jaw he blinked this eyes and shook his head. I think I came close to knocking him out. Anyway, I went in the house and called Cindy and told her about this and said, "Cindy I'm going to sell this horse, he damn near killed me. Do you want to buy him back? If you do, you don't have to pay for him all at once. Will $100.00 a month for three months be okay?"

She said, "Yes, Andy, I'll buy him back." So Tif and I decided it was the thing to do. She has always had a good head on her shoulders and she still does.

Tif had been to the veterinarian with us and Apache a time or two and she asked me to ask our vet if he would give her a job. She didn't want to be paid for her work, she just wanted to be around the animals. So I took her with me and we went to see our vet. He was a swell guy. He doctored both large and small animals, also boarded them and so on. I told him my granddaughter wanted to study to be a veterinarian. "Oh," he said, "You do, huh?"

She said, "Yes."

I then said, "Doc, she wants to work for you just to be around the animals."

Tif told him, "I'll empty your waste basket and sweep and mop the floors and whatever else you want me to do."

He said, "Well, Tiffany, I can't work you because of your young age (of twelve years), but you can come here and observe. Bring your lunch so you can stay all day when you come."

Grandma, and sometimes I, would take her over, about ten miles and then pick her up at noon and we would have our lunches at a little near-by park, then take her back. This went on for several weeks and she had some good stories to relate to us. We thought the world of this vet. He was a real man and a friend. He told her she would have to study a lot of science and math if she wanted to be a veterinarian. The idea of becoming a vet sort of waned in time, but her love for horses and dogs and cats is still as strong as ever.

When she returned to Albuquerque her mom found a riding stable that gave English Riding lessons and signed her up for lessons once a week. She loved it and got to be pretty good, even at jumps.

By now I had just about had this little four acre home place looking so good, just like I had manicured it. I had trimmed and burned brush until I was blue in the face! Growing vegetables. Bonnie canned them as well as fruit. I also bought a large upright freezer, as well as a chest type freezer to put it all in.

I shot two deer each year right there on the creek, standing right in my pickup under the large Live Oak tree on the creek bank. I would bleed them and gut them and then drive them to Johnson City about 20 or 30 miles to a deer processor and they would cut and package and freeze the meat for us — and into the freezer it would go.

One day I decided to do a little more to the outside of the house. The front porch was about eight feet deep and about fifty feet across the front of the house. All under the roof of the house. So I hired a friend of mine by the name of Charley Delancy and he and I built the nicest little three foot high porch railing out of 2" x 2" cedar posts with a frame across the top and bottom, then I painted it. It sure improved the appearance of our home. I had a large level front and side yards and back yard that I kept well mowed, then we all built a back yard fence from one side of the house in a half-moon shape out of cedar and I had three gates — one straight back from the house and in the center under a nice arbor with honeysuckle vines on it, and one on each side so we could go straight out to the garden or to the well house and garage or the pasture.

I bought a couple of miniature goats and it wasn't long until we had a half dozen or so. They were so cute and playful! My little grandson, Davis, Tiffany's little brother, would come down with his mom and dad, not to spend the summer like Tif had done, but to visit. He loved to play with these goats! He was five or six years old. I would let him ride on my mower with me and he enjoyed these visits and so did we.

I also bought six hens and a rooster from a neighbor of Charley Delancy's who raised fighting game chickens. We enjoyed them and the eggs were so very rich. Not quite as large as regular eggs but very good, usually there would be three each morning about as much as two regular chicken eggs. When it was time for the little hens to set, I would save about a dozen eggs for each hen and in 28 days I would have baby chickens all over the place. Cute as could be! The game hens were great little mothers. So with the long-horns, the little goats, the chickens, the dogs and two cats, we had quite a menagerie!

When we had about fifty or sixty new chickens full-grown, we decided to put them in our freezer, so I got my trusty hatchet and did some head chopping while the water got hot on an outside propane burner and we dipped them in four at a time and picked the feathers. I knew exactly how to do this from watching my grandmother Henderson clean and dress chickens when I was about six or seven years old when we lived on the farm with my grandparents during the Depression years.

This took a whole two days and we still have chicken and deer meat in our freezers as well as vegetables, and shelves full of canned fruit and vegetables.

We had some great neighbors. I mentioned the newly elected sheriff and his family just a quarter mile from our home and my banker just a quarter mile the other way. He and his wife worked at another bank, so we had good banking, which we put to use. Also, good police protection if we needed it. A highway patrolman also lived in the subdivision. I kept them all in fresh vegetables in season. So I was like the so-called "Franklin Park Circle Hero," so-to-speak.

Ruby and Vernon Alexander were our dearest friends there. They were just a year or so younger than Bonnie and me. He was Texas born and raised, but spent most of his working years as city engineer for the town of Greenville, Mississippi. He had graduated from Texas A&M as an engineer and Ruby was pure Texas as well as her Aggie husband. He helped me with any mechanical problems I had on my cars, mower, rototiller or anything. A wonderful man!

We had lots of relatives and friends come to visit us. Bonnie's brother, Bob Scott, who I told you about earlier, and all five of her living sisters came to visit and they took home lots of produce.

Oh, I must tell you about this! On September 27, 1994, it was our 50th wedding anniversary. We were not expecting any company. I was on my mower mowing the front lawn and looked up and here came four cars, one right behind the other, all honking their horns. The road curved around the twelve acres I had sold to Walt Schultz, so I could see them coming around the big sweeping curve across the pasture land. I thought to myself, "What in the hell is going on?" As they pulled into our big circle driveway that went completely around our house, I saw that it was all her sisters and their mates to celebrate our 50th anniversary! What a wonderful surprise! The party went on until the wee hours of the next morning. What a surprise!

Then I surprised my bride of fifty years with her present for us both. I told her we were going on a freighter cruise to New Zealand and Australia. We had taken one other cruise on a regular cruise line with Ruben and Betty Larson, our dear real estate friends from El Paso, years earlier, to Puerto Rico, St. Thomas, Jamaica, Nassau, and so on, but this one would be altogether different.

This freighter cruise was one of those huge container ships. It held hundreds of these large steel containers that you see on the railroad trains when you are traveling. The ship was the largest I had ever seen! As long as two football fields end-to-end, about 600 feet. They only carried six passengers. I had been wanting to go to New Zealand for several years and now was our chance.

The whole trip took us about six weeks. The name of our ship was the Columbus Victoria. It was German owned with German officers and a native islander crew from the Solomon Islands.

We boarded the ship at Long Beach, California. We had made the arrangements all by mail and telephone after we had spent three days in Malibu, California visiting with our friends Chuck and Pat Coutts. I was in "seventh heaven" --- being an old sea man!

We boarded her in the afternoon and got adjusted in our new quarters while they were finishing loading and we were notified by our steward, Walter Humner, that the Captain was throwing a "Welcome Aboard" party and dinner later that evening. Oh, what a lush meal! We started with wine and the main entrée was the best fish I had ever tasted. It was absolutely delicious and served with all kinds of side dishes.

The other two couples that we would share the ship with were Norman and Mary Crowfoot, a mining engineer and his wife, an artist. He had worked in mines all over the world. They were well traveled people who now lived in Tucson, Arizona. The other couple was Richard and Shirley Oakley. He was a retired United Airlines pilot. They lived in Florida aboard their boat, which was a large house boat. They were also characters! "Dick" had a hand held electronic sextant range finder and he could tell the Captain exactly where we were at sea. Our Captain was a really nice guy and he could hardly believe this. So, he would check him out on his instruments on the ship, and sure enough, Dick would be right. He got his ability to do this as an airline pilot and also from the trips he and his wife would take up and down the east coast of the U.S. in their house boat. Amazing! All in all, we enjoyed everyone on board. The passengers as well as the German officers.

At the Welcome Aboard dinner, I told the Captain, who was around 45 years old, that I had been a merchant seaman during World War II. I said, "You guys scared the living hell out of me several times during the war."

He responded quickly, "It wasn't me, I wasn't born yet."

I said, "Yes, I know, it wasn't you, but maybe your daddy, uncle or grandfather, perhaps." Anyway, all the officers were at the party. The Captain, First Mate, 2nd Mate and 3rd Mate, then the Chief Engineer, the 1st, 2nd, and 3rd Engineers. Eight officers in all, plus the combination Purser and Radio Operator. Then our Steward and the Cook. Both were great.

The Captain called the Chief Engineer over and introduced me to him and said, "Chief, this man was a ship engineer during World War II. I want you to give him a personal tour through your engine room in the morning."

The Chief said, "I will meet you in the morning." What an interesting tour it was! A huge engine, but not with the very loud noise like the ones I sailed on (the big diesel refrigerator ships during the war fifty years earlier). It was so modern and so clean. I can't remember how many tons of fuel the ship used an hour, but it was a very large amount.

The cook was great! He took all six of us passengers through his kitchen and food storage facilities. He was fifty-two and had been going to sea since he was twenty-six and was about ready to retire. What a wonderful cook he was! He and Bonnie exchanged recipes and stories. He had a native helper and dishwasher in the kitchen also.

Our steward was the best of all. Walter really took care of us. We had all of our meals in the officer's dining room at the same time with all of the men on board. Walter was our waiter. He prepared the menus with the cook, and took care of our cabin.

Our cabin was one large room with adjoining shower, a refrigerator, two beds, a nice couch, table and chairs, a large wardrobe closet and had chests of drawers under each bed. It was very nice and comfortable. There were also two large windows, about 2' x 3' offering a very nice view. It was air conditioned, of course, and also had an on-board telephone for ship use only.

The officer's lounge was large. This is where we had the Welcome Aboard party and the long table was used by us passengers and Captain for our coffee and tea snack breaks at 10:00 a.m. and again at 3:00 p.m. each day. Walter would serve us coffee or tea along with pie, cake, or cookies. We had many enjoyable conversations in this room.

One morning in particular I remember well. The Captain was in the lounge with his charts spread out on the table and said, "This is where we are right now." I looked at the spot he was pointing. We had been sailing for nine days and we hadn't seen one ship or plane or anything else since we got off the California coast. We were right in the middle of the Pacific Ocean. It takes sixteen days to go from California to New Zealand.

I said, "My God, what a lot of ocean!"

The Captain said, "Oh, don't worry. You are always within three or four miles from land."

I said, "What?"

"The chart shows us to be at a depth of 18,000 feet." He said.

I told him, "I don't think I feel any safer by this Captain!" And we all laughed.

We had such delicious meals and we had some good conversations with most of the officers, most of whom spoke good English. There was a small bar in the officer's lounge, but it was only open on special occasions. We could buy a bottle of booze and beer thru the Purser and there was a very nice selection of video tapes we could watch on the television in the officer's lounge. There was also a very well stocked library. I read a book on the life of J. Paul Getty while on this trip.

Oh, yes. We also had a small swimming pool on the aft deck. It was about five feet deep and about fourteen feet square. There was also a large swing, like an over-size porch swing. It was a very pleasant place to visit and watch the flying fish and porpoises. We could walk around the entire ship on deck — and did every morning. I so enjoyed this time.

We were approaching our first port in New Zealand, which was Auckland, after being at sea for sixteen days. It was a welcome sight. It was late afternoon when we docked and it took quite a while for the tug boats to nudge us into place at the dock with the Captain and the deck crew all working together with the tug boats to get us in a position to unload part of our big containers with the huge dock-side cranes. It was quite interesting to watch this. I got a lot of good pictures showing the tugs and big cranes operating.

Early the next morning, right after breakfast, us six passengers walked down the gangway to terra firma for the first time in over two weeks. It felt good. We walked a short distance to the port gates and walked into Auckland. We were surprised to see the beautiful modern buildings and the cleanliness of the city. No old junky, noisy cars honking. All just moving along very quietly. Much different than the traffic in the states. When a car gets old, noisy and smoking it is taken off the streets. No smog there. Even the busses are quiet and clean.

The three couples split up and we all went our separate ways. The people were so nice and friendly. We asked a young lady where the post office was. She smiled and said, "It's just down the street," and pointed. "About two blocks on the left, Love." We needed to make a phone call to confirm our future reservations in a couple or three weeks when we would return from Australia back to New Zealand. We would then catch a large tour bus and travel for a week seeing all of the coast and towns in the south island of New Zealand. Auckland is on the north island.

We asked a young man where we could find a telephone to make a long distance call. He asked, "Where are you folks from?"

I said, "Texas, U.S.A."

He smiled real big and said, "Real Texans. How nice to meet you. My favorite TV show is Walker, Texas Ranger. I watch it every week." He said, "Get in my car. I work for the hotel and you can use a phone there, and the girl will place the call for you right there." He was so nice and friendly and we couldn't have been treated any better!

We thanked him and left the hotel. It was noon and the office workers were on the sidewalks going to lunch. We got to see how the good looking young people dressed in New Zealand. Very modern, just like the states. We decided to go into the lobby of a large high-rise office building and we took an elevator up several floors, got off, looked around, then repeated this a few times on different floors. We really were enjoying our walking tour. We then did some bus sight-seeing and shopping, then back to the ship in time for supper. We were tired, but happy.

The next morning we were on our way to Sidney, Australia. We did pass several ships off-and-on that day. The weather was beautiful! I had taken lots of pictures while we were docking and also of the sights in Auckland. Mary Crowfoot was busy painting and Bonnie was making some of her handy work, a Native American decoration called a "Dream Catcher" for Walter to give to his "Mudder," and one for the Captain to give to his wife. I loved the sea and spent time walking the deck and watching the porpoises swimming just ahead of the ship's bow. This is what they like to do. I felt so at home and so at peace, it's hard to explain. It had been almost fifty years since I had spent this much time at sea, since 1945.

Almost every evening the Second Mate, a very friendly young man of probably thirty years old, would come to our cabin and play dominos with us. We did a lot of this while visiting. He spoke some English, not too much, but we had fun. A funny thing happened one day. It was his birthday, so he presented all the officer's and us six passengers with two bottles each of New Zealand beer. It was his birthday, but he gave the presents. Anyway, we all enjoyed them and had a little party in our cabin. He showed us a birthday present he had received from his wife. It had a colored picture of his beloved dogs. It was printed on the front of a tee shirt. Very nice.

Bonnie had bought a birthday card for him while we were in Auckland, which he really appreciated. Bonnie had me take it up to his cabin the next deck above us and when I knocked on his door, but there was no response. I bent down to slide it under his door and just then he stepped out the door of the First Mate's cabin and saw me and he asked me to join him and the First Mate to share a bottle of wine with them. I said, "Okay." He then picked up the phone and called our room and said, "Bonnie, the First Mate wants you to come to his cabin." This startled Bonnie at first, then she realized that it was probably where I was, so she said, "Okay." When she entered, all four of us had a good laugh, and enjoyed an hour of visiting.

The First Mate was the largest man I had ever seen! He had to be 6'8" tall and at least 300 pounds. He had a very black beard, but it was not bushy. He was very, very friendly. One day in the dining room after lunch I walked by his table and stopped to talk briefly and he asked, "How old do you think I am?"

I said, "About 45."

"I'm only 35." he said, and laughed. This was before the wine party in his room.

One day the Captain had all six of us passengers come up to the wheel house and chart room to show us the view out the front windows toward the ship's bow. What a sight! We all took a short turn at the wheel with him nearby. He showed us the ship's radar and how it worked and he explained the charts. He was a nice guy and we were having a ball! The islander crew kept the ship very clean. The colors of the exterior were red, black and white. Very well done.

It was mid-morning when we entered Sydney Bay and Harbour. It is well known as the world's most beautiful harbor. No doubt about it. A huge bridge passed over part of it with room for ships to pass under and the Sydney Opera House on the left hand side with beautiful skyscrapers behind it and on the right hand side, a mountain area covered with million dollar homes all along and running up the mountain. Beautiful beaches, sailboats, pleasure boats, and large sight-seeing boats with tables for food, drink and picture taking, which we did a lot.

Well, we spent two or three days in Sydney and enjoyed every minute. We walked just a couple of blocks from the ship, caught a taxi and were right in the heart of Sydney in about ten or fifteen minutes.

With our trip over, it's time to go back to our four little acres and great memories of our wonderful voyage to Australia and New Zealand that will last as long as we live.

When we left home to fly to Los Angeles to board our ship, I had our neighbor Jack Abercrombie drive us to the airport in our little Plymouth Horizon, our second car, and Jack picked us up six weeks later in the same car. I left our Lincoln Continental parked in our garage and locked my custom-made 30-06 deer rifle and scope in the trunk, just in case someone might break into our house. It was one of my most cherished possessions.

Back in 1949 I traded a full set of Lifetime Stainless Steel Cookware for this gun. The couple who I got it from lived in Clovis, New Mexico and the wife wanted the cookware so badly her husband traded me this rifle for her set. He had made it from a World War II Army 30-06 Springfield Rifle. He had made a beautiful walnut stock for it and it was a beauty. It was so accurate that even before I bought a $200 scope for it, I had already killed several deer and antelope with it. This size is the perfect caliber for an all-round rifle for deer, antelope, elk and bear. Like I said, it was one of my most prized possessions. A few years later I read in the paper where the fellow who made this wonderful gun of mine had gotten killed in a train wreck at Vaughn, New Mexico. He was a brakeman on the Santa Fe Railroad and was only in his mid-thirties when he died.

Anyway, later on when we moved to Los Alamos, N.M., I bought another one from a fellow named Ben Melton who was an employee at the Los Alamos Laboratory. I had sold the Meltons a home in White Rock in 1961 and Ben had made this rifle and it was identical to the one that I had bought in 1947 in Clovis. I got it for $100 and it was then that I bought the two $200 scopes and sheepskin lined cases for both rifles. I gave the second gun to Bonnie so that she could go hunting with me. Bonnie did not kill any deer, but she did kill an antelope with it. Tim and Andra both killed deer with it, though. Shortly before our big trip, Bonnie said, "Andy, I won't be hunting anymore, so I want you to sell my rifle so that I can buy a serger sewing machine with the money. So I did, and the gun and case brought $350. Anyway, when we were ready to leave on our trip, I put my rifle in the trunk of the Lincoln, locked the garage and we were gone.

When we got home and looked into my car, mice had gotten inside my Lincoln and they had built a nest and eaten up a lot of the upholstery and part of the leather case of the rifle! They got inside the car through the heater and then on into the trunk from inside the car. To make a long story short, the estimate to replace the car's interior was $4,300. Well, the insurance company did pay the claim after some haggling on my part as I explained that I had been insured with Allstate Insurance Company continuously since 1958 when I worked for Allstate for a short time selling insurance and had written my own policy. Now at the end of 1994 I explained that I had been insured with no lapse in coverage or premium payments and I had not scratched a fender, not one time and I hadn't had any losses during all of those 36 years. I had a few windshields and hubcaps replaced but not accidents. Well, they checked their records and decided to pay me the full $4,300.

I then drove the car to the Chrysler dealer in Burnet, Texas nearby and traded it to them for the nicest white 1990 Chrysler LeBaron, fully loaded and in excellent condition. With the trade-in and the $4,300 insurance check, I only had to pay out-of-pocket $1,650. The Lincoln was a 1985 model and had 132,000 miles on it. So, I made one hell of a deal!

I asked the salesman who in the world would trade in a car as nice as this LeBaron. "Well," he said, "This young school teacher had the car and it was needing new tires and they were so expensive that she just decided to trade cars." At that very moment I realized how the mentality of a little female school teacher works. Some people just can't keep from self-inflicting themselves. Huh?

Well, the rest of the story, as Paul Harvey says, is this: Today, January 3, 2003, this great little Chrysler LeBaron now has 229,000 miles on it! This is hard to believe, I know. But true. I have spent less than $4,000 on repairs on this car in the past eight years, and that includes a new $1,400 transmission! It still runs well and uses very little oil. Of course, I change the oil and filter, and lube it every 3,000 miles without fail. There is absolutely nothing wrong with the car now and I expect it to last me another 20,000 to 50,000 miles. Another good use of my sales ability was needed with the insurance company and I did perform, in my usual manner. Of course, the good driving record for 36 years was the real clincher to this deal, but the way I told them about it was handled quite delicately.

Over the years I have tried to teach my children and grandchildren the following: When you find yourself in a situation with a sour lemon, so-to-speak, then get to thinking about how to turn this lemon into a nice lemon pie. Good idea, huh?

When we drove into our yard from the airport in Austin I expected that the grass and weeds would be knee high, but to my amazement it was all mowed very nicely. Jack Abercrombie and Vernon Alexander had kept my grass mowed. I was delighted with the kind thing these two good neighbors had done.

I had paid my little friend Nicholas Brennaman $100 to water my orchard and keep my eighteen fruit trees alive. He had done a good job. He had never seen a $100 bill and I made this 14 year old boy very happy. He and I were real buddies, as you will see later on.

When the Texas economy had slumped to a low, I had bought three of the other lots in Hidden Oaks from the bank and had sold them on time-payment with a nice income coming in. One day my banker neighbor,

Steve Rogers, called me and said, "Andy, the bank still has two more of the off-water lots we need to sell. Would you be interested at $10,000 each like the two off-water lots you bought from us?"

I said, "No, Steve, I'm not interested in them at $10,000 each, but I will make you a firm offer of $5,000 each, cash." Oh, you should have heard him howl! I told him I had to hold the others way too long before they sold. In about a week or so, I got a call from him and he said the bank board decided to take my offer. So we closed the deal. In just a few months I sold one of them for $17,500 cash and a few months later I sold the other one for $14,000 on payments. About two years later it was paid off and the total came to $17,500 + $14,000 = $31,500. Not bad for a $10,000 investment.

Well, I decided right there and then that this $14,000 payoff on this last lot was going to be deposited in an account for Tiffany Jeanne Marie Riordan for her college education, and it still remains intact as she has not yet decided just what she wants to do with her life. The money is available when she does. She just hasn't found her place yet, as an old boy told me one time. I'm sure she will one of these days and the money is safe and drawing interest for her. She wanted to use it to buy a pickup but Grandma Bonnie said, "No, Tiffany, that money is for your education. You still have your little Ford Escort we bought for you."

I mentioned earlier about the sheriff living only about a quarter mile from us and my banker about the same distance in the opposite direction, but I didn't mention about our doctor, Phil McCurdy, living right next door to my banker. We were very good friends with him and his family. One of their daughters was Tiffany's age. They were such good neighbors. I kept them in plenty of vegetables, watermelon and cantaloupe every summer. So thinking about it a moment, I had plenty of good protection from Joe Pollick, the sheriff, good financial protection from Steve Rogers, my banker, and plenty of health protection from Dr. McCurdy, my doctor. That just about covers it all, I think.

I must tell you this good story now, about Phil McCurdy. One morning Bonnie was going to help me in the garden and our two dogs were each wanting her attention and our little miniature greyhound, Manhattan, tripped Bonnie and down she went. If you can imagine this, instead of her right foot pointing straight forward, it was pointing directly straight to the right. Oh, this hurt her! I looked at it and said, "I think it is just out of joint." I figured it could be popped back into place. So, I drove our car up right beside her and she laid down in the back seat. We went directly to the Burnet County Hospital and our doctor, Phil McCurdy was there. He x-rayed it and told us she had a small bone broken in her ankle. He said he was not qualified to set it, but he knew a specialist in Austin that was very good. His wife, Jill, had him work on her knee after she had injured it skiing in Colorado.

So he said, "Andy, I'll help you get her in your car again and take these x-rays to a doctor at Seton Hospital in Austin. I'll call his office and he will be expecting you."

Bonnie said, "Phil, I need to go by our house again as I have some spaghetti and sauce cooking on the stove."

Dr. Phil said, "Bonnie that's fifteen miles over to your house and fifteen miles back. You can be half way to Austin by then. I have to go back to my office in a few minutes. I'll stop by your house and turn your stove burner off."

"Here is the door key, Phil." She said, "Thank you very much."

I tell you this because these are the kind of people we had for neighbors in our little subdivision of Timber Ridge outside of Marble Falls, Texas. This is the way it was in the Hill Country of south central Texas. At this time Bonnie was working at the hospital gift shop as a volunteer Pink Lady, as they called them, one day a week. She looked forward to this day each week. There were two ladies that worked together each day and they all became good friends. Most of them were in their sixties or so. Once in a while I would drive over to Burnet and have lunch with them in the hospital cafeteria. One big happy family.

Anyway, this was a pretty serious operation. The doctor said it was the worst bone she could have broken in her foot. He operated and put in a stainless steel screw to hold it in place. Once in a while it hurts her a little, but not often.

We did enjoy our place so much. Nothing fancy, but we had made it very livable and we were super happy for the eight years we lived there. We had three couples we played dominoes with about every two weeks or so. They were wonderful people.

We had a home owners association for Timber Ridge and Vernon Alexander was our president. He took it as his personal responsibility to keep our gravel road graded. It was about a mile and a half to the black top at our entrance gate to the subdivision. They had bought an old road grader and Vernon, being a good mechanic, had it working good, so he was the only one who used it. He did a fine job, but the rough road and dust was getting to be a real nuisance.

Also the post office in Marble Falls would not deliver any mail to our subdivision because they said the road was too rough. Everyone had to drive seven miles to the post office and seven miles back. Of course, the ones who worked in Marble Falls could stop and pick theirs up on their way home. But some of us did not work in town, and it was a lot of trouble to get the mail. I asked Vernon about it and he said he had written several letters explaining this to the postmaster the past several years and had never received any answers. Well, I knew these twenty or thirty families were being abused, so I decided to see what I could do about it.

I was feeling extra good that next day when I went to town for our mail, so I walked up to the half door that is in the lobby that opens to the mail room if you have a problem. I rang the doorbell and asked to see the postmaster. He was a tall slim drink-of-water about my age with a necktie on and well-dressed and he said, "I am the postmaster. My name is Royce Nelson."

I said, "Mr. Nelson, my name is Andy Long. I live in Timber Ridge Subdivision and I am here to discuss with you why we cannot get mail delivered to our mailboxes like everyone else."

He said, "The road is too damn rough for us to deliver mail to you folks."

I said, "That rough road you are talking about is graded regularly so that is merely a figment of your imagination. I have gotten mail by rural delivery many times in my life even as far back as fifty years ago. The way I look at my mail delivery is that it is one of my rights as an American citizen in accordance with the Constitution of the United States. You have received many letters from Mr. Vernon Alexander of our subdivision and you have not even had the decency to answer a one of them."

He said, "You go back home and write me again and tell me how many families live there and the miles involved and I'll look it over."

"I will do that," I said, "and I want you to remember my name, Andy Long, and in two weeks if we have not heard from you I will be back to see you." With that I left and went to see Vernon and we wrote the letter the post master had asked for. The two weeks passed and one day I was feeling just right and I bounced into the post office and rang the door bell. The half door opened and one of the other employees said, "Can I help you?"

I said, "Yes, I'm here to see Mr. Nelson." He walked up to the half door and I said, "Do you remember me?"

He said, "I can't remember your name, but I do remember your face."

I said, "I told you specifically to remember my name and that I would be back to get an answer as to why we can't get mail delivery. You get your mail delivered, don't you? Well, I want mine delivered, too. By the time I drive seven miles to town and seven miles back home just to get my mail, I am so God Damn mad I am about to blow a head gasket. I demand some answers."

He said, "You can't talk to me this way."

I stopped him and said, "You dirty S.O.B.! I don't work for you like one of your employees do. By God, you work for me and a lot of other folks. I told you not to forget my name and if I don't get satisfaction I will go to the Postmaster General with this problem. I felt like punching him in the mouth. Oh, it was close! "You had better get busy as you don't have much time to solve our problem."

Well, it wasn't but about four or five days that my neighbor Vernon received a copy of a letter from Nelson to some lady in Austin and we waited to hear from her. When we did, she stated that Royce Nelson had retired from the Postal Service and she reported that as soon as we got street signs and mailboxes up they would start our regular mail delivery. That took about two weeks and our problem was solved.

At the next homeowner's meeting, which was twice a year, they wanted me to be president, but I declined as Vernon was doing an excellent job. I did commit to continue to be head "tail-twister" any time it became necessary.

I visited a lot with the Alexanders. Vernon was willing to help anyone with anything. He was a good mechanic and had lots of tools. So he was a great help to me with my cars, mower and roto-tiller. One day we were visiting them and Vernon said, "You know, Andy, I wonder what it would cost us to blacktop our roads in the subdivision? There are about two miles in all."

I said, "Let's analyze the situation. First, if we did pave the roads it would add at least $10,000 to the value of each of our homes." The road was private and each family owned to the center of the road in front of their home.

Vernon had been city engineer most of his working life in Greenville, Mississippi so he was experienced in working with street contractors and so on. So I suggested he get bids from two different contractors for a turn-key job and when he did we would take the best bid to our good neighbor, Steve Rogers the banker, and ask him if his bank would consider loaning our homeowner's association the money to pave our streets.

We did just that and Steve said, "Yes, we can make the loan if everyone agrees."

Well, some were reluctant but we held a special meeting when we got the cost estimate. We all voted, and on a majority vote we all finally agreed. I explained about how it would add to the value of our property the same as the mail delivery did when we got it. I gave a pretty convincing talk and I think the cost to each family was about $200 per year for the five year loan, and in a couple of months we had a very nice smooth paved road. We then sold our old grader and applied the money to the loan.

At the next meeting Vernon said, "Folks I have been president of the homeowners' association for about ten years now. I think it's time to have a new one." I refused to take it so Richard Bergman was elected by acclamation. He was a good man and would do a good job. And he did.

Several more houses were built in our subdivision and I attribute most of this happening to us having mail delivery and paved roads. So again, when good people have good ideas and proper planning, good things just seem to happen. Don't they?

We continued to have lots of company, long-time friends and relatives from all over and they all enjoyed old Andy and Bonnie and lots of vegetables when they left. We were having some of the best years of our life.

A few years had passed since the Texas economy had hit the skids and the real estate values had bounced back, as well as oil prices, and the economy was much better. The thing that helped our area the most was, surprisingly enough, an article that was written in a retirement magazine that said that the number two place in the U.S.A. to retire was in the beautiful Hill Country (as it was called in south central Texas), such as Marble Falls, Kerrville, Fredericksburg, and Johnson City (where Lyndon Johnson was born and raised and lived most of his life). The number one place to retire in the U.S.A., the article said, was somewhere in Arkansas. I think it was Mountain Home, Ark. Anyway, property values rebounded and people haven't stopped coming since.

I recognized what was happening, and one day I saw a real estate sign on 70 acres of ranch land on the road from the crossroads at Fairland, running a half-mile north to the entrance of Timber Ridge subdivision. It was just pasture land with trees and a large pond and was being used as pasture for cattle. Well, I thought that I might try and buy this 70 acres and split it into smaller tracks and sell it for homesites. The market was good for 10, 15 and 20 acre sites. People could have a well drilled and power was available, plus each lot would face onto a good blacktop road.

The 70 acres was owned by two friends who were bankers. They had owned it for a long time and one of them had just recently died. The one who died had been a banker for many years. His name was Counts. I had met him one time and he was a real nice old guy. The other one was named Pennington and he lived in south Texas. Counts had six heirs, mostly grandchildren, so herein lay some problems.

They had listed this 70 acres, which was surveyed out to be 69.94 acres, so we just say 70 acres. Anyway, they had listed it with John Mulkern, a very good land man type Realtor out of Austin. He was a young fellow around 35 or 40 years old. I called him and he came up to our house and we walked the land and, both being experienced Realtors, we hit it off really well right from the start.

The land fronted on two black top roads, at the crossroads at Fairland. I told John what I wanted to do with the land, and I told him I would let him help me sell it as he had a prospect or two. He was pleased with this as he could see a possible double commission. One from the partnership and one on my re-sales. So he was very cooperative. He said, "Andy, I suggest you sell two ten-acre tracts on the south end. Each would be square tracts facing the road and would extend about a quarter of a mile. Then you would have 50 acres left. The land runs about a half-mile north and faces west. This would give nice frontage on the black-top road and would be a quarter mile deep. This remaining fifty acres would make two 15-acre tracts and two 10-acre tracts, all a quarter of a mile deep. This would allow people to set their homes farther back from the road for privacy."

It was good flat rich land with nice trees, with several large ones. The depth of the water table was from 75 to 100 feet. John continued, "Andy, I have a buyer for the two 10-acre tracts but the heirs don't want to go through the trouble of selling it off piece-meal and they really don't understand how to do it. They just want to sell the whole 70 acres to one buyer."

I said, "John, this sounds real good to me. I'll buy the whole thing, then sell the 20 acres to your buyer. This will help me come up with less money to buy the rest of the 50 acres."

John asked, "How would we handle this?"

"I'll show you how to do it." I said. "We will have a simultaneous closing. It is a little complicated, but it can be done." We went to my bank and told them that what I wanted to do was borrow enough money to buy the fifty acres. "First I will have to buy the whole 70 acres and sell the 20 acre piece to a Mr. Robert Pancinie, using his money that he would pay me, to be my down payment on my 50 acres. Your bank will make me the loan on the fifty acres and all the money will be paid to the heirs for deeding me the whole 70 acres." Well, it took some talking before I convinced everyone, including the title company lady that it would work and that it was all legal if she would prepare the papers as I instructed her.

She agreed to try. She had never done this before. One morning she called me and said, "Andy, I figured out how to do this while I was laying awake last night. I think I can put it all together."

I said, "I'll prepare a letter of intent that I will sign spelling out that, indeed, I will buy the whole thing and then sell 20 acres to Mr. Pancinie." So it did happen and everyone involved learned a lesson from old Andy Long.

All were happy and Mr. Pancinie told us all at the simultaneous closing that his son was going to put in an herb farm and raise the best vegetables anywhere around. He said he had an engineer test the soil and the lady engineer who made the test told him it was the richest soil she had ever tested. I knew then why I had been growing such find garden vegetables on my land in Timber Ridge which was only a mile or so away.

My work was just beginning on the remaining 50 acres. This is when I talked to my good friend, neighbor and sheriff, Joe Pollick. I asked him if he would rent me his Ford tractor and brush hog attachment. He said, "Andy, you don't have to rent it, I'll loan it to you."

I said, "No, Joe, I'll pay you $100 per month. I expect to make some money when I sell the land and I want to make it look like a park or golf course." So the deal was made to rent it. It was a good thing as about a month later the transmission needed repairing so with the help of our other good friend and neighbor, Vernon Alexander, we got this job done with a trip to San Saba, Texas to the nearest Ford tractor place for the parts. It was like new again and Joe was happy.

I tackled one hell of a job! I was about 70 years old then and in good health and I would mount this machine around 7:00 in the morning, work till noon and then back at it all afternoon. I would hide the tractor and get in my pickup and drive home and do it all over again the next day. This took two or three months of hard work to get it all finished. There were lots of large cacti three or four feet tall, saplings and brush to mow, and lots of trees that had to be trimmed — and big brush piles of logs and dead trees.

All the neighbors in Timber Ridge would drive by on their way home and see me working and were all amazed at how this old piece of ugly land was being transformed, and how hard I was working. I had to tear out an old fence a half-mile long that had been there for probably a hundred years or so and pull out the old posts with a long piece of cable and my pickup.

It is time I told you the story about my old pickup. It is an interesting one. I had to have one to tackle this job and I saw one advertised in the local paper. A 1985 Dodge heavy duty half-ton pickup with only 36,000 miles. So Bonnie and I drove up to the village of Granite Shoals about five miles west of Marble Falls. An old man came out of his house and said his name was Peter Vanderlinden. He was a Dutchman from the Netherlands and he was 94 years old, he told me in broken English. He was asking $6,000 and I offered him $5,700 cash and we made a deal. Boy, oh, boy, what a good pickup! I was happy.

Peter was a good old man and we became instant friends. He still had a small car to drive and he lived alone in his little two bedroom house. One day he called me and said, "Do you like to play dominoes, Andy?"

I said, "Yes."

He said, "Come on over and we will play." He was very lonesome so I did. Well, I'm a pretty good domino player, but he beat me three out of four games. He was good.

I asked him one day if he was married and he said, "Not any more." He had married an old gal in Granite Shoals a few years back and he said he had put her on his checking account and one day she cleaned him out and left town.

He told me how he came to this country. He said that when he was a young man he went to Canada and got a job as a bicycle mechanic which was what he had done in the Netherlands. He later became an auto mechanic, then bought and sold cars in his own business. He later moved to Houston, Texas and contracted with the government doing repairs on government housing, hiring people to work for him and so on. You could see he wasn't lazy and didn't like anyone who was. This was the way he had pulled himself up "by his bootstraps," so-to-speak. I became quite fond of this old man as a friend. I always did have an affection for old people if they were good ones.

One day I stopped by to check on him and he was upset with the Police Dept. of Granite Shoals. He said he was charged $96 for not coming to a complete stop at a stop sign by a female police officer. He told her that he did slow down and saw no one was coming. She said, "Stop means stop." Well, with court costs the old man had to pay $96. What a shame.

Anyway, I called him one day and no answer, so I drove over about ten miles from our house and knocked, and no answer. I really got worried, so I tried the door knob and it wasn't locked so I went inside calling his name. No answer. I went to his bedroom and he was lying on the bed facing the wall. I reached over and touched his shoulder and to my surprise he turned half way over and looked at me. I was so relieved! I thought that he had died. He was in pretty bad shape, so I called a Catholic priest that he had mentioned to me had helped him with some business problems and told him how I had found Peter. He thanked me and said he would go to see him.

As I mentioned earlier, Bonnie was a volunteer Pink Lady at the Burnet County Hospital and a day or two later she told me that Peter was in the hospital, so I went to visit him. When I was leaving I told him that I would be back to see him again and he said to me, "Andy, don't wait too long."

A day or two later Peter was not in the hospital and Bonnie said he had either died or they had transferred him to another hospital where they had one of the urgent care units, but they wouldn't tell her where. I called the priest a few days later and he said that old Peter had passed on. Well, I named the old pickup "Peter."

Nicholas Brennaman, the young man, who had watered my orchard while we were on our long cruise, and I became very good friends. We had met when his family had moved to Texas and bought a home in Timber Ridge. They turned out to be some of our dearest friends and still are today. Doug Brennaman, the father, worked with the National Park Service and was a large man, about 6'3" or more, and 235 pounds with a bushy red beard and always smiling. The mother was a pretty thing and very nice and wonderful to her two sons. Nicholas, the oldest of the two, was about twelve years old when we met him and Jonathan was about four years old.

Nicholas was a chubby 5th grader and was the happiest little guy. He loved machinery and he loved to ride my mower and to roto-till my garden with me. In the summers he spent as much time at our place as he did at home. He really liked Bonnie as well as me and he would watch her cook when he was at our house. The best way to describe how we felt about Nick was he was just like a grandson to us both. You see I only have one grandson, Davis, who was then about five years old, and was Tiffany's little brother who lived in Albuquerque. We didn't get to see him very much so the Brennaman boys become our "surrogate" grandsons.

Doug's job was at the Johnson Ranch at Johnson City on the Llano River that was now a National Park. The mother's name was Nickie and she loved her little family very much. She got a job at our bank where I did my business. When they asked her if she knew anyone in town, she said she knew Andy and Bonnie Long and they hired her on the spot. She made them a very good and friendly employee.

When I started the work of cleaning up the fifty acres, Nick had a job. Boy, did we work! He learned to drive my pickup as he was about 14 years old then and was growing tall. He really loved to drive that old pickup! The 50 acres had several dirt trail roads running through it so he got a lot or practice.

I taught him about gardening, like my grandfather had taught me. He really learned how to work and we had a ball. It was good for me as I didn't get as lonesome as I would have working by myself. We would stop in at McDonald's in Marble Falls for a meal or ice cream whenever we had to make a trip to town for supplies. Once in a while we would drive old Peter to one of the surrounding towns and take in a sheep, goat and cattle auction and just have some fun. We worked that whole summer getting all the brush burned, the junk hauled off and the place all mowed.

One day later on we were driving around on the place and saw a deer. I kept my deer rifle in the pickup so I was ready. Nick got his first experience at watching me shoot a deer and dressing it out and we took it to Johnson City to have it processed, packaged and frozen. He really enjoyed all this.

The hard work on my fifty acres was really shaping up. A dozen huge piles of brush, logs and trimmings had been burned using diesel fuel. I must have used at least a barrel of it. I would buy it in two five gallon buckets at a time, then mow around every pile really good so as not to start a fire that would get out of hand. The piles would be 20 or 30 feet around and 10 feet high. I could only burn one at a time.

One pile not only had logs, brush and old fence posts, but a lot of various old junk that wouldn't burn as well. It was a huge pile. Nick said, "Andy, I'll have my dad come down and help us on Saturday on this last big pile when we burn it." Doug did help us and everything that would burn did burn. The other stuff we had to dispose of somehow. I called a guy that had a front-end loader and dump truck and he went to work and two days later all of the big old piles of scrap were gone. I then went to Home Depot in Austin and bought the largest hand held trimmer they had and started trimming the quarter mile of bar ditch out by hand. What a hard job! But it did look good and it had to be done if the property was going to sell.

I had to make an entrance into the property and there was already one good round concrete culvert about three feet in diameter across the bar ditch, so I set some gate posts and approach posts and bought an eighteen foot steel gate in order to have a main entrance. I painted the posts a forest green and filled the top of the posts with rounded up cement and stretched wire in the posts. It looked very proper for an entrance.

About 100 feet into the property there was an old dug well that was about four feet in diameter and about three feet high made of stone. It had a little water in the bottom of it, but had been abandoned years ago. I could see some possible danger there, so I decided to make a "lemon pie" out

Death of an Era

of this lemon. Bonnie's brother, Bob Scott of Galena, Kansas who I have mentioned before, came to visit us and he was a very capable guy. Well, we bought some lumber and a few shake shingles and built a little pitched roof over the well and it looked like a story book picture wishing well. I fastened some strong grated steel over the top of the stone and fastened a pulley with a rope and bucket above the steel grate that covered the well opening. Now we didn't have to worry about any of "momma's little darlings" falling into the well. It was strictly for looks and safety.

With this done, I was ready to call John Mulkern, the Austin realtor who had sold me the land, and have him sell some lots for me. I told him I would be trying to sell them also, but if he had any prospects I would pay him a commission. In the meantime I had my friend and neighbor and surveyor, Phillip Bergman, survey the fifty acres and make two fifteen acre tracts and two ten acre tracts.

One of the fifteen acre tracts on the south end of the fifty acres had the large pond on it. It sold to Edwin and Jeanie Cook for $55,000. They both worked for the University of Texas as a counselor and a secretary. The adjoining piece I sold myself to Stan Collier and his wife, Bonnie, for $53,000. John then sold the two ten acre tracts, twenty acres in all, for $60,000 to a fellow who worked as a salesman for the Xerox Corporation in Austin. He was married to a woman who we all figured had lots of money because he paid cash. The reason he bought the land was that he wanted to grow grapes. He was a Frenchman named Jacques Breix.

All this was happening near the end of 1995 and early 1996. Ed and Jeanne Cook were in love with their fifteen acre piece of land and I had gotten them in touch with a good home-builder who lived near us in Timber Ridge. He was helping them come up with a set of plans to build a new home on their land. They owned a house in Austin but they wanted to get out of the city. It was a second marriage for them both and they had not been married very long. They built a nice entrance coming off the road at the front end of their property and a nice fence separated it from my remaining fifteen acres. I introduced them to a water well driller and they got a real nice well. They were happy and by this time we had become good friends. They would always stop by to see us when they would come up to do some work on their land.

This was now the time period when big things were happening in the life of one of our twin granddaughters. Taña had graduated from the Fashion Institute of Technology (F.I.T.) in New York City, with two degrees — one in women's fashion and one in men's fashion. She took to it like a duck to water. Bonnie had been back to New York City to visit her and had a really nice time with not only Taña but also my sister's son, Mitch Stanfield, who had an apartment in New York City and a good job on Wall Street.

Taña graduated at the top of her class and had been chosen with a few other students to attend an important meeting in Raleigh, North Carolina to meet some "big wigs" who did the hiring of the brightest young students for their companies. This was quite an honor for Taña, so Grandma and I drove over to attend this big pow-wow in Raleigh. Taña was hired right on the spot by the Hanes Corporation and they started her out at $23,000 a year salary to work in their fashion sportswear department. We were all overjoyed with this.

A short time later we made another trip to meet Taña in Winston-Salem, North Carolina where she would be working at the Hanes Factory there. Tiffany was with us for the summer, so the three of us headed out together. The Hanes Company had rented a place for her in an apartment motel until she could get located so we had agreed to help her get situated. Taña was level-headed and quite skilled. She not only looked like her grandmother, she was just as capable. She rented a small U-Haul van, loaded her personal belongings and started driving from New York City to Winston-Salem, arriving on the same day we did from Texas.

First we helped her find a good little Plymouth Horizon to drive and we helped her buy it and get it financed. We then went to get the car insurance and her driver's license in North Carolina and to open a bank account, rent an apartment, and get all the furnishings she would need to keep house. This all took some real doing, but believe it or not, two days later we had it all done. This was such an adventure for this young lady who I called "my little Bonnie" once in a while as she looked and acted just like her Grandma. They loved each other dearly.

We got up early on Sunday morning and told her we were leaving to go home. Oh, she hated to see us leave, but Bonnie told her that she needed this day to fix her nails and hair and get used to being in her new apartment by herself and to be ready to start her new job the next day. Tiffany had been having a ball with all the excitement of Taña's settling in, so we decided to make a little vacation for us all on our return trip. Heading south from North Carolina to Atlanta, we spent the night there, then on the next morning to the panhandle of Florida and Panama City. It was a vacation paradise with miles of ocean front of the whitest sandy beaches. There were all kinds of amusement parks and things to do and we all played in the ocean and on the beach. Tif really enjoying herself and so did we.

We then continued on across the southern coast of Alabama and Mississippi into New Orleans where we spent the day sightseeing, riding a street car, visiting Bourbon Street and taking a ride on the Mississippi Queen, a large river cruise boat. The same one that we had taken earlier when we went to the World's Fair. This was just the vacation that we needed.

Then we headed across south Texas, and part of the time we were on a ferry boat with the car. We saw lots of off-shore oil platforms, and wells close up. Quite a sight for all three of us, and the Captain let Tif steer the ferry boat. This trip was taking place during the summer of 1995.

It wasn't long after Taña started working at Hanes that she mentioned her boyfriend, that she met at the Fashion Institute, was also looking for a job. Hanes really liked Taña and didn't want to take any chances that she might get married and move from Winston-Salem, so they told her to have her boyfriend come to Winston-Salem for an interview. He did, and they hired him right on the spot. His name is Carlos Martinez. His family all lived in Dallas, Texas where his father owned and ran a men's pants cutting factory and had been working with Haggar Pants Company for years. He was from a very nice family and we all liked them very much. What we had here were two young people with very good jobs, making good money and in love and moving into a larger apartment together. We could see that wedding bells were probably not far off.

Now, "Back to the Ranch" in Texas. The Cooks had gotten a price from the builder who had figured out how much the home they had designed would cost to build. I can't remember just how much it came to but their desires had overloaded their pocket book by quite a large amount. So they decided to wait a while before starting to build. In the meantime,

Stan Collier saw me one day on the property and he said, "Andy, I'm interested in buying your last fifteen acres, the piece between the Cook property and the Frenchman's property. I should have bought it all before you did as it joins my other land on the east side — about a hundred acres." He was pasturing cattle on it as well as quarrying top soil, which was rich and deep and selling it for $100 per dump truck load. He said he wanted to build a home for him and his new wife on this last fifteen acres and then open it up on the east end adjoining his other land. This made good sense to me, so I agreed to sell it for $3,500 an acre, for a total of $52,500. Stan said, "I'll pay you $5,000 down and $1,000 a month for five years at ten percent interest." So, we had a deal.

When you add it all up for the whole fifty acres, counting the $52,500 from Collier, the $55,000 from the Cooks and the $60,000 from the Frenchman, it came to $167,500. The cost of the land for the fifty acres was $79,000 for the land, and $15,482 for expenses including the sales commission, closing costs, tractor rental, fuel, repairs, labor and cleanup leaving a net profit of $73,018. This is considering of course that we held a note from Collier for $46,900, payable over five years at $1,000 per month, leaving cash to us of $26,188 for our risk and hard work. However, the $1,000 per month for five years sure came in handy over the five years and was paid off at the end of 2001.

The fifty acres looked great. The Frenchman's well came in good and he fenced off his twenty acres and started planting his grape orchard. He worked hard and spent a lot of money getting it fenced and planted. Some strange things were about to happen, however. In about three months the company that Jacque, the Frenchman, worked for, Xerox, gave him an ultimatum. "Either you get out of the grape farming business or you quit Xerox. You are spending far too much time trying to do both jobs. The decision is yours, Jacque." Well, his decision was to sell his twenty acres. He didn't have much choice and I imagine his wife was getting tired of putting her money into his grape raising venture. I think she considered it as poor judgment on his part. Old Stan Collier came to Jacque's rescue and bought the twenty acres from him.

The first thing we noticed was that Collier was digging a huge hole in the middle of his fifteen acres, right next door to the Cook's fifteen acres. The Cooks were devastated! They came to me asking for advice. I said,

"He is quarrying for top soil to sell and is hauling it all over this part of the state to golf courses and such, in the huge trucks. He was a big operator and owned several of these large trucks." I told the Cooks, "You could sue Collier but I don't imagine you can win. You would spend a lot of money on a lawsuit, too. In a way, Ed, this might be a blessing since you haven't started building your house yet. Maybe Collier would be interested in buying your land as I think he probably is the only one you can sell it to with his new quarry next door." They decided to take this advice and made a deal with Collier and were happy under the circumstances.

Shortly after this Ed Cook told me that he and his wife had found a home they liked and for less money than they were going to spend on the one they had planned to build. It was also a lot closer to their jobs in Austin. So everything worked out for the best. Ed was paying me by the month for his fifteen acres so when Collier bought his land, he cashed out the note that Ed owed me, so I was happy too. Collier now owned the entire fifty acres that adjoined his 100 acres. Strange things happen and I think it worked out best for all concerned (and Collier was still paying me $1,000 a month for his land for the next five years).

About this time Doug Brennaman decided to move his family to a new job with the National Park Service in South Dakota. We hated to see them go as we had become such friends and would miss the two boys very much. They had a little Ford Escort Station Wagon they were going to sell that was Nickie's car. She was the only one that drove it. It was a dandy and got about 40 miles per gallon of gasoline.

I told Doug to let me know how much the car dealers would pay him for it and I would pay him $300 more. He did and they offered him $4,000, so I paid him $4,300. Tif Riordan was going to turn 16 in September, so I made her the same deal I had made the twins several years earlier. She would get the car on her 16th birthday as a present if she didn't smoke, drink, or use drugs until she was 18. I put it all in writing and let her read it and told her if she violated the agreement the deal was off and the car would revert back to me. Right away she said, "Where do I sign, Gramps?" Her grandmother taught her how to drive in our little pasture which was very smooth and she was a very happy little girl and this made us happy too. She is still driving it and she is now 23 years old.

Another big event is about to happen. Taña and her boyfriend Carlos Martinez announced they were getting married in June. Taña came to see her grandmother and me and she and Bonnie went to Austin to pick out her wedding gown and accessories as our wedding gift to her. We also gave her a brand new set of Lifetime Stainless Steel Cookware that I had been saving for her wedding all these many years, still in the box it was in and unopened since I got out of the cookware business in 1961. It was now 1996 some 35 years later. Taña was 29 when she and Carlos got married. When I sold these sets of cookware they sold for $300. The same set now sells for $1,400. This shows you what inflation had done to all of us good folks, doesn't it?

The big wedding took place in Dallas, Texas where the Martinez family lived and the wedding was the largest that any of us had ever seen and it was beautiful, held in a big Catholic church in downtown Dallas. Taña had planned a wonderful wedding celebration and all of Bonnie's sisters attended along with her brother, Bob. Mitch Stanfield flew in from New York City with his new wife and step-daughter, Taña's mother and step-father came from El Paso and her father, Tim, and the Riordan family drove in from Albuquerque together.

The newlyweds moved into their new two-story home surrounded by large pine trees in a gorgeous setting. They were on their way to a wonderful happy family life. Both were still working for Hanes, having been promoted and both were traveling a great deal going to cities like New York, Las Vegas, Chicago, Los Angeles, and Miami as well as trips to Paris, London, Egypt, San Salvador and other places for fashion shows, manufacturing plants for material selection, photo shoots and the like. Taña called on some of their largest buyers such as J.C. Pennys and WalMart, etc. She was promoted to Senior Designer in their sportswear department. Her greatest claim to fame at that time was that she was chosen to design the jackets for the Olympians to wear when they received their gold, silver, and bronze medals for the Olympics held in Australia. She gave her grandmother one of the jackets and it is one of her most prized possessions.

The Brennaman family spent a summer and winter in South Dakota and by then had just about enough of it. They put Doug to work on the big presidential faces at Mount Rushmore, cleaning and renovating them, using a rope chair swinging high above the ground which he didn't care for much, and in the winter he was working on the snow plows keeping the roads open in temperatures of –10° to –20° F. Man, that's cold. We were not surprised to hear from them that they were moving back to Texas. They had sold their home in Timber Ridge when they left, so they bought a place just outside of Johnson City so that Doug would not have to commute thirty miles to work at the historic Lyndon B. Johnson Memorial Park and home. We were delighted to see them and he promised Nicholas that he would not have to change schools until he graduated from high school. Nicholas was in the 10th grade and had lost his baby fat and was not the chubby little boy he had been. He was now about 6' tall and slim, but still his happy, smiling self. Jonathan was in the 4th grade and a great little kid, also.

Nicholas told me one day that his dad was looking for a pickup that he could buy for him. I got to thinking about my pickup that we had used to clean up the 50 acres and how much Nick had loved to drive it, so I told Doug that I didn't need it anymore and would sell it to him if Nicholas wanted it. It now had about 40,000 miles on it, just 4,000 more than when I bought it for $5,700. I made Doug a deal for it for $4,000, which he knew was a real bargain. On Nicholas's 16th birthday we met the Brennaman family for breakfast on a Saturday morning in Marble Falls. As soon as breakfast was over, Nickie handed Nicholas his gift box and inside was a set of keys. We all went out to the parking lot where I had parked the pickup and as he saw my pickup said to me, "Andy, did you drive your pickup to meet us for breakfast?"

I said, "No, our car is over there, see it?" Bonnie had followed me in our car so she could drive us home.

Nicholas said, "That is your pickup, I know that pickup!"

"Try that key you have in your hand and see if it works," I told him. It did, of course, and he was one very happy young man.

"I'm going to name it 'old Andy'," he said.

I had a big 10 gallon cowboy hat that I had hardly ever worn and I had it laying in the seat and I said, "There is my birthday present to you, Nicholas, try it on and see how it fits." So I had bought a car from them for Tiffany's 16th birthday and they had bought one from me for Nicholas's 16th birthday. Nicholas and Jonathan would drive up and see us quite often and we were always glad to see them.

Going into 1997 we had just about done all we could to make our place look sharp. New paint, new fences, garden planted and trees trimmed. I had all 600 feet of creek frontage mowed and trimmed and it looked like a picture with the clear water and waterfalls, like something out of a storybook all up along the stream. I had painted all 100 fence posts white on all four sides and it was so pretty. We all were enjoying our new paved road and our mail delivery. I had sold all the parcels of land that I had and about all I had to do now was mow every other week and play with my longhorns, little goats, chickens and dogs, and take care of my orchard and garden. I had been a busy guy for a 73 year old.

Bonnie and I were both very active for our age and I stayed very busy with my garden and keeping our little acreage and home beautiful and in good repair. Bonnie canned a lot and froze a lot of vegetables too and she loved her volunteer job at the hospital gift shop. I watched a lot of baseball on our satellite TV, especially the Chicago Cubs and the Atlanta Braves, my two favorite teams.

We decided to join the First Christian Church in Burnet, Texas which we enjoyed. There were quite a few nice people, along with a few old crabs. One couple, Audi and Mary Alice Ross, were movers and shakers in the church and we became excellent friends. Really our kind of people. They were from Kansas City, Missouri and he had retired when they drove thru Texas on a trip and came across Burnet and liked it so much that they bought a home and moved there. Audi had been a radio operator on a bomber during World War II. They had been shot down during an air raid over the Balkans at a large oil storage depot the Germans had there. They were able to land in Italy and were lucky to be alive. We enjoyed these people so much. We would play dominoes every Thursday — at their home one week, then ours the next. This went on for a couple of years. What a joy, and with good conversation.

They were "take charge" kind of people. Audi was the greeter at the church door every Sunday morning and Mary Alice was very active and out-going in her church work. They delivered meals-on-wheels every Wednesday in Burnet. We are still good friends, even though we moved away.

Well, a lot of American people were concerned with the Y2K — the year 2000 turn of the century. There was a lot of talk about all the computers failing when the calendar went from 1999 to 2000. By us not owning a computer at this time we didn't really understand just how much of a problem the country might be in. I have always been a deep thinker and liked to plan ahead, just in case there is a crisis. So we started stockpiling all kinds of food staples, cases of vegetables and meats in canned goods as well as gallons of canned wheat and rice — also medicines and first aid products. We had large new 30 gallon plastic garbage cans for water storage, eight large six gallon plastic cans for gasoline and oil storage, as well as kerosene for lights and lamps and fuel, flash lights and batteries. We had two large freezers and two refrigerators with freezers for meat and all kinds of frozen food. I bought six five-gallon propane storage bottles as well as camp stoves that used propane. I decided to be safe rather than sorry, and most of this could be used in time if it was not utilized for an emergency.

During the year of 1998 I was having trouble with my ears and eyes. So I was fitted with hearing aids and had cataracts removed from my eyes. Also my doctor, Phil McCurdy, discovered I had the onset of diabetes. He had it under control with medication without having to use insulin or needles, thank God. Also I was having bladder trouble, so he sent me to a very good urologist in Austin and he gave me a ream job, with a sort of roto-rooter up the old tool. He removed a large amount of stuff from my bladder, about a cup full. He did a good job. I was so concerned about this problem as my dear old dad had died of prostate cancer and I was really worried. I spent the day and night in the hospital after the surgery in Austin and the next morning the doctor came in my room and the first words he spoke were, "No cancer."

I said, "Doc, these are the sweetest words I have ever heard." In due time, I completely recovered, after a year of regular visits to the doctor.

Well, Marble Falls was 650 miles from Albuquerque and that was a two-day trip for us to go to visit our children and grandchildren. Tim and Andra said, "Dad, we think it's time for you to be closer to us." (Tim had been making the thirteen hour drive regularly for several years and a deer, during rutting season, had totaled his Ford Probe on the way to Christmas in 1997.)

We said, "Good idea." However, I felt we would be practically house-bound with the Albuquerque traffic. Andra suggested we look at

Alamogordo. She called the Chamber of Commerce there and had a package sent to us in Marble Falls. I read it very carefully and it sounded pretty good. This was about the middle of February 1999.

I called my old friend, Bobby Jones, in Altus, Oklahoma and asked him if he would like to take a trip with me to Alamogordo, New Mexico and "Jonesy" was ready to go anywhere, anytime. He was nearly blind from his prison camp experience during World War II. I told him I would pick him up in Altus and then we took off early and drove all the way across west Texas and stayed the night at Artesia, New Mexico, near the Texas/New Mexico border. The next morning we drove northwest into the Sacramento Mountains, which provided us with some fabulous views. We stopped at Cloudcroft, a picturesque town of 9,100 feet elevation. It is a summer tourist area and a ski resort in the winter.

The mountains are covered with huge pine trees and the town is over a hundred years old. As the west was settled the need for lots of railroad cross-ties was great and these huge trees provided them. A railroad line had been built through these scenic mountains to haul the railroad ties down, so this was a pretty thriving little town. They later added passenger cars to the railroad and a thriving vacation business emerged. A large lodge was built, that is absolutely fabulous, to house the large number of vacationers that would go there for the cool climate in the summer. The lodge is still there and is still doing a brisk business year round. It is a favorite place for conventions, having the world's highest golf course. Though the railroad is no longer there, a very good highway provides access for local residents and visitors now — with lots of summer homes and condos.

Jonesy, as I called Bobby, since meeting him in 1952, was really enjoying the trip. It was his first time to see Cloudcroft so we drove around a while, visited the lodge and then drove down the mountain seventeen miles to Alamogordo, a drop in elevation to 4,300 feet.

We checked into a motel around noon and proceeded to tour Alamogordo. We were so surprised to see how clean and neat this New Mexico town of around 40,000 people was. One thing unusual is there are more Anglos who reside there than in any other town in New Mexico other than Albuquerque and Los Alamos, because Holloman Air Force Base is there as well as nearby White Sands Missile Range. A good number of the 40,000 people living in Alamogordo are members of the military or retired military.

During World War II and the Viet Nam War this air base was a helicopter training area as well as the secret missile testing site. The air base now is the only one in the U.S. that is the home base for the Stealth Fighter plane. The Stealth Bomber base is in Missouri. The town has a considerable German population because German pilots are trained here to fly the F-16 fighter planes. There is now a large German school for children of the German trainees so that the children can keep up with their education while Daddy is taking his flight training. Tim became friends with our neighbor Dan Goebbel who was an instructor for the German pilots, and would take him to fly the F-16 flight simulator at Holloman, which he enjoyed immensely.

The Germans love Alamogordo because the sun shines almost all the time. Hardly any clouds — just beautiful, endless blue sky. Quite a difference in the weather than what they have in Germany, where there are lots of clouds and poor visibility and congestion. We have miles and miles of open territory which is excellent for flight training.

Alamogordo sits in the middle of Tularosa Basin which is an ancient inland sea between two mountain ranges. It is sixty-four miles northeast of Las Cruces, New Mexico, eighty-four miles north of El Paso, Texas, and 200 miles south, south-east of Albuquerque. Jonesy and I both really fell in love with this town. There were hundreds of very nice brick homes, almost all of which were built after World War II, on wide paved streets, with sidewalks on both sides. Plus a four-lane highway to Las Cruces and El Paso. I told Jonesy that I thought the town was so perfectly laid out and the climate here was so exceptional that when the airmens' retirement time came, they stayed. This was where their children grew up and married. A lot of these retired airmen decided to run for political office and it gave the town a more well-rounded type of people that were more progressive folks than you usually see in New Mexico. He thought I was right.

We visited Holloman Air Force Base and both of us being former military, they allowed us to drive through, but not get out of our car. All of the buildings and on-base housing were brick, permanent construction, and, all in all, a beautiful base. We also visited the International Space Museum which was really something! Inspired by Colonel Stapp, the world's fastest man. who tested the high speed sled while at White Sands Missile Range. He lived here and retired here, and passed away a few years ago.

Two days after arriving, I decided that if we were going to relocate from Marble Falls, Texas, that this place was the right place to do so.

We then drove northeast up the mountains to the resort town of Ruidoso, New Mexico, famous for the world's richest quarter horse race every year at their race track. I think half of the people who live in west Texas and New Mexico come here in the summer time as well as for skiing in the winter on the 12,000 foot peak of Sierra Blanca Mountain. Remember me writing about my venture with my Realtor friend, Jim Wimberley, in trying to put together a deal to build a hotel and lease it to the Hilton? Jonesy and I located Jim Wimberley on this trip and had a great visit. It had been almost twenty-five years since we had seen each other. He was pleased that I was considering moving to Alamogordo and that we could renew our friendship. He was still in the real estate business which had grown considerably.

It was now February 25, 1999. The clouds were gathering and I told Jonesy we had better get on over the mountain as I had seen two feet of snow fall at one time in this area, so we had a great lunch and headed for Roswell, New Mexico, about seventy miles northeast. We got into Roswell about dusk and it was spitting a little snow. We got checked into a nice motel right next door to a good restaurant, had supper and called my friend and former New Mexico Real Estate Commission member, Ron Meyer. He was so glad to hear from me as I hadn't seen him in thirty years either. He came over to our motel with a fifth of good whiskey and the three of us talked until midnight. What a treat for me and Ron! He was also still in the real estate business, mostly selling and managing large ranches, and was very successful. He had been appointed by Governor Bruce King as a regent on the board of the New Mexico Military Academy. He was a quality guy and a good friend.

We awoke to a BIG surprise! As we opened the motel door, there was ten inches of snow on the top of my car! Fortunately, the restaurant was next door, so we just walked through the snow to breakfast and again for lunch. Later that afternoon we drove through the snow to downtown Roswell where the U.F.O. Museum was located. After going through it, we were completely convinced that the flying saucer story was true, seeing a short movie of it and the people involved at the time when the U.F.O. crashed near Roswell in 1947.

Alamagordo, New Mexico

The next morning we braved the snow-packed highway east of Roswell until we got to the Texas line and out of the snow-covered roads, had lunch in Lubbock, Texas, and continued on to Jonesy's home in Altus, Oklahoma just before dark. The next day found me back home that afternoon full of good things to tell Bonnie about what I had seen in Alamogordo.

I told Bonnie all that Jonesy and I had seen and that as far as I was concerned, I would like to make the move to Alamogordo. I said it was only a four hour drive to Albuquerque to see our kids and grandkids instead of the thirteen hour trips which took two days. I told her how nice and clean the whole town was and that all the homes had block walls on all three sides of the lots, and that there were alleyways for trash pickup and utility meters. Just like all the homes had when we were growing up. The walled yards were really nice for privacy. Most of the yards had palm trees and desert landscaping as well as some grass. Really a pretty town.

The climate was great — it rarely got to 100 degrees in the summer and it rarely got below 30 degrees in the winter — and the sun shone every day. They had only one snow in the past two years and it was gone before noon. They had started construction on a new super hospital that would serve the military base as well as the county. They claimed that it would be second only to the one in Rochester, Minnesota. Bonnie told me she had received a letter from a real estate lady with the ReMax Company there telling us she would be glad to show us around town and look at any homes we wanted to see. The Chamber of Commerce had given her our name and address from the inquiry we had made when we received the brochure we got from them.

Bonnie and I decided that we would talk to our son and daughter and plan for them and Andra's family to all meet us in Alamogordo for an Easter weekend and see if all of us liked the town enough for Gram and Gramps to move there. We did just that and we all agreed. We looked it all over for two days and all thought that we should sell out in Texas and move to Alamogordo as soon as possible, as the spring of the year is the best time to sell property.

I took all of us up the mountain to Cloudcroft and we had an Easter buffet lunch at the lodge there, my treat. Fabulous food! There were seven of us and the bill came to $150, but it was so good and the service was great. None of us have forgotten it. Everyone was excited about getting us old folks back closer together.

We returned to Marble Falls and started in earnest getting our place there ready to sell. I put a sign up: "Longhorns for Sale" and about an hour later one of our neighbors stopped and asked me how much I would take for all four — Bill, Hillary, Chelsea and Buddy. I said, "I'll take $300 each for the three full grown ones and $100 for little Buddy. $1,000 for all four of them, and I'll throw in the four little miniature goats for good measure."

"Well," she said, "You have a deal."

I asked, "Don't you want to wait and talk to your husband?"

And she answered, "No, he likes them as much as I do."

So I told her, "Well, if he changes your mind, I'll give you your money back."

She agreed, paid me half and said, "I'll pay you the rest when we pick them up. My husband will have to build a fence for them first." Her husband was a boss at a large fence building company out of Austin, and they even contracted to build chain link fences along the freeways and so on, so he really knew how to build good fences. It took a couple of months for him to build a really good-looking fence and I fed and looked after the cattle until they were ready. I couldn't have found a better home for my Longhorns, and I was well pleased.

The big job of selling our place in Timber Ridge was necessary before we bought a home in Alamogordo, so I started slicking it up. I planted my garden that spring and shortly it was looking very good. I set out thirty-six tomato plants and plenty of everything else. I had it looking great. I had the yard and creek banks looking good, and painted the trim on our rock house and our orchard was in full bloom and looking great. I knew very well how to get a place ready to sell and it was shaping up really well.

I wrote the lady Realtor, Elaine Tucker, that I had received the letter from, and told her that we would be out to look at the homes she had listed and set a date when we would be there. Around the middle of June, 1999, we called her to confirm and headed for New Mexico. It was around 600 miles, so we always would go half way to Fort Stockton, then drive on in the next day. We gave Elaine a phone call when we got into town and the next day started looking at homes. We told her our price range was around $100,000 so she started showing us homes in the northeast part of town. There were hundreds of really nice brick homes in this part of town, valued anywhere from $100,000 to $150,000. I was looking for a bargain, naturally, and I told her this. She understood very well as she had been selling real estate for 27 years and was just 50 years old. I said to her, "You must have started selling very young."

She said, "Yes, I did. I was the youngest licensed real estate salesman in the state when I first got my license when I was 21 years old." I was pleased to hear this and she was handling us like a pro, and this pleased us both.

The second day we found a great house that had been on the market for a year or so. It wasn't slick and shiny as most of the others were. I said, "Elaine, what's the deal with this home?"

She said, "Andy, the fellow that owned this home worked for the Border Patrol and lived here with his invalid father. Just the two of them. He was transferred to the Albuquerque area, so the government bought his home, which is commonplace in cases like this, so he could go ahead and move." There was nothing structurally wrong. It was a large brick home with four bedrooms and 2,300 sq. ft. plus a two-car garage on a large lot with block walls and located on 10th Street, one of the nicest areas. However, the house needed painting inside and outside. The yard was overgrown and the carpet was soiled and was out-of-date. The house was 16 to 18 years old and when the average buyer saw it, they got turned off. Of course, when I saw it, I knew why it hadn't sold and it didn't bother me much. I knew that if I could buy it at the right price, I would have an excellent deal. Elaine said, "Andy, the appraisal was $124,500 and this was what it was listed for."

I said, "Elaine, it will never sell for that in its present condition." She agreed. "Let's look around and see some more homes, there's no great rush."

We spent enough time looking and we now had to go back home and sell our place before we could buy. I told her when we sold our house I might make an offer on this house. "Okay, Andy and Bonnie, I will stay in touch," she said. With this, we headed back home to start advertising our home in Timber Ridge and pass the word to our friends and neighbors about our upcoming move.

The garden and orchard was in picking time. Bonnie and I got started canning and freezing all we would need to add to our Y-2-K stockpile. I wrote an ad for our local paper that I think was the best real estate ad I ever wrote. I headed it: "A Little Bit of Heaven on Backbone Creek." I have mentioned this several times so far and I'll say it again, you make your money on real estate when you buy. Then work like hell in improving it and wait for the market to come back and you will recapture your investment and get well paid for your work and also make a good profit. That is what it is all about. You must understand all this, for sure, to make it happen.

As you know, I bought this place so 'right' at the auction, then added more land and worked like hell improving it. The next thing that happened even surprised us.

One morning the phone rang and I talked to a fellow named Tom Taylor. He wanted to know if he could come out to look at the place that morning. I said, "Sure." So in an hour or so, he was there and it started raining. I got two umbrellas and he began looking. He was so fascinated with the live stream that was running — so pretty he just couldn't believe it. We spent an hour looking at the land and garden and the large garage with its shop space and small office where I had all four walls filled completely with pictures of my keepsakes, letters, certificates and pictures of friends and relatives. I was so proud of all this and he was very impressed with it all.

He took off and said, "I'll see you tomorrow morning." I told him that the price of the whole place, including my new riding mower, roto-tiller and utility trailer, which came to around $3,000, was $159,500. Indeed, he did show up the next morning and I had a really good prospect! We sat down at the kitchen table and I asked him where he worked. He said he was a commercial Realtor. Well, this surprised me as he said he was a bachelor but was planning on getting married soon. He said, "I work with large companies and travel over several states finding locations for them to build large store buildings, like Home Depot, Lowe's, supermarket sites and the like." He said his office was at Horseshoe Bay, which was a resort location close to Marble Falls on Lake L.B.J.

So here are two Realtors trying to deal with each other, each of us had mutual respect for each other and were enjoying the exercise. I told him the place was free and clear and he would need to get a new loan. His answer was, "No problem. My sister is the manager of a savings and loan in south Texas. All we need is an appraisal and a survey. That will be done easily enough." He then said, "Mr. Long, I'll give you $150,000 for the place." I told him that wouldn't buy it, but that $155,000 would. He said, "We have a deal."

I said, "Let's shake on that." He agreed and said he would prepare the contract subject to him getting his loan. I agreed and, by golly, I had sold it to the first guy that had looked at the place. It had appreciated a lot from what we had done to it, plus having a new blacktop road and mail delivery and the other improvements. We had sold it to the very first prospect I had showed it to. How about that?!!

Every few days he would bring one of his friends to show them the place. The first thing he would do was to look to see if the creek was still running. I would always give him a sack of tomatoes and cucumbers and squash and a watermelon. He was a happy man. And so was I.

We called Elaine Tucker, the Alamogordo Realtor, and gave her the good news and she had some good news for us. She said, "Andy, the government agency in Washington, D.C. has decided to get new appraisals on the home you liked and they had three different appraisals done. The house had been appraised at $124,500 and had been on the market a long time and hadn't sold. So they listed it again with the lowest of the three new appraisals, which was $118,500." Well, this was good news, as it was getting closer to the price that we wanted to spend on a home.

I said, "Elaine, we will be back out to buy a home from you so keep looking for a good one."

She said, "Okay, Andy, we'll find you a good one." We had become good friends by now.

Taña, one of our darling twin granddaughters, wanted to go with us and help us decide which house to buy, so she and Bonnie got in our Chrysler and I got in our second car, a 1987 Lincoln Towncar which we had loaded jam-packed full of breakable things like good dishes, pictures, statues, paintings and things that we didn't want to haul in the U-Haul trucks with our furniture. I drove the Lincoln and Taña and Bonnie followed me. Two days later we arrived and met with Elaine early and started looking again.

She showed us a couple of listings she had that we hadn't seen before, that were newly on the market, but they didn't turn us on. So I said, "Elaine, drive us by that big house on 10th Street again and let's take another look at it." A surprise is coming. As we started to turn into the driveway there were two pickups backed up to the open garage door. They were cutting carpet padding for the house. I said, "Oh, hell, it looks like it has been sold and they are going to lay new carpet. Oh, damn."

Elaine said, "Maybe not, let me call the listing agent and find out." Well, she dialed on her cell phone and they said, "No, it's not sold yet, but the people in Washington that decided to re-price the home at the lowest of the three appraisals, also had the entire house painted inside plus the outside trim (the rest of the house was brick) and they are ready to have new carpet installed in the whole house. It is still for sale, but it is priced $6,000 less and with a new paint job and new carpet."

Elaine said, "Folks, what a break!" She called them back and asked, "Is it possible to pick out different carpet instead of what they are planning to install?" They said, "Yes, if you hurry up." We immediately drove to the carpet store and picked out different carpet that was $450 more in price so we agreed to pay the difference. Elaine asked, "Are you ready to write a contract?"

I said, "Yes, I am ready to make an offer."

"Make an offer?" she said.

"Yes, Elaine, you write up an offer for $112,000."

She said, "Andy, they will never accept that."

I said, "Elaine, never mind. Do as I say and we will see."

I didn't really expect them to accept my offer of $112,000 but I expected they might counter-offer $115,000. So we went to Elaine's office and she sent a fax to Washington D.C. with the $112,000 offer. We all cooled our heels for about three hours and then we got a reply from the Washington bureaucracy. They said, "The least we will take is $116,900.00, but you won't have to pay for the carpet upgrade."

Well, old Elaine was really surprised! She said, "Andy, I can't believe it. You have made the best buy of the year!"

I said, "Elaine I am a great believer in the fact that you never know what you can get unless you only ask." We were paying cash, of course, and they knew it, so this helped a lot in making the deal. The contract was subject to our house closing in Marble Falls and the Washington people said, "If it doesn't close for some reason or other, we will have to charge you for the $450 carpet upgrade as they were already installing it in the house." Well, our house was to close the next morning, so we had the title company in Marble Falls wire our money to the title company that would be closing the deal in Alamogordo.

So, Elaine Tucker saw how an old real estate 'wheeler dealer' operates. After all, to date I had only been doing this for the past thirty-nine years at that time. Every time we see Elaine now she says, "Andy, if you ever sell that house it will bring around $140,000."

I said, "Elaine, remember this. In real estate you make your money when you buy." Well, we got the deal closed and had a pretty big chunk of dough left over from the sale of our house in Timber Ridge. We were all so happy with our deal. Taña especially because she wanted us to get a nice place that wouldn't work us as hard as we had been doing in Texas for the past nine years. Also, we would be close to El Paso, Texas, just eighty-four miles from her mother and stepfather. When she and her husband flew into El Paso at Christmas they would be able to come and see us too. Plus it was only a four hour drive to Albuquerque where her dad and aunt lived.

Later that day we made all our utility deposits and the next morning we headed back to Marble Falls, leaving our stuffed Lincoln Towncar at Elaine's house out in the country until we came back to move into our new home.

It was now the first week of August 1999. The house we were moving out of was only about 200 sq. ft. smaller than our new home, so we had enough furniture to fit comfortably in it. Tim had a lot of his things that had been stored in our over-sized garage, so we decided we would load his things in the biggest U-Haul truck first and when we unloaded our things in Alamogordo, he could drive the truck on into Albuquerque, unload his things and turn the truck back in there. I hired four guys to help Tim, Bonnie and I to move our things out of the house into the truck: Nicholas and his dad, Doug, and Charlie and Ron Delancy, all strong guys to help us load our furniture and things.

We started early and planned to load it all in one day and leave very early the next morning. We could see one truck was not going to hold it all, so we got two big 24 foot long trucks. When we got both of them filled up we still needed a fourteen foot U-Haul trailer, too. I had made a deal with Doug and Nicholas to pay them $100 each to help us load. They didn't want to take the money, but I insisted as they worked very hard until 8:00 p.m. that night, in 110 degree heat.

The deal I made with Charlie was that I would pay him $300 plus his expenses for motel and food for him and his son and his wife, Helen, who was a great gal. She would drive their pickup and follow Charlie in one of the trucks, and pull the 14-foot trailer. That way they would have their pickup to drive back to Marble Falls in. The Delancy's had us three stay all night at their house and leave at 4:00 a.m. the next morning. Tim drove the other big U-Haul and Bonnie and I followed all of them in our Chrysler. Quite a caravan!

We worked until 10:00 p.m. and cleaned the house after we got everything loaded so it would be nice and clean for our buyer, Tom Taylor. We filled up with gas and it was about midnight when we got to bed. We were all exhausted!

We only had three hours of sleep before we headed out. I don't know when I had been so tired, as we all felt I'm sure. We made it to Ft. Stockton by noon and we had lunch. It was August 9, 1999 and August in Texas is no picnic! It was hot! But, we didn't have any trouble at all and we drove into our new home's driveway and parked the trucks and trailer in the drive and on the street.

I had made arrangements with Elaine Tucker to have her son and two other high school football players help us unload our things the next morning. We had a good supper at the Western Sizzler Steakhouse and all bedded down for the night. I told Charlie that they didn't need to help unload and they could go ahead and start back early and get in before dark and that we had plenty of help to unload. They decided to go up the mountain to Cloudcroft and over the mountains and on down the other side into west Texas. This way they could see some of the beautiful mountain country.

After breakfast we drove to the house to start unloading. Only two of the big boys showed up. They said the other one had football practice, so this left only Bonnie, Tim and me and the two high school boys to unload the two trucks and the trailer! Ole "Gung Ho" Tim bounced up on the back bumper of the first truck and reached up high for the strap to open the big door on the truck. As he was pulling hard on the strap, we don't know exactly what happened, he just blacked out and fell backwards off the truck bumper that was about two feet above the driveway and hit the back of his head right where the garage floor joins the driveway and sticks up about an inch above the driveway!

I was standing right there and so was Bonnie and the two boys. I looked at him and he wasn't moving and his eyes were open and I said, "My God, Bonnie, our boy is dead!" Oh, what a shock! We were just stunned!

About ten seconds later his eyes batted and we realized he was not dead and Tim said, "Okay, boys, let's get started." It had just knocked him out or he blacked out but we were so grateful he wasn't dead!

He was lying in a pool of blood, however, and we said, "Lay real still, son, Mom is going to take you to the hospital." It was down 10th Street about one-half mile, so we got him in the car and Bonnie took off to the emergency room. I was beside myself. I went next door and called Elaine, told her what had happened and she drove to the hospital so she could be with Bonnie as she was as shook as I was, of course. We were very fortunate to be as close to the hospital as we were, it was just about a five minute drive.

They x-rayed Tim's head and fortunately, his skull was not fractured, so that afternoon they released him and Bonnie took him to our motel. He stayed in bed for two days. We are so lucky to have our son still alive! When he fell backwards, his height plus the two feet the truck was off the ground meant his head fell eight feet before it hit the concrete. I had accused him of being hard-headed many times, but I never knew it was that hard! His sister, Andra, thinks that he was saved partially because he wore his hair in a long ponytail and his hair cushioned the fall. (Later, it was found that he had acquired 3 hernias during the loading in the Texas summer and, with three hours of sleep combined with the 16 hour drive, he had pushed himself to the limit.)

With Tim under doctor's orders to not unload, it was up to the two boys, Bonnie and I to unload the trucks! We all four worked two full days and when the boys finished and they had done such a good job that

I tipped each with a $100 bill in addition to their $6.00 per hour. They were happy.

Well, we had spent about $2,500 on this move including rental of the trucks and fuel, paying everyone, the hotel rooms and food on the road, etc., but it would have been about $4,500 if we had hired a moving company to move us. It was hard work but we had done it before and Bonnie and I have been used to hard work all our lives. We were very careful and we didn't have any serious damage to our furniture.

After we got the house straightened up my attention turned to the outside work. The front yard was desert landscaping, the ground cover was gravel and lots of greenery in shrubs and evergreen bushes and trees. Very attractive, but overgrown, so I hired a landscape man and he spent the day trimming and cleaning up. $75 later it looked very good. In our neighborhood there were lots of palm trees and large cactus type plants but we didn't have any palms or cactus.

Looking up the street to the east it was only three blocks to the foot of the Sacramento Mountains and they were high and parallel to the east side of the whole town, north to south. This was absolutely a perfect location for us — views to the north, the east, and the south. The famous national observatory, "Sunspot Solar Observatory" was on top of the Sacramento Mountains near Cloudcroft and was in view at an altitude of some 12,000 plus ft. What a sight!

Our view to the north and the east from the backyard was perfect when they set off fireworks on the 4th of July; we had "grandstand "seats. (We missed it the first year as we didn't move in until the 10th of August. We spent Bonnie's birthday on the 11th still moving into the house.)

Each year in September there is a local hot air balloon festival and the balloons would fly right over our yard and across from downtown west to the mountains east of us. We could look up at them and wave and they would wave back. With our field glasses you could see everyone's faces. It is quite a celebration and the balloonists would come from as far away as New Zealand. It's not a "rinkey-dink" thing and is enjoyed by everyone in town. Alamogordo also puts on some local rodeos here each year and they are pretty good as this is cowboy country and quite a few families have saddle horses to enjoy.

The International Space Museum in Alamogordo is a wonderful place to tour. There are many large pictures of the various scientists that started the space exploration program. There are numerous full-sized satellites on display as well as huge full-sized rockets of all kinds in an outside display. It is terrific and is very educational and interesting to see it all. It is only about five years old as I write this. One of the displays is the capsule that John Glenn was in when he made the first trip into space that made him famous. You can even sit in it and have someone take your picture. How about that! Not many places will let you do that sort of thing.

We also have an air show every summer here for two days on a Saturday and Sunday. They open the base and it is a big wonderful show. All the different kinds of aircraft — small ones and very large ones. We see some terrific air acrobatics. This draws people from far and wide. The airbase is the industry that keeps this town going strong and I think it will be here for ever and ever. There are lots of good quality educated people and exceptional schools and hospital facilities.

One interesting thing that happened when we first arrived, we needed to find a good family doctor, one like we had in Phil McCurdy in Marble Falls, Texas. We called all of them that were listed in the phone book and every one of them were booked up. One day at the pharmacy in our big WalMart Superstore, Bonnie asked how she could get a family doctor to take care of us. The pharmacist said, "There is a new doctor that has come to town, and his wife is also a doctor with him that works with the women." So a phone call to them produced two very good doctors for both Bonnie and me. After a few visits we were tickled to death to have gotten started with them. Their names were Dan and Kay Moezzi. They were both around 35 years old and very pleasant to talk to.

My first visit was fine and he gave me a complete physical. I asked him how his name was pronounced and he said, "Mo Easy."

I said to him, "Irish, no doubt." He looked sort of dumb-founded and then I smiled and he realized that I was just kidding.

Then he said, "No, Persian." We both laughed and we were on common ground.

The nurse took my electrocardiogram and Dr. Moezzi came later and asked, "Mr. Long, how old are you?"

I said, "I'm seventy-five."

Dr. Moezzi said, "I can't believe this! I'm going to write down on this piece of paper what age of heart you have."

I was puzzled. I said, "What's wrong, doc?"

He said, "Nothing. Take a look at this number I wrote down here." He had written 14 years. "I just can't believe it."

I said, "No shit?"

He said, "No shit." With that we both laughed. From that day on we were good friends. It wasn't long before he got my diabetes in better shape by changing my medication and monitoring it better. He was really pleased with my blood pressure, which averages around 130 to 140 over 75 or 80 with an 85 pulse rate, which is excellent for my age.

Bonnie had gotten a computer and she would get some great jokes in her email (as far as I was concerned) so whenever I had an appointment I would take him a sealed envelope of four or five really good jokes which he loved getting. One day he said, "Andy, you make my day." He started working on my cholesterol, which was somewhat high and he now has it in pretty good shape, too. He and Kay had three little boys when they came here, now three years later they have five little boys.

I told him one day, "Dan, one of these days after you get those boys educated you can open your own clinic. Each one can specialize in a different kind of doctoring and all you will need to do is work the cash register and keep their books." He just laughed. Isn't it wonderful to have this kind of rapport with your doctor? We think so! He loves doctor jokes and lawyer jokes, especially. Dr. Kay has improved Bonnie's health and she is very happy with her also.

One of the first things we had to do after moving in was to get new New Mexico driver's licenses. Well, I knew my eyes were getting worse, especially driving at night (and that's why I didn't want to move to Albuquerque from Marble Falls — I just couldn't take the traffic). I failed my driver's test! I could not read that small print when I took the eye exam. I had to go to an eye doctor and they made a report, and the driver's license people sent it to Santa Fe. After several months they finally issued me one for local driving in the daytime only and it had to be renewed every year.

In the fall of 1999, I was still driving on my first one-year temporary license, so I was still able to drive, and the traffic in Alamogordo was not bad like it is in Albuquerque or El Paso. So the shocker about not being able to drive hadn't set in quite yet. That first fall was beautiful weather and we enjoyed taking drives up in the mountains and enjoying ourselves very much.

When the next year rolled around, I took the test again after having my glasses changed. They would not even consider issuing a temporary license. So my good "iron horse" of a wife, Bonnie Jeanne, has to do all the driving now. For just a minute think about this, I had been driving a car for 65 years and never had a serious accident that was my fault and now to be told that I can no longer drive a car, well, that is absolutely terrible. Just because I can't read the fine print on a damn chart. I can see cars, people, dogs and bicycles darn well, and just because I can't see this fine print on a chart I don't have a license. I'm pretty bitter about it, but I realize that my eyesight is slowly getting worse and I am now resolved to just being a "back seat" driver and letting Bonnie handle the driving from now on. I just sit there and tell her how she should do it, while punching holes in the floorboard of the passenger seat. Not much fun!

Tim would come down quite often as he was single and had a great job in Albuquerque that allowed him to work three twelve-hour days and have four days off in a row. He would drive to Alamogordo on Sunday and not have to drive home until Wednesday, then he worked Thursday, Friday and Saturday. He said it was the next best thing to being retired. Tim enjoyed seeing us and besides that he got his weekly laundry washed and plenty of home-cooked meals.

My garage was jam-packed with tools and the like, as well as box after box of records that I had been storing. I even had boxes of old order books that were filled with my cookware sales as far back as 1949! That is when we moved to Albuquerque from Baton Rouge, Louisiana. Remember when the moving truck turned over and burned and we lost all of our furniture, keepsakes, and everything else we owned up to that time? Since then I had all my sales records, including my cookware sales, up until the fall of 1961 when we moved to Los Alamos and started selling houses in White Rock. Then I started keeping all of my sales records on selling and building houses plus the blueprints and all the legal papers. They really added up to one hell of a lot of boxes!

I never knew when the I.R.S. was going to check on us, and they did on several occasions over the years. Our wonderful friend and accountant,

Joe Sisneros, did a super job for us and the I.R.S. never ever found anything that we had done wrong as far as taxes were concerned. Thanks, of course, to the fine job that Joe did for us every year. From the year 1962 until the year 2000, which is thirty-eight years, they tried several times to stick us, but thanks to Joe's good work and our records, they never found a thing — not that they didn't try, mind you. We did, however, pay one hell of a lot in taxes! We were Joe's best clients and he was very well paid. Some years we paid him as much as $4,000 per year. That was a lot more then than $4,000 is today because of inflation. But we were glad to do it as it gave us peace of mind and we were making money beyond our wildest dreams.

Anyway, I still had all these records and order books in the garage. Tim said, "Dad, why don't you and I build you a storage shed for your lawnmower and tools in the back yard?" So we bought one to assemble from the True Value store and I then had everything I needed for the yard right where I needed them. By the way, our back yard is fabulous! Large and flat and with a six foot tall concrete block privacy fence. It had a terrific view of the mountains to the north and east and also had a large seedless mulberry tree right in the middle of it. I had room for a real small garden, only big enough to grow tomatoes, cucumbers, squash and bell peppers and only about 4 plants of each. I just had no need for a large garden like we had in Texas. We still have lots of canned food that Bonnie had canned as well as food in two large freezers.

We were ready for Y-2-K, if all the "soothsayers" were correct that the first day of January in 2000 was going to send all of the computers crashing. As we know now, that didn't happen, however, there was an awful lot of work done by a lot of people at a lot of companies during 1998 and 1999 that kept those computers from going down. I thank God it didn't happen as predicted, but we were well prepared just in case.

I was getting sort of bored now that I didn't have much to do except to water and mow my yard, and I had been going full bore for a long, long time. So, I told Bonnie when I saw a little house for sale in the newspaper for $39,500, "Mom, why don't we buy this little house and slick it up and sell it on contract? We can carry the contract ourselves and have some extra income." We still had a pretty good chunk of money in the local bank that we had after we bought our home here as we had made a bundle on the place we sold in Timber Ridge and from the land sales we had there. The bank was only paying us 3% interest and that is not good.

So, to tell the story, we did buy this little house. I made an offer on it of $36,000 instead of the asking price. I had looked it over well and it was a good solid little house, but it did need several things done to it. The lot was pretty large and flat, but the backyard was a mess. It didn't have a blade of grass. It had a small garden area, but nothing planted and it was full of weeds. Me being a seasoned old real estate guy, I didn't see it like it was, I could see it like it would be when I got through with it.

One of Elaine Tucker's sales gals that worked with her had bought it at a foreclosure sale and hadn't done hardly anything to it. She had bought it dirt cheap, I imagine, but didn't know how to fix it up to make it so someone would want to buy it. The little place had two nice trees in the front yard and two large shade trees in the backyard. It had concrete block walls on each side of the lot, but none across the back. The view across the back yard and alley into the neighbor behind was terrible; a couple of old cars and other trash, etc., in their yard, so I figured that a new block wall and a nice gate had to be constructed.

I knew I was going to have to hire someone to help me, so again I called on Elaine Tucker for help. She said, "Andy, we hire a guy by the name of Leonard Smith to do our little fix-up jobs. He can carpenter, plumb, wire and paint and he only charges $8.00 per hour."

I told Elaine, "That's is exactly who I need to help me slick up this little house so I can sell it." So I called Leonard and he met me at the house that next morning.

When we arrived and got out of the car we were met by the old man next door, who was about my age and a heavy-set old boy. The first thing out of his mouth was "How much did you pay for the place?"

I said, "Mister, I don't discuss that type of thing with anyone other than my wife."

"Are you going to sell it or rent it?" He asked.

"I haven't decided for sure yet," I said.

"Well," He told me, "They have had a lot of trouble with the sewer line in the back yard and it stank so bad I had to call the police to make them fix it. So if it happens again, I will be calling the police on you."

I thought to myself, "What an old ass-hole for a neighbor!" Well, Leonard and I walked up to my front door and I said to him, "That old bastard is just jealous because he didn't buy this house himself."

Well, the old boy heard me say this and he said, "I heard that! And you had better be careful messing with me or I will call the police on you!"

I said, "Mister, you don't scare me one damn bit. I'll fight you with words or fists, it doesn't make any difference to me." By this time I had walked over to the fence between our driveways and I asked him, "Are you an ass-hole?"

He looked me right in the eye and said, "Yes."

So, I said, "Well, I don't have anything to do with ass-holes. This is all I'm going to say to you." I turned and walked up to the house and unlocked the front door. Well, Leonard and I started making a list of the things that needed to be done. Paint the walls, fix the switch on the air conditioner and put in new kitchen countertops, for starters.

The stove was one of those little two foot square four burner apartment type stoves, so I planned on replacing it with a good, full-size stove and buying a good used refrigerator also. I opened the door to the small utility room and a step down of about eight inches and a big wide crack across the concrete floor. It was a mess! I told Leonard the first thing I am going to do is check the washer's water drain. Well, we did and, indeed, it was stopped up bad. Well, this told me exactly what the problem was that the old neighbor next door was upset about. A call to a plumber with a Roto-Rooter worked wonders! There was a large shade tree about fifteen feet outside the back door and the plumber pulled out six feet of compacted tree roots the full-size of the sewer line, and the drainage problem was solved.

I told Leonard that when we had a concrete truck come out to pour the concrete footing for the block wall we would have to have built, we would pour a four inch thick new floor for the utility room. I said, "Leonard, there is quite a bit of work here. Can you do it all except lay the blocks for the block wall?"

He said, "Yes," and we got started. I was his boss but also his laborer and helper. I contracted a Mexican fellow to build the wall and they did it in nothing flat. About two days and labor and material was around $1,200. Leonard built a nice 12 foot wide gate in the back wall that we painted it a nice tile red.

While he was working inside the house, I started cleaning up the front and back yards. About all we had to do in the front yard was trim the two trees and water the grass frequently. I also replaced the front walk from the porch to the mailbox with 12" x 12" x 2" concrete slab blocks which Tim put in place. This was my job as well as raking and bagging the refuse into large black plastic trash bags. And there was lots of it! I must have bagged 25 or 30 of these bags full and carried them out to the trash container in the alley. Leaves and weeds and all kinds of trash. I spaded up the small garden space and got it ready to plant. It was still too early to plant a garden, but I got it ready to plant.

I painted the iron pipe clothes line posts a pretty forest green color and bought white plastic clothesline wire and I-bolts and stretched it good and tight. It did turn out real pretty. I then had that backyard as clean as a whistle with a new block wall and gate that completed all three sides of the fence. I bought five fruit trees — one apple, one peach, one plum and two cherry. It was now the prettiest little back yard in the neighborhood.

Leonard and I had worked every day for two or three weeks and it was really shaping up. I also had to build some nice shelves in the utility room and that old ugly lemon utility room looked like a pretty lemon pie, so to speak. We were just about finished with this little house and it looked like a doll house — nothing like it did when I bought it about a month earlier.

The house had three bedrooms, two small ones and a large one at the other end of the house. The master bedroom had once been the garage and had been converted some time earlier. The two small bedrooms had hardwood floors and the large one was carpeted with nice drapes on the windows and French doors that opened into the living room. This made it very saleable, as you will soon see.

Leonard and I were putting the finishing touches on the place and I said, "Leonard, we need a five foot wide gate at the back corner of the house between the house and the block wall between our lot and the neighbor's wall. Why don't we drill anchor bolt holes and put in lead anchors to hinge the new gate."

He said, "Okay."

So when we were just ready to start, the old man next door had been looking out his window watching us work and he came out and said, "You are not going to attach that gate to my wall."

I said, "I damn sure am, it's a party wall, isn't it?"

He said, "No, it's not. It is all mine."

So I said, "See that iron pin in the ground right in the center of the end of the block wall, that tells me that it is a party wall."

"Well, it's not. I put that pin in the ground when I put my chain link fence in. That separates our property." He said.

"Have it your way, you sorry old S.O.B. I think you're a liar, but I will not attach my gate post to your wall."

He said, "You better not or I'll call the cops."

I told him, "I've just about had it with you and if you don't quit f***ing with me, you are going to get yourself hurt."

He said, "I doubt that."

I said, "You had better get yourself back in your house or you'll find out." This old fart had been throwing his weight around with all the neighbors, I think, but he had picked on the wrong guy this time. I just took my post hole digger and dug a two foot deep hole and went and bought a 4"x4"x 8' wood post and set it right next to the wall and attached the gate hinges to the post and it worked just fine.

While Leonard and I were finishing up the building of the gate, I said, "Leonard, I wonder what that old boy would think if he knew I was the middle weight boxing champion of the Pacific Fleet during World War II from 1943 to 1945?"

Leonard said, "You were?"

I said, "Sure. I could tear this old man's ass up if I wanted to." Old Leonard laughed and laughed. The reason I told Leonard this lie was I knew the old man was standing just the other side of the block wall, listening to what we were talking about. I told Leonard later that day that what I said was just a lie, but I wanted to really shake the old fart up!

Well, I painted the two gates and the little house was pretty as a picture — and it was time to put an ad in the paper. My record remained intact. I sold it to the first prospect that looked at it. A couple by the names of Fernando and Mary Martinez. They had three children, a 15 year old girl, a nine year old boy and a 3 year old little girl. Just right for the three bedrooms, which would work out just fine. The two girls would share a bedroom and the little boy would have a room of his own — and mom and dad had a nice big master bedroom. Oh, you have never seen a happier couple! They had been living in a small trailer all their married life. It was a joy to work with them. I had no qualms about selling the place to this Mexican couple. Fernando had been working for the railroad for years and Mary was a school teacher. When they came back to look at the house the second time, I had bought a nice piece of white nylon rope and had made a swing for the little girls in the back yard on the big shade tree. Oh, how she loved it.

This was their first home. Fernando had just gotten a job at our local sawmill and had quit his job on the railroad, so he could be at home and watch his children grow up. He would get his retirement pay from the railroad very soon and this would make their down payment, and with both of them working they could handle the monthly payments which were just a little more than what they had been paying rent on their trailer house.

It made my heart feel good to sell the house to a very deserving little family. I think this sort of thing is what kept me in the home building and selling business for so many years. It was a wonderful way to make a living and the satisfaction I received from the people buying homes was a real joy. I used to tell people that when a wife and mother gets a home of her own, it is the most emotional thing that happens to a family other than having their first child. It was certainly true in this case.

When I tallied up all the costs, including the purchase price and all the things we did to make a house a home, I put an asking price of $49,500 on the house, 10 percent down and a 10 year loan came to a $4,500 down payment and $496 per month payment. Fernando said, "Mr. Long, that is as cheap as I could rent a house, and I can make the down payment with my retirement money." The deal was made and we were all very happy.

It wasn't long until the saw mill shut down and Fernando and a lot of other men were laid off. Well, this was too bad, but they took it in stride and he got another job with a different railroad company and he said he even gets to drive the train some. They have never missed a payment and the old sore-head neighbor's house had started to sink for some reason or another and they had moved.

I have had a saying for a long time that says: "Good things happen to good people. And bad things happen to bad people." I've seen it happen several times in my long life.

Well, old Andy and Bonnie had added about another $500 per month to their income instead of drawing 3% interest on our money in the bank. So, once again, I have to say, "Andy Long is my name and real estate is my game."

I would like to say one thing to the young people reading my story. I have said it several times and I still practice it. It is this: "First plan your work, then work your plan." It works one hell of a lot better. Then, stay focused on what you want to accomplish. All that a lot of young people I have seen want to do is have fun. Well, I've never seen it written down anywhere that says all we have to do is have fun. In fact, it is time to say that a man or woman with a suitable purpose, who is willing to stay with it, cannot help but win at most any worthwhile thing they really want to do. Now, there! End of sermon!

Oh, yes! Always try to be calm and cheerful, except in rare cases when you run into someone like the old man that was a self-proclaimed "asshole" that lived next door to the little house. Life is much too short to put up with those kinds of people! Thank God they don't come along too often.

Well, another three or four months passed since I had bought the little house, and the payments were coming in regularly. The spring and summer is great here in Alamogordo. The spring is kind of windy, but the summers are a delight! There is little or no humidity here and there is always a clear, blue sky. It's nice to see the Stealth Fighters streak across the sky. The high temperature in the summer is usually in the high eighties or low nineties. It only breaks 100 degrees two or three times each summer and is always cool in the shade. We have a large covered patio where we have breakfast nearly every morning up until Christmas — a real delight, along with a great view of the mountains.

I must tell you about another real plus. That is about our two neighbors, the ones to the east and the ones to the west. On the west side of us is Mr. and Mrs. Scott Murray and their teenage daughter. Scott is a policeman and is the finest, nicest policeman I have ever met. His mother lives in Oklahoma and is part Indian, so I guess this might have something to do with that (ha, ha!). He even waters my small garden and lawn when we take a trip. Once he even mowed my big backyard! Of course, this earned him a case of beer (I had a hard time getting him to accept it though). I had told him that I would share the vegetables with him from my garden, which I did. We couldn't have asked for a better neighbor.

On the other side of us was Dan and Laura Gobel and their eight-year old daughter, Danielle. Dan was a recently retired fighter pilot from the air base here. He was now working at the base training the young ones, both American and German, on the F-4 jets. He even took Tim to "fly" the F-4 flight simulator on base several times where they could see the Stealth fighters take off and land. You might say we "fell in love with all three of them." Dan and I hit it off right away, and so did Bonnie and Laura. Danielle was a little doll and smart as she could be. My little grandson, Davis, and her were the same age and they had a ball when Andra and her family came to visit. for a few days.

I was staying in touch with some of my old friends in New Mexico while we lived in Texas. Some of them were Wes Trask, Jim Wimberley, and Bruce King. Bruce and I have been exchanging Christmas and birthday cards ever since he was first elected Governor of the State of New Mexico when I also ran for State Representative for Los Alamos County back in 1968. My God, that has now been over 30 years! How time flies when you are having fun, so the saying goes. Now we are staying in touch with the friends we had in Marble Falls and just enjoying a good, well-deserved, rest.

I had a phone call one day from Bill Sontag's daughter, Terri Sontag, who lives in Wichita. Terri lived with Bill during his last years taking care of him. He was now 93 years old. We had known each other since 1947, some 54 years. Terri told me, "Andy, dad is very sick. The doctor says he doesn't have long to live."

I said, "Can he talk?"

She replied, "Yes, but not very loud. He wants to talk to you." Well, we had a short visit and I told him we would be back to see him right away.

Bill told me, "Oh, good, I'll be waiting." We left the following morning and did not want to go in on him late that night, so we stayed overnight in Greenville, Kansas, just outside Wichita. While Bonnie drove most of the way that day on the long drive, I decided to write out a eulogy. I called it, "A Tribute To A Friend."

The previous year when Bill Sontag turned 90 years old we had attended his birthday party and Bonnie had taken a picture of him and me together and we had some large colored prints of it made. Tim drove into Wichita from Los Alamos that morning, driving most of the night after getting off work the day before. All of Bill's children were there as well as his sister. I had Bonnie's nephew type out my tribute to Bill, which was a full 8 1/2" x 11" page long, the same size as the picture. We made six copies of each for all six of his children. I thought I would keep it in order to give the eulogy at his funeral.

Anyway, back to the present, we got out to his house around 9:00 a.m. and they had him dressed and laying back in a big Lazy-Boy chair. He could hardly whisper, but we talked some, but not too much, as he was so weak and he knew he was going. We visited with the children, all of whom we had known for years. They all remembered Bill's 90th birthday party when I gave a nice talk about what his life had done for my life all the time I had known him. I had worked with him for 13 years before we moved to Los Alamos, New Mexico in 1961 and he and his wife had visited with us several times while we lived there doing our real estate building and development and he had told me many times how proud he was of Bonnie and me and what we had accomplished. He told me many times in those late years that I was the best salesman he had ever had.

To give you an idea of how close we were, his son said that Bill had told him that when all the kids were here that he could rest easy. Bill, Jr. told me that he said, "Bill, they are not all here yet."

Bill, Jr. said, "Who is not here, Dad?"

Bill said, "Andy is not here yet."

"Dad, Andy called and will be here at the house in a little while." He told him. Well, when we arrived that morning I was so glad that we made it in time to talk to him a little bit for our last good-bye.

I left to get the copy of a "Tribute To A Friend" and six copies of the large picture and told the children that we would be back that afternoon. They all say, "Okay, Andy." When we got back at 2:00 p.m. they told us that Bill had gone into a coma around 1:00 p.m. and he had passed away. I was so glad that I had gotten to speak to him that one last time.

The funeral was held two days later. They asked me if I would like to give the Eulogy and I had thought that I might, but by this time I just knew that I would break down and I thought that I had better not do it. I explained this to his son and he knew how close his Dad and I had been all those years and he understood. The funeral went well and we all drove about twenty miles to the little town of Layton, Kansas where his parents and his wife, Maxine, who had died of cancer about 15 years previously, were buried. Bill and I had visited the family cemetery every time we came back to the Scott reunion at Thanksgiving. We would always get together for breakfast the day after Thanksgiving and spend the day together driving over to Layton where Bill was born and raised on a farm and ranch. Bill had bought a large ranch and ran cattle on it for several years after he retired from the cookware business and went back to his roots — always living in Wichita and Derby, Kansas nearby. He had become a multi-millionaire but you would not have known it. He was one of the best men I had ever known.

When we lived in Texas those nine years. Bill drove down to see us in Marble Falls when he was in his late 80's. It was about 550 miles from Wichita. He and I would drive on down to Brownsville, Texas and visit the summer and winter place he had once owned. We had visited Maxine and him there several times when the children were small. We would stay three or four days and enjoy the beach and talk about old times. The last trip we had made there, Bill was 87 years old and had just bought himself a brand new Jaguar. He let me drive it from Marble Falls to Brownsville and back. I worried about him getting back to Wichita, but he made it just fine.

When we moved back to New Mexico and lived here in Alamogordo, we would call each other about once a month and have a long visit and look forward to another time we would see each other after the Scott reunion on the day after Thanksgiving.

We just love living in Alamogordo. I think it has the very best climate in the whole world. It's about 30,000 population plus around 10,000 at the base, so it is just the right size. All the stores we need without any of the wild traffic. Just five minutes to downtown to the supermarkets, WalMart, banks, post office, doctor's office, and hospital. We live on East 10th Street, three blocks to the base of the Sacramento Mountains where the cutest little Fire Station is located and looking out our big living room window we look straight south on Sunshine Street and as the mountains curve back a little we have a clear view of a mountain scene called "the sleeping lady." We have an unobstructed view up Sunshine Street of all the front lawns and beautiful landscaping on all the houses on both sides of the street. It is quite pleasant and very picturesque.

I was beginning to feel a little "restless" again for something to do, so one day I was driving around and saw a small house for sale on one of the prettiest streets in town. It was a boulevard street with a thirty-foot space between the two streets, one going each way. In this center space were big mature pecan trees. The street was called Pecan Drive.

There was a convenience store just across the street and to the right two doors down. "Very convenient," I thought to myself. It was about four blocks to the senior citizen's center. What a pleasant location for some retired couple to live. I called Elaine Tucker and said, "Elaine, I am interested in this house." She gave me the lowdown on it: it seems the couple that owned it bought it to fix up and sell. Well, when they got it about half-finished, they got a divorce. The wife ended up with this house. She didn't have the money or the know-how to finish fixing it up, so she put it on the market "as is."

Well, it just wasn't going to sell in this condition and it had been on the market for a year and a half. The asking price was $36,000 — but no offers. Well, Bonnie and I looked it over thoroughly and it was in good shape inside. It had a new bathroom, new furnace, new air conditioner and new carpet in the two bedrooms and living room. The kitchen had new lower cabinets, but no upper cabinets and no stove or refrigerator either. The yard was a complete mess. It had a one-car carport and a large utility room which was also a mess. The yard had a good block wall on three sides and a 12' x 12' concrete pad for a storage shed. There was a small garden area and two old dead peach trees in the back yard. This was December 2000. I could see the house was a solid one, but I would have to spend quite a bit of money to slick it up.

Elaine said, "Andy, she just lowered the price to $33,500 from $36,000."

I said, "Elaine, I will make an offer of cash money for $26,000 and close on January 2nd, 2001."

She said, "Andy, she won't take it, but I'll try." Well, I figured I would probably have to pay $30,000 to get it, but the offer was made for $26,000 and two days later Elaine called and said, "Andy, the lady said if she could close before Christmas she would accept your offer of $26,000."

I told Elaine, "Sure. Let's close it on December 20th." And we did.

I called Leonard Smith and he and I went to work. We first started on the yard and to build a storage shed. We worked a week or so building a really nice shed out of plywood, all painted up, and then we got rid of the old dead trees, raked and cleaned up the garden area and both the front and back yards and got rid of an awful lot of trash.

One day Leonard told me his wife was complaining that he was just spending too much time working long hours and said, "Andy, you are going to have to get someone else to help you." As it was, he had only been able to work with me after 4:00 p.m. weekdays and on Saturday, so I really needed someone who could work full-time. I got lucky when I called a guy that I hired to haul me in a load of top soil.

I asked him, "Do you do carpentry work?"

And he said, "Sure." I found a real jewel in Mike Westerbur.

Mike could do it all! He and I worked steady for a month or so. He laid new sheet vinyl floor covering in the kitchen and utility room, and also painted the utility room and hung a new back door. He installed a new hot water tank and I bought new upper kitchen cabinets just like the lower ones in the kitchen. I bought a very good kitchen range with a self-cleaning oven and a real nice refrigerator with an ice maker.

We installed five new ceiling fans, new kitchen curtains and drapes and the inside just sparkled. We installed a new back patio 12'x 18' and I started seeding and sprigging the front and back yards on my hands and knees. Talk about hard work for this old man! But things were shaping up inside and out. I watered the new lawns every day and trimmed up the large climbing rose bushes in the front yard and a beautiful lilac bush in the back yard I then planted five fruit trees in the back yard. Twelve tomato plants, four squash plants, four cucumber plants, and some pepper plants.

By the time we got all the other work done, the roses were blooming, the lilac was in full bloom, the fruit trees were blooming and the garden had started to bloom and the new front and back yards were green and pretty. I strung the clothesline on the newly painted clothesline poles. As an old cowboy once said, "It was as pretty as a diamond in a goat's ass." I prefer to say it looked like a pretty little doll house. It was now ready for me to write an appropriate ad for the local newspaper.

I started this ad with the heading, "Color Me Love" and went on to describe it. Again I sold it to the first couple that looked at it. I priced it at the same amount that I had sold the other house for last year, $49,500, with a $5,000 down payment and a $45,500 loan for 10 years at 10% interest, payable at $500 per month. The key to all of this is that people were paying this much for rent and not getting anything but a bunch of rent receipts.

The couple was so happy. It was a second marriage for both of them and they were very much in love. Randy worked at the White Sands Missile Range, he built the little drone airplanes that we are hearing so much about at this time. He had been working there for several years and he was a rock-solid guy and his wife, Pam, was a living doll. Bonnie and I had another "real love affair" with these folks.

The money we used to buy these two houses had been in the bank drawing 3% interest and now we are getting 9 percent interest for 10 years and the buyers will have a home paid for. This is why the real estate business is so worthwhile. Everyone benefits. And once again I'll say, you make your money when you buy.

Now, let me tell you the rest of the story. Since I didn't owe anything on either of these houses, when I sold them, we carried the notes ourselves. We sold them on real estate contracts, rather than on a note and mortgage. What this means is this: in the event they don't make their payments as agreed, we don't have to go through a foreclosure suit. This only takes 90 days or more, if necessary. At the closing the seller gives the buyer a deed and the buyer also gives the seller a deed. These deeds both are held in escrow by an escrow company or agency. In the event the buyer fails to pay, all the seller has to do is file the deed at the court house that the buyer has already given him. It simply eliminates a lot of red tape, and time and expense, by not having to go through foreclosure.

If the buyer pays his monthly payments as agreed, then when he makes his last payment the escrow agent releases the deed they have been holding in escrow during the ten year contract. The home is now theirs, free and clear. The seller does not even have to be in contact with the buyer and listen to any sob stories about their payments that they send every month. They make their payment directly to the escrow company and the escrow company takes out their fee to handle the transaction and sends the seller's monthly payment check to the seller. It is a wonderful arrangement for all concerned.

In the event you should get hold of a dead-beat, it makes it very simple for the seller to get the house back. Of course, there is a certain grace period should the buyer run into unexpected hardship. The nice thing about this escrow deal is, that if the seller should move or leave town, the escrow company simply sends their check to them at their new address. The key is for the seller to make sure the buyer has a good credit record when the deal is made.

I wanted to explain this in detail, because who knows, some of you folks who read this may want to sell some property on a real estate contract and all you have to do is go to a title insurance company and they will prepare the necessary paperwork for you and the buyer to sign and they will make the arrangements with the escrow agency for you. The real estate laws do vary from state to state so be sure to check with a good real estate attorney before using this method. Andy Long is my name and real estate is my game, right?

Mike Westerbur and I became good friends and when I need anything done around our place I just call Mike and he always does a good job for us. We go trout fishing together and he is quite a good hunter. He and his wife killed a nice deer that next fall and I told Mike that I had killed several deer, but with my failing eyesight, I just could not see the crosshairs on my rifle scope. So I asked Mike if I bought a license and went with him, if he shot a deer for me I would split it with him. Mike said, "Okay, Andy. Good idea. I have a married daughter in Albuquerque that could use some deer meat, so I will even dress the deer out and cut it up for you, ready to put in your freezer."

It is now 2002 and I decided I was just not up to trying to remodel any more houses. I turned 77 this past November, so it's time to stop this hard work and enjoy myself. Mike introduced me to a small trout lake at Carrizozo, a small town about 50 miles north of Alamogordo. The State Fish and Game Department starts stocking it with trout in the fall and stops in the spring, in April. Then they stock it with catfish. It's a put and take situation, but they are fun to catch. The limit is five fish per person on trout and two catfish per person. The catfish are around 12"-16" and the trout are from 9"-14". The largest trout I have caught there was 16" — he was a dandy.

Tim and I go fishing a lot and Bonnie and I go quite a bit also. I have to depend on someone to drive me now, as I explained earlier. We sometimes fish at Fenton Lake in the Jemez Mountains (pronounced hay-mez) near Los Alamos, when it is stocked with large trout, like we had done when we lived there from 1961–1981. This is near the famous Valle Grande volcano crater ("Valles Caldera" as it is now formally called) – magnificent country!

My general health is pretty good considering my age. I have had diabetes for about 10 years, but it is under control with pills and I don't have to take insulin shots, thank God! The diabetes along with the macular degeneration (my eye problem) and, of course, my hearing aids which I need and am thankful for, is all that's wrong with me in the spring of 2002.

Bonnie and I decided to take a trip back to Marble Falls and visit several families that we had enjoyed knowing, namely Jim and Betty Nations, Ruby and Vernon Alexander, our neighbors in Timber Ridge and Audi and Mary Alice Ross, our domino playing friends, and Charlie and Helen Delancy, that had done a lot of work for me and the ones that helped us move to Alamogordo, and especially the Brennamans — Doug, Nickie, Nicholas and Jonathan. Nicholas is graduating this year, so we wanted to attend his graduation, and we did. We had a wonderful time, and even stayed overnight with three of these families.

We made the trip just fine. Bonnie did almost all the driving. Once in a while on I-10 which is all four-lane, I would drive for a while when the traffic was very light, and all the cars were going in the same direction. I just didn't dare drive up a two-lane highway with cars coming both ways. I'm a pretty gutsy guy, as most of you know, but I am not at all stupid. We had a wonderful time with all of these good folks. You never know just how long we all have to live, you know?

About the only other big thing that has happened this year of 2002 was Bonnie and I decided we both needed false teeth. We both had partial plates for many years and we were now experiencing some more tooth problems. We heard that in Juarez, Mexico we could both get a full set of false teeth for $2,000 each. In Alamogordo it would be double or triple this amount. So, for a total of $4,000 we are in good shape now. This was happening around the time the terrorists destroyed the Twin Towers and attacked the Pentagon in Washington, D.C. The last time we went to Juarez was just after September 11th, so the border practically closed as security became very tight when re-entering the U.S. at El Paso.

In the process of getting our dental work done, we made about a dozen trips from El Paso to Alamogordo, about 100 miles each way. This is how it worked: we would drive about two hours to the International Bridge crossing the Rio Grande River, park the car in a secured parking lot, then walk about two blocks, catch the bus to Juarez about a quarter mile over the bridge and at the end of the bridge the bus would stop and we would walk across the street to the dental office. The facility was so nice and clean — and sanitary. There was never a thought of anything bad. The people were all very nice and polite. There were always six or eight people in the waiting room. Several of the people spoke English. The doctor did not, but he had a great interpreter who did and this worked out very well.

I asked the doctor how long he had been practicing and he said eleven years. I asked him how long he had to go to school at the University of Mexico City and he said six years. It is only four years in the U.S. He really knew his business and was very nice and thorough. His interpreter and I became friends and he enjoyed my jokes and would pass them on to the doctor in Spanish. We always had a good time. His name was Jesus (pronounced hay-soos). Bonnie also enjoyed everyone at the office.

When we would leave to come back home, they would drive us back to our car, but after September 11th, it took about an hour and a half to get back into the U.S., and by another route as they had to inspect every car going into the U.S. We would usually walk back across the bridge which took about 30 minutes to get to our car. This all took about a year from the time we started, but we enjoyed it and we both are very happy with our new teeth. Well, you can see that I am up-to-date with the history of my long life when all I have to write about is my new false teeth.

The Kelley's came to visit us and Elmer and I went trout fishing four days in a row and we played all the dominoes we could and really enjoyed our visit, as we always do with these great friends.

The greatest things that have taken place recently is that our dear, dear twin granddaughters each had a baby boy this year! Taña and Carlos Martinez's little boy, Nicolas Carlos, was born February 7, 2002 and Katae and Grant Phelps little boy, Jarvis Phineas, was born September 19, 2002, just eight months apart. Tim could not be prouder!! They are just about a year old as of this writing, and we are great-grandparents at last.

About all I have to do now is watch the grass grow, take care of my small garden, walk the dogs, pet the cat, and fuss with (at) this old Grandma I live with. The best things I have to look forward to are going trout fishing and watching my favorite baseball teams, the Chicago Cubs and the Atlanta Braves, beat their opponents on my big screen TV. It was necessary for us to get one this year as I just could not see the regular size TV well enough — it sure is a blessing.

We do enjoy taking mountain drives through the Lincoln National Forest and the Sacramento Mountains, especially when we have company visit us. We usually take them to the Apache Indian Casino, outside of Ruidoso, for a little recreation and some good food, which is enjoyed by all. There is horse racing there that opens on Memorial Day and closes each year on Labor Day. Ruidoso is a great summer resort as it is always nice and cool all summer long. There is also a nice trout lake there which is stocked all year round, as the lake water is always cool. Tim, Bonnie and I enjoy fishing there.

So we are enjoying ourselves as much as possible at our age. At this writing it is May 9, 2003. Bonnie will be 78 on August 11th and I will be 79 November 17th this fall. We will celebrate our 59th wedding anniversary on September 27th. What a roll we have had! Two years after our wedding in 1944 we had a new baby boy on September 17th, 1946, Timothy Edward Long. Then on March 13, 1951 along came Andra Jeanne Long, a beautiful baby girl.

Years later, twin granddaughters came on December 10, 1967 to Timothy and Juanita Long: Mary Antaña Long and Kathy Jeanne Long. Now each of them have baby boys of their own.

Andra and her husband, Richard Riordan have a beautiful daughter, Tiffany Jeanne Marie, who will be 22 years old September 1st, and on November 23, 1991 along came Davis Grayson Riordan my only grandson.

That makes eight children, grandchildren and great-grandchildren in all. So surely Andrew Long and Bonnie Scott have done what our good Lord expected us to do — reproduce and multiply. Each one is a real winner, and I say that without reservation. We are so proud of each and every one of our family.

Now, dear relatives and friends, as our days dwindle down to a precious few, so do our friends and loved ones. During this recent past two years we have lost my dear first cousin on my Dad's side, Annabel Shattuck of Bartlesville, Oklahoma. She was 87 years old. She was a wonderful woman. We also lost our dear friends of many years, Lloyd Howard and his wife, Anna Lou, of El Reno, Oklahoma. We first met them in 1948. It was 53 years we knew Lloyd and 34 years we knew Anna Lou. They were wonderful people. Then we lost Nadyne Harbour. We first met her and Jack in Los Alamos in the 1960's. They visited us in Alamogordo this past year. We had many good times together. I have written about all these people in this story.

One of the friends I hated most to lose was Wes Trask, a dear, dear friend. He was a brilliant engineer in Los Alamos and did lots of work for my building company over many years, as well as traveling with me on the big job in Joplin, Missouri, also included in this story. Bonnie and I, and Tim and Andra attended his funeral in Albuquerque last summer. We were such good friends and had gone fishing together many times. I told his wife, Lucille, and his son, Charles, at the funeral that Wes Trask was one of the best men I have ever known. Her answer was, "Andy, he felt the same way about you." And the tears flowed.

So as the years dwindle down to a precious few, so do our dear friends and relatives. Thank the Lord there is no expiration date on memories!

May 20, 2004

Andrew E. "Andy" Long

(November 17, 1924 -- September 23, 2013)

579

Contact Info:

Libre Arts
PO Box 2001
Santa Fe, NM 87504